California Laws and Regulations Related to the Practice of Optometry and Opticianry

2024 Edition

Published November, 2024
by Gold Rush Publishing, Springfield, IL.

This book is a compilation of the applicable laws and regulations regarding the practice of optometry and opticianry in the State of California. While every effort has been made to ensure that the book is current and accurate, readers are advised that the applicable laws and regulations are subject to revision. Should any difference or discrepancy occur, duly enacted laws or regulations shall take precedence over the information contained herein. Information is current as of October 24, 2024. Please refer to the reference sources below for any changes made after that date.

Reference sources:

California Laws - www.leginfo.legislature.ca.gov/faces/codes.xhtml
California Code of Regulations - www.govt.westlaw.com/calregs
Code of Federal Regulations - www.ecfr.gov

First Edition, Paperback
Published November, 2024

ISBN-13: 978-1-890305-47-5

Published by Gold Rush Publishing
Springfield, IL 62702
http://goldrushpub.com

Cover design by Mark Arsenault. Cover image by Gary Cassel via Pixabay.

CONTENTS

BUSINESS AND PROFESSIONS CODE

GENERAL PROVISIONS **11**
DIVISION 1: DEPARTMENT OF CONSUMER AFFAIRS **19**
CHAPTER 1: THE DEPARTMENT 19
CHAPTER 1.5: UNLICENSED ACTIVITY ENFORCEMENT 49
CHAPTER 2: THE DIRECTOR OF CONSUMER AFFAIRS 52
CHAPTER 3: FUNDS OF THE DEPARTMENT 61
CHAPTER 4: CONSUMER AFFAIRS 67
ARTICLE 3: POWERS AND DUTIES 67
ARTICLE 3.6: UNIFORM STANDARDS REGARDING SUBSTANCE-ABUSING HEALING ARTS LICENSEES 69
ARTICLE 4: REPRESENTATION OF CONSUMERS 72
ARTICLE 5: CONSUMER COMPLAINTS 72
CHAPTER 6: PUBLIC MEMBERS 75
CHAPTER 7: LICENSEE 77
DIVISION 1.2 JOINT COMMITTEE ON BOARDS, COMMISSIONS, AND CONSUMER PROTECTION **79**
CHAPTER 1: REVIEW OF BOARDS UNDER THE DEPARTMENT OF CONSUMER AFFAIRS 79
DIVISION 1.5: DENIAL, SUSPENSION & REVOCATION OF LICENSES **81**
CHAPTER 1: GENERAL PROVISIONS 81
CHAPTER 2: DENIAL OF LICENSES 83
CHAPTER 3: SUSPENSION AND REVOCATION OF LICENSES 89
CHAPTER 4: PUBLIC REPROVALS 99
CHAPTER 5: EXAMINATION SECURITY 101
DIVISION 2: HEALING ARTS **103**
CHAPTER 1: GENERAL PROVISIONS 103
ARTICLE 1: RECORDS 103
ARTICLE 1.5: ADVOCACY FOR APPROPRIATE HEALTH CARE 104
ARTICLE 2: EYEGLASSES 111
ARTICLE 4: FRAUDS OF MEDICAL RECORDS 111
ARTICLE 6: UNEARNED REBATES, REFUNDS, AND DISCOUNTS 113
ARTICLE 7.5: HEALTH CARE PRACTITIONERS 137
ARTICLE 8: SELECTION OF HEALING ARTS PRACTITIONER 142
ARTICLE 9: INACTIVE LICENSE 142
ARTICLE 10: FEDERAL PERSONNEL AND TRIBAL HEALTH PROGRAMS 143
ARTICLE 10.5: UNPROFESSIONAL CONDUCT 146
ARTICLE 11: PROFESSIONAL REPORTING 148
ARTICLE 12: INSURANCE FRAUD 165
ARTICLE 12.5: MENTAL ILLNESS OR PHYSICAL ILLNESS 167
ARTICLE 13: STANDARDS FOR LICENSURE OR CERTIFICATION 169
CHAPTER 1.5: EXEMPTION FROM LICENSURE 171
CHAPTER 5: MEDICINE 173
ARTICLE 3: LICENSE REQUIRED AND EXEMPTIONS 173
ARTICLE 12. ENFORCEMENT 173
CHAPTER 5.4: PRESCRIPTION LENSES AND OPHTHALMIC AND OPTOMETRIC ASSISTANTS 177
CHAPTER 5.45: NONRESIDENT CONTACT LENS 183

CHAPTER 5.5: REGISTERED DISPENSING OPTICIANS 185
ARTICLE 1: GENERAL PROVISIONS 185
ARTICLE 1.5: SPECTACLE LENS DISPENSING 194
ARTICLE 2: CONTACT LENS DISPENSING 196
ARTICLE 2.5. NONRESIDENT OPHTHALMIC LENS DISPENSERS 198
ARTICLE 2.7. REGISTERED DISPENSING OPTHALMIC BUSINESSES 201
ARTICLE 3. FISCAL PROVISIONS 203
CHAPTER 7. OPTOMETRY 205
ARTICLE 1. GENERAL PROVISIONS 205
ARTICLE 2. ADMINISTRATION 205
ARTICLE 3. ADMISSION TO PRACTICE 211
ARTICLE 4. REGISTRATION 226
ARTICLE 5. REVOCATION AND SUSPENSION 234
ARTICLE 6. OFFENSES AGAINST THE CHAPTER 240
ARTICLE 7. REVENUE 241
ARTICLE 8. OPTOMETRIC CORPORATIONS 245

CALIFORNIA CODE OF REGULATIONS

TITLE 16: PROFESSIONAL AND VOCATIONAL REGULATIONS 247
DIVISION 13.5. REGISTERED DISPENSING OPTICIANS OF THE CALIFORNIA STATE BOARD OF OPTOMETRY 247
ARTICLE 1. GENERAL PROVISIONS 247
ARTICLE 2. APPLICATIONS 249
ARTICLE 3. PRESCRIPTIONS FOR OPHTHALMIC DEVICES 250
ARTICLE 4. CHANGES OF BUSINESS NAME, BUSINESS ADDRESS, OR OWNERSHIP 250
ARTICLE 5. ADVERTISING 251
ARTICLE 6. FEES 252
ARTICLE 7. ENFORCEMENT 253
ARTICLE 8. OPTICAL DISPENSING EDUCATIONAL PROGRAMS [REPEALED] 258
DIVISION 15: BOARD OF OPTOMETRY 261
ARTICLE 1. GENERAL PROVISIONS 261
ARTICLE 2. LOCATION OF PRACTICE 262
ARTICLE 2.5. SPONSORED FREE HEALTH-CARE EVENTS — REQUIREMENTS FOR EXEMPTION [REPEALED] 266
ARTICLE 3. PROFESSIONAL RULES 267
ARTICLE 4. SANITARY AND/OR HYGIENIC FACILITIES—STANDARDS GOVERNING SERVICES 273
ARTICLE 5. APPLICATION FOR LICENSURE EXAMINATION 276
ARTICLE 5.1. FINGERPRINT REQUIREMENTS 278
ARTICLE 6. EXAMINATIONS 280
ARTICLE 6.5. CONTINUING OPTOMETRIC EDUCATION 283
ARTICLE 7. OPTOMETRIC CORPORATIONS 288
ARTICLE 8. TOPICAL PHARMACEUTICAL AGENTS 291
ARTICLE 9. APPLICATION PROCESSING TIMELINES 293
ARTICLE 10. PRESCRIPTIONS 294
ARTICLE 11. THERAPEUTIC PHARMACEUTICAL AGENTS 295
ARTICLE 12. ENFORCEMENT 301
ARTICLE 12.5. CITATIONS AND FINES 302
ARTICLE 13 - MOBILE OPTOMETRIC OFFICES 306

CORPORATIONS CODE

TITLE 1: CORPORATIONS 317
DIVISION 3 CORPORATIONS FOR SPECIFIC PURPOSES 317
PART 4: PROFESSIONAL CORPORATIONS 317

EDUCATION CODE

TITLE 2: ELEMENTARY & SECONDARY EDUCATION 327
DIVISION 4: INSTRUCTION AND SERVICES 327
PART 27: PUPILS 327
CHAPTER 9: PUPIL AND PERSONNEL HEALTH 327
ARTICLE 4: PHYSICAL EXAMINATION 327
PART 28: GENERAL INSTRUCTIONAL PROGRAMS 331
CHAPTER 4: PROHIBITED INSTRUCTIONS 331
ARTICLE 3: SOLICITATIONS 331

GOVERNMENT CODE

TITLE 1: GENERAL 333
DIVISION 7: MISCELLANEOUS 333
CHAPTER 3.5: INSPECTION OF PUBLIC RECORDS [REPEALED] 333
ARTICLE 1: GENERAL PROVISIONS 333
DIVISION 10. ACCESS TO PUBLIC RECORDS 349
PART 1. GENERAL PROVISIONS 349
CHAPTER 1. PRELIMINARY PROVISIONS 349
ARTICLE 1. SHORT TITLES 349
ARTICLE 2. EFFECT OF RECODIFICATION 349
CHAPTER 2. DEFINITIONS 351
PART 2. DISCLOSURE AND EXEMPTIONS GENERALLY 355
CHAPTER 1. RIGHT OF ACCESS TO PUBLIC RECORDS 355
CHAPTER 2. GENERAL RULES GOVERNING DISCLOSURE 357
ARTICLE 1. NONDISCRIMINATION 357
ARTICLE 2. VOLUNTARY DISCLOSURE 357
ARTICLE 3. DISCLOSURE TO DISTRICT ATTORNEY AND RELATED MATTERS 358
CHAPTER 3. GENERAL RULES GOVERNING EXEMPTIONS FROM DISCLOSURE 361
ARTICLE 1. JUSTIFICATION FOR WITHHOLDING OF RECORD 361
ARTICLE 2. SOCIAL SECURITY NUMBERS AND RELATED MATTERS 361
PART 3. PROCEDURES AND RELATED MATTERS 363
CHAPTER 1. REQUEST FOR A PUBLIC RECORD 363
ARTICLE 1. GENERAL PRINCIPLES 363
ARTICLE 2. PROCEDURAL REQUIREMENTS GENERALLY 363
ARTICLE 3. INFORMATION IN ELECTRONIC FORMAT 365
ARTICLE 4. DUTY TO ASSIST IN FORMULATING REQUEST 366
CHAPTER 2. AGENCY REGULATIONS, GUIDELINES, SYSTEMS, AND SIMILAR MATTERS 367
ARTICLE 1. AGENCY REGULATIONS AND GUIDELINES 367
ARTICLE 2. INTERNET RESOURCES 368
ARTICLE 3. CATALOG OF ENTERPRISE SYSTEMS 368
PART 4. ENFORCEMENT 371
CHAPTER 1. GENERAL PRINCIPLES 371

CHAPTER 2. ENFORCEMENT PROCEDURE 373
ARTICLE 1. PETITION TO SUPERIOR COURT 373
ARTICLE 2. WRIT REVIEW AND CONTEMPT 373
PART 5. SPECIFIC TYPES OF PUBLIC RECORDS 375
CHAPTER 5. HEALTH CARE 375
ARTICLE 1. ACCREDITATION 375
ARTICLE 2. ADVANCE HEALTH CARE DIRECTIVE AND RELATED MATTERS 375
ARTICLE 3. CONTRACTS AND NEGOTIATIONS 375
ARTICLE 6. WEBSITES AND RELATED MATTERS 380
CHAPTER 8. LITIGATION RECORDS AND SIMILAR MATTERS 381
CHAPTER 10. PERSONAL INFORMATION AND CUSTOMER RECORDS 383
CHAPTER 11. PRELIMINARY DRAFTS AND SIMILAR MATERIALS 385
CHAPTER 12. PRIVATE INDUSTRY 387
CHAPTER 13. PRIVATE RECORDS, PRIVILEGED MATERIALS, AND OTHER RECORDS PROTECTED BY LAW FROM DISCLOSURE 389
PART 6. OTHER EXEMPTIONS FROM DISCLOSURE 391
CHAPTER 1. INTRODUCTORY PROVISIONS 391
CHAPTER 2. ALPHABETICAL LIST 392
PART 7. OPERATIVE DATE 417
TITLE 2: GOVERNMENT OF THE STATE OF CALIFORNIA 419
DIVISION 3: EXECUTIVE DEPARTMENT 419
PART 1: STATE DEPARTMENT AND AGENCIES 419
CHAPTER 1: STATE AGENCIES 419
ARTICLE 9: MEETINGS 419
PART 2.8: DEPARTMENT OF FAIR EMPLOYMENT AND HOUSING 443
CHAPTER 4: DEFINITIONS 443
CHAPTER 6: DISCRIMINATION PROHIBITED 449
ARTICLE 1: UNLAWFUL PRACTICES, GENERALLY 449
TITLE 3 GOVERNMENT OF COUNTIES 455
DIVISION 2: OFFICERS 455
PART 3: OTHER OFFICERS 455
CHAPTER 1: DISTRICT ATTORNEY 455
ARTICLE 1: DUTIES AS PUBLIC PROSECUTOR 455

HEALTH AND SAFETY CODE

DIVISION 2 LICENSING PROVISIONS 457
CHAPTER 2.2: HEALTH CARE SERVICE PLANS 457
ARTICLE 5: STANDARDS 457
ARTICLE 9: MISCELLANEOUS 460
DIVISION 10: UNIFORM CONTROLLED SUBSTANCES ACT 465
CHAPTER 1: GENERAL PROVISIONS AND DEFINITIONS 465
CHAPTER 4: PRESCRIPTIONS 467
ARTICLE 1: REQUIREMENTS OF PRESCRIPTIONS 467
CHAPTER 5: USE OF CONTROLLED SUBSTANCES 477
ARTICLE 1: LAWFUL MEDICAL USE OTHER THAN TREATMENT OF ADDICTS 477
DIVISION 106: PERSONAL HEALTH CARE (INCLUDING MATERNAL, CHILD, AND ADOLESCENT) 479
PART 1: GENERAL ADMINISTRATION 479
CHAPTER 1: PATIENT ACCESS TO HEALTH RECORDS 479

LABOR CODE

DIVISION 3: EMPLOYMENT RELATIONS 489
CHAPTER 2: EMPLOYERS, EMPLOYEES AND DEPENDENTS 489
ARTICLE 1. THE CONTRACT OF EMPLOYMENT 489
ARTICLE 1.5. WORKER STATUS: EMPLOYEES 489
DIVISION 4: WORKERS' COMPENSATION AND INSURANCE 505
PART 1: SCOPE AND OPERATION 505
CHAPTER 2: EMPLOYERS, EMPLOYEES AND DEPENDENTS 505
ARTICLE 2: EMPLOYEES 505

PENAL CODE

PART 4: PREVENTION OF CRIMES AND APPREHENSION OF CRIMINALS 507
TITLE 1: INVESTIGATION AND CONTROL OF CRIMES AND CRIMINALS 507
CHAPTER 2: CONTROL OF CRIMES AND CRIMINALS 507
ARTICLE 2.5: CHILD ABUSE AND NEGLECT REPORTING ACT 507

CODE OF FEDERAL REGULATIONS

TITLE 16: COMMERCIAL PRACTICES 523
CHAPTER 1: FEDERAL TRADE COMMISSION 523
SUBCHAPTER C: REGULATIONS UNDER SPECIFIC ACTS OF CONGRESS . 523
PART 315. CONTACT LENS RULE 523
SUBCHAPTER D: TRADE REGULATION RULES 531
PART 456. OPHTHALMIC PRACTICE RULES (EYEGLASS RULE) 531

BUSINESS AND PROFESSIONS CODE

GENERAL PROVISIONS

6. CERTIFICATION UNDER REPEALED ACTS

All persons who, at the time this code goes into effect, are entitled to a certificate under any act repealed by this code, are thereby entitled to a certificate under the provisions of this code so far as the provisions of this code are applicable.

(Enacted by Stats. 1937, Ch. 399.)

7. CONVICTION UNDER REPEALED ACTS

Any conviction for a crime under any act repealed by this code, which crime is continued as a public offense by this code, constitutes a conviction under this code for any purpose for which it constituted a conviction under the act repealed.

(Enacted by Stats. 1937, Ch. 399.)

7.5. "CONVICTION"; WHEN AN ACTION BY BOARD FOLLOWING ESTABLISHMENT OF CONVICTION MAY BE TAKEN; PROHIBITION AGAINST DENIAL OF LICENSURE; APPLICATION OF SECTION

(a) A conviction within the meaning of this code means a judgment following a plea or verdict of guilty or a plea of nolo contendere or finding of guilt. Any action which a board is permitted to take following the establishment of a conviction may be taken when the time for appeal has elapsed, or the judgment of conviction has been affirmed on appeal or when an order granting probation is made suspending the imposition of sentence. However, a board may not deny a license to an applicant who is otherwise qualified pursuant to subdivision (b) or (c) of Section 480.

(b) (1) Nothing in this section shall apply to the licensure of persons pursuant to Chapter 4 (commencing with Section 6000) of Division 3.

(2) This section does not in any way modify or otherwise affect the existing authority of the following entities in regard to licensure:

(A) The State Athletic Commission.

(B) The Bureau for Private Postsecondary Education.

(C) The California Horse Racing Board.

(c) Except as provided in subdivision (b), this section controls over and supersedes the definition of conviction contained within individual practice acts under this code.

(d) This section shall become operative on July 1, 2020.

(Repealed and added by Stats. 2018, Ch. 995, Sec. 2. (AB 2138) Effective January 1, 2019. Section operative July 1, 2020, by its own provisions.)

12.5. VIOLATION OF REGULATION ADOPTED PURSUANT TO CODE PROVISION; ISSUANCE OF CITATION

Whenever in any provision of this code authority is granted to issue a citation for a violation of any provision of this code, that authority also includes the authority to issue a citation for the violation of any regulation adopted pursuant to any provision of this code.

(Added by Stats. 1986, Ch. 1379, Sec. 1.)

22. "BOARD"; "BUREAU"

"Board," as used in any provision of this code, refers to the board in which the administration of the provision is vested, and unless otherwise expressly provided, shall include "bureau," "commission," "committee," "department," "division," "examining committee," "program," and "agency."

(Amended by Stats. 2010, Ch. 670, Sec. 1. (AB 2130) Effective January 1, 2011.)

23. "DEPARTMENT"

"Department," unless otherwise defined, refers to the Department of Consumer Affairs.

Wherever the laws of this state refer to the Department of Professional and Vocational Standards, the reference shall be construed to be to the Department of Consumer Affairs.

(Amended by Stats. 1971, Ch. 716.)

23.5. "DIRECTOR"

"Director," unless otherwise defined, refers to the Director of Consumer Affairs.

Wherever the laws of this state refer to the Director of Professional and Vocational Standards, the reference shall be construed to be to the Director of Consumer Affairs.

(Amended by Stats. 1971, Ch. 716.)

23.6. "APPOINTING POWER"

"Appointing power," unless otherwise defined, refers to the Director of Consumer Affairs.

(Amended by Stats. 1971, Ch. 716.)

23.7. "LICENSE"

Unless otherwise expressly provided, "license" means license, certificate, registration, or other means to engage in a business or profession regulated by this code or referred to in Section 1000 or 3600.

(Added by Stats. 1994, Ch. 26, Sec. 1. Effective March 30, 1994.)

23.8. "LICENSEE"

"Licensee" means any person authorized by a license, certificate, registration, or other means to engage in a business or profession regulated by this code or referred to in Sections 1000 and 3600.

Any reference to licentiate in this code shall be deemed to refer to licensee.

(Amended by Stats. 2019, Ch. 351, Sec. 1. (AB 496) Effective January 1, 2020.)

24. SEVERABILITY PROVISION

If any provision of this code, or the application thereof, to any person or circumstance, is held invalid, the remainder of the code, or the application of such provision to other persons or circumstances, shall not be affected thereby.

(Enacted by Stats. 1937, Ch. 399.)

27. INFORMATION TO BE PROVIDED ON INTERNET; ENTITIES IN DEPARTMENT OF CONSUMER AFFAIRS REQUIRED TO COMPLY

(a) Each entity specified in subdivisions (c), (d), and (e) shall provide on the internet information regarding the status of every license issued by that entity in accordance with the California Public Records Act (Division 10 (commencing with Section 7920.000) of Title 1 of the Government Code) and the Information Practices Act of 1977 (Chapter 1 (commencing with Section 1798) of Title 1.8 of Part 4 of Division 3 of the Civil Code). The public information to be provided on the internet shall include information on suspensions and revocations of licenses issued by the entity and other related enforcement action, including accusations filed pursuant to the Administrative Procedure Act (Chapter 3.5 (commencing with Section 11340) of Part 1 of Division 3 of Title 2 of the Government Code) taken by the entity relative to persons, businesses, or facilities subject to licensure or regulation by the entity. The information may not include personal information, including home telephone number, date of birth, or social security number. Each entity shall disclose a licensee's address of record. However, each entity shall allow a licensee to provide a post office box number or other alternate address, instead of the licensee's home address, as the address of record. This section shall not preclude an entity from also requiring a licensee, who has provided a post office box number or other alternative mailing address as the licensee's address of record, to provide a physical business address or residence address only for the entity's internal administrative use and not for disclosure as the licensee's address of record or disclosure on the internet.

(b) In providing information on the internet, each entity specified in subdivisions (c) and (d) shall comply with the Department of Consumer Affairs' guidelines for access to public records.

(c) Each of the following entities within the Department of Consumer Affairs shall comply with the requirements of this section:

(1) The Board for Professional Engineers, Land Surveyors, and Geologists shall disclose information on its registrants and licensees.

(2) The Bureau of Automotive Repair shall disclose information on its licensees, including automotive repair dealers, smog check stations, smog check inspectors and repair technicians, and vehicle safety systems inspection stations and technicians.

(3) The Bureau of Household Goods and Services shall disclose information on its licensees, registrants, and permitholders.

(4) The Cemetery and Funeral Bureau shall disclose information on its licensees, including cemetery brokers, cemetery salespersons, cemetery managers, crematory managers, cemetery authorities, crematories, cremated remains disposers, embalmers, funeral establishments, and funeral directors.

(5) The Professional Fiduciaries Bureau shall disclose information on its licensees.

(6) The Contractors State License Board shall disclose information on its licensees and registrants in accordance with Chapter 9 (commencing with Section 7000) of Division 3. In addition to information related to licenses as specified in subdivision (a), the board shall also disclose information provided to the board by the Labor Commissioner pursuant to Section 98.9 of the Labor Code.

(7) The Bureau for Private Postsecondary Education shall disclose information on private postsecondary institutions under its jurisdiction, including disclosure of notices to comply issued pursuant to Section 94935 of the Education Code.

(8) The California Board of Accountancy shall disclose information on its licensees and registrants.

(9) The California Architects Board shall disclose information on its licensees, including architects and landscape architects.

(10) The State Athletic Commission shall disclose information on its licensees and registrants.

(11) The State Board of Barbering and Cosmetology shall disclose information on its licensees.

(12) The Acupuncture Board shall disclose information on its licensees.

(13) The Board of Behavioral Sciences shall disclose information on its licensees and registrants.

(14) The Dental Board of California shall disclose information on its licensees.

(15) The California State Board of Optometry shall disclose information on its licensees and registrants.

(16) The Board of Psychology shall disclose information on its licensees, including psychologists and registered psychological associates.

(17) The Veterinary Medical Board shall disclose information on its licensees, registrants, and permitholders.

(d) The State Board of Chiropractic Examiners shall disclose information on its licensees.

(e) The Structural Pest Control Board shall disclose information on its licensees, including applicators, field representatives, and operators in the areas of fumigation, general pest and wood destroying pests and organisms, and wood roof cleaning and treatment.

(f) "Internet" for the purposes of this section has the meaning set forth in paragraph (6) of subdivision (f) of Section 17538.

(Amended by Stats. 2023, Ch. 681, Sec. 1. (AB 1263) Effective January 1, 2024.)

29.5. ADDITIONAL QUALIFICATIONS FOR LICENSURE

In addition to other qualifications for licensure prescribed by the various acts of boards under the department, applicants for licensure and licensees renewing their licenses shall also comply with Section 17520 of the Family Code.

(Amended by Stats. 2003, Ch. 607, Sec. 1. Effective January 1, 2004.)

30. PROVISION OF FEDERAL EMPLOYER IDENTIFICATION NUMBER OR SOCIAL SECURITY NUMBER BY LICENSEE

(a) (1) Notwithstanding any other law, any board, as defined in Section 22, the State Bar of California, and the Department of Real Estate shall, at the time of issuance of the license, require that the applicant provide its federal employer identification number, if the applicant is a partnership, or the applicant's social security number for all other applicants.

(2) (A) In accordance with Section 135.5, a board, as defined in Section 22, the State Bar of California, and the Department of Real Estate shall require either the individual taxpayer identification number or social security number if the applicant is an individual for a license or certificate, as defined in subparagraph (2) of subdivision (e), and for purposes of this subdivision.

(B) In implementing the requirements of subparagraph (A), a licensing board shall not require an individual to disclose either citizenship status or immigration status for purposes of licensure.

(C) A licensing board shall not deny licensure to an otherwise qualified and eligible individual based solely on the individual's citizenship status or immigration status.

(D) The Legislature finds and declares that the requirements of this subdivision are consistent with subsection (d) of Section 1621 of Title 8 of the United States Code.

(b) A licensee failing to provide the federal employer identification number, or the individual taxpayer identification number or social security number shall be reported by the licensing board to the

Franchise Tax Board. If the licensee fails to provide that information after notification pursuant to paragraph (1) of subdivision (b) of Section 19528 of the Revenue and Taxation Code, the licensee shall be subject to the penalty provided in paragraph (2) of subdivision (b) of Section 19528 of the Revenue and Taxation Code.

(c) In addition to the penalty specified in subdivision (b), a licensing board shall not process an application for an initial license unless the applicant provides its federal employer identification number, or individual taxpayer identification number or social security number where requested on the application.

(d) A licensing board shall, upon request of the Franchise Tax Board or the Employment Development Department, furnish to the board or the department, as applicable, the following information with respect to every licensee:

(1) Name.

(2) Address or addresses of record.

(3) Federal employer identification number if the licensee is a partnership, or the licensee's individual taxpayer identification number or social security number for all other licensees.

(4) Type of license.

(5) Effective date of license or a renewal.

(6) Expiration date of license.

(7) Whether license is active or inactive, if known.

(8) Whether license is new or a renewal.

(e) For the purposes of this section:

(1) "Licensee" means a person or entity, other than a corporation, authorized by a license, certificate, registration, or other means to engage in a business or profession regulated by this code or referred to in Section 1000 or 3600.

(2) "License" includes a certificate, registration, or any other authorization needed to engage in a business or profession regulated by this code or referred to in Section 1000 or 3600.

(3) "Licensing board" means any board, as defined in Section 22, the State Bar of California, and the Department of Real Estate.

(f) The reports required under this section shall be filed on magnetic media or in other machine-readable form, according to standards furnished by the Franchise Tax Board or the Employment Development Department, as applicable.

(g) Licensing boards shall provide to the Franchise Tax Board or the Employment Development Department the information required by this section at a time that the board or the department, as applicable, may require.

(h) Notwithstanding Chapter 3.5 (commencing with Section 6250) of Division 7 of Title 1 of the Government Code, a federal employer identification number, individual taxpayer identification number, or social security number furnished pursuant to this section shall not be deemed to be a public record and shall not be open to the public for inspection.

(i) A deputy, agent, clerk, officer, or employee of a licensing board described in subdivision (a), or any former officer or employee or other individual who, in the course of their employment or duty, has or has had access to the information required to be furnished under this section, shall not disclose or make known in any manner that information, except as provided pursuant to this section, to the Franchise Tax Board, the Employment Development Department, the Office of the Chancellor of the California Community Colleges, a collections agency contracted to collect funds owed to the State Bar by licensees pursuant to Sections 6086.10 and 6140.5, or as provided in subdivisions (j) and (k).

(j) It is the intent of the Legislature in enacting this section to utilize the federal employer identification number, individual taxpayer identification number, or social security number for the purpose of establishing the identification of persons affected by state tax laws, for purposes of compliance with Section 17520 of the Family Code, for purposes of measuring employment outcomes of students who participate in career technical education programs offered by the California Community Colleges, and for purposes of collecting funds owed to the State Bar by licensees pursuant to Section 6086.10 and Section 6140.5 and, to that end, the information furnished pursuant to this section shall be used exclusively for those purposes.

(k) If the board utilizes a national examination to issue a license, and if a reciprocity agreement or comity exists between the State of California and the state requesting release of the individual taxpayer identification number or social security number, any deputy, agent, clerk, officer, or employee of any licensing board described in subdivision (a) may release an individual taxpayer identification number or social security number to an examination or licensing entity, only for the purpose of verification of licensure or examination status.

(l) For the purposes of enforcement of Section 17520 of the Family Code, and notwithstanding any other law, a board, as defined in Section 22, the State Bar of California, and the Department of Real Estate shall at the time of issuance of the license require that each licensee provide the individual taxpayer identification number or social security number of each individual listed on the license and any person who qualifies for the license. For the purposes of this subdivision, "licensee" means an entity that is issued a license by any board, as defined in Section 22, the State Bar of California, the Department of Real Estate, and the Department of Motor Vehicles.

(m) The department shall, upon request by the Office of the Chancellor of the California Community Colleges, furnish to the chancellor's office, as applicable, the following information with respect to every licensee:

(1) Name.

(2) Federal employer identification number if the licensee is a partnership, or the licensee's individual taxpayer identification number or social security number for all other licensees.

(3) Date of birth.

(4) Type of license.

(5) Effective date of license or a renewal.

(6) Expiration date of license.

(n) The department shall make available information pursuant to subdivision (m) only to allow the chancellor's office to measure employment outcomes of students who participate in career technical education programs offered by the California Community Colleges and recommend how these programs may be improved. Licensure information made available by the department pursuant to this section shall not be used for any other purpose.

(o) The department may make available information pursuant to subdivision (m) only to the extent that making the information available complies with state and federal privacy laws.

(p) The department may, by agreement, condition or limit the availability of licensure information pursuant to subdivision (m) in order to ensure the security of the information and to protect the privacy rights of the individuals to whom the information pertains.

(q) All of the following apply to the licensure information made available pursuant to subdivision (m):

(1) It shall be limited to only the information necessary to accomplish the purpose authorized in subdivision (n).

(2) It shall not be used in a manner that permits third parties to personally identify the individual or individuals to whom the information pertains.

(3) Except as provided in subdivision (n), it shall not be shared with or transmitted to any other party or entity without the consent of the individual or individuals to whom the information pertains.

(4) It shall be protected by reasonable security procedures and practices appropriate to the nature of the information to protect that information from unauthorized access, destruction, use, modification, or disclosure.

(5) It shall be immediately and securely destroyed when no longer needed for the purpose authorized in subdivision (n).

(r) The department or the chancellor's office may share licensure information with a third party who contracts to perform the function described in subdivision (n), if the third party is required by contract to follow the requirements of this section.

(Amended by Stats. 2019, Ch. 351, Sec. 6. (AB 496) Effective January 1, 2020.)

31. COMPLIANCE WITH JUDGMENT OF ORDER FOR SUPPORT UPON ISSUANCE OR RENEWAL OF LICENSE

(a) As used in this section, "board" means any entity listed in Section 101, the entities referred to in Sections 1000 and 3600, the State Bar, the Department of Real Estate, and any other state agency that issues a license, certificate, or registration authorizing a person to engage in a business or profession.

(b) Each applicant for the issuance or renewal of a license, certificate, registration, or other means to engage in a business or profession regulated by a board who is not in compliance with a judgment or order for support shall be subject to Section 17520 of the Family Code.

(c) "Compliance with a judgment or order for support" has the meaning given in paragraph (4) of subdivision (a) of Section 17520 of the Family Code.

(d) Each licensee or applicant whose name appears on a list of the 500 largest tax delinquencies pursuant to Section 7063 or 19195 of the Revenue and Taxation Code shall be subject to Section 494.5.

(e) Each application for a new license or renewal of a license shall indicate on the application that the law allows the California Department of Tax and Fee Administration and the Franchise Tax Board to share taxpayer information with a board and requires the licensee to pay the licensee's state tax obligation and that the licensee's license may be suspended if the state tax obligation is not paid.

(f) For purposes of this section, "tax obligation" means the tax imposed under, or in accordance with, Part 1 (commencing with Section 6001), Part 1.5 (commencing with Section 7200), Part 1.6 (commencing with Section 7251), Part 1.7 (commencing with Section 7280), Part 10 (commencing with Section 17001), or Part 11 (commencing with Section 23001) of Division 2 of the Revenue and Taxation Code.

(Amended by Stats. 2019, Ch. 351, Sec. 7. (AB 496) Effective January 1, 2020.)

35. PROVISIONS IN RULES AND REGULATIONS FOR EVALUATION EXPERIENCE OBTAINED IN THE ARMED SERVICES

It is the policy of this state that, consistent with the provision of high-quality services, persons with skills, knowledge, and experience obtained in the armed services of the United States should be permitted to apply this learning and contribute to the employment needs of the state at the maximum level of responsibility and skill for which they are qualified. To this end, rules and regulations of boards provided for in this code shall provide for methods of evaluating education, training, and experience obtained in the armed services, if applicable to the requirements of the business, occupation, or profession regulated. These rules and regulations shall also specify how this education, training, and experience may be used to meet the licensure requirements for the particular business, occupation, or profession regulated. Each board shall consult with the Department of Veterans Affairs and the Military Department before adopting these rules and regulations.

Each board shall perform the duties required by this section within existing budgetary resources of the agency within which the board operates.

(Amended by Stats. 2010, Ch. 214, Sec. 1. (AB 2783) Effective January 1, 2011.)

40. EXPERT CONSULTANT AGREEMENTS

(a) Subject to the standards described in Section 19130 of the Government Code, any board, as defined in Section 22, the State Board of Chiropractic Examiners, or the Osteopathic Medical Board of California may enter into an agreement with an expert consultant to do any of the following:

(1) Provide an expert opinion on enforcement-related matters, including providing testimony at an administrative hearing.

(2) Assist the board as a subject matter expert in examination development, examination validation, or occupational analyses.

(3) Evaluate the mental or physical health of a licensee or an applicant for a license as may be necessary to protect the public health and safety.

(b) An executed contract between a board and an expert consultant shall be exempt from the provisions of Part 2 (commencing with Section 10100) of Division 2 of the Public Contract Code.

(c) Each board shall establish policies and procedures for the selection and use of expert consultants.

(d) Nothing in this section shall be construed to expand the scope of practice of an expert consultant providing services pursuant to this section.

(Added by Stats. 2011, Ch. 339, Sec. 1. (SB 541) Effective September 26, 2011.)

DIVISION 1: DEPARTMENT OF CONSUMER AFFAIRS

CHAPTER 1: THE DEPARTMENT

100. ESTABLISHMENT

There is in the state government, in the Business, Consumer Services, and Housing Agency, a Department of Consumer Affairs.

(Amended by Stats. 2012, Ch. 147, Sec. 1. (SB 1039) Effective January 1, 2013. Operative July 1, 2013, by Sec. 23 of Ch. 147.)

101. COMPOSITION OF DEPARTMENT

The department is comprised of the following:

(a) The Dental Board of California.

(b) The Medical Board of California.

(c) The California State Board of Optometry.

(d) The California State Board of Pharmacy.

(e) The Veterinary Medical Board.

(f) The California Board of Accountancy.

(g) The California Architects Board.

(h) The State Board of Barbering and Cosmetology.

(i) The Board for Professional Engineers, Land Surveyors, and Geologists.

(j) The Contractors State License Board.

(k) The Bureau for Private Postsecondary Education.

(l) The Bureau of Household Goods and Services.

(m) The Board of Registered Nursing.

(n) The Board of Behavioral Sciences.

(o) The State Athletic Commission.

(p) The Cemetery and Funeral Bureau.

(q) The Bureau of Security and Investigative Services.

(r) The Court Reporters Board of California.

(s) The Board of Vocational Nursing and Psychiatric Technicians.

(t) The Landscape Architects Technical Committee.

(u) The Division of Investigation.

(v) The Bureau of Automotive Repair.

(w) The Respiratory Care Board of California.

(x) The Acupuncture Board.

(y) The Board of Psychology.

(z) The Podiatric Medical Board of California.

(aa) The Physical Therapy Board of California.

(ab) The Arbitration Review Program.

(ac) The Physician Assistant Board.

(ad) The Speech-Language Pathology and Audiology and Hearing Aid Dispensers Board.

(ae) The California Board of Occupational Therapy.

(af) The Osteopathic Medical Board of California.

(ag) The California Board of Naturopathic Medicine.

(ah) The Dental Hygiene Board of California.

(ai) The Professional Fiduciaries Bureau.

(aj) The State Board of Chiropractic Examiners.

(ak) The Bureau of Real Estate Appraisers.

(al) The Structural Pest Control Board.

(am) Any other boards, offices, or officers subject to its jurisdiction by law.

(Amended by Stats. 2022, Ch. 414, Sec. 1. (AB 2685) Effective January 1, 2023.)

101.6. PURPOSE

The boards, bureaus, and commissions in the department are established for the purpose of ensuring that those private businesses and professions deemed to engage in activities which have potential impact upon the public health, safety, and welfare are adequately regulated in order to protect the people of California.

To this end, they establish minimum qualifications and levels of competency and license persons desiring to engage in the occupations they regulate upon determining that such persons possess the requisite skills and qualifications necessary to provide safe and effective services to the public, or register or otherwise certify persons in order to identify practitioners and ensure performance according to set and accepted professional standards. They provide a means for redress of grievances by investigating allegations of unprofessional conduct, incompetence, fraudulent action, or unlawful activity brought to their attention by members of the public and institute disciplinary action against persons licensed or registered under the provisions of this code when such action is warranted. In addition, they conduct periodic checks of licensees, registrants, or otherwise certified persons in order to ensure compliance with the relevant sections of this code.

(Added by Stats. 1980, Ch. 375, Sec. 1.)

101.7. MEETING OF BOARDS; REGULAR AND SPECIAL

(a) Notwithstanding any other provision of law, boards shall meet at least two times each calendar year. Boards shall meet at least once each calendar year in northern California and once each calendar year in southern California in order to facilitate participation by the public and its licensees.

(b) The director has discretion to exempt any board from the requirement in subdivision (a) upon a showing of good cause that the board is not able to meet at least two times in a calendar year.

(c) The director may call for a special meeting of the board when a board is not fulfilling its duties.

(d) An agency within the department that is required to provide a written notice pursuant to subdivision (a) of Section 11125 of the Government Code, may provide that notice by regular mail, email, or by both regular mail and email. An agency shall give a person who requests a notice the option of receiving the notice by regular mail, email, or by both regular mail and email. The agency shall comply with the requester's chosen form or forms of notice.

(e) An agency that plans to webcast a meeting shall include in the meeting notice required pursuant to subdivision (a) of Section 11125 of the Government Code a statement of the board's intent to webcast the meeting. An agency may webcast a meeting even if the agency fails to include that statement of intent in the notice.

(Amended by Stats. 2019, Ch. 351, Sec. 9. (AB 496) Effective January 1, 2020.)

102.3. INTERAGENCY AGREEMENT TO DELEGATE DUTIES TO CERTAIN REPEALED BOARDS; TECHNICAL COMMITTEES FOR REGULATION OF PROFESSIONS UNDER DELEGATED AUTHORITY; RENEWAL OF AGREEMENT

(a) The director may enter into an interagency agreement with an appropriate entity within the Department of Consumer Affairs as provided for in Section 101 to delegate the duties, powers, purposes, responsibilities, and jurisdiction that have been succeeded and vested with the department, of a board, as defined in Section 477, which became inoperative and was repealed in accordance with Chapter 908 of the Statutes of 1994.

(b) (1) Where, pursuant to subdivision (a), an interagency agreement is entered into between the director and that entity, the entity receiving the delegation of authority may establish a technical committee to regulate, as directed by the entity, the profession subject to the authority that has been delegated. The entity may delegate to the technical committee only those powers that it received pursuant to the interagency agreement with the director. The technical committee shall have only those powers that have been delegated to it by the entity.

(2) Where the entity delegates its authority to adopt, amend, or repeal regulations to the technical committee, all regulations adopted, amended, or repealed by the technical committee shall be subject to the review and approval of the entity.

(3) The entity shall not delegate to a technical committee its authority to discipline a licensee who has violated the provisions of the applicable chapter of the Business and Professions Code that is subject to the director's delegation of authority to the entity.

(c) An interagency agreement entered into, pursuant to subdivision (a), shall continue until such time as the licensing program administered by the technical committee has undergone a review by the Assembly Committee on Business and Professions and the Senate Committee on Business, Professions and Economic Development to evaluate and determine whether the licensing program has demonstrated a public need for its continued existence. Thereafter, at the director's discretion, the interagency agreement may be renewed.

(Amended by Stats. 2019, Ch. 351, Sec. 10. (AB 496) Effective January 1, 2020.)

103. COMPENSATION AND REIMBURSEMENT FOR EXPENSES

Each member of a board, commission, or committee created in the various chapters of Division 2 (commencing with Section 500) and Division 3 (commencing with Section 5000), and in Chapter 2 (commencing with Section 18600) and Chapter 3 (commencing with Section 19000) of Division 8, shall receive the moneys specified in this section when authorized by the respective provisions.

Each such member shall receive a per diem of one hundred dollars ($100) for each day actually spent in the discharge of official duties, and shall be reimbursed for traveling and other expenses necessarily incurred in the performance of official duties.

The payments in each instance shall be made only from the fund from which the expenses of the agency are paid and shall be subject to the availability of money.

Notwithstanding any other provision of law, no public officer or employee shall receive per diem salary compensation for serving on those boards, commissions, or committees on any day when the officer or employee also received compensation for the officer or employee's regular public employment.

(Amended by Stats. 2019, Ch. 351, Sec. 11. (AB 496) Effective January 1, 2020.)

104. DISPLAY OF LICENSES OR REGISTRATIONS

All boards or other regulatory entities within the department's jurisdiction that the department determines to be health-related may adopt regulations to require licensees to display their licenses or registrations in the locality in which they are treating patients, and to inform patients as to the identity of the regulatory agency they may contact if they have any questions or complaints regarding the licensee. In complying with this requirement, those boards may take into consideration the particular settings in which licensees practice, or other circumstances which may make the displaying or providing of information to the consumer extremely difficult for the licensee in their particular type of practice.

(Added by Stats. 1998, Ch. 991, Sec. 1. Effective January 1, 1999.)

105. OATH OF OFFICE

Members of boards in the department shall take an oath of office as provided in the Constitution and the Government Code.

(Added by Stats. 1949, Ch. 829.)

105.5. TENURE OF MEMBERS OF BOARDS ETC., WITHIN THE DEPARTMENT

Notwithstanding any other provision of this code, each member of a board, commission, examining committee, or other similarly constituted agency within the department shall hold office until the appointment and qualification of that member's successor or until one year shall have elapsed since the expiration of the term for which the member was appointed, whichever first occurs.

(Amended by Stats. 2019, Ch. 351, Sec. 12. (AB 496) Effective January 1, 2020.)

106. REMOVAL OF BOARD MEMBERS

The appointing authority has power to remove from office at any time any member of any board appointed by the appointing authority for continued neglect of duties required by law, or for incompetence, or unprofessional or dishonorable conduct. Nothing in this section shall be construed as a limitation or restriction on the power of the appointing authority conferred on the appointing authority by any other provision of law to remove any member of any board.

(Amended by Stats. 2019, Ch. 351, Sec. 13. (AB 496) Effective January 1, 2020.)

106.5. REMOVAL OF MEMBER OF LICENSING BOARD FOR DISCLOSURE OF EXAMINATION INFORMATION

Notwithstanding any other provision of law, the Governor may remove from office a member of a board or other licensing entity in the department if it is shown that such member has knowledge of the specific questions to be asked on the licensing entity's next examination and directly or indirectly discloses any such question or questions in advance of or during the examination to any applicant for that examination.

The proceedings for removal shall be conducted in accordance with the provisions of Chapter 5 of Part 1 of Division 3 of Title 2 of the Government Code, and the Governor shall have all the powers granted therein.

(Added by Stats. 1977, Ch. 482.)

107. EXECUTIVE OFFICERS

Pursuant to subdivision (e) of Section 4 of Article VII of the California Constitution, each board may appoint a person exempt from civil service, who shall be designated as an executive officer unless the licensing act of the particular board designates the person as a registrar, and may fix that person's salary, with the approval of the Department of Human Resources pursuant to Section 19825 of the Government Code.

(Amended by Stats. 2020, Ch. 370, Sec. 1. (SB 1371) Effective January 1, 2021.)

107.5. OFFICIAL SEALS

If any board in the department uses an official seal pursuant to any provision of this code, the seal shall contain the words "State of California" and "Department of Consumer Affairs" in addition to the title of the board, and shall be in a form approved by the director.

(Amended by Stats. 1971, Ch. 716.)

108. STATUS AND POWERS OF BOARDS

Each of the boards comprising the department exists as a separate unit, and has the functions of setting standards, holding meetings, and setting dates thereof, preparing and conducting examinations, passing upon applicants, conducting investigations of violations of laws under its jurisdiction, issuing citations and holding hearings for the revocation of licenses, and the imposing of penalties following those hearings, insofar as these powers are given by statute to each respective board.

(Amended by Stats. 2008, Ch. 179, Sec. 1. Effective January 1, 2009.)

108.5. WITNESS FEES AND EXPENSES

In any investigation, proceeding, or hearing that any board, commission, or officer in the department is empowered to institute, conduct, or hold, any witness appearing at the investigation, proceeding, or hearing whether upon a subpoena or voluntarily, may be paid the sum of twelve dollars ($12) per day for every day in actual attendance at the investigation, proceeding, or hearing and for the witness's actual, necessary, and reasonable expenses and those sums shall be a legal charge against the funds of the respective board, commission, or officer; provided further, that no witness appearing other than at the instance of the board, commission, or officer may be compensated out of the fund.

The board, commission, or officer shall determine the sums due to any witness and enter the amount on its minutes.

(Amended by Stats. 2019, Ch. 351, Sec. 15. (AB 496) Effective January 1, 2020.)

109. REVIEW OF DECISIONS; INVESTIGATIONS

(a) The decisions of any of the boards comprising the department with respect to setting standards, conducting examinations, passing candidates, and revoking licenses, are not subject to review by the director, but are final within the limits provided by this code which are applicable to the particular board, except as provided in this section.

(b) The director may initiate an investigation of any allegations of misconduct in the preparation, administration, or scoring of an examination which is administered by a board, or in the review of qualifications which are a part of the licensing process of any board. A request for investigation shall be made by the director to the Division of Investigation through the chief of the division or to any law enforcement agency in the jurisdiction where the alleged misconduct occurred.

(c) The director may intervene in any matter of any board where an investigation by the Division of Investigation discloses probable cause to believe that the conduct or activity of a board, or its members or employees constitutes a violation of criminal law.

The term "intervene," as used in paragraph (c) of this section may include, but is not limited to, an application for a restraining order or injunctive relief as specified in Section 123.5, or a referral or request for criminal prosecution. For purposes of this section, the director shall be deemed to have standing under Section 123.5 and shall seek representation of the Attorney General, or other appropriate counsel in the event of a conflict in pursuing that action.

(Amended by Stats. 1991, Ch. 1013, Sec. 1.)

110. RECORDS AND PROPERTY

The department shall have possession and control of all records, books, papers, offices, equipment, supplies, funds, appropriations, land and other property—real or personal—now or hereafter held for the benefit or use of all of the bodies, offices or officers comprising the department. The title to all property held by any of these bodies, offices or officers for the use and benefit of the state, is vested in the State of California to be held in the possession of the department.

Except as authorized by a board, the department shall not have the possession and control of examination questions prior to submission to applicants at scheduled examinations.

(Amended by Stats. 1996, Ch. 829, Sec. 1. Effective January 1, 1997.)

111. COMMISSIONERS ON EXAMINATION

Unless otherwise expressly provided, any board may, with the approval of the appointing power, appoint qualified persons, who shall be designated as commissioners on examination, to give the whole or any portion of any examination. A commissioner on examination need not be a member of the board but shall have the same qualifications as one and shall be subject to the same rules.

(Amended by Stats. 2019, Ch. 351, Sec. 16. (AB 496) Effective January 1, 2020.)

112. PUBLICATION AND SALE OF DIRECTORIES OF AUTHORIZED PERSONS

Notwithstanding any other provision of this code, no agency in the department, with the exception of the Board for Professional Engineers and Land Surveyors, shall be required to compile, publish, sell, or otherwise distribute a directory. When an agency deems it necessary to compile and publish a directory, the agency shall cooperate with the director in determining its form and content, the time and frequency of its publication, the persons to whom it is to be sold or otherwise distributed, and its price if it is sold. Any agency that requires the approval of the director for the compilation, publication, or distribution of a directory, under the law in effect at the time the amendment made to this section at the 1970 Regular Session of the Legislature becomes effective, shall continue to require that approval. As used in this section, "directory" means a directory, roster, register, or similar compilation of the names of persons who hold a license, certificate, permit, registration, or similar indicia of authority from the agency.

(Amended by Stats. 1998, Ch. 59, Sec. 3. Effective January 1, 1999.)

113. CONFERENCES; TRAVELING EXPENSES

Upon recommendation of the director, officers, and employees of the department, and the officers, members, and employees of the boards, committees, and commissions comprising it or subject to its jurisdiction may confer, in this state or elsewhere, with officers or employees of this state, its political subdivisions, other states, or the United States, or with other persons, associations, or organizations as may be of assistance to the department, board, committee, or commission in the conduct of its work. The officers, members, and employees shall be entitled to their actual traveling expenses incurred in pursuance hereof, but when these expenses are incurred with respect to travel outside of the state, they shall be subject to the approval of the Governor and the Director of Finance.

(Amended by Stats. 2001, Ch. 159, Sec. 2. Effective January 1, 2002.)

114. REINSTATEMENT OF EXPIRED LICENSE OF LICENSEE SERVING IN MILITARY

(a) Notwithstanding any other provision of this code, any licensee or registrant of any board, commission, or bureau within the department whose license expired while the licensee or registrant was on active duty as a member of the California National Guard or the United States Armed Forces, may, upon application, reinstate their license or registration without examination or penalty, provided that all of the following requirements are satisfied:

(1) The licensee or registrant's license or registration was valid at the time they entered the California National Guard or the United States Armed Forces.

(2) The application for reinstatement is made while serving in the California National Guard or the United States Armed Forces, or not later than one year from the date of discharge from active service or return to inactive military status.

(3) The application for reinstatement is accompanied by an affidavit showing the date of entrance into the service, whether still in the service, or date of discharge, and the renewal fee for the current renewal period in which the application is filed is paid.

(b) If application for reinstatement is filed more than one year after discharge or return to inactive status, the applicant, in the discretion of the licensing agency, may be required to pass an examination.

(c) If application for reinstatement is filed and the licensing agency determines that the applicant has not actively engaged in the practice of the applicant's profession while on active duty, then the licensing agency may require the applicant to pass an examination.

(d) Unless otherwise specifically provided in this code, any licensee or registrant who, either part time or full time, practices in this state the profession or vocation for which the licensee or registrant is licensed or registered shall be required to maintain their license in good standing even though the licensee or registrant is in military service.

For the purposes in this section, time spent by a licensee in receiving treatment or hospitalization in any veterans' facility during which the licensee is prevented from practicing the licensee's profession or vocation shall be excluded from said period of one year.

(Amended by Stats. 2019, Ch. 351, Sec. 17. (AB 496) Effective January 1, 2020.)

114.3. WAIVER OF FEES AND REQUIREMENTS FOR ACTIVE DUTY MEMBERS OF ARMED FORCES AND NATIONAL GUARD

(a) Notwithstanding any other law, every board, as defined in Section 22, within the department shall waive the renewal fees, continuing education requirements, and other renewal requirements as determined by the board, if any are applicable, for a licensee or registrant called to active duty as a member of the United States Armed Forces or the California National Guard if all of the following requirements are met:

(1) The licensee or registrant possessed a current and valid license with the board at the time the licensee or registrant was called to active duty.

(2) The renewal requirements are waived only for the period during which the licensee or registrant is on active duty service.

(3) Written documentation that substantiates the licensee or registrant's active duty service is provided to the board.

(b) For purposes of this section, the phrase "called to active duty" shall have the same meaning as "active duty" as defined in Section 101 of Title 10 of the United States Code and shall additionally include individuals who are on active duty in the California National Guard, whether due to proclamation of a state of insurrection pursuant to Section 143 of the Military and Veterans Code or due to a proclamation of a state extreme emergency or when the California National Guard is otherwise on active duty pursuant to Section 146 of the Military and Veterans Code.

(c) (1) Except as specified in paragraph (2), the licensee or registrant shall not engage in any activities requiring a license during the period that the waivers provided by this section are in effect.

(2) If the licensee or registrant will provide services for which the licensee or registrant is licensed while on active duty, the board shall convert the license status to military active and no private practice of any type shall be permitted.

(d) In order to engage in any activities for which the licensee or registrant is licensed once discharged from active duty, the licensee or registrant shall meet all necessary renewal requirements as determined by the board within six months from the licensee's or registrant's date of discharge from active duty service.

(e) After a licensee or registrant receives notice of the licensee or registrant's discharge date, the licensee or registrant shall notify the board of their discharge from active duty within 60 days of receiving their notice of discharge.

(f) A board may adopt regulations to carry out the provisions of this section.

(g) This section shall not apply to any board that has a similar license renewal waiver process statutorily authorized for that board.

(Amended by Stats. 2022, Ch. 386, Sec. 1. (SB 1237) Effective January 1, 2023.)

115. APPLICABILITY OF SECTION 1

The provisions of Section 114 of this code are also applicable to a licensee or registrant whose license or registration was obtained while in the armed services.

(Added by Stats. 1951, Ch. 1577.)

115.4. EXPEDITION OF LICENSURE PROCESS FOR ACTIVE DUTY MEMBERS OF THE U.S. ARMED FORCES

(a) Notwithstanding any other law, on and after July 1, 2016, a board within the department shall expedite, and may assist, the initial licensure process for an applicant who supplies satisfactory evidence to the board that the applicant has served as an active duty member of the Armed Forces of the United States and was honorably discharged.

(b) Notwithstanding any other law, on and after July 1, 2024, a board within the department shall expedite, and may assist, the initial licensure process for an applicant who supplies satisfactory evidence to the board that the applicant is an active duty member of a regular component of the Armed Forces of the United States enrolled in the United States Department of Defense SkillBridge program as authorized under Section 1143(e) of Title 10 of the United States Code.

(c) A board may adopt regulations necessary to administer this section in accordance with the provisions of Chapter 3.5 (commencing with Section 11340) of Part 1 of Division 3 of Title 2 of the Government Code.

(Amended by Stats. 2023, Ch. 348, Sec. 1. (AB 883) Effective January 1, 2024.)

115.5. EXPEDITION OF LICENSURE PROCESS FOR SPOUSES AND DOMESTIC PARTNERS OF ACTIVE DUTY MEMBER OF THE U.S. ARMED FORCES

(a) A board within the department shall expedite the licensure process and waive the licensure application fee and the initial or original license fee charged by the board for an applicant who meets both of the following requirements:

(1) Supplies evidence satisfactory to the board that the applicant is married to, or in a domestic partnership or other legal union with, an active duty

member of the Armed Forces of the United States who is assigned to a duty station in this state under official active duty military orders.

(2) Holds a current license in another state, district, or territory of the United States in the profession or vocation for which the applicant seeks a license from the board.

(b) A board may adopt regulations necessary to administer this section.

(c) This section shall become operative on July 1, 2022.

(Repealed (in Sec. 1) and added by Stats. 2021, Ch. 367, Sec. 2. (SB 607) Effective January 1, 2022. Operative July 1, 2022, by its own provisions.)

115.6. TEMPORARY LICENSES

(a) (1) Except as provided in subdivision (j), a board within the department shall, after appropriate investigation, issue a temporary license to practice a profession or vocation to an applicant who meets the requirements set forth in subdivisions (c) and (d).

(2) Revenues from fees for temporary licenses issued by the California Board of Accountancy shall be credited to the Accountancy Fund in accordance with Section 5132.

(b) The board may conduct an investigation of an applicant for purposes of denying or revoking a temporary license issued pursuant to this section. This investigation may include a criminal background check.

(c) An applicant seeking a temporary license pursuant to this section shall meet the following requirements:

(1) The applicant shall supply evidence satisfactory to the board that the applicant is married to, or in a domestic partnership or other legal union with, an active duty member of the Armed Forces of the United States who is assigned to a duty station in this state under official active duty military orders.

(2) The applicant shall hold a current, active, and unrestricted license that confers upon the applicant the authority to practice, in another state, district, or territory of the United States, the profession or vocation within the same scope for which the applicant seeks a temporary license from the board.

(3) The applicant shall submit an application to the board that shall include a signed affidavit attesting to the fact that the applicant meets all of the requirements for the temporary license, and that the information submitted in the application is accurate, to the best of the applicant's knowledge. The application shall also include written verification from the applicant's original licensing jurisdiction stating that the applicant's license is in good standing in that jurisdiction.

(4) The applicant shall not have committed an act in any jurisdiction that would have constituted grounds for denial, suspension, or revocation of the license under this code at the time the act was committed. A violation of this paragraph may be grounds for the denial or revocation of a temporary license issued by the board.

(5) The applicant shall not have been disciplined by a licensing entity in another jurisdiction and shall not be the subject of an unresolved complaint, review procedure, or disciplinary proceeding conducted by a licensing entity in another jurisdiction.

(6) (A) The applicant shall, upon request by a board, furnish a full set of fingerprints for purposes of conducting a criminal background check.

(B) The board shall request a fingerprint-based criminal history information check from the Department of Justice in accordance with subdivision (u) of Section 11105 of the Penal Code and the Department of Justice shall furnish state or federal criminal history information in accordance with subdivision (p) of Section 11105 of the Penal Code.

(d) The applicant shall pass a California law and ethics examination if otherwise required by the board for the profession or vocation for which the applicant seeks licensure.

(e) Except as specified in subdivision (g), a board shall issue a temporary license pursuant to this section within 30 days of receiving documentation that the applicant has met the requirements specified in subdivisions (c) and (d) if the results of the criminal background check do not show grounds for denial.

(f) (1) A temporary license issued pursuant to this section may be immediately terminated upon a finding that the temporary licenseholder failed to meet any of the requirements described in subdivision (c) or (d) or provided substantively inaccurate information that would affect the person's eligibility for temporary licensure. Upon termination of the temporary license, the board shall issue a notice of termination that shall require the temporary licenseholder to immediately cease the practice of the licensed profession upon receipt.

(2) Notwithstanding any other law, if, after notice and an opportunity to be heard, a board finds that a temporary licenseholder engaged in unprofessional conduct or any other act that is a cause for discipline by the board, the board shall revoke the temporary license.

(g) An applicant seeking a temporary license as a civil engineer, geotechnical engineer, structural engineer, land surveyor, professional geologist, professional geophysicist, certified engineering geologist, or certified hydrogeologist pursuant to this section shall successfully pass the appropriate California-specific examination or examinations required for licensure in those respective professions by the Board for Professional Engineers, Land Surveyors, and Geologists. The board shall issue a temporary license pursuant to this subdivision within 30 days of receiving documentation that the applicant has met the requirements specified in this subdivision and subdivisions (c) and (d) if the results of the criminal background check do not show grounds for denial.

(h) A temporary license issued pursuant to this section is nonrenewable and shall expire 12 months after issuance, upon issuance or denial of a standard license, upon issuance or denial of a license by endorsement, or upon issuance or denial of an expedited license pursuant to Section 115.5, whichever occurs first.

(i) A board shall submit to the department for approval, if necessary to implement this section, draft regulations necessary to administer this section. These regulations shall be adopted pursuant to the Administrative Procedure Act (Chapter 3.5 (commencing with Section 11340) of Part 1 of Division 3 of Title 2 of the Government Code).

(j) (1) This section shall not apply to a board that has a process in place by which an out-of-state licensed applicant in good standing who is married to, or in a domestic partnership or other legal union with, an active duty member of the Armed Forces of the United States is able to receive expedited, temporary authorization to practice while meeting state-specific requirements for a period of at least one year or is able to receive an expedited license by endorsement with no additional requirements superseding those described in subdivisions (c) and (d).

(2) This section shall apply only to the extent that it does not amend an initiative or violate constitutional requirements.

(k) This section shall become operative on July 1, 2023.

(Repealed (in Sec. 1) and added by Stats. 2021, Ch. 693, Sec. 2. (AB 107) Effective

January 1, 2022. Operative July 1, 2023, by its own provisions.)

115.8. MILITARY AND SPOUSE LICENSURE

The Department of Consumer Affairs shall compile information on military and spouse licensure into an annual report for the Legislature, which shall be submitted in conformance with Section 9795 of the Government Code. The report shall include all of the following for each license type of each board:

(a) The number of applications for a temporary license submitted by military spouses per fiscal year, pursuant to Section 115.6.

(b) The number of applications for expedited licenses received from honorably discharged military members and military spouses pursuant to Sections 115.4 and 115.5.

(c) The number of licenses issued and denied per fiscal year pursuant to Sections 115.4, 115.5, and 115.6.

(d) The number of licenses issued pursuant to Section 115.6 that were suspended or revoked per fiscal year.

(e) The number of applications for waived renewal fees received and granted pursuant to Section 114.3 per fiscal year.

(f) The average length of time between application and issuance of licenses pursuant to Sections 115.4, 115.5, and 115.6.

(Amended by Stats. 2023, Ch. 510, Sec. 1. (SB 887) Effective January 1, 2024.)

115.9. PUBLISHING LICENSING OPTIONS AVAILABLE TO MILITARY SPOUSES

The department and each board within the department shall publish information pertinent to all licensing options available to military spouses on the home page of the internet website of the department or board, as applicable, including, but not limited to, the following:

(a) The process for expediting applications for military spouses.

(b) The availability of temporary licensure, the requirements for obtaining a temporary license, and length of time a temporary license is active.

(c) The requirements for full, permanent licensure by endorsement or credential for out-of-state applicants.

(Added by Stats. 2021, Ch. 693, Sec. 4. (AB 107) Effective January 1, 2022.)

115.10. DEFINITIONS

(a) For purposes of this section, the following definitions apply:

(1) "Applicant" means a servicemember or a spouse of a servicemember.

(2) "Board" means an entity described in Section 101.

(3) "Professional license" means an individual professional license and does not include a business or entity license.

(4) "Registering authority" means a board or the Department of Real Estate, as applicable.

(5) "Spouse" means an individual who is married to, or who is in a domestic partnership or other legal union with, a military servicemember.

(b) Notwithstanding any other law, a registering authority shall register an applicant who satisfies all of the following requirements:

(1) The applicant holds a professional license in good standing in another state, district, or territory of the United States that confers on the applicant the authority to practice a profession or vocation within a similar scope of practice as that regulated by the registering authority.

(2) The applicant relocated to this state because of military orders for military service within this state and the

applicant submits to the registering authority a copy of the military orders.

(3) The applicant performed at least one activity within the scope and under the authority of their professional license during the two years immediately preceding the relocation to this state.

(4) For an applicant who is licensed within the same professional discipline in more than one jurisdiction, both of the following:

(A) The applicant maintains each license in good standing.

(B) The applicant submits to the registering authority written verification from, or documentation printed from an online licensing system for, each jurisdiction that the applicant's license is in good standing in the jurisdiction.

(5) The applicant submits to the registering authority written verification from, or documentation printed from an online licensing system for, the applicant's original licensing jurisdiction that the applicant's license is in good standing in that jurisdiction.

(6) For an applicant that is a spouse, the applicant submits evidence to the registering authority that the applicant is married to, or in a domestic partnership or other legal union with, a servicemember who is subject to military orders described in paragraph (2).

(7) The applicant submits to the registering authority their California address of record and an affidavit attesting to both of the following:

(A) The applicant meets all of the requirements for registration under this section.

(B) The information submitted to the registering authority pursuant to this section is accurate to the best of the applicant's knowledge.

(c) (1) The registering authority shall register an applicant within 30 days of receiving all applicable documentation described in subdivision (b).

(2) The registering authority shall not register an applicant who fails to provide all applicable documentation described in subdivision (b) and shall deem the applicant's request for registration incomplete.

(d) For each person registered pursuant to this section, the registering authority shall post all of the following on the registering authority's internet website:

(1) The person's name.

(2) The person's California address of record.

(3) The person's registration status.

(4) The state name and license number of each license from each original licensing jurisdiction.

(e) A person registered pursuant to this section shall be deemed to be a licensee of the registering authority for purposes of the laws administered by that registering authority relating to standards of practice, discipline, and continuing education for the duration of the military orders described in paragraph (2) of subdivision (b), and the registration shall expire when those military orders expire.

(f) A registering authority may take appropriate enforcement action against a person registered pursuant to this section, including, but not limited to, revoking or suspending the registration of a person who does not meet the requirements of subdivision (b) or the laws applicable to licensees pursuant to subdivision (e).

(g) A registering authority shall not collect or require a fee for registration pursuant to this section.

(h) A registering authority may develop and publish guidance to implement this section.

(Added by Stats. 2023, Ch. 196, Sec. 1. (SB 143) Effective September 13, 2023.)

116. AUDIT AND REVIEW OF DISCIPLINARY PROCEEDINGS; REPORT TO LEGISLATURE

(a) The director may audit and review, upon the director's own initiative, or upon the request of a consumer or licensee, inquiries and complaints regarding licensees, dismissals of disciplinary cases, the opening, conduct, or closure of investigations, informal conferences, and discipline short of formal accusation by the Medical Board of California, the allied health professional boards, and the Podiatric Medical Board of California. The director may make recommendations for changes to the disciplinary system to the appropriate board, the Legislature, or both.

(b) The director shall report to the Chairpersons of the Senate Business, Professions and Economic Development Committee and the Assembly Business and Professions Committee annually, commencing March 1, 1995, regarding the director's findings from any audit, review, or monitoring and evaluation conducted pursuant to this section.

(Amended by Stats. 2019, Ch. 351, Sec. 21. (AB 496) Effective January 1, 2020.)

118. EFFECT OF WITHDRAWAL OF APPLICATIONS; EFFECT OF SUSPENSION, FORFEITURE, ETC., OF LICENSE

(a) The withdrawal of an application for a license after it has been filed with a board in the department shall not, unless the board has consented in writing to such withdrawal, deprive the board of its authority to institute or continue a proceeding against the applicant for the denial of the license upon any ground provided by law or to enter an order denying the license upon any such ground.

(b) The suspension, expiration, or forfeiture by operation of law of a license issued by a board in the department, or its suspension, forfeiture, or cancellation by order of the board or by order of a court of law, or its surrender without the written consent of the board, shall not, during any period in which it may be renewed, restored, reissued, or reinstated, deprive the board of its authority to institute or continue a disciplinary proceeding against the licensee upon any ground provided by law or to enter an order suspending or revoking the license or otherwise taking disciplinary action against the licensee on any such ground.

(c) As used in this section, "board" includes an individual who is authorized by any provision of this code to issue, suspend, or revoke a license, and "license" includes "certificate," "registration," and "permit."

(Added by Stats. 1961, Ch. 1079.)

119. MISDEMEANORS PERTAINING TO USE OF LICENSES

Any person who does any of the following is guilty of a misdemeanor:

(a) Displays or causes or permits to be displayed or has in the person's possession either of the following:

(1) A canceled, revoked, suspended, or fraudulently altered license.

(2) A fictitious license or any document simulating a license or purporting to be or have been issued as a license.

(b) Lends the person's license to any other person or knowingly permits the use thereof by another.

(c) Displays or represents any license not issued to the person as being the person's license.

(d) Fails or refuses to surrender to the issuing authority upon its lawful written demand any license, registration, permit, or certificate which has been suspended, revoked, or canceled.

(e) Knowingly permits any unlawful use of a license issued to the person.

(f) Photographs, photostats, duplicates, manufactures, or in any way reproduces any license or facsimile thereof in a manner that it could be mistaken for a valid license, or displays or has in the person's possession any such photograph, photostat, duplicate, reproduction, or facsimile unless authorized by this code.

(g) Buys or receives a fraudulent, forged, or counterfeited license knowing that it is fraudulent, forged, or counterfeited. For purposes of this subdivision, "fraudulent" means containing any misrepresentation of fact.

As used in this section, "license" includes "certificate," "permit," "authority," and "registration" or any other indicia giving authorization to engage in a business or profession regulated by this code or referred to in Section 1000 or 3600.

(Amended by Stats. 2019, Ch. 351, Sec. 22. (AB 496) Effective January 1, 2020.)

121. PRACTICE DURING PERIOD BETWEEN RENEWAL AND RECEIPT OF EVIDENCE OF RENEWAL

No licensee who has complied with the provisions of this code relating to the renewal of the licensee's license prior to expiration of such license shall be deemed to be engaged illegally in the practice of the licensee's business or profession during any period between such renewal and receipt of evidence of such renewal which may occur due to delay not the fault of the applicant.

As used in this section, "license" includes "certificate," "permit," "authorization," and "registration," or any other indicia giving authorization, by any agency, board, bureau, commission, committee, or entity within the Department of Consumer Affairs, to engage in a business or profession regulated by this code or by the board referred to in the Chiropractic Act or the Osteopathic Act.

(Amended by Stats. 2019, Ch. 351, Sec. 24. (AB 496) Effective January 1, 2020.)

121.5. APPLICATION OF FEES TO LICENSES REGISTRATIONS LAWFULLY INACTIVATED

Except as otherwise provided in this code, the application of delinquency fees or accrued and unpaid renewal fees for the renewal of expired licenses or registrations shall not apply to licenses or registrations that have lawfully been designated as inactive or retired.

(Added by Stats. 2001, Ch. 435, Sec. 1. Effective January 1, 2002.)

122. FEE FOR ISSUANCE OF DUPLICATE CERTIFICATE

Except as otherwise provided by law, the department and each of the boards, bureaus, committees, and commissions within the department may charge a fee for the processing and issuance of a duplicate copy of any certificate of licensure or other form evidencing licensure or renewal of licensure. The fee shall be in an amount sufficient to cover all costs incident to the issuance of the duplicate certificate or other form but shall not exceed twenty-five dollars ($25).

(Added by Stats. 1986, Ch. 951, Sec. 1.)

123. CONDUCT CONSTITUTING SUBVERSION OF LICENSING EXAMINATION; PENALTIES AND DAMAGES

It is a misdemeanor for any person to engage in any conduct which subverts or attempts to subvert any licensing examination or the administration of an examination, including, but not limited to:

(a) Conduct which violates the security of the examination materials; removing from the examination room any examination materials without authorization; the unauthorized reproduction by any means of any portion of the actual licensing examination; aiding by any means the unauthorized reproduction of any portion of the actual licensing examination; paying or using professional or paid examination-takers for the purpose of reconstructing any portion of the licensing examination; obtaining examination questions or other examination material, except by specific authorization either before, during, or after an examination; or using or purporting to use any examination questions or materials which were improperly removed or taken from any examination for the purpose of instructing or preparing any applicant for examination; or selling, distributing, buying, receiving, or having unauthorized possession of any portion of a future, current, or previously administered licensing examination.

(b) Communicating with any other examinee during the administration of a licensing examination; copying answers from another examinee or permitting one's answers to be copied by another examinee; having in one's possession during the administration of the licensing examination any books, equipment, notes, written or printed materials, or data of any kind, other than the examination materials distributed, or otherwise authorized to be in one's possession during the examination; or impersonating any examinee or having an impersonator take the licensing examination on one's behalf.

Nothing in this section shall preclude prosecution under the authority provided for in any other provision of law.

In addition to any other penalties, a person found guilty of violating this section, shall be liable for the actual damages sustained by the agency administering the examination not to exceed ten thousand dollars ($10,000) and the costs of litigation.

(c) If any provision of this section or the application thereof to any person or circumstances is held invalid, that invalidity shall not affect other provisions or applications of the section that can be given effect without the invalid provision or application, and to this end the provisions of this section are severable.

(Amended by Stats. 1991, Ch. 647, Sec. 1.)

123.5. ENJOINING VIOLATIONS

Whenever any person has engaged, or is about to engage, in any acts or practices which constitute, or will constitute, a violation of Section 123, the superior court in and for the county wherein the acts or practices take place, or are about to take place, may issue an injunction, or other appropriate order, restraining such conduct on application of a board, the Attorney General or the district attorney of the county.

The proceedings under this section shall be governed by Chapter 3 (commencing with Section 525) of Title 7 of Part 2 of the Code of Civil Procedure.

The remedy provided for by this section shall be in addition to, and not a limitation on, the authority provided for in any other provision of law.

(Added by renumbering Section 497 by Stats. 1989, Ch. 1022, Sec. 4.)

124. MANNER OF NOTICE

Notwithstanding subdivision (c) of Section 11505 of the Government Code, whenever written notice, including a notice, order, or document served pursuant to Chapter 3.5 (commencing with Section 11340), Chapter 4 (commencing with Section 11370), or Chapter 5 (commencing with Section 11500), of Part 1 of Division 3 of Title 2 of the Government Code, is required to be given by any board in the department, the notice may be given by regular mail addressed to the last known address of the licensee or by personal service, at the option of the board.

(Amended by Stats. 2019, Ch. 351, Sec. 25. (AB 496) Effective January 1, 2020. Operative July 1, 1997, by its own provisions.)

125. MISDEMEANOR OFFENSES BY LICENSEES

Any person, licensed under Division 1 (commencing with Section 100), Division 2 (commencing with Section 500), or Division 3 (commencing with Section 5000) is guilty of a misdemeanor and subject to the disciplinary provisions of this code applicable to them, who conspires with a person not so licensed to violate any provision of this code, or who, with intent to aid or assist that person in violating those provisions does either of the following:

(a) Allows their license to be used by that person.

(b) Acts as their agent or partner.

(Amended by Stats. 2019, Ch. 351, Sec. 26. (AB 496) Effective January 1, 2020.)

125.3. DIRECTION TO LICENTIATE VIOLATING LICENSING ACT TO PAY COSTS OF INVESTIGATION AND ENFORCEMENT

(a) Except as otherwise provided by law, in any order issued in resolution of a disciplinary proceeding before any board within the department or before the Osteopathic Medical Board, upon request of the entity bringing the proceeding, the administrative law judge may direct a licensee found to have committed a violation or violations of the licensing act to pay a sum not to exceed the reasonable costs of the investigation and enforcement of the case.

(b) In the case of a disciplined licensee that is a corporation or a partnership, the order may be made against the licensed corporate entity or licensed partnership.

(c) A certified copy of the actual costs, or a good faith estimate of costs where actual costs are not available, signed by the entity bringing the proceeding or its designated representative shall be prima facie evidence of reasonable costs of investigation and prosecution of the case. The costs shall include the amount of investigative and enforcement costs up to the date of the hearing, including, but not limited to, charges imposed by the Attorney General.

(d) The administrative law judge shall make a proposed finding of the amount of reasonable costs of investigation and prosecution of the case when requested pursuant to subdivision (a). The finding of the administrative law judge with regard to costs shall not be reviewable by the board to increase the cost award. The board may reduce or eliminate the cost award, or remand to the administrative law judge if the proposed

decision fails to make a finding on costs requested pursuant to subdivision (a).

(e) If an order for recovery of costs is made and timely payment is not made as directed in the board's decision, the board may enforce the order for repayment in any appropriate court. This right of enforcement shall be in addition to any other rights the board may have as to any licensee to pay costs.

(f) In any action for recovery of costs, proof of the board's decision shall be conclusive proof of the validity of the order of payment and the terms for payment.

(g) (1) Except as provided in paragraph (2), the board shall not renew or reinstate the license of any licensee who has failed to pay all of the costs ordered under this section.

(2) Notwithstanding paragraph (1), the board may, in its discretion, conditionally renew or reinstate for a maximum of one year the license of any licensee who demonstrates financial hardship and who enters into a formal agreement with the board to reimburse the board within that one-year period for the unpaid costs.

(h) All costs recovered under this section shall be considered a reimbursement for costs incurred and shall be deposited in the fund of the board recovering the costs to be available upon appropriation by the Legislature.

(i) Nothing in this section shall preclude a board from including the recovery of the costs of investigation and enforcement of a case in any stipulated settlement.

(j) This section does not apply to any board if a specific statutory provision in that board's licensing act provides for recovery of costs in an administrative disciplinary proceeding.

(Amended by Stats. 2021, Ch. 649, Sec. 1. (SB 806) Effective January 1, 2022.)

125.5. ENJOINING VIOLATIONS; RESTITUTION ORDERS

(a) The superior court for the county in which any person has engaged or is about to engage in any act which constitutes a violation of a chapter of this code administered or enforced by a board within the department may, upon a petition filed by the board with the approval of the director, issue an injunction or other appropriate order restraining such conduct. The proceedings under this section shall be governed by Chapter 3 (commencing with Section 525) of Title 7 of Part 2 of the Code of Civil Procedure. As used in this section, "board" includes commission, bureau, division, agency and a medical quality review committee.

(b) The superior court for the county in which any person has engaged in any act which constitutes a violation of a chapter of this code administered or enforced by a board within the department may, upon a petition filed by the board with the approval of the director, order such person to make restitution to persons injured as a result of such violation.

(c) The court may order a person subject to an injunction or restraining order, provided for in subdivision (a) of this section, or subject to an order requiring restitution pursuant to subdivision (b), to reimburse the petitioning board for expenses incurred by the board in its investigation related to its petition.

(d) The remedy provided for by this section shall be in addition to, and not a limitation on, the authority provided for in any other section of this code.

(Amended by Stats. 1982, Ch. 517, Sec 1.)

125.6. UNLAWFUL DISCRIMINATION BY LICENSEES

(a) (1) With regard to an applicant, every person who holds a license under the provisions of this code is subject to disciplinary action under the disciplinary provisions of this code applicable to that person if, because of any characteristic listed or defined in subdivision (b) or (e) of Section 51 of the Civil Code, the person refuses to perform the licensed activity or aids or incites the refusal to perform that licensed activity by another licensee, or if, because of any characteristic listed or defined in subdivision (b) or (e) of Section 51 of the Civil Code, the person makes any discrimination, or restriction in the performance of the licensed activity.

(2) Nothing in this section shall be interpreted to prevent a physician or health care professional licensed pursuant to Division 2 (commencing with Section 500) from considering any of the characteristics of a patient listed in subdivision (b) or (e) of Section 51 of the Civil Code if that consideration is medically necessary and for the sole purpose of determining the appropriate diagnosis or treatment of the patient.

(3) Nothing in this section shall be interpreted to apply to discrimination by employers with regard to employees or prospective employees, nor shall this section authorize action against any club license issued pursuant to Article 4 (commencing with Section 23425) of Chapter 3 of Division 9 because of discriminatory membership policy.

(4) The presence of architectural barriers to an individual with physical disabilities that conform to applicable state or local building codes and regulations shall not constitute discrimination under this section.

(b) (1) Nothing in this section requires a person licensed pursuant to Division 2 (commencing with Section 500) to permit an individual to participate in, or benefit from, the licensed activity of the licensee where that individual poses a direct threat to the health or safety of others. For this purpose, the term "direct threat" means a significant risk to the health or safety of others that cannot be eliminated by a modification of policies, practices, or procedures or by the provision of auxiliary aids and services.

(2) Nothing in this section requires a person licensed pursuant to Division 2 (commencing with Section 500) to perform a licensed activity for which the person is not qualified to perform.

(c) (1) "Applicant," as used in this section, means a person applying for licensed services provided by a person licensed under this code.

(2) "License," as used in this section, includes "certificate," "permit," "authority," and "registration" or any other indicia giving authorization to engage in a business or profession regulated by this code.

(Amended by Stats. 2019, Ch. 351, Sec. 28. (AB 496) Effective January 1, 2020.)

125.7. RESTRAINING ORDERS

In addition to the remedy provided for in Section 125.5, the superior court for the county in which any licensee licensed under Division 2 (commencing with Section 500), or any initiative act referred to in that division, has engaged or is about to engage in any act that constitutes a violation of a chapter of this code administered or enforced by a board referred to in Division 2 (commencing with Section 500), may, upon a petition filed by the board and accompanied by an affidavit or affidavits in support thereof and a memorandum of points and authorities, issue a temporary restraining order or other appropriate order restraining the licensee from engaging in the business or profession for which the person is licensed or from any part thereof, in accordance with this section.

(a) If the affidavits in support of the petition show that the licensee has engaged or is about to engage in acts or omissions constituting a violation of a chapter of this code and if the court is satisfied that permitting the licensee to continue to engage in the business or profession for which the license was issued will endanger the public health, safety, or welfare, the court may issue an order temporarily restraining the licensee from engaging in the profession for which he or she is licensed.

(b) The order may not be issued without notice to the licensee unless it appears from facts shown by the affidavits that serious injury would result to the public before the matter can be heard on notice.

(c) Except as otherwise specifically provided by this section, proceedings under this section shall be governed by Chapter 3 (commencing with Section 525) of Title 7 of Part 2 of the Code of Civil Procedure.

(d) When a restraining order is issued pursuant to this section, or within a time to be allowed by the superior court, but in any case not more than 30 days after the restraining order is issued, an accusation shall be filed with the board pursuant to Section 11503 of the Government Code or, in the case of a licensee of the State Department of Health Services, with that department pursuant to Section 100171 of the Health and Safety Code. The accusation shall be served upon the licensee as provided by Section 11505 of the Government

Code. The licensee shall have all of the rights and privileges available as specified in Chapter 5 (commencing with Section 11500) of Part 1 of Division 3 of Title 2 of the Government Code. However, if the licensee requests a hearing on the accusation, the board shall provide the licensee with a hearing within 30 days of the request and a decision within 15 days of the date the decision is received from the administrative law judge, or the court may nullify the restraining order previously issued. Any restraining order issued pursuant to this section shall be dissolved by operation of law at the time the board's decision is subject to judicial review pursuant to Section 1094.5 of the Code of Civil Procedure.

(e) The remedy provided for in this section shall be in addition to, and not a limitation upon, the authority provided by any other provision of this code.

(Amended by Stats. 1998, Ch. 878, Sec. 1.5. Effective January 1, 1999.)

125.8. TEMPORARY ORDER RESTRAINING LICENSEE ENGAGED OR ABOUT TO ENGAGE IN VIOLATION OF LAW

In addition to the remedy provided for in Section 125.5, the superior court for the county in which any licensee licensed under Division 3 (commencing with Section 5000) or Chapter 2 (commencing with Section 18600) or Chapter 3 (commencing with Section 19000) of Division 8 has engaged or is about to engage in any act which constitutes a violation of a chapter of this code administered or enforced by a board referred to in Division 3 (commencing with Section 5000) or Chapter 2 (commencing with Section 18600) or Chapter 3 (commencing with Section 19000) of Division 8 may, upon a petition filed by the board and accompanied by an affidavit or affidavits in support thereof and a memorandum of points and authorities, issue a temporary restraining order or other appropriate order restraining the licensee from engaging in the business or profession for which the person is licensed or from any part thereof, in accordance with the provisions of this section.

(a) If the affidavits in support of the petition show that the licensee has engaged or is about to engage in acts or omissions constituting a violation of a chapter of this code and if the court is satisfied that permitting the licensee to continue to engage in the business or profession for which the license was issued will endanger the public health, safety, or welfare, the court may issue an order temporarily restraining the licensee from engaging in the profession for which he is licensed.

(b) Such order may not be issued without notice to the licensee unless it appears from facts shown by the affidavits that serious injury would result to the public before the matter can be heard on notice.

(c) Except as otherwise specifically provided by this section, proceedings under this section shall be governed by Chapter 3 (commencing with Section 525) of Title 7 of Part 2 of the Code of Civil Procedure.

(d) When a restraining order is issued pursuant to this section, or within a time to be allowed by the superior court, but in any case not more than 30 days after the restraining order is issued, an accusation shall be filed with the board pursuant to Section 11503 of the Government Code. The accusation shall be served upon the licensee as provided by Section 11505 of the Government Code. The licensee shall have all of the rights and privileges available as specified in Chapter 5 (commencing with Section 11500) of Part 1 of Division 3 of Title 2 of the Government Code; however, if the licensee requests a hearing on the accusation, the board must provide the licensee with a hearing within 30 days of the request and a decision within 15 days of the date of the conclusion of the hearing, or the court may nullify the restraining order previously issued. Any restraining order issued pursuant to this section shall be dissolved by operation of law at such time the board's decision is subject to judicial review pursuant to Section 1094.5 of the Code of Civil Procedure.

(Amended by Stats. 1982, Ch. 517, Sec. 3.)

125.9. SYSTEM FOR ISSUANCE OF CITATIONS TO LICENSEES; CONTENTS; FINES

(a) Except with respect to persons regulated under Chapter 11 (commencing with Section 7500), any board, bureau, or commission within the department, the State Board of Chiropractic Examiners, and the Osteopathic Medical Board of California, may establish, by regulation, a system for the issuance to a licensee of a citation which may contain an order of abatement or an order to pay an administrative fine assessed by the board, bureau, or commission where the licensee is in violation of the applicable licensing act or any regulation adopted pursuant thereto.

(b) The system shall contain the following provisions:

(1) Citations shall be in writing and shall describe with particularity the nature of the violation, including specific reference to the provision of law determined to have been violated.

(2) Whenever appropriate, the citation shall contain an order of abatement fixing a reasonable time for abatement of the violation.

(3) In no event shall the administrative fine assessed by the board, bureau, or commission exceed five thousand dollars ($5,000) for each inspection or each investigation made with respect to the violation, or five thousand dollars ($5,000) for each violation or count if the violation involves fraudulent billing submitted to an insurance company, the Medi-Cal program, or Medicare. In assessing a fine, the board, bureau, or commission shall give due consideration to the appropriateness of the amount of the fine with respect to factors such as the gravity of the violation, the good faith of the licensee, and the history of previous violations.

(4) A citation or fine assessment issued pursuant to a citation shall inform the licensee that if the licensee desires a hearing to contest the finding of a violation, that hearing shall be requested by written notice to the board, bureau, or commission within 30 days of the date of issuance of the citation or assessment. If a hearing is not requested pursuant to this section, payment of any fine shall not constitute an admission of the violation charged. Hearings shall be held pursuant to Chapter 5 (commencing with Section 11500) of Part 1 of Division 3 of Title 2 of the Government Code.

(5) Failure of a licensee to pay a fine or comply with an order of abatement, or both, within 30 days of the date of assessment or order, unless the citation is being appealed, may result in disciplinary action being taken by the board, bureau, or commission. Where a citation is not contested and a fine is not paid, the full amount of the assessed fine shall be added to the fee for renewal of the license. A license shall not be renewed without payment of the renewal fee and fine.

(c) The system may contain the following provisions:

(1) A citation may be issued without the assessment of an administrative fine.

(2) Assessment of administrative fines may be limited to only particular violations of the applicable licensing act.

(d) Notwithstanding any other provision of law, if a fine is paid to satisfy an assessment based on the finding of a violation, payment of the fine and compliance with the order of abatement, if applicable, shall be represented as satisfactory resolution of the matter for purposes of public disclosure.

(e) Administrative fines collected pursuant to this section shall be deposited in the special fund of the particular board, bureau, or commission.

(Amended by Stats. 2020, Ch. 312, Sec. 3. (SB 1474) Effective January 1, 2021.)

126. SUBMISSION OF REPORTS TO GOVERNOR

Notwithstanding any other provision of this code, any board, commission, examining committee, or other similarly constituted agency within the department required prior to the effective date of this section to submit reports to the Governor under any provision of this code shall not be required to submit such reports.

(Added by Stats. 1967, Ch. 660.)

127. SUBMISSION OF REPORTS TO DIRECTOR

Notwithstanding any other provision of this code, the director may require such reports from any board, commission, examining committee, or other similarly constituted agency within the department as the director deems reasonably necessary on any phase of their operations.

(Amended by Stats. 2019, Ch. 351, Sec. 30. (AB 496) Effective January 1, 2020.)

128. SALE OF EQUIPMENT, SUPPLIES, OR SERVICES FOR USE IN VIOLATION OF LICENSING REQUIREMENTS

Notwithstanding any other provision of law, it is a misdemeanor to sell equipment, supplies, or services to any person with knowledge that the equipment, supplies, or services are to be used in the performance of a service or contract in violation of the licensing requirements of this code.

The provisions of this section shall not be applicable to cash sales of less than one hundred dollars ($100).

For the purposes of this section, "person" includes, but is not limited to, a company, partnership, limited liability company, firm, or corporation.

For the purposes of this section, "license" includes certificate or registration.

A violation of this section shall be punishable by a fine of not less than one thousand dollars ($1,000) and by imprisonment in the county jail not exceeding six months.

(Amended by Stats. 1994, Ch. 1010, Sec. 1. Effective January 1, 1995.)

128.5. REDUCTION OF LICENSE FEES IN EVENT OF SURPLUS FUNDS

(a) Notwithstanding any other provision of law, if at the end of any fiscal year, an agency within the Department of Consumer Affairs, except the agencies referred to in subdivision (b), has unencumbered funds in an amount that equals or is more than the agency's operating budget for the next two fiscal years, the agency shall reduce license or other fees, whether the license or other fees be fixed by statute or may be determined by the agency within limits fixed by statute, during the following fiscal year in an amount that will reduce any surplus funds of the agency to an amount less than the agency's operating budget for the next two fiscal years.

(b) Notwithstanding any other provision of law, if at the end of any fiscal year, the California Architects Board, the Board of Behavioral Sciences, the Veterinary Medical Board, the Court Reporters Board of California, the Medical Board of California, the Board of Vocational Nursing and Psychiatric Technicians, or the Bureau of Security and Investigative Services has unencumbered funds in an amount that equals or is more than the agency's operating budget for the next two fiscal years, the agency shall reduce license or other fees, whether the license or other fees be fixed by statute or may be determined by the agency within limits fixed by statute, during the following fiscal year in an amount that will reduce any surplus funds of the agency to an amount less than the agency's operating budget for the next two fiscal years.

(Amended by Stats. 2009, Ch. 308, Sec. 3. (SB 819) Effective January 1, 2010.)

129. HANDLING OF COMPLAINTS; REPORTS TO LEGISLATURE

(a) As used in this section, "board" means every board, bureau, commission, committee, and similarly constituted agency in the department that issues licenses.

(b) Each board shall, upon receipt of any complaint respecting an individual licensed by the board, notify the complainant of the initial administrative action taken on the complainant's complaint within 10 days of receipt. Each board shall notify the complainant of the final action taken on the complainant's complaint. There shall be a notification made in every case in which the complainant is known. If the complaint is not within the jurisdiction of the board or if the board is unable to dispose satisfactorily of the complaint, the board shall transmit the complaint together with any evidence or information it has concerning the complaint to the agency, public or private, whose authority in the opinion of the board will provide the most effective means to secure the relief sought. The board shall notify the complainant of this action and of any other means that may be available to the complainant to secure relief.

(c) The board shall, when the board deems it appropriate, notify the person against whom the complaint is made of the nature of the complaint, may request appropriate relief for the complainant, and may meet and confer with the complainant and the licensee in order to mediate the complaint. Nothing in this subdivision shall be construed as authorizing or requiring any board to set or to modify any fee charged by a licensee.

(d) It shall be the continuing duty of the board to ascertain patterns of complaints and to report on all actions taken with respect to those patterns of complaints to the director and to the Legislature at least once per year. The board shall evaluate those complaints dismissed for lack of jurisdiction or no violation and recommend to the director and to the Legislature at least once per year the statutory changes it deems necessary to implement the board's functions and responsibilities under this section.

(e) It shall be the continuing duty of the board to take whatever action it deems necessary, with the approval of the director, to inform the public of its functions under this section.

(f) Notwithstanding any other law, upon receipt of a child custody evaluation report submitted to a court pursuant to Chapter 6 (commencing with Section 3110) of Part 2 of Division 8 of the Family Code, the board shall notify the noncomplaining party in the underlying custody dispute, who is a subject of that report, of the pending investigation.

(Amended by Stats. 2019, Ch. 351, Sec. 31. (AB 496) Effective January 1, 2020.)

130. TERMS OF OFFICE OF AGENCY MEMBERS

(a) Notwithstanding any other law, the term of office of any member of an agency designated in subdivision (b) shall be for a term of four years expiring on June 1.

(b) Subdivision (a) applies to the following boards or committees:

(1) The Medical Board of California.

(2) The Podiatric Medical Board of California.

(3) The Physical Therapy Board of California.

(4) The Board of Registered Nursing, except as provided in subdivision (c) of Section 2703.

(5) The Board of Vocational Nursing and Psychiatric Technicians.

(6) The California State Board of Optometry.

(7) The California State Board of Pharmacy.

(8) The Veterinary Medical Board.

(9) The California Architects Board.

(10) The Landscape Architect Technical Committee.

(11) The Board for Professional Engineers and Land Surveyors.

(12) The Contractors State License Board.

(13) The Board of Behavioral Sciences.

(14) The Court Reporters Board of California.

(15) The State Athletic Commission.

(16) The Osteopathic Medical Board of California.

(17) The Respiratory Care Board of California.

(18) The Acupuncture Board.

(19) The Board of Psychology.

(20) The Structural Pest Control Board.

(Amended by Stats. 2021, Ch. 630, Sec. 3. (AB 1534) Effective January 1, 2022.)

131. MAXIMUM NUMBER OF TERMS

Notwithstanding any other provision of law, no member of an agency designated in subdivision (b) of Section 130 or member of a board, commission, committee, or similarly constituted agency in the department shall serve more than two consecutive full terms.

(Amended by Stats. 1987, Ch. 850, Sec. 5.)

132. REQUIREMENTS FOR INSTITUTION OR JOINDER OF LEGAL ACTION BY STATE AGENCY AGAINST OTHER STATE OR FEDERAL AGENCY

No board, commission, examining committee, or any other agency within the department may institute or join any legal action against any other agency within the state or federal government without the permission of the director.

Prior to instituting or joining in a legal action against an agency of the state or federal government, a board, commission, examining committee, or any other agency within the department shall present a written request to the director to do so.

Within 30 days of receipt of the request, the director shall communicate the director's approval or denial of the request and the director's reasons for approval or denial to the requesting agency in writing. If the director does not act within 30 days, the request shall be deemed approved.

A requesting agency within the department may override the director's denial of its request to institute or join a legal action against a state or federal agency by a two-thirds vote of the members of the board, commission, examining committee, or other agency, which vote shall include the vote of at least one public member of that board, commission, examining committee, or other agency.

(Amended by Stats. 2019, Ch. 351, Sec. 33. (AB 496) Effective January 1, 2020.)

134. PRORATION OF LICENSE FEES

When the term of any license issued by any agency in the department exceeds one year, initial license fees for licenses which are issued during a current license term shall be prorated on a yearly basis.

(Amended by Stats. 1978, Ch. 1161.)

135. REEXAMINATION OF APPLICANTS

No agency in the department shall, on the basis of an applicant's failure to successfully complete prior examinations, impose any additional limitations, restrictions, prerequisites, or requirements on any applicant who wishes to participate in subsequent examinations except that any examining agency which allows an applicant conditional credit for successfully completing a divisible part of an examination may require that an applicant be reexamined in those parts successfully completed if such applicant has not successfully completed all parts of the examination within a required period of time established by the examining agency. Nothing in this section, however, requires the exemption of such applicant from the regular fees and requirements normally associated with examinations.

(Added by Stats. 1974, Ch. 743.)

135.4 EXPEDITING LICENSURE PROCESS FOR REFUGEES GRANTED ASYLUM

(a) Notwithstanding any other law, a board within the department shall expedite, and may assist, the initial licensure process for an applicant who supplies satisfactory evidence to the board that they have been admitted to the United States as a refugee under Section 1157 of Title 8 of the United States Code, have been granted asylum by the Secretary of Homeland Security or the Attorney General of the United States pursuant to Section 1158 of Title 8 of the United States Code, or they have a special immigrant visa (SIV) that has been granted a status under Section 1244 of Public Law 110-181, under Public Law 109-163, or under Section 602(b) of Title VI of Division F of Public Law 111-8.

(b) Nothing in this section shall be construed as changing existing licensure requirements. A person applying for expedited licensure under subdivision (a) shall meet all applicable statutory and regulatory licensure requirements.

(c) A board may adopt regulations necessary to administer this section.

(Added by Stats. 2020, Ch. 186, Sec. 1. (AB 2113) Effective January 1, 2021.)

135.5 LICENSURE BASED ON IMMIGRATION STATUS

(a) The Legislature finds and declares that it is in the best interests of the State of California to provide persons who are not lawfully present in the United States with the state benefits provided by all licensing acts of entities within the department, and therefore enacts this section pursuant to subsection (d) of Section 1621 of Title 8 of the United States Code.

(b) Notwithstanding subdivision (a) of Section 30, and except as required by subdivision (e) of Section 7583.23, no entity within the department shall deny licensure to an applicant based on his or her citizenship status or immigration status.

(c) Every board within the department shall implement all required regulatory or procedural changes necessary to implement this section no later than January 1, 2016. A board may implement the provisions of this section at any time prior to January 1, 2016.

(Added by Stats. 2014, Ch. 752, Sec. 2. (SB 1159) Effective January 1, 2015.)

136. NOTIFICATION OF CHANGE OF ADDRESS; PUNISHMENT FOR FAILURE TO COMPLY

(a) Each person holding a license, certificate, registration, permit, or other authority to engage in a profession or occupation issued by a board within the department shall notify the issuing board at its principal office of any change in the person's mailing address within 30 days after the change, unless the board has specified by regulations a shorter time period.

(b) Except as otherwise provided by law, failure of a licensee to comply with the requirement in subdivision (a) constitutes grounds for the issuance of a citation and administrative fine, if the board has the authority to issue citations and administrative fines.

(Amended by Stats. 2019, Ch. 351, Sec. 34. (AB 496) Effective January 1, 2020.)

137. REGULATIONS REQUIRING INCLUSION OF LICENSE NUMBERS IN ADVERTISING, ETC.

Any agency within the department may promulgate regulations requiring licensees to include their license numbers in any advertising, soliciting, or other presentments to the public.

However, nothing in this section shall be construed to authorize regulation of any person not a licensee who engages in advertising, solicitation, or who makes any other presentment to the public on behalf of a licensee. Such a person shall incur no liability pursuant to this section for communicating in any advertising, soliciting, or other presentment to the public a licensee's license number exactly as provided by the licensee or for failure to communicate such number if none is provided by the licensee.

(Amended by Stats. 2019, Ch. 351, Sec. 35. (AB 496) Effective January 1, 2020.)

138. NOTICE THAT PRACTITIONER IS LICENSED; EVALUATION OF LICENSING EXAMINATION

Every board in the department, as defined in Section 22, shall initiate the process of adopting regulations on or before June 30, 1999, to require its licensees, as defined in Section 23.8, to provide notice to their clients or customers that the practitioner is licensed by this state. A board shall be exempt from the requirement to adopt regulations pursuant to this section if the board has in place, in statute or regulation, a requirement that provides for consumer notice of a practitioner's status as a licensee of this state.

(Amended by Stats. 2019, Ch. 351, Sec. 36. (AB 496) Effective January 1, 2020.)

139. POLICY FOR EXAMINATION DEVELOPMENT AND VALIDATION AND OCCUPATIONAL ANALYSIS

(a) The Legislature finds and declares that occupational analyses and examination validation studies are fundamental components of licensure programs. It is the intent of the Legislature that the policy developed by the department pursuant to subdivision (b) be used by the fiscal, policy, and sunset review committees of the Legislature in their annual reviews of these boards, programs, and bureaus.

(b) Notwithstanding any other provision of law, the department shall develop, in consultation with the boards, programs, bureaus, and divisions under its jurisdiction, and the Osteopathic Medical Board of California and the State Board of Chiropractic Examiners, a policy regarding examination development and validation, and occupational analysis. The department shall finalize and distribute this policy by September 30, 1999, to each of the boards, programs, bureaus, and divisions under its jurisdiction and to the Osteopathic Medical Board of California and the State Board of Chiropractic Examiners. This policy shall be submitted in draft form at least 30 days prior to that date to the appropriate fiscal, policy, and sunset review committees of the Legislature for review. This policy shall address, but shall not be limited to, the following issues:

(1) An appropriate schedule for examination validation and occupational analyses, and circumstances under which more frequent reviews are appropriate.

(2) Minimum requirements for psychometrically sound examination validation, examination development, and occupational analyses, including

standards for sufficient number of test items.

(3) Standards for review of state and national examinations.

(4) Setting of passing standards.

(5) Appropriate funding sources for examination validations and occupational analyses.

(6) Conditions under which boards, programs, and bureaus should use internal and external entities to conduct these reviews.

(7) Standards for determining appropriate costs of reviews of different types of examinations, measured in terms of hours required.

(8) Conditions under which it is appropriate to fund permanent and limited term positions within a board, program, or bureau to manage these reviews.

(c) Every regulatory board and bureau, as defined in Section 22, and every program and bureau administered by the department, the Osteopathic Medical Board of California, and the State Board of Chiropractic Examiners, shall submit to the director on or before December 1, 1999, and on or before December 1 of each subsequent year, its method for ensuring that every licensing examination administered by or pursuant to contract with the board is subject to periodic evaluation. The evaluation shall include

(1) a description of the occupational analysis serving as the basis for the examination; (2) sufficient item analysis data to permit a psychometric evaluation of the items; (3) an assessment of the appropriateness of prerequisites for admittance to the examination; and (4) an estimate of the costs and personnel required to perform these functions. The evaluation shall be revised and a new evaluation submitted to the director whenever, in the judgment of the board, program, or bureau, there is a substantial change in the examination or the prerequisites for admittance to the examination.

(d) The evaluation may be conducted by the board, program, or bureau, the Office of Professional Examination Services of the department, the Osteopathic Medical Board of California, or the State Board of Chiropractic Examiners or pursuant to a contract with a qualified private testing firm. A board, program, or bureau that provides for development or administration of a licensing examination pursuant to contract with a public or private entity may rely on an occupational analysis or item analysis conducted by that entity. The department shall compile this information, along with a schedule specifying when examination validations and occupational analyses shall be performed, and submit it to the appropriate fiscal, policy, and sunset review committees of the Legislature by September 30 of each year.

It is the intent of the Legislature that the method specified in this report be consistent with the policy developed by the department pursuant to subdivision (b).

(Amended by Stats. 2009, Ch. 307, Sec. 1. (SB 821) Effective January 1, 2010.)

139.5 PUBLISHING LICENSE APPLICATIONS

Beginning July 1, 2021, each board, as defined in Section 22, within the department that issues a license shall do both of the following on at least a quarterly basis:

(a) Prominently display on its internet website one of the following:

(1) The current average timeframes for processing initial and renewal license applications.

(2) The combined current average timeframe for processing both initial and renewal license applications.

(b) Prominently display on its internet website one of the following:

(1) The current average timeframes for processing each license type that the board administers.

(2) The combined current average timeframe for processing all license types that the board administers.

(Added by Stats. 2020, Ch. 131, Sec. 1. (SB 878) Effective January 1, 2021.)

140. DISCIPLINARY ACTION; LICENSEE'S FAILURE TO RECORD CASH TRANSACTIONS IN PAYMENT OF EMPLOYEE WAGES

Any board, as defined in Section 22, which is authorized under this code to take disciplinary action against a person who holds a license may take disciplinary action upon the ground that the licensee has failed to record and preserve for not less than three years, any and all cash transactions involved in the payment of employee wages by a licensee. Failure to make these records available to an authorized representative of the board may be made grounds for disciplinary action. In any action brought and sustained by the board which involves a violation of this section and any regulation adopted thereto, the board may assess the licensee with the actual investigative costs incurred, not to exceed two thousand five hundred dollars ($2,500).

Failure to pay those costs may result in revocation of the license. Any moneys collected pursuant to this section shall be deposited in the respective fund of the board.

(Added by Stats. 1984, Ch. 1490, Sec. 2. Effective September 27, 1984.)

141. DISCIPLINARY ACTION BY FOREIGN JURISDICTION; GROUNDS OR DISCIPLINARY ACTION BY STATE LICENSING BOARD

(a) For any licensee holding a license issued by a board under the jurisdiction of the department, a disciplinary action taken by another state, by any agency of the federal government, or by another country for any act substantially related to the practice regulated by the California license, may be a ground for disciplinary action by the respective state licensing board. A certified copy of the record of the disciplinary action taken against the licensee by another state, an agency of the federal government, or another country shall be conclusive evidence of the events related therein.

(b) Nothing in this section shall preclude a board from applying a specific statutory provision in the licensing act administered by that board that provides for discipline based upon a disciplinary action taken against the licensee by another state, an agency of the federal government, or another country.

(Added by Stats. 1994, Ch. 1275, Sec. 2. Effective January 1, 1995.)

142. AUTHORITY TO SYNCHRONIZE RENEWAL DATES OF LICENSES; ABANDONMENT DATE FOR APPLICATION; DELINQUENCY FEE

This section shall apply to the bureaus and programs under the direct authority of the director, and to any board that, with the prior approval of the director, elects to have the department administer one or more of the licensing services set forth in this section.

(a) Notwithstanding any other provision of law, each bureau and program may synchronize the renewal dates of licenses granted to applicants with more than one license issued by the bureau or program. To the extent practicable, fees shall be prorated or adjusted so that no applicant shall be required to pay a greater or lesser fee than he or she would have been required to pay if the change in renewal dates had not occurred.

(b) Notwithstanding any other provision of law, the abandonment date for an application that has been returned to the applicant as incomplete shall be 12 months from the date of returning the application.

(c) Notwithstanding any other provision of law, a delinquency, penalty, or late fee shall be assessed if the renewal fee is not postmarked by the renewal expiration date.

(Added by Stats. 1998, Ch. 970, Sec. 2. Effective January 1, 1999.)

143. PROOF OF LICENSE AS CONDITION OF BRINGING ACTION FOR COLLECTION OF COMPENSATION

(a) No person engaged in any business or profession for which a license is required under this code governing the department or any board, bureau, commission, committee, or program within the department, may bring or maintain any action, or recover in law or equity in any action, in any court of this state for the collection of compensation for the performance of any act or contract for which a license is required without alleging and proving that he or she was duly licensed at all times during the performance of that act or contract, regardless of the merits of the cause of action brought by the person.

(b) The judicial doctrine of substantial compliance shall not apply to this section.

(c) This section shall not apply to an act or contract that is considered to qualify as lawful practice of a licensed occupation or profession pursuant to Section 121.

(Added by Stats. 1990, Ch. 1207, Sec. 1.5.)

143.5. PROVISION IN AGREEMENTS TO SETTLE CERTAIN CAUSES OF ACTION PROHIBITED; ADOPTION OF REGULATIONS; EXEMPTIONS

(a) No licensee who is regulated by a board, bureau, or program within the Department of Consumer Affairs, nor an entity or person acting as an authorized agent of a licensee, shall include or permit to be included a provision in an agreement to settle a civil dispute, whether the agreement is made before or after the commencement of a civil action, that prohibits the other party in that dispute from contacting, filing a complaint with, or cooperating with the department, board, bureau, or program within the Department of Consumer Affairs that regulates the licensee or that requires the other party to withdraw a complaint from the department, board, bureau, or program within the Department of Consumer Affairs that regulates the licensee. A provision of that nature is void as against public policy, and any licensee who includes or permits to be included a provision of that nature In a settlement agreement is subject to disciplinary action by the board, bureau, or program.

(b) Any board, bureau, or program within the Department of Consumer Affairs that takes disciplinary action against a licensee or licensees based on a complaint or report that has also been the subject of a civil action and that has been settled for monetary damages providing for full and final satisfaction of the parties may not require its licensee or licensees to pay any additional sums to the benefit of any plaintiff in the civil action.

(c) As used in this section, "board" shall have the same meaning as defined in Section 22, and "licensee" means a person who has been granted a license, as that term is defined in Section 23.7.

(d) Notwithstanding any other law, upon granting a petition filed by a licensee or authorized agent of a licensee pursuant to Section 11340.6 of the Government Code, a board, bureau, or program within the Department of Consumer Affairs may, based upon evidence and legal authorities cited in the petition, adopt a regulation that does both of the following:

(1) Identifies a code section or jury instruction in a civil cause of action that

has no relevance to the board's, bureau's, or program's enforcement responsibilities such that an agreement to settle such a cause of action based on that code section or jury instruction otherwise prohibited under subdivision (a) will not impair the board's, bureau's, or program's duty to protect the public.

(2) Exempts agreements to settle such a cause of action from the requirements of subdivision (a).

(e) This section shall not apply to a licensee subject to Section 2220.7.

(Added by Stats. 2012, Ch. 561, Sec. 1. (AB 2570) Effective January 1, 2013.)

144. REQUIREMENT OF FINGERPRINTS FOR CRIMINAL RECORD CHECKS; APPLICABILITY

(a) Notwithstanding any other law, an agency designated in subdivision (b) shall require an applicant to furnish to the agency a full set of fingerprints for purposes of conducting criminal history record checks. Any agency designated in subdivision (b) may obtain and receive, at its discretion, criminal history information from the Department of Justice and the United States Federal Bureau of Investigation.

(b) Subdivision (a) applies to the following:

(1) California Board of Accountancy.

(2) State Athletic Commission.

(3) Board of Behavioral Sciences.

(4) Court Reporters Board of California.

(5) Dental Board of California.

(6) California State Board of Pharmacy.

(7) Board of Registered Nursing.

(8) Veterinary Medical Board.

(9) Board of Vocational Nursing and Psychiatric Technicians of the State of California.

(10) Respiratory Care Board of California.

(11) Physical Therapy Board of California.

(12) Physician Assistant Board.

(13) Speech-Language Pathology and Audiology and Hearing Aid Dispensers Board.

(14) Medical Board of California.

(15) California State Board of Optometry.

(16) Acupuncture Board.

(17) Cemetery and Funeral Bureau.

(18) Bureau of Security and Investigative Services.

(19) Division of Investigation.

(20) Board of Psychology.

(21) California Board of Occupational Therapy.

(22) Structural Pest Control Board.

(23) Contractors State License Board.

(24) Naturopathic Medicine Committee.

(25) Professional Fiduciaries Bureau.

(26) Board for Professional Engineers, Land Surveyors, and Geologists.

(27) Podiatric Medical Board of California.

(28) Osteopathic Medical Board of California.

(29) California Architects Board, beginning January 1, 2021.

(30) Landscape Architects Technical Committee, beginning January 1, 2022.

(31) Bureau of Household Goods and Services with respect to household movers as described in Chapter 3.1 (commencing with Section 19225) of Division 8.

(c) For purposes of paragraph (26) of subdivision (b), the term "applicant" shall be limited to an initial applicant who has never been registered or licensed by the board or to an applicant for a new licensure or registration category.

(Amended by Stats. 2021, Ch. 630, Sec. 4.5. (AB 1534) Effective January 1, 2022.)

144.5. BOARD AUTHORIZED TO RECEIVE CRIMINAL RECORD AND RELATED DOCUMENTATION

Notwithstanding any other law, a board described in Section 144 may request, and is authorized to receive, from a local or state agency certified records of all arrests and convictions, certified records regarding probation, and any and all other related documentation needed to complete an applicant or licensee investigation. A local or state agency may provide those records to the board upon request.

(Added by Stats. 2013, Ch. 516, Sec. 1. (SB 305) Effective January 1, 2014.)

144.6. MINIMUM HOURS OF EDUCATION

(a) For purposes of Section 668.14 of Title 34 of the Code of Federal Regulations, the required minimum number of hours, or the equivalent, established in this state for education programs that qualify persons for any license issued by a board within the department shall be equal to the number of clock or credit hours, or the equivalent, that the education program provides as of the effective date of this section.

(b) For an education program approved by a board within the department as of the effective date of this section that submits to the applicable board, no later than July 1, 2026, a request to modify the program to reduce the program clock or credit hours, or the equivalent, the applicable board shall, no later than January 1, 2027, complete its review of the requested modification.

(c) This section shall remain in effect only until January 1, 2027, and as of that date is repealed.

(Added by Stats. 2024, Ch. 41, Sec. 1. (SB 164) Effective June 29, 2024. Repealed as of January 1, 2027, by its own provisions.)

CHAPTER 1.5: UNLICENSED ACTIVITY ENFORCEMENT

145. LEGISLATIVE FINDINGS AND DECLARATIONS

The Legislature finds and declares that:

(a) Unlicensed activity in the professions and vocations regulated by the Department of Consumer Affairs is a threat to the health, welfare, and safety of the people of the State of California.

(b) The law enforcement agencies of the state should have sufficient, effective, and responsible means available to enforce the licensing laws of the state.

(c) The criminal sanction for unlicensed activity should be swift, effective, appropriate, and create a strong incentive to obtain a license.

(Added by Stats. 1992, Ch. 1135, Sec. 2. Effective January 1, 1993.)

146. VIOLATIONS CLASSIFIED AS INFRACTIONS

(a) Notwithstanding any other provision of law, a violation of any code section listed in subdivision (c) is an infraction subject to the procedures described in Sections 19.6 and 19.7 of the Penal Code when either of the following applies:

(1) A complaint or a written notice to appear in court pursuant to Chapter 5C (commencing with Section 853.5) of Title 3 of Part 2 of the Penal Code is filed in court charging the offense as an infraction unless the defendant, at the time they are arraigned, after being advised of their rights, elects to have the case proceed as a misdemeanor.

(2) The court, with the consent of the defendant and the prosecution, determines that the offense is an infraction in which event the case shall proceed as if the defendant has been arraigned on an infraction complaint.

(b) Subdivision (a) does not apply to a violation of the code sections listed in subdivision (c) if the defendant has had their license, registration, or certificate previously revoked or suspended.

(c) The following sections require registration, licensure, certification, or other authorization in order to engage in certain businesses or professions regulated by this code:

(1) Section 2474.

(2) Sections 2052 and 2054.

(3) Section 2570.3.

(4) Section 2630.

(5) Section 2903.

(6) Section 3575.

(7) Section 3660.

(8) Sections 3760 and 3761.

(9) Section 4080.

(10) Section 4825.

(11) Section 4935.

(12) Section 4980.

(13) Section 4989.50.

(14) Section 4996.

(15) Section 4999.30.

(16) Section 5536.

(17) Section 6530 or 6532.

(18) Section 6704.

(19) Section 6980.10.

(20) Section 7317.

(21) Section 7502 or 7592.

(22) Section 7520.

(23) Section 7617 or 7641.

(24) Subdivision (a) of Section 7872.

(25) Section 8016.

(26) Section 8505.

(27) Section 8725.

(28) Section 9681.

(29) Section 9840.

(30) Subdivision (c) of Section 9891.24.

(31) Section 19049.

(d) Notwithstanding any other law, a violation of any of the sections listed in subdivision (c), which is an infraction, is punishable by a fine of not less than two hundred fifty dollars ($250) and not more than one thousand dollars ($1,000). No portion of the minimum fine may be suspended by the court unless as a condition of that suspension the defendant is required to submit proof of a current valid license, registration, or certificate for the profession or vocation that was the basis for their conviction.

(Amended by Stats. 2023, Ch. 680, Sec. 1. (AB 1262) Effective January 1, 2024.)

147. AUTHORITY TO ISSUE WRITTEN NOTICE TO APPEAR IN COURT

(a) Any employee designated by the director shall have the authority to issue a written notice to appear in court pursuant to Chapter 5c (commencing with Section 853.5) of Title 3 of Part 2 of the Penal Code. Employees so designated are not peace officers and are not entitled to safety member retirement benefits, as a result of such designation. The employee's authority is limited to the issuance of written notices to appear for infraction violations of provisions of this code and only when the violation is committed in the presence of the employee.

(b) There shall be no civil liability on the part of, and no cause of action shall arise against, any person, acting pursuant to subdivision (a) and within the scope of his or her authority, for false arrest or false imprisonment arising out of any arrest which is lawful or which the person, at the time of such arrest, had reasonable cause to believe was lawful.

(Added by Stats. 1992, Ch. 1135, Sec. 2. Effective January 1, 1993.)

148. ESTABLISHMENT OF ADMINISTRATIVE CITATION SYSTEM

Any board, bureau, or commission within the department may, in addition to the administrative citation system authorized by Section 125.9, also establish, by regulation, a similar system for the issuance of an administrative citation to an unlicensed person who is acting in the capacity of a licensee or registrant under the jurisdiction of that board, bureau, or commission. The administrative citation system authorized by this section shall meet the requirements of Section 125.9 and may not be applied to an unlicensed person who is otherwise exempted from the provisions of the applicable licensing act. The establishment of an administrative citation system for unlicensed activity does not preclude the use of other enforcement statutes for unlicensed activities at the discretion of the board, bureau, or commission.

(Added by Stats. 1992, Ch. 1135, Sec. 2. Effective January 1, 1993.)

149. ENFORCEMENT OF UNLICENSED ADVERTISING

(a) If, upon investigation, an agency designated in Section 101 has probable cause to believe that a person is advertising with respect to the offering or performance of services, without being properly licensed by or registered with the agency to offer or perform those services, the agency may issue a citation under Section 148 containing an order of correction that requires the violator to do both of the following:

(1) Cease the unlawful advertising.

(2) Notify the telephone company furnishing services to the violator to disconnect the telephone service furnished to any telephone number contained in the unlawful advertising.

(b) This action is stayed if the person to whom a citation is issued under subdivision (a) notifies the agency in writing that he or she intends to contest the citation. The agency shall afford an opportunity for a hearing, as specified in Section 125.9.

(c) If the person to whom a citation and order of correction is issued under subdivision (a) fails to comply with the order of correction after that order is final, the agency shall inform the Public Utilities Commission of the violation and the Public Utilities Commission shall require the telephone corporation furnishing services to that person to disconnect the telephone service furnished to any telephone number contained in the unlawful advertising.

(d) The good faith compliance by a telephone corporation with an order of the Public Utilities Commission to terminate service issued pursuant to this section shall constitute a complete defense to any civil or criminal action brought against the telephone corporation arising from the termination of service.

(Amended by Stats. 2014, Ch. 395, Sec. 2. (SB 1243) Effective January 1, 2015.)

CHAPTER 2: THE DIRECTOR OF CONSUMER AFFAIRS

150. DESIGNATION

The department is under the control of a civil executive officer who is known as the Director of Consumer Affairs.

(Amended by Stats. 1971, Ch. 716.)

151. APPOINTMENT AND TENURE; SALARY AND TRAVELING EXPENSES

The director is appointed by the Governor and holds office at the Governor's pleasure. The director shall receive the annual salary provided for by Chapter 6 (commencing with Section 11550) of Part 1 of Division 3 of Title 2 of the Government Code, and the director's necessary traveling expenses.

(Amended by Stats. 2019, Ch. 351, Sec. 38. (AB 496) Effective January 1, 2020.)

152. DEPARTMENTAL ORGANIZATION

For the purpose of administration, the reregistration and clerical work of the department is organized by the director, subject to the approval of the Governor, in such manner as the director deems necessary to properly segregate and conduct the work of the department.

(Amended by Stats. 2020, Ch. 370, Sec. 2. (SB 1371) Effective January 1, 2021.)

152.5. EXTENSION OF RENEWAL DATES

For purposes of distributing the reregistration work of the department uniformly throughout the year as nearly as practicable, the boards in the department may, with the approval of the director, extend by not more than six months the date fixed by law for the renewal of any license, certificate or permit issued by them, except that in such event any renewal fee which may be involved shall be prorated in such manner that no person shall be required to pay a greater or lesser fee than would have been required had the change in renewal dates not occurred.

(Added by Stats. 1959, Ch. 1707.)

152.6. ESTABLISHMENT OF LICENSE PERIODS AND RENEWAL DATES

Notwithstanding any other provision of this code, each board within the department shall, in cooperation with the director, establish such license periods and renewal dates for all licenses in such manner as best to distribute the renewal work of all boards throughout each year and permit the most efficient, and economical use of personnel and equipment. To the extent practicable, provision shall be made for the proration or other adjustment of fees in such manner that no person shall be required to pay a greater or lesser fee than the person would have been required to pay if the change in license periods or renewal dates had not occurred.

As used in this section "license" includes "certificate," "permit," "authority," "registration," and similar indicia of authority to engage in a business or profession, and "board" includes "board," "bureau," "commission," "committee," and an individual who is authorized to renew a license.

(Amended by Stats. 2019, Ch. 351, Sec. 40. (AB 496) Effective January 1, 2020.)

153. INVESTIGATIONS

The director may investigate the work of the boards in the department and may obtain a copy of all records and full and complete data in all official matters in possession of the boards and their members, officers, or employees, other than examination questions prior to submission to applicants at scheduled examinations.

(Amended by Stats. 2019, Ch. 351, Sec. 41. (AB 496) Effective January 1, 2020.)

153.5. INTERIM EXECUTIVE OFFICER

In the event that a newly authorized board replaces an existing or a previous board, the director may appoint an interim executive officer for the board who shall serve temporarily until the new board appoints a permanent executive officer.

(Added by Stats. 2002, Ch. 1079, Sec. 1. Effective September 29, 2002.)

154. MATTER RELATING TO EMPLOYEES OF BOARDS

Any and all matters relating to employment, tenure or discipline of employees of any board, agency or commission, shall be initiated by said board, agency or commission, but all such actions shall, before reference to the State Personnel Board, receive the approval of the appointing power.

To effect the purposes of Division 1 of this code and each agency of the department, employment of all personnel shall be in accord with Article XXIV of the Constitution, the law and rules and regulations of the State Personnel Board. Each board, agency or commission, shall select its employees from a list of eligibles obtained by the appointing power from the State Personnel Board. The person selected by the board, agency or commission to fill any position or vacancy shall thereafter be reported by the board, agency or commission, to the appointing power.

(Amended by Stats. 1945, Ch. 1276.)

154.2. AUTHORITY TO EMPLOY INDIVIDUALS TO PERFORM INVESTIGATIVE SERVICES OR TO SERVE AS EXPERTS

(a) The healing arts boards within Division 2 (commencing with Section 500) may employ individuals, other than peace officers, to perform investigative services.

(b) The healing arts boards within Division 2 (commencing with Section 500) may employ individuals to serve as experts.

(Added by Stats. 2010, Ch. 719, Sec. 1. (SB 856) Effective October 19, 2010.)

154.3 SUBMITTING FINGERPRINTS TO THE DEPARTMENT OF JUSTICE

(a) Pursuant to subdivision (u) of Section 11105 of the Penal Code, the department shall submit to the Department of Justice fingerprint images and related information required by the Department of Justice for an employee, prospective employee, contractor, subcontractor, or volunteer. The Department of Justice shall provide a state- or federal-level response pursuant to subdivision (p) of Section 11105 of the Penal Code.

(b) Pursuant to subdivision (u) of Section 11105 of the Penal Code, the department shall submit to the Department of Justice fingerprint images and related information required by the Department of Justice for all peace officer employees and prospective peace officer employees of the department. The Department of Justice shall provide a state- or federal-level response pursuant to subdivision (k) of Section 11105 of the Penal Code.

(Added by Stats. 2024, Ch. 997, Sec. 1. (AB 179) Effective September 30, 2024.)

154.5. LEGAL ASSISTANCE OF EXPERTS AIDING IN INVESTIGATIONS OF LICENSEES

If a person, not a regular employee of a board under this code, including the Board of Chiropractic Examiners and the Osteopathic Medical Board of California, is hired or under contract to provide expertise to the board in the evaluation of an applicant or the conduct of a licensee, and that person is named as a defendant in a civil action arising out of the evaluation or any opinions rendered, statements made, or testimony given to the board or its representatives, the board shall provide for representation required to defend the defendant in that civil action. The board shall not be liable for any judgment rendered against the person.

The Attorney General shall be utilized in the action and his or her services shall be a charge against the board.

(Amended by Stats. 1991, Ch. 359, Sec. 3.)

155. EMPLOYMENT OF INVESTIGATORS; INSPECTORS AS EMPLOYEES OR UNDER CONTRACT

(a) In accordance with Section 159.5, the director may employ such investigators, inspectors, and deputies as are necessary properly to investigate and prosecute all violations of any law, the enforcement of which is charged to the department or to any board, agency, or commission in the department.

(b) It is the intent of the Legislature that inspectors used by boards, bureaus, or commissions in the department shall not be required to be employees of the Division of Investigation, but may either be employees of, or under contract to, the boards, bureaus, or commissions. Contracts for services shall be consistent with Article 4.5 (commencing with Section 19130) of Chapter 6 of Part 2 of Division 5 of Title 2 of the Government Code. All civil service employees currently employed as inspectors whose functions are transferred as a result of this section shall retain their positions, status, and rights in accordance with Section 19994.10 of the Government Code and the State Civil Service Act (Part 2 (commencing with Section 18500) of Division 5 of Title 2 of the Government Code).

(c) Nothing in this section limits the authority of, or prohibits, investigators in the Division of Investigation in the conduct of inspections or investigations of any licensee, or in the conduct of investigations of any officer or employee of a board or the department at the specific request of the director or his or her designee.

(Amended by Stats. 1985, Ch. 1382, Sec. 1.)

156. CONTRACTUAL AUTHORITY

(a) The director may, for the department and at the request and with the consent of a board within the department on whose behalf the contract is to be made, enter into contracts pursuant to Chapter 3 (commencing with Section 11250) of Part 1 of Division 3 of Title 2 of the Government Code or Chapter 2 (commencing with Section 10290) of Part 2 of Division 2 of the Public Contract Code for and on behalf of any board within the department.

(b) In accordance with subdivision (a), the director may, in his or her discretion, negotiate and execute contracts for examination purposes, which include provisions that hold harmless a contractor where liability resulting from a contract between a board in the department and the contractor is traceable to the state or its officers, agents, or employees.

(c) The director shall report progress on release 3 entities' transition to a new licensing technology platform to all the appropriate committees of the Legislature by December 31 of each year. Progress reports shall include updated plans and timelines for completing all of the following:

(1) Business process documentation.

(2) Cost benefit analyses of information technology options.

(3) Information technology system development and implementation.

(4) Any other relevant steps needed to meet the IT needs of release 3 entities.

(5) Any other information as the Legislature may request.

(Amended by Stats. 2017, Ch. 429, Sec. 2. (SB 547) Effective January 1, 2018.)

156.1. RETENTION OF RECORDS BY PROVIDERS OF SERVICES RELATED TO TREATMENT OF ALCOHOL OR DRUG IMPAIRMENT

(a) Notwithstanding any other law, individuals or entities contracting with the department or any board within the department for the provision of services relating to the treatment and rehabilitation of licensees impaired by alcohol or dangerous drugs shall retain all records and documents pertaining to those services until such time as these records and documents have been reviewed for audit by the department. These records and documents shall be retained for three years from the date of the last treatment or service rendered to that licensee, after which time the records and documents may be purged and destroyed by the contract vendor. This provision shall supersede any other law relating to the purging or destruction of records pertaining to those treatment and rehabilitation programs.

(b) Unless otherwise expressly provided by statute or regulation, all records and documents pertaining to services for the treatment and rehabilitation of licensees impaired by alcohol or dangerous drugs provided by any contract vendor to the department or to any board within the department shall be kept confidential and are not subject to discovery or subpoena.

(c) With respect to all other contracts for services with the department, or any board within the department other than those set forth in subdivision (a), the director or chief deputy director may request an examination and audit by the department's internal auditor of all performance under the contract. For this purpose, all documents and records of the contract vendor in connection with such performance shall be retained by the vendor for a period of three years after final payment under the contract. Nothing in this section shall affect the authority of the State Auditor to conduct any examination or audit under the terms of Section 8546.7 of the Government Code.

(Amended by Stats. 2019, Ch. 351, Sec. 42. (AB 496) Effective January 1, 2020.)

156.5. LEASES OF EXAMINATION OR MEETING PURPOSES

The director may negotiate and execute for the department and for its component agencies, rental agreements for short-term hiring of space and furnishings for examination or meeting purposes. The director may, in his or her discretion, negotiate and execute contracts for that space which include provisions which hold harmless the provider of the space where liability resulting from use of the space under the contract is traceable to the state or its officers, agents, or employees.

Notwithstanding any other provision of law, the director may, in his or her discretion, advance payments as deposits to reserve and hold examination or meeting space. Any such agreement is subject to the approval of the legal office of the Department of General Services.

(Amended by Stats. 1988, Ch. 1448, Sec. 1.5.)

157. EXPENSES IN CRIMINAL PROSECUTION AND UNPROFESSIONAL CONDUCT PROCEEDINGS

Expenses incurred by any board or on behalf of any board in any criminal prosecution or unprofessional conduct proceeding constitute proper charges against the funds of the board.

(Added by Stats. 1937, Ch. 474.)

158. REFUNDS TO APPLICANTS

With the approval of the Director of Consumer Affairs, the boards and commissions comprising the department or subject to its jurisdiction may make refunds to applicants who are found ineligible to take the examinations or whose credentials are insufficient to entitle them to certificates or licenses.

Notwithstanding any other law, any application fees, license fees, or penalties imposed and collected illegally, by mistake, inadvertence, or error shall be refunded. Claims authorized by the department shall be filed with the State Controller, and the Controller shall draw a warrant against the fund of the agency in payment of the refund.

(Amended by Stats. 2019, Ch. 351, Sec. 43. (AB 496) Effective January 1, 2020.)

159. ADMINISTRATION OF OATHS

The members and the executive officer of each board, agency, bureau, division, or commission have power to administer oaths and affirmations in the performance of any business of the board, and to certify to official acts.

(Added by Stats. 1947, Ch. 1350.)

159.5. DIVISION OF INVESTIGATION; TRANSFER AGENCY PERSONNEL

(a) (1) There is in the department the Division of Investigation. The division is in the charge of a person with the title of chief of the division.

(2) Except as provided in Section 160, investigators who have the authority of peace officers, as specified in subdivision (a) of Section 160 and in subdivision (a) of Section 830.3 of the Penal Code, shall be in the division and shall be appointed by the director.

(b) (1) There is in the Division of Investigation the Health Quality Investigation Unit. The primary responsibility of the unit is to investigate violations of law or regulation within the jurisdiction of the Medical Board of California, the Podiatric Medical Board of California, the Board of Psychology, the Osteopathic Medical Board of California, the Physician Assistant Board, or any entities under the jurisdiction of the Medical Board of California.

(2) The Medical Board of California shall not be charged an hourly rate for the performance of investigations by the unit.

(Amended by Stats. 2019, Ch. 351, Sec. 44. (AB 496) Effective January 1, 2020.)

160. PEACE OFFICER STATUS OF INVESTIGATORS

(a) The chief and all investigators of the Division of Investigation of the department and all investigators of the Dental Board of California have the authority of peace officers while engaged in exercising the powers granted or performing the duties imposed upon them or the division in investigating the laws administered by the various boards comprising the department or commencing directly or indirectly any criminal prosecution arising from any investigation conducted under these laws. All persons herein referred to shall be deemed to be acting within the scope of employment with respect to all acts and matters set forth in this section.

(b) The Division of Investigation of the department and the Dental Board of California may employ individuals, who are not peace officers, to provide investigative services.

(c) This section shall become operative on July 1, 2014.

(Repealed (in Sec. 2) and added by Stats. 2013, Ch. 515, Sec. 3. (SB 304) Effective January 1, 2014. Section operative July 1, 2014, by its own provisions.)

161. SALE OF COPIES OF PUBLIC RECORDS

The department, or any board in the department, may, in accordance with the California Public Records Act (Division 10 (commencing with Section 7920.000) of Title 1 of the Government Code) and the Information Practices Act of 1977 (Chapter 1 (commencing with Section 1798) of Title 1.8 of Part 4 of Division 3 of the Civil Code), make available to the public copies of any part of its respective public records, or compilations, extracts, or summaries of information contained in its public records, at a charge sufficient to pay the actual cost thereof. That charge shall be determined by the director with the approval of the Department of General Services.

(Amended by Stats. 2021, Ch. 615, Sec. 3. (AB 474) Effective January 1, 2022. Operative January 1, 2023, pursuant to Section 463 of Stats. 2021, Ch. 615.)

162. EVIDENTIARY EFFECT OF CERTIFICATE OF RECORDS OFFICER AS TO LICENSE, ETC.

The certificate of the officer in charge of the records of any board in the department that any person was or was not on a specified date, or during a specified period of time, licensed, certified or registered under the provisions of law administered by the board, or that the license, certificate or registration of any person was revoked or under suspension, shall be admitted in any court as prima facie evidence of the facts therein recited.

(Added by Stats. 1949, Ch. 355.)

163. FEE FOR CERTIFICATION OF RECORDS, ETC.

Except as otherwise expressly provided by law, the department and each board in the department shall charge a fee of two dollars ($2) for the certification of a copy of any record, document, or paper in its custody or for the certification of any document evidencing the content of any such record, document or paper.

(Amended by Stats. 1963, Ch. 590.)

163.5. DELINQUENCY FEES; REINSTATEMENT FEES

Except as otherwise provided by law, the delinquency, penalty, or late fee for any licensee within the Department of Consumer Affairs shall be 50 percent of the renewal fee for such license in effect on the date of the renewal of the license, but not less than twenty-five dollars ($25) nor more than one hundred fifty dollars ($150).

A delinquency, penalty, or late fee shall not be assessed until 30 days have elapsed from the date that the licensing agency mailed a notice of renewal to the licensee at the licensee's last known address of record. The notice shall specify the date for timely renewal, and that failure to renew in a timely fashion shall result in the assessment of a delinquency, penalty, or late fee.

In the event a reinstatement or like fee is charged for the reinstatement of a license, the reinstatement fee shall be 150 percent of the renewal fee for such license in effect on the date of the reinstatement of the license, but not more than twenty-five dollars ($25) in excess of the renewal fee, except that in the event that such a fee is fixed by statute at less than 150 percent of the renewal fee and less than the renewal fee plus twenty-five dollars ($25), the fee so fixed shall be charged.

(Amended by Stats. 1985, Ch. 587, Sec. 1.)

164. FORM AND CONTENT OF LICENSE, CERTIFICATE, PERMIT, OR SIMILAR INDICIA OF AUTHORITY

The form and content of any license, certificate, permit, or similar indicia of authority issued by any agency in the department, including any document evidencing renewal of a license, certificate, permit, or similar indicia of authority, shall be determined by the director after consultation with and consideration of the views of the agency concerned.

(Amended by Stats. 1987, Ch. 850, Sec. 6.)

165. PROHIBITION AGAINST SUBMISSION OF FISCAL IMPACT ANALYSIS RELATING TO PENDING LEGISLATION WITHOUT PRIOR SUBMISSION TO DIRECTOR FOR COMMENT

Notwithstanding any other provision of law, no board, bureau, committee, commission, or program in the Department of Consumer Affairs shall submit to the Legislature any fiscal impact analysis relating to legislation pending before the Legislature until the analysis has been submitted to the Director of Consumer Affairs, or his or her designee, for review and comment. The boards, bureaus, committees, commissions, and programs shall include the comments of the director when submitting any fiscal impact analysis to the Legislature. This section shall not be construed to prohibit boards, bureaus, committees, commissions, and programs from responding to direct requests for fiscal data from Members of the Legislature or their staffs. In those instances it shall be the responsibility of boards, bureaus, committees, commissions, and programs to also transmit that information to the director, or his or her designee, within five working days.

(Added by Stats. 1984, Ch. 268, Sec. 0.2. Effective June 30, 1984.)

166. DEVELOPMENT OF GUIDELINES FOR MANDATORY CONTINUING EDUCATION PROGRAMS

The director shall, by regulation, develop guidelines to prescribe components for mandatory continuing education programs administered by any board within the department.

(a) The guidelines shall be developed to ensure that mandatory continuing education is used as a means to create a more competent licensing population, thereby enhancing public protection. The guidelines shall require mandatory continuing education programs to address, at least, the following:

(1) Course validity.

(2) Occupational relevancy.

(3) Effective presentation.

(4) Actual attendance.

(5) Material assimilation.

(6) Potential for application.

(b) The director shall consider educational principles, and the guidelines shall prescribe mandatory continuing education program formats to include, but not be limited to, the following:

(1) The specified audience.

(2) Identification of what is to be learned.

(3) Clear goals and objectives.

(4) Relevant learning methods (participatory, hands-on, or clinical setting).

(5) Evaluation, focused on the learner and the assessment of the intended learning outcomes (goals and objectives).

(c) Any board within the department that, after January 1, 1993, proposes a mandatory continuing education program for its licensees shall submit the proposed program to the director for review to assure that the program contains all the elements set forth in this section and complies with the guidelines developed by the director.

(d) Any board administering a mandatory continuing education program that proposes to amend its current program shall do so in a manner consistent with this section.

(e) Any board currently administering a mandatory continuing education program shall review the components and requirements of the program to determine the extent to which they are consistent with the guidelines developed under this section. The board shall submit a report of their findings to the director. The report shall identify the similarities and differences of its mandatory continuing education program. The report shall include any board-specific needs to explain the variation from the director's guidelines.

(f) Any board administering a mandatory continuing education program, when accepting hours for credit which are obtained out of state, shall ensure that the course for which credit is given is administered in accordance with the guidelines addressed in subdivision (a).

(g) Nothing in this section or in the guidelines adopted by the director shall be construed to repeal any requirements for continuing education programs set forth in any other provision of this code.

(Amended by Stats. 1994, Ch. 146, Sec. 1. Effective January 1, 1995.)

CHAPTER 3: FUNDS OF THE DEPARTMENT

201. LEVY FOR ADMINISTRATIVE EXPENSES

(a) (1) A charge for the estimated administrative expenses of the department, not to exceed the available balance in any appropriation for any one fiscal year, may be levied in advance on a pro rata share basis against any of the boards, bureaus, commissions, divisions, and agencies, at the discretion of the director and with the approval of the Department of Finance.

(2) The department shall submit a report of the accounting of the pro rata calculation of administrative expenses to the appropriate policy committees of the Legislature on or before July 1, 2015, and on or before July 1 of each subsequent year.

(b) The department shall conduct a one-time study of its current system for prorating administrative expenses to determine if that system is the most productive, efficient, and cost-effective manner for the department and the agencies comprising the department. The study shall include consideration of whether some of the administrative services offered by the department should be outsourced or charged on an as- needed basis and whether the agencies should be permitted to elect not to receive and be charged for certain administrative services. The department shall include the findings in its report pursuant to paragraph (2) of subdivision (a) that it is required to submit on or before July 1, 2015.

(Amended by Stats. 2014, Ch. 395, Sec. 4. (SB 1243) Effective January 1, 2015.)

205. PROFESSIONS AND VOCATIONS FUND (REPEALED JULY 1, 2026)

(a) There is in the State Treasury the Professions and Vocations Fund. The fund shall consist of the following special funds:

(1) Accountancy Fund.

(2) California Architects Board Fund.

(3) Athletic Commission Fund.

(4) Barbering and Cosmetology Contingent Fund.

(5) Cemetery and Funeral Fund.

(6) Contractors License Fund.

(7) State Dentistry Fund.

(8) Home Furnishings and Thermal Insulation Fund.

(9) California Architects Board-Landscape Architects Fund.

(10) Contingent Fund of the Medical Board of California.

(11) Optometry Fund.

(12) Pharmacy Board Contingent Fund.

(13) Physical Therapy Fund.

(14) Private Security Services Fund.

(15) Professional Engineer's, Land Surveyor's, and Geologist's Fund.

(16) Consumer Affairs Fund.

(17) Behavioral Sciences Fund.

(18) Licensed Midwifery Fund.

(19) Court Reporters' Fund.

(20) Veterinary Medical Board Contingent Fund.

(21) Vocational Nursing and Psychiatric Technicians Fund.

(22) Electronic and Appliance Repair Fund.

(23) Acupuncture Fund.

(24) Physician Assistant Fund.

(25) Board of Podiatric Medicine Fund.

(26) Psychology Fund.

(27) Respiratory Care Fund.

(28) Speech-Language Pathology and Audiology and Hearing Aid Dispensers Fund.

(29) Board of Registered Nursing Fund.

(30) Animal Health Technician Examining Committee Fund.

(31) State Dental Hygiene Fund.

(32) Structural Pest Control Fund.

(33) Structural Pest Control Education and Enforcement Fund.

(34) Structural Pest Control Research Fund.

(35) Household Movers Fund.

(36) Household Goods and Services Fund.

(b) For accounting and recordkeeping purposes, the Professions and Vocations Fund shall be deemed to be a single special fund, and each of the several special funds therein shall constitute and be deemed to be a separate account in the Professions and Vocations Fund. Each account or fund shall be available for expenditure only for the purposes as are now or may hereafter be provided by law.

(c) This section shall remain in effect only until July 1, 2026, and as of that date is repealed.

(Amended by Stats. 2023, Ch. 508, Sec. 1. (SB 814) Effective January 1, 2024. Repealed as of July 1, 2026, by its own provisions. See later operative version added by Sec. 2 of Stats. 2023, Ch. 508.)

205. PROFESSIONS AND VOCATIONS FUND (OPERATIVE JULY 1, 2026)

(a) There is in the State Treasury the Professions and Vocations Fund. The fund shall consist of the following special funds:

(1) Accountancy Fund.

(2) California Architects Board Fund.

(3) Athletic Commission Fund.

(4) Barbering and Cosmetology Contingent Fund.

(5) Cemetery and Funeral Fund.

(6) Contractors License Fund.

(7) State Dentistry Fund.

(8) California Architects Board-Landscape Architects Fund.

(9) Contingent Fund of the Medical Board of California.

(10) Optometry Fund.

(11) Pharmacy Board Contingent Fund.

(12) Physical Therapy Fund.

(13) Private Security Services Fund.

(14) Professional Engineer's, Land Surveyor's, and Geologist's Fund.

(15) Consumer Affairs Fund.

(16) Behavioral Sciences Fund.

(17) Licensed Midwifery Fund.

(18) Court Reporters' Fund.

(19) Veterinary Medical Board Contingent Fund.

(20) Vocational Nursing and Psychiatric Technicians Fund.

(21) Acupuncture Fund.

(22) Physician Assistant Fund.

(23) Board of Podiatric Medicine Fund.

(24) Psychology Fund.

(25) Respiratory Care Fund.

(26) Speech-Language Pathology and Audiology and Hearing Aid Dispensers Fund.

(27) Board of Registered Nursing Fund.

(28) Animal Health Technician Examining Committee Fund.

(29) State Dental Hygiene Fund.

(30) Structural Pest Control Fund.

(31) Structural Pest Control Education and Enforcement Fund.

(32) Structural Pest Control Research Fund.

(33) Household Goods and Services Fund.

(b) For accounting and recordkeeping purposes, the Professions and Vocations Fund shall be deemed to be a single special fund, and each of the several special funds therein shall constitute and be deemed to be a separate account in the Professions and Vocations Fund. Each account or fund shall be available for expenditure only for the purposes as are now or may hereafter be provided by law.

(c) This section shall become operative on July 1, 2026.

(Repealed (in Sec. 1) and added by Stats. 2023, Ch. 508, Sec. 2. (SB 814) Effective January 1, 2024. Operative July 1, 2026, by its own provisions.)

205.3. DISPENSING OPTICIANS FUND MEANING

Whenever any reference is made in any provision of this code to the "Dispensing Opticians Fund," it means the Optometry Fund. All moneys within the Dispensing Opticians Fund shall be deposited into the Optometry Fund by July 1, 2022. On July 1, 2022, the Dispensing Opticians Fund shall be abolished.

(Added by Stats. 2020, Ch. 121, Sec. 2. (AB 896) Effective September 24, 2020.)

206. DISHONORED CHECK TENDERED FOR PAYMENT OF FINE, FEE, OR PENALTY

Notwithstanding any other provision of law, any person tendering a check for payment of a fee, fine, or penalty that was subsequently dishonored, shall not be granted a license, or other authority that they were seeking, until the applicant pays the amount outstanding from the dishonored payment together with the applicable fee, including any delinquency fee. The board may require the person whose check was returned unpaid to make payment of all fees by cashier's check or money order.

(Added by Stats. 1994, Ch. 26, Sec. 12. Effective March 30, 1994.)

207. APPROPRIATION REQUIRED

(a) Notwithstanding any other provision of law, the money in any fund described in Section 205 that is attributable to administrative fines, civil penalties, and criminal penalties imposed by a regulating entity, or cost recovery by a regulating entity from enforcement actions and case settlements, shall not be continuously appropriated. The money in each fund that is not continuously appropriated shall be available for expenditure as provided in this code only upon appropriation by the Legislature.

(b) Notwithstanding any other provision of law, the annual Budget Act may appropriate, in a single budget item for each individual fund described in subdivision (a) of Section 205, the entire amount available for expenditure in the budget year for that fund. That appropriation may include funds that are continuously appropriated and funds that are not continuously appropriated.

(Amended by Stats. 2015, Ch. 428, Sec. 3. (AB 177) Effective January 1, 2016.)

208. CURES FUND (INOPERATIVE APRIL 1, 2025)

(a) Beginning April 1, 2023, a Controlled Substance Utilization Review and Evaluation System (CURES) fee of nine dollars ($9) shall be assessed annually on each of the licensees specified in subdivision (b) to pay the reasonable costs associated with operating and maintaining CURES for the purpose of regulating those licensees. The fee assessed pursuant to this subdivision shall be billed and collected by the regulating agency of each licensee at the time of the licensee's license renewal. If the reasonable regulatory cost of operating and maintaining CURES is less than nine dollars ($9) per licensee, the Department of Consumer Affairs may, by regulation, reduce the fee established by this section to the reasonable regulatory cost.

(b) (1) Licensees authorized pursuant to Section 11150 of the Health and Safety Code to prescribe, order, administer, furnish, or dispense Schedule II, Schedule III, or Schedule IV controlled substances or pharmacists licensed pursuant to Chapter 9 (commencing with Section 4000) of Division 2.

(2) Licensees issued a license that has been placed in a retired or inactive status pursuant to a statute or regulation are exempt from the CURES fee requirement in subdivision (a). This exemption shall not apply to licensees whose license has been placed in a retired or inactive status if the licensee is at any time authorized to prescribe, order, administer, furnish, or dispense Schedule II, Schedule III, or Schedule IV controlled substances.

(3) Wholesalers, third-party logistics providers, nonresident wholesalers, and nonresident third-party logistics providers of dangerous drugs licensed pursuant to Article 11 (commencing with Section 4160) of Chapter 9 of Division 2.

(4) Nongovernmental clinics licensed pursuant to Article 13 (commencing with Section 4180) and Article 14 (commencing with Section 4190) of Chapter 9 of Division 2.

(5) Nongovernmental pharmacies licensed pursuant to Article 7 (commencing with Section 4110) of Chapter 9 of Division 2.

(c) The funds collected pursuant to subdivision (a) shall be deposited in the CURES Fund, which is hereby created within the State Treasury. Moneys in the CURES Fund shall, upon appropriation by the Legislature, be available to the Department of Consumer Affairs to reimburse the Department of Justice for costs to operate and maintain CURES for the purposes of regulating the licensees specified in subdivision (b).

(d) The Department of Consumer Affairs shall contract with the Department of Justice on behalf of the Medical Board of California, the Dental Board of California, the California State Board of Pharmacy, the Veterinary Medical Board, the Board of Registered Nursing, the Physician Assistant Board, the Osteopathic Medical Board of California, the Naturopathic Medicine Committee of the Osteopathic Medical Board, the State Board of Optometry, and the Podiatric Medical Board of California to operate and maintain CURES for the purposes of regulating the licensees specified in subdivision (b).

(e) This section shall become operative on April 1, 2023.

(f) This section shall become inoperative on April 1, 2025, and, as of January 1, 2026, is repealed.

(Amended by Stats. 2024, Ch. 41, Sec. 2. (SB 164) Effective June 29, 2024. Inoperative April 1, 2025, by its own provisions. Repealed as of January 1, 2026, by its own provisions. See later operative version added by Sec. 3 of Stats. 2024, Ch. 41.)

208. CURES FUND (OPERATIVE APRIL 1, 2025)

(a) Beginning April 1, 2025, a Controlled Substance Utilization Review and Evaluation System (CURES) fee of fifteen dollars ($15) shall be assessed annually on each of the licensees specified in subdivision (b) to pay the reasonable costs associated with operating and maintaining CURES for the purpose of regulating those licensees. The fee assessed pursuant to this subdivision shall be billed and collected by the regulating agency of each licensee at the time of the licensee's license renewal. If the reasonable regulatory cost of operating and maintaining CURES is less than fifteen dollars ($15) per licensee, the Department of Consumer Affairs may, by regulation, reduce the fee established by this section to the reasonable regulatory cost.

(b) (1) Licensees authorized pursuant to Section 11150 of the Health and Safety Code to prescribe, order, administer, furnish, or dispense Schedule II, Schedule III, or Schedule IV controlled substances or pharmacists licensed pursuant to Chapter 9 (commencing with Section 4000) of Division 2.

(2) Licensees issued a license that has been placed in a retired or inactive status pursuant to a statute or regulation are exempt from the CURES fee requirement in subdivision (a). This exemption shall not apply to licensees whose license has been placed in a retired or inactive status if the licensee is at any time authorized to prescribe, order, administer, furnish, or dispense Schedule II, Schedule III, or Schedule IV controlled substances.

(3) Wholesalers, third-party logistics providers, nonresident wholesalers, and nonresident third-party logistics providers of dangerous drugs licensed pursuant to Article 11 (commencing with Section 4160) of Chapter 9 of Division 2.

(4) Nongovernmental clinics licensed pursuant to Article 13 (commencing with Section 4180) and Article 14 (commencing with Section 4190) of Chapter 9 of Division 2.

(5) Nongovernmental pharmacies licensed pursuant to Article 7 (commencing with Section 4110) of Chapter 9 of Division 2.

(c) The funds collected pursuant to subdivision (a) shall be deposited in the CURES Fund, which is hereby created within the State Treasury. Moneys in the CURES Fund shall, upon appropriation by the Legislature, be available to the Department of Consumer Affairs to reimburse the Department of Justice for costs to operate and maintain CURES for the purposes of regulating the licensees specified in subdivision (b).

(d) The Department of Consumer Affairs shall contract with the Department of Justice on behalf of the Medical Board of California, the Dental Board of California, the California State Board of Pharmacy, the Veterinary Medical Board, the Board of Registered Nursing, the Physician Assistant Board, the Osteopathic Medical Board of California, the Naturopathic Medicine Committee of the Osteopathic Medical Board, the State Board of Optometry, and the Podiatric Medical Board of California to operate and maintain CURES for the purposes of regulating the licensees specified in subdivision (b).

(e) This section shall become operative on April 1, 2025.

(Repealed (in Sec. 2) and added by Stats. 2024, Ch. 41, Sec. 3. (SB 164) Effective June 29, 2024. Operative April 1, 2025, by its own provisions.)

209. ACCESS TO THE CURES PRESCRIPTION DRUG MONITORING PROGRAM

The Department of Justice, in conjunction with the Department of Consumer Affairs and the boards and committees identified in subdivision (d) of Section 208, shall do all of the following:

(a) Identify and implement a streamlined application and approval process to provide access to the CURES Prescription Drug Monitoring Program (PDMP) database for licensed health care practitioners eligible to prescribe, order, administer, furnish, or dispense Schedule II, Schedule III, or Schedule IV controlled substances and for pharmacists. Every reasonable effort shall be made to implement a streamlined application and approval process that a licensed health care practitioner or pharmacist can complete at the time that they are applying for licensure or renewing their license.

(b) Identify necessary procedures to enable licensed health care practitioners and pharmacists with access to the CURES PDMP to delegate their authority to access reports from the CURES PDMP.

(c) Develop a procedure to enable health care practitioners who do not have a federal Drug Enforcement Administration (DEA) number to opt out of applying for access to the CURES PDMP.

(Amended by Stats. 2019, Ch. 677, Sec. 2. (AB 528) Effective January 1, 2020.)

CHAPTER 4: CONSUMER AFFAIRS

ARTICLE 3: POWERS AND DUTIES

310. DIRECTOR'S POWERS AND DUTIES

The director shall have the following powers and it shall be his duty to:

(a) Recommend and propose the enactment of such legislation as necessary to protect and promote the interests of consumers.

(b) Represent the consumer's interests before federal and state legislative hearings and executive commissions.

(c) Assist, advise, and cooperate with federal, state, and local agencies and officials to protect and promote the interests of consumers.

(d) Study, investigate, research, and analyze matters affecting the interests of consumers.

(e) Hold public hearings, subpoena witnesses, take testimony, compel the production of books, papers, documents, and other evidence, and call upon other state agencies for information.

(f) Propose and assist in the creation and development of consumer education programs.

(g) Promote ethical standards of conduct for business and consumers and undertake activities to encourage public responsibility in the production, promotion, sale and lease of consumer goods and services.

(h) Advise the Governor and Legislature on all matters affecting the interests of consumers.

(i) Exercise and perform such other functions, powers and duties as may be deemed appropriate to protect and promote the interests of consumers as directed by the Governor or the Legislature.

(j) Maintain contact and liaison with consumer groups in California and nationally.

(Amended by Stats. 1975, Ch. 1262.)

312. REPORT TO GOVERNOR AND LEGISLATURE

(a) The director shall submit to the Governor and the Legislature on or before January 1, 2003, and annually thereafter, a report of programmatic and statistical information regarding the activities of the department and its constituent entities for the previous fiscal year. The report shall include information concerning the director's activities pursuant to Section 326, including the number and general patterns of consumer complaints and the action taken on those complaints.

(b) The report shall include information relative to the performance of each constituent entity, including, but not limited to, length of time for a constituent entity to reach each of the following milestones in the enforcement process:

(1) Average number of days from when a constituent entity receives a complaint until the constituent entity assigns an investigator to the complaint.

(2) Average number of days from a constituent entity opening an investigation conducted by the constituent entity staff or the Division of Investigation to closing the investigation regardless of outcome.

(3) Average number of days from a constituent entity closing an investigation to imposing formal discipline.

(c) A report submitted pursuant to subdivision (a) shall be submitted in compliance with Section 9795 of the Government Code.

(Amended by Stats. 2014, Ch. 395, Sec. 6. (SB 1243) Effective January 1, 2015.)

313.1. COMPLIANCE WITH SECTION AS REQUIREMENT FOR EFFECTIVENESS OF SPECIFIED RULES OR REGULATIONS; SUBMISSION OF RECORDS; AUTHORITY FOR DISAPPROVAL

(a) Notwithstanding any other provision of law to the contrary, no rule or regulation, except those relating to examinations and qualifications for licensure, and no fee change proposed or promulgated by any of the boards, commissions, or committees within the department, shall take effect pending compliance with this section.

(b) The director shall be formally notified of and shall be provided a full opportunity to review, in accordance with the requirements of Article 5 (commencing with Section 11346) of Chapter 3.5 of Part 1 of Division 3 of Title 2 of the Government Code, and this section, all of the following:

(1) All notices of proposed action, any modifications and supplements thereto, and the text of proposed regulations.

(2) Any notices of sufficiently related changes to regulations previously noticed to the public, and the text of proposed regulations showing modifications to the text.

(3) Final rulemaking records.

(c) The submission of all notices and final rulemaking records to the director and the completion of the director's review, as authorized by this section, shall be a precondition to the filing of any rule or regulation with the Office of Administrative Law. The Office of Administrative Law shall have no jurisdiction to review a rule or regulation subject to this section until after the completion of the director's review and only then if the director has not disapproved it. The filing of any document with the Office of Administrative Law shall be accompanied by a certification that the board, commission, or committee has complied with the requirements of this section.

(d) Following the receipt of any final rulemaking record subject to subdivision (a), the director shall have the authority for a period of 30 days to disapprove a proposed rule or regulation on the ground that it is injurious to the public health, safety, or welfare.

(e) Final rulemaking records shall be filed with the director within the one-year notice period specified in Section 11346.4 of the Government Code. If necessary for compliance with this section, the one-year notice period may be extended, as specified by this subdivision.

(1) In the event that the one-year notice period lapses during the director's 30-day review period, or within 60 days following the notice of the director's disapproval, it may be extended for a maximum of 90 days.

(2) If the director approves the final rulemaking record or declines to take action on it within 30 days, the board, commission, or committee shall have five days from the receipt of the record from the director within which to file it with the Office of Administrative Law.

(3) If the director disapproves a rule or regulation, it shall have no force or effect unless, within 60 days of the notice of disapproval, (A) the disapproval is overridden by a unanimous vote of the members of the board, commission, or committee, and (B) the board, commission, or committee files the final rulemaking record with the Office of Administrative Law in compliance with this section and the procedures required by Chapter 3.5 (commencing with Section 11340) of Part 1 of Division 3 of Title 2 of the Government Code.

(f) Nothing in this section shall be construed to prohibit the director from affirmatively approving a proposed rule, regulation, or fee change at any time within the 30-day period after it has been submitted to him or her, in which event it shall become effective upon compliance with this section and the procedures required by Chapter 3.5 (commencing with Section 11340) of Part 1 of Division 3 of Title 2 of the Government Code.

(Amended by Stats. 1994, Ch. 26, Sec. 13. Effective March 30, 1994.)

313.2. ADOPTION OF REGULATIONS IN CONFORMANCE WITH AMERICANS WITH DISABILITIES ACT

The director shall adopt regulations to implement, interpret, and make specific the provisions of the Americans with Disabilities Act (P.L. 101-336), as they relate to the examination process for professional licensing and certification programs under the purview of the department.

(Added by Stats. 1992, Ch. 1289, Sec. 3. Effective January 1, 1993.)

314. PROHIBITING EARN AND LEARN PROGRAMS

(a) The department or board shall not approve an accrediting entity that prohibits earn and learn programs for training in a profession licensed or certified by the board. A board shall use licensing or certification standards that authorize the use of earn and learn training.

(b) Notwithstanding subdivision (a), the department and its boards shall not be required to establish a mandate specifying an accrediting entity must provide earn and learn programs for training in a profession licensed or certified by a board.

(c) As used in this section, "earn and learn" has the same meaning as defined in subdivision (q) of Section 14005 of the Unemployment Insurance Code.

(d) This section shall become operative on January 1, 2024.

(Added by Stats. 2021, Ch. 477, Sec. 2. (AB 1273) Effective January 1, 2022. Operative January 1, 2024, by its own provisions.)

ARTICLE 3.6: UNIFORM STANDARDS REGARDING SUBSTANCE-ABUSING HEALING ARTS LICENSEES

315. ESTABLISHMENT OF SUBSTANCE ABUSE COORDINATION COMMITTEE; MEMBERS; DUTIES

(a) For the purpose of determining uniform standards that will be used by healing arts boards in dealing with substance-abusing licensees, there is established in the Department of Consumer Affairs the Substance Abuse Coordination Committee. The committee shall be comprised of the executive officers of the department's healing arts boards established pursuant to Division 2 (commencing with Section 500), the State Board of Chiropractic Examiners, the Osteopathic Medical Board of California, and a designee of the State Department of Health Care Services. The Director of Consumer Affairs shall chair the committee and may invite individuals or stakeholders who have particular expertise in the area of substance abuse to advise the committee.

(b) The committee shall be subject to the Bagley-Keene Open Meeting Act (Article 9 (commencing with Section 11120) of Division 3 of Title 2 of the Government Code).

(c) By January 1, 2010, the committee shall formulate uniform and specific standards in each of the following areas that each healing arts board shall use in dealing with substance-abusing licensees, whether or not a board chooses to have a formal diversion program:

(1) Specific requirements for a clinical diagnostic evaluation of the licensee,

including, but not limited to, required qualifications for the providers evaluating the licensee.

(2) Specific requirements for the temporary removal of the licensee from practice, in order to enable the licensee to undergo the clinical diagnostic evaluation described in paragraph (1) and any treatment recommended by the evaluator described in paragraph (1) and approved by the board, and specific criteria that the licensee must meet before being permitted to return to practice on a full- time or part-time basis.

(3) Specific requirements that govern the ability of the licensing board to communicate with the licensee's employer about the licensee's status and condition.

(4) Standards governing all aspects of required testing, including, but not limited to, frequency of testing, randomness, method of notice to the licensee, number of hours between the provision of notice and the test, standards for specimen collectors, procedures used by specimen collectors, the permissible locations of testing, whether the collection process must be observed by the collector, backup testing requirements when the licensee is on vacation or otherwise unavailable for local testing, requirements for the laboratory that analyzes the specimens, and the required maximum timeframe from the test to the receipt of the result of the test.

(5) Standards governing all aspects of group meeting attendance requirements, including, but not limited to, required qualifications for group meeting facilitators, frequency of required meeting attendance, and methods of documenting and reporting attendance or nonattendance by licensees.

(6) Standards used in determining whether inpatient, outpatient, or other type of treatment is necessary.

(7) Worksite monitoring requirements and standards, including, but not limited to, required qualifications of worksite monitors, required methods of monitoring by worksite monitors, and required reporting by worksite monitors.

(8) Procedures to be followed when a licensee tests positive for a banned substance.

(9) Procedures to be followed when a licensee is confirmed to have ingested a banned substance.

(10) Specific consequences for major violations and minor violations. In particular, the committee shall consider the use of a "deferred prosecution" stipulation similar to the stipulation described in Section 1000 of the Penal Code, in which the licensee admits to self- abuse of drugs or alcohol and surrenders his or her license. That agreement is deferred by the agency unless or until the licensee commits a major violation, in which case it is revived and the license is surrendered.

(11) Criteria that a licensee must meet in order to petition for return to practice on a full-time basis.

(12) Criteria that a licensee must meet in order to petition for reinstatement of a full and unrestricted license.

(13) If a board uses a private-sector vendor that provides diversion services, standards for immediate reporting by the vendor to the board of any and all noncompliance with any term of the diversion contract or probation; standards for the vendor's approval process for providers or contractors that provide diversion services, including, but not limited to, specimen collectors, group meeting facilitators, and worksite monitors; standards requiring the vendor to disapprove and discontinue the use of providers or contractors that fail to provide effective or timely diversion services; and standards for a licensee's termination from

the program and referral to enforcement.

(14) If a board uses a private-sector vendor that provides diversion services, the extent to which licensee participation in that program shall be kept confidential from the public.

(15) If a board uses a private-sector vendor that provides diversion services, a schedule for external independent audits of the vendor's performance in adhering to the standards adopted by the committee.

(16) Measurable criteria and standards to determine whether each board's method of dealing with substance-abusing licensees protects patients from harm and is effective in assisting its licensees in recovering from substance abuse in the long term.

(d) Notwithstanding any other law, by January 1, 2019, the committee shall review the existing criteria for Uniform Standard #4 established pursuant to paragraph (4) of subdivision (c). The committee's review and findings shall determine whether the existing criteria for Uniform Standard #4 should be updated to reflect recent developments in testing research and technology. The committee shall consider information from, but not limited to, the American Society of Addiction Medicine, and other sources of best practices.

(Amended by Stats. 2017, Ch. 600, Sec. 1. (SB 796) Effective January 1, 2018.)

315.2. CEASE PRACTICE ORDER

(a) A board, as described in Section 315, shall order a licensee of the board to cease practice if the licensee tests positive for any substance that is prohibited under the terms of the licensee's probation or diversion program.

(b) An order to cease practice under this section shall not be governed by the provisions of Chapter 5 (commencing with Section 11500) of Part 1 of Division 3 of Title 2 of the Government Code.

(c) A cease practice order under this section shall not constitute disciplinary action.

(d) This section shall have no effect on the Board of Registered Nursing pursuant to Article 3.1 (commencing with Section 2770) of Chapter 6 of Division 2.

(Added by Stats. 2010, Ch. 517, Sec. 2. (SB 1172) Effective January 1, 2011.)

315.4. CEASE PRACTICE ORDER FOR VIOLATION OF PROBATION OR DIVERSION PROGRAM

(a) A board, as described in Section 315, may adopt regulations authorizing the board to order a licensee on probation or in a diversion program to cease practice for major violations and when the board orders a licensee to undergo a clinical diagnostic evaluation pursuant to the uniform and specific standards adopted and authorized under Section 315.

(b) An order to cease practice under this section shall not be governed by the provisions of Chapter 5 (commencing with Section 11500) of Part 1 of Division 3 of Title 2 of the Government Code.

(c) A cease practice order under this section shall not constitute disciplinary action.

(d) This section shall have no effect on the Board of Registered Nursing pursuant to Article 3.1 (commencing with Section 2770) of Chapter 6 of Division 2.

(Added by Stats. 2010, Ch. 517, Sec. 3. (SB 1172) Effective January 1, 2011.)

ARTICLE 4: REPRESENTATION OF CONSUMERS

320. INTERVENTION IN ADMINISTRATIVE OR JUDICIAL PROCEEDINGS

Whenever there is pending before any state commission, regulatory agency, department, or other state agency, or any state or federal court or agency, any matter or proceeding which the director finds may affect substantially the interests of consumers within California, the director, or the Attorney General, may intervene in such matter or proceeding in any appropriate manner to represent the interests of consumers. The director, or any officer or employee designated by the director for that purpose, or the Attorney General, may thereafter present to such agency, court, or department, in conformity with the rules of practice and procedure thereof, such evidence and argument as he shall determine to be necessary, for the effective protection of the interests of consumers.

(Amended by Stats. 1975, Ch. 1262.)

321. COMMENCEMENT OF LEGAL PROCEEDINGS

Whenever it appears to the director that the interests of the consumers of this state are being damaged, or may be damaged, by any person who engaged in, or intends to engage in, any acts or practices in violation of any law of this state, or any federal law, the director or any officer or employee designated by the director, or the Attorney General, may commence legal proceedings in the appropriate forum to enjoin such acts or practices and may seek other appropriate relief on behalf of such consumers.

(Added by Stats. 1975, Ch. 1262.)

ARTICLE 5: CONSUMER COMPLAINTS

325. ACTIONABLE COMPLAINTS

It shall be the duty of the director to receive complaints from consumers concerning (a) unfair methods of competition and unfair or deceptive acts or practices undertaken by any person in the conduct of any trade or commerce; (b) the production, distribution, sale, and lease of any goods and services undertaken by any person which may endanger the public health, safety, or welfare; (c) violations of provisions of this code relating to businesses and professions licensed by any agency of the department, and regulations promulgated pursuant thereto; (d) student concerns related to the Bureau for Private Postsecondary Education's performance of its responsibilities, including concerns that arise related to the Bureau for Private Postsecondary Education's handling of a complaint or its administration of the Student Tuition Recovery Fund, established in Article 14 (commencing with Section 94923) of Chapter 8 of Part 59 of Division 10 of Title 3 of the Education Code; and (e) other matters consistent with the purposes of this chapter, whenever appropriate.

(Amended by Stats. 2016, Ch. 593, Sec. 1. (SB 1192) Effective January 1, 2017.)

326. PROCEEDINGS ON RECEIPT OF COMPLAINT

(a) Upon receipt of any complaint pursuant to Section 325, the director may notify the person against whom the complaint is made of the nature of the complaint and may request appropriate relief for the consumer.

(b) The director shall also transmit any valid complaint to the local, state or federal agency whose authority provides the most effective means to secure the relief.

The director shall, if appropriate, advise the consumer of the action taken on the complaint and of any other means which may be available to the consumer to secure relief.

(c) If the director receives a complaint or receives information from any source indicating a probable violation of any law, rule, or order of any regulatory agency of the state, or if a pattern of complaints from consumers develops, the director shall transmit any complaint he or she considers to be valid to any appropriate law enforcement or regulatory agency and any evidence or information he or she may have concerning the probable violation or pattern of complaints or request the Attorney General to undertake appropriate legal action. It shall be the continuing duty of the director to discern patterns of complaints and to ascertain the nature and extent of action taken with respect to the probable violations or pattern of complaints.

(Amended by Stats. 1989, Ch. 1360, Sec. 1.)

328. COMPLAINT PRIORITIZATION GUIDELINES

(a) In order to implement the Consumer Protection Enforcement Initiative of 2010, the director, through the Division of Investigation, shall implement "Complaint Prioritization Guidelines" for boards to utilize in prioritizing their respective complaint and investigative workloads. The guidelines shall be used to determine the referral of complaints to the division and those that are retained by the health care boards for investigation.

(b) Neither the Medical Board of California nor the Podiatric Medical Board of California shall be required to utilize the guidelines implemented pursuant to subdivision (a).

(c) On or before July 1, 2019, the director shall amend the guidelines implemented pursuant to subdivision (a) to include the category of "allegations of serious harm to a minor" under the "urgent" or "highest priority" level.

(Amended by Stats. 2019, Ch. 351, Sec. 47. (AB 496) Effective January 1, 2020.)

CHAPTER 6: PUBLIC MEMBERS

450. QUALIFICATIONS GENERALLY

In addition to the qualifications provided in the respective chapters of this code, a public member or a lay member of any board shall not be, nor shall they have been within the period of five years immediately preceding their appointment, any of the following:

(a) An employer, or an officer, director, or substantially full-time representative of an employer or group of employers, of any licensee of a board, except that this subdivision shall not preclude the appointment of a person who maintains infrequent employer status with a licensee, or maintains a client, patient, or customer relationship with a licensee that does not constitute more than 2 percent of the practice or business of the licensee.

(b) A person maintaining a contractual relationship with a licensee of a board that would constitute more than 2 percent of the practice or business of the licensee, or an officer, director, or substantially full- time representative of that person or group of persons.

(c) An employee of a licensee of a board, or a representative of the employee, except that this subdivision shall not preclude the appointment of a person who maintains an infrequent employee relationship or renders professional or related services to a licensee if the employment or service does not constitute more than 2 percent of the employment or practice of the member of the board.

(Amended by Stats. 2019, Ch. 351, Sec. 48. (AB 496) Effective January 1, 2020.)

450.2. AVOIDING CONFLICT OF INTEREST

In order to avoid a potential for a conflict of interest, a public member of a board shall not:

(a) Be a current or past licensee of that board.

(b) Be a close family member of a licensee of that board.

(Added by Stats. 2002, Ch. 1150, Sec. 1.2. Effective January 1, 2003.)

450.3. CONFLICTING PECUNIARY INTERESTS

No public member shall either at the time of their appointment or during their tenure in office have any financial interest in any organization subject to regulation by the board, commission, or committee of which they are a member.

(Amended by Stats. 2019, Ch. 351, Sec. 49. (AB 496) Effective January 1, 2020.)

450.5. PRIOR INDUSTRIAL AND PROFESSIONAL PURSUITS

A public member, or a lay member, at any time within five years immediately preceding his or her appointment, shall not have been engaged in pursuits which lie within the field of the industry or profession, or have provided representation to the industry or profession, regulated by the board of which he or she is a member, nor shall he or she engage in those pursuits or provide that representation during his or her term of office.

(Amended by Stats. 2003, Ch. 563, Sec. 2. Effective January 1, 2004.)

450.6. AGE

Notwithstanding any other section of law, a public member may be appointed without regard to age so long as the public member has reached the age of majority prior to appointment.

(Added by Stats. 1976, Ch. 1188.)

451. DELEGATION OF DUTIES

If any board shall as a part of its functions delegate any duty or responsibility to be performed by a single member of such board, such delegation shall not be made solely to any public member or any lay member of the board in any of the following instances:

(a) The actual preparation of, the administration of, and the grading of, examinations.

(b) The inspection or investigation of licentiates, the manner or method of practice or doing business, or their place of practice or business.

Nothing in this section shall be construed as precluding a public member or a lay member from participating in the formation of policy relating to the scope of the activities set forth in subdivisions (a) and (b) or in the approval, disapproval or modification of the action of its individual members, nor preclude such member from participating as a member of a subcommittee consisting of more than one member of the board in the performance of any duty.

(Added by Stats. 1961, Ch. 2232.)

452. "BOARD"

"Board," as used in this chapter, includes a board, advisory board, commission, examining committee, committee or other similarly constituted body exercising powers under this code.

(Amended by Stats. 1976, Ch. 1188.)

453. TRAINING AND ORIENTATION PROGRAM FOR NEW BOARD MEMBERS

Every newly appointed board member shall, within one year of assuming office, complete a training and orientation program offered by the department regarding, among other things, his or her functions, responsibilities, and obligations as a member of a board. The department shall adopt regulations necessary to establish this training and orientation program and its content.

(Added by Stats. 2002, Ch. 1150, Sec. 1.4. Effective January 1, 2003.)

CHAPTER 7: LICENSEE

460. POWERS OF LOCAL GOVERNMENT ENTITIES

(a) No city, county, or city and county shall prohibit a person or group of persons, authorized by one of the agencies in the Department of Consumer Affairs or an entity established pursuant to this code by a license, certificate, or other means to engage in a particular business, from engaging in that business, occupation, or profession or any portion of that business, occupation, or profession.

(b) (1) No city, county, or city and county shall prohibit a healing arts professional licensed with the state under Division 2 (commencing with Section 500) or licensed or certified by an entity established pursuant to this code from engaging in any act or performing any procedure that falls within the professionally recognized scope of practice of that licensee.

(2) This subdivision shall not be construed to prohibit the enforcement of a local ordinance in effect prior to January 1, 2010, related to any act or procedure that falls within the professionally recognized scope of practice of a healing arts professional licensed under Division 2 (commencing with Section 500).

(c) This section shall not be construed to prevent a city, county, or city and county from adopting or enforcing any local ordinance governing zoning, business licensing, or reasonable health and safety requirements for establishments or businesses of a healing arts professional licensed under Division 2 (commencing with Section 500) or licensed or certified by an entity established under this code or a person or group of persons described in subdivision (a).

(d) Nothing in this section shall prohibit any city, county, or city and county from levying a business license tax solely for revenue purposes, nor any city or county from levying a license tax solely for the purpose of covering the cost of regulation.

(Amended by Stats. 2014, Ch. 406, Sec. 1. (AB 1147) Effective January 1, 2015.)

461. ASKING APPLICANT TO REVEAL ARREST RECORD PROHIBITED

No public agency, state or local, shall, on an initial application form for any license, certificate or registration, ask for or require the applicant to reveal a record of arrest that did not result in a conviction or a plea of nolo contendere. A violation of this section is a misdemeanor.

This section shall apply in the case of any license, certificate or registration provided for by any law of this state or local government, including, but not limited to, this code, the Corporations Code, the Education Code, and the Insurance Code.

(Added by Stats. 1975, Ch. 883.)

462. INACTIVE CATEGORY OF LICENSURE

(a) Any of the boards, bureaus, commissions, or programs within the department may establish, by regulation, a system for an inactive category of licensure for persons who are not actively engaged in the practice of their profession or vocation.

(b) The regulation shall contain the following provisions:

(1) The holder of an inactive license issued pursuant to this section shall not engage in any activity for which a license is required.

(2) An inactive license issued pursuant to this section shall be renewed during the same time period in which an active license is renewed. The holder of an inactive license need not comply with any continuing education requirement for renewal of an active license.

(3) The renewal fee for a license in an active status shall apply also for a

renewal of a license in an inactive status, unless a lesser renewal fee is specified by the board.

(4) In order for the holder of an inactive license issued pursuant to this section to restore his or her license to an active status, the holder of an inactive license shall comply with all the following:

(A) Pay the renewal fee.

(B) If the board requires completion of continuing education for renewal of an active license, complete continuing education equivalent to that required for renewal of an active license, unless a different requirement is specified by the board.

(c) This section shall not apply to any healing arts board as specified in Section 701.

(Added by Stats. 1994, Ch. 26, Sec. 14. Effective March 30, 1994.)

464. ESTABLISHING A SYSTEM FOR RETIRED LICENSURE

(a) Any of the boards within the department may establish, by regulation, a system for a retired category of licensure for persons who are not actively engaged in the practice of their profession or vocation.

(b) The regulation shall contain the following:

(1) A retired license shall be issued to a person with either an active license or an inactive license that was not placed on inactive status for disciplinary reasons.

(2) The holder of a retired license issued pursuant to this section shall not engage in any activity for which a license is required, unless the board, by regulation, specifies the criteria for a retired licensee to practice his or her profession or vocation.

(3) The holder of a retired license shall not be required to renew that license.

(4) The board shall establish an appropriate application fee for a retired license to cover the reasonable regulatory cost of issuing a retired license.

(5) In order for the holder of a retired license issued pursuant to this section to restore his or her license to an active status, the holder of that license shall meet all the following:

(A) Pay a fee established by statute or regulation.

(B) Certify, in a manner satisfactory to the board, that he or she has not committed an act or crime constituting grounds for denial of licensure.

(C) Comply with the fingerprint submission requirements established by regulation.

(D) If the board requires completion of continuing education for renewal of an active license, complete continuing education equivalent to that required for renewal of an active license, unless a different requirement is specified by the board.

(E) Complete any other requirements as specified by the board by regulation.

(c) A board may upon its own determination, and shall upon receipt of a complaint from any person, investigate the actions of any licensee, including a person with a license that either restricts or prohibits the practice of that person in his or her profession or vocation, including, but not limited to, a license that is retired, inactive, canceled, revoked, or suspended.

(d) Subdivisions (a) and (b) shall not apply to a board that has other statutory authority to establish a retired license.

(Added by Stats. 2016, Ch. 473, Sec. 1. (AB 2859) Effective January 1, 2017.)

DIVISION 1.2 JOINT COMMITTEE ON BOARDS, COMMISSIONS, AND CONSUMER PROTECTION

CHAPTER 1: REVIEW OF BOARDS UNDER THE DEPARTMENT OF CONSUMER AFFAIRS

473. JOINT COMMITTEE ON BOARDS, COMMISSIONS, AND CONSUMER PROTECTION ESTABLISHED; MEMBERS; POWERS AND DUTIES; STAFF; TERMINATION [SECTION REPEALED 2011.]

473.1. APPLICATION OF DIVISION [SECTION REPEALED 2011.]

473.2. SUBMISSION OF ANALYSIS AND REPORT TO COMMITTEE [SECTION REPEALED 2011.]

473.3. PUBLIC HEARINGS PRIOR TO TERMINATION, CONTINUATION, OR REESTABLISHMENT OF ANY BOARD; REVIEW OF BUREAU FOR PRIVATE POSTSECONDARY AND VOCATIONAL EDUCATION AND BUREAU OF AUTOMOTIVE REPAIR [SECTION REPEALED 2011.].

473.4. EVALUATION OF BOARDS AND REGULATORY PROGRAMS; DETERMINATION OF NEED FOR CONTINUED EXISTENCE [SECTION REPEALED 2011.].

473.5. REPORT [SECTION REPEALED 2011.].

473.6. REFERRAL OF PROPOSALS TO CREATE NEW LICENSURE CATEGORIES, CHANGE REQUIREMENTS, OR CREATE NEW LICENSING BOARD TO JOINT COMMITTEE [SECTION REPEALED 2011.].

DIVISION 1.5: DENIAL, SUSPENSION & REVOCATION OF LICENSES

CHAPTER 1: GENERAL PROVISIONS

475. APPLICABILITY OF DIVISION

(a) Notwithstanding any other provisions of this code, the provisions of this division shall govern the denial of licenses on the grounds of:

(1) Knowingly making a false statement of material fact, or knowingly omitting to state a material fact, in an application for a license.

(2) Conviction of a crime.

(3) Commission of any act involving dishonesty, fraud or deceit with the intent to substantially benefit himself or another, or substantially injure another.

(4) Commission of any act which, if done by a licentiate of the business or profession in question, would be grounds for suspension or revocation of license.

(b) Notwithstanding any other provisions of this code, the provisions of this division shall govern the suspension and revocation of licenses on grounds specified in paragraphs (1) and (2) of subdivision (a).

(c) A license shall not be denied, suspended, or revoked on the grounds of a lack of good moral character or any similar ground relating to an applicant's character, reputation, personality, or habits.

(Amended by Stats. 1992, Ch. 1289, Sec. 5. Effective January 1, 1993.)

476. EXEMPTIONS

(a) Except as provided in subdivision (b), nothing in this division shall apply to the licensure or registration of persons pursuant to Chapter 4 (commencing with Section 6000) of Division 3, or pursuant to Division 9 (commencing with Section 23000) or pursuant to Chapter 5 (commencing with Section 19800) of Division 8.

(b) Section 494.5 shall apply to the licensure of persons authorized to practice law pursuant to Chapter 4 (commencing with Section 6000) of Division 3, and the licensure or registration of persons pursuant to Chapter 5 (commencing with Section 19800) of Division 8 or pursuant to Division 9 (commencing with Section 23000).

(Amended by Stats. 2011, Ch. 455, Sec. 2. (AB 1424) Effective January 1, 2012.)

477. "BOARD"; "LICENSE"

As used in this division:

(a) "Board" includes "bureau," "commission," "committee," "department," "division," "examining committee," "program," and "agency."

(b) "License" includes certificate, registration or other means to engage in a business or profession regulated by this code.

(Amended by Stats. 1991, Ch. 654, Sec. 5.)

478. "APPLICATION"; "MATERIAL"

(a) As used in this division, "application" includes the original documents or writings filed and any other supporting documents or writings including supporting documents provided or filed contemporaneously, or later, in support of the application whether provided or filed by the applicant or by any other person in support of the application.

(b) As used in this division, "material" includes a statement or omission substantially related to the qualifications, functions, or duties of the business or profession.

(Added by Stats. 1992, Ch. 1289, Sec. 6. Effective January 1, 1993.)

CHAPTER 2: DENIAL OF LICENSES

480. GROUNDS FOR DENIAL; EFFECT OF OBTAINING CERTIFICATE OF REHABILITATION [EFFECTIVE JANUARY 1, 2023]

(a) Notwithstanding any other provision of this code, a board may deny a license regulated by this code on the grounds that the applicant has been convicted of a crime or has been subject to formal discipline only if either of the following conditions are met:

(1) The applicant has been convicted of a crime within the preceding seven years from the date of application that is substantially related to the qualifications, functions, or duties of the business or profession for which the application is made, regardless of whether the applicant was incarcerated for that crime, or the applicant has been convicted of a crime that is substantially related to the qualifications, functions, or duties of the business or profession for which the application is made and for which the applicant is presently incarcerated or for which the applicant was released from incarceration within the preceding seven years from the date of application. However, the preceding seven-year limitation shall not apply in either of the following situations:

(A) The applicant was convicted of a serious felony, as defined in Section 1192.7 of the Penal Code or a crime for which registration is required pursuant to paragraph (2) or (3) of subdivision (d) of Section 290 of the Penal Code.

(B) The applicant was convicted of a financial crime currently classified as a felony that is directly and adversely related to the fiduciary qualifications, functions, or duties of the business or profession for which the application is made, pursuant to regulations adopted by the board, and for which the applicant is seeking licensure under any of the following:

(i) Chapter 6 (commencing with Section 6500) of Division 3.

(ii) Chapter 9 (commencing with Section 7000) of Division 3.

(iii) Chapter 11.3 (commencing with Section 7512) of Division 3.

(iv) Licensure as a funeral director or cemetery manager under Chapter 12 (commencing with Section 7600) of Division 3.

(v) Division 4 (commencing with Section 10000).

(2) The applicant has been subjected to formal discipline by a licensing board in or outside California within the preceding seven years from the date of application based on professional misconduct that would have been cause for discipline before the board for which the present application is made and that is substantially related to the qualifications, functions, or duties of the business or profession for which the present application is made. However, prior disciplinary action by a licensing board within the preceding seven years shall not be the basis for denial of a license if the basis for that disciplinary action was a conviction that has been dismissed pursuant to Section 1203.4, 1203.4a, 1203.41, 1203.42, or 1203.425 of the Penal Code or a comparable dismissal or expungement. Formal discipline that occurred earlier than seven years preceding the date of application may be grounds for denial of a license only if the formal discipline was for conduct that, if committed in this state by a physician and surgeon licensed pursuant to Chapter 5 (commencing with Section 2000) of Division 2, would have constituted an act of sexual abuse,

misconduct, or relations with a patient pursuant to Section 726 or sexual exploitation as defined in subdivision (a) of Section 729.

(b) Notwithstanding any other provision of this code, a person shall not be denied a license on the basis that the person has been convicted of a crime, or on the basis of acts underlying a conviction for a crime, if that person has obtained a certificate of rehabilitation under Chapter 3.5 (commencing with Section 4852.01) of Title 6 of Part 3 of the Penal Code, has been granted clemency or a pardon by a state or federal executive, or has made a showing of rehabilitation pursuant to Section 482.

(c) Notwithstanding any other provision of this code, a person shall not be denied a license on the basis of any conviction, or on the basis of the acts underlying the conviction, that has been dismissed pursuant to Section 1203.4, 1203.4a, 1203.41, 1203.42, or 1203.425 of the Penal Code, or a comparable dismissal or expungement. An applicant who has a conviction that has been dismissed pursuant to Section 1203.4, 1203.4a, 1203.41, or 1203.42 of the Penal Code shall provide proof of the dismissal if it is not reflected on the report furnished by the Department of Justice.

(d) Notwithstanding any other provision of this code, a board shall not deny a license on the basis of an arrest that resulted in a disposition other than a conviction, including an arrest that resulted in an infraction, citation, or a juvenile adjudication.

(e) A board may deny a license regulated by this code on the ground that the applicant knowingly made a false statement of fact that is required to be revealed in the application for the license. A board shall not deny a license based solely on an applicant's failure to disclose a fact that would not have been cause for denial of the license had it been disclosed.

(f) A board shall follow the following procedures in requesting or acting on an applicant's criminal history information:

(1) A board issuing a license pursuant to Chapter 3 (commencing with Section 5500), Chapter 3.5 (commencing with Section 5615), Chapter 10 (commencing with Section 7301), Chapter 20 (commencing with Section 9800), or Chapter 20.3 (commencing with Section 9880), of Division 3, or Chapter 3 (commencing with Section 19000) or Chapter 3.1 (commencing with Section 19225) of Division 8 may require applicants for licensure under those chapters to disclose criminal conviction history on an application for licensure.

(2) Except as provided in paragraph (1), a board shall not require an applicant for licensure to disclose any information or documentation regarding the applicant's criminal history. However, a board may request mitigating information from an applicant regarding the applicant's criminal history for purposes of determining substantial relation or demonstrating evidence of rehabilitation, provided that the applicant is informed that disclosure is voluntary and that the applicant's decision not to disclose any information shall not be a factor in a board's decision to grant or deny an application for licensure.

(3) If a board decides to deny an application for licensure based solely or in part on the applicant's conviction history, the board shall notify the applicant in writing of all of the following:

(A) The denial or disqualification of licensure.

(B) Any existing procedure the board has for the applicant to challenge the decision or to request reconsideration.

(C) That the applicant has the right to appeal the board's decision.

(D) The processes for the applicant to request a copy of the applicant's complete conviction history and question the accuracy or completeness of the record pursuant to Sections 11122 to 11127 of the Penal Code.

(g) (1) For a minimum of three years, each board under this code shall retain application forms and other documents submitted by an applicant, any notice provided to an applicant, all other communications received from and provided to an applicant, and criminal history reports of an applicant.

(2) Each board under this code shall retain the number of applications received for each license and the number of applications requiring inquiries regarding criminal history. In addition, each licensing authority shall retain all of the following information:

(A) The number of applicants with a criminal record who received notice of denial or disqualification of licensure.

(B) The number of applicants with a criminal record who provided evidence of mitigation or rehabilitation.

(C) The number of applicants with a criminal record who appealed any denial or disqualification of licensure.

(D) The final disposition and demographic information, consisting of voluntarily provided information on race or gender, of any applicant described in subparagraph (A), (B), or (C).

(3) (A) Each board under this code shall annually make available to the public through the board's internet website and through a report submitted to the appropriate policy committees of the Legislature deidentified information collected pursuant to this subdivision. Each board shall ensure confidentiality of the individual applicants.

(B) A report pursuant to subparagraph (A) shall be submitted in compliance with Section 9795 of the Government Code.

(h) "Conviction" as used in this section shall have the same meaning as defined in Section 7.5.

(i) This section does not in any way modify or otherwise affect the existing authority of the following entities in regard to licensure:

(1) The State Athletic Commission.

(2) The Bureau for Private Postsecondary Education.

(3) The California Horse Racing Board.

(Amended by Stats. 2022, Ch. 453, Sec. 1. (AB 1636) Effective January 1, 2023.)

481. CRIME AND JOB-FITNESS CRITERIA [INOPERATIVE JULY 1, 2020]

(a) Each board under the provisions of this code shall develop criteria to aid it, when considering the denial, suspension or revocation of a license, to determine whether a crime or act is substantially related to the qualifications, functions, or duties of the business or profession it regulates.

(b) This section shall become inoperative on July 1, 2020, and, as of January 1, 2021, is repealed.

(Amended by Stats. 2018, Ch. 995, Sec. 6. (AB 2138) Effective January 1, 2019. Section inoperative July 1, 2020. Repealed as of January 1, 2021, by its own provisions. See later operative version added by Stats. 2018, Ch. 995.)

481. CRIME AND JOB-FITNESS CRITERIA [OPERATIVE JULY 1, 2020]

(a) Each board under this code shall develop criteria to aid it, when considering the denial, suspension, or revocation of a license, to determine whether a crime is substantially related to the qualifications, functions, or duties of the business or profession it regulates.

(b) Criteria for determining whether a crime is substantially related to the qualifications, functions, or duties of the business or profession a board regulates shall include all of the following:

(1) The nature and gravity of the offense.

(2) The number of years elapsed since the date of the offense.

(3) The nature and duties of the profession in which the applicant seeks licensure or in which the licensee is licensed.

(c) A board shall not deny a license based in whole or in part on a conviction without considering evidence of rehabilitation submitted by an applicant pursuant to any process established in the practice act or regulations of the particular board and as directed by Section 482.

(d) Each board shall post on its Internet Web site a summary of the criteria used to consider whether a crime is considered to be substantially related to the qualifications, functions, or duties of the business or profession it regulates consistent with this section.

(e) This section does not in any way modify or otherwise affect the existing authority of the following entities in regard to licensure:

(1) The State Athletic Commission.

(2) The Bureau for Private Postsecondary Education.

(3) The California Horse Racing Board.

(f) This section shall become operative on July 1, 2020.

(Repealed and added by Stats. 2018, Ch. 995, Sec. 7. (AB 2138) Effective January 1, 2019. Section operative July 1, 2020, by its own provisions.).

482. REHABILITATION CRITERIA [INOPERATIVE JULY 1, 2020]

(a) Each board under the provisions of this code shall develop criteria to evaluate the rehabilitation of a person when:

(1) Considering the denial of a license by the board under Section 480; or

(2) Considering suspension or revocation of a license under Section 490.

(b) Each board shall take into account all competent evidence of rehabilitation furnished by the applicant or licensee.

(c) This section shall become inoperative on July 1, 2020, and, as of January 1, 2021, is repealed.

(Amended by Stats. 2018, Ch. 995, Sec. 8. (AB 2138) Effective January 1, 2019. Section inoperative July 1, 2020. Repealed as of January 1, 2021, by its own provisions. See later operative version added by Stats. 2018, Ch. 995.)

482. REHABILITATION CRITERIA [OPERATIVE JULY 1, 2020]

(a) Each board under this code shall develop criteria to evaluate the rehabilitation of a person when doing either of the following:

(1) Considering the denial of a license by the board under Section 480.

(2) Considering suspension or revocation of a license under Section 490.

(b) Each board shall consider whether an applicant or licensee has made a showing of rehabilitation if either of the following are met:

(1) The applicant or licensee has completed the criminal sentence at issue without a violation of parole or probation.

(2) The board, applying its criteria for rehabilitation, finds that the applicant is rehabilitated.

(c) This section does not in any way modify or otherwise affect the existing authority of the following entities in regard to licensure:

(1) The State Athletic Commission.

(2) The Bureau for Private Postsecondary Education.

(3) The California Horse Racing Board.

(d) This section shall become operative on July 1, 2020.

(Repealed and added by Stats. 2018, Ch. 995, Sec. 9. (AB 2138) Effective January 1, 2019. Section operative July 1, 2020, by its own provisions.)

484. ATTESTATION TO GOOD MORAL CHARACTER OF APPLICANT

No person applying for licensure under this code shall be required to submit to any licensing board any attestation by other persons to his good moral character.

(Amended by Stats. 1974, Ch. 1321.)

485. PROCEDURE UPON DENIAL

Upon denial of an application for a license under this chapter or Section 496, the board shall do either of the following:

(a) File and serve a statement of issues in accordance with Chapter 5 (commencing with Section 11500) of Part 1 of Division 3 of Title 2 of the Government Code.

(b) Notify the applicant that the application is denied, stating (1) the reason for the denial, and (2) that the applicant has the right to a hearing under Chapter 5 (commencing with Section 11500) of Part 1 of Division 3 of Title 2 of the Government Code if written request for hearing is made within 60 days after service of the notice of denial. Unless written request for hearing is made within the 60-day period, the applicant's right to a hearing is deemed waived.

Service of the notice of denial may be made in the manner authorized for service of summons in civil actions, or by registered mail addressed to the applicant at the latest address filed by the applicant in writing with the board in his or her application or otherwise. Service by mail is complete on the date of mailing.

(Amended by Stats. 1997, Ch. 758, Sec. 2.3. Effective January 1, 1998.)

486. CONTENTS OF DECISION OR NOTICE

Where the board has denied an application for a license under this chapter or Section 496, it shall, in its decision, or in its notice under subdivision (b) of Section 485, inform the applicant of the following:

(a) The earliest date on which the applicant may reapply for a license which shall be one year from the effective date of the decision, or service of the notice under subdivision (b) of Section 485, unless the board prescribes an earlier date or a later date is prescribed by another statute.

(b) That all competent evidence of rehabilitation presented will be considered upon a reapplication.

Along with the decision, or the notice under subdivision (b) of Section 485, the board shall serve a copy of the criteria relating to rehabilitation formulated under Section 482.

(Amended by Stats. 1997, Ch. 758, Sec. 2.4. Effective January 1, 1998.)

487. HEARING; TIME [CURRENT]

If a hearing is requested by the applicant, the board shall conduct such hearing within 90 days from the date the hearing is requested unless the applicant shall request or agree in writing to a postponement or continuance of the hearing. Notwithstanding the above, the Office of Administrative Hearings may order, or on a showing of good cause, grant a request for, up to 45 additional days within which to conduct a hearing, except in cases involving alleged examination or licensing fraud, in which cases the period may be up to 180 days. In no case shall more than two such orders be made or requests be granted.

(Amended by Stats. 1986, Ch. 220, Sec. 1. Effective June 30, 1986.)

488. HEARING REQUEST [INOPERATIVE JULY 1, 2020]

(a) Except as otherwise provided by law, following a hearing requested by an applicant pursuant to subdivision (b) of Section 485, the board may take any of the following actions:

(1) Grant the license effective upon completion of all licensing requirements by the applicant.

(2) Grant the license effective upon completion of all licensing requirements by the applicant, immediately revoke the license, stay the revocation, and impose probationary conditions on the license, which may include suspension.

(3) Deny the license.

(4) Take other action in relation to denying or granting the license as the board in its discretion may deem proper.

(b) This section shall become inoperative on July 1, 2020, and, as of January 1, 2021, is repealed.

(Amended by Stats. 2018, Ch. 995, Sec. 10. (AB 2138) Effective January 1, 2019. Section inoperative July 1, 2020. Repealed as of January 1, 2021, by its own provisions. See later operative version added by Stats. 2018, Ch. 995.)

488. HEARING REQUEST [OPERATIVE JULY 1, 2020]

(a) Except as otherwise provided by law, following a hearing requested by an applicant pursuant to subdivision (b) of Section 485, the board may take any of the following actions:

(1) Grant the license effective upon completion of all licensing requirements by the applicant.

(2) Grant the license effective upon completion of all licensing requirements by the applicant, immediately revoke the license, stay the revocation, and impose probationary conditions on the license, which may include suspension.

(3) Deny the license.

(4) Take other action in relation to denying or granting the license as the board in its discretion may deem proper.

(b) This section does not in any way modify or otherwise affect the existing authority of the following entities in regard to licensure:

(1) The State Athletic Commission.

(2) The Bureau for Private Postsecondary Education.

(3) The California Horse Racing Board.

(c) This section shall become operative on July 1, 2020.

(Repealed and added by Stats. 2018, Ch. 995, Sec. 11. (AB 2138) Effective January 1, 2019. Section operative July 1, 2020, by its own provisions.)

489. DENIAL OF APPLICATION WITHOUT A HEARING

Any agency in the department which is authorized by law to deny an application for a license upon the grounds specified in Section 480 or 496, may without a hearing deny an application upon any of those grounds, if within one year previously, and after proceedings conducted in accordance with Chapter 5 (commencing with Section 11500) of Part 1 of Division 3 of Title 2 of the Government Code, that agency has denied an application from the same applicant upon the same ground.

(Amended by Stats. 1997, Ch. 758, Sec. 2.5. Effective January 1, 1998.)

CHAPTER 3: SUSPENSION AND REVOCATION OF LICENSES

490. GROUNDS FOR SUSPENSION OR REVOCATION; DISCIPLINE FOR SUBSTANTIALLY RELATED CRIME; CONVICTION; LEGISLATIVE FINDINGS

(a) In addition to any other action that a board is permitted to take against a licensee, a board may suspend or revoke a license on the ground that the licensee has been convicted of a crime, if the crime is substantially related to the qualifications, functions, or duties of the business or profession for which the license was issued.

(b) Notwithstanding any other provision of law, a board may exercise any authority to discipline a licensee for conviction of a crime that is independent of the authority granted under subdivision (a) only if the crime is substantially related to the qualifications, functions, or duties of the business or profession for which the licensee's license was issued.

(c) A conviction within the meaning of this section means a plea or verdict of guilty or a conviction following a plea of nolo contendere. An action that a board is permitted to take following the establishment of a conviction may be taken when the time for appeal has elapsed, or the judgment of conviction has been affirmed on appeal, or when an order granting probation is made suspending the imposition of sentence, irrespective of a subsequent order under Section 1203.4 of the Penal Code.

(d) The Legislature hereby finds and declares that the application of this section has been made unclear by the holding in Petropoulos v. Department of Real Estate (2006) 142 Cal.App.4th 554, and that the holding in that case has placed a significant number of statutes and regulations in question, resulting in potential harm to the consumers of California from licensees who have been convicted of crimes. Therefore, the Legislature finds and declares that this section establishes an independent basis for a board to impose discipline upon a licensee, and that the amendments to this section made by Chapter 33 of the Statutes of 2008 do not constitute a change to, but rather are declaratory of, existing law.

(Amended by Stats. 2010, Ch. 328, Sec. 2. (SB 1330) Effective January 1, 2011.)

490.5. SUSPENSION OF LICENSE FOR FAILURE TO COMPLY WITH CHILD SUPPORT ORDER

A board may suspend a license pursuant to Section 17520 of the Family Code if a licensee is not in compliance with a child support order or judgment.

(Amended by Stats. 2010, Ch. 328, Sec. 3. (SB 1330) Effective January 1, 2011.)

491. PROCEDURE UPON SUSPENSION OR REVOCATION

Upon suspension or revocation of a license by a board on one or more of the grounds specified in Section 490, the board shall:

(a) Send a copy of the provisions of Section 11522 of the Government Code to the ex-licensee.

(b) Send a copy of the criteria relating to rehabilitation formulated under Section 482 to the ex-licensee.

(Amended by Stats. 1975, Ch. 678.)

492. EFFECT OF COMPLETION OF DRUG DIVERSION PROGRAM ON DISCIPLINARY ACTION OR DENIAL OF LICENSE

Notwithstanding any other provision of law, successful completion of any diversion program under the Penal Code, or successful completion of an alcohol and drug problem assessment program under Article 5 (commencing with Section 23249.50) of Chapter 12 of Division 11 of the Vehicle Code, shall not prohibit any agency established under Division 2 (commencing with Section 500) of this code, or any initiative act referred to in that division, from taking disciplinary action against a licensee or from denying a license for professional misconduct, notwithstanding that evidence of that misconduct may be recorded in a record pertaining to an arrest.

This section shall not be construed to apply to any drug diversion program operated by any agency established under Division 2 (commencing with Section 500) of this code, or any initiative act referred to in that division.

(Amended by Stats. 1994, Ch. 26, Sec. 15. Effective March 30, 1994.)

493. EVIDENTIARY EFFECT OF RECORD OF CONVICTION OF CRIME SUBSTANTIALLY RELATED TO LICENSEE'S QUALIFICATIONS, FUNCTIONS AND DUTIES

(a) Notwithstanding any other law, in a proceeding conducted by a board within the department pursuant to law to deny an application for a license or to suspend or revoke a license or otherwise take disciplinary action against a person who holds a license, upon the ground that the applicant or the licensee has been convicted of a crime substantially related to the qualifications, functions, and duties of the licensee in question, the record of conviction of the crime shall be conclusive evidence of the fact that the conviction occurred, but only of that fact.

(b) (1) Criteria for determining whether a crime is substantially related to the qualifications, functions, or duties of the business or profession the board regulates shall include all of the following:

(A) The nature and gravity of the offense.

(B) The number of years elapsed since the date of the offense.

(C) The nature and duties of the profession.

(2) A board shall not categorically bar an applicant based solely on the type of conviction without considering evidence of rehabilitation.

(c) As used in this section, "license" includes "certificate," "permit," "authority," and "registration."

(d) This section does not in any way modify or otherwise affect the existing authority of the following entities in regard to licensure:

(1) The State Athletic Commission.

(2) The Bureau for Private Postsecondary Education.

(3) The California Horse Racing Board.

(e) This section shall become operative on July 1, 2020.

(Repealed and added by Stats. 2018, Ch. 995, Sec. 13. (AB 2138) Effective January 1, 2019. Section operative July 1, 2020, by its own provisions.)

494. INTERIM SUSPENSION OR RESTRICTION ORDER

(a) A board or an administrative law judge sitting alone, as provided in subdivision (h), may, upon petition, issue an interim order suspending any licentiate or imposing license restrictions, including, but not limited to, mandatory biological fluid testing, supervision, or remedial training. The petition shall include affidavits that demonstrate, to the satisfaction of the board, both of the following:

(1) The licentiate has engaged in acts or omissions constituting a violation of this code or has been convicted of a crime substantially related to the licensed activity.

(2) Permitting the licentiate to continue to engage in the licensed activity, or permitting the licentiate to continue in the licensed activity without restrictions, would endanger the public health, safety, or welfare.

(b) No interim order provided for in this section shall be issued without notice to the licentiate unless it appears from the petition and supporting documents that serious injury would result to the public before the matter could be heard on notice.

(c) Except as provided in subdivision (b), the licentiate shall be given at least 15 days' notice of the hearing on the petition for an interim order. The notice shall include documents submitted to the board in support of the petition. If the order was initially issued without notice as provided in subdivision (b), the licentiate shall be entitled to a hearing on the petition within 20 days of the issuance of the interim order without notice. The licentiate shall be given notice of the hearing within two days after issuance of the initial interim order, and shall receive all documents in support of the petition. The failure of the board to provide a hearing within 20 days following the issuance of the interim order without notice, unless the licentiate waives his or her right to the hearing, shall result in the dissolution of the interim order by operation of law.

(d) At the hearing on the petition for an interim order, the licentiate may:

(1) Be represented by counsel.

(2) Have a record made of the proceedings, copies of which shall be available to the licentiate upon payment of costs computed in accordance with the provisions for transcript costs for judicial review contained in Section 11523 of the Government Code.

(3) Present affidavits and other documentary evidence.

(4) Present oral argument.

(e) The board, or an administrative law judge sitting alone as provided in subdivision (h), shall issue a decision on the petition for interim order within five business days following submission of the matter. The standard of proof required to obtain an interim order pursuant to this section shall be a preponderance of the evidence standard. If the interim order was previously issued without notice, the board shall determine whether the order shall remain in effect, be dissolved, or modified.

(f) The board shall file an accusation within 15 days of the issuance of an interim order. In the case of an interim order issued without notice, the time shall run from the date of the order issued after the noticed hearing. If the licentiate files a Notice of Defense, the hearing shall be held within 30 days of the agency's receipt of the Notice of Defense. A decision shall be rendered on the accusation no later than 30 days after submission of the matter. Failure to comply with any of the requirements in this subdivision shall dissolve the interim order by operation of law.

(g) Interim orders shall be subject to judicial review pursuant to Section 1094.5 of the Code of Civil Procedure and shall be heard only in the superior court in and for the Counties of Sacramento, San Francisco, Los Angeles, or San Diego. The review of an interim order shall be limited to a determination of whether the board abused its discretion in the issuance of the interim order. Abuse of discretion is established if the respondent board has not proceeded in the manner required by law, or if the court determines that the interim order is not supported by substantial evidence in light of the whole record.

(h) The board may, in its sole discretion, delegate the hearing on any petition for an interim order to an administrative law judge in the Office of Administrative Hearings. If the board hears the noticed petition itself, an administrative law judge shall preside at the hearing, rule on the admission and exclusion of evidence, and advise the board on matters of law. The board shall exercise all other powers relating to the conduct of the hearing but may delegate any or all of them to the administrative law judge.

When the petition has been delegated to an administrative law judge, he or she shall sit alone and exercise all of the powers of the board relating to the conduct of the hearing. A decision issued by an administrative law judge sitting alone shall be final when it is filed with the board. If the administrative law judge issues an interim order without notice, he or she shall preside at the noticed hearing, unless unavailable, in which case another administrative law judge may hear the matter. The decision of the administrative law judge sitting alone on the petition for an interim order is final, subject only to judicial review in accordance with subdivision (g).

(i) Failure to comply with an interim order issued pursuant to subdivision (a) or (b) shall constitute a separate cause for disciplinary action against any licentiate, and may be heard at, and as a part of, the noticed hearing provided for in subdivision

(f). Allegations of noncompliance with the interim order may be filed at any time prior to the rendering of a decision on the accusation. Violation of the interim order is established upon proof that the licentiate was on notice of the interim order and its terms, and that the order was in effect at the time of the violation. The finding of a violation of an interim order made at the hearing on the accusation shall be reviewed as a part of any review of a final decision of the agency.

If the interim order issued by the agency provides for anything less than a complete suspension of the licentiate from his or her business or profession, and the licentiate violates the interim order prior to the hearing on the accusation provided for in subdivision (f), the agency may, upon notice to the licentiate and proof of violation, modify or expand the interim order.

(j) A plea or verdict of guilty or a conviction after a plea of nolo contendere is deemed to be a conviction within the meaning of this section. A certified record of the conviction shall be conclusive evidence of the fact that the conviction occurred. A board may take action under this section notwithstanding the fact that an appeal of the conviction may be taken.

(k) The interim orders provided for by this section shall be in addition to, and not a limitation on, the authority to seek injunctive relief provided in any other provision of law.

(l) In the case of a board, a petition for an interim order may be filed by the executive officer. In the case of a bureau or program, a petition may be filed by the chief or program administrator, as the case may be.

(m) "Board," as used in this section, shall include any agency described in Section 22, and any allied health agency within the jurisdiction of the Medical Board of California. Board shall also include the Osteopathic Medical Board of California and the State Board of Chiropractic Examiners. The provisions of this section shall not be applicable to the Medical Board of California, the Board of Podiatric Medicine, or the State Athletic Commission.

(Amended by Stats. 1994, Ch. 1275, Sec. 4. Effective January 1, 1995.)

494.5. AGENCY ACTIONS WHEN LICENSEE IS ON CERTIFIED LIST; DEFINITIONS; COLLECTION AND DISTRIBUTION OF CERTIFIED LISTS INFORMATION; TIMING; NOTICES; CHALLENGES BY APPLICANTS AND LICENSEES; RELEASE FORMS; INTERAGENCY AGREEMENTS; FEES; REMEDIES; INQUIRIES AND DISCLOSURE OF INFORMATION; SEVERABILITY

(a) (1) Except as provided in paragraphs (2), (3), and (4), a state governmental licensing entity shall refuse to issue, reactivate, reinstate, or renew a license and shall suspend a license if a licensee's name is included on a certified list.

(2) The Department of Motor Vehicles shall suspend a license if a licensee's name is included on a certified list. Any reference in this section to the issuance, reactivation, reinstatement, renewal, or denial of a license shall not apply to the Department of Motor Vehicles.

(3) The State Bar of California may recommend to refuse to issue, reactivate, reinstate, or renew a license and may recommend to suspend a license if a licensee's name is included on a certified list. The word "may" shall be substituted for the word "shall" relating to the issuance of a temporary license, refusal to issue, reactivate, reinstate, renew, or suspend a license in this section for licenses under the jurisdiction of the California Supreme Court.

(4) The Department of Alcoholic Beverage Control may refuse to issue, reactivate, reinstate, or renew a license, and may suspend a license, if a licensee's name is included on a certified list.

(b) For purposes of this section:

(1) "Certified list" means either the list provided by the State Board of Equalization or the list provided by the Franchise Tax Board of persons whose names appear on the lists of the 500 largest tax delinquencies pursuant to Section 7063 or 19195 of the Revenue and Taxation Code, as applicable.

(2) "License" includes a certificate, registration, or any other authorization to engage in a profession or occupation issued by a state governmental licensing entity. "License" includes a driver's license issued pursuant to Chapter 1 (commencing with Section 12500) of Division 6 of the Vehicle Code. "License" excludes a vehicle registration issued pursuant to Division 3 (commencing with Section 4000) of the Vehicle Code.

(3) "Licensee" means an individual authorized by a license to drive a motor vehicle or authorized by a license, certificate, registration, or other authorization to engage in a profession or occupation issued by a state governmental licensing entity.

(4) "State governmental licensing entity" means any entity listed in Section 101, 1000, or 19420, the office of the Attorney General, the Department of Insurance, the Department of Motor Vehicles, the State Bar of California, the Department of Real Estate, and any other state agency, board, or commission that issues a license, certificate, or registration authorizing an individual to engage in a profession or occupation, including any certificate, business or occupational license, or permit or license issued by the Department of Motor Vehicles or the Department of the California Highway Patrol. "State governmental licensing entity" shall not include the Contractors State License Board.

(c) The State Board of Equalization and the Franchise Tax Board shall each submit its respective certified list to every state governmental licensing entity. The certified lists shall include the name, social security number or taxpayer identification number, and the last known address of the persons identified on the certified lists.

(d) Notwithstanding any other law, each state governmental licensing entity shall collect the social security number or the federal taxpayer identification number from all applicants for the purposes of matching the names of the certified lists provided by the State Board of Equalization and the Franchise Tax Board to applicants and licensees.

(e) (1) Each state governmental licensing entity shall determine whether an applicant or licensee is on the most recent certified list provided by the State Board of Equalization and the Franchise Tax Board.

(2) If an applicant or licensee is on either of the certified lists, the state governmental licensing entity shall immediately provide a preliminary notice to the applicant or licensee of the entity's intent to suspend or withhold issuance or renewal of the license. The preliminary notice shall be delivered personally or by mail to the applicant's or licensee's last known mailing address on file with the state governmental licensing entity within 30 days of receipt of the certified list. Service by mail shall be completed in accordance with Section 1013 of the Code of Civil Procedure.

(A) The state governmental licensing entity shall issue a temporary license valid for a period of 90 days to any applicant whose name is on a certified list if the applicant is otherwise eligible for a license.

(B) The 90-day time period for a temporary license shall not be extended. Only one temporary license shall be issued during a regular license term and the term of the temporary license shall coincide with the first 90 days of the regular license term. A license for the full term or the remainder of the license term may be issued or renewed only upon compliance with this section.

(C) In the event that a license is suspended or an application for a license or the renewal of a license is denied pursuant to this section, any funds paid by the applicant or licensee shall not be refunded by the state governmental licensing entity.

(f) (1) A state governmental licensing entity shall refuse to issue or shall suspend a license pursuant to this section no sooner than 90 days and no later than 120 days of the mailing of the preliminary notice described in paragraph (2) of subdivision (e), unless the state governmental licensing entity has received a release pursuant to subdivision (h). The procedures in the administrative adjudication provisions of the Administrative Procedure Act (Chapter 4.5 (commencing with Section 11400) and Chapter 5 (commencing with Section 11500) of Part 1 of Division 3 of Title 2 of the Government Code) shall not apply to the denial or suspension of, or refusal to renew, a license or the issuance of a temporary license pursuant to this section.

(2) Notwithstanding any other law, if a board, bureau, or commission listed in Section 101, other than the Contractors State License Board, fails to take action in accordance with this section, the Department of Consumer Affairs shall issue a temporary license or suspend or refuse to issue, reactivate, reinstate, or renew a license, as appropriate.

(g) Notices shall be developed by each state governmental licensing entity. For an applicant or licensee on the State Board of Equalization's certified list, the notice shall include the address and telephone number of the State Board of Equalization, and shall emphasize the necessity of obtaining a release from the State Board of Equalization as a condition for the issuance, renewal, or continued valid status of a license or licenses. For an applicant or licensee on the Franchise Tax Board's certified list, the notice shall include the address and telephone number of the Franchise Tax Board, and shall emphasize the necessity of obtaining a release from the Franchise Tax Board as a condition for the issuance, renewal, or continued valid status of a license or licenses.

(1) The notice shall inform the applicant that the state governmental licensing entity shall issue a temporary license, as provided in subparagraph (A) of paragraph (2) of subdivision (e), for 90 calendar days if the applicant is

otherwise eligible and that upon expiration of that time period, the license will be denied unless the state governmental licensing entity has received a release from the State Board of Equalization or the Franchise Tax Board, whichever is applicable.

(2) The notice shall inform the licensee that any license suspended under this section will remain suspended until the state governmental licensing entity receives a release along with applications and fees, if applicable, to reinstate the license.

(3) The notice shall also inform the applicant or licensee that if an application is denied or a license is suspended pursuant to this section, any moneys paid by the applicant or licensee shall not be refunded by the state governmental licensing entity. The state governmental licensing entity shall also develop a form that the applicant or licensee shall use to request a release by the State Board of Equalization or the Franchise Tax Board. A copy of this form shall be included with every notice sent pursuant to this subdivision.

(h) If the applicant or licensee wishes to challenge the submission of their name on a certified list, the applicant or licensee shall make a timely written request for release to the State Board of Equalization or the Franchise Tax Board, whichever is applicable. The State Board of Equalization or the Franchise Tax Board shall immediately send a release to the appropriate state governmental licensing entity and the applicant or licensee, if any of the following conditions are met:

(1) The applicant or licensee has complied with the tax obligation, either by payment of the unpaid taxes or entry into an installment payment agreement, as described in Section 6832 or 19008 of the Revenue and Taxation Code, to satisfy the unpaid taxes.

(2) The applicant or licensee has submitted a request for release not later than 45 days after the applicant's or licensee's receipt of a preliminary notice described in paragraph (2) of subdivision (e), but the State Board of Equalization or the Franchise Tax Board, whichever is applicable, will be unable to complete the release review and send notice of its findings to the applicant or licensee and state governmental licensing entity within 45 days after the State Board of Equalization's or the Franchise Tax Board's receipt of the applicant's or licensee's request for release. Whenever a release is granted under this paragraph, and, notwithstanding that release, the applicable license or licenses have been suspended erroneously, the state governmental licensing entity shall reinstate the applicable licenses with retroactive effect back to the date of the erroneous suspension and that suspension shall not be reflected on any license record.

(3) The applicant or licensee is unable to pay the outstanding tax obligation due to a current financial hardship. "Financial hardship" means financial hardship as determined by the State Board of Equalization or the Franchise Tax Board, whichever is applicable, where the applicant or licensee is unable to pay any part of the outstanding liability and the applicant or licensee is unable to qualify for an installment payment arrangement as provided for by Section 6832 or Section 19008 of the Revenue and Taxation Code. In order to establish the existence of a financial hardship, the applicant or licensee shall submit any information, including information related to reasonable business and personal expenses, requested by the State Board of Equalization or the Franchise Tax Board, whichever is applicable, for purposes of making that determination.

(i) An applicant or licensee is required to act with diligence in responding to notices from the state governmental licensing entity and the State Board of Equalization or the Franchise Tax Board with the recognition that the temporary license will lapse or the license suspension will go into effect after 90 days and that the State Board of Equalization or the Franchise Tax Board must have time to act within that period. An applicant's or licensee's delay in acting, without good cause, which directly results in the inability of the State Board of Equalization or the Franchise Tax Board, whichever is applicable, to complete a review of the applicant's or licensee's request for release shall not constitute the diligence required under this section which would justify the issuance of a release. An applicant or licensee shall have the burden of establishing that they diligently responded to notices from the state governmental licensing entity or the State Board of Equalization or the Franchise Tax Board and that any delay was not without good cause.

(j) The State Board of Equalization or the Franchise Tax Board shall create release forms for use pursuant to this section. When the applicant or licensee has complied with the tax obligation by payment of the unpaid taxes, or entry into an installment payment agreement, or establishing the existence of a current financial hardship as defined in paragraph (3) of subdivision (h), the State Board of Equalization or the Franchise Tax Board, whichever is applicable, shall mail a release form to the applicant or licensee and provide a release to the appropriate state governmental licensing entity. Any state governmental licensing entity that has received a release from the State Board of Equalization and the Franchise Tax Board pursuant to this subdivision shall process the release within five business days of its receipt. If the State Board of Equalization or the Franchise Tax Board determines subsequent to the issuance of a release that the licensee has not complied with their installment payment agreement, the State Board of Equalization or the Franchise Tax Board, whichever is applicable, shall notify the state governmental licensing entity and the licensee in a format prescribed by the State Board of Equalization or the Franchise Tax Board, whichever is applicable, that the licensee is not in compliance and the release shall be rescinded. The State Board of Equalization and the Franchise Tax Board may, when it is economically feasible for the state governmental licensing entity to develop an automated process for complying with this subdivision, notify the state governmental licensing entity in a manner prescribed by the State Board of Equalization or the Franchise Tax Board, whichever is applicable, that the licensee has not complied with the installment payment agreement. Upon receipt of this notice, the state governmental licensing entity shall immediately notify the licensee on a form prescribed by the state governmental licensing entity that the licensee's license will be suspended on a specific date, and this date shall be no longer than 30 days from the date the form is mailed. The licensee shall be further notified that the license will remain suspended until a new release is issued in accordance with this subdivision.

(k) The State Board of Equalization and the Franchise Tax Board may enter into interagency agreements with the state governmental licensing entities necessary to implement this section.

(l) Notwithstanding any other law, a state governmental licensing entity, with the approval of the appropriate department director or governing body, may impose a fee on a licensee whose license has been suspended pursuant to this section. The fee shall not exceed the amount necessary for the state governmental licensing entity to cover its costs in carrying out the provisions of this section. Fees imposed pursuant to this section shall be deposited in the fund in which other fees imposed by the state governmental licensing entity are deposited and shall be available to that entity upon appropriation in the annual Budget Act.

(m) The process described in subdivision (h) shall constitute the sole administrative remedy for contesting the issuance of a temporary license or the denial or suspension of a license under this section.

(n) Any state governmental licensing entity receiving an inquiry as to the licensed status of an applicant or licensee who has had a license denied or suspended under this section or who has been granted a temporary license under this section shall respond that the license was denied or suspended or the temporary license was issued only because the licensee appeared on a list of the 500 largest tax delinquencies pursuant to Section 7063 or 19195 of the Revenue and Taxation Code. Information collected pursuant to this section by any state agency, board, or department shall be subject to the Information Practices Act of 1977 (Chapter 1 (commencing with Section 1798) of Title 1.8 of Part 4 of Division 3 of the Civil Code). Any state governmental licensing entity that discloses on its internet website or other publication that the licensee has had a license denied or suspended under this section or has been granted a temporary license under this section shall prominently disclose, in bold and adjacent to the information regarding the status of the license, that the only reason the license was denied, suspended, or temporarily issued is because the licensee failed to pay taxes.

(o) Any rules and regulations issued pursuant to this section by any state agency, board, or department may be adopted as emergency regulations in accordance with the rulemaking provisions of the Administrative Procedure Act (Chapter 3.5 (commencing with Section 11340) of Part 1 of Division 3 of Title 2 of the Government Code). The adoption of these regulations shall be deemed an emergency and necessary for the immediate preservation of the public peace, health, and safety, or general welfare. The regulations shall become effective immediately upon filing with the Secretary of State.

(p) The State Board of Equalization, the Franchise Tax Board, and state governmental licensing entities, as appropriate, shall adopt regulations as necessary to implement this section.

(q) (1) Neither the state governmental licensing entity, nor any officer, employee, or agent, or former officer, employee, or agent of a state governmental licensing entity, may disclose or use any information obtained from the State Board of Equalization or the Franchise Tax Board, pursuant to this section, except to inform the public of the denial, refusal to renew, or suspension of a license or the issuance of a temporary license pursuant to this section. The release or other use of information received by a state governmental licensing entity pursuant to this section, except as authorized by this section, is punishable as a misdemeanor. This subdivision may not be interpreted to prevent the State Bar of California from filing a request with the Supreme Court of California to suspend a member of the bar pursuant to this section.

(2) A suspension of, or refusal to renew, a license or issuance of a temporary license pursuant to this section does not constitute denial or discipline of a licensee for purposes of any reporting requirements to the National Practitioner Data Bank and shall not be reported to the National Practitioner Data Bank or the Healthcare Integrity and Protection Data Bank.

(3) Upon release from the certified list, the suspension or revocation of the applicant's or licensee's license shall be purged from the state governmental

licensing entity's internet website or other publication within three business days. This paragraph shall not apply to the State Bar of California.

(r) If any provision of this section or the application thereof to any person or circumstance is held invalid, that invalidity shall not affect other provisions or applications of this section that can be given effect without the invalid provision or application, and to this end the provisions of this section are severable.

(s) All rights to review afforded by this section to an applicant shall also be afforded to a licensee.

(t) Unless otherwise provided in this section, the policies, practices, and procedures of a state governmental licensing entity with respect to license suspensions under this section shall be the same as those applicable with respect to suspensions pursuant to Section 17520 of the Family Code.

(u) No provision of this section shall be interpreted to allow a court to review and prevent the collection of taxes prior to the payment of those taxes in violation of the California Constitution.

(v) This section shall apply to any licensee whose name appears on a list of the 500 largest tax delinquencies pursuant to Section 7063 or 19195 of the Revenue and Taxation Code on or after July 1, 2012.

(Amended by Stats. 2020, Ch. 312, Sec. 9. (SB 1474) Effective January 1, 2021.)

494.6 SUSPENSION OR REVOCATION OF LICENSES FOR VIOLATIONS OF SECTION 244 OF LABOR CODE

(a) A business license regulated by this code may be subject to suspension or revocation if the licensee has been determined by the Labor Commissioner or the court to have violated subdivision (b) of Section 244 of the Labor Code and the court or Labor Commissioner has taken into consideration any harm such a suspension or revocation would cause to employees of the licensee, as well as the good faith efforts of the licensee to resolve any alleged violations after receiving notice.

(b) Notwithstanding subdivision (a), a licensee of an agency within the Department of Consumer Affairs who has been found by the Labor Commissioner or the court to have violated subdivision (b) of Section 244 of the Labor Code may be subject to disciplinary action by his or her respective licensing agency.

(c) An employer shall not be subject to suspension or revocation under this section for requiring a prospective or current employee to submit, within three business days of the first day of work for pay, an I-9 Employment Eligibility Verification form.

(Amended by Stats. 2014, Ch. 71, Sec. 1. (SB 1304) Effective January 1, 2015.)

CHAPTER 4: PUBLIC REPROVALS

495. PUBLIC REPROVAL OF LICENTIATE OR CERTIFICATE HOLDER FOR ACT CONSTITUTING GROUNDS FOR SUSPENSION OR REVOCATION OF LICENSE OR CERTIFICATE; PROCEEDINGS

Notwithstanding any other provision of law, any entity authorized to issue a license or certificate pursuant to this code may publicly reprove a licentiate or certificate holder thereof, for any act that would constitute grounds to suspend or revoke a license or certificate. Any proceedings for public reproval, public reproval and suspension, or public reproval and revocation shall be conducted in accordance with Chapter 5 (commencing with Section 11500) of Part 1 of Division 3 of Title 2 of the Government Code, or, in the case of a licensee or certificate holder under the jurisdiction of the State Department of Health Services, in accordance with Section 100171 of the Health and Safety Code.

(Amended by Stats. 1997, Ch. 220, Sec. 2. Effective August 4, 1997.)

CHAPTER 5: EXAMINATION SECURITY

496. GROUND FOR DENIAL, SUSPENSION, OR REVOCATION OF LICENSE

A board may deny, suspend, revoke, or otherwise restrict a license on the ground that an applicant or licensee has violated Section 123 pertaining to subversion of licensing examinations.

(Repealed and added by Stats. 1989, Ch. 1022, Sec. 3.)

498. FRAUD, DECEIT OR MISREPRESENTATION AS GROUNDS FOR ACTION AGAINST LICENSE

A board may revoke, suspend, or otherwise restrict a license on the ground that the licensee secured the license by fraud, deceit, or knowing misrepresentation of a material fact or by knowingly omitting to state a material fact.

(Added by Stats. 1992, Ch. 1289, Sec. 8. Effective January 1, 1993.)

499. ACTION AGAINST LICENSE BASED ON LICENTIATE'S ACTIONS REGARDING APPLICATION OF ANOTHER

A board may revoke, suspend, or otherwise restrict a license on the ground that the licensee, in support of another person's application for license, knowingly made a false statement of a material fact or knowingly omitted to state a material fact to the board regarding the application.

(Added by Stats. 1992, Ch. 1289, Sec. 9. Effective January 1, 1993.)

DIVISION 2: HEALING ARTS

CHAPTER 1: GENERAL PROVISIONS

ARTICLE 1: RECORDS

502. COLLECTION OF LICENSEE AND REGISTRANT WORKFORCE DATA

(a) Notwithstanding any other law, both of the following apply:

(1) The Board of Registered Nursing, the Board of Vocational Nursing and Psychiatric Technicians of the State of California, the Physician Assistant Board, and the Respiratory Care Board of California shall collect workforce data from their respective licensees and registrants as specified in subdivision (b) for future workforce planning at least biennially. The data shall be collected at the time of electronic license or registration renewal for those boards that utilize electronic renewals for licensees or registrants.

(2) All other boards that are not listed in paragraph (1) that regulate healing arts licensees or registrants under this division shall request workforce data from their respective licensees and registrants as specified in subdivision (b) for future workforce planning at least biennially. The data shall be requested at the time of electronic license or registration renewal for those boards that utilize electronic renewals for licensees or registrants.

(b) In conformance with specifications under subdivision (d), the workforce data collected or requested by each board about its licensees and registrants shall include, at a minimum, all of the following information:

(1) Anticipated year of retirement.

(2) Area of practice or specialty.

(3) City, county, and ZIP Code of practice.

(4) Date of birth.

(5) Educational background and the highest level attained at time of licensure or registration.

(6) Gender or gender identity.

(7) Hours spent in direct patient care, including telehealth hours as a subcategory, training, research, and administration.

(8) Languages spoken.

(9) National Provider Identifier.

(10) Race or ethnicity.

(11) Type of employer or classification of primary practice site among the types of practice sites specified by the board, including, but not limited to, clinic, hospital, managed care organization, or private practice.

(12) Work hours.

(13) Sexual orientation.

(14) Disability status.

(c) Each board shall maintain the confidentiality of the information it receives from licensees and registrants under this section and shall only release information in an aggregate form that cannot be used to identify an individual other than as specified in subdivision (e).

(d) The Department of Consumer Affairs, in consultation with the Department of Health Care Access and Information, shall specify for each board subject to this section the specific information and data that will be collected or requested pursuant to subdivision (b). The Department of Consumer Affairs' identification and specification of this information and data shall be exempt until June 30, 2023, from the requirements of the Administrative Procedure Act (Chapter 3.5 (commencing with Section 11340) of Part 1 of Division 3 of Title 2 of the Government Code).

(e) Each board, or the Department of Consumer Affairs on its behalf, shall, beginning on July 1, 2022, and quarterly thereafter, provide the individual licensee and registrant data it collects pursuant to this section to the Department of Health Care Access and Information in a manner directed by the Department of Health Care Access and Information, including license or registration number and associated license or registration information. The Department of Health Care Access and Information shall maintain the confidentiality of the licensee and registrant information it receives and shall only release information in an aggregate form that cannot be used to identify an individual.

(f) A licensee or registrant shall not be required to provide the information listed in subdivision (b) as a condition for license or registration renewal, and licensees or registrants shall not be subject to discipline for not providing the information listed in subdivision (b).

(g) This section does not alter or affect mandatory reporting requirements for licensees or registrants established pursuant to this division, including, but not limited to, Sections 1715.5, 1902.2, 2425.3, and 2455.2.

(Added by Stats. 2021, Ch. 143, Sec. 4. (AB 133) Effective July 27, 2021.)

ARTICLE 1.5: ADVOCACY FOR APPROPRIATE HEALTH CARE

510. PROTECTION AGAINST RETALIATION FOR PHYSICIAN WHO "ADVOCATE FOR MEDICALLY APPROPRIATE HEALTH CARE"

(a) The purpose of this section is to provide protection against retaliation for health care practitioners who advocate for appropriate health care for their patients pursuant to Wickline v. State of California 192 Cal. App. 3d 1630.

(b) It is the public policy of the State of California that a health care practitioner be encouraged to advocate for appropriate health care for his or her patients. For purposes of this section, "to advocate for appropriate health care" means to appeal a payer's decision to deny payment for a service pursuant to the reasonable grievance or appeal procedure established by a medical group, independent practice association, preferred provider organization, foundation, hospital medical staff and governing body, or payer, or to protest a decision, policy, or practice that the health care practitioner, consistent with that degree of learning and skill ordinarily possessed by reputable health care practitioners with the same license or certification and practicing according to the applicable legal standard of care, reasonably believes impairs the health care practitioner's ability to provide appropriate health care to his or her patients.

(c) The application and rendering by any individual, partnership, corporation, or other organization of a decision to terminate an employment or other contractual relationship with or otherwise penalize a health care practitioner principally for advocating for appropriate health care consistent with that degree of learning and skill ordinarily possessed by reputable health care practitioners with the same license or certification and practicing according to the applicable legal standard of care violates the public policy of this state.

(d) This section shall not be construed to prohibit a payer from making a determination not to pay for a particular medical treatment or service, or the services of a type of health care practitioner, or to prohibit a medical group, independent practice association, preferred provider organization, foundation, hospital medical staff, hospital governing body acting pursuant to Section 809.05, or payer from enforcing reasonable peer review or utilization review protocols or determining whether a health care practitioner has complied with those protocols.

(e) (1) Except as provided in paragraph (2), appropriate health care in a hospital licensed pursuant to Section 1250 of the Health and Safety Code shall be defined by the appropriate hospital committee and approved by the hospital medical staff and the governing body, consistent with that degree of learning and skill ordinarily possessed by reputable health care practitioners with the same license or certification and practicing according to the applicable legal standard of care.

(2) To the extent the issue is under the jurisdiction of the medical staff and its committees, appropriate health care in a hospital licensed pursuant to Section 1250 of the Health and Safety Code shall be defined by the hospital medical staff and approved by the governing body, consistent with that degree of learning and skill ordinarily possessed by reputable health care practitioners with the same license or certification and practicing according to the applicable legal standard of care.

(f) Nothing in this section shall be construed to prohibit the governing body of a hospital from taking disciplinary actions against a health care practitioner as authorized by Sections 809.05, 809.4, and 809.5.

(g) Nothing in this section shall be construed to prohibit the appropriate licensing authority from taking disciplinary actions against a health care practitioner.

(h) For purposes of this section, "health care practitioner" means a person who is described in subdivision (f) of Section 900 and who is either (1) a licentiate as defined in Section 805, or (2) a party to a contract with a payer whose decision, policy, or practice is subject to the advocacy described in subdivision (b), or (3) an individual designated in a contract with a payer whose decision, policy, or practice is subject to the advocacy described in subdivision (b), where the individual is granted the right to appeal denials of payment or authorization for treatment under the contract.

(i) Nothing in this section shall be construed to revise or expand the scope of practice of any health care practitioner, or to revise or expand the types of health care practitioners who are authorized to obtain medical staff privileges or to submit claims for reimbursement to payers.

(j) The protections afforded health care practitioners by this section shall be in addition to the protections available under any other law of this state.

(Added by Stats. 1994, Ch. 1119, Sec. 1. Effective January 1, 1995.)

511. PROSCRIPTION ON PAYMENT TO HEALTH CARE PRACTITIONER TO DENY, LIMIT, OR DELAY SERVICES

(a) No subcontract between a physician and surgeon, physician and surgeon group, or other licensed health care practitioner who contracts with a health care service plan or health insurance carrier, and another physician and surgeon, physician and surgeon group, or licensed health care practitioner, shall contain any incentive plan that includes a specific payment made, in any type or form, to a physician and surgeon, physician and surgeon group, or other licensed health care practitioner as an inducement to deny, reduce, limit, or delay specific, medically necessary, and appropriate services covered under the contract with the health care service plan or health insurance carrier and provided with respect to a specific enrollee or groups of enrollees with similar medical conditions.

(b) Nothing in this section shall be construed to prohibit subcontracts that contain incentive plans that involve general payments such as capitation payments or shared risk agreements that are not tied to specific medical decisions involving specific enrollees or groups of enrollees with similar medical conditions.

(Added by Stats. 1996, Ch. 1014, Sec. 1. Effective January 1, 1997.)

511.1. DISCLOSURE RELATING TO HEALTH CARE PROVIDER'S PARTICIPATION IN NETWORK; DISCLOSURES BY CONTRACTING AGENT CONVEYING ITS LIST OF CONTRACTED HEALTH CARE PROVIDERS AND REIMBURSEMENT RATES; ELECTION BY PROVIDER TO BE EXCLUDED FROM LIST; DEMONSTRATION BY PAYOR OF THE ENTITLEMENT TO PAY CONTRACTED RATE

(a) In order to prevent the improper selling, leasing, or transferring of a health care provider's contract, it is the intent of the Legislature that every arrangement that results in a payor paying a health care provider a reduced rate for health care services based on the health care provider's participation in a network or panel shall be disclosed to the provider in advance and that the payor shall actively encourage beneficiaries to use the network, unless the health care provider agrees to provide discounts without that active encouragement.

(b) Beginning July 1, 2000, every contracting agent that sells, leases, assigns, transfers, or conveys its list of contracted health care providers and their contracted reimbursement rates to a payor, as defined in subparagraph (A) of paragraph (3) of subdivision (d), or another contracting agent shall, upon entering or renewing a provider contract, do all of the following:

(1) Disclose whether the list of contracted providers may be sold, leased, transferred, or conveyed to other payors or other contracting agents, and specify whether those payors or contracting agents include workers' compensation insurers or automobile insurers.

(2) Disclose what specific practices, if any, payors utilize to actively encourage a payor's beneficiaries to use the list of contracted providers when obtaining medical care that entitles a payor to claim a contracted rate. For purposes of this paragraph, a payor is deemed to have actively encouraged its beneficiaries to use the list of contracted providers if one of the following occurs:

(A) The payor's contract with subscribers or insureds offers beneficiaries direct financial incentives to use the list of contracted providers when obtaining medical care. "Financial incentives" means reduced copayments, reduced deductibles, premium discounts directly attributable to the use of a provider panel, or financial penalties directly attributable to the nonuse of a provider panel.

(B) The payor provides information directly to its beneficiaries, who are parties to the contract, or, in the case of workers' compensation insurance, the employer, advising them of the existence of the list of contracted providers through the use of a variety of advertising or marketing approaches that supply the names, addresses, and telephone numbers of contracted providers to beneficiaries in advance of their selection of a health care provider, which approaches may include, but are not limited to, the use of provider directories, or the use of toll-free telephone numbers or internet web site addresses supplied directly to every beneficiary. However, internet web site addresses alone shall not be deemed to satisfy the requirements of this subparagraph. Nothing in this subparagraph shall prevent contracting agents or payors from providing only listings of providers located within a reasonable geographic range of a beneficiary.

(3) Disclose whether payors to which the list of contracted providers may be sold, leased, transferred, or conveyed may be permitted to pay a provider's contracted rate without actively encouraging the payors' beneficiaries to use the list of contracted providers when obtaining medical care. Nothing in this subdivision shall be construed to require a payor to actively encourage the payor's beneficiaries to use the list of contracted providers when obtaining medical care in the case of an emergency.

(4) Disclose, upon the initial signing of a contract, and within 30 calendar days of receipt of a written request from a provider or provider panel, a payor summary of all payors currently eligible to claim a provider's contracted rate due to the provider's and payor's respective written agreements with any contracting agent.

(5) Allow providers, upon the initial signing, renewal, or amendment of a provider contract, to decline to be included in any list of contracted providers that is sold, leased, transferred, or conveyed to payors that do not actively encourage the payors' beneficiaries to use the list of contracted providers when obtaining medical care as described in paragraph (2). Each provider's election under this paragraph shall be binding on the contracting agent with which the provider has the contract and on any other contracting agent that buys, leases, or otherwise obtains the list of contracted providers. A provider shall not be excluded from any list of contracted providers that is sold, leased, transferred, or conveyed to payors that actively encourage the payors' beneficiaries to use the list of contracted providers when obtaining medical care, based upon the provider's refusal to be included on any list of contracted providers that is sold, leased, transferred, or conveyed to payors that do not actively encourage the payors' beneficiaries to use the list of contracted providers when obtaining medical care.

(6) Nothing in this subdivision shall be construed to impose requirements or regulations upon payors, as defined in subparagraph (A) of paragraph (3) of subdivision (d).

(c) Beginning July 1, 2000, a payor, as defined in subparagraph (B) of paragraph (3) of subdivision (d), shall do all of the following:

(1) Provide an explanation of benefits or explanation of review that identifies the name of the plan or network that has a written agreement signed by the provider whereby the payor is entitled, directly or indirectly, to pay a preferred rate for the services rendered.

(2) Demonstrate that it is entitled to pay a contracted rate within 30 business days of receipt of a written request from a provider who has received a claim payment from the payor. The failure of a payor to make the demonstration within 30 business days shall render the payor responsible for the amount that the payor would have been required to pay pursuant to the contract between the payor and the beneficiary, which amount shall be due

and payable within 10 business days of receipt of written notice from the provider, and shall bar the payor from taking any future discounts from that provider without the provider's express written consent until the payor can demonstrate to the provider that it is entitled to pay a contracted rate as provided in this paragraph. A payor shall be deemed to have demonstrated that it is entitled to pay a contracted rate if it complies with either of the following:

(A) Discloses the name of the network that has a written agreement with the provider whereby the provider agrees to accept discounted rates, and describes the specific practices the payor utilizes to comply with paragraph (2) of subdivision (b).

(B) Identifies the provider's written agreement with a contracting agent whereby the provider agrees to be included on lists of contracted providers sold, leased, transferred, or conveyed to payors that do not actively encourage beneficiaries to use the list of contracted providers pursuant to paragraph (5) of subdivision (b).

(d) For the purposes of this section, the following terms have the following meanings:

(1) "Beneficiary" means:

(A) For workers' compensation insurance, an employee seeking health care services for a work-related injury.

(B) For automobile insurance, those persons covered under the medical payments portion of the insurance contract.

(C) For group or individual health services covered through a health care service plan contract, including a specialized health care service plan contract, or a policy of disability insurance that covers hospital, medical, or surgical benefits, a subscriber, an enrollee, a policyholder, or an insured.

(2) "Contracting agent" means a third-party administrator or trust not licensed under the Health and Safety Code, the Insurance Code, or the Labor Code, a self-insured employer, a preferred provider organization, or an independent practice association, while engaged, for monetary or other consideration, in the act of selling, leasing, transferring, assigning, or conveying, a provider or provider panel to provide health care services to beneficiaries. For purposes of this section, a contracting agent shall not include a health care service plan, including a specialized health care service plan, an insurer licensed under the Insurance Code to provide disability insurance that covers hospital, medical, or surgical benefits, automobile insurance, or workers' compensation insurance, or a self-insured employer.

(3) (A) For purposes of subdivision (b), "payor" means a health care service plan, including a specialized health care service plan, an insurer licensed under the Insurance Code to provide disability insurance that covers hospital, medical, or surgical benefits, automobile insurance, workers' compensation insurance, or a self-insured employer that is responsible to pay for health care services provided to beneficiaries.

(B) For purposes of subdivision (c), "payor" means only those entities that provide coverage for hospital, medical, or surgical benefits that are not regulated under the Health and Safety Code, the Insurance Code, or the Labor Code.

(4) "Payor summary" means a written summary that includes the payor's name and the type of plan, including, but not limited to, a group health plan, an automobile insurance plan, and a workers' compensation insurance plan.

(5) "Provider" means any of the following:

(A) Any person licensed or certified pursuant to this division.

(B) Any person licensed pursuant to the Chiropractic Initiative Act or the Osteopathic Initiative Act.

(C) Any person licensed pursuant to Chapter 2.5 (commencing with Section 1440) of Division 2 of the Health and Safety Code.

(D) A clinic, health dispensary, or health facility licensed pursuant to Division 2 (commencing with Section 1200) of the Health and Safety Code.

(E) Any entity exempt from licensure pursuant to Section 1206 of the Health and Safety Code.

(e) This section shall become operative on July 1, 2000.

(Amended by Stats. 2000, Ch. 1069, Sec. 1. Effective January 1, 2001.)

511.3. RIGHTS AND OBLIGATIONS OF PROVIDER UPON SALE, LEASE OR TRANSFER OF HEALTH PROVIDERS CONTRACT TO PAYOR

(a) When a contracting agent sells, leases, or transfers a health provider's contract to a payor, the rights and obligations of the provider shall be governed by the underlying contract between the health care provider and the contracting agent.

(b) For purposes of this section, the following terms shall have the following meanings:

(1) "Contracting agent" has the meaning set forth in paragraph (2) of subdivision (d) of Section 511.1.

(2) "Payor" has the meaning set forth in paragraph (3) of subdivision (d) of Section 511.1.

(Amended by Stats. 2004, Ch. 183, Sec. 1. Effective January 1, 2005.)

511.4. INFORMATION PROVIDED IN ELECTRONIC FORMAT

(a) A contracting agent, as defined in paragraph (2) of subdivision (d) of Section 511.1, shall beginning July 1, 2006, prior to contracting, annually thereafter on or before the contract anniversary date, and, in addition, upon the contracted provider's written request, disclose to contracting providers all of the following information in an electronic format:

(1) The amount of payment for each service to be provided under the contract, including any fee schedules or other factors or units used in determining the fees for each service. To the extent that reimbursement is made pursuant to a specified fee schedule, the contract shall incorporate that fee schedule by reference, including the year of the schedule. For any proprietary fee schedule, the contract shall include sufficient detail that payment amounts related to that fee schedule can be accurately predicted.

(2) The detailed payment policies and rules and nonstandard coding methodologies used to adjudicate claims, which shall, unless otherwise prohibited by state law, do all of the following:

(A) When available, be consistent with Current Procedural Terminology (CPT), and standards accepted by nationally recognized medical societies and organizations, federal regulatory bodies, and major credentialing organizations.

(B) Clearly and accurately state what is covered by any global payment provisions for both professional and institutional services, any global payment provisions for all services necessary as part of a course of treatment in an institutional setting, and any other global arrangements, such as per diem hospital payments.

(C) At a minimum, clearly and accurately state the policies regarding all of the following:

(i) Consolidation of multiple services or charges and payment adjustments due to coding changes.

(ii) Reimbursement for multiple procedures.

(iii) Reimbursement for assistant surgeons.

(iv) Reimbursement for the administration of immunizations and injectable medications.

(v) Recognition of CPT modifiers.

(b) The information disclosures required by this section shall be in sufficient detail and in an understandable format that does not disclose proprietary trade secret information or violate copyright law or patented processes, so that a reasonable person with sufficient training, experience, and competence in claims processing can determine the payment to be made according to the terms of the contract.

(c) A contracting agent may disclose the fee schedules mandated by this section through the use of a Web site, so long as it provides written notice to the contracted provider at least 45 days prior to implementing a Web site transmission format or posting any changes to the information on the Web site.

(Added by Stats. 2005, Ch. 441, Sec. 2. Effective January 1, 2006.)

512. CONTRACT TO RESTRICT HEALTH CARE PROVIDER'S ADVERTISING

(a) Except as provided in subdivisions (b) and (c), no contract that is issued, amended, renewed, or delivered on or after January 1, 1999, between any person or entity, including, but not limited to, any group of physicians and surgeons, any medical group, any independent practice association (IPA), or any preferred provider organization (PPO), and a health care provider shall contain provisions that prohibit, restrict, or limit the health care provider from advertising.

(b) Nothing in this section shall be construed to prohibit the establishment of reasonable guidelines in connection with the activities regulated pursuant to this division, including those to prevent advertising that is, in whole or in part, untrue, misleading, deceptive, or otherwise inconsistent with this division or the rules and regulations promulgated thereunder. For advertisements mentioning a provider's participation in a plan or product line of any person or entity, nothing in this section shall be construed to prohibit requiring each advertisement to contain a disclaimer to the effect that the provider's services may be covered for some, but not all, plans or product lines of that person or entity, or that the person or entity may cover some, but not all, provider services.

(c) Nothing in this section is intended to prohibit provisions or agreements intended to protect service marks, trademarks, trade secrets, or other confidential information or property. If a health care provider participates on a provider panel or network as a result of a direct contractual arrangement with a person or entity, including, but not limited to, any group of physicians and surgeons, any medical group, any independent practice association, or any preferred provider organization, that, in turn, has entered into a direct contractual arrangement with another person or entity, pursuant to which enrollees, subscribers, insureds, and other beneficiaries of that other person or entity may receive covered services from the health care provider, then nothing in this section is intended to prohibit reasonable provisions or agreements in the direct contractual arrangement between the health care provider and the person or entity that protect the name or trade name of the other person or entity or require that the health care provider obtain the consent of the person or entity prior to the use of the name or trade name of the person or entity in any advertising by the health care provider.

(d) Nothing in this section shall be construed to impair or impede the authority of any state department to regulate advertising, disclosure, or solicitation pursuant to this division.

(Added by Stats. 1998, Ch. 523, Sec. 2. Effective January 1, 1999.)

ARTICLE 2: EYEGLASSES

525. WHEN SHATTER-RESISTANT MATERIALS REQUIRED

No dispensing optician, optometrist, or physician and surgeon shall dispense, prescribe, or sell any eyeglasses for use of a person whose sight is limited to one eye, a person who is a member of the California Highway Patrol or of a county sheriff's office, a city police officer, a person who is a firefighter employed by the fire department of a city, county, city and county, or fire protection district and who normally wears such glasses for on-duty employment, or a person who is under 18 years of age, unless such eyeglasses are made with case-hardened lenses, with lenses made of laminated glass, with lenses made of resin material, or with lenses made of any other material resistant to shattering and which shall not be installed in frames manufactured of flammable material.

(Amended by Stats. 2021, Ch. 630, Sec. 7. (AB 1534) Effective January 1, 2022.)

526. SCIENTER AS ELEMENT OF OFFENSE

A dispensing optician, optometrist, or physician and surgeon shall not be subject to disciplinary action under this article unless they are informed by the person obtaining the eyeglasses or they have personal knowledge that the eyeglasses are for a person whose sight is limited to one eye, a person who is a member of the California Highway Patrol or of a county sheriff's office, a city police officer, or a firefighter employed by the fire department of a city, county, city and county, or fire protection district, or a person who is under 18 years of age.

A dispensing optician, optometrist, or physician and surgeon is not required under this article to make any independent investigation of the occupation of the person for whom eyeglasses are intended or as to whether or not the sight of such person is limited to one eye.

(Amended by Stats. 2021, Ch. 630, Sec. 8. (AB 1534) Effective January 1, 2022.)

527. DISCIPLINARY ACTION

Any dispensing optician, optometrist, or physician and surgeon who violates this article is subject to disciplinary action by the board that issues their license, registration, or certificate to engage in practice.

(Amended by Stats. 2021, Ch. 630, Sec. 9. (AB 1534) Effective January 1, 2022.)

ARTICLE 4: FRAUDS OF MEDICAL RECORDS

580. SALE OR BARTER OF DEGREE, CERTIFICATE, OR TRANSCRIPT

No person, company, or association shall sell or barter or offer to sell or barter any medical degree, podiatric degree, or osteopathic degree, or chiropractic degree, or any other degree which is required for licensure, certification, or registration under this division, or any degree, certificate, transcript, or any other writing, made or purporting to be made pursuant to any laws regulating the licensing and registration or issuing of a certificate to physicians and surgeons, podiatrists, osteopathic physicians, chiropractors, persons lawfully engaged in any other system or mode of treating the sick or afflicted, or to any other person licensed, certified, or registered under this division.

(Amended by Stats. 1986, Ch. 220, Sec. 2. Effective June 30, 1986.)

581. PURCHASE OR FRAUDULENT ALTERATION OF DIPLOMA OR OTHER WRITINGS

No person, company, or association shall purchase or procure by barter or by any unlawful means or method, or have in possession any diploma, certificate, transcript, or any other writing with intent that it shall be used as evidence of the holder's qualifications to practice as a physician and surgeon, osteopathic physician, podiatrist, any other system or mode of treating the sick or afflicted, as provided in the Medical Practice Act, Chapter 5 (commencing with Section 2000), or to practice as any other licentiate under this division or in any fraud of the law regulating this practice or, shall with fraudulent intent, alter in a material regard, any such diploma, certificate, transcript, or any other writing.

(Amended by Stats. 1986, Ch. 220, Sec. 3. Effective June 30, 1986.)

582. USE OF ILLEGALLY OBTAINED, ALTERED, OR COUNTERFEIT DIPLOMA, CERTIFICATE, OR TRANSCRIPT

No person, company, or association shall use or attempt to use any diploma, certificate, transcript, or any other writing which has been purchased, fraudulently issued, illegally obtained, counterfeited, or materially altered, either as a certificate or as to character or color of certificate, to practice as a physician and surgeon, podiatrist, osteopathic physician, or a chiropractor, or to practice any other system or mode of treating the sick or afflicted, as provided in the Medical Practice Act, Chapter 5 (commencing with Section 2000) or to practice as any other licentiate under this division.

(Amended by Stats. 1986, Ch. 220, Sec. 4. Effective June 30, 1986.)

583. FALSE STATEMENTS IN DOCUMENTS OR WRITINGS

No person shall in any document or writing required of an applicant for examination, license, certificate, or registration under this division, the Osteopathic Initiative Act, or the Chiropractic Initiative Act, willfully make a false statement in a material regard.

(Amended by Stats. 1986, Ch. 220, Sec. 5. Effective June 30, 1986.)

584. VIOLATION OF EXAMINATION SECURITY; IMPERSONATION

No person shall violate the security of any examination, as defined in subdivision (a) of Section 123, or impersonate, attempt to impersonate, or solicit the impersonation of, another in any examination for a license, certificate, or registration to practice as provided in this division, the Osteopathic Initiative Act, or the Chiropractic Initiative Act, or under any other law providing for the regulation of any other system or method of treating the sick or afflicted in this state.

(Amended by Stats. 1989, Ch. 1022, Sec. 5.)

585. PUNISHMENT

Any person, company, or association violating the provisions of this article is guilty of a felony and upon conviction thereof shall be punishable by a fine of not less than two thousand dollars ($2,000) nor more than six thousand dollars ($6,000), or by imprisonment pursuant to subdivision (h) of Section 1170 of the Penal Code. The enforcement remedies provided under this article are not exclusive and shall not preclude the use of any other criminal, civil, or administrative remedy.

(Amended by Stats. 2011, Ch. 15, Sec. 2. (AB 109) Effective April 4, 2011. Operative October 1, 2011, by Sec. 636 of Ch. 15, as amended by Stats. 2011, Ch. 39, Sec. 68.)

ARTICLE 6: UNEARNED REBATES, REFUNDS, AND DISCOUNTS

650. REBATES FOR PATIENT REFERRALS

(a) Except as provided in Chapter 2.3 (commencing with Section 1400) of Division 2 of the Health and Safety Code, the offer, delivery, receipt, or acceptance by any person licensed under this division or the Chiropractic Initiative Act of any rebate, refund, commission, preference, patronage dividend, discount, or other consideration, whether in the form of money or otherwise, as compensation or inducement for referring patients, clients, or customers to any person, irrespective of any membership, proprietary interest, or coownership in or with any person to whom these patients, clients, or customers are referred is unlawful.

(b) The payment or receipt of consideration for services other than the referral of patients that is based on a percentage of gross revenue or similar type of contractual arrangement shall not be unlawful if the consideration is commensurate with the value of the services furnished or with the fair rental value of any premises or equipment leased or provided by the recipient to the payer.

(c) The offer, delivery, receipt, or acceptance of any consideration between a federally qualified health center, as defined in Section 1396d(l)(2)(B) of Title 42 of the United States Code, and any individual or entity providing goods, items, services, donations, loans, or a combination thereof to the health center entity pursuant to a contract, lease, grant, loan, or other agreement, if that agreement contributes to the ability of the health center entity to maintain or increase the availability, or enhance the quality, of services provided to a medically underserved population served by the health center, shall be authorized only to the extent sanctioned or permitted by federal law.

(d) Except as provided in Chapter 2.3 (commencing with Section 1400) of Division 2 of the Health and Safety Code and in Sections 654.1 and 654.2 of this code, it shall not be unlawful for any person licensed under this division to refer a person to any laboratory, pharmacy, clinic, including entities exempt from licensure pursuant to Section 1206 of the Health and Safety Code, or health care facility solely because the licensee has a proprietary interest or coownership in the laboratory, pharmacy, clinic, or health care facility, provided, however, that the licensee's return on investment for that proprietary interest or coownership shall be based upon the amount of the capital investment or proportional ownership of the licensee which ownership interest is not based on the number or value of any patients referred. Any referral excepted under this section shall be unlawful if the prosecutor proves that there was no valid medical need for the referral.

(e) Except as provided in Chapter 2.3 (commencing with Section 1400) of Division 2 of the Health and Safety Code and in Sections 654.1 and 654.2 of this code, it shall not be unlawful to provide nonmonetary remuneration, in the form of hardware, software, or information technology and training services, as described in subsections (x) and (y) of Section 1001.952 of Title 42 of the Code of Federal Regulations, as amended October 4, 2007, as published in the Federal Register (72 Fed. Reg. 56632 and 56644), and as subsequently amended.

(f) "Health care facility" means a general acute care hospital, acute psychiatric hospital, skilled nursing facility, intermediate care facility, and any other health facility licensed by the State Department of Public Health under Chapter 2 (commencing with Section 1250) of Division 2 of the Health and Safety Code.

(g) Notwithstanding this section or any other law, the payment or receipt of consideration for advertising, wherein a licensee offers or sells services through a third-party advertiser, shall not constitute a referral of patients when the third-party advertiser does not itself recommend, endorse, or otherwise select a licensee. The fee paid to the third-party advertiser shall be commensurate with the service provided by the third-party advertiser. If the licensee determines, after consultation with the purchaser of the service, that the service provided by the licensee is inappropriate for the purchaser or if the purchaser elects not to receive the service for any reason and requests a refund, the purchaser shall receive a refund of the full purchase price as determined by the terms of the advertising service agreement between the third-party advertiser and the licensee. The licensee shall disclose in the advertisement that a consultation is required and that the purchaser will receive a refund if ineligible to receive the service. This subdivision shall not apply to basic health care services, as defined in subdivision (b) of Section 1345 of the Health and Safety Code, or essential health benefits, as defined in Section 1367.005 of the Health and Safety Code and Section 10112.27 of the Insurance Code. The entity that provides the advertising shall be able to demonstrate that the licensee consented in writing to the requirements of this subdivision. A third-party advertiser shall make available to prospective purchasers advertisements for services of all licensees then advertising through the third-party advertiser in the applicable geographic region. In any advertisement offering a discount price for a service, the licensee shall also disclose the regular, nondiscounted price for that service.

(h) To the extent consistent with federal law, regulations, or guidance, the payment or receipt of consideration for internet-based advertising, appointment booking, or any service that provides information and resources to prospective patients of licensees shall not constitute a referral of a patient if the internet-based service provider does not recommend or endorse a specific licensee to a prospective patient.

(i) A violation of this section is a public offense and is punishable upon a first conviction by imprisonment in a county jail for not more than one year, or by imprisonment pursuant to subdivision (h) of Section 1170 of the Penal Code, or by a fine not exceeding fifty thousand dollars ($50,000), or by both that imprisonment and fine. A second or subsequent conviction is punishable by imprisonment pursuant to subdivision (h) of Section 1170 of the Penal Code, or by that imprisonment and a fine of fifty thousand dollars ($50,000).

(Amended by Stats. 2021, Ch. 439, Sec. 3. (AB 457) Effective January 1, 2022.)

650.01. UNLAWFUL REFERRALS; DEFINITIONS

(a) Notwithstanding Section 650, or any other provision of law, it is unlawful for a licensee to refer a person for laboratory, diagnostic nuclear medicine, radiation oncology, physical therapy, physical rehabilitation, psychometric testing, home infusion therapy, or diagnostic imaging goods or services if the licensee or their immediate family has a financial interest with the person or in the entity that receives the referral.

(b) For purposes of this section and Section 650.02, the following shall apply:

(1) "Diagnostic imaging" includes, but is not limited to, all X-ray, computed axial tomography, magnetic resonance imaging nuclear medicine, positron emission tomography, mammography, and ultrasound goods and services.

(2) A "financial interest" includes, but is not limited to, any type of ownership interest, debt, loan, lease, compensation, remuneration, discount, rebate, refund, dividend, distribution, subsidy, or other form of direct or indirect payment, whether in money or otherwise, between a licensee and a person or entity to whom the licensee refers a person for a good or service specified in subdivision (a). A financial interest also exists if there is an indirect financial relationship between a licensee and the referral recipient including, but not limited to, an arrangement whereby a licensee has an ownership interest in an entity that leases property to the referral recipient. Any financial interest transferred by a licensee to any person or entity or otherwise established in any person or entity for the purpose of avoiding the prohibition of this section shall be deemed a financial interest of the licensee. For purposes of this paragraph, "direct or indirect payment" shall not include a royalty or consulting fee received by a physician and surgeon who has completed a recognized residency training program in orthopedics from a manufacturer or distributor as a result of their research and development of medical devices and techniques for that manufacturer or distributor. For purposes of this paragraph, "consulting fees" means those fees paid by the manufacturer or distributor to a physician and surgeon who has completed a recognized residency training program in orthopedics only for their ongoing services in making refinements to their medical devices or techniques marketed or distributed by the manufacturer or distributor, if the manufacturer or distributor does not own or control the facility to which the physician is referring the patient. A "financial interest" shall not include the receipt of capitation payments or other fixed amounts that are prepaid in exchange for a promise of a licensee to provide specified health care services to specified beneficiaries. A "financial interest" shall not include the receipt of remuneration by a medical director of a hospice, as defined in Section 1746 of the Health and Safety Code, for specified services if the arrangement is set out in writing, and specifies all services to be provided by the medical director, the term of the arrangement is for at least one year, and the compensation to be paid over the term of the arrangement is set in advance, does not exceed fair market value, and is not determined in a manner that takes into account the volume or value of any referrals or other business generated between parties.

(3) For the purposes of this section, "immediate family" includes the spouse and children of the licensee, the parents of the licensee, and the spouses of the children of the licensee.

(4) "Licensee" means all of the following:

(A) A physician as defined in Section 3209.3 of the Labor Code.

(B) A nurse practitioner practicing pursuant to Section 2837.103 or 2837.104.

(C) A certified nurse-midwife as described in Article 2.5 (commencing with Section 2746) of Chapter 6, acting within their scope of practice.

(5) "Licensee's office" means either of the following:

(A) An office of a licensee in solo practice.

(B) An office in which services or goods are personally provided by the licensee or by employees in that office, or personally by independent contractors in that office, in accordance with other provisions of law.

Employees and independent contractors shall be licensed or certified when licensure or certification is required by law.

(6) "Office of a group practice" means an office or offices in which two or more licensees are legally organized as a partnership, professional corporation, or not-for-profit corporation, licensed pursuant to subdivision (a) of Section 1204 of the Health and Safety Code, for which all of the following apply:

(A) Each licensee who is a member of the group provides substantially the full range of services that the licensee routinely provides, including medical care, consultation, diagnosis, or treatment through the joint use of shared office space, facilities, equipment, and personnel.

(B) Substantially all of the services of the licensees who are members of the group are provided through the group and are billed in the name of the group and amounts so received are treated as receipts of the group, except in the case of a multispecialty clinic, as defined in subdivision (l) of Section 1206 of the Health and Safety Code, physician services are billed in the name of the multispecialty clinic and amounts so received are treated as receipts of the multispecialty clinic.

(C) The overhead expenses of, and the income from, the practice are distributed in accordance with methods previously determined by members of the group.

(c) It is unlawful for a licensee to enter into an arrangement or scheme, such as a cross-referral arrangement, that the licensee knows, or should know, has a principal purpose of ensuring referrals by the licensee to a particular entity that, if the licensee directly made referrals to that entity, would be in violation of this section.

(d) No claim for payment shall be presented by an entity to any individual, third party payer, or other entity for a good or service furnished pursuant to a referral prohibited under this section.

(e) No insurer, self-insurer, or other payer shall pay a charge or lien for any good or service resulting from a referral in violation of this section.

(f) A licensee who refers a person to, or seeks consultation from, an organization in which the licensee has a financial interest, other than as prohibited by subdivision (a), shall disclose the financial interest to the patient, or the parent or legal guardian of the patient, in writing, at the time of the referral or request for consultation.

(1) If a referral, billing, or other solicitation is between one or more licensees who contract with a multispecialty clinic pursuant to subdivision (l) of Section 1206 of the Health and Safety Code or who conduct their practice as members of the same professional corporation or partnership, and the services are rendered on the same physical premises, or under the same professional corporation or partnership name, the requirements of this subdivision may be met by posting a conspicuous disclosure statement at the registration area or by providing a patient with a written disclosure statement.

(2) If a licensee is under contract with the Department of Corrections or the California Youth Authority, and the patient is an inmate or parolee of either respective department, the requirements of this subdivision shall be satisfied by disclosing financial interests to either the Department of Corrections or the California Youth Authority.

(g) A violation of subdivision (a) shall be a misdemeanor. In the case of a licensee who is a physician and surgeon, the Medical Board of California shall review the facts and circumstances of any conviction pursuant to subdivision (a) and take appropriate disciplinary action if the licensee has committed unprofessional conduct. In the case of a licensee who is a certified nurse-midwife, the Board of Registered Nursing shall review the facts and circumstances of any conviction pursuant to subdivision (a) and take appropriate disciplinary action if the licensee has committed unprofessional conduct. Violations of this section may also be subject to civil penalties of up to five thousand dollars ($5,000) for each offense, which may be enforced by the Insurance Commissioner, Attorney General, or a district attorney. A violation of subdivision (c), (d), or (e) is a public offense and is punishable upon conviction by a fine not exceeding fifteen thousand dollars ($15,000) for each violation and appropriate disciplinary action, including revocation of professional licensure, by the Medical Board of California, the Board of Registered Nursing, or other appropriate governmental agency.

(h) This section shall not apply to referrals for services that are described in and covered by Sections 139.3 and 139.31 of the Labor Code.

(i) This section shall become operative on January 1, 1995.

(Amended by Stats. 2020, Ch. 265, Sec. 1.5. (AB 890) Effective January 1, 2021.)

650.02. EXCEPTIONS TO REFERRAL PROHIBITION

The prohibition of Section 650.01 shall not apply to or restrict any of the following:

(a) A licensee may refer a patient for a good or service otherwise prohibited by subdivision (a) of Section 650.01 if the licensee's regular practice is located where there is no alternative provider of the service within either 25 miles or 40 minutes traveling time, via the shortest route on a paved road. If an alternative provider commences furnishing the good or service for which a patient was referred pursuant to this subdivision, the licensee shall cease referrals under this subdivision within six months of the time at which the licensee knew or should have known that the alternative provider is furnishing the good or service. A licensee who refers to or seeks consultation from an organization in which the licensee has a financial interest under this subdivision shall disclose this interest to the patient or the patient's parents or legal guardian in writing at the time of referral.

(b) A licensee, when the licensee or his or her immediate family has one or more of the following arrangements with another licensee, a person, or an entity, is not prohibited from referring a patient to the licensee, person, or entity because of the arrangement:

(1) A loan between a licensee and the recipient of the referral, if the loan has commercially reasonable terms, bears interest at the prime rate or a higher rate that does not constitute usury, is adequately secured, and the loan terms are not affected by either party's referral of any person or the volume of services provided by either party.

(2) A lease of space or equipment between a licensee and the recipient of the referral, if the lease is written, has commercially reasonable terms, has a fixed periodic rent payment, has a term of one year or more, and the lease payments are not affected by either party's referral of any person or the volume of services provided by either party.

(3) Ownership of corporate investment securities, including shares, bonds, or other debt instruments that may be purchased on terms generally available to the public and that are traded on a licensed securities exchange or NASDAQ, do not base profit distributions or other transfers of value on the licensee's referral of persons to the corporation, do not have a separate

class or accounting for any persons or for any licensees who may refer persons to the corporation, and are in a corporation that had, at the end of the corporation's most recent fiscal year, or on average during the previous three fiscal years, stockholder equity exceeding seventy-five million dollars ($75,000,000).

(4) Ownership of shares in a regulated investment company as defined in Section 851(a) of the federal Internal Revenue Code, if the company had, at the end of the company's most recent fiscal year, or on average during the previous three fiscal years, total assets exceeding seventy-five million dollars ($75,000,000).

(5) A one-time sale or transfer of a practice or property or other financial interest between a licensee and the recipient of the referral if the sale or transfer is for commercially reasonable terms and the consideration is not affected by either party's referral of any person or the volume of services provided by either party.

(6) A personal services arrangement between a licensee or an immediate family member of the licensee and the recipient of the referral if the arrangement meets all of the following requirements:

(A) It is set out in writing and is signed by the parties.

(B) It specifies all of the services to be provided by the licensee or an immediate family member of the licensee.

(C) The aggregate services contracted for do not exceed those that are reasonable and necessary for the legitimate business purposes of the arrangement.

(D) A person who is referred by a licensee or an immediate family member of the licensee is informed in writing of the personal services arrangement that includes information on where a person may go to file a complaint against the licensee or the immediate family member of the licensee.

(E) The term of the arrangement is for at least one year.

(F) The compensation to be paid over the term of the arrangement is set in advance, does not exceed fair market value, and is not determined in a manner that takes into account the volume or value of any referrals or other business generated between the parties.

(G) The services to be performed under the arrangement do not involve the counseling or promotion of a business arrangement or other activity that violates any state or federal law.

(c) (1) A licensee may refer a person to a health facility, as defined in Section 1250 of the Health and Safety Code, or to any facility owned or leased by a health facility, if the recipient of the referral does not compensate the licensee for the patient referral, and any equipment lease arrangement between the licensee and the referral recipient complies with the requirements of paragraph (2) of subdivision (b).

(2) Nothing shall preclude this subdivision from applying to a licensee solely because the licensee has an ownership or leasehold interest in an entire health facility or an entity that owns or leases an entire health facility.

(3) A licensee may refer a person to a health facility for any service classified as an emergency under subdivision (a) or (b) of Section 1317.1 of the Health and Safety Code.

(4) A licensee may refer a person to any organization that owns or leases a health facility licensed pursuant to subdivision (a), (b), or (f) of Section 1250 of the Health and Safety Code if the licensee is not compensated for the patient referral, the licensee does not receive any payment from the recipient of the referral that is based or

determined on the number or value of any patient referrals, and any equipment lease arrangement between the licensee and the referral recipient complies with the requirements of paragraph (2) of subdivision (b). For purposes of this paragraph, the ownership may be through stock or membership, and may be represented by a parent holding company that solely owns or controls both the health facility organization and the affiliated organization.

(d) A licensee may refer a person to a nonprofit corporation that provides physician services pursuant to subdivision (l) of Section 1206 of the Health and Safety Code if the nonprofit corporation is controlled through membership by one or more health facilities or health facility systems and the amount of compensation or other transfer of funds from the health facility or nonprofit corporation to the licensee is fixed annually, except for adjustments caused by physicians joining or leaving the groups during the year, and is not based on the number of persons utilizing goods or services specified in Section 650.01.

(e) A licensee compensated or employed by a university may refer a person for a physician service, to any facility owned or operated by the university, or to another licensee employed by the university, provided that the facility or university does not compensate the referring licensee for the patient referral. In the case of a facility that is totally or partially owned by an entity other than the university, but that is staffed by university physicians, those physicians may not refer patients to the facility if the facility compensates the referring physicians for those referrals.

(f) The prohibition of Section 650.01 shall not apply to any service for a specific patient that is performed within, or goods that are supplied by, a licensee's office, or the office of a group practice. Further, the provisions of Section 650.01 shall not alter, limit, or expand a licensee's ability to deliver, or to direct or supervise the delivery of, in-office goods or services according to the laws, rules, and regulations governing his or her scope of practice.

(g) The prohibition of Section 650.01 shall not apply to cardiac rehabilitation services provided by a licensee or by a suitably trained individual under the direct or general supervision of a licensee, if the services are provided to patients meeting the criteria for Medicare reimbursement for the services.

(h) The prohibition of Section 650.01 shall not apply if a licensee is in the office of a group practice and refers a person for services or goods specified in Section 650.01 to a multispecialty clinic, as defined in subdivision (l) of Section 1206 of the Health and Safety Code.

(i) The prohibition of Section 650.01 shall not apply to health care services provided to an enrollee of a health care service plan licensed pursuant to the Knox-Keene Health Care Service Plan Act of 1975 (Chapter 2.2 (commencing with Section 1340) of Division 2 of the Health and Safety Code).

(j) The prohibition of Section 650.01 shall not apply to a request by a pathologist for clinical diagnostic laboratory tests and pathological examination services, a request by a radiologist for diagnostic radiology services, or a request by a radiation oncologist for radiation therapy if those services are furnished by, or under the supervision of, the pathologist, radiologist, or radiation oncologist pursuant to a consultation requested by another physician.

(k) This section shall not apply to referrals for services that are described in and covered by Sections 139.3 and 139.31 of the Labor Code.

(l) This section shall become operative on January 1, 1995.

(Amended by Stats. 2002, Ch. 309, Sec. 1. Effective January 1, 2003.)

651. DISSEMINATION OF FALSE OR MISLEADING INFORMATION CONCERNING PROFESSIONAL SERVICES OR PRODUCTS; PERMISSIBLE ADVERTISING

(a) It is unlawful for any person licensed under this division or under any initiative act referred to in this division to disseminate or cause to be disseminated any form of public communication containing a false, fraudulent, misleading, or deceptive statement, claim, or image for the purpose of or likely to induce, directly or indirectly, the rendering of professional services or furnishing of products in connection with the professional practice or business for which he or she is licensed. A "public communication" as used in this section includes, but is not limited to, communication by means of mail, television, radio, motion picture, newspaper, book, list or directory of healing arts practitioners, Internet, or other electronic communication.

(b) A false, fraudulent, misleading, or deceptive statement, claim, or image includes a statement or claim that does any of the following:

(1) Contains a misrepresentation of fact.

(2) Is likely to mislead or deceive because of a failure to disclose material facts.

(3) (A) Is intended or is likely to create false or unjustified expectations of favorable results, including the use of any photograph or other image that does not accurately depict the results of the procedure being advertised or that has been altered in any manner from the image of the actual subject depicted in the photograph or image.

(B) Use of any photograph or other image of a model without clearly stating in a prominent location in easily readable type the fact that the photograph or image is of a model is a violation of subdivision (a). For purposes of this paragraph, a model is anyone other than an actual patient, who has undergone the procedure being advertised, of the licensee who is advertising for his or her services.

(C) Use of any photograph or other image of an actual patient that depicts or purports to depict the results of any procedure, or presents "before" and "after" views of a patient, without specifying in a prominent location in easily readable type size what procedures were performed on that patient is a violation of subdivision (a). Any "before" and "after" views (i) shall be comparable in presentation so that the results are not distorted by favorable poses, lighting, or other features of presentation, and (ii) shall contain a statement that the same "before" and "after" results may not occur for all patients.

(4) Relates to fees, other than a standard consultation fee or a range of fees for specific types of services, without fully and specifically disclosing all variables and other material factors.

(5) Contains other representations or implications that in reasonable probability will cause an ordinarily prudent person to misunderstand or be deceived.

(6) Makes a claim either of professional superiority or of performing services in a superior manner, unless that claim is relevant to the service being performed and can be substantiated with objective scientific evidence.

(7) Makes a scientific claim that cannot be substantiated by reliable, peer reviewed, published scientific studies.

(8) Includes any statement, endorsement, or testimonial that is likely to mislead or deceive because of a failure to disclose material facts.

(c) Any price advertisement shall be exact, without the use of phrases, including, but not limited to, "as low as," "and up," "lowest prices," or words or phrases of similar import. Any advertisement that refers to services, or costs for services, and that uses words of comparison shall be based on verifiable data substantiating the comparison. Any person so advertising shall be prepared to provide information sufficient to establish the accuracy of that comparison. Price advertising shall not be fraudulent, deceitful, or misleading, including statements or advertisements of bait, discount, premiums, gifts, or any statements of a similar nature. In connection with price advertising, the price for each product or service shall be clearly identifiable. The price advertised for products shall include charges for any related professional services, including dispensing and fitting services, unless the advertisement specifically and clearly indicates otherwise.

(d) Any person so licensed shall not compensate or give anything of value to a representative of the press, radio, television, or other communication medium in anticipation of, or in return for, professional publicity unless the fact of compensation is made known in that publicity.

(e) Any person so licensed may not use any professional card, professional announcement card, office sign, letterhead, telephone directory listing, medical list, medical directory listing, or a similar professional notice or device if it includes a statement or claim that is false, fraudulent, misleading, or deceptive within the meaning of subdivision (b).

(f) Any person so licensed who violates this section is guilty of a misdemeanor. A bona fide mistake of fact shall be a defense to this subdivision, but only to this subdivision.

(g) Any violation of this section by a person so licensed shall constitute good cause for revocation or suspension of his or her license or other disciplinary action.

(h) Advertising by any person so licensed may include the following:

(1) A statement of the name of the practitioner.

(2) A statement of addresses and telephone numbers of the offices maintained by the practitioner.

(3) A statement of office hours regularly maintained by the practitioner.

(4) A statement of languages, other than English, fluently spoken by the practitioner or a person in the practitioner's office.

(5) (A) A statement that the practitioner is certified by a private or public board or agency or a statement that the practitioner limits his or her practice to specific fields.

(B) A statement of certification by a practitioner licensed under Chapter 7 (commencing with Section 3000) shall only include a statement that he or she is certified or eligible for certification by a private or public board or parent association recognized by that practitioner's licensing board.

(C) A physician and surgeon licensed under Chapter 5 (commencing with Section 2000) by the Medical Board of California may include a statement that he or she limits his or her practice to specific fields, but shall not include a statement that he or she is certified or eligible for certification by a private or public board or parent association, including, but not limited to, a multidisciplinary board or association, unless that board or association is (i) an American Board of Medical Specialties member board, (ii) a board or association with equivalent requirements approved by that physician's and surgeon's licensing board prior to January 1, 2019, or (iii) a board or association with an Accreditation Council for Graduate Medical Education approved postgraduate training program that provides complete training in that specialty or subspecialty. A physician and surgeon licensed under Chapter 5 (commencing with Section 2000) by the Medical Board of California who is certified by an organization other than a board or association referred to in clause (i), (ii), or (iii) shall not use the term "board certified" in reference to that certification, unless the physician and surgeon is also licensed under Chapter 4 (commencing with Section 1600) and the use of the term "board certified" in reference to that certification is in accordance with subparagraph (A). A physician and surgeon licensed under Chapter 5 (commencing with Section 2000) by the Medical Board of California who is certified by a board or association referred to in clause (i), (ii), or (iii) shall not use the term "board certified" unless the full name of the certifying board is also used and given comparable prominence with the term "board certified" in the statement.

For purposes of this subparagraph, a "multidisciplinary board or association" means an educational certifying body that has a psychometrically valid testing process, as determined by the Medical Board of California, for certifying medical doctors and other health care professionals that is based on the applicant's education, training, and experience. A multidisciplinary board or association approved by the Medical Board of California prior to January 1, 2019, shall retain that approval.

For purposes of the term "board certified," as used in this subparagraph, the terms "board" and "association" mean an organization that is an American Board of Medical Specialties member board, an organization with equivalent requirements approved by a physician's and surgeon's licensing board prior to January 1, 2019, or an organization with an Accreditation Council for Graduate Medical Education approved postgraduate training program that provides complete training in a specialty or subspecialty.

(D) A doctor of podiatric medicine licensed under Article 22 (commencing with Section 2460) of Chapter 5 by the California Board of Podiatric Medicine may include a statement that he or she is certified or eligible or qualified for certification by a private or public board or parent association, including, but not limited to, a multidisciplinary board or association, if that board or association meets one of the following requirements:

(i) is approved by the Council on Podiatric Medical Education, (ii) is a board or association with equivalent requirements approved by the California Board of Podiatric Medicine, or (iii) is a board or association with the Council on Podiatric Medical Education approved postgraduate training programs that provide training in podiatric medicine and podiatric surgery. A doctor of podiatric medicine licensed under Article 22 (commencing with Section 2460) of Chapter 5 by the California Board of Podiatric Medicine who is certified by a board or association referred to in clause (i), (ii), or (iii) shall not use the term "board certified" unless the full name of the certifying board is also used and given comparable prominence with the term "board certified" in the statement. A doctor of podiatric medicine licensed under Article 22 (commencing with Section 2460) of Chapter 5 by the California Board of Podiatric Medicine who is certified by an organization other than a board or association referred to in clause (i), (ii), or (iii) shall not use the term "board certified" in reference to that certification.

For purposes of this subparagraph, a "multidisciplinary board or association" means an educational certifying body that has a psychometrically valid testing process, as determined by the California Board of Podiatric Medicine, for certifying doctors of podiatric medicine that is based on the applicant's education, training, and experience. For purposes of the term "board certified," as used in this subparagraph, the terms "board" and "association" mean an organization that is a Council on Podiatric Medical Education approved board, an organization with equivalent requirements approved by the California Board of Podiatric Medicine, or an organization with a Council on Podiatric Medical Education approved postgraduate training program that provides training in podiatric medicine and podiatric surgery.

The California Board of Podiatric Medicine shall adopt regulations to establish and collect a reasonable fee from each board or association applying for recognition pursuant to this subparagraph, to be deposited in the State Treasury in the Podiatry Fund, pursuant to Section 2499. The fee shall not exceed the cost of administering this subparagraph.

(6) A statement that the practitioner provides services under a specified private or public insurance plan or health care plan.

(7) A statement of names of schools and postgraduate clinical training programs from which the practitioner has graduated, together with the degrees received.

(8) A statement of publications authored by the practitioner.

(9) A statement of teaching positions currently or formerly held by the practitioner, together with pertinent dates.

(10) A statement of his or her affiliations with hospitals or clinics.

(11) A statement of the charges or fees for services or commodities offered by the practitioner.

(12) A statement that the practitioner regularly accepts installment payments of fees.

(13) Otherwise lawful images of a practitioner, his or her physical facilities, or of a commodity to be advertised.

(14) A statement of the manufacturer, designer, style, make, trade name, brand name, color, size, or type of commodities advertised.

(15) An advertisement of a registered dispensing optician may include statements in addition to those specified in paragraphs (1) to (14), inclusive, provided that any statement shall not violate subdivision (a), (b), (c), or (e) or any other section of this code.

(16) A statement, or statements, providing public health information encouraging preventive or corrective care.

(17) Any other item of factual information that is not false, fraudulent, misleading, or likely to deceive.

(i) Each of the healing arts boards and examining committees within Division 2 shall adopt appropriate regulations to enforce this section in accordance with Chapter 3.5 (commencing with Section 11340) of Part 1 of Division 3 of Title 2 of the Government Code.

Each of the healing arts boards and committees and examining committees within Division 2 shall, by regulation, define those efficacious services to be advertised by businesses or professions under their jurisdiction for the purpose of determining whether advertisements are false or misleading. Until a definition for that service has been issued, no advertisement for that service shall be disseminated. However, if a definition of a service has not been issued by a board or committee within 120 days of receipt of a request from a licensee, all those holding the license may advertise the service.

Those boards and committees shall adopt or modify regulations defining what services may be advertised, the manner in which defined services may be advertised, and restricting advertising that would promote the inappropriate or excessive use of health services or commodities. A board or committee shall not, by regulation, unreasonably prevent truthful, nondeceptive price or otherwise lawful forms of advertising of services or commodities, by either outright prohibition or imposition of onerous disclosure requirements. However, any member of a board or committee acting in good faith in the adoption or enforcement of any regulation shall be deemed to be acting as an agent of the state.

(j) The Attorney General shall commence legal proceedings in the appropriate forum to enjoin advertisements disseminated or about to be disseminated in violation of this section and seek other appropriate relief to enforce this section. Notwithstanding any other provision of law, the costs of enforcing this section to the respective licensing boards or committees may be awarded against any licensee found to be in violation of any provision of this section. This shall not diminish the power of district attorneys, county counsels, or city attorneys pursuant to existing law to seek appropriate relief.

(k) A physician and surgeon licensed pursuant to Chapter 5 (commencing with Section 2000) by the Medical Board of California or a doctor of podiatric medicine licensed pursuant to Article 22 (commencing with Section 2460) of Chapter 5 by the California Board of Podiatric Medicine who knowingly and intentionally violates this section may be cited and assessed an administrative fine not to exceed ten thousand dollars ($10,000) per event. Section 125.9 shall govern the issuance of this citation and fine except that the fine limitations prescribed in paragraph (3) of subdivision (b) of Section 125.9 shall not apply to a fine under this subdivision.

(Amended by Stats. 2017, Ch. 775, Sec. 6. (SB 798) Effective January 1, 2018.)

651.3. HEALTH CARE SERVICE PLAN INFORMATION AND ADVERTISING; PROHIBITION AGAINST CONTRACTING ENTITY DERIVING PROFIT FROM PLAN

(a) Any labor organization, bona fide employee group or bona fide employee association having contracted health care services from a health care service plan under the Knox-Keene Health Care Service Plan Act of 1975 (commencing with Section 1340 of the Health and Safety Code) may inform its members as to the benefits available and the charges therefor.

(b) Any new or revised written advertising or solicitation, or any form of evidence of coverage adopted by a health care service plan under the Knox-Keene Health Care Service Plan Act of 1975 (commencing with Section 1340 of the Health and Safety Code) for distribution to members pursuant to subdivision (a) shall comply with the provisions of the Knox- Keene Health Care Service Plan Act of 1975 and the regulations thereunder.

(c) Any labor organization, bona fide employee group or bona fide employee association, contracting for a health care service plan under this section, shall not derive any profit from such plan.

Nothing contained in this section shall be construed as authorizing a provider of medical assistance, including a prepaid health plan, under the Medi-Cal Act or the Waxman-Duffy Prepaid Health Plan Act to advertise in violation of any of the provisions of such acts and regulations developed thereto.

(Amended by Stats. 1981, Ch. 662, Sec. 1.)

652. VIOLATIONS BY LICENSEES

Violation of this article in the case of a licensed person constitutes unprofessional conduct and grounds for suspension or revocation of his or her license by the board by whom he or she is licensed, or if a license has been issued in connection with a place of business, then for the suspension or revocation of the place of business in connection with which the violation occurs. The proceedings for suspension or revocation shall be conducted in accordance with Chapter 5 (commencing with Section 11500) of Part 1 of Division 3 of Title 2 of the Government Code, and each board shall have all the powers granted therein. However, in the case of a licensee of the State Department of Health Services, the proceedings shall be conducted in accordance with Section 110171 of the Health and Safety Code. In addition, any violation constitutes a misdemeanor as to any and all persons offering, delivering, receiving, accepting, or participating in any rebate, refund, commission, preference, patronage dividend, unearned discount, or consideration, whether or not licensed under this division, and is punishable by imprisonment in the county jail not exceeding six months, by a fine not exceeding two thousand five hundred dollars ($2,500), or by both the imprisonment and fine.

(Amended by Stats. 1997, Ch. 220, Sec. 3. Effective August 4, 1997.)

652.5. VIOLATION OF ARTICLE

Except as otherwise provided in this article, any violation of this article constitutes a misdemeanor as to any and all persons, whether or not licensed under this division, and is punishable by imprisonment in the county jail not exceeding six months, or by a fine not exceeding two thousand five hundred dollars ($2,500), or by both the imprisonment and fine.

(Amended by Stats. 1994, Ch. 1206, Sec. 6. Effective January 1, 1995.)

653. "PERSON"

The word "person" as used in this article includes an individual, firm, partnership, association, corporation, limited liability company, or cooperative association.

(Amended by Stats. 1994, Ch. 1010, Sec. 3. Effective January 1, 1995.)

654. LICENSEES' CO-OWNERSHIP ARRANGEMENTS

No person licensed under Chapter 5 (commencing with Section 2000) of this division may have any membership, proprietary interest or coownership in any form in or with any person licensed under Chapter 5.5 (commencing with Section 2550) of this division to whom patients, clients or customers are referred or any profit-sharing arrangements.

(Amended by Stats. 1979, Ch. 688.)

654.2. REFERRALS TO ORGANIZATION IN WHICH LICENSEE OR FAMILY HAS SIGNIFICANT BENEFICIAL INTEREST; REQUIRED DISCLOSURE STATEMENT

(a) It is unlawful for any person licensed under this division or under any initiative act referred to in this division to charge, bill, or otherwise solicit payment from a patient on behalf of, or refer a patient to, an organization in which the licensee, or the licensee's immediate family, has a significant beneficial interest, unless the licensee first discloses in writing to the patient, that there is such an interest and advises the patient that the patient may choose any organization for the purpose of obtaining the services ordered or requested by the licensee.

(b) The disclosure requirements of subdivision (a) may be met by posting a conspicuous sign in an area which is likely to be seen by all patients who use the facility or by providing those patients with a written disclosure statement. Where referrals, billings, or other solicitations are between licensees who contract with multispecialty clinics pursuant to subdivision (l) of Section 1206 of the Health and Safety Code or who conduct their practice as members of the same professional corporation or partnership, and the services are rendered on the same physical premises, or under the same professional corporation or partnership name, the requirements of subdivision (a) may be met by posting a conspicuous disclosure statement at a single location which is a common area or registration area or by providing those patients with a written disclosure statement.

(c) On and after July 1, 1987, persons licensed under this division or under any initiative act referred to in this division shall disclose in writing to any third-party payer for the patient, when requested by the payer, organizations in which the licensee, or any member of the licensee's immediate family, has a significant beneficial interest and to which patients are referred. The third-party payer shall not request this information from the provider more than once a year.

Nothing in this section shall be construed to serve as the sole basis for the denial or delay of payment of claims by third party payers.

(d) For the purposes of this section, the following terms have the following meanings:

(1) "Immediate family" includes the spouse and children of the licensee, the parents of the licensee and licensee's spouse, and the spouses of the children of the licensee.

(2) "Significant beneficial interest" means any financial interest that is equal to or greater than the lesser of the following:

(A) Five percent of the whole.

(B) Five thousand dollars ($5,000).

(3) A third-party payer includes any health care service plan, self-insured employee welfare benefit plan, disability insurer, nonprofit hospital service plan, or private group or indemnification insurance program.

A third party payer does not include a prepaid capitated plan licensed under the Knox-Keene Health Care Service Plan Act of 1975 or Chapter 11a (commencing with Section 11491) of Part 2 of Division 2 of the Insurance Code.

(e) This section shall not apply to a "significant beneficial interest" which is limited to ownership of a building where the space is leased to the organization at the prevailing rate under a straight lease agreement or to any interest held in publicly traded stocks.

(f) (1) This section does not prohibit the acceptance of evaluation specimens for proficiency testing or referral of specimens or assignment from one clinical laboratory to another clinical laboratory, either licensed or exempt under this chapter, if the report indicates clearly the name of the laboratory performing the test.

(2) This section shall not apply to relationships governed by other provisions of this article nor is this section to be construed as permitting relationships or interests that are prohibited by existing law on the effective date of this section.

(3) The disclosure requirements of this section shall not be required to be given to any patient, customer, or his or her representative, if the licensee, organization, or entity is providing or arranging for health care services pursuant to a prepaid capitated contract with the State Department of Health Services.

(Amended by Stats. 1986, Ch. 881, Sec. 1.)

654.3. DEFINITIONS

(a) For purposes of this section, the following definitions shall apply:

(1) "Arrange for" and "establish" mean the act of a licensee, or an employee

or agent of that licensee, receiving application information from the applicant and submitting it to the lender for approval or rejection.

(2) "Deferred interest provision" means a contractual provision that allows for interest to be charged on portions of the original balance that have already been paid off.

(3) "Licensee" means an individual, firm, partnership, association, corporation, limited liability company, or cooperative association licensed under this division or under any initiative act or division referred to in this division.

(4) "Licensee's office" means either of the following:

(A) An office of a licensee in solo practice.

(B) An office in which services or goods are personally provided by the licensee or by employees in that office, or personally by independent contractors in that office, in accordance with law. Employees and independent contractors shall be licensed or certified when licensure or certification is required by law.

(5) "Open-end credit" means credit extended by a creditor under a plan in which the creditor reasonably contemplates repeated transactions, the creditor may impose a finance charge from time to time on an outstanding unpaid balance, and the amount of credit that may be extended to the debtor during the term of the plan, up to any limit set by the creditor, is generally made available to the extent that any outstanding balance is repaid.

(6) (A) "Patient" includes, but is not limited to, the patient's parent or other legal representative.

(B) In veterinary medical settings, "patient" means one of the following, as indicated by context:

(i) If the patient is receiving the services, the owned animal of a client.

(ii) If the patient is agreeing to or paying for services, the client owner of an animal patient.

(b) (1) It is unlawful for a licensee, or employee or agent of that licensee, to arrange for or establish an open-end credit or loan that contains a deferred interest provision.

(2) This subdivision shall not be construed as prohibiting a licensee, or employee or agent of a licensee, from doing any of the following:

(A) Charging treatment or costs to an open-end credit or loan that is lawfully extended by a third party, including those that contain deferred interest provisions.

(B) Arranging for or establishing an open- end credit or loan that does any of the following:

(i) Offers a promotional period during which a debtor may avoid the payment of interest in connection with an open-end credit plan.

(ii) At the end of a promotional period, charges interest on any unpaid balance remaining at that time.

(iii) Imposes a late fee on a debtor who fails to pay the minimum amount due during any payment period.

(c) (1) It is unlawful for a licensee, or employee or agent of that licensee, to charge treatment or costs to an open-end credit or loan, that is extended by a third party and that is arranged for, or established in, that licensee's office, more than 30 days before the date upon which the treatment is rendered or costs are incurred.

(2) This subdivision does not apply to orthodontic treatment provided by a licensed dentist who may charge incremental fees throughout the course of treatment.

(d) It is unlawful for a licensee, or employee or agent of that licensee, to charge treatment or costs to an open-end credit or loan that is extended by a third party and that is arranged for, or established in, that licensee's office without first providing the patient with a treatment plan, as required by subdivision (h), and a list of which treatment and services are being charged in advance of rendering treatment or incurring costs.

(e) It is unlawful for a licensee, or employee or agent of a licensee, to complete any portion of an application for credit or a loan extended by a third party for the patient or otherwise arrange for or establish an application that is not completely filled out by the patient.

(f) A licensee shall, within 15 business days of a patient's request, refund to the lender any payment received through credit or a loan extended by a third party that is arranged for, or established in, that licensee's office for treatment that has not been rendered or costs that have not been incurred.

(g) A licensee, or an employee or agent of that licensee, shall not arrange for or establish credit or a loan extended by a third party for a patient without first providing the following written or electronic notice, on one page or screen, respectively, in at least 14-point type, and obtaining a signature from the patient:

"Credit or Loan for Health Care Services

The attached application and information is for a credit card or loan to help you pay for your health care treatment. You should know that:

You are applying for a credit card or a loan for $__.

You do not have to apply for the credit card or the loan. You may request a different place and additional time to review, fill out, and sign the application. You may pay your health care provider for treatment in another manner.

This credit card or loan is not a payment plan with the provider's office. It is credit with, or a loan made by, [name of company issuing the credit card or loan]. Your health care provider does not work for this company.

Before applying for this credit card or loan, you have the right to a written treatment plan from your health care provider. This plan must include the expected treatment to be provided and the estimated costs of each service. If you have insurance, the treatment plan must tell you how much your insurance is expected to cover. If you are a Medi-Cal patient seeking services from a Medi-Cal provider, your treatment plan must tell you if Medi-Cal will cover a different service to treat your condition. If you only want services covered by Medi-Cal, you should not sign up for this credit card or loan.

Your health care provider cannot charge your credit card or loan account before you start treatment.

You have the right to have your credit card or loan account refunded for any charges for treatment you did not get. However, your provider does not have to refund the amount they spent to prepare for your treatment. Your health care provider must refund the amount of the charges to the lender within 15 business days of your request. The lender must take refunded charges off your account.

Please read carefully the terms and conditions of this credit card or loan.

You may be required to pay interest rates on the amount charged to the credit card or the amount of the loan. If you pay late, you may have to pay a penalty and a higher interest rate.

You may use this credit card or loan to pay for future health care services.

If you do not pay the money that you owe on the credit card or loan, your missed payments can be reported and could hurt your credit rating. You could also be sued.

[Patient's Signature]"

(h) Before arranging for or establishing credit or a loan extended by a third party, a licensee shall give a patient a written treatment plan that complies with all of the following:

(1) The treatment plan shall include each anticipated service to be provided and the estimated cost of each service.

(2) If a patient is covered by a private or government medical benefit plan or medical insurance from which the licensee takes assignment of benefits, the treatment plan shall indicate the patient's private or government-estimated share of cost for each service.

(3) If the licensee accepts Medi-Cal, the treatment plan for a Medi-Cal patient shall indicate if Medi-Cal would cover an alternate, medically necessary service as defined in Section 14059.5 of the Welfare and Institutions Code. The treatment plan shall indicate that the Medi-Cal patient has a right to ask for only services covered by Medi-Cal and that the licensee agrees to follow Medi-Cal rules to secure Medi-Cal covered services before treatment.

(4) If the licensee does not take assignment of benefits from a patient's medical benefit plan or insurance, the treatment plan shall indicate that the treatment may or may not be covered by a patient's medical benefit or insurance plan, and that the patient has the right to confirm medical benefit or insurance information from the patient's plan, insurer, or employer before beginning treatment.

(i) A licensee, or an employee or agent of that licensee, shall not arrange for or establish credit or a loan extended by a third party for a patient with whom the licensee, or an employee or agent of that licensee, communicates primarily in a language other than English that is one of the Medi-Cal threshold languages, unless the written notice information required by subdivision (g) is also provided in that language.

(j) (1) A licensee, or an employee or agent of that licensee, shall not arrange for or establish credit or a loan that is extended by a third party for a patient under either of the following circumstances:

(A) The patient has been administered or is under the influence of general anesthesia, conscious sedation, or nitrous oxide.

(B) The patient is in a treatment area, including, but not limited to, an exam room, surgical room, or other area where medical treatment is administered, unless the patient agrees to fill out and sign the application to arrange for or establish credit or a loan in the treatment area.

(2) Paragraph (1) shall not apply to veterinary medicine. Any credit or loan application offered to an owner of an animal shall be filled out by the owner.

(k) A patient who suffers any damage as a result of the use or employment by any person of a method, act, or practice that willfully violates this section may seek the relief provided by Chapter 4 (commencing with Section 1780) of Title 1.5 of Part 4 of Division 3 of the Civil Code.

(l) The rights, remedies, and penalties set forth in this article are cumulative, and shall not supersede the rights, remedies, or penalties established under other laws.

(m) This section shall become operative on July 1, 2020.

(Repealed (in Sec. 1) and added by Stats. 2019, Ch. 856, Sec. 2. (SB 639) Effective January 1, 2020. Section operative July 1, 2020, by its own provisions.)

655. PROHIBITION OF BUSINESS ARRANGEMENTS BETWEEN OPTOMETRISTS AND OPTICIANS OR PERSONS IN OPTICAL PRODUCT BUSINESS

(a) For the purposes of this section, the following terms have the following meanings:

(1) "Health plan" means a health care service plan licensed pursuant to the Knox-Keene Health Care Service Plan Act of 1975 (Chapter 2.2 (commencing with Section 1340) of Division 2 of the Health and Safety Code).

(2) "Optical company" means a person or entity that is engaged in the manufacture, sale, or distribution to physicians and surgeons, optometrists, health plans, or dispensing opticians of lenses, frames, optical supplies, or optometric appliances or devices or kindred products.

(3) "Optometrist" means a person licensed pursuant to Chapter 7 (commencing with Section 3000) or an optometric corporation, as described in Section 3160.

(4) "Physician and surgeon" means a person licensed by the Medical Board of California or the Osteopathic Medical Board of California under Chapter 5 (commencing with Section 2000) or a medical corporation that is authorized to render professional services, as defined in Section 13401 of the Corporations Code.

(5) "Registered dispensing optician" means a person or entity licensed pursuant to Chapter 5.5 (commencing with Section 2550).

(6) "Therapeutic ophthalmic product" means lenses or other products that provide direct treatment of eye disease or visual rehabilitation for diseased eyes.

(b) No optometrist may have any membership, proprietary interest, coownership, or any profit-sharing arrangement, either by stock ownership, interlocking directors, trusteeship, mortgage, or trust deed, with any registered dispensing optician or any optical company, except as otherwise permitted under this section.

(c) (1) A registered dispensing optician or an optical company may operate, own, or have an ownership interest in a health plan so long as the health plan does not directly employ optometrists to provide optometric services directly to enrollees of the health plan, and may directly or indirectly provide products and services to the health plan or its contracted providers or enrollees or to other optometrists. For purposes of this section, an optometrist may be employed by a health plan as a clinical director for the health plan pursuant to Section 1367.01 of the Health and Safety Code or to perform services related to utilization management or quality assurance or other similar related services that do not require the optometrist to directly provide health care services to enrollees. In addition, an optometrist serving as a clinical director may not employ optometrists to provide health care services to enrollees of the health plan for which the optometrist is serving as clinical director. For the purposes of this section, the health plan's utilization management and quality assurance programs that are consistent with the Knox-Keene Health Care Service Plan Act of 1975 (Chapter 2.2 (commencing with Section 1340) of Division 2 of the Health and Safety Code) do not constitute providing health care services to enrollees.

(2) The registered dispensing optician or optical company shall not interfere with the professional judgment of the optometrist.

(3) The Department of Managed Health Care shall forward to the California State Board of Optometry any complaints received from consumers

that allege that an optometrist violated the Optometry Practice Act (Chapter 7 (commencing with Section 3000)). The Department of Managed Health Care and the California State Board of Optometry shall enter into an Inter-Agency Agreement regarding the sharing of information related to the services provided by an optometrist that may be in violation of the Optometry Practice Act that the Department of Managed Health Care encounters in the course of the administration of the Knox-Keene Health Care Service Plan Act of 1975 (Chapter 2.2 (commencing with Section 1340) of Division 2 of the Health and Safety Code).

(d) An optometrist, a registered dispensing optician, a physician and surgeon, an optical company, or a health plan may execute a lease, sublease, or other written agreement with an optometrist, if all of the following conditions are contained in a written agreement establishing the landlord-tenant relationship:

(1) (A) The practice shall be owned by the optometrist and in every phase be under the optometrist's exclusive control, including the selection and supervision of optometric staff, the scheduling of patients, the amount of time the optometrist spends with patients, fees charged for optometric products and services, the examination procedures and treatment provided to patients, and the optometrist's contracting with managed care organizations.

(B) Subparagraph (A) shall not preclude a lease from including commercially reasonable terms that: (i) require the provision of optometric services at the leased space during certain days and hours, (ii) restrict the leased space from being used for the sale or offer for sale of spectacles, frames, lenses, contact lenses, or other ophthalmic products, except that the optometrist shall be permitted to sell therapeutic ophthalmic products if the registered dispensing optician, physician and surgeon, health plan, or optical company located on or adjacent to the optometrist's leased space does not offer any substantially similar therapeutic ophthalmic products for sale, (iii) require the optometrist to contract with a health plan network, health plan, or health insurer, or (iv) permit the landlord to directly or indirectly provide furnishings and equipment in the leased space.

(2) The optometrist's records shall be the sole property of the optometrist. Only the optometrist and those persons with written authorization from the optometrist shall have access to the patient records and the examination room, except as otherwise provided by law.

(3) The optometrist's leased space shall be definite and distinct from space occupied by other occupants of the premises, have a sign designating that the leased space is occupied by an independent optometrist or optometrists and be accessible to the optometrist after hours or in the case of an emergency, subject to the facility's general accessibility. This paragraph shall not require a separate entrance to the optometrist's leased space.

(4) All signs and displays shall be separate and distinct from that of the other occupants and shall have the optometrist's name and the word "optometrist" prominently displayed in connection therewith. This paragraph shall not prohibit the optometrist from advertising the optometrist's practice location with reference to other occupants or prohibit the optometrist or registered dispensing optician from advertising their participation in any health plan's network or the health plan's products in which the optometrist or registered dispensing optician participates.

(5) There shall be no signs displayed on any part of the premises or in any

advertising indicating that the optometrist is employed or controlled by the registered dispensing optician, health plan, or optical company.

(6) Except for a statement that an independent doctor of optometry is located in the leased space, in-store pricing signs and as otherwise permitted by this subdivision, the registered dispensing optician or optical company shall not link its advertising with the optometrist's name, practice, or fees.

(7) Notwithstanding paragraphs (4) and (6), this subdivision shall not preclude a health plan from advertising its health plan products and associated premium costs and any copayments, coinsurance, deductibles, or other forms of cost sharing, or the names and locations of the health plan's providers, including any optometrists or registered dispensing opticians that provide professional services, in compliance with the Knox-Keene Health Care Service Plan Act of 1975 (Chapter 2.2 (commencing with Section 1340) of Division 2 of the Health and Safety Code).

(8) A health plan that advertises its products and services in accordance with paragraph (7) shall not advertise the optometrist's fees for products and services that are not included in the health plan's contract with the optometrist.

(9) The optometrist shall not be precluded from collecting fees for services that are not included in a health plan's products and services, subject to any patient disclosure requirements contained in the health plan's provider agreement with the optometrist or that are not otherwise prohibited by the Knox-Keene Health Care Service Plan Act of 1975 (Chapter 2.2 (commencing with Section 1340) of Division 2 of the Health and Safety Code).

(10) The term of the lease shall be no less than one year and shall not require the optometrist to contract exclusively with a health plan. The optometrist may terminate the lease according to the terms of the lease. The landlord may terminate the lease for the following reasons:

(A) The optometrist's failure to maintain a license to practice optometry or the imposition of restrictions, suspension or revocation of the optometrist's license, or if the optometrist or the optometrist's employee is or becomes ineligible to participate in state or federal government-funded programs.

(B) Termination of any underlying lease where the optometrist has subleased space, or the optometrist's failure to comply with the underlying lease provisions that are made applicable to the optometrist.

(C) If the health plan is the landlord, the termination of the provider agreement between the health plan and the optometrist, in accordance with the Knox-Keene Health Care Service Plan Act of 1975 (Chapter 2.2 (commencing with Section 1340) of Division 2 of the Health and Safety Code).

(D) Other reasons pursuant to the terms of the lease or permitted under the Civil Code.

(11) The landlord shall act in good faith in terminating the lease and in no case shall the landlord terminate the lease for reasons that constitute interference with the practice of optometry.

(12) Lease or rent terms and payments shall not be based on number of eye exams performed, prescriptions written, patient referrals, or the sale or promotion of the products of a registered dispensing optician or an optical company.

(13) The landlord shall not terminate the lease solely because of a report, complaint, or allegation filed by the optometrist against the landlord, a registered dispensing optician, or a health plan, to the California State Board of

Optometry or the Department of Managed Health Care or any law enforcement or regulatory agency.

(14) The landlord shall provide the optometrist with written notice of the scheduled expiration date of a lease at least 60 days prior to the scheduled expiration date. This notice obligation shall not affect the ability of either party to terminate the lease pursuant to this section. The landlord may not interfere with an outgoing optometrist's efforts to inform the optometrist's patients, in accordance with customary practice and professional obligations, of the relocation of the optometrist's practice.

(15) The California State Board of Optometry may inspect, upon request, an individual lease agreement pursuant to its investigational authority, and if such a request is made, the landlord or tenant, as applicable, shall promptly comply with the request. Failure or refusal to comply with the request for lease agreements within 30 days of receiving the request constitutes unprofessional conduct and is grounds for disciplinary action by the appropriate regulatory agency. This section shall not affect the Department of Managed Health Care's authority to inspect all books and records of a health plan pursuant to Section 1381 of the Health and Safety Code.

Any financial information contained in the lease submitted to a regulatory entity, pursuant to this paragraph, shall be considered confidential trade secret information that is exempt from disclosure under the California Public Records Act (Division 10 (commencing with Section 7920.000) of Title 1 of the Government Code).

(16) This subdivision shall not be applicable to the relationship between any optometrist employee and the employer medical group, or the relationship between a medical group exclusively contracted with a health plan regulated by the Department of Managed Health Care and that health plan.

(e) No registered dispensing optician may have any membership, proprietary interest, coownership, or profit-sharing arrangement either by stock ownership, interlocking directors, trusteeship, mortgage, or trust deed, with an optometrist, except as permitted under this section.

(f) Nothing in this section shall prohibit a person licensed under Chapter 5 (commencing with Section 2000) or its professional corporation from contracting with or employing optometrists, ophthalmologists, or optometric assistants and entering into a contract or landlord-tenant relationship with a health plan, an optical company, or a registered dispensing optician, in accordance with Sections 650 and 654 of this code.

(g) Any violation of this section constitutes a misdemeanor as to such person licensed under Chapter 7 (commencing with Section 3000) of this division and as to any and all persons, whether or not so licensed under this division, who participate with such licensed person in a violation of any provision of this section.

(h) (1) Notwithstanding any other law and in addition to any action available to the California State Board of Optometry, the California State Board of Optometry may issue a citation containing an order of abatement, an order to pay an administrative fine, or both, to an optical company, an optometrist, or a registered dispensing optician for a violation of this section. The administrative fine shall not exceed fifty thousand dollars ($50,000) per administrative action. Notwithstanding any other law and in addition to any action available to the Medical Board of California or the Osteopathic Medical Board of California, the Medical Board of California or the Osteopathic Medical Board of California may issue a citation containing an order of abatement, an order to pay an administrative fine, or both, to a physician and surgeon for a violation of this section. In assessing the amount of the fine, the board shall give due consideration to all of the following:

(A) The gravity of the violation.

(B) The good faith of the cited person or entity.

(C) The history of previous violations of the same or similar nature.

(D) Evidence that the violation was or was not willful.

(E) The extent to which the cited person or entity has cooperated with the board's investigation.

(F) The extent to which the cited person or entity has mitigated or attempted to mitigate any damage or injury caused by the violation.

(G) Any other factors as justice may require.

(2) A citation or fine assessment issued pursuant to a citation shall inform the cited person or entity that if a hearing is desired to contest the finding of a violation, that hearing shall be requested by written notice to the board within 30 days of the date of issuance of the citation or assessment. If a hearing is not requested pursuant to this section, payment of any fine shall not constitute an admission of the violation charged. Hearings shall be held pursuant to Chapter 5 (commencing with Section 11500) of Part 1 of Division 3 of Title 2 of the Government Code.

(3) The board shall adopt regulations to implement a system for the issuance of citations, administrative fines, and orders of abatement authorized by this section. The regulations shall include provisions for both of the following:

(A) The issuance of a citation without an administrative fine.

(B) The opportunity for a cited person or entity to have an informal conference with the executive officer of the board in addition to the hearing described in paragraph (2).

(4) The failure of a licensee to pay a fine within 30 days of the date of assessment, unless the citation is being appealed, may result in disciplinary action being taken by the board. Where a citation is not contested and a fine is not paid, the full amount of the assessed fine shall be added to the fee for renewal of the license. A license shall not be renewed without payment of the renewal fee and fine.

(5) Notwithstanding any other law, if a fine is paid to satisfy an assessment based on the finding of a violation, payment of the fine shall be represented as satisfactory resolution of the matter for purposes of public disclosure.

(i) Administrative fines collected pursuant to this section shall be deposited in the fund of the board that has issued the fine. It is the intent of the Legislature that moneys collected as fines and deposited in the fund be used by the board primarily for enforcement purposes.

(j) Any complaints against a physician and surgeon for violations of this section shall be referred to the physician and surgeon's licensing board.

(k) This section shall become operative on January 1, 2023.

(Amended (as added by Stats. 2021, Ch. 630, Sec. 11) by Stats. 2022, Ch. 28, Sec. 2. (SB 1380) Effective January 1, 2023.)

655.5. PROCEDURE FOR BILLING FOR SERVICES PERFORMED BY OUTSIDE LABORATORY

(a) It is unlawful for any person licensed under this division or under any initiative act referred to in this division, or any clinical laboratory, or any health facility when billing for a clinical laboratory of the facility, to charge, bill, or otherwise solicit payment from any patient, client, or customer for any clinical laboratory service not actually rendered by the person or clinical laboratory or under his, her or its direct supervision unless the patient, client, or customer is apprised at the first time of the charge, billing, or solicitation of the name, address, and charges of the clinical laboratory performing the service. The first such written charge, bill, or other solicitation of payment shall separately set forth the name, address, and charges of the clinical laboratory concerned and shall clearly show whether or not the charge is included in the total of the account, bill, or charge. This subdivision shall be satisfied if the required disclosures are made to the third-party payer of the patient, client, or customer. If the patient is responsible for submitting the bill for the charges to the third-party payer, the bill provided to the patient for that purpose shall include the disclosures required by this section. This subdivision shall not apply to a clinical laboratory of a health facility or a health facility when billing for a clinical laboratory of the facility nor to a person licensed under this division or under any initiative act referred to in this division if the standardized billing form used by the facility or person requires a summary entry for all clinical laboratory charges. For purposes of this subdivision, "health facility" has the same meaning as defined in Section 1250 of the Health and Safety Code.

(b) Commencing July 1, 1994, a clinical laboratory shall provide to each of its referring providers, upon request, a schedule of fees for services provided to patients of the referring provider. The schedule shall be provided within two working days after the clinical laboratory receives the request. For the purposes of this subdivision, a "referring provider" means any provider who has referred a patient to the clinical laboratory in the preceding six-month period. Commencing July 1, 1994, a clinical laboratory that provides a list of laboratory services to a referring provider or to a potential referring provider shall include a schedule of fees for the laboratory services listed.

(c) It is also unlawful for any person licensed under this division or under any initiative act referred to in this division to charge additional charges for any clinical laboratory service that is not actually rendered by the licensee to the patient and itemized in the charge, bill, or other solicitation of payment. This section shall not be construed to prohibit any of the following:

(1) Any itemized charge for any service actually rendered to the patient by the licensee.

(2) Any summary charge for services actually rendered to a patient by a health facility, as defined in Section 1250 of the Health and Safety Code, or by a person licensed under this division or under any initiative act referred to in this division if the standardized billing form used by the facility or person requires a summary entry for all clinical laboratory charges.

(d) As used in this section, the term "any person licensed under this division" includes a person licensed under paragraph (1) of subdivision (a) of Section 1265, all wholly owned subsidiaries of the person, a parent company that wholly owns the person, and any subsidiaries wholly owned by the same parent that wholly owns the person. "Wholly owned" means ownership directly or through one or more subsidiaries. This section shall not apply to billings by a person licensed under paragraph (1) of subdivision (a) of Section 1265 when the person licensed under paragraph (1) of subdivision (a) of Section 1265 bills for services performed by any laboratory owned or operated by the person licensed under paragraph (1) of subdivision (a) of Section 1265.

(e) This section shall not apply to any person or clinical laboratory who or which contracts directly with a health care service plan licensed pursuant to Section 1349 of the Health and Safety Code, if the services are to be provided to members of the plan on a prepaid basis and without additional charge or liability on account thereof.

(f) A violation of this section is a public offense and is punishable upon a first conviction by imprisonment in a county jail for not more than one year, or by imprisonment pursuant to subdivision (h) of Section 1170 of the Penal Code, or by a fine not exceeding ten thousand dollars ($10,000), or by both that imprisonment and fine. A second or subsequent conviction is punishable by imprisonment pursuant to subdivision (h) of Section 1170 of the Penal Code.

(g) (1) Notwithstanding subdivision (f), a violation of this section by a physician and surgeon for a first offense shall be subject to the exclusive remedy of reprimand by the Medical Board of California if the transaction that is the subject of the violation involves a charge for a clinical laboratory service that is less than the charge would have been if the clinical laboratory providing the service billed a patient, client, or customer directly for the clinical laboratory service, and if that clinical laboratory charge is less than the charge listed in the clinical laboratory's schedule of fees pursuant to subdivision (b).

(2) Nothing in this subdivision shall be construed to permit a physician and surgeon to charge more than he or she was charged for the laboratory service by the clinical laboratory providing the service unless the additional charge is for service actually rendered by the physician and surgeon to the patient.

(Amended by Stats. 2011, Ch. 15, Sec. 5. (AB 109) Effective April 4, 2011. Operative October 1, 2011, by Sec. 636 of Ch. 15, as amended by Stats. 2011, Ch. 39, Sec. 68.)

656. INJUNCTIONS

Whenever any person has engaged, or is about to engage, in any acts or practices that constitute, or will constitute, a violation of this article, the superior court in and for the county wherein the acts or practices take place, or are about to take place, may issue an injunction, or other appropriate order, restraining the conduct on application of the California State Board of Optometry, the Medical Board of California, the California Board of Podiatric Medicine, the Osteopathic Medical Board of California, the Attorney General, or the district attorney of the county.

The proceedings under this section shall be governed by Chapter 3 (commencing with Section 525) of Title 7 of Part 2 of the Code of Civil Procedure.

The remedy provided for in this section shall be in addition to, and not a limitation upon, the authority provided by any other provision of this code.

(Amended by Stats. 2021, Ch. 630, Sec. 12. (AB 1534) Effective January 1, 2022.)

657. LEGISLATIVE FINDINGS AND DECLARATIONS; DISCOUNTS FOR PROMPT PAYMENT OF HEALTH OR MEDICAL CLAIMS

(a) The Legislature finds and declares all of the following:

(1) Californians spend more than one hundred billion dollars ($100,000,000,000) annually on health care.

(2) In 1994, an estimated 6.6 million of California's 32 million residents did not have any health insurance and were ineligible for Medi-Cal.

(3) Many of California's uninsured cannot afford basic, preventative health care resulting in these residents relying on emergency rooms for urgent health care, thus driving up health care costs.

(4) Health care should be affordable and accessible to all Californians.

(5) The public interest dictates that uninsured Californians have access to basic, preventative health care at affordable prices.

(b) To encourage the prompt payment of health or medical care claims, health care providers are hereby expressly authorized to grant discounts in health or medical care claims when payment is made promptly within time limits prescribed by the health care providers or institutions rendering the service or treatment.

(c) Notwithstanding any provision in any health care service plan contract or insurance contract to the contrary, health care providers are hereby expressly authorized to grant discounts for health or medical care provided to any patient the health care provider has reasonable cause to believe is not eligible for, or is not entitled to, insurance reimbursement, coverage under the Medi-Cal program, or coverage by a health care service plan for the health or medical care provided. Any discounted fee granted pursuant to this section shall not be deemed to be the health care provider's usual, customary, or reasonable fee for any other purposes, including, but not limited to, any health care service plan contract or insurance contract.

(d) "Health care provider," as used in this section, means any person licensed or certified pursuant to Division 2 (commencing with Section 500) of the Business and Professions Code, or licensed pursuant to the Osteopathic Initiative Act, or the Chiropractic Initiative Act, or licensed pursuant to Chapter 2.5 (commencing with Section 1440) of Division 2 of the Health and Safety Code; and any clinic, health dispensary, or health facility, licensed pursuant to Division 2 (commencing with Section 1200) of the Health and Safety Code.

(Amended by Stats. 1998, Ch. 20, Sec. 1. Effective April 14, 1998.)

ARTICLE 7.5: HEALTH CARE PRACTITIONERS

680. HEALTH CARE PRACTITIONER'S DISCLOSURE OF NAME AND LICENSE STATUS

(a) Except as otherwise provided in this section, a health care practitioner shall disclose, while working, his or her name and practitioner's license status, as granted by this state, on a name tag in at least 18-point type. A health care practitioner in a practice or an office, whose license is prominently displayed, may opt to not wear a name tag. If a health care practitioner or a licensed clinical social worker is working in a psychiatric setting or in a setting that is not licensed by the state, the employing entity or agency shall have the discretion to make an exception from the name tag requirement for individual safety or therapeutic concerns. In the interest of public safety and consumer awareness, it shall be unlawful for any person to use the title "nurse" in reference to himself or herself and in any capacity, except for an individual who is a registered nurse or a licensed vocational nurse, or as otherwise provided in Section 2800. Nothing in this section shall prohibit a certified nurse assistant from using his or her title.

(b) Facilities licensed by the State Department of Social Services, the State Department of Public Health, or the State Department of Health Care Services shall develop and implement policies to ensure that health care practitioners providing care in those facilities are in compliance with subdivision (a). The State Department of Social Services, the State Department of Public Health, and the State Department of Health Care Services shall verify through periodic inspections that the policies required pursuant to subdivision (a) have been developed and implemented by the respective licensed facilities.

(c) For purposes of this article, "health care practitioner" means any person who engages in acts that are the subject of licensure or regulation under this division or under any initiative act referred to in this division.

(Amended by Stats. 2013, Ch. 23, Sec. 1. (AB 82) Effective June 27, 2013.)

680.5. ADDITIONAL DISCLOSURES OF SPECIFIED INFORMATION; APPLICABILITY

(a) (1) A health care practitioner licensed under Division 2 (commencing with Section 500) shall communicate to a patient his or her name, state-granted practitioner license type, and highest level of academic degree, by one or both of the following methods:

(A) In writing at the patient's initial office visit.

(B) In a prominent display in an area visible to patients in his or her office.

(2) An individual licensed under Chapter 6 (commencing with Section 2700) or Chapter 9 (commencing with Section 4000) is not required to disclose the highest level of academic degree he or she holds.

(b) A person licensed under Chapter 5 (commencing with Section 2000) or under the Osteopathic Act, who is certified by (1) an American Board of Medical Specialties member board, (2) a board or association with requirements equivalent to a board described in paragraph (1) approved by that person's medical licensing authority, or (3) a board or association with an Accreditation Council for Graduate Medical Education approved postgraduate training program that provides complete training in the person's specialty or subspecialty, shall disclose the name of the board or association by either method described in subdivision (a).

(c) A health care practitioner who chooses to disclose the information required by subdivisions (a) and (b) pursuant to subparagraph (A) of paragraph (1) of subdivision (a) shall present that information in at least 24-point type in the following format:

HEALTH CARE PRACTITIONER INFORMATION

1. Name and license.

2. Highest level of academic degree.

3. Board certification (ABMS/MBC).

(d) This section shall not apply to the following health care practitioners:

(1) A person who provides professional medical services to enrollees of a health care service plan that exclusively contracts with a single medical group in a specific geographic area to provide or arrange for professional medical services for the enrollees of the plan.

(2) A person who works in a facility licensed under Section 1250 of the Health and Safety Code or in a clinical laboratory licensed under Section 1265.

(3) A person licensed under Chapter 3 (commencing with Section 1200), Chapter 7.5 (commencing with Section 3300), Chapter 8.3 (commencing with Section 3700), Chapter 11 (commencing with Section 4800), Chapter 13 (commencing with Section 4980), Chapter 14 (commencing with Section 4990.1), or Chapter 16 (commencing with Section 4999.10).

(e) A health care practitioner, who provides information regarding health care services on an Internet Web site that is directly controlled or administered by that health care practitioner or his or her office personnel, shall prominently display on that Internet Web site the information required by this section.

(Amended by Stats. 2011, Ch. 381, Sec. 5. (SB 146) Effective January 1, 2012.)

683. REPORTING NAME AND LICENSE NUMBER OF LICENSE PROHIBITED FROM PRACTICING

(a) A board shall report, within 10 working days, to the State Department of Health Care Services the name and license number of a person whose license has been revoked, suspended, surrendered, made inactive by the licensee, or placed in another category that prohibits the licensee from practicing their profession. The purpose of the reporting requirement is to prevent reimbursement by the state for Medi-Cal and Denti-Cal services provided after the cancellation of a provider's professional license.

(b) "Board," as used in this section, means the Dental Board of California, the Medical Board of California, the Board of Psychology, the California State Board of Optometry, the California State Board of Pharmacy, the Osteopathic Medical Board of California, the State Board of Chiropractic Examiners, the Board of Behavioral Sciences, the California Board of Podiatric Medicine, and the California Board of Occupational Therapy.

(c) This section shall become operative on January 1, 2015.

(Amended by Stats. 2021, Ch. 630, Sec. 13. (AB 1534) Effective January 1, 2022.)

686. PROVIDING SERVICES VIA TELEHEALTH

A health care practitioner licensed under Division 2 (commencing with Section 500) providing services via telehealth shall be subject to the requirements and definitions set forth in Section 2290.5, to the practice act relating to his or her licensed profession, and to the regulations adopted by a board pursuant to that practice act.

(Added by Stats. 2012, Ch. 782, Sec. 1. (AB 1733) Effective January 1, 2013.)

688. ELECTRONC DATA PRESCRIPTIONS

(a) A health care practitioner authorized to issue a prescription pursuant to Section 4040 shall have the capability to issue an electronic data transmission prescription, as defined under Section 4040, on behalf of a patient and to transmit that electronic data transmission prescription to a pharmacy selected by the patient.

(b) (1) A pharmacy, pharmacist, or other practitioner authorized under California law to dispense or furnish a prescription pursuant to Section 4040 shall have the capability to receive an electronic data transmission prescription on behalf of a patient.

(2) A pharmacy, pharmacist, or other practitioner authorized under California law to dispense or furnish a prescription pursuant to Section 4040 shall not refuse to dispense or furnish an electronic data transmission prescription solely because the prescription was not submitted via, or is not compatible with, the proprietary software of the pharmacy, pharmacist, or other dispensing practitioner.

(3) A pharmacy, pharmacist, or other practitioner authorized under California law to dispense or furnish a prescription pursuant to Section 4040 may decline to dispense or furnish an electronic data transmission prescription submitted via a software that fails to meet any of the following:

(A) Adheres to the National Council for Prescription Drug Programs SCRIPT standard, as modified from time to time.

(B) Complies with the prescription content requirements set forth in Section 4040.

(C) For a controlled substance prescription, complies with Parts 1300, 1304, 1306, and 1311 of Title 21 of the Code of Federal Regulations, as amended from time to time.

(D) Complies with the federal Health Insurance Portability and Accountability Act of 1996, the California Confidentiality of Medical Information Act, or the security and confidentiality requirements prescribed to by the pharmacy, pharmacist, or other practitioner authorized pursuant to Section 4040.

(c) For a prescription for a controlled substance, as defined by Section 4021, generation and transmission of the electronic data transmission prescription shall comply with Parts 1300, 1304, 1306, and 1311 of Title 21 of the Code of Federal Regulations, as amended from time to time.

(d) A prescription prescribed by a health care practitioner shall be issued as an electronic data transmission prescription. This subdivision shall not apply to prescriptions issued pursuant to subdivision (e).

(e) Subdivision (d) shall not apply to any of the following:

(1) The prescription is issued pursuant to Section 11159.2 of the Health and Safety Code.

(2) An electronic data transmission prescription is unavailable due to a temporary technological or electrical failure. For purposes of this paragraph, "temporary technological or electrical failure" means failure of a computer system, application, or device, or the loss of electrical power to that system, application, or device, or any other service interruption affecting the certified electronic data transmission prescription application used to transmit the prescription.

(3) The prescribing health care practitioner is issuing a prescription to be dispensed by a pharmacy located outside California.

(4) (A) The prescription is issued in a hospital emergency department or urgent care clinic and one or more of the following conditions are present:

(i) The patient resides outside California.

(ii) The patient resides outside the geographic area of the hospital.

(iii) The patient is homeless or indigent and does not have a preferred pharmacy.

(iv) The prescription is issued at a time when a patient's regular or preferred pharmacy is likely to be closed.

(B) Under any of the conditions described in subparagraph (A), a prescription shall be electronically issued but does not require electronic transmission and may be provided directly to the patient.

(5) The prescription is issued by a veterinarian.

(6) The prescription is for eyeglasses or contact lenses.

(7) The prescription is issued by a prescribing health care practitioner serving as a volunteer in a free clinic and receives no remuneration for their services.

(8) The prescribing health care practitioner and the dispenser are the same entity.

(9) The prescription is issued by a prescribing health care practitioner under circumstances whereby the practitioner reasonably determines that it would be impractical for the patient to obtain substances prescribed by an electronic data transmission prescription in a timely manner, and the delay would adversely impact the patient's medical condition.

(10) The prescription that is issued includes elements not covered by the latest version of the National Council for Prescription Drug Programs' SCRIPT standard, as amended from time to time.

(11) (A) The prescriber registers with the California State Board of Pharmacy in a manner and format determined by the board, stating that they meet one or more of the following criteria:

(i) Their practice is located in the area of an emergency or disaster declared by a federal, state, or local government.

(ii) They issue 100 or fewer prescriptions per calendar year.

(iii) They are unable to issue electronic data transmission prescriptions due to circumstances beyond their control.

(B) The prescriber shall annually submit the registration required in subparagraph (A) to the California State Board of Pharmacy and maintain documentation of the circumstances qualifying them for exemption under subparagraph (A).

(C) The California State Board of Pharmacy shall post a list of prescribers meeting the requirements of subparagraph (A) on its internet website.

(f) A health care practitioner who issues a prescription for a controlled substance but does not transmit the prescription as an electronic data transmission prescription shall document the reason in the patient's medical record as soon as practicable and within 72 hours of the end of the technological or electrical failure that prevented the electronic data transmission of the prescription.

(g) (1) A pharmacy that receives an electronic data transmission prescription from a prescribing health care practitioner who has issued the prescription but has not dispensed the medication to the patient shall, at the request of the patient or a person authorized to make a request on behalf of the patient, immediately transfer or forward the electronic data transmission prescription to an alternative pharmacy designated by the requester, unless one of the following applies:

(A) The action would result in a violation of any state or federal law.

(B) The action is not supported by the latest version of the National Council for Prescription Drug Programs SCRIPT standard, as amended from time to time.

(2) If a pharmacy is prohibited from transferring or forwarding electronic data transmission prescriptions, as specified in paragraph (1), to a designated alternative pharmacy, and that prohibition is subsequently removed, then that pharmacy shall implement, within one year from the date the prohibition is removed, the necessary provisions to allow for the transferring or forwarding of an electronic data transmission prescription.

(h) If a pharmacy, or its staff, is aware than an attempted transmission of an electronic data transmission prescription failed, is incomplete, or is otherwise not appropriately received, the pharmacy shall immediately notify the prescribing health care practitioner.

(i) A pharmacist who receives a written, oral, or faxed prescription shall not be required to verify that the prescription properly falls under one of the exceptions in subdivision (e). Pharmacists may continue to dispense medications from legally valid written, oral, or fax prescriptions pursuant to this division.

(j) A health care practitioner, pharmacist, or pharmacy who fails to meet the applicable requirements of this section shall be referred to the appropriate state professional licensing board solely for administrative sanctions, as deemed appropriate by that board. This section does not create a private right of action against a health care practitioner. This section does not limit a health care practitioner's liability for the negligent failure to diagnose or treat a patient.

(k) This section shall not apply to a health care practitioner, pharmacist, or pharmacy when providing health care services to an inmate, individual on parole, or youth under the jurisdiction of the Department of Corrections and Rehabilitation.

(Amended by Stats. 2022, Ch. 518, Sec. 1. (AB 852) Effective January 1, 2023.)

ARTICLE 8: SELECTION OF HEALING ARTS PRACTITIONER

690. PATIENT'S SELECTION OF OPTOMETRIST OR PHYSICIAN RENDERING VISION CARE UNDER STATE-SUPPORTED PROGRAMS

(a) Except as provided in Section 4601 of the Labor Code and Section 2627 of the Unemployment Insurance Code, neither the administrators, agents, or employees of any program supported, in whole or in part, by funds of the State of California, nor any state agency, county, or city of the State of California, nor any officer, employee, agent, or governing board of a state agency, county, or city in the performance of its, his, or her duty, duties, function, or functions, shall prohibit any person, who is entitled to vision care that may be rendered by either an optometrist or a physician and surgeon within the scope of his or her license, from selecting a duly licensed member of either profession to render the service, provided the member has not been removed or suspended from participation in the program for cause.

(b) Whenever any person has engaged, or is about to engage, in any acts or practices that constitute, or will constitute, a violation of this section, the superior court in and for the county wherein the acts or practices take place, or are about to take place, may issue an injunction, or other appropriate order, restraining the conduct on application of the Attorney General, the district attorney of the county, or any person aggrieved.

For purposes of this subdivision, "person aggrieved" means the person who seeks the particular medical or optometric services mentioned in this section, or the holder of any certificate who is discriminated against in violation of this section.

(c) Nothing contained in this section shall prohibit any agency operating a program of services, including, but not limited to, a program established pursuant to Article 5 (commencing with Section 123800) of Chapter 3 of Part 2 of Division 106 of the Health and Safety Code, from preparing lists of healing arts licensees and requiring patients to select a licensee on the list as a condition to payment by the program for the services, except that if the lists are established and a particular service may be performed by either a physician and surgeon or an optometrist the list shall contain a sufficient number of licensees so as to assure the patients an adequate choice.

(Amended by Stats. 2006, Ch. 538, Sec. 1. Effective January 1, 2007.)

ARTICLE 9: INACTIVE LICENSE

700. LEGISLATIVE INTENT

It is the intent of the Legislature to establish in this article an inactive category of health professionals' licensure. Such inactive licenses or certificates are intended to allow a person who has a license or certificate in one of the healing arts, but who is not actively engaged in the practice of his or her profession, to maintain licensure or certification in a nonpracticing status.

(Added by Stats. 1977, Ch. 410.)

701. ISSUANCE

(a) As used in this article, "board" refers to any healing arts board, division, or examining committee which licenses or certifies health professionals.

(b) Each healing arts board referred to in this division shall issue, upon application and payment of the normal renewal fee, an inactive license or certificate to a current holder of an active license or certificate whose license or certificate is not suspended, revoked, or otherwise punitively restricted by that board.

(Amended by Stats. 2018, Ch. 249, Sec. 1. (AB 1659) Effective January 1, 2019.)

702. HOLDING PROHIBITED FROM ENGAGING IN ACTIVE LICENSE ACTIVITY

The holder of an inactive healing arts license or certificate issued pursuant to this article shall not do any of the following:

(a) Engage in any activity for which an active license or certificate is required.

(b) Represent that he or she has an active license.

(Amended by Stats. 2018, Ch. 249, Sec. 2. (AB 1659) Effective January 1, 2019.)

703. RENEWAL; FEES

(a) An inactive healing arts license or certificate issued pursuant to this article shall be renewed during the same time period at which an active license or certificate is renewed. In order to renew a license or certificate issued pursuant to this article, the holder thereof need not comply with any continuing education requirement for renewal of an active license or certificate.

(b) The renewal fee for a license or certificate in an active status shall apply also for renewal of a license or certificate in an inactive status, unless a lower fee has been established by the issuing board.

(Amended by Stats. 2018, Ch. 249, Sec. 3. (AB 1659) Effective January 1, 2019.)

704. RESTORATION TO ACTIVE STATUS

In order for the holder of an inactive license or certificate issued pursuant to this article to restore his or her license or certificate to an active status, the holder of an inactive license or certificate shall comply with all the following:

(a) Pay the renewal fee; provided, that the renewal fee shall be waived for a physician and surgeon who certifies to the Medical Board of California that license restoration is for the sole purpose of providing voluntary, unpaid service to a public agency, not-for-profit agency, institution, or corporation which provides medical services to indigent patients in medically underserved or critical-need population areas of the state.

(b) If the board requires completion of continuing education for renewers of an active license or certificate, complete continuing education equivalent to that required for a single license renewal period.

(Amended by Stats. 1999, Ch. 631, Sec. 2. Effective January 1, 2000.)

ARTICLE 10: FEDERAL PERSONNEL AND TRIBAL HEALTH PROGRAMS

710. APPLICABILITY OF SKILLS OBTAINED IN ARMED SERVICES TO SATISFYING PROFESSIONAL REQUIREMENTS

It is the policy of the State of California that, consistent with high quality health care services, persons with skills, knowledge and experience obtained in the armed services of the United States should be permitted to apply such learning and contribute to the health manpower needs of the state at the maximum level of responsibility and skill for which they are qualified.

To this end, the rules and regulations of boards under this division shall provide for methods of evaluating education, training, and experience obtained in military service if such training is applicable to the requirements of that profession.

(Added by Stats. 1969, Ch. 1592.)

715. LICENSES TO PRACTICE IN STATE

Unless otherwise required by federal law or regulation, no board under this division which licenses dentists, physicians and surgeons, podiatrists, or nurses may require a person to obtain or maintain any license to practice a profession or render services in the State of California if one of the following applies:

(a) The person practicing a profession or rendering services does so exclusively as an employee of a department, bureau, office, division, or similarly constituted agency of the federal government, and provides medical services exclusively on a federal reservation or at any facility wholly supported by and maintained by the United States government.

(b) The person practicing a profession or rendering services does so solely pursuant to a contract with the federal government on a federal reservation or at any facility wholly supported and maintained by the United States government.

(c) The person practicing a profession or rendering services does so pursuant to, or as a part of a program or project conducted or administered by a department, bureau, office, division, or similarly constituted agency of the federal government which by federal statute expressly exempts persons practicing a profession or rendering services as part of the program or project from state laws requiring licensure.

(Amended by Stats. 1986, Ch. 220, Sec. 7.5. Effective June 30, 1986.)

716. DENIAL OF LICENSE; DISCIPLINARY ACTION AGAINST HOLDER OF STATE LICENSE

Notwithstanding any other provision of law, a board under this division may deny issuance of a license to an applicant or take disciplinary action against the holder of a California license for acts or omissions committed by the applicant or licensee in the course of professional practice or rendering services described in Section 715 if both of the following apply:

(a) The acts or omissions committed by the applicant or licensee constituted grounds for denial or discipline pursuant to the laws of this state governing licensees or applicants for licensure for the profession or vocation in question.

(b) The acts or omissions constituting the basis for denial or discipline by the agency were not authorized, exempted or rendered inconsistent by federal statute.

(Added by Stats. 1983, Ch. 239, Sec. 3.)

717. CONSTRUCTION OF ARTICLE

This article is not intended to address the scope of practice of a dentist, physician and surgeon, or nurse licensed under this division, and nothing in this article shall be construed to restrict, expand, alter, or modify the existing scope of practice established by federal statute or regulation.

(Added by Stats. 1983, Ch. 239, Sec. 4.)

718. PARTICIPATION IN RESIDENCY, FELLOWSHIP OR CLINICAL TRAINING PROGRAM

A physician and surgeon who is not licensed in this state but who is a commissioned officer on active duty in the medical corps of any branch of the armed forces of the United States may engage in the practice of medicine as part of a residency, fellowship, or clinical training program if all the following conditions are met:

(a) The residency, fellowship, or clinical training program is conducted by a branch of the armed forces of the United States at a health facility on a federal reservation and limited in enrollment to military physicians on active duty in the medical corps of a branch of the armed forces of the United States.

(b) The residency, fellowship, or clinical training program, as part of its program, contracts with or affiliates with a similar program in or at a health facility not on a federal reservation to offer specific courses or training not available at the facility located on the federal reservation.

(c) The officers enrolled in the residency, fellowship, or clinical training program restrict their practice only to patients who are seen as part of their duties in the program.

(d) The compensation received by the officers enrolled in the residency, fellowship, or clinical training program is limited to their regular pay and allowances as commissioned officers.

(e) The officers enrolled in the training programs or portions of training programs not conducted on a federal reservation shall register with the Division of Licensing of the Medical Board of California on a form provided by the division.

(Amended by Stats. 1989, Ch. 886, Sec. 9.)

719. EMPLOYMENT OF HEALTH CARE PRACTITIONER LICENSED IN ANOTHER STATE BY TRIBAL HEALTH PROGRAM (AB 1896)

(a) A person who is licensed as a health care practitioner in any other state and is employed by a tribal health program, as defined in Section 1603 of Title 25 of the United States Code, shall be exempt from any licensing requirement described in this division with respect to acts authorized under the person's license where the tribal health program performs the services described in the contract or compact of the tribal health program under the Indian Self-Determination and Education Assistance Act (25 U.S.C. Sec. 450 et seq.).

(b) For purposes of this section, "health care practitioner" means any person who engages in acts that are the subject of licensure or regulation under the law of any other state.

(Added by Stats. 2012, Ch. 119, Sec. 2. (AB 1896) Effective January 1, 2013. See similar section added by Stats. 2012, Ch. 799.)

719. EMPLOYMENT OF HEALTH CARE PRACTITIONER LICENSED IN ANOTHER STATE BY TRIBAL HEALTH PROGRAM (SB 1575)

(a) A person who possesses a current, valid license as a health care practitioner in any other state and is employed by a tribal health program, as defined in Section 1603 of Title 25 of the United States Code, shall be exempt from any licensing requirement described in this division with respect to acts authorized under the person's license where the tribal health program performs the services described in the contract or compact of the tribal health program under the Indian Self-Determination and Education Assistance Act (25 U.S.C. Sec. 450 et seq.).

(b) For purposes of this section, "health care practitioner" means any person who engages in acts that are the subject of licensure or regulation under the law of any other state.

(Added by Stats. 2012, Ch. 799, Sec. 1. (SB 1575) Effective January 1, 2013.)

ARTICLE 10.5: UNPROFESSIONAL CONDUCT

725. EXCESSIVE PRESCRIBING OR TREATMENT; TREATMENT FOR INTRACTABLE PAIN

(a) Repeated acts of clearly excessive prescribing, furnishing, dispensing, or administering of drugs or treatment, repeated acts of clearly excessive use of diagnostic procedures, or repeated acts of clearly excessive use of diagnostic or treatment facilities as determined by the standard of the community of licensees is unprofessional conduct for a physician and surgeon, dentist, podiatrist, psychologist, physical therapist, chiropractor, optometrist, speech- language pathologist, or audiologist.

(b) Any person who engages in repeated acts of clearly excessive prescribing or administering of drugs or treatment is guilty of a misdemeanor and shall be punished by a fine of not less than one hundred dollars ($100) nor more than six hundred dollars ($600), or by imprisonment for a term of not less than 60 days nor more than 180 days, or by both that fine and imprisonment.

(c) A practitioner who has a medical basis for prescribing, furnishing, dispensing, or administering dangerous drugs or prescription controlled substances shall not be subject to disciplinary action or prosecution under this section.

(d) No physician and surgeon shall be subject to disciplinary action pursuant to this section for treating intractable pain in compliance with Section 2241.5.

(Amended by Stats. 2007, Ch. 130, Sec. 2. Effective January 1, 2008.)

726. COMMISSION OF ACT OF SEXUAL ABUSE OR MISCONDUCT WITH PATIENT OR CLIENT

(a) The commission of any act of sexual abuse, misconduct, or relations with a patient, client, or customer constitutes unprofessional conduct and grounds for disciplinary action for any person licensed under this division or under any initiative act referred to in this division.

(b) This section shall not apply to consensual sexual contact between a licensee and his or her spouse or person in an equivalent domestic relationship when that licensee provides medical treatment, other than psychotherapeutic treatment, to his or her spouse or person in an equivalent domestic relationship.

(Amended by Stats. 2015, Ch. 510, Sec. 3. (AB 179) Effective January 1, 2016.)

727. APPLICABILITY OF EVIDENCE CODE PROVISIONS

The provisions of subdivision (2) of Section 1103 of the Evidence Code shall apply in disciplinary proceedings brought against a licensee for acts in violation of Section 726.

(Added by renumbering Section 731 by Stats. 1981, Ch. 714, Sec. 4.)

731. VIOLATIONS AT WORK AS UNPROFESSIONAL CONDUCT

(a) Any person licensed, certified, registered, or otherwise subject to regulation pursuant to this division who engages in, or who aids or abets in, a violation of Section 266h, 266i, 315, 316, or 318 of, or subdivision (a) or (b) of Section 647 of, the Penal Code occurring in the work premises of, or work area under the direct professional supervision or control of, that person, shall be guilty of unprofessional conduct. The license, certification, or registration of that person shall be subject to denial, suspension, or revocation by the appropriate regulatory entity under this division.

(b) In addition to any penalty provided under any other provision of law, a violation of subdivision (a) shall subject the person to a civil penalty in an amount not to exceed two thousand five hundred dollars

($2,500) for the first offense, and not to exceed five thousand dollars ($5,000) for each subsequent offense, which may be assessed and recovered in a civil action brought by any district attorney. If the action is brought by a district attorney, the penalty recovered shall be paid to the treasurer of the county in which the judgment was entered.

(Added by Stats. 1998, Ch. 971, Sec. 2. Effective January 1, 1999.)

733. HEALTH CARE LICENTIATE REQUIRED TO DISPENSE DRUGS AND DEVICES PURSUANT TO LAWFUL ORDER OR PRESCRIPTION; SPECIFIED EXCEPTIONS; VIOLATIONS AS UNPROFESSIONAL CONDUCT

(a) A licentiate shall not obstruct a patient in obtaining a prescription drug or device that has been legally prescribed or ordered for that patient. A violation of this section constitutes unprofessional conduct by the licentiate and shall subject the licentiate to disciplinary or administrative action by his or her licensing agency.

(b) Notwithstanding any other law, a licentiate shall dispense drugs and devices, as described in subdivision (a) of Section 4024, pursuant to a lawful order or prescription unless one of the following circumstances exists:

(1) Based solely on the licentiate's professional training and judgment, dispensing pursuant to the order or the prescription is contrary to law, or the licentiate determines that the prescribed drug or device would cause a harmful drug interaction or would otherwise adversely affect the patient's medical condition.

(2) The prescription drug or device is not in stock. If an order, other than an order described in Section 4019, or prescription cannot be dispensed because the drug or device is not in stock, the licentiate shall take one of the following actions:

(A) Immediately notify the patient and arrange for the drug or device to be delivered to the site or directly to the patient in a timely manner.

(B) Promptly transfer the prescription to another pharmacy known to stock the prescription drug or device that is near enough to the site from which the prescription or order is transferred, to ensure the patient has timely access to the drug or device.

(C) Return the prescription to the patient and refer the patient. The licentiate shall make a reasonable effort to refer the patient to a pharmacy that stocks the prescription drug or device that is near enough to the referring site to ensure that the patient has timely access to the drug or device.

(3) The licentiate refuses on ethical, moral, or religious grounds to dispense a drug or device pursuant to an order or prescription. A licentiate may decline to dispense a prescription drug or device on this basis only if the licentiate has previously notified his or her employer, in writing, of the drug or class of drugs to which he or she objects, and the licentiate's employer can, without creating undue hardship, provide a reasonable accommodation of the licentiate's objection. The licentiate's employer shall establish protocols that ensure that the patient has timely access to the prescribed drug or device despite the licentiate's refusal to dispense the prescription or order. For purposes of this section, "reasonable accommodation" and "undue hardship" shall have the same meaning as applied to those terms pursuant to subdivision (l) of Section 12940 of the Government Code.

(c) For the purposes of this section, "prescription drug or device" has the same meaning as the definition in Section 4022.

(d) This section applies to emergency contraception drug therapy and self-administered hormonal contraceptives described in Section 4052.3.

(e) This section imposes no duty on a licentiate to dispense a drug or device pursuant to a prescription or order without payment for the drug or device, including payment directly by the patient or through a third-party payer accepted by the licentiate or payment of any required copayment by the patient.

(f) The notice to consumers required by Section 4122 shall include a statement that describes patients' rights relative to the requirements of this section.

(Amended by Stats. 2013, Ch. 469, Sec. 1. (SB 493) Effective January 1, 2014.)

ARTICLE 11: PROFESSIONAL REPORTING

800. CENTRAL FILES OR LICENSEES' INDIVIDUAL HISTORICAL RECORDS

(a) The Medical Board of California, the Podiatric Medical Board of California, the Board of Psychology, the Dental Board of California, the Dental Hygiene Board of California, the Osteopathic Medical Board of California, the State Board of Chiropractic Examiners, the Board of Registered Nursing, the Board of Vocational Nursing and Psychiatric Technicians of the State of California, the California State Board of Optometry, the Veterinary Medical Board, the Board of Behavioral Sciences, the Physical Therapy Board of California, the California State Board of Pharmacy, the Speech-Language Pathology and Audiology and Hearing Aid Dispensers Board, the California Board of Occupational Therapy, the Acupuncture Board, and the Physician Assistant Board shall each separately create and maintain a central file of the names of all persons who hold a license, certificate, or similar authority from that board. Each central file shall be created and maintained to provide an individual historical record for each licensee with respect to the following information:

(1) Any conviction of a crime in this or any other state that constitutes unprofessional conduct pursuant to the reporting requirements of Section 803.

(2) Any judgment or settlement requiring the licensee or the licensee's insurer to pay any amount of damages in excess of three thousand dollars ($3,000) for any claim that injury or death was proximately caused by the licensee's negligence, error, or omission in practice, or by rendering unauthorized professional services, pursuant to the reporting requirements of Section 801 or 802.

(3) Any public complaints for which provision is made pursuant to subdivision (b).

(4) Disciplinary information reported pursuant to Section 805, including any additional exculpatory or explanatory statements submitted by the licentiate pursuant to subdivision (f) of Section 805. If a court finds, in a final judgment, that the peer review resulting in the 805 report was conducted in bad faith and the licensee who is the subject of the report notifies the board of that finding, the board shall include that finding in the central file. For purposes of this paragraph, "peer review" has the same meaning as defined in Section 805.

(5) Information reported pursuant to Section 805.01, including any explanatory or exculpatory information submitted by the licensee pursuant to subdivision (b) of that section.

(b) (1) Each board shall prescribe and promulgate forms on which members of the public and other licensees or certificate holders may file written complaints to the board alleging any act of misconduct in, or connected with, the performance of professional services by the licensee.

(2) If a board, or division thereof, a committee, or a panel has failed to act upon

a complaint or report within five years, or has found that the complaint or report is without merit, the central file shall be purged of information relating to the complaint or report.

(3) Notwithstanding this subdivision, the Board of Psychology, the Board of Behavioral Sciences, and the Respiratory Care Board of California shall maintain complaints or reports as long as each board deems necessary.

(c) (1) The contents of any central file that are not public records under any other provision of law shall be confidential except that the licensee involved, or the licensee's counsel or representative, may inspect and have copies made of the licensee's complete file except for the provision that may disclose the identity of an information source. For the purposes of this section, a board may protect an information source by providing a copy of the material with only those deletions necessary to protect the identity of the source or by providing a summary of the substance of the material. Whichever method is used, the board shall ensure that full disclosure is made to the subject of any personal information that could reasonably in any way reflect or convey anything detrimental, disparaging, or threatening to a licensee's reputation, rights, benefits, privileges, or qualifications, or be used by a board to make a determination that would affect a licensee's rights, benefits, privileges, or qualifications. The information required to be disclosed pursuant to Section 803.1 shall not be considered among the contents of a central file for the purposes of this subdivision.

(2) The licensee may, but is not required to, submit any additional exculpatory or explanatory statement or other information that the board shall include in the central file.

(3) Each board may permit any law enforcement or regulatory agency when required for an investigation of unlawful activity or for licensing, certification, or regulatory purposes to inspect and have copies made of that licensee's file, unless the disclosure is otherwise prohibited by law.

(4) These disclosures shall effect no change in the confidential status of these records.

(Amended by Stats. 2021, Ch. 630, Sec. 14. (AB 1534) Effective January 1, 2022.)

801. INSURERS' REPORTS OF MALPRACTICE SETTLEMENTS OR ARBITRATION AWARDS; INSURED'S WRITTEN CONSENT TO SETTLEMENT

(a) Except as provided in Section 801.01 and subdivisions (b), (c), (d), and (e) of this section, every insurer providing professional liability insurance to a person who holds a license, certificate, or similar authority from or under any agency specified in subdivision (a) of Section 800 shall send a complete report to that agency as to any settlement or arbitration award over three thousand dollars ($3,000) of a claim or action for damages for death or personal injury caused by that person's negligence, error, or omission in practice, or by his or her rendering of unauthorized professional services. The report shall be sent within 30 days after the written settlement agreement has been reduced to writing and signed by all parties thereto or within 30 days after service of the arbitration award on the parties.

(b) Every insurer providing professional liability insurance to a person licensed pursuant to Chapter 13 (commencing with Section 4980), Chapter 14 (commencing with Section 4990), or Chapter 16 (commencing with Section 4999.10) shall send a complete report to the Board of Behavioral Sciences as to any settlement or arbitration award over ten thousand dollars ($10,000) of a claim or action for damages for death or personal injury caused by that person's negligence, error, or omission in practice, or by his or her rendering of unauthorized professional services. The report shall be sent within 30 days after the written settlement agreement has been reduced to writing and signed by all parties thereto or within 30 days after service of the arbitration award on the parties.

(c) Every insurer providing professional liability insurance to a dentist licensed pursuant to Chapter 4 (commencing with Section 1600) shall send a complete report to the Dental Board of California as to any settlement or arbitration award over ten thousand dollars ($10,000) of a claim or action for damages for death or personal injury caused by that person's negligence, error, or omission in practice, or rendering of unauthorized professional services. The report shall be sent within 30 days after the written settlement agreement has been reduced to writing and signed by all parties thereto or within 30 days after service of the arbitration award on the parties.

(d) Every insurer providing liability insurance to a veterinarian licensed pursuant to Chapter 11 (commencing with Section 4800) shall send a complete report to the Veterinary Medical Board of any settlement or arbitration award over ten thousand dollars ($10,000) of a claim or action for damages for death or injury caused by that person's negligence, error, or omission in practice, or rendering of unauthorized professional service. The report shall be sent within 30 days after the written settlement agreement has been reduced to writing and signed by all parties thereto or within 30 days after service of the arbitration award on the parties.

(e) Every insurer providing professional liability insurance to a person licensed pursuant to Chapter 6 (commencing with Section 2700) shall send a complete report to the Board of Registered Nursing as to any settlement or arbitration award over ten thousand dollars ($10,000) of a claim or action for damages for death or personal injury caused by that person's negligence, error, or omission in practice, or by his or her rendering of unauthorized professional services. The report shall be sent within 30 days after the written settlement agreement has been reduced to writing and signed by all parties thereto or within 30 days after service of the arbitration award on the parties.

(f) The insurer shall notify the claimant, or if the claimant is represented by counsel, the insurer shall notify the claimant's attorney, that the report required by subdivision (a), (b), or (c) has been sent to the agency. If the attorney has not received this notice within 45 days after the settlement was reduced to writing and signed by all of the parties, the arbitration award was served on the parties, or the date of entry of the civil judgment, the attorney shall make the report to the agency.

(g) Notwithstanding any other provision of law, no insurer shall enter into a settlement without the written consent of the insured, except that this prohibition shall not void any settlement entered into without that written consent. The requirement of written consent shall only be waived by both the insured and the insurer.

(h) For purposes of this section, "insurer" means the following:

(1) The insurer providing professional liability insurance to the licensee.

(2) The licensee, or his or her counsel, if the licensee does not possess professional liability insurance.

(3) A state or local governmental agency, including, but not limited to, a joint powers authority, that self-insures the licensee. As used in this paragraph, "state governmental agency" includes, but is not limited to, the University of California.

(Amended by Stats. 2017, Ch. 520, Sec. 1. (SB 799) Effective January 1, 2018.)

801.01. REPORTING REQUIREMENTS

The Legislature finds and declares that the filing of reports with the applicable state agencies required under this section is essential for the protection of the public. It is the intent of the Legislature that the reporting requirements set forth in this section be interpreted broadly in order to expand reporting obligations.

(a) A complete report shall be sent to the Medical Board of California, the Osteopathic Medical Board of California, the California Board of Podiatric Medicine, or the Physician Assistant Board with respect to a licensee of the board as to the following:

(1) A settlement over thirty thousand dollars ($30,000) or arbitration award of any amount or a civil judgment of any amount, whether or not vacated by a settlement after entry of the judgment, that was not reversed on appeal, of a claim or action for damages for death or personal injury caused by the licensee's alleged negligence, error, or omission in practice, or by the licensee's rendering of unauthorized professional services.

(2) A settlement over thirty thousand dollars ($30,000), if the settlement is based on the licensee's alleged negligence, error, or omission in practice, or on the licensee's rendering of unauthorized professional services, and a party to the settlement is a corporation, medical group, partnership, or other corporate entity in which the licensee has an ownership interest or that employs or contracts with the licensee.

(b) The report shall be sent by any of the following:

(1) The insurer providing professional liability insurance to the licensee.

(2) The licensee, or the licensee's counsel.

(3) A state or local governmental agency that self-insures the licensee. For purposes of this section, "state governmental agency" includes, but is not limited to, the University of California.

(c) The entity, person, or licensee obligated to report pursuant to subdivision (b) shall send the complete report if the judgment, settlement agreement, or arbitration award is entered against or paid by the employer of the licensee and not entered against or paid by the licensee. "Employer," as used in this paragraph, means a professional corporation, a group practice, a health care facility or clinic licensed or exempt from licensure under the Health and Safety Code, a licensed health care service plan, a medical care foundation, an educational institution, a professional institution, a professional school or college, a general law corporation, a public entity, or a nonprofit organization that employs, retains, or contracts with a licensee referred to in this section. Nothing in this paragraph shall be construed to authorize the employment of, or contracting with, any licensee in violation of Section 2400.

(d) The report shall be sent to the Medical Board of California, the Osteopathic Medical Board of California, the California Board of Podiatric Medicine, or the Physician Assistant Board as appropriate, within 30 days after the written settlement agreement has been reduced to writing and signed by all parties thereto, within 30 days after service of the arbitration award on the parties, or within 30 days after the date of entry of the civil judgment.

(e) The entity, person, or licensee required to report under subdivision (b) shall notify the claimant or the claimant's counsel, if the claimant is represented by counsel, that the report has been sent to the Medical Board of California, the Osteopathic Medical Board of California, the California Board of Podiatric Medicine, or the Physician Assistant Board. If the claimant or the claimant's counsel has not received this notice within 45 days after the settlement was reduced to writing and signed by all of the parties or the arbitration award was served on the parties or the date of entry of the civil judgment, the claimant or the claimant's counsel shall make the report to the appropriate board.

(f) Failure to substantially comply with this section is a public offense punishable by a fine of not less than five hundred dollars ($500) and not more than five thousand dollars ($5,000).

(g) (1) The Medical Board of California, the Osteopathic Medical Board of California, the California Board of Podiatric Medicine, and the Physician Assistant Board may develop a prescribed form for the report.

(2) The report shall be deemed complete only if it includes the following information:

(A) The name and last known business and residential addresses of every plaintiff or claimant involved in the matter, whether or not the person received an award under the settlement, arbitration, or judgment.

(B) The name and last known business and residential addresses of every licensee who was alleged to have acted improperly, whether or not that person was a named defendant in the action and whether or not that person was required to pay any damages pursuant to the settlement, arbitration award, or judgment.

(C) The name, address, and principal place of business of every insurer providing professional liability insurance to any person described in subparagraph (B), and the insured's policy number.

(D) The name of the court in which the action or any part of the action was filed, and the date of filing and case number of each action.

(E) A description or summary of the facts of each claim, charge, or allegation, including the date of occurrence and the licensee's role in the care or professional services provided to the patient with respect to those services at issue in the claim or action.

(F) The name and last known business address of each attorney who represented a party in the settlement, arbitration, or civil action, including the name of the client the attorney represented.

(G) The amount of the judgment, the date of its entry, and a copy of the judgment; the amount of the arbitration award, the date of its service on the parties, and a copy of the award document; or the amount of the settlement and the date it was reduced to writing and signed by all parties and a copy of the settlement agreement. If an otherwise reportable settlement is entered into after a reportable judgment or arbitration award is issued, the report shall include both a copy of the settlement agreement and a copy of the judgment or award.

(H) The specialty or subspecialty of the licensee who was the subject of the claim or action.

(I) Any other information the Medical Board of California, the Osteopathic Medical Board of California, the California Board of Podiatric Medicine, or the Physician Assistant Board may, by regulation, require.

(3) Every professional liability insurer, self-insured governmental agency, or licensee or the licensee's counsel that makes a report under this section and has received a copy of any written or electronic patient medical or hospital records prepared by the treating physician and surgeon, podiatrist, or physician assistant, or the staff of the treating physician and surgeon, podiatrist, or hospital, describing the medical condition, history, care, or treatment of the person whose death or injury is the subject of the report, or a copy of any deposition in the matter that discusses the care, treatment, or medical condition of the person, shall include with the report, copies of the records and depositions, subject to reasonable costs to be paid by the Medical Board of California, the Osteopathic Medical Board of California, the California Board of Podiatric Medicine, or the Physician Assistant Board. If confidentiality is required by court order and, as a result, the reporter is unable to provide the records and depositions, documentation to that effect shall accompany the

original report. The applicable board may, upon prior notification of the parties to the action, petition the appropriate court for modification of any protective order to permit disclosure to the board. A professional liability insurer, self-insured governmental agency, or licensee or the licensee's counsel shall maintain the records and depositions referred to in this paragraph for at least one year from the date of filing of the report required by this section.

(h) If the board, within 60 days of its receipt of a report filed under this section, notifies a person named in the report, that person shall maintain for the period of three years from the date of filing of the report any records that person has as to the matter in question and shall make those records available upon request to the board to which the report was sent.

(i) Notwithstanding any other provision of law, no insurer shall enter into a settlement without the written consent of the insured, except that this prohibition shall not void any settlement entered into without that written consent. The requirement of written consent shall only be waived by both the insured and the insurer.

(j) (1) A state or local governmental agency that self-insures licensees shall, prior to sending a report pursuant to this section, do all of the following with respect to each licensee who will be identified in the report:

(A) Before deciding that a licensee will be identified, provide written notice to the licensee that the agency intends to submit a report in which the licensee may be identified, based on the licensee's role in the care or professional services provided to the patient that were at issue in the claim or action. This notice shall describe the reasons for notifying the licensee. The agency shall include with this notice a reasonable opportunity for the licensee to review a copy of records to be used by the agency in deciding whether to identify the licensee in the report.

(B) Provide the licensee with a reasonable opportunity to provide a written response to the agency and written materials in support of the licensee's position. If the licensee is identified in the report, the agency shall include this response and materials in the report submitted to a board under this section if requested by the licensee.

(C) At least 10 days prior to the expiration of the 30-day reporting requirement under subdivision (d), provide the licensee with the opportunity to present arguments to the body that will make the final decision or to that body's designee. The body shall review the care or professional services provided to the patient with respect to those services at issue in the claim or action and determine the licensee or licensees to be identified in the report and the amount of the settlement to be apportioned to the licensee.

(2) Nothing in this subdivision shall be construed to modify either the content of a report required under this section or the timeframe for filing that report.

(k) For purposes of this section, "licensee" means a licensee of the Medical Board of California, the Osteopathic Medical Board of California, the California Board of Podiatric Medicine, or the Physician Assistant Board.

(Amended by Stats. 2021, Ch. 649, Sec. 2. (SB 806) Effective January 1, 2022.)

801.1. REPORTS OF SETTLEMENTS OR ARBITRATION AWARDS FOR DAMAGES FOR DEATH OR PERSONAL INJURY

(a) Every state or local governmental agency that self-insures a person who holds a license, certificate, or similar authority from or under any agency specified in subdivision (a) of Section 800 (except a person licensed pursuant to Chapter 3 (commencing with Section 1200) or Chapter 5 (commencing with Section 2000) or the Osteopathic Initiative Act) shall send a complete report to that agency as to any settlement or arbitration award over three thousand dollars ($3,000) of a claim or action for damages for death or personal injury caused by that person's negligence, error, or omission in practice, or rendering of unauthorized professional services. The report shall be sent within 30 days after the written settlement agreement has been reduced to writing and signed by all parties thereto or within 30 days after service of the arbitration award on the parties.

(b) Every state or local governmental agency that self-insures a person licensed pursuant to Chapter 13 (commencing with Section 4980), Chapter 14 (commencing with Section 4990), or Chapter 16 (commencing with Section 4999.10) shall send a complete report to the Board of Behavioral Science Examiners as to any settlement or arbitration award over ten thousand dollars ($10,000) of a claim or action for damages for death or personal injury caused by that person's negligence, error, or omission in practice, or rendering of unauthorized professional services.

The report shall be sent within 30 days after the written settlement agreement has been reduced to writing and signed by all parties thereto or within 30 days after service of the arbitration award on the parties.

(Amended by Stats. 2011, Ch. 381, Sec. 7. (SB 146) Effective January 1, 2012.)

802. REPORTS OF MALPRACTICE SETTLEMENTS OR ARBITRATION AWARDS INVOLVING UNINSURED LICENSEES; PENALTIES FOR NONCOMPLIANCE

(a) Every settlement, judgment, or arbitration award over three thousand dollars ($3,000) of a claim or action for damages for death or personal injury caused by negligence, error or omission in practice, or by the unauthorized rendering of professional services, by a person who holds a license, certificate, or other similar authority from an agency specified in subdivision (a) of Section 800 (except a person licensed pursuant to Chapter 3 (commencing with Section 1200) or Chapter 5 (commencing with Section 2000) or the Osteopathic Initiative Act) who does not possess professional liability insurance as to that claim shall, within 30 days after the written settlement agreement has been reduced to writing and signed by all the parties thereto or 30 days after service of the judgment or arbitration award on the parties, be reported to the agency that issued the license, certificate, or similar authority. A complete report shall be made by appropriate means by the person or his or her counsel, with a copy of the communication to be sent to the claimant through his or her counsel if the person is so represented, or directly if he or she is not. If, within 45 days of the conclusion of the written settlement agreement or service of the judgment or arbitration award on the parties, counsel for the claimant (or if the claimant is not represented by counsel, the claimant himself or herself) has not received a copy of the report, he or she shall himself or herself make the complete report.

Failure of the licensee or claimant (or, if represented by counsel, their counsel) to comply with this section is a public offense punishable by a fine of not less than fifty dollars ($50) or more than five hundred dollars ($500). Knowing and intentional failure to comply with this section or conspiracy or collusion not to comply with this section, or to hinder or impede any other person in the compliance, is a public offense punishable by a fine of not less than five thousand dollars ($5,000) nor more than fifty thousand dollars ($50,000).

(b) Every settlement, judgment, or arbitration award over ten thousand dollars ($10,000) of a claim or action for damages for death or personal injury caused by negligence, error or omission in practice, or by the unauthorized rendering of professional services, by a marriage and family therapist, a clinical social worker, or a professional clinical counselor licensed pursuant to Chapter 13 (commencing with Section 4980), Chapter 14 (commencing with Section 4990), or Chapter 16 (commencing with Section 4999.10), respectively, who does not possess professional liability insurance as to that claim shall within 30 days after the written settlement agreement has been reduced to writing and signed by all the parties thereto or 30 days after service of the judgment or arbitration award on the parties be reported to the agency that issued the license, certificate, or similar authority. A complete report shall be made by appropriate means by the person or his or her counsel, with a copy of the communication to be sent to the claimant through his or her counsel if he or she is so represented, or directly if he or she is not. If, within 45 days of the conclusion of the written settlement agreement or service of the judgment or arbitration award on the parties, counsel for the claimant (or if he or she is not represented by counsel, the claimant himself or herself) has not received a copy of the report, he or she shall himself or herself make a complete report. Failure of the marriage and family therapist, clinical social worker, or professional clinical counselor or claimant (or, if represented by counsel, his or her counsel) to comply with this section is a public offense punishable by a fine of not less than fifty dollars ($50) nor more than five hundred dollars ($500). Knowing and intentional failure to comply with this section, or conspiracy or collusion not to comply with this section or to hinder or impede any other person in that compliance, is a public offense punishable by a fine of not less than five thousand dollars ($5,000) nor more than fifty thousand dollars ($50,000).

(Amended by Stats. 2011, Ch. 381, Sec. 8. (SB 146) Effective January 1, 2012.)

803. REPORT OF CRIME OR LIABILITY FOR DEATH OR INJURY ON PART OF SPECIFIED LICENSEES TO LICENSING AGENCY

(a) Except as provided in subdivision (b), within 10 days after a judgment by a court of this state that a person who holds a license, certificate, or other similar authority from the Board of Behavioral Sciences or from an agency mentioned in subdivision (a) of Section 800 (except a person licensed pursuant to Chapter 3 (commencing with Section 1200)) has committed a crime, or is liable for any death or personal injury resulting in a judgment for an amount in excess of thirty thousand dollars ($30,000) caused by his or her negligence, error or omission in practice, or his or her rendering unauthorized professional services, the clerk of the court that rendered the judgment shall report that fact to the agency that issued the license, certificate, or other similar authority.

(b) For purposes of a physician and surgeon, osteopathic physician and surgeon, doctor of podiatric medicine, or physician assistant, who is liable for any death or personal injury resulting in a judgment of any amount caused by his or her negligence, error or omission in practice, or his or her rendering unauthorized professional services, the clerk of the court that rendered the judgment shall report that fact to the agency that issued the license.

(Amended by Stats. 2012, Ch. 332, Sec. 5. (SB 1236) Effective January 1, 2013.)

803.1. DISCLOSURE OF ENFORCEMENT ACTIONS

(a) Notwithstanding any other law, the Medical Board of California, the Osteopathic Medical Board of California, the California Board of Podiatric Medicine, and the Physician Assistant Board shall disclose to an inquiring member of the public information regarding any enforcement actions taken against a licensee, including a former licensee, by the board or by another state or jurisdiction, including all of the following:

(1) Temporary restraining orders issued.

(2) Interim suspension orders issued.

(3) Revocations, suspensions, probations, or limitations on practice ordered by the board, including those made part of a probationary order or stipulated agreement.

(4) Public letters of reprimand issued.

(5) Infractions, citations, or fines imposed.

(b) Notwithstanding any other law, in addition to the information provided in subdivision (a), the Medical Board of California, the Osteopathic Medical Board of California, the California Board of Podiatric Medicine, and the Physician Assistant Board shall disclose to an inquiring member of the public all of the following:

(1) Civil judgments in any amount, whether or not vacated by a settlement after entry of the judgment, that were not reversed on appeal and arbitration awards in any amount of a claim or action for damages for death or personal injury caused by the licensee's negligence, error, or omission in practice, or by rendering unauthorized professional services.

(2) (A) All settlements in the possession, custody, or control of the board shall be disclosed for a licensee in the low-risk category if there are three or more settlements for that licensee within the last 10 years, except for settlements by a licensee regardless of the amount paid where (i) the settlement is made as a part of the settlement of a class claim, (ii) the licensee paid in settlement of the class claim the same amount as the other licensees in the same class or similarly situated licensees in the same class, and (iii) the settlement was paid in the context of a case where the complaint that alleged class liability on behalf of the licensee also alleged a products liability class action cause of action. All settlements in the possession, custody, or control of the board shall be disclosed for a licensee in the high-risk category if there are four or more settlements for that licensee within the last 10 years except for settlements by a licensee regardless of the amount paid where (i) the settlement is made as a part of the settlement of a class claim, (ii) the licensee paid in settlement of the class claim the same amount as the other licensees in the same class or similarly situated licensees in the same class, and (iii) the settlement was paid in the context of a case where the complaint that alleged class liability on behalf of the licensee also alleged a products liability class action cause of action. Classification of a licensee in either a "high-risk category" or a "low-risk category" depends upon the specialty or subspecialty practiced by the licensee and the designation assigned to that specialty or subspecialty by the Medical Board of California, as described in subdivision (f). For the purposes of this paragraph, "settlement" means a settlement of an action described in paragraph (1) entered into by the licensee on or after January 1, 2003, in an amount of thirty thousand dollars ($30,000) or more.

(B) The board shall not disclose the actual dollar amount of a settlement but shall put the number and amount of the settlement in context by doing the following:

(i) Comparing the settlement amount to the experience of other licensees within the same specialty or subspecialty, indicating if it is below average, average, or above average for the most recent 10-year period.

(ii) Reporting the number of years the licensee has been in practice.

(iii) Reporting the total number of licensees in that specialty or subspecialty, the number of those who have entered into a settlement agreement, and the percentage that number represents of the total number of licensees in the specialty or subspecialty.

(3) Current American Board of Medical Specialties certification or board equivalent as certified by the Medical Board of California, the Osteopathic Medical Board of California, or the California Board of Podiatric Medicine.

(4) Approved postgraduate training.

(5) Status of the license of a licensee. By January 1, 2004, the Medical Board of California, the Osteopathic Medical Board of California, and the California Board of Podiatric Medicine shall adopt regulations defining the status of a licensee. The board shall employ this definition when disclosing the status of a licensee pursuant to Section 2027.

(6) Any summaries of hospital disciplinary actions that result in the termination or revocation of a licensee's staff privileges for medical disciplinary cause or reason, unless a court finds, in a final judgment, that the peer review resulting in the disciplinary action was conducted in bad faith and the licensee notifies the board of that finding. In addition, any exculpatory or explanatory statements submitted by the licentiate electronically pursuant to subdivision (f) of Section 805 shall be disclosed. For purposes of this paragraph, "peer review" has the same meaning as defined in Section 805.

(c) Notwithstanding any other law, the Medical Board of California, the Osteopathic Medical Board of California, the California Board of Podiatric Medicine, and the Physician Assistant Board shall disclose to an inquiring member of the public information received regarding felony convictions of a licensee.

(d) The Medical Board of California, the Osteopathic Medical Board of California, the California Board of Podiatric Medicine, and the Physician Assistant Board may formulate appropriate disclaimers or explanatory statements to be included with any information released, and may by regulation establish categories of information that need not be disclosed to an inquiring member of the public because that information is unreliable or not sufficiently related to the licensee's professional practice. The Medical Board of California, the Osteopathic Medical Board of California, the California Board of Podiatric Medicine, and the Physician Assistant Board shall include the following statement when disclosing information concerning a settlement:

"Some studies have shown that there is no significant correlation between malpractice history and a licensee's competence. At the same time, the State of California believes that consumers should have access to malpractice information. In these profiles, the State of California has given you information about both the malpractice settlement history for the licensee's specialty and the licensee's history of settlement payments only if in the last 10 years, the licensee, if in a low-risk specialty, has three or more settlements or the licensee, if in a high-risk specialty, has four or more settlements. The State of California has excluded some class action lawsuits because those cases are commonly related to systems issues such as product liability, rather than questions of individual professional competence and because they are brought on a class basis where the economic incentive for settlement is great. The State of California has placed payment amounts into three statistical categories: below average, average, and above average compared to others in the licensee's specialty. To make the best health care decisions, you should view this information in perspective. You could miss an opportunity for high-quality care by selecting a licensee based solely on malpractice history.

When considering malpractice data, please keep in mind:

Malpractice histories tend to vary by specialty. Some specialties are more likely than others to be the subject of litigation. This report compares licensees only to the members of their specialty, not to all licensees, in order to make an individual licensee's history more meaningful.

This report reflects data only for settlements made on or after January 1, 2003. Moreover, it includes information concerning those settlements for a 10-year period only. Therefore, you should know that a licensee may have made settlements in the 10 years immediately preceding January 1, 2003, that are not included in this report. After January 1, 2013, for licensees practicing less than 10 years, the data covers their total years of practice. You should take into account the effective date of settlement disclosure as well as how long the licensee has been in practice when considering malpractice averages.

The incident causing the malpractice claim may have happened years before a payment is finally made. Sometimes, it takes a long time for a malpractice lawsuit to settle. Some licensees work primarily with high-risk patients. These licensees may have malpractice settlement histories that are higher than average because they specialize in cases or patients who are at very high risk for problems.

Settlement of a claim may occur for a variety of reasons that do not necessarily reflect negatively on the professional competence or conduct of the licensee. A payment in settlement of a medical malpractice action or claim should not be construed as creating a presumption that medical malpractice has occurred.

You may wish to discuss information in this report and the general issue of malpractice with the licensee."

(e) The Medical Board of California, the Osteopathic Medical Board of California, the California Board of Podiatric Medicine, and the Physician Assistant Board shall, by regulation, develop standard terminology that accurately describes the different types of disciplinary filings and actions to take against a licensee as described in paragraphs (1) to (5), inclusive, of subdivision (a). In providing the public with information about a licensee via the internet pursuant to Section 2027, the Medical Board of California, the Osteopathic Medical Board of California, the California Board of Podiatric Medicine, and the Physician Assistant Board shall not use the terms "enforcement," "discipline," or similar language implying a sanction unless the licensee has been the subject of one of the actions described in paragraphs (1) to (5), inclusive, of subdivision (a).

(f) The Medical Board of California shall adopt regulations no later than July 1, 2003, designating each specialty and subspecialty practice area as either high risk or low risk. In promulgating these regulations, the board shall consult with commercial underwriters of medical malpractice insurance companies, health care systems that self-insure physicians and surgeons, and representatives of the California medical specialty societies. The board shall utilize the carriers' statewide data to establish the two risk categories and the averages required by subparagraph (B) of paragraph (2) of subdivision (b). Prior to issuing regulations, the board shall convene public meetings with the medical malpractice carriers, self-insurers, and specialty representatives.

(g) The Medical Board of California, the Osteopathic Medical Board of California, the California Board of Podiatric Medicine, and the Physician Assistant Board shall provide each licensee, including a former licensee under subdivision (a), with a copy of the text of any proposed public disclosure authorized by this section prior to release of the disclosure to the public. The licensee shall have 10 working days from the date the board provides the copy of the proposed public disclosure to propose corrections of factual inaccuracies. Nothing in this section shall prevent the board from disclosing information to the public prior to the expiration of the 10-day period.

(h) Pursuant to subparagraph (A) of paragraph (2) of subdivision (b), the specialty or subspecialty information required by this section shall group licensees by specialty board recognized pursuant to paragraph (5) of subdivision (h) of Section 651 unless a different grouping would be more valid and the board, in its statement of reasons for its regulations, explains why the validity of the grouping would be more valid.

(Amended by Stats. 2019, Ch. 456, Sec. 1. (SB 786) Effective January 1, 2020.)

803.5. NOTICE TO BOARD OF FILING CHARGING LICENSEE WITH FELONY; TRANSMITTAL OF COPY OF CONVICTION

(a) The district attorney, city attorney, or other prosecuting agency shall notify the Medical Board of California, the Osteopathic Medical Board of California, the California Board of Podiatric Medicine, the State Board of Chiropractic Examiners, the Physician Assistant Board, or other appropriate allied health board, and the clerk of the court in which the charges have been filed, of any filings against a licensee of that board charging a felony immediately upon obtaining information that the defendant is a licensee of the board. The notice shall identify the licensee and describe the crimes charged and the facts alleged. The prosecuting agency shall also notify the clerk of the court in which the action is pending that the defendant is a licensee, and the clerk shall record prominently in the file that the defendant holds a license from one of the boards described above.

(b) The clerk of the court in which a licensee of one of the boards is convicted of a crime shall, within 48 hours after the conviction, transmit a certified copy of the record of conviction to the applicable board.

(Amended by Stats. 2012, Ch. 332, Sec. 7. (SB 1236) Effective January 1, 2013.)

803.6. TRANSMITTAL OF FELONY PRELIMINARY HEARING TRANSCRIPT CONCERNING LICENSEE TO BOARD; TRANSMITTAL OF PROBATION REPORT

(a) The clerk of the court shall transmit any felony preliminary hearing transcript concerning a defendant licensee to the Medical Board of California, the Osteopathic Medical Board of California, the California Board of Podiatric Medicine, the Physician Assistant Board, or other appropriate allied health board, as applicable, where the total length of the transcript is under 800 pages and shall notify the appropriate board of any proceeding where the transcript exceeds that length.

(b) In any case where a probation report on a licensee is prepared for a court pursuant to Section 1203 of the Penal Code, a copy of that report shall be transmitted by the probation officer to the board.

(Amended by Stats. 2012, Ch. 332, Sec. 8. (SB 1236) Effective January 1, 2013.)

804. FORM AND CONTENT OF REPORT

(a) Any agency to whom reports are to be sent under Section 801, 801.1, 802, or 803, may develop a prescribed form for the making of the reports, usage of which it may, but need not, by regulation, require in all cases.

(b) A report required to be made by Sections 801, 801.1, or 802 shall be deemed complete only if it includes the following information: (1) the name and last known business and residential addresses of every plaintiff or claimant involved in the matter, whether or not each plaintiff or claimant recovered anything; (2) the name and last known business and residential addresses of every physician or provider of health care services who was claimed or alleged to have acted improperly, whether or not that person was a named defendant and whether or not any recovery or judgment was had against that person; (3) the name, address, and principal place of business of every insurer providing professional liability insurance as to any person named in (2), and the insured's policy number; (4) the name of the court in which the action or any part of the action was filed along with the date of filing and docket number of each action; (5) a brief description or summary of the facts upon which each claim, charge or judgment rested including the date of occurrence; (6) the names and last known business and residential addresses of every person who acted as counsel for any party in the litigation or negotiations, along with an identification of the party whom said person represented; (7) the date and amount of final judgment or settlement; and (8) any other information the agency to whom the reports are to be sent may, by regulation, require.

(c) Every person named in the report, who is notified by the board within 60 days of the filing of the report, shall maintain for the period of three years from the filing of the report any records he or she has as to the matter in question and shall make those available upon request to the agency with which the report was filed.

(Amended by Stats. 2006, Ch. 223, Sec. 14. Effective January 1, 2007.)

805. DEFINITIONS

(a) As used in this section, the following terms have the following definitions:

(1) (A) "Peer review" means both of the following:

(i) A process in which a peer review body reviews the basic qualifications, staff privileges, employment, medical outcomes, or professional conduct of licentiates to make recommendations for quality improvement and education, if necessary, in order to do either or both of the following:

(I) Determine whether a licentiate may practice or continue to practice in a health care facility, clinic, or other setting providing medical services, and, if so, to determine the parameters of that practice.

(II) Assess and improve the quality of care rendered in a health care facility, clinic, or other setting providing medical services.

(ii) Any other activities of a peer review body as specified in subparagraph (B).

(B) "Peer review body" includes:

(i) A medical or professional staff of any health care facility or clinic licensed under Division 2 (commencing with Section 1200) of the Health and Safety Code or of a facility certified to participate in the federal Medicare program as an ambulatory surgical center.

(ii) A health care service plan licensed under Chapter 2.2 (commencing with Section 1340) of Division 2 of the Health and Safety Code or a disability insurer that contracts with licentiates to provide services at alternative rates of payment pursuant to Section 10133 of the Insurance Code.

(iii) Any medical, psychological, marriage and family therapy, social work, professional clinical counselor, dental, midwifery, or podiatric professional society having as members at least 25 percent of the eligible licentiates in the area in which it functions (which must include at least one county), which is not organized for profit and which has been determined to be exempt from taxes pursuant to Section 23701 of the Revenue and Taxation Code.

(iv) A committee organized by any entity consisting of or employing more than 25 licentiates of the same class that functions for the purpose of reviewing the quality of professional care provided by members or employees of that entity.

(2) "Licentiate" means a physician and surgeon, doctor of podiatric medicine, clinical psychologist, marriage and family therapist, clinical social worker, professional clinical counselor, dentist, licensed midwife, physician assistant, or nurse practitioner practicing pursuant to

Section 2837.103 or 2837.104. "Licentiate" also includes a person authorized to practice medicine pursuant to Section 2113 or 2168.

(3) "Agency" means the relevant state licensing agency having regulatory jurisdiction over the licentiates listed in paragraph (2).

(4) "Staff privileges" means any arrangement under which a licentiate is allowed to practice in or provide care for patients in a health facility. Those arrangements shall include, but are not limited to, full staff privileges, active staff privileges, limited staff privileges, auxiliary staff privileges, provisional staff privileges, temporary staff privileges, courtesy staff privileges, locum tenens arrangements, and contractual arrangements to provide professional services, including, but not limited to, arrangements to provide outpatient services.

(5) "Denial or termination of staff privileges, membership, or employment" includes failure or refusal to renew a contract or to renew, extend, or reestablish any staff privileges, if the action is based on medical disciplinary cause or reason.

(6) "Medical disciplinary cause or reason" means that aspect of a licentiate's competence or professional conduct that is reasonably likely to be detrimental to patient safety or to the delivery of patient care.

(7) "805 report" means the written report required under subdivision (b).

(b) The chief of staff of a medical or professional staff or other chief executive officer, medical director, or administrator of any peer review body and the chief executive officer or administrator of any licensed health care facility or clinic shall file an 805 report with the relevant agency within 15 days after the effective date on which any of the following occur as a result of an action of a peer review body:

(1) A licentiate's application for staff privileges or membership is denied or rejected for a medical disciplinary cause or reason.

(2) A licentiate's membership, staff privileges, or employment is terminated or revoked for a medical disciplinary cause or reason.

(3) Restrictions are imposed, or voluntarily accepted, on staff privileges, membership, or employment for a cumulative total of 30 days or more for any 12-month period, for a medical disciplinary cause or reason.

(c) If a licentiate takes any action listed in paragraph (1), (2), or (3) after receiving notice of a pending investigation initiated for a medical disciplinary cause or reason or after receiving notice that their application for membership or staff privileges is denied or will be denied for a medical disciplinary cause or reason, the chief of staff of a medical or professional staff or other chief executive officer, medical director, or administrator of any peer review body and the chief executive officer or administrator of any licensed health care facility or clinic where the licentiate is employed or has staff privileges or membership or where the licentiate applied for staff privileges or membership, or sought the renewal thereof, shall file an 805 report with the relevant agency within 15 days after the licentiate takes the action.

(1) Resigns or takes a leave of absence from membership, staff privileges, or employment.

(2) Withdraws or abandons their application for staff privileges or membership.

(3) Withdraws or abandons their request for renewal of staff privileges or membership.

(d) For purposes of filing an 805 report, the signature of at least one of the individuals indicated in subdivision (b) or (c) on the completed form shall constitute compliance with the requirement to file the report.

(e) An 805 report shall also be filed within 15 days following the imposition of summary suspension of staff privileges, membership, or employment, if the summary suspension remains in effect for a period in excess of 14 days.

(f) (1) A copy of the 805 report, and a notice advising the licentiate of their right to submit additional statements or other information, electronically or otherwise, pursuant to Section 800, shall be sent by the peer review body to the licentiate named in the report. The notice shall also advise the licentiate that information submitted electronically will be publicly disclosed to those who request the information.

(2) The information to be reported in an 805 report shall include the name and license number of the licentiate involved, a description of the facts and circumstances of the medical disciplinary cause or reason, and any other relevant information deemed appropriate by the reporter.

(3) A supplemental report shall also be made within 30 days following the date the licentiate is deemed to have satisfied any terms, conditions, or sanctions imposed as disciplinary action by the reporting peer review body. In performing its dissemination functions required by Section 805.5, the agency shall include a copy of a supplemental report, if any, whenever it furnishes a copy of the original 805 report.

(4) If another peer review body is required to file an 805 report, a health care service plan is not required to file a separate report with respect to action attributable to the same medical disciplinary cause or reason. If the Medical Board of California or a licensing agency of another state revokes or suspends, without a stay, the license of a physician and surgeon, a peer review body is not required to file an 805 report when it takes an action as a result of the revocation or suspension. If the California Board of Podiatric Medicine or a licensing agency of another state revokes or suspends, without a stay, the license of a doctor of podiatric medicine, a peer review body is not required to file an 805 report when it takes an action as a result of the revocation or suspension. If the Board of Registered Nursing or a licensing agency of another state revokes or suspends, without a stay, the license of a nurse practitioner, a peer review body is not required to file an 805 report when it takes an action as a result of the revocation or suspension.

(g) The reporting required by this section shall not act as a waiver of confidentiality of medical records and committee reports. The information reported or disclosed shall be kept confidential except as provided in subdivision (c) of Section 800 and Sections 803.1 and 2027, provided that a copy of the report containing the information required by this section may be disclosed as required by Section 805.5 with respect to reports received on or after January 1, 1976.

(h) The Medical Board of California, the California Board of Podiatric Medicine, the Osteopathic Medical Board of California, the Dental Board of California, and the Board of Registered Nursing shall disclose reports as required by Section 805.5.

(i) An 805 report shall be maintained electronically by an agency for dissemination purposes for a period of three years after receipt.

(j) No person shall incur any civil or criminal liability as the result of making any report required by this section.

(k) A willful failure to file an 805 report by any person who is designated or otherwise required by law to file an 805 report is punishable by a fine not to exceed one hundred thousand dollars ($100,000) per violation. The fine may be imposed in any civil or administrative action or proceeding brought by or on behalf of any agency having regulatory jurisdiction over the person regarding whom the report was or should have been filed. If the person who is designated or otherwise required to file an 805 report is a licensed physician and surgeon, the action or proceeding shall be brought by the Medical Board of California. If the person who is designated or otherwise required to file an 805 report is a licensed doctor of podiatric medicine, the action or proceeding shall be brought by the California Board of Podiatric Medicine. If the person who is designated or otherwise required to file an 805 report is a licensed nurse practitioner, the action or proceeding shall be brought by the Board of Registered Nursing. The fine shall be paid to that agency but not expended until appropriated by the Legislature. A violation of this subdivision may constitute unprofessional conduct by the licentiate. A person who is alleged to have violated this subdivision may assert any defense available at law. As used in this subdivision, "willful" means a voluntary and intentional violation of a known legal duty.

(l) Except as otherwise provided in subdivision (k), any failure by the administrator of any peer review body, the chief executive officer or administrator of any health care facility, or any person who is designated or otherwise required by law to file an 805 report, shall be punishable by a fine that under no circumstances shall exceed fifty thousand dollars ($50,000) per violation. The fine may be imposed in any civil or administrative action or proceeding brought by or on behalf of any agency having regulatory jurisdiction over the person regarding whom the report was or should have been filed. If the person who is designated or otherwise required to file an 805 report is a licensed physician and surgeon, the action or proceeding shall be brought by the Medical Board of California. If the person who is designated or otherwise required to file an 805 report is a licensed doctor of podiatric medicine, the action or proceeding shall be brought by the California Board of Podiatric Medicine. If the person who is designated or otherwise required to file an 805 report is a licensed nurse practitioner, the action or proceeding shall be brought by the Board of Registered Nursing. The fine shall be paid to that agency but not expended until appropriated by the Legislature. The amount of the fine imposed, not exceeding fifty thousand dollars ($50,000) per violation, shall be proportional to the severity of the failure to report and shall differ based upon written findings, including whether the failure to file caused harm to a patient or created a risk to patient safety; whether the administrator of any peer review body, the chief executive officer or administrator of any health care facility, or any person who is designated or otherwise required by law to file an 805 report exercised due diligence despite the failure to file or whether they knew or should have known that an 805 report would not be filed; and whether there has been a prior failure to file an 805 report. The amount of the fine imposed may also differ based on whether a health care facility is a small or rural hospital as defined in Section 124840 of the Health and Safety Code.

(m) A health care service plan licensed under Chapter 2.2 (commencing with Section 1340) of Division 2 of the Health and Safety Code or a disability insurer that negotiates and enters into a contract with licentiates to provide services at alternative rates of payment pursuant to Section 10133 of the Insurance Code, when determining participation with the plan or insurer, shall evaluate, on a case-by-case basis, licentiates who are the subject of an 805 report, and not automatically exclude or deselect these licentiates.

(Amended by Stats. 2020, Ch. 265, Sec. 2. (AB 890) Effective January 1, 2021.)

805.8. REPORTING ALLEGATIONS OF SEXUAL ABUSE OR MISCONDUCT

(a) As used in this section, the following terms shall have the following meanings:

(1) "Agency" means the relevant state licensing agency with regulatory

jurisdiction over a healing arts licensee listed in paragraph (2).

(2) "Healing arts licensee" or "licensee" means a licensee licensed under Division 2 (commencing with Section 500) or any initiative act referred to in that division. "Healing arts licensee" or "licensee" also includes a person authorized to practice medicine pursuant to Sections 2064.5, 2113, and 2168.

(3) "Health care facility" means a clinic or health facility licensed or exempt from licensure pursuant to Division 2 (commencing with Section 1200) of the Health and Safety Code.

(4) "Other entity" includes, but is not limited to, a postsecondary educational institution as defined in Section 66261.5 of the Education Code.

(5) "Sexual misconduct" means inappropriate contact or communication of a sexual nature.

(b) A health care facility or other entity that makes any arrangement under which a healing arts licensee is allowed to practice or provide care for patients shall file a report of any allegation of sexual abuse or sexual misconduct made against a healing arts licensee by a patient, if the patient or the patient's representative makes the allegation, in writing, to the agency within 15 days of receiving the written allegation of sexual abuse or sexual misconduct. An arrangement under which a licensee is allowed to practice or provide care for patients includes, but is not limited to, full staff privileges, active staff privileges, limited staff privileges, auxiliary staff privileges, provisional staff privileges, temporary staff privileges, courtesy staff privileges, locum tenens arrangements, and contractual arrangements to provide professional services, including, but not limited to, arrangements to provide outpatient services.

(c) The report provided pursuant to subdivision (b) shall be kept confidential and shall not be subject to discovery, except that the information may be reviewed as provided in subdivision (c) of Section 800 and may be disclosed in any subsequent disciplinary hearing conducted pursuant to the Administrative Procedure Act (Chapter 5 (commencing with Section 11500) of Part 1 of Division 3 of Title 2 of the Government Code).

(d) A willful failure to file the report described in subdivision (b) shall be punishable by a fine, not to exceed one hundred thousand dollars ($100,000) per violation, that shall be paid by the health care facility or other entity subject to subdivision (b). The fine may be imposed in any civil or administrative action or proceeding brought by or on behalf of any agency having regulatory jurisdiction over the licensee regarding whom the report was or should have been filed. If the person who is designated or otherwise required to file the report under this section is a licensed physician and surgeon, the action or proceeding shall be brought by the Medical Board of California. If the person who is designated or otherwise required to file the report required under this section is a licensed doctor of podiatric medicine, the action or proceeding shall be brought by the Podiatric Medical Board of California. The fine shall be paid to that agency, but not expended until appropriated by the Legislature. A violation of this subdivision may constitute unprofessional conduct by the licensee. A person who is alleged to have violated this subdivision may assert any defense available at law. As used in this subdivision, "willful" means a voluntary and intentional violation of a known legal duty.

(e) Except as provided in subdivision (c), any failure to file the report described in subdivision (b) is punishable by a fine, not to exceed fifty thousand dollars ($50,000) per violation, that shall be paid by the health care facility or other entity subject to subdivision (b). The fine may be imposed in any civil or administrative action or proceeding brought by or on behalf of any agency having regulatory jurisdiction over the person regarding whom the report was or should have been filed. If the person who is designated or otherwise required to file the report required under this section is a licensed physician and surgeon, the action or proceeding shall be brought by the Medical Board of California. If the person who is designated or otherwise required to file the report required under this section is a licensed doctor of podiatric medicine, the action or proceeding shall be brought by the Podiatric Medical Board of California. The fine shall be paid to that agency, but not expended until appropriated by the Legislature. The amount of the fine imposed, not exceeding fifty thousand dollars ($50,000) per violation, shall be proportional to the severity of the failure to report and shall differ based upon written findings, including whether the failure to file caused harm to a patient or created a risk to patient safety; whether any person who is designated or otherwise required by law to file the report required under this section exercised due diligence despite the failure to file or whether the person knew or should have known that a report required under this section would not be filed; whether there has been a prior failure to file a report required under this section; and whether a report was filed with another state agency or law enforcement. The amount of the fine imposed may also differ based on whether a health care facility is a small or rural hospital, as defined in Section 124840 of the Health and Safety Code.

(f) A person, including an employee or individual contracted or subcontracted to provide health care services, a health care facility, or other entity shall not incur any civil or criminal liability as a result of making a report required by this section.

(g) The agency shall investigate the circumstances underlying a report received pursuant to this section.

(Amended by Stats. 2020, Ch. 370, Sec. 4. (SB 1371) Effective January 1, 2021.)

806. STATISTICAL REPORTS AND RECOMMENDATIONS TO LEGISLATURE

Each agency in the department receiving reports pursuant to the preceding sections shall prepare a statistical report based upon these records for presentation to the Legislature not later than 30 days after the commencement of each regular session of the Legislature, including by the type of peer review body, and, where applicable, type of health care facility, the number of reports received and a summary of administrative and disciplinary action taken with respect to these reports and any recommendations for corrective legislation if the agency considers legislation to be necessary.

(Amended by Stats. 2001, Ch. 614, Sec. 8. Effective January 1, 2002.)

ARTICLE 12: INSURANCE FRAUD

810. GROUNDS FOR DISCIPLINARY ACTION AGAINST HEALTH CARE PROFESSIONAL

(a) It shall constitute unprofessional conduct and grounds for disciplinary action, including suspension or revocation of a license or certificate, for a health care professional to do any of the following in connection with their professional activities:

(1) Knowingly present or cause to be presented any false or fraudulent claim for the payment of a loss under a contract of insurance.

(2) Knowingly prepare, make, or subscribe any writing, with intent to present or use the same, or to allow it to be presented or used in support of any false or fraudulent claim.

(b) It shall constitute cause for revocation or suspension of a license or certificate for a health care professional to engage in any conduct prohibited under Section

1871.4 of the Insurance Code or Section 549 or 550 of the Penal Code.

(c) (1) It shall constitute cause for automatic suspension of a license or certificate issued pursuant to Chapter 4 (commencing with Section 1600), Chapter 5 (commencing with Section 2000), Chapter 6.6 (commencing with Section 2900), Chapter 7 (commencing with Section 3000), or Chapter 9 (commencing with Section 4000), or pursuant to the Chiropractic Act or the Osteopathic Act, if a licensee or certificate holder has been convicted of any felony involving fraud committed by the licensee or certificate holder in conjunction with providing benefits covered by worker's compensation insurance, or has been convicted of any felony involving Medi-Cal fraud committed by the licensee or certificate holder in conjunction with the Medi-Cal program, including the Denti-Cal element of the Medi-Cal program, pursuant to Chapter 7 (commencing with Section 14000), or Chapter 8 (commencing with Section 14200), of Part 3 of Division 9 of the Welfare and Institutions Code. The board shall convene a disciplinary hearing to determine whether or not the license or certificate shall be suspended, revoked, or some other disposition shall be considered, including, but not limited to, revocation with the opportunity to petition for reinstatement, suspension, or other limitations on the license or certificate as the board deems appropriate.

(2) It shall constitute cause for automatic suspension and for revocation of a license or certificate issued pursuant to Chapter 4 (commencing with Section 1600), Chapter 5 (commencing with Section 2000), Chapter 6.6 (commencing with Section 2900), Chapter 7 (commencing with Section 3000), or Chapter 9 (commencing with Section 4000), or pursuant to the Chiropractic Act or the Osteopathic Act, if a licensee or certificate holder has more than one conviction of any felony arising out of separate prosecutions involving fraud committed by the licensee or certificate holder in conjunction with providing benefits covered by worker's compensation insurance, or in conjunction with the Medi-Cal program, including the Denti-Cal element of the Medi-Cal program pursuant to Chapter 7 (commencing with Section 14000), or Chapter 8 (commencing with Section 14200), of Part 3 of Division 9 of the Welfare and Institutions Code. The board shall convene a disciplinary hearing to revoke the license or certificate and an order of revocation shall be issued unless the board finds mitigating circumstances to order some other disposition.

(3) It is the intent of the Legislature that paragraph (2) apply to a licensee or certificate holder who has one or more convictions prior to January 1, 2004, as provided in this subdivision.

(4) Nothing in this subdivision shall preclude a board from suspending or revoking a license or certificate pursuant to any other provision of law.

(5) "Board," as used in this subdivision, means the Dental Board of California, the Medical Board of California, the California Board of Podiatric Medicine, the Board of Psychology, the California State Board of Optometry, the California State Board of Pharmacy, the Osteopathic Medical Board of California, and the State Board of Chiropractic Examiners.

(6) "More than one conviction," as used in this subdivision, means that the licensee or certificate holder has one or more convictions prior to January 1, 2004, and at least one conviction on or after that date, or the licensee or certificate holder has two or more convictions on or after January 1, 2004. However, a licensee or certificate holder who has one or more convictions prior to January 1, 2004, but who has no convictions and is currently licensed or holds a certificate after that date, does not have "more than one conviction" for the purposes of this subdivision.

(d) As used in this section, health care professional means any person licensed or certified pursuant to this division, or licensed pursuant to the Osteopathic Initiative Act, or the Chiropractic Initiative Act.

(Amended by Stats. 2021, Ch. 630, Sec. 15. (AB 1534) Effective January 1, 2022.)

ARTICLE 12.5: MENTAL ILLNESS OR PHYSICAL ILLNESS

820. EXAMINATION OF LICENTIATE FOR MENTAL ILLNESS OR PHYSICAL ILLNESS AFFECTING COMPETENCY

Whenever it appears that any person holding a license, certificate or permit under this division or under any initiative act referred to in this division may be unable to practice his or her profession safely because the licentiate's ability to practice is impaired due to mental illness, or physical illness affecting competency, the licensing agency may order the licentiate to be examined by one or more physicians and surgeons or psychologists designated by the agency. The report of the examiners shall be made available to the licentiate and may be received as direct evidence in proceedings conducted pursuant to Section 822.

(Amended by Stats. 1989, Ch. 1104, Sec. 1.7.)

821. EFFECT OF LICENTIATE'S FAILURE TO COMPLY WITH ORDER FOR EXAMINATION

The licentiate's failure to comply with an order issued under Section 820 shall constitute grounds for the suspension or revocation of the licentiate's certificate or license.

(Added by Stats. 1982, Ch. 1183, Sec. 1.)

822. ACTION BY LICENSING AGENCY

If a licensing agency determines that its licentiate's ability to practice his or her profession safely is impaired because the licentiate is mentally ill, or physically ill affecting competency, the licensing agency may take action by any one of the following methods:

(a) Revoking the licentiate's certificate or license.

(b) Suspending the licentiate's right to practice.

(c) Placing the licentiate on probation.

(d) Taking such other action in relation to the licentiate as the licensing agency in its discretion deems proper.

The licensing agency shall not reinstate a revoked or suspended certificate or license until it has received competent evidence of the absence or control of the condition which caused its action and until it is satisfied that with due regard for the public health and safety the person's right to practice his or her profession may be safely reinstated.

(Added by Stats. 1982, Ch. 1183, Sec. 1.)

823. REINSTATEMENT OF LICENTIATE

Notwithstanding any other provisions of law, reinstatement of a licentiate against whom action has been taken pursuant to Section 822 shall be governed by the procedures in this article. In reinstating a certificate or license which has been revoked or suspended under Section 822, the licensing agency may impose terms and conditions to be complied with by the licentiate after the certificate or license has been reinstated. The authority of the licensing agency to impose terms and conditions includes, but is not limited to, the following:

(a) Requiring the licentiate to obtain additional professional training and to pass an examination upon the completion of the training.

(b) Requiring the licentiate to pass an oral, written, practical, or clinical examination, or any combination thereof to determine his or her present fitness to engage in the practice of his or her profession.

(c) Requiring the licentiate to submit to a complete diagnostic examination by one or more physicians and surgeons or psychologists appointed by the licensing agency. If the licensing agency requires the licentiate to submit to such an examination, the licensing agency shall receive and consider any other report of a complete diagnostic examination given by one or more physicians and surgeons or psychologists of the licentiate's choice.

(d) Requiring the licentiate to undergo continuing treatment.

(e) Restricting or limiting the extent, scope or type of practice of the licentiate.

(Added by Stats. 1982, Ch. 1183, Sec 1.)

824. OPTIONS OPEN TO LICENSING AGENCY WHEN PROCEEDING AGAINST LICENTIATE

The licensing agency may proceed against a licentiate under either Section 820, or 822, or under both sections.

(Added by Stats. 1982, Ch. 1183, Sec. 1.)

826. FORMAT OF PROCEEDINGS UNDER SECTION 821 AND 822; RIGHTS AND POWERS

The proceedings under Sections 821 and 822 shall be conducted in accordance with Chapter 5 (commencing with Section 11500) of Part 1 of Division 3 of Title 2 of the Government Code, and the licensing agency and the licentiate shall have all the rights and powers granted therein.

(Added by Stats. 1982, Ch. 1183, Sec. 1.)

827. AUTHORITY OF LICENSING AGENCY TO CONVENE IN CLOSED SESSION

Notwithstanding the provisions of Article 9 (commencing with Section 11120) of Chapter 1 of Part 1 of Division 3 of Title 2 of the Government Code, relating to public meetings, the licensing agency may convene in closed session to consider any evidence relating to the licentiate's mental or physical illness obtained pursuant to the proceedings under Section 820. The licensing agency shall only convene in closed session to the extent that it is necessary to protect the privacy of a licentiate.

(Added by Stats. 1982, Ch. 1183, Sec. 1.)

828. DETERMINATION OF INSUFFICIENT EVIDENCE TO BRING ACTION AGAINST LICENTIATE; EFFECT ON RECORDS OF PROCEEDINGS

If the licensing agency determines, pursuant to proceedings conducted under Section 820, that there is insufficient evidence to bring an action against the licentiate pursuant to Section 822, then all licensing agency records of the proceedings, including the order for the examination, investigative reports, if any, and the report of the physicians and surgeons or psychologists, shall be kept confidential and are not subject to discovery or subpoena. If no further proceedings are conducted to determine the licentiates fitness to practice during a period of five years from the date of the determination by the licensing agency of the proceeding pursuant to Section 820, then the licensing agency shall purge and destroy all records pertaining to the proceedings. If new proceedings are instituted during the five- year period against the licentiate by the licensing agency, the records, including the report of the physicians and surgeons or psychologists, may be used in the proceedings and shall be available to the respondent pursuant to the provisions of Section 11507.6 of the Government Code.

(Added by Stats. 1982, Ch. 1183, Sec. 1.)

ARTICLE 13: STANDARDS FOR LICENSURE OR CERTIFICATION

850. DELEGATION OF LICENSING STANDARDS; PROHIBITIONS

No healing arts licensing board or examining committee under the Department of Consumer Affairs shall by regulation require an applicant for licensure or certification to be a member of, to be certified by, to be eligible to be certified or registered by, or otherwise meet the standards of a specified private voluntary association or professional society except as provided for in this article.

(Added by Stats. 1978, Ch. 1106.)

850.1. NO DENIAL FOR ACTIONS BASED ON ANOTHER STATE'S LAW THAT INTERFERES WITH A PERSON'S RIGHT TO RECEIVE SENSITIVE SERVICES LAWFUL IN CALIFORNIA

(a) A healing arts board shall not deny an application for licensure or suspend, revoke, or otherwise impose discipline upon a licensee or health practitioner subject to this division on the basis of a civil judgment, criminal conviction, or disciplinary action in another state if that judgment, conviction, or disciplinary action is based solely on the application of another state's law that interferes with a person's right to receive sensitive services that would be lawful if provided in this state, regardless of the patient's location.

(b) This section does not apply to a civil judgment, criminal conviction, or disciplinary action imposed in another state based upon conduct in another state that would subject an applicant, licensee, or health care practitioner subject to this division to a similar claim, charge, or action under the laws of this state.

(c) For purposes of this section:

(1) "Healing arts board" means any board, division, or examining committee in the Department of Consumer Affairs that licenses or certifies health professionals.

(2) "Sensitive services" has the same meaning as in Section 56.05 of the Civil Code.

(Added by Stats. 2023, Ch. 258, Sec. 2. (AB 1707) Effective January 1, 2024. See same-numbered section added by Stats. 2023, Ch. 260.)

850.1. NO DENIAL FOR ACTIONS BASED ON ANOTHER STATE'S LAW THAT INTERFERES WITH A PERSON'S RIGHT TO RECEIVE SENSITIVE SERVICES LAWFUL IN CALIFORNIA

(a) A healing arts board shall not deny an application for licensure or suspend, revoke, or otherwise impose discipline upon a licensee or health care practitioner subject to this division on the basis of a civil judgment, criminal conviction, or disciplinary action in another state if that judgment, conviction, or disciplinary action is based solely on the application of another state's law that interferes with a person's right to receive sensitive services that would be lawful if provided in this state, regardless of the patient's location.

(b) This section does not apply to a civil judgment, criminal conviction, or disciplinary action imposed in another state based upon conduct in another state that would subject an applicant, licensee, or health care practitioner subject to this division to a similar claim, charge, or action under the laws of this state.

(c) For purposes of this section:

(1) "Healing arts board" means any board, division, or examining committee in the Department of Consumer Affairs that licenses or certifies health professionals.

(2) "Sensitive services" has the same meaning as in Section 56.05 of the Civil Code.

(Added by Stats. 2023, Ch. 260, Sec. 2. (SB 345) Effective January 1, 2024. See same-numbered section added by Stats. 2023, Ch. 258)

851. AUTHORIZED DELEGATION OF HEALING ARTS LICENSING STANDARDS

A healing arts licensure board or examining committee may by regulation require an applicant for licensure or certification to meet the standards of a specified private voluntary association or professional society when either of the following conditions is met:

(a) There is direct statutory authority or requirement that the board or examining committee utilize the standards of the specified private voluntary association or professional society; or

(b) The board or examining committee specifies in the regulation the amount of education, training, experience, examinations, or other requirements of the private voluntary association or professional society, which standards shall be consistent with the provisions of law regulating such licensees, and the board or examining committee adopts such standards in public hearing. The board or examining committee may, by regulation, require an applicant to successfully complete an examination conducted by or created by a relevant national certification association, testing firm, private voluntary association, or professional society.

Nothing in this section authorizes the Medical Board of California to limit the licensure of physicians and surgeons by specialty.

(Amended by Stats. 1989, Ch. 886, Sec. 15.)

856. CPR AND AED TRAINING APPLICABLE TOWARD ANNUAL CONTINUING EDUCATION CREDITS REQUIRED FOR LICENSE RENEWAL

(a) (1) A person licensed pursuant to this division who is required to complete continuing education units as a condition of renewing his or her license may, once per renewal cycle, apply one unit of continuing education credit, pursuant to paragraph (2), towards that requirement for attending a course that results in the licensee becoming a certified instructor of cardiopulmonary resuscitation (CPR) or the proper use of an automated external defibrillator (AED).

(2) A licensee may only apply continuing education credit for attending one of the following courses:

(A) An instructional program developed by the American Heart Association.

(B) An instructional program developed by the American Red Cross.

(C) An instructional program that is nationally recognized and based on the most current national evidence-based emergency cardiovascular care guidelines for the performance of CPR and the use of an AED.

(b) A person licensed pursuant to this division who is required to complete continuing education units as a condition of renewing his or her license may, once per renewal cycle, apply up to two units of continuing education credit towards that requirement for conducting CPR or AED training sessions for employees of school districts and community college districts in the state.

(c) For purposes of this section, "unit" means any measurement for continuing education, such as hours or course credits.

(d) This section shall only apply to a person licensed under this division if the applicable licensing board's laws or regulations establishing continuing education requirements include the courses or activities described in subdivisions (a) and (b).

(Added by Stats. 2015, Ch. 360, Sec. 1. (AB 333) Effective January 1, 2016.)

CHAPTER 1.5: EXEMPTION FROM LICENSURE

900. REQUIREMENTS FOR EXEMPTION IMMUNITY FROM LIABILITY

(a) Nothing in this division applies to a health care practitioner licensed in another state or territory of the United States who offers or provides health care for which he or she is licensed, if the health care is provided only during a state of emergency as defined in subdivision (b) of Section 8558 of the Government Code, which emergency overwhelms the response capabilities of California health care practitioners and only upon the request of the Director of the Emergency Medical Services Authority.

(b) The director shall be the medical control and shall designate the licensure and specialty health care practitioners required for the specific emergency and shall designate the areas to which they may be deployed.

(c) Health care practitioners shall provide, upon request, a valid copy of a professional license and a photograph identification issued by the state in which the practitioner holds licensure before being deployed by the director.

(d) Health care practitioners deployed pursuant to this chapter shall provide the appropriate California licensing authority with verification of licensure upon request.

(e) Health care practitioners providing health care pursuant to this chapter shall have immunity from liability for services rendered as specified in Section 8659 of the Government Code.

(f) For the purposes of this section, "health care practitioner" means any person who engages in acts which are the subject of licensure or regulation under this division or under any initiative act referred to in this division.

(g) For purposes of this section, "director" means the Director of the Emergency Medical Services Authority who shall have the powers specified in Division 2.5 (commencing with Section 1797) of the Health and Safety Code.

(Amended by Stats. 2010, Ch. 270, Sec. 1. (AB 2699) Effective January 1, 2011.)

901. (REPEALED JANUARY 1, 2014) EXEMPTION FROM LICENSURE REQUIREMENTS FOR SERVICES PROVIDED UNDER ENUMERATED CIRCUMSTANCES; PRIOR AUTHORIZATION; STEPS NECESSARY FOR SPONSORING ENTITY; REPORT; LIST OF HEALTH CARE PRACTITIONERS PROVIDING HEALTH CARE SERVICES UNDER THIS SECTION; COMPLIANCE

CHAPTER 5: MEDICINE

ARTICLE 3: LICENSE REQUIRED AND EXEMPTIONS

2071. RECOMMENDATIONS REGARDING STANDARDS FROM APPROPRIATE AGENCIES

The board shall adopt and administer regulations that establish standards for technical supportive services that may be performed by a medical assistant. Nothing in this section shall prohibit the board from amending or repealing regulations covering medical assistants. The board shall, prior to the adoption of any regulations, request recommendations regarding these standards from appropriate public agencies, including, but not limited to, the California State Board of Optometry, the Board of Registered Nursing, the Board of Vocational Nursing and Psychiatric Technicians, the Laboratory Field Services division of the State Department of Public Health, those divisions of the State Department of Education that pertain to private postsecondary education and career and vocational preparation, the Chancellor of the California Community Colleges, the California Board of Podiatric Medicine, the Physician Assistant Examining Committee, and the Physical Therapy Board of California. The board shall also request recommendations regarding these standards from associations of medical assistants, physicians and surgeons, nurses, doctors of podiatric medicine, physician assistants, physical therapists, laboratory technologists, optometrists, and others as the board finds appropriate, including, but not limited to, the California Optometric Association, the California Nurses Association, the California Medical Association, the California Society of Medical Assistants, the California Medical Assistants Association, and the California Physical Therapy Association. Nothing in this section shall be construed to supersede or modify that portion of the Administrative Procedure Act that relates to the procedure for the adoption of regulations and which is set forth in Article 5 (commencing with Section 11346) of Chapter 3.5 of Part 1 of Division 3 of Title 2 of the Government Code.

(Amended by Stats. 2021, Ch. 630, Sec. 16. (AB 1534) Effective January 1, 2022.)

2074. EMPLOYMENT OF OPHTHALMOLOGIST BY OPTOMETRIST

Nothing in this chapter shall prohibit the employment of a licensed physician and surgeon practicing in the specialty of ophthalmology by an optometrist licensed under the provisions of Chapter 7 (commencing with Section 3000) or by an optometric corporation certificated under that chapter.

(Added by Stats. 1980, Ch. 1313, Sec 2.)

ARTICLE 12. ENFORCEMENT

2290.5. DEFINITIONS

(a) For purposes of this division, the following definitions apply:

(1) "Asynchronous store and forward" means the transmission of a patient's medical information from an originating site to the health care provider at a distant site.

(2) "Distant site" means a site where a health care provider who provides health care services is located while providing these services via a telecommunications system.

(3) "Health care provider" means any of the following:

(A) A person who is licensed under this division.

(B) An associate marriage and family therapist or marriage and family therapist trainee functioning pursuant to Section 4980.43.3.

(C) A qualified autism service provider or qualified autism service professional certified by a national entity pursuant to Section 1374.73 of the Health and Safety Code and Section 10144.51 of the Insurance Code.

(D) An associate clinical social worker functioning pursuant to Section 4996.23.2.

(E) An associate professional clinical counselor or clinical counselor trainee functioning pursuant to Section 4999.46.3.

(4) "Originating site" means a site where a patient is located at the time health care services are provided via a telecommunications system or where the asynchronous store and forward service originates.

(5) "Synchronous interaction" means a real-time interaction between a patient and a health care provider located at a distant site.

(6) "Telehealth" means the mode of delivering health care services and public health via information and communication technologies to facilitate the diagnosis, consultation, treatment, education, care management, and self-management of a patient's health care. Telehealth facilitates patient self-management and caregiver support for patients and includes synchronous interactions and asynchronous store and forward transfers.

(b) Before the delivery of health care via telehealth, the health care provider initiating the use of telehealth shall inform the patient about the use of telehealth and obtain verbal or written consent from the patient for the use of telehealth as an acceptable mode of delivering health care services and public health. The consent shall be documented.

(c) This section does not preclude a patient from receiving in-person health care delivery services during a specified course of health care and treatment after agreeing to receive services via telehealth.

(d) The failure of a health care provider to comply with this section shall constitute unprofessional conduct. Section 2314 shall not apply to this section.

(e) This section does not alter the scope of practice of a health care provider or authorize the delivery of health care services in a setting, or in a manner, not otherwise authorized by law.

(f) All laws regarding the confidentiality of health care information and a patient's rights to the patient's medical information shall apply to telehealth interactions.

(g) All laws and regulations governing professional responsibility, unprofessional conduct, and standards of practice that apply to a health care provider under the health care provider's license shall apply to that health care provider while providing telehealth services.

(h) This section shall not apply to a patient under the jurisdiction of the Department of Corrections and Rehabilitation or any other correctional facility.

(i) (1) Notwithstanding any other law and for purposes of this section, the governing body of the hospital whose patients are receiving the telehealth services may grant privileges to, and verify and approve credentials for, providers of telehealth services based on its medical staff recommendations that rely on information provided by the distant-site hospital or telehealth entity, as described in Sections 482.12, 482.22, and 485.616 of Title 42 of the Code of Federal Regulations.

(2) By enacting this subdivision, it is the intent of the Legislature to authorize a hospital to grant privileges to, and verify and approve credentials for,

providers of telehealth services as described in paragraph (1).

(3) For the purposes of this subdivision, "telehealth" shall include "telemedicine" as the term is referenced in Sections 482.12, 482.22, and 485.616 of Title 42 of the Code of Federal Regulations.

(Amended by Stats. 2022, Ch. 520, Sec. 1. (AB 1759) Effective January 1, 2023.)

CHAPTER 5.4: PRESCRIPTION LENSES AND OPHTHALMIC AND OPTOMETRIC ASSISTANTS

2540. MEASURE OF RANGE OF VISION; DETERMINE PRESCRIPTION OF LENSES

No person other than a physician and surgeon or optometrist may measure the powers or range of human vision or determine the accommodative and refractive status of the human eye or the scope of its functions in general or prescribe ophthalmic devices.

(Amended by Stats. 2006, Ch. 148, Sec. 2. Effective January 1, 2007.)

2541. PRESCRIPTION OPHTHALMIC DEVICE DEFINED

A prescription ophthalmic device includes each of the following:

(a) Any spectacle or contact lens ordered by a physician and surgeon or optometrist, that alters or changes the visual powers of the human eye.

(b) Any contact lens described in paragraph (1) of subdivision (n) of Section 520 of the federal Food, Drug, and Cosmetic Act (21 U.S.C. Sec. 360j and following).

(c) Any plano contact lens that is marketed or offered for sale in this state. "Plano contact lens" means a zero-power or noncorrective contact lens intended to change the appearance of the normal eye in a decorative fashion.

(Amended by Stats. 2006, Ch. 148, Sec. 3. Effective January 1, 2007.)

2541.1. SPECTACLE LENS PRESCRIPTION REQUIREMENTS

(a) A spectacle lens prescription shall include all of the following:

(1) The dioptric power of the lens. When the prescription needed by the patient has not changed since the previous examination, the prescriber may write on the prescription form "copy lenses currently worn" instead.

(2) The expiration date of the prescription.

(3) The date of the issuance of the prescription.

(4) The name, address, telephone number, prescriber's license number, and signature of the prescribing optometrist or physician and surgeon.

(5) The name of the person to whom the prescription is issued.

(b) The expiration date of a spectacle lens prescription shall not be less than two years and shall not exceed four years from the date of issuance unless the patient's history or current circumstances establish a reasonable probability of changes in the patient's vision of sufficient magnitude to necessitate reexamination earlier than two years, or presence or probability of visual abnormalities related to ocular or systemic disease indicates, the need for reexamination of the patient earlier than two years. In no circumstances shall the expiration date be shorter than the period of time recommended by the prescriber for reexamination of the patient. Establishing an expiration date that is not consistent with this section shall be regarded as unprofessional conduct by the board that issued the prescriber's certificate to practice.

(c) The prescriber of a spectacle lens shall orally inform the patient of the expiration date of a spectacle lens prescription at the time the prescription is issued. The expiration date of a prescription may be extended by the prescriber and transmitted by telephone, electronic mail, or any other means of communication. An oral prescription for a spectacle lens shall be reduced to writing and a copy of that writing shall be sent to the prescriber prior to the delivery of the lenses to the person to whom the prescription is issued.

(d) A prescriber of a spectacle lens shall abide by the rules pertaining to spectacle lens prescriptions and eye examinations adopted by the Federal Trade Commission found in Part 456 of Title 16 of the Code of Federal Regulations.

(e) An expired prescription may be filled if all of the following conditions exist:

(1) The patient's spectacles are lost, broken, or damaged to a degree that renders them unusable.

(2) Upon dispensing a prescription pursuant to this subdivision, the person dispensing shall recommend that the patient return to the optometrist or physician and surgeon who issued the prescription for an eye examination and provide the prescriber with a written notification of the prescription that was filled.

(Amended by Stats. 2021, Ch. 630, Sec. 17. (AB 1534) Effective January 1, 2022.)

2541.2. RELEASE OF CONTACT LENS PRESCRIPTION TO PATIENT; EXPIRATION DATE OF PRESCRIPTION; VIOLATION OF SECTION UNPROFESSIONAL CONDUCT

(a)(1) The expiration date of a contact lens prescription shall not be less than one year and shall not exceed two years from the date of issuance, unless the patient's history or current circumstances establish a reasonable probability of changes in the patient's vision of sufficient magnitude to necessitate reexamination earlier than one year, or the presence or probability of visual abnormalities related to ocular or systemic disease indicate the need for reexamination of the patient earlier than one year. If the expiration date of a prescription is less than one year, the health-related reasons for the limitation shall be documented in the patient's medical record. In no circumstances shall the prescription expiration date be less than the period of time recommended by the prescriber for reexamination of the patient.

(2) For the purposes of this subdivision, the date of issuance is the date the patient receives a copy of the prescription.

(3) Establishing an expiration date that is not consistent with this section shall be regarded as unprofessional conduct by the board that issued the prescriber's license to practice.

(b) Upon completion of the eye examination or, if applicable, the contact lens fitting process for a patient as described in subdivision (f), a prescriber or a registered dispensing optician shall provide the patient with a copy of the patient's contact lens prescription signed by the prescriber, unless the prescription meets the standards set forth in subdivision (c).

(c) A prescriber shall retain professional discretion regarding the release of the contact lens prescription for patients who wear the following types of contact lenses:

(1) Rigid gas permeables.

(2) Bitoric gas permeables.

(3) Bifocal gas permeables.

(4) Keratoconus lenses.

(5) Custom designed lenses that are manufactured for an individual patient and are not mass produced.

(d) If a patient places an order with a contact lens seller other than a physician and surgeon, an optometrist, or a registered dispensing optician, the prescriber or his or her authorized agent shall, upon request of the contact lens seller and in the absence of the actual prescription, attempt to promptly confirm the information contained in the prescription through direct communication with the contact lens seller.

(e) The contact lens prescription shall include sufficient information for the complete and accurate filling of a prescription, including, but not limited to, the power, the material or manufacturer or both, the base curve or appropriate designation, the diameter when appropriate, and an appropriate expiration date. When a provider prescribes a private label contact lens for a patient, the prescription shall include the name of the manufacturer, the trade name of the private label brand, and, if applicable, the trade name of the equivalent national brand.

(f) The contact lens fitting process begins after the initial comprehensive eye examination, and includes an examination to determine the lens specifications, an initial evaluation of the fit of the lens on the patient's eye, except in the case of a renewal prescription of an established patient, and followup examinations that are medically necessary, and ends when the prescriber or registered dispensing optician determines that an appropriate fit has been achieved, or in the case of a prescription renewal for an established patient, the prescriber determines that there is no change in the prescription.

(g) The payment of professional fees for the eye exam, fitting, and evaluation may be required prior to the release of the prescription, but only if the prescriber would have required immediate payment from the patient had the examination revealed that no ophthalmic devices were required. A prescriber or registered dispensing optician shall not charge the patient any fee as a condition to releasing the prescription to the patient. A prescriber may charge an additional fee for verifying ophthalmic devices dispensed by another seller if the additional fee is imposed at the time the verification is performed.

(h) A prescriber shall not condition the availability of an eye examination, a contact lens fitting, or the release of a contact lens prescription on a requirement that the patient agree to purchase contact lenses from that prescriber. A registered dispensing optician shall not condition the availability of a contact lens fitting on a requirement that the patient agrees to purchase contact lenses from that registered dispensing optician.

(i) A prescriber or a registered dispensing optician shall not place on the contact lens prescription, deliver to the patient, or require a patient to sign a form or notice waiving or disclaiming the liability or responsibility of the prescriber or registered dispensing optician for the accuracy of the ophthalmic devices dispensed by another seller. This prohibition against waivers and disclaimers shall not impose liability on a prescriber or registered dispensing optician for the ophthalmic devices dispensed by another seller pursuant to the prescriber's prescription.

(j) The willful failure or refusal of a prescriber to comply with the provisions of this section shall constitute grounds for professional discipline, including, but not limited to, the imposition of a fine or the suspension or revocation of the prescriber's license. The Medical Board of California, the Osteopathic Medical Board of California, and the California State Board of Optometry shall adopt regulations, to implement this subdivision, including, but not limited to, standards for processing complaints each receives regarding this subdivision.

(k) For the purposes of this section, "prescriber" means a physician and surgeon or an optometrist.

(l) Nothing in this section shall be construed to expand the scope of practice of a registered dispensing optician as defined in Sections 2542, 2543, and Chapter 5.5 (commencing with Section 2550).

(Amended by Stats. 2021, Ch. 630, Sec. 18. (AB 1534) Effective January 1, 2022.)

2541.3. QUALITY STANDARDS FOR PRESCRIPTION OPHTHALMIC DEVICES; ENFORCEMENT

(a) The State Department of Public Health, the California State Board of

Optometry, and the Medical Board of California shall prepare and adopt quality standards and adopt regulations relating to prescription ophthalmic devices, including, but not limited to, lenses, frames, and contact lenses. In promulgating these rules and regulations, the department and the boards shall adopt the current standards of the American National Standards Institute regarding ophthalmic materials. Nothing in this section shall prohibit the department and the boards from jointly adopting subsequent standards that are equivalent or more stringent than the current standards of the American National Standards Institute regarding ophthalmic materials.

(b) No individual or group that deals with prescription ophthalmic devices, including, but not limited to, distributors, registered dispensing opticians or ophthalmic businesses, manufacturers, laboratories, optometrists, or ophthalmologists shall sell, dispense, or furnish any prescription ophthalmic device that does not meet the minimum standards set by the State Department of Public Health, the California State Board of Optometry, or the Medical Board of California.

(c) Any violation of the regulations adopted by the State Department of Public Health, the California State Board of Optometry, or the Medical Board of California pursuant to this section shall be a misdemeanor.

(d) Any optometrist, ophthalmologist, or dispensing optician who violates the regulations adopted by the State Department of Public Health, the California State Board of Optometry, the Medical Board of California, or the Osteopathic Medical Board of California pursuant to this section shall be subject to disciplinary action by the individual's licensing board.

(e) The California State Board of Optometry, the Medical Board of California, or the Osteopathic Medical Board of California may send any prescription ophthalmic device to the State Department of Public Health for testing as to whether or not the device meets established standards adopted pursuant to this section, which testing shall take precedence over any other prescription ophthalmic device testing being conducted by the department. The department may conduct the testing in its own facilities or may contract with any other facility to conduct the testing.

(Amended by Stats. 2021, Ch. 630, Sec. 19. (AB 1534) Effective January 1, 2022.)

2541.6. PURCHASE OF PRESCRIPTION OPHTHALMIC DEVICES WITH STATE FUNDS

No prescription ophthalmic device that does not meet the standards adopted by the State Department of Public Health, the California State Board of Optometry, the Medical Board of California, or the Osteopathic Medical Board of California under Section 2541.3 shall be purchased with state funds.

(Amended by Stats. 2021, Ch. 630, Sec. 20. (AB 1534) Effective January 1, 2022.)

2542. DUTIES OF REGISTERED DISPENSING OPTICIANS

A registered dispensing optician shall dispense contact lenses, including plano contact lenses, only on the valid prescription of a physician and surgeon or optometrist, and acting on the advice, direction, and responsibility of the physician and surgeon or optometrist. The registrant shall also comply with the requirements of Section 2560. A registered dispensing optician shall not dispense a contact lens or lenses, or a plano contact lens or lenses, unless the prescription specifically refers to and authorizes contact lenses. A registered dispensing optician shall not fit a generic type of contact lens or mode of wear for a contact lens contrary to the type or mode, if any, referred to in the prescription.

(Amended by Stats. 2021, Ch. 630, Sec. 21. (AB 1534) Effective January 1, 2022.)

2543. DISPENSATION OR FURNISHING OF LENSES; DECEPTIVE MARKETING

(a) Except as provided in the Nonresident Ophthalmic Lens Dispenser Registration Act (Article 2.5 (commencing with Section 2564.70)), the right to dispense, sell, or furnish prescription ophthalmic devices at retail or to the person named in a prescription is limited exclusively to licensed physicians and surgeons, licensed optometrists, and registered dispensing opticians as provided in this division. This section shall not be construed to affect licensing requirements pursuant to Section 111615 of the Health and Safety Code.

(b) It shall be considered a deceptive marketing practice for:

(1) Any physician and surgeon, optometrist, or registered dispensing optician to publish or cause to be published any advertisement or sales presentation relating to contact lenses that represents that contact lenses may be obtained without confirmation of a valid prescription.

(2) Any individual or entity who offers for sale plano contact lenses, as defined in subdivision (c) of Section 2541, to represent by any means that those lenses may be lawfully obtained without an eye examination or confirmation of a valid prescription, or may be dispensed or furnished to a purchaser without complying with the requirements of Section 2562, except as provided in Article 2.5 (commencing with Section 2564.70).

(Amended by Stats. 2021, Ch. 630, Sec. 22. (AB 1534) Effective January 1, 2022.)

2544. FITTING OF LENSES; ADDITIONAL PROCEDURES BY ASSISTANT

(a) Notwithstanding any other provision of law, an assistant in any setting where optometry or ophthalmology is practiced who is acting under the direct responsibility and supervision of an optometrist or a physician and surgeon may fit prescription lenses. Under the direct responsibility and supervision of an optometrist or ophthalmologist, an assistant in any setting where optometry or ophthalmology is practiced may also do the following:

(1) Prepare patients for examination.

(2) Collect preliminary patient data, including taking a patient history.

(3) Perform simple noninvasive testing of visual acuity, pupils, and ocular motility.

(4) Perform automated visual field testing.

(5) Perform ophthalmic photography and digital imaging.

(6) Perform tonometry.

(7) Perform lensometry.

(8) Perform nonsubjective auto refraction.

(9) Perform preliminary subjective refraction procedures in connection with finalizing subjective refraction procedures performed by an ophthalmologist or optometrist, subject to the following conditions:

(A) The assistant shall have at least 45 hours of documented training in subjective refraction procedures acceptable to the supervising ophthalmologist or optometrist, which may include performing preliminary subjective refraction procedures consistent with this paragraph to accomplish that training.

(B) Any preliminary subjective refraction procedures shall be performed as follows:

(i) When the supervising physician and surgeon or optometrist is physically present at the location where the procedures are being performed, and not involving telehealth services.

(ii) In conjunction with an in-person examination being performed by the supervising physician and surgeon or optometrist.

(iii) With a supervisory ratio of no more than three assistants per supervising ophthalmologist or optometrist during the supervisor's work shift.

(C) An assistant performing preliminary subjective refraction procedures may utilize appropriate related equipment, including, but not limited to, a phoropter, trial lenses, and a retinoscope, solely for the purpose of performing those procedures.

(D) An assistant may not prescribe glasses or contact lenses, and nothing in this section shall be interpreted as authorizing those activities.

(10) Administer cycloplegics, mydriatics, and topical anesthetics that are not controlled substances, for ophthalmic purposes.

(11) Perform pachymetry, keratometry, A scan and B scan ultrasound testing, and electrodiagnostic testing.

(b) For the purposes of this section, "setting" includes, but is not limited to, any facility licensed by the State Department of Public Health or the State Department of Social Services.

(c) Nothing in this section shall be construed to authorize activities that corporations and other artificial legal entities are prohibited from conducting by Section 2400.

(Amended by Stats. 2022, Ch. 596, Sec. 2. (AB 2574) Effective January 1, 2023.)

2545. INJUNCTION; FINES

(a) Whenever a person or corporation has engaged, or is about to engage, in any acts or practices which constitute, or will constitute, an offense against this chapter, the superior court in and for the county wherein the acts or practices take place, or are about to take place, may issue an injunction, or other appropriate order, restraining the conduct on application of the California State Board of Optometry, the Medical Board of California, the Osteopathic Medical Board of California, the Attorney General, or the district attorney of the county.

The proceedings under this section shall be governed by Chapter 3 (commencing with Section 525) of Title 7 of Part 2 of the Code of Civil Procedure.

(b) (1) A person or corporation who violates any of the provisions of this chapter shall be subject to a fine of not less than two hundred fifty dollars ($250) nor more than thirty-five thousand dollars ($35,000) per violation. The fines collected pursuant to this section from licensed physicians and surgeons shall be available upon appropriation to the Medical Board of California or the Osteopathic Medical Board of California for the purposes of administration and enforcement. The fines collected pursuant to this section from licensed optometrists and registered dispensing opticians shall be deposited into the Optometry Fund and shall be available upon appropriation to the California State Board of Optometry for the purposes of administration and enforcement.

(2) The Medical Board of California, the Osteopathic Medical Board of California, and the California State Board of Optometry shall adopt regulations implementing this section and shall consider the following factors, including, but not limited to, applicable enforcement penalties, prior conduct, gravity of the offense, and the manner in which complaints will be processed.

(3) The proceedings under this section shall be conducted in accordance with the provisions of Chapter 5 (commencing with Section 11500) of Part 1 of Division 3 of Title 2 of the Government Code.

(Amended by Stats. 2021, Ch. 630, Sec. 24. (AB 1534) Effective January 1, 2022.)

CHAPTER 5.45: NONRESIDENT CONTACT LENS

2546 – [RENUMBERED]

(Renumbered as Ca. Bus. and Prof. Code 2564.70 by Stats 2021 ch 630 (AB 1534),s 26, eff. 1/1/2022.)

2546.1 – [RENUMBERED]

(Renumbered as Ca. Bus. and Prof. Code 2564.71 by Stats 2021 ch 630 (AB 1534),s 27, eff. 1/1/2022.)

2546.2 – [REPEALED]

(Repealed by Stats 2021 ch 630 (AB 1534),s 28, eff. 1/1/2022.)

2546.3 – [RENUMBERED]

(Renumbered as Ca. Bus. and Prof. Code 2564.73 by Stats 2021 ch 630 (AB 1534),s 29, eff. 1/1/2022.)

2546.4 – [RENUMBERED]

(Renumbered as Ca. Bus. and Prof. Code 2564.74 by Stats 2021 ch 630 (AB 1534),s 30, eff. 1/1/2022.)

2546.5 – [RENUMBERED]

(Renumbered as Ca. Bus. and Prof. Code 2564.75 by Stats 2021 ch 630 (AB 1534),s 31, eff. 1/1/2022.)

2546.6 – [RENUMBERED]

(Renumbered as Ca. Bus. and Prof. Code 2564.76 by Stats 2021 ch 630 (AB 1534),s 32, eff. 1/1/2022.)

2546.7 – [RENUMBERED]

(Renumbered as Ca. Bus. and Prof. Code 2564.77 by Stats 2021 ch 630 (AB 1534),s 33, eff. 1/1/2022.)

2546.8 – [RENUMBERED]

(Renumbered as Ca. Bus. and Prof. Code 2564.78 by Stats 2021 ch 630 (AB 1534),s 34, eff. 1/1/2022.)

2546.9 – [RENUMBERED]

(Renumbered as Ca. Bus. and Prof. Code 2564.79 by Stats 2021 ch 630 (AB 1534),s 35, eff. 1/1/2022.)

2546.10 – [RENUMBERED]

(Renumbered as Ca. Bus. and Prof. Code 2564.80 by Stats 2021 ch 630 (AB 1534),s 36, eff. 1/1/2022.)

CHAPTER 5.5: REGISTERED DISPENSING OPTICIANS

ARTICLE 1: GENERAL PROVISIONS

2550. DEFINITIONS

For purposes of this chapter, the following definitions shall apply:

(a) "Adjust" and "adjusting" includes the following acts, either singly or in combination with others: adapting or manipulation of the ophthalmic device to fit the face of the consumer, pursuant and incidental to the filling of any prescription for lenses, spectacles, eyeglasses, contact lens, plano contact lens, and other ophthalmic devices as specified in Section 2541, and prescriptions.

(b) "Board" means the California State Board of Optometry.

(c) "Dispensing optician," "registered dispensing optician," and "registrant" mean any of the following individuals that are registered with the board:

(1) "Spectacle lens dispenser" means an individual who is registered with the board pursuant to Article 1.5 (commencing with Section 2559.1).

(2) "Contact lens dispenser" means an individual who is registered with the board pursuant to Article 2 (commencing with Section 2560).

(3) "Nonresident ophthalmic lens dispenser" means an entity that is registered with the board pursuant to Article 2.5 (commencing with Section 2564.70) which offers, advertises, and performs optical services to the general public.

(4) "Registered dispensing ophthalmic business" means an entity that is registered with the board pursuant to Article 2.7 (commencing with Section 2564.90) that offers, advertises, and performs optical services for the general public.

(d) "Fit" and "fitting" mean doing any of the following acts, either singly or in combination with others, before the act of adjusting: designing, taking measurements to determine the size, shape, or specifications, and replacing the prescribed optical aids, pursuant and incidental to the filling of any prescription for lenses, spectacles, eyeglasses, contact lens, plano contact lens, and other ophthalmic devices as specified in Section 2541.

(e) "Ophthalmic lens" or "ophthalmic device" means any prescription lenses, spectacles, eyeglasses, contact lens, other ophthalmic devices that alter or change the visual powers of the human eye, or any prescription plano contact lens ordered by a physician and surgeon or optometrist.

(f) "Prescription" means an order made by a licensed physician and surgeon or licensed optometrist pursuant to Section 2541.1 or 2541.2.

(g) "Unregistered individual" means an individual who is not registered with the board pursuant to this chapter. The unregistered individual may perform any of the following:

(1) Fitting and adjusting of spectacle lenses under the direct responsibility and supervision of a duly registered spectacle lens dispenser pursuant to Section 2559.1.

(2) Fitting and adjusting of contact lenses under the direct responsibility and supervision of a duly registered contact lens dispenser pursuant to Section 2560.

(Added by Stats. 2021, Ch. 630, Sec. 38. (AB 1534) Effective January 1, 2022.)

2550.1. APPLICATION OF PROVISIONS

The provisions of this chapter shall not apply to an individual who is acting under the direct responsibility and supervision of a physician and surgeon or optometrist, pursuant to Section 2544, in any setting where optometry or ophthalmology is practiced.

(Repealed and added by Stats. 2021, Ch. 630, Sec. 40. (AB 1534) Effective January 1, 2022.)

2551 – [RENUMBERED]

(Renumbered as Ca. Bus. and Prof. Code 2564.91 by Stats 2021 ch 630 (AB 1534),s 41, eff. 1/1/2022.)

2552. CONTENTS AND VERIFICATION OF APPLICATIONS

(a) Each application made pursuant to this chapter shall be verified under oath by the person required to sign the application and shall designate the name, address, and direct business telephone number of the applicant's employee who will be responsible for handling customer inquiries and complaints with respect to the business address for which registration is applied. An applicant shall report any changes to this information in writing to the board within 14 days.

(b) The applicant shall furnish such additional information or proof, oral or written, which the board may request, including information and proof relating to the provisions of Division 1.5 (commencing with Section 475).

(c) The board shall promptly notify any applicant if, as of the 30th day following the submission of an application under this chapter, the application and supporting documentation are not substantially complete and in proper form. The notification shall be in writing, shall state specifically what documents or other information are to be supplied by the applicant to the board, and shall be sent to the applicant by certified, electronic, or registered mail. Within 30 days of the applicant's submission of the requested documents or information to the board, the board shall notify the applicant by certified, electronic, or registered mail if the board requires additional documents or information.

(Amended by Stats. 2021, Ch. 630, Sec. 42. (AB 1534) Effective January 1, 2022.)

2552.2. POSTING CITATION ISSUED FOR AN ORDER OF ABATEMENT

(a) A citation issued for an order of abatement in accordance with Sections 1399.275 and 1399.277 of Title 16 of the California Code of Regulations shall be posted on the front of the place of business of the dispensing optician. The citation shall remain posted until the violation has been corrected. The dispensing optician must also prominently post and make available its notice on any internet website it maintains that provides information about its services.

(b) A dispensing optician that has been issued a citation for an order of abatement in accordance with Sections 1399.275 and 1399.277 of Title 16 of the California Code of Regulations shall notify all optometrists with which it has entered into a lease or other contract within 10 calendar days of being served with the order of abatement.

(Added by Stats. 2021, Ch. 630, Sec. 43. (AB 1534) Effective January 1, 2022.)

2553. REGISTRATION OF APPLICANTS; DISPLAY OF CERTIFICATES

Each certificate of registration shall be at all times displayed in a conspicuous place at the certified place of business. The certificate shall not be transferable, but on application to the board there may be registered a change of address of the certificate.

(Amended by Stats. 2021, Ch. 630, Sec. 44. (AB 1534) Effective January 1, 2022.)

2553.1 – [RENUMBERED]

(Renumbered as Ca. Bus. and Prof. Code 2564.94 by Stats 2021 ch 630 (AB 1534),s 45, eff. 1/1/2022.)

2553.5. LOCATIONS FOR FITTING AND ADJUSTING OF SPECTACLE LENSES AND FRAMES; DISCLOSURE OF REGISTRANT'S REGULAR BUSINESS ADDRESS

(a) A registered dispensing optician may fit and adjust spectacle lenses and frames or take facial measurements in any of the following locations:

(1) A health facility as defined in Section 1250 of the Health and Safety Code for a person admitted to that facility or an employee of that facility.

(2) A business location as defined in subdivision (f) for an employee or independent contractor of the person operating the business at that location.

(3) Any certified place of business pursuant to Section 2564.93.

(b) A registered dispensing optician who fits and adjusts spectacle lenses at a health facility or business location shall provide to the patient written information disclosing the registrant's regular business address, certificate of registration number, phone number, and the name and phone number of the person designated by the licensee to receive complaints and inquiries, as specified in Section 2554.

(c) Nothing in this section shall be deemed to permit a registered dispensing optician or registered contact lens dispenser to fit or adjust contact lenses at a health facility or at a business location, as defined in subdivision (e).

(d) A registered spectacle lens dispenser may fit and adjust spectacle lenses at a health facility or at a business location, as defined in subdivision (e), only if the dispenser is in personal attendance at a certified place of business pursuant to Section 2564.93 at least 40 percent of the dispenser's regular working hours each week.

(e) "Business location" means the place at which any business employs more than 25 persons at any single business address, but shall not include a health facility, as defined in Section 1250 of the Health and Safety Code, or a certified place of business as specified in Section 2564.93.

(f) This section shall not affect the requirements regarding fitting and adjusting as set forth in Sections 2559.1 and 2560.

(Amended by Stats. 2021, Ch. 630, Sec. 46. (AB 1534) Effective January 1, 2022.)

2553.6. EFFECT OF INTERMINGLING PROPRIETARY INTERESTS

(a) The board shall deny any application for registration under this chapter if any person licensed as a physician and surgeon, for whom the applicant, in accordance with Section 2564.90, proposes to fill any prescription, has any proprietary interest, or has designated or arranged for any other person to have any proprietary interest in or with the applicant.

(b) (1) The board may, in accordance with Section 2555, suspend, revoke, or refuse to renew the certificate of any individual or firm under this chapter, if such individual or firm, after the effective date of this section, fills, or has filled, while holding a certificate issued pursuant to this chapter, any prescription issued by any person licensed under Chapter 5 (commencing with Section 2000) who has any proprietary interest, or has designated or arranged for any other person to have any proprietary interest, in or with such individual or firm.

(2) Such penalties shall be in addition to, and not to the exclusion of, any other remedies or penalties provided by law.

(3) "Proprietary interest," for the purposes of this section, means any membership, coownership, stock ownership, legal or beneficial interest, any other proprietary interest, or profit-sharing arrangement, designated or

arranged or held, directly or indirectly in any form, in or with any individual or firm applying for registration or registered under this chapter, except stock ownership in a corporation which is listed on a stock exchange regulated by the Securities and Exchange Commission if the stock is acquired in a transaction conducted through such stock exchange.

(c) This section shall apply only to a dispensing optician required to be registered pursuant to Chapter 5.5 (commencing with Section 2550) and shall not be construed to modify Section 2557, or to affect the fitting of prescription lenses by an assistant pursuant to Section 2544.

(Amended by Stats. 2021, Ch. 630, Sec. 47. (AB 1534) Effective January 1, 2022.)

2553.7. WHEN REGISTRATIONS OF DISPENSING OPTICIANS AND LENS DISPENSERS SHALL EXPIRE

(a) Registrations shall expire at midnight on the last day of the month in which the license was issued during the second year of a two-year term if not renewed.

(b) Except as otherwise provided by Section 114, any registration under this chapter may be renewed at any time within three years after its expiration by filing an application for renewal or reactivation on a form prescribed by the board, paying all accrued and unpaid renewal fees or reactivation fees as determined by the board and by paying any delinquency fees prescribed by the board. If the registration under this chapter is not renewed three years after its expiration, the registration shall be considered cancelled and may not be reinstated or renewed.

(Amended by Stats. 2021, Ch. 630, Sec. 48. (AB 1534) Effective January 1, 2022.)

2554. DESIGNATION OF EMPLOYEE RESPONSIBLE FOR HANDLING CUSTOMER COMPLAINTS

Each registrant shall conspicuously and prominently display at each registered location the following consumer information:

"Eye doctors are required to provide patients with a copy of their ophthalmic lens prescriptions as follows:

Spectacle prescriptions: Release upon completion of exam.

Contact lens prescriptions: Release upon completion of exam or upon completion of the fitting process.

Patients may take their prescription to any eye doctor or registered dispensing optician to be filled.

The California State Board of Optometry regulates optometrists and registered dispensing opticians. The California State Board of Optometry receives and investigates all consumer complaints involving the practice of optometry and registered dispensing opticians. Complaints involving a California-licensed optometrist or a registered dispensing optician should be directed to:

California State Board of Optometry
Department of Consumer Affairs
2450 Del Paso Road, Suite 105
Sacramento, CA 95834
Phone: 1-866-585-2666 or (916) 575-7170
Email: optometry@dca.ca.gov
Internet website: www.optometry.ca.gov"

(Amended by Stats. 2021, Ch. 630, Sec. 49. (AB 1534) Effective January 1, 2022.)

2555. SUSPENSION AND REVOCATION OF CERTIFICATES

Certificates issued under this chapter may in the discretion of the board be suspended or revoked or subjected to terms and conditions of probation for violating or attempting to violate this chapter, Chapter 5.4 (commencing with Section

2540) or any regulation adopted under this chapter or, Chapter 5.4 (commencing with Section 2540), or Section 651, 654, or 655, or for incompetence, gross negligence, or repeated similar negligent acts performed by the registrant or by an employee of the registrant. The proceedings shall be conducted in accordance with Chapter 5 (commencing with Section 11500) of Part 1 of Division 3 of Title 2 of the Government Code, and the board shall have all the powers granted therein.

(Amended by Stats. 2021, Ch. 630, Sec. 50. (AB 1534) Effective January 1, 2022.)

2555.1. DISCIPLINARY ACTION UPON CONVICTION OF CHARGE RELATED TO QUALIFICATIONS FUNCTIONS, AND DUTIES OF DISPENSING OPTICIAN

(a) In the discretion of the board, a certificate issued under this chapter may be suspended or revoked if an individual certificate holder or persons having any proprietary interest who will engage in dispensing operations, have been convicted of a crime substantially related to the qualifications, functions, and duties of a dispensing optician. The record of conviction or a certified copy thereof shall be conclusive evidence of the conviction.

(b) A plea or verdict of guilty or a conviction following a plea of nolo contendere made to a charge substantially related to the qualifications, functions, and duties of a dispensing optician is deemed to be a conviction within the meaning of this article. The board may order the certificate suspended or revoked, or may decline to issue a certificate, when the time for appeal has elapsed, or the judgment of conviction has been affirmed on appeal or when an order granting probation is made suspending the imposition of sentence, irrespective of a subsequent order under the provisions of Section 1203.4 of the Penal Code allowing such person to withdraw their plea of guilty and to enter a plea of not guilty, or setting aside the verdict of guilty, or dismissing the accusation, information, or indictment.

(c) The proceeding under this section shall be conducted in accordance with Chapter 5 (commencing with Section 11500) of Part 1 of Division 3 of Title 2 of the Government Code, and the board shall have all the powers granted therein.

(Amended by Stats. 2021, Ch. 630, Sec. 51. (AB 1534) Effective January 1, 2022.)

2555.5. UNPROFESSIONAL CONDUCT BY REGISTRANTS OR APPLICANT

The board may take action against any registrant who is charged with unprofessional conduct and may deny an application for a registration if the applicant has committed unprofessional conduct. In addition to other provisions of this article, unprofessional conduct includes, but is not limited to, all of the following:

(a) Violating, attempting to violate, conspiring to violate, or directly or indirectly assisting in or abetting the violation of any provision of this chapter or any of the rules and regulations adopted by the board pursuant to this chapter.

(b) Gross negligence.

(c) Repeated negligent acts. To be repeated, there must be two or more negligent acts or omissions.

(d) Incompetence.

(e) The commission of fraud, misrepresentation, or any act involving dishonesty or corruption that is substantially related to the qualifications, functions, or duties of a registered optician.

(f) Any action or conduct that would have warranted the denial of a registration.

(g) The use of advertising relating to opticianry that violates Section 651 or 17500.

(h) Denial of licensure, revocation, suspension, restriction, or any other disciplinary action against a health care professional license, registration, or permit by another state or territory of the United States, by any other governmental agency, or by another California health care professional licensing board. A certified copy of the decision or judgment shall be conclusive evidence of that action.

(i) Procuring the registrant's registration by fraud, misrepresentation, or mistake.

(j) Making or giving any false statement or information in connection with the application for issuance of a license.

(k) Conviction of a felony or of any offense substantially related to the qualifications, functions, and duties of a registered dispensing optician, in which event the record of the conviction shall be conclusive evidence thereof.

(l) Administering to oneself any controlled substance or using any of the dangerous drugs specified in Section 4022, or using alcoholic beverages to the extent, or in a manner, as to be dangerous or injurious to the person applying for a license or holding a registration under this chapter, or to any other person, or to the public, or, to the extent that the use impairs the ability of the person applying for or holding a license to conduct with safety to the public the practice authorized by the license, or the conviction of a misdemeanor or felony involving the use, consumption, or self-administration of any of the substances referred to in this subdivision, or any combination thereof.

(m) (1) Committing or soliciting an act punishable as a sexually related crime, if that act or solicitation is substantially related to the qualifications, functions, or duties of an optician.

(2) Committing any act of sexual abuse, misconduct, or relations with a patient. The commission of and conviction for any act of sexual abuse, sexual misconduct, or attempted sexual misconduct, whether or not with a patient, shall be considered a crime substantially related to the qualifications, functions, or duties of a registrant. This paragraph shall not apply to sexual contact between any person licensed under this chapter and the registrant's spouse or person in an equivalent domestic relationship when that registrant provides optometry treatment to the registrant's spouse or person in an equivalent domestic relationship.

(3) Conviction of a crime that requires the person to register as a sex offender pursuant to Chapter 5.5 (commencing with Section 290) of Title 9 of Part 1 of the Penal Code. A conviction within the meaning of this paragraph means a plea or verdict of guilty or a conviction following a plea of nolo contendere. A conviction described in this paragraph shall be considered a crime substantially related to the qualifications, functions, or duties of a registrant.

(n) The failure to maintain adequate and accurate records relating to the provision of services to one's patients.

(o) Performing, or holding oneself out as being able to perform, or offering to perform, any professional services beyond the scope of the license authorized by this chapter.

(p) The practice of functions defined in this chapter without a valid, unrevoked, unexpired registration.

(q) The employing, directly or indirectly, of any suspended or unregistered individual to perform any work for which an optician registration is required.

(r) Permitting another person to use the registration for any purpose.

(s) Altering with fraudulent intent a registration issued by the board, or using a fraudulently altered license, permit, certification, or any registration issued by the board.

(t) Except for good cause, the knowing failure to protect patients by failing to follow infection control guidelines of the board, thereby risking transmission of bloodborne infectious diseases from optician to patient, from patient to patient, or from patient to optician. In administering this subdivision, the board shall consider the standards, regulations, and guidelines of the State Department of Public Health developed pursuant to Section 1250.11 of the Health and Safety Code and the standards, guidelines, and regulations pursuant to the California Occupational Safety and Health Act of 1973 (Part 1 (commencing with Section 6300) of Division 5 of the Labor Code) for preventing the transmission of HIV, hepatitis B, and other bloodborne pathogens in health care settings.

(u) Dispensing ophthalmic lenses without a current prescription.

(Added by Stats. 2021, Ch. 630, Sec. 52. (AB 1534) Effective January 1, 2022.)

2556. UNLAWFUL PRACTICES

(a) Except as authorized by Section 655, it is unlawful for a registered dispensing optician or a person who engages in the business of, or holds himself or herself out to be, a dispensing optician to do any of the following: to advertise the furnishing of, or to furnish, the services of an optometrist or a physician and surgeon, to directly employ an optometrist or physician and surgeon for the purpose of any examination or treatment of the eyes, or to duplicate or change lenses without a prescription or order from a person duly licensed to issue the same. For the purposes of this section, "furnish" does not mean to enter into a landlord-tenant relationship of any kind.

(b) Notwithstanding Section 125.9, the board may, by regulation, impose and issue administrative fines and citations for a violation of this section or Section 655, which may be assessed in addition to any other applicable fines, citations, or administrative or criminal actions.

(Amended by Stats. 2018, Ch. 703, Sec. 22. (SB 1491) Effective January 1, 2019.)

2556.1. LICENSED OPTOMETRISTS AND REGISTERED DISPENSING OPTICIANS IN A COLOCATED SETTING SHALL REPORT TO BOARD

All licensed optometrists and registered dispensing opticians who are in a colocated setting shall report the business relationship to the California State Board of Optometry, as determined by the board. The California State Board of Optometry shall have the authority to inspect any premises at which the business of a registered dispensing optician is colocated with the practice of an optometrist, for the purposes of determining compliance with Section 655. The inspection may include the review of any written lease agreement between the registered dispensing optician and the optometrist or between the optometrist and the health plan. Failure to comply with the inspection or any request for information by the board may subject the party to disciplinary action. The board shall provide a copy of its inspection results, if applicable, to the Department of Managed Health Care.

(Amended by Stats. 2021, Ch. 630, Sec. 53. (AB 1534) Effective January 1, 2022.)

2556.2. REGISTERED DISPENSING OPTICIANS NOT SUBJECT TO ACTION FOR CONDUCT PROHIBITED BY SECTION 2556 OR SECTION 655

(a) Notwithstanding any other law, subsequent to the effective date of this section and until January 1, 2019, any individual, corporation, or firm operating as a registered dispensing optician under this chapter before the effective date of this section, or an employee of such an entity, shall not be subject to any action for engaging in conduct prohibited by Section 2556 or Section 655 as those sections existed prior to the effective date of this bill, except that a registrant shall be subject to discipline for duplicating or changing lenses without a prescription or order from a person duly licensed to issue the same.

(b) Nothing in this section shall be construed to imply or suggest that a person registered under this chapter is in violation of or in compliance with the law.

(c) This section shall not apply to any business relationships prohibited by Section 2556 commencing registration or operations on or after the effective date of this section.

(d) Subsequent to the effective date of this section and until January 1, 2019, nothing in this section shall prohibit an individual, corporation, or firm operating as a registered dispensing optician from engaging in a business relationship with an optometrist licensed pursuant to Chapter 7 (commencing with Section 3000) before the effective date of this section at locations registered with the Medical Board of California before the effective date of this section.

(e) This section does not apply to any administrative action pending, litigation pending, cause for discipline, or cause of action accruing prior to September 1, 2015.

(f) Any registered dispensing optician or optical company that owns a health plan that employs optometrists, subject to this section, shall comply with the following milestones:

(1) By January 1, 2017, 15 percent of its locations shall no longer employ an optometrist.

(2) By August 1, 2017, 45 percent of its locations shall no longer employ an optometrist.

(3) By January 1, 2019, 100 percent of its locations shall no longer employ an optometrist.

(g) Any registered dispensing optician or optical company that owns a health plan that employs optometrists shall report to the California State Board of Optometry in writing as to whether it has met each of the milestones in subdivision (f) within 30 days of each milestone. The California State Board of Optometry shall provide those reports as soon as it receives them to the director and the Legislature. The report to the Legislature shall be submitted in compliance with Section 9795 of the Government Code.

(h) (1) Notwithstanding any other law and in addition to any action available to the California State Board of Optometry, the California State Board of Optometry may issue a citation containing an order of abatement, an order to pay an administrative fine, or both, to an optical company, an optometrist, or a registered dispensing optician for a violation of this section. The administrative fine shall not exceed fifty thousand dollars ($50,000). In assessing the amount of the fine, the board shall give due consideration to all of the following:

(A) The gravity of the violation.

(B) The good faith of the cited person or entity.

(C) The history of previous violations of the same or similar nature.

(D) Evidence that the violation was or was not willful.

(E) The extent to which the cited person or entity has cooperated with the board's investigation.

(F) The extent to which the cited person or entity has mitigated or attempted to mitigate any damage or injury caused by the violation.

(G) Any other factors as justice may require.

(2) A citation or fine assessment issued pursuant to a citation shall inform the cited person or entity that if a hearing is desired to contest the finding of a violation, that hearing shall be requested by written notice to the board within 30 days of the date of issuance of the citation or assessment. If a hearing is not requested pursuant to this section, payment of any fine shall not constitute an admission of the violation charged. Hearings shall be held

pursuant to Chapter 5 (commencing with Section 11500) of Part 1 of Division 3 of Title 2 of the Government Code.

(3) The board shall adopt regulations to implement a system for the issuance of citations, administrative fines, and orders of abatement authorized by this section. The regulations shall include provisions for both of the following:

(A) The issuance of a citation without an administrative fine.

(B) The opportunity for a cited person or entity to have an informal conference with the executive officer of the board in addition to the hearing described in paragraph (2).

(4) The failure of a licensee to pay a fine within 30 days of the date of assessment, unless the citation is being appealed, may result in disciplinary action being taken by the board. Where a citation is not contested and a fine is not paid, the full amount of the assessed fine shall be added to the fee for renewal of the license. A license shall not be renewed without payment of the renewal fee and fine.

(5) Notwithstanding any other law, if a fine is paid to satisfy an assessment based on the finding of a violation, payment of the fine shall be represented as satisfactory resolution of the matter for purposes of public disclosure.

(i) Administrative fines collected pursuant to this section shall be deposited in the Optometry Fund. It is the intent of the Legislature that moneys collected as fines and deposited in the fund be used by the board primarily for enforcement purposes.

(Amended by Stats. 2021, Ch. 630, Sec. 54. (AB 1534) Effective January 1, 2022.)

2556.5. USE OF "DISPENSING OPTICIAN"

Any person who holds himself out as a "dispensing optician" or "registered dispensing optician" or who uses any other term or letters indicating or implying that he is registered and holds a certificate under the terms of this law without having at the time of so doing a valid, unrevoked certificate, as provided in this chapter, is guilty of a misdemeanor.

(Added by Stats. 1953, Ch. 1144.)

2557. EXEMPT PRACTITIONERS; EXEMPT SALES

This chapter shall not affect any person licensed as an optometrist under Chapter 7 of Division II of this code, or any physician and surgeon licensed under Chapter 5 of Division II of this code. Such exemption shall not apply to any optometrist or physician and surgeon exclusively engaged in the business of filling prescriptions for physicians and surgeons. This chapter does not prohibit the sale of goggles, sun glasses, colored glasses, or occupational protective eye devices if they do not have refractive values nor do the provisions of this chapter prohibit the sale of complete ready-to-wear eyeglasses as merchandise.

(Added by Stats. 1939, Ch. 955.)

2557.1. SUSPENSION OR REVOCATION OF CERTIFICATES

A certificate issued to a registered spectacle or contact lens dispenser may in the discretion of the board be suspended or revoked for violating or attempting to violate any provision of this chapter or any regulation adopted under this chapter, or for incompetence, gross negligence, or repeated similar negligent acts performed by the certificate holder. A certificate may also be suspended or revoked if the individual certificate holder has been convicted of a felony as provided in Section 2555.1.

Any proceedings under this section shall be conducted in accordance with Chapter 5 (commencing with Section 11500) of Part 1 of Division 3 of Title 2 of the

Government Code, and the board shall have all the powers granted therein.

(Added by Stats. 2021, Ch. 630, Sec. 55. (AB 1534) Effective January 1, 2022.)

2558. PUNISHMENT FOR MISDEMEANOR VIOLATIONS; RULE MAKING AUTHORITY

Any person who violates any of the provisions of this chapter is guilty of a misdemeanor and, upon conviction thereof, shall be punished by imprisonment in the county jail not less than 10 days nor more than one year, or by a fine of not less than two hundred dollars ($200) nor more than one thousand dollars ($1,000) or by both such fine and imprisonment.

The board may adopt, amend, or repeal, in accordance with the Administrative Procedure Act, any regulations as are reasonably necessary to carry out this chapter.

(Amended by Stats. 2016, Ch. 489, Sec. 20. (SB 1478) Effective January 1, 2017.)

2558.1. PRESCRIPTION REQUIREMENTS

A registered dispensing optician shall not dispense a spectacle lens or contact lens prescription unless the prescription meets the requirements of Section 2541.1. A registered dispensing optician shall not dispense a spectacle lens prescription after the expiration date of the prescription unless so authorized pursuant to subdivision (e) of Section 2541.1. A person violating this section shall not be guilty of a misdemeanor pursuant to Section 2558. A violation of this section shall be considered unprofessional conduct by the board. A registered dispensing optician may defend this proceeding by establishing that the expiration date of the prescription was not established consistent with Section 2541.1. Nothing in this section shall be construed to authorize a registered dispensing optician to fill a prescription after the expiration date or to make any judgment regarding the appropriateness of the expiration date.

(Added by Stats. 2021, Ch. 630, Sec. 56. (AB 1534) Effective January 1, 2022.)

2558.2.

Any individual, corporation, or firm operating as a registered dispensing optician under this chapter who demonstrates a willful disregard for the provisions of this chapter is guilty of a misdemeanor.

(Added by Stats. 2021, Ch. 630, Sec. 57. (AB 1534) Effective January 1, 2022.)

2559. INJUNCTIONS

Whenever any person has engaged, or is about to engage, in any acts or practices which constitute, or will constitute, a violation of any provision of this chapter, or Chapter 5.4 (commencing with Section 2540), the superior court in and for the county wherein the acts or practices take place, or are about to take place, may issue an injunction, or other appropriate order, restraining such conduct on application of the board, the Attorney General, or the district attorney of the county.

The proceedings under this section shall be governed by Chapter 3 (commencing with Section 525) of Title 7 of Part 2 of the Code of Civil Procedure.

(Amended by Stats. 2016, Ch. 489, Sec. 21. (SB 1478) Effective January 1, 2017.)

ARTICLE 1.5: SPECTACLE LENS DISPENSING

2559.1. RIGHT TO PRACTICE

(a) An individual shall not fit and adjust spectacle lenses unless that individual complies with the registration requirement of Section 2564.90, and unless either of the following applies:

(1) The individual is a duly registered spectacle lens dispenser as provided in Section 2559.2.

(2) The individual is an unregistered individual who performs the fitting and adjusting under the direct responsibility and supervision of a duly registered spectacle lens dispenser whose certificate of registration is then conspicuously and prominently displayed on the premises.

(b) A supervising registered optician shall be physically present on the registered premises when an unregistered individual fits and adjusts spectacle lenses.

(c) The board shall not take action for a violation of subdivision (b) if either of the following apply:

(1) A supervising registered optician was not physically present on the registered premises due to reasonably unanticipated circumstances, including, but not limited to, illness, injury, family emergency, or the supervising registered optician's termination or resignation, and reasonable action was taken to have another supervising registered optician be physically present on the registered premises.

(2) A supervising registered spectacle lens dispenser was not physically present due to a legally required employee meal or break period.

(Amended by Stats. 2021, Ch. 630, Sec. 58. (AB 1534) Effective January 1, 2022.)

2559.2. APPLICATIONS; REGISTRATION OF APPLICANTS; DISPLAY OF CERTIFICATE

(a) An individual shall apply for registration as a registered spectacle lens dispenser on forms prescribed by the board. The board shall register an individual as a registered spectacle lens dispenser upon satisfactory proof that the individual has passed the registry examination of the American Board of Opticianry or any successor agency to that board. In the event the board should determine, after hearing, that the registry examination is not appropriate to determine entry level competence as a spectacle lens dispenser or is not designed to measure specific job performance requirements, the board may thereafter prescribe or administer a written examination that meets those specifications. If an applicant for renewal has not engaged in the full-time or substantial part-time practice of fitting and adjusting spectacle lenses but has maintained their American Board of Opticianry and National Contact Lens Examiners registration or practiced within another state within the last three years then the board may require the applicant to take and pass the examination referred to in this section as a condition of registration. Any examination prescribed or administered by the board shall be given at least twice each year on dates publicly announced at least 90 days before the examination dates. The board is authorized to contract for administration of an examination.

(b) The board may deny registration where there are grounds for denial under the provisions of Division 1.5 (commencing with Section 475).

(c) The board shall issue a certificate to each qualified individual stating that the individual is a registered spectacle lens dispenser.

(d) A registered spectacle lens dispenser is authorized to fit and adjust spectacle lenses at any place of business holding a certificate of registration under Section 2564.93 or at any location where the practice of ophthalmology or optometry is practiced. The certificate of the registered spectacle lens dispenser shall be displayed in a conspicuous place at the place of business where the registered dispenser is fitting and adjusting.

(Amended by Stats. 2021, Ch. 630, Sec. 59. (AB 1534) Effective January 1, 2022.)

2559.3. SUSPENSION AND REVOCATION OF CERTIFICATES

A certificate issued to a registered spectacle lens dispenser may, in the discretion of the board, be suspended or revoked for violating or attempting to violate any provision of this chapter or any regulation adopted under this chapter, or for incompetence, gross negligence, or repeated similar negligent acts performed by the certificate holder. A certificate may also be suspended or revoked if the individual certificate holder has been convicted of a felony as provided in Section 2555.1.

Any proceedings under this section shall be conducted in accordance with Chapter 5 (commencing with Section 11500) of Part 1 of Division 3 of Title 2 of the Government Code, and the board shall have all the powers granted therein.

(Amended by Stats. 2016, Ch. 489, Sec. 23. (SB 1478) Effective January 1, 2017.)

2559.4. APPLICATION OF ARTICLE

This article shall not apply to an assistant fitting spectacle lenses pursuant to Section 2544 if the assistant is acting under the direct responsibility and supervision of a physician and surgeon or optometrist who engages in the practice of fitting spectacle lenses for his or her patients.

(Amended by Stats. 2010, Ch. 604, Sec. 3. (AB 2683) Effective January 1, 2011.)

2559.5 – [REPEALED]

(Repealed by Stats 2021 ch 630 (AB 1534),s 60, eff. 1/1/2022.)

2559.6 – [REPEALED]

(Repealed by Stats 2021 ch 630 (AB 1534),s 61, eff. 1/1/2022.)

ARTICLE 2: CONTACT LENS DISPENSING

2560. REGISTRATION; TRAINEES

An individual shall not fit and adjust contact lenses, including plano contact lenses, unless that individual complies with the registration requirement of Section 2564.90, and unless either of the following applies:

(a) The individual is a duly registered contact lens dispenser as provided in Section 2561.

(b) The individual is an unregistered individual who performs the fitting and adjusting under the direct responsibility and supervision of a duly registered contact lens dispenser who is then physically present on the registered premises. In no event shall a registered contact lens dispenser supervise more than three unregistered individuals.

(Amended by Stats. 2021, Ch. 630, Sec. 62. (AB 1534) Effective January 1, 2022.)

2561. QUALIFICATIONS FOR REGISTRATION; DENIAL OF REGISTRATION

An individual shall apply for registration as a registered contact lens dispenser on forms prescribed by the board. The board shall register an individual as a registered contact lens dispenser upon satisfactory proof that the individual has passed the contact lens registry examination of the National Committee of Contact Lens Examiners or any successor agency to that committee. In the event the board should ever find after hearing that the registry examination is not appropriate to determine entry level competence as a contact lens dispenser or is not designed to measure specific job performance requirements, the board may thereafter from time to time prescribe or administer a written examination that meets those specifications. If an applicant for renewal has not engaged in the full-time or substantial part-time practice of fitting and adjusting contact lenses within the last five years then the board may require the applicant to take and pass the examination referred to in this section as a condition of registration. Any examination administered by the board shall be given at least twice each year on dates publicly announced at least 90 days before the examination dates. The board is authorized to contract with the National Committee of Contact Lens Examiners or any successor agency to that committee to provide that the registry examination is given at least twice each year on dates publicly announced at least 90 days before the examination dates.

The board may deny registration where there are grounds for denial under the provisions of Division 1.5 (commencing with Section 475).

The board shall issue a certificate to each qualified individual stating that the individual is a registered contact lens dispenser.

A registered contact lens dispenser may use that designation, but shall not hold himself or herself out in advertisements or otherwise as a specialist in fitting and adjusting contact lenses.

(Amended by Stats. 2016, Ch. 489, Sec. 25. (SB 1478) Effective January 1, 2017.)

2562. EVALUATION BY PRESCRIBING PHYSICIAN

Upon satisfactory completion of the fitting of contact lenses, but in no event more than 60 days after receipt of the prescription, a registered contact lens dispenser shall direct the person named in the prescription to return to the prescribing physician and surgeon or optometrist for an evaluation.

(Added by Stats. 1982, Ch. 418, Sec. 8.)

2563. SUSPENSION OR REVOCATION OF CERTIFICATE

A certificate issued to a registered contact lens dispenser may in the discretion of the board be suspended or revoked for violating or attempting to violate any provision of this chapter or any regulation adopted under this chapter, or for incompetence, gross negligence, or repeated similar negligent acts performed by the certificate holder. A certificate may also be suspended or revoked if the individual certificate holder has been convicted of a felony as provided in Section 2555.1.

Any proceedings under this section shall be conducted in accordance with Chapter 5 (commencing with Section 11500) of Part 1 of Division 3 of Title 2 of the Government Code, and the board shall have all the powers granted therein.

(Amended by Stats. 2016, Ch. 489, Sec. 26. (SB 1478) Effective January 1, 2017.)

2564. ASSISTANT FITTING CONTACT LENSES UNDER SUPERVISION OF PHYSICIAN OR OPTOMETRIST

The provisions of this article shall not apply to an assistant fitting contact lenses while acting under the direct responsibility and supervision of a physician and surgeon or optometrist who engages in the practice of fitting contact lenses for his or her patients under Section 2544.

(Amended by Stats. 2010, Ch. 604, Sec. 4. (AB 2683) Effective January 1, 2011.)

2564.5. HANDWASHING FACILITIES

A registered dispensing optician fitting contact lenses shall maintain accessible handwashing facilities on the premises and those facilities shall be used before each fitting of contact lenses. For purposes of this section, "accessible handwashing facilities" means a clean and sanitary sink with clean running water, disinfectant soap, and adequate drying devices such as a towel or electric hand dryer, which is physically separate from a lavatory or bathroom and is accessible to all relevant persons.

(Amended by Stats. 2021, Ch. 630, Sec. 64. (AB 1534) Effective January 1, 2022.)

2564.6. COMPLIANCE WITH 2541.2.

A registered dispensing optician shall comply with the applicable provisions of Section 2541.2.

(Added by Stats. 2002, Ch. 814, Sec. 7. Effective January 1, 2003.)

ARTICLE 2.5. NONRESIDENT OPHTHALMIC LENS DISPENSERS

2564.70

This act may be cited as the "Nonresident Ophthalmic Lens Dispenser Registration Act."

(Added by renumbering Section 2546 by Stats. 2021, Ch. 630, Sec. 26. (AB 1534) Effective January 1, 2022.)

2564.71

(a) A person located outside California shall not ship, mail, furnish, or deliver in any manner, ophthalmic lenses at retail to a patient at a California address unless the person is registered with the California State Board of Optometry.

(b) With regard to any person subject to registration pursuant to this section, only spectacle lenses and replacement contact lenses provided pursuant to a valid prescription as described in Section 2564.76 may be shipped, mailed, furnished, or delivered directly to a patient.

(Added by renumbering Section 2546.1 by Stats. 2021, Ch. 630, Sec. 27. (AB 1534) Effective January 1, 2022.)

2564.73

The board may adopt, amend, or repeal any rules and regulations that are reasonably necessary to carry out this article.

(Added by renumbering Section 2546.3 by Stats. 2021, Ch. 630, Sec. 29. (AB 1534) Effective January 1, 2022.)

2564.74

(a) Application for registration as a nonresident ophthalmic lens dispenser shall be made on forms prescribed by the board, accompanied by the fee prescribed by this article, and shall bear the signature of the individual, or individuals if a copartnership, or the president or secretary if a corporation, and shall contain the name or fictitious or assumed name, if applicable, under which the person proposes to do business, location of the business, registration number issued by the board, if applicable, and the designation of an agent for service of process in California.

(b) The board shall be notified in writing within 30 days of any change of name or fictitious or assumed name, location of business, corporate officer, or agent of service.

(Added by renumbering Section 2546.4 by Stats. 2021, Ch. 630, Sec. 30. (AB 1534) Effective January 1, 2022.)

2564.75

In order to obtain and maintain registration, a nonresident ophthalmic lens dispenser shall:

(a) Be in good standing and either registered or otherwise authorized in the state or jurisdiction in which the selling facility is located and from which the ophthalmic lenses are sold.

(b) Comply with all directions and requests for information made by the board as authorized under this article.

(c) Maintain records of ophthalmic lenses shipped, mailed, furnished, or delivered to patients in California for a period of at least three years.

(d) Provide a toll-free telephone service for responding to patient questions and complaints during the applicant's regular hours of operation, but in no event less than six days per week and 40 hours per week. The toll-free number shall be included in literature provided with each mailed ophthalmic lens prescription. All questions relating to eye care for the lens prescribed shall be referred back to the ophthalmic lens prescriber.

(e) Provide the following or a substantially equivalent written notification to the patient whenever contact lenses are supplied:

WARNING: IF YOU ARE HAVING ANY UNEXPLAINED EYE DISCOMFORT, WATERING, VISION CHANGE, OR REDNESS, REMOVE YOUR LENSES IMMEDIATELY AND CONSULT YOUR EYE CARE PRACTITIONER BEFORE WEARING YOUR LENSES AGAIN.

(f) Disclose in any price advertisement any required membership fees or enrollment fees and indicate that shipping costs may apply unless the advertisement specifically and clearly states otherwise.

(g) Provide a toll-free telephone number, facsimile line, and email address that are dedicated to prescribers and their authorized agents for the purposes of confirmation of ophthalmic lens prescriptions. These numbers, along with an email address, shall be included in any communication with the prescriber when requesting confirmation of an ophthalmic lens prescription.

(h) It shall be considered a deceptive marketing practice for any nonresident ophthalmic lens dispenser to publish or cause to be published any advertisement or sales presentation relating to ophthalmic lenses representing that ophthalmic lenses may be obtained without confirmation of a valid prescription.

(Added by renumbering Section 2546.5 by Stats. 2021, Ch. 630, Sec. 31. (AB 1534) Effective January 1, 2022.)

2564.76

(a) Ophthalmic lenses may be sold only upon receipt of a written prescription or a copy of a written prescription and may be sold in quantities consistent with the prescription's established expiration date and the standard packaging of the manufacturer or vendor. If the written prescription or a copy of it is not available to the dispenser, the dispenser shall confirm the prescription by direct communication with the prescriber or the prescriber's authorized agent before furnishing, shipping, mailing, or delivering any lens, and maintain a record of the communication. A prescription shall be deemed confirmed upon the occurrence of one of the following:

(1) The prescriber or the prescriber's agent confirms the prescription by communication with the dispenser.

(2) The prescriber fails to communicate with the dispenser within eight business hours after the dispenser requests confirmation, or the prescriber fails to communicate with the dispenser by the next business day on or before the same time of day that the dispenser requested confirmation, whichever is sooner. For purposes of this paragraph, "business day" means each day except a Sunday or a federal holiday.

(b) If a prescriber communicates with a dispenser before the time period described in paragraph (2) of subdivision (a) elapses and informs the dispenser that the ophthalmic lens prescription is invalid, the dispenser shall not fill the prescription. The prescriber shall specify in the communication with the dispenser the basis for invalidating the prescription.

(c) A dispenser shall not alter any of the specifications of an ophthalmic lens prescription, other than the color, or substitute a different manufacturer, brand, or other physical property of the lens.

(d) Notwithstanding the provisions of this section, if the ophthalmic lens is manufactured by a company, but sold under multiple private labels by that same company to individual providers, the dispenser may fill the prescription with an ophthalmic lens manufactured by that company if the ophthalmic lens prescription and the related parameters are not substituted, changed, or altered for a different manufacturer or brand.

(Added by renumbering Section 2546.6 by Stats. 2021, Ch. 630, Sec. 32. (AB 1534) Effective January 1, 2022.)

2564.77

(a) A certificate may be denied, to the extent authorized by Section 480, or suspended, revoked, or otherwise subjected to discipline for any of the following:

(1) Incompetence, gross negligence, or repeated similar negligent acts performed by the registrant or any employee of the registrant.

(2) An act of dishonesty or fraud.

(3) Committing any act or being convicted of a crime constituting grounds for denial of licensure or registration under Section 480.

(4) Any violation of Section 2564.75 or 2564.76.

(b) The proceedings shall be conducted in accordance with Chapter 5 (commencing with Section 11500) of Part 1 of Division 3 of Title 2 of the Government Code, and the board shall have all powers granted therein.

(Added by renumbering Section 2546.7 by Stats. 2021, Ch. 630, Sec. 33. (AB 1534) Effective January 1, 2022.)

2564.78

Every registration issued to a nonresident ophthalmic lens dispenser shall expire 24 months after the initial date of issuance. To renew an unexpired registration, the registrant shall, before the time at which the license would otherwise expire, apply for renewal on a form prescribed by the board, and pay the renewal fee prescribed by this article.

(Added by renumbering Section 2546.8 by Stats. 2021, Ch. 630, Sec. 34. (AB 1534) Effective January 1, 2022.)

2564.79

The amount of fees prescribed in connection with the registration of nonresident ophthalmic lens dispensers is that established by the following schedule:

(a) The application fee for a nonresident ophthalmic lens dispenser shall be a minimum of one hundred fifty dollars ($150) and shall not exceed two hundred dollars ($200).

(b) The initial registration fee shall be a minimum of two hundred dollars ($200) and shall not exceed three hundred dollars ($300).

(c) The renewal fee shall be a minimum of two hundred dollars ($200) and shall not exceed three hundred dollars ($300).

(d) The delinquency fee shall be a minimum of fifty dollars ($50) and shall not exceed seventy-five dollars ($75).

(e) The fee for replacement of a lost, stolen, or destroyed registration shall be twenty-five dollars ($25).

(f) The California State Board of Optometry may periodically revise and fix by regulation the fees specified in subdivisions (a), (b), (c), and (d), and these revised fees shall not exceed the reasonable regulatory cost.

(g) The fees collected pursuant to this chapter shall be deposited in the Optometry Fund, and shall be available, upon appropriation, to the California State Board of Optometry for the purposes of this chapter.

(Added by renumbering Section 2546.9 by Stats. 2021, Ch. 630, Sec. 35. (AB 1534) Effective January 1, 2022.)

2564.80

(a) Any person who violates any of the provisions of this chapter shall be subject to a fine of not less than one thousand dollars ($1,000) nor more than thirty-five thousand dollars ($35,000) per violation. The fines collected pursuant to this section shall be available upon appropriation to the California State Board of Optometry for the purposes of administration and enforcement.

(b) The California State Board of Optometry shall adopt regulations implementing this section and shall consider the following factors, including, but not limited to, applicable enforcement penalties, prior conduct, gravity of the offense, and the manner in which complaints will be processed.

(c) The proceedings under this section shall be conducted in accordance with the provisions of Chapter 5 (commencing with Section 11500) of Part 1 of Division 3 of Title 2 of the Government Code.

(Added by renumbering Section 2546.10 by Stats. 2021, Ch. 630, Sec. 36. (AB 1534) Effective January 1, 2022.)

ARTICLE 2.7. REGISTERED DISPENSING OPTHALMIC BUSINESSES

2564.90

Individuals, corporations, and firms engaged in the business of filling prescriptions of physicians and surgeons licensed by the Medical Board of California or the Osteopathic Medical Board of California, or optometrists licensed by the California State Board of Optometry for prescription lenses and kindred products shall be known as dispensing ophthalmic businesses and shall not engage in that business unless registered with the California State Board of Optometry.

(Added by renumbering Section 2550 by Stats. 2021, Ch. 630, Sec. 37. (AB 1534) Effective January 1, 2022.)

2564.91

(a) Individuals, corporations, and firms shall make application for registration and shall not engage in that business defined in Section 2564.90 before being issued a certificate of registration.

(b) Application for that registration shall be on forms prescribed by the board, shall bear the signature of the individual, or general partners if a partnership, or the president or secretary if a corporation or firm, and shall contain the name under which they propose to do business and the business address.

(c) Corporations and firms shall be organized and exist pursuant to the General Corporation Law (Division 1 (commencing with Section 100) of Title 1 of the Corporations Code) and shall not be limited liability companies within the meaning of Title 2.6 of the Corporations Code.

(d) If applicable, the application shall include a list of officers in the corporation, firm, or partnership and a copy of the articles of incorporation submitted to the Secretary of State.

(e) Separate applications shall be made for each place of business and each application shall be accompanied by the application fee prescribed by Section 2565.

(Added by renumbering Section 2551 by Stats. 2021, Ch. 630, Sec. 41. (AB 1534) Effective January 1, 2022.)

2564.92

(a) Each application shall be verified under oath by the person required to sign the application and shall designate the name, address, and direct business telephone number of the applicant's employee who will be responsible for handling customer inquiries and complaints with respect to the business address for which registration is applied. Any changes to this information shall be reported in writing to the board within 14 days.

(b) The applicant shall furnish such additional information or proof, oral or written, which the board may request, including information and proof relating to the provisions of Division 1.5 (commencing with Section 475).

(c) The board shall promptly notify an applicant if, as of the 30th day following the submission of an application under this chapter, the application and supporting documentation are not substantially complete and in proper form. The notification shall be in writing, shall state specifically what documents or other information are to be supplied by the applicant to the board, and shall be sent to the applicant by certified, electronic, or registered mail. Within 30 days of the applicant's submission of the requested documents or information to the board, the board shall notify the applicant by certified, electronic, or registered mail if the board requires additional documents or information.

(Added by Stats. 2021, Ch. 630, Sec. 67. (AB 1534) Effective January 1, 2022.)

2564.93

(a) If the board, after investigation, approves the application, it shall register the applicant and issue to the applicant a certificate of dispensing ophthalmic business. A separate certificate of registration shall be required for each address where the business is to be conducted.

(b) A certificate authorizes the applicant, its agents, and employees, acting therefor, to engage in the business defined in Section 2564.90 provided that the fitting and adjusting of spectacle lenses is performed in compliance with Article 1.5 (commencing with Section 2559.1) and the fitting and adjusting of contact lenses is performed in compliance with Article 2 (commencing with Section 2560). Only individuals registered with the board pursuant to those sections shall perform those supervisory functions.

(Added by Stats. 2021, Ch. 630, Sec. 68. (AB 1534) Effective January 1, 2022.)

2564.94

(a) If a registered dispensing ophthalmic business sells or transfers ownership of their place of business, both of the following requirements shall be satisfied:

(1) The registered dispensing ophthalmic business selling or transferring ownership of the business shall return the certificate of registration to the board no later than 10 calendar days after the change of ownership is completed. This registered dispensing ophthalmic business shall be responsible for complying with all laws relating to the dispensing ophthalmic business until the notice described in paragraph (2) is received by the board.

(2) The registered dispensing ophthalmic business assuming ownership of the business shall record with the board a written notice of the change of ownership, providing all information required by the board. This notice shall be filed with the board no later than 10 calendar days after the change of ownership is completed.

(3) The registered dispensing ophthalmic business assuming ownership of the business shall apply for a new certificate of registration from the board no later than 10 calendar days after the change of ownership is completed.

(b) This section does not apply to a change of location of business by a registered dispensing optician.

(Added by renumbering Section 2553.1 by Stats. 2021, Ch. 630, Sec. 45. (AB 1534) Effective January 1, 2022.)

ARTICLE 3. FISCAL PROVISIONS

2565

The amount of fees prescribed in connection with the registration of dispensing ophthalmic businesses shall be as set forth in this section.

(a) The application fee for registration shall be a minimum of one hundred fifty dollars ($150) and shall not exceed two hundred dollars ($200).

(b) The initial registration fee shall be a minimum of two hundred dollars ($200) and shall not exceed three hundred dollars ($300).

(c) The renewal fee shall be a minimum of two hundred dollars ($200) and shall not exceed three hundred dollars ($300).

(d) The delinquency fee shall be a minimum of fifty dollars ($50) and shall not exceed seventy-five dollars ($75).

(e) The fee for replacement of a lost, stolen, or destroyed certificate shall be twenty-five dollars ($25).

(f) The California State Board of Optometry may periodically revise and fix by regulation the fees specified in subdivisions (a), (b), (c), and (d), and these revised fees shall not exceed the reasonable regulatory cost.

(Amended by Stats. 2021, Ch. 630, Sec. 69. (AB 1534) Effective January 1, 2022.)

2566

The amount of fees prescribed in connection with certificates for contact lens dispensers is as follows:

(a) The application fee for a registered contact lens dispenser shall be a minimum of one hundred fifty dollars ($150) and shall not exceed two hundred dollars ($200).

(b) The initial registration fee shall be a minimum of two hundred dollars ($200) and shall not exceed three hundred dollars ($300).

(c) The biennial fee for the renewal of certificates shall be a minimum of two hundred dollars ($200) and shall not exceed three hundred dollars ($300).

(d) The delinquency fee shall be a minimum of fifty dollars ($50) and shall not exceed seventy-five dollars ($75).

(e) The California State Board of Optometry may by regulation provide for a refund of a portion of the application fee to applicants who do not meet the requirements for registration.

(f) The California State Board of Optometry may periodically revise and fix by regulation the fees specified in subdivisions (a), (b), (c), and (d), and these revised fees shall not exceed the reasonable regulatory cost.

(g) The fee for replacement of a lost, stolen, or destroyed certificate is twenty-five dollars ($25).

(Amended by Stats. 2021, Ch. 630, Sec. 70. (AB 1534) Effective January 1, 2022.)

2566.1

The amount of fees prescribed in connection with certificates for spectacle lens dispensers shall be as set forth in this section:

(a) The application for registration fee shall be a minimum of one hundred fifty dollars ($150) and shall not exceed two hundred dollars ($200).

(b) The initial registration fee shall be a minimum of two hundred dollars ($200) and shall not exceed three hundred dollars ($300).

(c) The renewal fee shall be a minimum of two hundred dollars ($200) and shall not exceed three hundred dollars ($300).

(d) The delinquency fee shall be a minimum of fifty dollars ($50) and shall not exceed seventy-five dollars ($75).

(e) The fee for replacement of a lost, stolen, or destroyed certificate is twenty-five dollars ($25).

(f) The California State Board of Optometry may periodically revise and fix by regulation the fees specified in subdivisions (a), (b), (c), and (d), and these revised fees shall not exceed the reasonable regulatory cost.

(Amended by Stats. 2021, Ch. 630, Sec. 71. (AB 1534) Effective January 1, 2022.)

2566.2

Every registration issued to a dispensing ophthalmic business, contact lens dispenser, and spectacle lens dispenser shall expire 24 months after the initial date of issuance or renewal. To renew an unexpired registration, the registrant shall, before the time at which the license would otherwise expire, apply for renewal on a form prescribed by the board, and pay the renewal fee prescribed by this chapter.

(Amended by Stats. 2021, Ch. 630, Sec. 72. (AB 1534) Effective January 1, 2022.)

2567

(a) All fees collected from persons registered or seeking registration under this chapter shall be paid into the Optometry Fund, and shall be available, upon appropriation, to the California State Board of Optometry for the purposes of this chapter. Any moneys within the Contingent Fund of the Medical Board of California collected pursuant to this chapter shall be deposited in the Optometry Fund. Any moneys within the Dispensing Opticians Fund collected pursuant to this chapter shall be deposited in the Optometry Fund.

(b) The board may employ, subject to civil service regulations, whatever additional clerical assistance is necessary for the administration of this chapter.

(Amended by Stats. 2021, Ch. 630, Sec. 73. (AB 1534) Effective January 1, 2022.)

2568

The board shall report to the Controller at the beginning of each month for the month preceding the amount and source of all revenue received by it pursuant to this chapter, and shall pay the entire amount thereof to the Treasurer for deposit in the Optometry Fund.

(Amended by Stats. 2020, Ch. 121, Sec. 8. (AB 896) Effective September 24, 2020.)

CHAPTER 7. OPTOMETRY

ARTICLE 1. GENERAL PROVISIONS

3000

This chapter constitutes the chapter on optometry. It shall be known and may be cited as the Optometry Practice Act.

(Repealed and added by Stats. 2004, Ch. 426, Sec. 2. Effective January 1, 2005.)

3001

As used in this chapter, an ophthalmic lens is any lens which has a spherical, cylindrical, or prismatic power or value.

(Amended by Stats. 2021, Ch. 630, Sec. 75. (AB 1534) Effective January 1, 2022.)

3002

As used in this chapter, a trial frame or test lens is any frame or lens used in testing the eye, which is not sold and is not for sale to clients.

(Added by Stats. 1937, Ch. 423.)

3003

As used in this chapter, "optometrist" means a person who is licensed to practice optometry in this state under the authority of this chapter.

(Added by Stats. 2004, Ch. 426, Sec. 3. Effective January 1, 2005.)

3004

(a) As used in this chapter, "board" means the California State Board of Optometry.

(b) Any reference in this code or any other code to the "State Board of Optometry" shall be deemed to refer to the "California State Board of Optometry."

(Amended by Stats. 2021, Ch. 630, Sec. 76. (AB 1534) Effective January 1, 2022.)

3005

As used in this chapter, "place of practice" means any location where optometry is practiced.

(Added by Stats. 2004, Ch. 426, Sec. 5. Effective January 1, 2005.)

3006

As used in this chapter, the term "advertise" and any of its variants include the use of a newspaper, magazine, the Internet, or other publication, book, notice, circular, pamphlet, letter, handbill, poster, bill, sign, placard, card, label, tag, window display, store sign, radio announcement, or any other means or methods now or hereafter employed to bring to the attention of the public the practice of optometry or the prescribing, fitting, or sale, in connection therewith, of lenses, frames, or other accessories or appurtenances.

(Amended by Stats. 2017, Ch. 564, Sec. 2. (AB 1708) Effective January 1, 2018.)

3007

An optometrist shall retain a patient's records for a minimum of seven years from the date he or she completes treatment of the patient. If the patient is a minor, the patient's records shall be retained for a minimum of seven years from the date he or she completes treatment of the patient and at least until the patient reaches 19 years of age.

(Added by Stats. 2007, Ch. 276, Sec. 1. Effective January 1, 2008.)

ARTICLE 2. ADMINISTRATION

3010.1

Protection of the public shall be the highest priority for the California State Board of Optometry in exercising its licensing, regulatory, and disciplinary functions.

Whenever the protection of the public is inconsistent with other interests sought to be promoted, the protection of the public shall be paramount.

(Amended by Stats. 2021, Ch. 630, Sec. 77. (AB 1534) Effective January 1, 2022.)

3010.5

(a) There is in the Department of Consumer Affairs a California State Board of Optometry in which the enforcement of this chapter is vested. The board consists of 11 members, five of whom shall be public members and one of the nonpublic members shall be an individual registered as a dispensing optician, spectacle lens dispenser, or contact lens dispenser. The registered dispensing member shall be registered pursuant to Chapter 5.5 (commencing with Section 2550) and in good standing with the board.

Six members of the board shall constitute a quorum.

(b) The board shall, with respect to conducting investigations, inquiries, and disciplinary actions and proceedings, have the authority previously vested in the board as created pursuant to former Section 3010. The board may enforce any disciplinary actions undertaken by that board.

(c) This section shall remain in effect only until January 1, 2026, and as of that date is repealed. Notwithstanding any other law, the repeal of this section renders the board subject to review by the appropriate policy committees of the Legislature.

(Amended by Stats. 2021, Ch. 630, Sec. 78. (AB 1534) Effective January 1, 2022. Repealed as of January 1, 2026, by its own provisions.)

3011

(a) Members of the board, except the public members and the registered dispensing member, shall be appointed only from persons who are registered optometrists of the State of California and actually engaged in the practice of optometry at the time of appointment or who are members of the faculty of a school of optometry. The public members shall not be a licentiate of the board or of any other board under this division or of any board referred to in Sections 1000 and 3600.

No person except the registered dispensing member, including the public members, shall be eligible to membership on the board who is a stockholder in or owner of or a member of the board of trustees of any school of optometry or who shall be financially interested, directly or indirectly, in any concern manufacturing or dealing in optical supplies at wholesale.

No person shall serve as a member of the board for more than two consecutive terms.

A member of the faculty of a school of optometry may be appointed to the board; however, no more than two faculty members of schools of optometry may be on the board at any one time. Faculty members of the board shall not serve as public members.

(b) The amendments to this section by the act adding this subdivision shall apply to appointments made on or after January 1, 2016.

(Amended by Stats. 2016, Ch. 31, Sec. 5. (SB 836) Effective June 27, 2016.)

3013

(a) Each member of the board shall hold office for a term of four years, and shall serve until the appointment and qualification of his or her successor or until one year shall have elapsed since the expiration of the term for which he or she was appointed, whichever first occurs.

(b) Vacancies occurring shall be filled by appointment for the unexpired term.

(c) The Governor shall appoint three of the public members, five members qualified as provided in Section 3011, and the registered dispensing member as provided in Section 3010.5. The Senate Committee on Rules and the Speaker of the Assembly shall each appoint a public member.

(d) No board member serving between January 1, 2000, and June 1, 2002, inclusive, shall be eligible for reappointment.

(e) For initial appointments made on or after January 1, 2003, one of the public members appointed by the Governor and two of the professional members shall serve terms of one year. One of the public members appointed by the Governor and two of the professional members shall serve terms of three years. The remaining public member appointed by the Governor and the remaining two professional members shall serve terms of four years. The public members appointed by the Senate Committee on Rules and the Speaker of the Assembly shall each serve for a term of four years.

(f) The initial appointment of a registered dispensing optician, spectacle lens dispenser, or contact lens dispenser member shall replace the optometrist member whose term expired on June 1, 2015.

(g) The amendments to this section by the act adding this subdivision shall apply to appointments made on or after January 1, 2016.

(Amended by Stats. 2016, Ch. 31, Sec. 6. (SB 836) Effective June 27, 2016.)

3014

The board shall elect from its membership a president, a vice president, and a secretary who shall hold office for one year or until the election and qualification of a successor.

(Amended by Stats. 2004, Ch. 426, Sec. 9. Effective January 1, 2005.)

3014.6

(a) The board may appoint a person exempt from civil service who shall be designated as an executive officer and who shall exercise the powers and perform the duties delegated by the board and vested in him or her by this chapter.

(b) This section shall remain in effect only until January 1, 2026, and as of that date is repealed.

(Amended by Stats. 2021, Ch. 630, Sec. 79. (AB 1534) Effective January 1, 2022. Repealed as of January 1, 2026, by its own provisions.)

3016

Each member of the board shall receive a per diem and expenses as provided in Section 103.

(Amended by Stats. 2004, Ch. 426, Sec. 11. Effective January 1, 2005.)

3017

The board shall hold regular meetings every calendar quarter.

Special meetings shall be held upon request of a majority of the members of the board or upon the call of the president.

(Amended by Stats. 2004, Ch. 426, Sec. 12. Effective January 1, 2005.)

3018

The board shall keep an accurate record of all of its licensees, proceedings, and meetings.

(Amended by Stats. 2004, Ch. 426, Sec. 13. Effective January 1, 2005.)

3019

The board shall keep a record of all prosecutions for violations of this chapter and of all applications for licensure and examination.

(Amended by Stats. 2004, Ch. 426, Sec. 14. Effective January 1, 2005.)

3020

(a) There shall be established under the California State Board of Optometry a dispensing optician committee to advise and make recommendations to the board regarding the regulation of dispensing opticians, spectacle lens dispensers, and contact lens dispensers, registered pursuant to Chapter 5.5 (commencing with Section 2550). The committee shall consist of five members, one of whom shall be a registered dispensing optician registered pursuant to Chapter 5.5 (commencing with Section 2550), one of whom shall be a spectacle lens dispenser or contact lens dispenser registered pursuant to Chapter 5.5 (commencing with Section 2550), two of whom shall be public members, and one of whom shall be a member of the board. Initial appointments to the committee shall be made by the board. The board shall stagger the terms of the initial members appointed. The filling of vacancies on the committee shall be made by the board upon recommendations by the committee.

(b) The committee shall be responsible for:

(1) Recommending registration standards and criteria for the registration of dispensing opticians, nonresident contact lens sellers, spectacle lens dispensers, and contact lens dispensers.

(2) Reviewing of the disciplinary guidelines relating to registered dispensing opticians, nonresident contact lens sellers, spectacle lens dispensers, and contact lens dispensers.

(3) Recommending to the board changes or additions to regulations adopted pursuant to Chapter 5.5 (commencing with Section 2550).

(4) Carrying out and implementing all responsibilities and duties imposed upon it pursuant to this chapter or as delegated to it by the board.

(c) The committee shall meet at least twice a year and as needed in order to conduct its business.

(d) Recommendations by the committee regarding scope of practice or regulatory changes or additions shall be approved, modified, or rejected by the board within 90 days of submission of the recommendation to the board. If the board rejects or significantly modifies the intent or scope of the recommendation, the committee may request that the board provide its reasons in writing for rejecting or significantly modifying the recommendation, which shall be provided by the board within 30 days of the request.

(e) After the initial appointments by the board pursuant to subdivision (a), the Governor shall appoint the registered dispensing optician members and the public members. The committee shall submit a recommendation to the board regarding which board member should be appointed to serve on the committee, and the board shall appoint the member to serve. Committee members shall serve a term of four years except for the initial staggered terms. A member may be reappointed, but no person shall serve as a member of the committee for more than two consecutive terms.

(Amended by Stats. 2021, Ch. 630, Sec. 80. (AB 1534) Effective January 1, 2022.)

3021

The board shall have rulemaking authority with respect to Chapter 5.5 (commencing with Section 2550) in accordance with Section 3025. Regulations adopted pursuant to Chapter 5.5 (commencing with Section 2550) by the Medical Board of California prior to the effective date of this section shall continue to be valid, except that any reference to the board or division contained therein shall be construed to mean the California State Board of Optometry, unless the context determines otherwise.

(Amended by Stats. 2021, Ch. 630, Sec. 81. (AB 1534) Effective January 1, 2022.)

3023

For the purposes of this chapter, the board shall accredit schools, colleges, and universities in or out of this state providing optometric education, that it finds giving a sufficient program of study for the preparation of optometrists.

(Amended by Stats. 2004, Ch. 426, Sec. 18. Effective January 1, 2005.)

3023.1

(a) The nonresident contact lens seller program established under Chapter 5.45 (commencing with Section 2546) and the registered dispensing optician, spectacle lens dispensing, and contact lens dispensing programs established under Chapter 5.5 (commencing with Section 2550) are hereby transferred from the jurisdiction of the Medical Board of California and placed under the jurisdiction of the State Board of Optometry.

(b) All the duties, powers, purposes, responsibilities, and jurisdictions of the Medical Board of California under Chapter 5.45 (commencing with Section 2546) and Chapter 5.5 (commencing with Section 2550) shall be transferred to the State Board of Optometry.

(c) For the performance of the duties and the exercise of the powers vested in the board under Chapter 5.45 (commencing with Section 2546) and Chapter 5.5 (commencing with Section 2550), the State Board of Optometry shall have possession and control of all records, papers, offices, equipment, supplies, or other property, real or personal, held for the benefit or use by the Medical Board of California.

(Added by Stats. 2015, Ch. 405, Sec. 16. (AB 684) Effective January 1, 2016.)

3024

The board may grant or refuse to grant an optometrist license as provided in this chapter and may revoke or suspend the license of any optometrist for any of the causes specified in this chapter.

It shall have the power to administer oaths and to take testimony in the exercise of these functions.

(Amended by Stats. 2013, Ch. 473, Sec. 4. (SB 821) Effective January 1, 2014.)

3025

The board may make and promulgate rules and regulations governing procedure of the board, the admission of applicants for examination for a license as an optometrist, and the practice of optometry. All of those rules and regulations shall be in accordance with and not inconsistent with the provisions of this chapter. The rules and regulations shall be adopted, amended, or repealed in accordance with the provisions of the Administrative Procedure Act.

(Amended by Stats. 2013, Ch. 473, Sec. 5. (SB 821) Effective January 1, 2014.)

3025.1

The board may adopt rules and regulations that are, in its judgment, reasonable and necessary to ensure that optometrists have the knowledge to adequately protect the public health and safety by establishing educational requirements for admission to the examinations for licensure.

(Amended by Stats. 2010, Ch. 653, Sec. 12. (SB 1489) Effective January 1, 2011.)

3025.2

The board may adopt rules and regulations that are, in its judgment, reasonable and necessary to ensure that optometrists have the knowledge to adequately protect the public health and safety by governing its accreditation of schools, colleges, and universities that provide optometric education. In promulgating these rules and regulations, or in extending accreditation, the board may, to the extent that it deems consistent with the purposes of this chapter, recognize, accept, or adopt the advice, recommendation, accreditation, or approval of a nationally recognized accrediting agency or organization.

(Added by Stats. 2004, Ch. 426, Sec. 21. Effective January 1, 2005.)

3025.5

The board may adopt regulations prescribing minimum standards governing the optometric services offered or performed, the equipment, or the sanitary conditions, in all offices for the practice of optometry, which are necessary to protect the health and safety of persons availing themselves of the services offered or performed in such offices.

(Added by Stats. 1963, Ch. 1464.)

3025.6

The board may adopt regulations clarifying the level of training and the level of supervision of assistants.

(Added by Stats. 2002, Ch. 1150, Sec. 20. Effective January 1, 2003.)

3025.7

Except as provided in Sections 3102 and 3103, nothing contained in Section 651.3 shall be construed as authorizing the board to adopt, amend, or repeal rules and regulations relating to price fixing or advertising of commodities.

(Amended by Stats. 2005, Ch. 393, Sec. 1. Effective January 1, 2006.)

3026

The board may adopt and use a common seal and establish a permanent office or offices.

(Added by Stats. 1937, Ch. 423.)

3027

The board shall employ an executive officer and other necessary assistance in the carrying out of the provisions of this chapter.

The executive officer shall perform the duties delegated by the board and shall be responsible to it for the accomplishment of those duties. The executive officer shall not be a member of the board. With the approval of the Director of Finance, the board shall fix the salary of the executive officer. The executive officer shall be entitled to traveling and other necessary expenses in the performance of the executive officer's duties.

(Amended by Stats. 2021, Ch. 630, Sec. 82. (AB 1534) Effective January 1, 2022.)

3028

The Attorney General shall act as the legal counsel for the board and his or her services shall be a charge against it.

(Added by Stats. 2004, Ch. 426, Sec. 26. Effective January 1, 2005.)

3030

(a) The board, or its designated agent, may at any time inspect either of the following:

(1) Any premise in which optometric services, as defined in Section 3041, are provided or reasonably suspected of being provided.

(2) Any premise in which the services of dispensing, adjusting, or fitting of contact lenses or spectacle lenses are provided or reasonably suspected of being provided.

(b) Nothing in this section shall be construed to grant the board jurisdiction over the practice of medicine.

(Amended by Stats. 2017, Ch. 564, Sec. 5. (AB 1708) Effective January 1, 2018.)

ARTICLE 3. ADMISSION TO PRACTICE

3040

(a) It is unlawful for a person to engage in the practice of optometry or to advertise or hold himself or herself out as an optometrist without a valid, unrevoked California optometrist license. The practice of optometry includes the performing or controlling of any acts set forth in Section 3041.

(b) In any prosecution for a violation of this section, the use of test cards, test lenses, or of trial frames is prima facie evidence of the practice of optometry.

(Amended by Stats. 2018, Ch. 703, Sec. 24. (SB 1491) Effective January 1, 2019.)

3041

(a) The practice of optometry includes the diagnosis, prevention, treatment, and management of disorders and dysfunctions of the visual system, as authorized by this chapter, as well as the provision of habilitative or rehabilitative optometric services, and is the doing of any or all of the following:

(1) The examination of the human eyes and their adnexa, including through the use of all topical and oral diagnostic pharmaceutical agents that are not controlled substances, and the analysis of the human vision system, either subjectively or objectively.

(2) The determination of the powers or range of human vision and the accommodative and refractive states of the human eyes, including the scope of their functions and general condition.

(3) The prescribing, using, or directing the use of any optical device in connection with ocular exercises, visual training, vision training, or orthoptics.

(4) The prescribing, fitting, or adaptation of contact and spectacle lenses to, the human eyes, including lenses that may be classified as drugs or devices by any law of the United States or of this state, and diagnostic or therapeutic contact lenses that incorporate a medication or therapy the optometrist is certified to prescribe or provide.

(5) For an optometrist certified pursuant to Section 3041.3, diagnosing and preventing conditions and diseases of the human eyes and their adnexa, and treating nonmalignant conditions and diseases of the anterior segment of the human eyes and their adnexa, including ametropia and presbyopia:

(A) Using or prescribing, including for rational off-label purposes, topical and oral prescription and nonprescription therapeutic pharmaceutical agents that are not controlled substances and are not antiglaucoma agents or limited or excluded by subdivision (b). For purposes of this section, “controlled substance” has the same meaning as used in the California Uniform Controlled Substances Act (Division 10 (commencing with Section 11000) of the Health and Safety Code) and the United States Uniform Controlled Substances Act (21 U.S.C. Sec. 801 et seq.).

(B) Prescribing the oral analgesic controlled substance codeine with compounds, hydrocodone with compounds, and tramadol as listed in the California Uniform Controlled Substances Act (Division 10 (commencing with Section 11000) of the Health and Safety Code) and the United States Uniform Controlled Substances Act (21 U.S.C. Sec. 801 et seq.), limited to three days, with referral to an ophthalmologist if the pain persists.

(C) If also certified under subdivision (c), using or prescribing topical and oral antiglaucoma agents for the medical treatment of all primary open-angle, exfoliation, pigmentary, and steroid-induced glaucomas in persons 18 years of age or over. In the case of steroid-induced glaucoma, the prescriber of the steroid medication shall be promptly notified if the prescriber did not refer the patient to the optometrist for treatment.

(D) If also certified under subdivision (d), independent initiation and administration of immunizations for influenza, herpes zoster virus, pneumococcus, and SARS-CoV-2 in compliance with individual Advisory Committee on Immunization Practices (ACIP) vaccine recommendations published by the federal Centers for Disease Control and Prevention (CDC) in persons 18 years of age or over.

(E) Utilizing the following techniques and instrumentation necessary for the diagnosis of conditions and diseases of the eye and adnexa:

(i) Laboratory tests or examinations ordered from an outside facility.

(ii) Laboratory tests or examinations performed in a laboratory with a certificate of waiver under the federal Clinical Laboratory Improvement Amendments of 1988 (CLIA) (42 U.S.C. Sec. 263a; Public Law 100-578), which shall also be allowed for:

(I) Detecting indicators of possible systemic disease that manifests in the eye for the purpose of facilitating appropriate referral to or consultation with a physician and surgeon.

(II) Detecting the presence of SARS-CoV-2 virus.

(iii) Skin testing performed in an office to diagnose ocular allergies, limited to the superficial layer of the skin.

(iv) X-rays ordered from an outside facility.

(v) Other imaging studies ordered from an outside facility subject to prior consultation with an appropriate physician and surgeon.

(vi) Other imaging studies performed in an office, including those that utilize laser or ultrasound technology, but excluding those that utilize radiation.

(F) Performing the following procedures, which are excluded from restrictions imposed on the performance of surgery by paragraph (6) of subdivision (b), unless explicitly indicated:

(i) Corneal scraping with cultures.

(ii) Debridement of corneal epithelium not associated with band keratopathy.

(iii) Mechanical epilation.

(iv) Collection of blood by skin puncture or venipuncture for laboratory testing authorized by this subdivision.

(v) Suture removal subject to co-management requirements in paragraph (7) of subdivision (b).

(vi) Treatment or removal of sebaceous cysts by expression.

(vii) Lacrimal punctal occlusion using plugs, or placement of a stent or similar device in a lacrimal canaliculus intended to deliver a medication the optometrist is certified to prescribe or provide.

(viii) Foreign body and staining removal from the cornea, eyelid, and conjunctiva with any appropriate instrument. Removal of corneal foreign bodies and any related stain shall, as relevant, be limited to that which is nonperforating, no deeper than the midstroma, and not reasonably anticipated to require surgical repair.

(ix) Lacrimal irrigation and dilation in patients 12 years of age or over, excluding probing of the nasolacrimal tract. The board shall certify any optometrist who graduated from an accredited school of optometry before May 1, 2000, to perform this procedure after submitting proof of satisfactory completion of 10 procedures under the supervision of an ophthalmologist as confirmed by the ophthalmologist. Any optometrist who graduated from an accredited school of optometry on or after May 1, 2000, shall be exempt from the certification requirement contained in this paragraph.

(x) Administration of oral fluorescein for the purpose of ocular angiography.

(xi) Intravenous injection for the purpose of performing ocular angiography at the direction of an ophthalmologist as part of an active treatment plan in a setting where a physician and surgeon is immediately available.

(xii) Use of noninvasive devices delivering intense pulsed light therapy or low-level light therapy that do not rely on laser technology, limited to treatment of conditions and diseases of the adnexa.

(xiii) Use of an intranasal stimulator in conjunction with treatment of dry eye syndrome.

(G) Using additional noninvasive medical devices or technology that:

(i) Have received a United States Food and Drug Administration approved indication for the diagnosis or treatment of a condition or disease authorized by this chapter. A licensee shall successfully complete any clinical training imposed by a related manufacturer prior to using any of those noninvasive medical devices or technologies.

(ii) Have been approved by the board through regulation for the rational treatment of a condition or disease authorized by this chapter. Any regulation under this paragraph shall require a licensee to successfully complete an appropriate amount of clinical training to qualify to use each noninvasive medical device or technology approved by the board pursuant to this paragraph.

(b) Exceptions or limitations to the provisions of subdivision (a) are as follows:

(1) Treatment of the following is excluded from the practice of optometry in a patient under 18 years of age, unless explicitly allowed otherwise:

(A) Anterior segment inflammation, which shall not exclude treatment of:

(i) The conjunctiva.

(ii) Nonmalignant ocular surface disease, including dry eye syndrome.

(iii) Contact lens-related inflammation of the cornea.

(iv) An infection of the cornea.

(B) Conditions or diseases of the sclera.

(2) Use of any oral prescription steroid anti-inflammatory medication for a patient under 18 years of age shall be done pursuant to a documented, timely consultation with an appropriate physician and surgeon.

(3) Use of any nonantibiotic oral prescription medication for a patient under five years of age shall be done pursuant to a documented, prior consultation with an appropriate physician and surgeon.

(4) The following classes of agents are excluded from the practice of optometry unless they have an explicit United States Food and Drug Administration-approved indication for treatment of a

condition or disease authorized under this section:

(A) Antiamoebics.

(B) Antineoplastics.

(C) Coagulation modulators.

(D) Hormone modulators.

(E) Immunomodulators.

(5) The following are excluded from authorization under subparagraph (G) of paragraph (5) of subdivision (a):

(A) A laboratory test or imaging study.

(B) Any noninvasive device or technology that constitutes surgery under paragraph (6).

(6) Performing surgery is excluded from the practice of optometry. "Surgery" means any act in which human tissue is cut, altered, or otherwise infiltrated by any means. It does not mean an act that solely involves the administration or prescribing of a topical or oral therapeutic pharmaceutical.

(7) (A) Treatment with topical and oral medications authorized in subdivision (a) related to an ocular surgery shall be comanaged with the ophthalmologist that performed the surgery, or another ophthalmologist designated by that surgeon, during the customary preoperative and postoperative period for the procedure. For purposes of this subparagraph, this may involve treatment of ocular inflammation in a patient under 18 years of age.

(B) Where published, the postoperative period shall be the "global" period established by the federal Centers for Medicare and Medicaid Services, or, if not published, a reasonable period not to exceed 90 days.

(C) Such comanaged treatment may include addressing agreed-upon complications of the surgical procedure occurring in any ocular or adnexal structure with topical and oral medications authorized in subdivision (a). For patients under 18 years of age, this subparagraph shall not apply unless the patient's primary care provider agrees to allowing comanagement of complications.

(c) An optometrist certified pursuant to Section 3041.3 shall be certified to medically treat authorized glaucomas under this chapter after meeting the following requirements:

(1) For licensees who graduated from an accredited school of optometry on or after May 1, 2008, submission of proof of graduation from that institution.

(2) For licensees who were certified to treat glaucoma under this section before January 1, 2009, submission of proof of completion of that certification program.

(3) For licensees who completed a didactic course of not less than 24 hours in the diagnosis, pharmacological, and other treatment and management of glaucoma, submission of proof of satisfactory completion of the case management requirements for certification established by the board.

(4) For licensees who graduated from an accredited school of optometry on or before May 1, 2008, and who are not described in paragraph (2) or (3), submission of proof of satisfactory completion of the requirements for certification established by the board under Chapter 352 of the Statutes of 2008.

(d) An optometrist certified pursuant to Section 3041.3 shall be certified to administer authorized immunizations, as described in subparagraph (D) of paragraph (5) of subdivision (a), after the optometrist meets all of the following requirements:

(1) Completes an immunization training program endorsed by the federal Centers for Disease Control and Prevention (CDC) or the Accreditation Council for Pharmacy Education that, at a minimum, includes hands-on injection technique, clinical evaluation of

indications and contraindications of vaccines, and the recognition and treatment of emergency reactions to vaccines, and maintains that training.

(2) Is certified in basic life support.

(3) Complies with all state and federal recordkeeping and reporting requirements, including providing documentation to the patient's primary care provider and entering information in the appropriate immunization registry designated by the immunization branch of the State Department of Public Health.

(4) Applies for an immunization certificate in accordance with Section 3041.5.

(e) Other than for prescription ophthalmic devices described in subdivision (b) of Section 2541, any dispensing of a therapeutic pharmaceutical agent by an optometrist shall be without charge.

(f) An optometrist licensed under this chapter is subject to the provisions of Section 2290.5 for purposes of practicing telehealth.

(g) For the purposes of this chapter, all of the following definitions shall apply:

(1) "Adnexa" means the eyelids and muscles within the eyelids, the lacrimal system, and the skin extending from the eyebrows inferiorly, bounded by the medial, lateral, and inferior orbital rims, excluding the intraorbital extraocular muscles and orbital contents.

(2) "Anterior segment" means the portion of the eye anterior to the vitreous humor, including its overlying soft tissue coats.

(3) "Ophthalmologist" means a physician and surgeon, licensed under Chapter 5 (commencing with Section 2000) of Division 2 of the Business and Professions Code, specializing in treating eye disease.

(4) "Physician and surgeon" means a physician and surgeon licensed under Chapter 5 (commencing with Section 2000) of Division 2 of the Business and Professions Code.

(5) "Prevention" means use or prescription of an agent or noninvasive device or technology for the purpose of inhibiting the development of an authorized condition or disease.

(6) "Treatment" means use of or prescription of an agent or noninvasive device or technology to alter the course of an authorized condition or disease once it is present.

(h) In an emergency, an optometrist shall stabilize, if possible, and immediately refer any patient who has an acute attack of angle closure to an ophthalmologist.

(Amended by Stats. 2022, Ch. 596, Sec. 3. (AB 2574) Effective January 1, 2023.)

3041.1

An optometrist diagnosing or treating eye disease shall be held to the same standard of care to which physicians and surgeons and osteopathic physicians and surgeons are held. An optometrist shall consult with and, if necessary, refer to a physician and surgeon or other appropriate health care provider when a situation or condition occurs that is beyond the optometrist's scope of practice. Consultations, referrals, and notifications required by this section shall be documented in the patient record.

(Amended by Stats. 2017, Ch. 549, Sec. 3. (AB 443) Effective January 1, 2018.)

3041.2

The California State Board of Optometry shall, by regulation, establish educational and examination requirements for licensure to ensure the competence of optometrists to practice pursuant to this chapter. Satisfactory completion of the educational and examination requirements shall be a condition for the issuance of an original optometrist license or certifications pursuant to this chapter.

(Amended by Stats. 2021, Ch. 630, Sec. 83. (AB 1534) Effective January 1, 2022.)

3041.3

(a) In order to be certified to use therapeutic pharmaceutical agents and authorized to diagnose and treat the conditions listed in subdivisions (b) and (d) of Section 3041, an optometrist shall apply for a certificate from the board and meet all requirements imposed by the board.

(b) The board shall grant a therapeutic pharmaceutical agents (TPA) certification to any applicant who graduated from a California accredited school of optometry prior to January 1, 1996, is licensed as an optometrist in California, and meets all of the following requirements:

(1) Completes a preceptorship of no less than 65 hours, during a period of not less than two months nor more than one year, with either a TPA-certified optometrist in good standing or a physician and surgeon board-certified in ophthalmology in good standing. The training received during the preceptorship shall be on the diagnosis, treatment, and management of ocular and systemic disease. The preceptor shall certify completion of the preceptorship using a form approved by the board. The individual serving as the preceptor shall schedule no more than three optometrist applicants for each of the required 65 hours of the preceptorship program. This paragraph shall not be construed to limit the total number of optometrist applicants for whom an individual may serve as a preceptor, and is intended only to ensure the quality of the preceptorship by requiring that the preceptor schedule the training so that each applicant optometrist completes each of the 65 hours of the preceptorship while scheduled with no more than two other optometrist applicants.

(2) Successfully completes a minimum of 100 hours of directed and accredited education in ocular and systemic diseases within two years prior to meeting the requirements of paragraph (1).

(3) Passes the National Board of Examiners in Optometry's "Treatment and Management of Ocular Disease" examination or, in the event this examination is no longer offered, its equivalent, as determined by the California State Board of Optometry.

(c) The board shall grant a therapeutic pharmaceutical agents certification to any applicant who graduated from a California accredited school of optometry on or after January 1, 1996, who is licensed as an optometrist in California, and who passes all sections of the National Board of Examiners in Optometry's national board examination or its equivalent, as determined by the California State Board of Optometry.

(d) The board shall grant a therapeutic pharmaceutical agents certification to any applicant who is an optometrist who obtained their license outside of California if they meet all of the requirements for an optometrist licensed in California to be granted a therapeutic pharmaceutical agents certification.

(1) In order to obtain a therapeutic pharmaceutical agents certification, any optometrist who obtained their license outside of California and graduated from an accredited school of optometry prior to January 1, 1996, shall be required to fulfill the requirements set forth in subdivision (b). In order for the applicant to be eligible for therapeutic pharmaceutical agents certification, the education the applicant received at the accredited out-of-state school of optometry shall be equivalent to the education provided by any accredited school of optometry in California for persons who graduate before

January 1, 1996. For those out-of-state applicants who request that any of the requirements contained in subdivision (b) be waived based on fulfillment of the requirement in another state, if the board determines that the completed requirement was equivalent to that required in California, the requirement shall be waived.

(2) In order to obtain a therapeutic pharmaceutical agents certification, any optometrist who obtained their license outside of California and who graduated from an accredited school of optometry on or after January 1, 1996, shall be required to fulfill the requirements set forth in subdivision (c). In order for the applicant to be eligible for therapeutic pharmaceutical agents certification, the education the applicant received by the accredited out-of-state school of optometry shall be equivalent to the education provided by any accredited school of optometry for persons who graduate on or after January 1, 1996. For those out-of-state applicants who request that any of the requirements contained in subdivision (c) be waived based on fulfillment of the requirement in another state, if the board determines that the completed requirement was equivalent to that required in California, the requirement shall be waived.

(3) The California State Board of Optometry shall decide all issues relating to the equivalency of an optometrist's education or training under this subdivision.

(Amended by Stats. 2021, Ch. 630, Sec. 84. (AB 1534) Effective January 1, 2022.)

3041.5

(a) A person requesting to be certified to administer immunizations pursuant to Section 3041 shall apply for a certificate from the board pursuant to an application that shall be in substantially the following form:

"Application for Optometrists to Administer Immunizations

Per California Business and Professions Code 3041(g), you must have a current California Optometrist License and have a Therapeutic Pharmaceutical Agents (TPA) license type to be eligible for a certificate to administer immunizations. "Immunization" means the administration of immunizations for influenza, herpes zoster virus, pneumococcus, and SARS-CoV-2 in compliance with individual Advisory Committee on Immunization Practices (ACIP) vaccine recommendations published by the federal Centers for Disease Control and Prevention (CDC) for persons 18 years of age or older.

If eligible, you must also meet and maintain the following requirements for an immunization certificate:

1. Complete an immunization training program endorsed by the CDC or the Accreditation Council for Pharmacy Education that, at a minimum, includes hands-on injection technique, clinical evaluation of indications and contraindications of vaccines, and the recognition and treatment of emergency reactions to vaccines, and maintain that training.

2. Be certified in basic life support.

3. Comply with all state and federal recordkeeping and reporting requirements, including providing documentation to the patient's primary care provider and entering information in the appropriate immunization registry designated by the immunization branch of the California State Department of Public Health.

To apply for an immunization certificate, provide documentation for items #1 and #2 above with your application. All documentation must be provided, or the application will be rejected.

First, Middle, and Last Name: _____

Email address: _____

License No. : _____

1. I declare under penalty of perjury under the laws of the State of California that the information provided on this form and the attached documents or other requested proof of completion is true and accurate. I understand and agree that any misstatements of material facts may be cause for denial of the Application for Optometrists to Administer Immunizations and disciplinary action by the California State Board of Optometry.

AND

2. I declare under penalty of perjury under the laws of the State of California that I will comply with all state and federal recordkeeping and reporting requirements, including providing documentation to the patient's primary care provider and entering information in the appropriate immunization registry designated by the immunization branch of the California State Department of Public Health.

Optometrist Signature: ____________

Date:______________"

(b) The application for an immunization certificate set forth in subdivision (a) shall be accompanied by an application fee of fifty dollars ($50), or a fee in an amount as determined by the board, not to exceed the reasonable cost of administering this section.

(c) After the effective date of this section, the board may modify the Application for Optometrists to Administer Immunizations set forth in subdivision (a) by regulation in accordance with Section 3025.

(Added by Stats. 2021, Ch. 654, Sec. 2. (AB 691) Effective October 8, 2021.)

3042

The provisions of this chapter do not prevent a licensed physician and surgeon from treating or fitting glasses to the human eye, or from doing any act within the practice of optometry, or a licensed physician and surgeon or optometrist from filling prescriptions or orders, nor do they prevent the replacing, duplicating or repairing of ophthalmic lenses, frames, or fittings by persons qualified to write or fill prescriptions or orders under the provisions of this chapter, nor prevent the doing of the mechanical work upon those lenses, frames, or fittings by an assistant, nor prevent an assistant acting under the responsibility and direction of a physician and surgeon or an optometrist from using any optical device in connection with ocular exercises, vision training, or orthoptics, or acts set forth in Section 2544.

It is unlawful for a person to dispense, replace, or duplicate an ophthalmic lens without a prescription or order from a licensed physician and surgeon or optometrist.

(Amended by Stats. 2004, Ch. 426, Sec. 30. Effective January 1, 2005.)

3042.5

(a) The practice of persons actually enrolled as undergraduate or graduate students of optometry in the clinical departments of schools or colleges of optometry accredited by the board shall be exempt from the provisions of this chapter; provided, however, that such practice shall be entirely confined to the operations of the clinical department of the accredited school or college of optometry and shall be carried on only in pursuing the study of optometry.

(b) The board may grant, for specified periods, exemption from the provisions of this chapter to any person who is licensed in another state or country and who is employed as a clinician or instructor by an accredited school or college of optometry. Such exemption from the provisions of this chapter shall extend only to practice which is conducted for educational purposes and which is confined to the clinical department of the accredited school or college employing the person to whom the exemption is granted.

(Added by Stats. 1955, Ch. 110.)

3043

The provisions of this chapter do not prohibit the sale of goggles, sun glasses, colored glasses or occupational eye-protective devices if they do not have refractive values nor do the provisions of this chapter prohibit the sale of complete ready to wear eyeglasses as merchandise by any person not holding himself out as competent to examine, test or prescribe for the human eye or its refractive errors.

(Added by Stats. 1937, Ch. 423.)

3044

A person over the age of 18 years desiring to engage in the practice of optometry in this state may file an application for examination and an application for licensure. The application shall be accompanied by the fee required by this chapter.

(Amended by Stats. 2004, Ch. 426, Sec. 31. Effective January 1, 2005.)

3045

Applications shall be verified by the oath of the applicant and shall contain information and evidence satisfactory to the board showing the eligibility of the applicant.

(Amended by Stats. 2004, Ch. 426, Sec. 32. Effective January 1, 2005.)

3046

In order to obtain a license to practice optometry in California, an applicant shall have graduated from an accredited school of optometry, passed the required examinations for licensure, not have met any of the grounds for denial established in Section 480, and not be currently required to register as a sex offender pursuant to Section 290 of the Penal Code. The proceedings under this section shall be in accordance with Chapter 5 (commencing with Section 11500) of Part 1 of Division 3 of Title 2 of the Government Code.

(Amended by Stats. 2013, Ch. 516, Sec. 14. (SB 305) Effective January 1, 2014.)

3046.1

(a) The board shall issue a temporary license to practice optometry to any person who applies for and is eligible for licensure pursuant to Section 3046, but who is unable to immediately take the Section III - Clinical Skills Examination developed by the National Board of Examiners in Optometry (NBEO), required for licensure under this chapter, due to the state of emergency, proclaimed by the Governor on March 4, 2020, in response to the COVID-19 pandemic. In addition to Section 3046, the person shall also satisfy all of the following conditions:

(1) The person has never been previously licensed to practice optometry in any state in the United States.

(2) The person pays to the board the applicable fee of one hundred dollars ($100), or a fee in an amount as determined by the board, not to exceed the reasonable cost of administering this section and submits an application to be a temporary licensee, as described in subdivision (j), to the board.

(3) The person has received approval from their accredited school of optometry that the person meets the educational requirements to practice optometry.

(4) The person satisfies all other conditions to licensure established by this chapter.

(b) A person holding a temporary license shall be subject to the same rights and restrictions that are afforded to a person holding a valid, unrevoked

California optometrist license, except as set forth in this section. For the purposes of this chapter, "temporary licensee" means a person holding a temporary license pursuant to this section.

(c) A temporary licensee shall practice under the direct supervision of a supervising optometrist. For the purposes of this chapter, "supervising optometrist" means a California licensed optometrist that has been licensed for a minimum of five years and has been certified for the treatment of glaucoma, pursuant to subdivision (e) of Section 3041, and submits an application to be a supervising optometrist, as described in subdivision (k), to the board. A licensed physician practicing ophthalmology may also supervise a temporary licensee and shall be subject to all of the same reporting requirements as set forth in this section.

(d) Notwithstanding any other law, a temporary licensee may perform services as authorized by this chapter if both of the following requirements are met:

(1) The temporary licensee renders the services under the direct supervision of a supervising optometrist who is not subject to a disciplinary condition imposed by the board prohibiting that supervision or prohibiting the employment of a temporary licensee.

(2) The supervising optometrist is legally and professionally responsible for the actions of the temporary licensee.

(e) For the purposes of this chapter, "direct supervision" means that a supervising optometrist oversees the activities of, and accepts responsibility for, the services rendered by a temporary licensee. Direct supervision, as defined in this subdivision, requires that the supervising optometrist be physically present and immediately available in the facility or office in which the optometric services are being provided when the temporary licensee is with a patient.

(f) The supervising optometrist shall have a formal written procedure in place by which patients are informed that an optometrist with a temporary license will be performing the services. Additionally, the patient shall be informed that the supervising optometrist will be supervising the temporary licensee and the supervising optometrist will be identified to the patient. The temporary licensee shall note in the medical record the patient's consent to this process prior to performing services authorized by this chapter.

(g) During the timeframe in which the temporary licensee holds a temporary license, the temporary licensee shall not open their own optometric office or place of practice.

(h) The temporary license shall expire either upon the date that the temporary licensee completes all of the requirements for licensure or six months after the date the state of emergency, proclaimed by the Governor on March 4, 2020, in response to the COVID-19 pandemic has ended, pursuant to Section 8629 of the Government Code, whichever occurs first.

(i) The supervising optometrist shall submit in writing to the board any violations of this chapter committed by the temporary licensee within 14 days of becoming aware of the violation.

(j) A person requesting to be a temporary licensee shall apply to the board pursuant to an application that shall be in substantially the following form, and may include any other information the board deems appropriate to safeguard the public from substandard optometric care, fraud, or other violation of this chapter:

"Application for Temporary License

Pursuant to Section 3046.1 of the Business and Professions Code, the board shall issue a temporary license to practice optometry to any person who applies for and is eligible for licensure pursuant to Section 3046 of the Business and Professions Code, but who is unable to immediately take the Section III - Clinical Skills Examination developed by the National Board of Examiners in Optometry (NBEO), required for licensure under this chapter, due to the state of emergency, proclaimed by the Governor on March 4, 2020, in response to the COVID-19 pandemic. If eligible, you must also meet and maintain the following requirements to be a temporary licensee:

(1) Never been previously licensed to practice optometry in any state in the United States; and

(2) Receive confirmation via transcript or other correspondence from your accredited school of optometry that you meet the educational requirements to practice optometry.

To apply to be a temporary licensee, provide documentation for item (2) above with your application. All documentation must be provided, or the application will be rejected.

First, Middle, and Last Name:

Address (City, State, Zip Code):

Phone Number:

Email Address:

Social Security or ITIN number:

Date of Birth:

Name of School of Optometry:

Address of School of Optometry (City, State, Zip Code, Country):

Date Degree Conferred:

Name and License Number of Supervising Optometrist:

Date you completed the CLRE:

Regulations require the submission of fingerprints prior to issuance of the temporary license. Due to a change in the regulations, fingerprints are now checked by the Department of Justice (DOJ) and the Federal Bureau of Investigation (FBI). Live Scan is required for California residents and a Manual Fingerprint Card is required for non-California residents.

I declare under penalty of perjury under the laws of the State of California that the information provided on this form and the attached documents or other requested proof of completion is true and accurate. I understand and agree that any misstatements of material facts may be cause for denial of the Application for Temporary License and disciplinary action by the State Board of Optometry.

Applicant Signature:

Date: "

(k) A person requesting to be a supervising optometrist shall apply to the board pursuant to an application that shall be in substantially the following form, and may include any other information the board deems appropriate to safeguard the public from substandard optometric care, fraud, or other violation of this chapter:

"Application to be a Supervising Optometrist

Pursuant to Section 3046.1 of the Business and Professions Code, an individual may act as supervising optometrist to a temporary licensee, as defined in that section, if they meet the following conditions:

(1) Has been licensed for a minimum of five years; and

(2) Has been certified for the treatment of glaucoma pursuant to subdivision (e) of Section 3041.

To apply to be a supervising optometrist, provide documentation for items (1) and (2) above with your application. All documentation must be provided, or the application will be rejected.

First, Middle, and Last Name:

Address of Record:

Phone Number:

Email Address:

License Number:

Name of temporary licensee whom you will be supervising:

1. I declare under penalty of perjury under the laws of the State of California that the information provided on this form and the attached documents or other requested proof of completion is true and accurate. I understand and agree that any misstatements of material facts may be cause for denial of the application to be a Supervising Optometrist and disciplinary action by the State Board of Optometry.

AND

2. I declare under penalty of perjury under the laws of the State of California that I will comply with all duties as a supervising optometrist set forth in Section 3046.1 of the Business and Professions Code, and that pursuant to that section, I am legally and professionally responsible for the actions of the temporary licensee which may result in action being taken against my license in cases of temporary licensee misconduct.

Applicant Signature:

Date: "

(l) The board shall not be required to adopt regulations pursuant to the Administrative Procedure Act (Chapter 3.5 (commencing with Section 11340) of Part 1 of Division 3 of Title 2 of the Government Code) to carry out this section.

(Amended by Stats. 2022, Ch. 28, Sec. 4. (SB 1380) Effective January 1, 2023.)

3047

(a) The board shall develop an interface with the National Practitioner Data Bank for the purpose of conducting inquiries on applicants for licensure, applicants for renewal of licensure, and current licensees.

(b) The board shall limit its inquiries to both of the following:

(1) Whether an applicant or current licensee has been subject to discipline.

(2) Whether an applicant or current licensee has been the subject of an action required to be reported to the National Practitioner Data Bank by federal law.

(c) On and after July 1, 2018, the board shall charge, in addition to the fees in Section 3152, an applicant for licensure and an applicant for renewal of licensure four dollars ($4) for the purposes of this section.

(Amended by Stats. 2018, Ch. 571, Sec. 17. (SB 1480) Effective January 1, 2019.)

3051

All applicants for examination for an optometrist license in accordance with the educational and examination requirements adopted pursuant to Section 3023.1 shall show the board by satisfactory evidence that he or she has received education in child abuse detection and the detection of alcoholism and other chemical substance dependency. This section shall apply only to applicants who matriculate in a school of optometry on or after September 1, 1997.

(Amended by Stats. 2013, Ch. 473, Sec. 8. (SB 821) Effective January 1, 2014.)

3053

All examinations shall be practical in character, designed to ascertain applicants' fitness to practice the profession of optometry and conducted in the English language. The board may by rule or regulation accept the examination given by other agencies or organizations which it deems equivalent to the examination required to determine an applicant's fitness to practice optometry.

(Amended by Stats. 1978, Ch. 872.)

3054

The passing grades for the licensure examination shall be based on psychometrically sound principles of establishing minimum qualifications and levels of competency. If an applicant fails to pass any section of the examination, he or she may be examined in any succeeding examination held during the next five years only in those sections in which he or she failed to obtain a passing grade.

(Amended by Stats. 2004, Ch. 426, Sec. 37. Effective January 1, 2005.)

3055

The board shall issue a license to an applicant who meets the requirements of this chapter, including the payment of the prescribed licensure, certification, or renewal fee, and who meets any other requirement in accordance with state law. A license or certificate issued under the chapter shall be subject to renewal as prescribed by the board and shall expire unless renewed in that manner. The board may provide for the late renewal of a license or certificate as provided for in Section 163.5.

(Repealed and added by Stats. 2004, Ch. 426, Sec. 39. Effective January 1, 2005.)

3056

(a) The board may issue a license to practice optometry to a person who meets all of the following qualifications:

(1) Has a degree as a doctor of optometry issued by an accredited school or college of optometry.

(2) Is currently licensed in another state.

(3) Is currently a full-time faculty member of an accredited California school or college of optometry and has served in that capacity for a period of at least five continuous years.

(4) Has attained, at an accredited California school or college of optometry, the academic rank of professor, associate professor, or clinical professor, except that the status of adjunct or affiliated faculty member shall not be deemed sufficient.

(5) Has successfully passed the board's jurisprudence examination.

(6) Is in good standing, with no past or pending malpractice awards or judicial or administrative actions.

(7) Has met the minimum continuing education requirements set forth in Section 3059 for the current and preceding year.

(8) Has met the requirements of Section 3041.3 regarding the use of therapeutic pharmaceutical agents under subdivision (d) of Section 3041.

(9) Has never had his or her license to practice optometry revoked or suspended.

(10) (A) Is not subject to denial based on any of the grounds listed in Section 480.

(B) Is not currently required to register as a sex offender pursuant to Section 290 of the Penal Code.

(11) Pays an application fee in an amount equal to the application fee prescribed by the board pursuant to Section 3152.

(12) Files an application on a form prescribed by the board.

(b) Any license issued pursuant to this section shall expire as provided in Section 3146, and may be renewed as provided in this chapter, subject to the same conditions as other licenses issued under this chapter.

(c) The term "in good standing," as used in this section, means that a person under this section:

(1) Is not currently under investigation nor has been charged with an offense for any act substantially related to the practice of optometry by any public agency, nor entered into any consent

agreement or subject to an administrative decision that contains conditions placed by an agency upon a person's professional conduct or practice, including any voluntary surrender of license, nor been the subject of an adverse judgment resulting from the practice of optometry that the board determines constitutes evidence of a pattern of incompetence or negligence.

(2) Has no physical or mental impairment related to drugs or alcohol, and has not been found mentally incompetent by a physician so that the person is unable to undertake the practice of optometry in a manner consistent with the safety of a patient or the public.

(Amended by Stats. 2017, Ch. 549, Sec. 6. (AB 443) Effective January 1, 2018.)

3057

(a) The board may issue a license to practice optometry to a person who meets all of the following requirements:

(1) Has a degree as a doctor of optometry issued by an accredited school or college of optometry.

(2) Has successfully passed the licensing examination for an optometric license in another state.

(3) Submits proof that he or she is licensed in good standing as of the date of application in every state where he or she holds a license, including compliance with continuing education requirements.

(4) Is not subject to disciplinary action as set forth in subdivision (h) of Section 3110. If the person has been subject to disciplinary action, the board shall review that action to determine if it presents sufficient evidence of a violation of this chapter to warrant the submission of additional information from the person or the denial of the application for licensure.

(5) Has furnished a signed release allowing the disclosure of information from the National Practitioner Data Bank and, if applicable, the verification of registration status with the federal Drug Enforcement Administration. The board shall review this information to determine if it presents sufficient evidence of a violation of this chapter to warrant the submission of additional information from the person or the denial of the application for licensure.

(6) Has never had his or her license to practice optometry revoked or suspended in any state where the person holds a license. This paragraph shall become inoperative on July 1, 2018.

(7) (A) Is not subject to denial of an application for licensure based on any of the grounds listed in Section 480.

(B) Is not currently required to register as a sex offender pursuant to Section 290 of the Penal Code.

(8) Has met the minimum continuing education requirements set forth in Section 3059 for the current and preceding year.

(9) Has met the certification requirements of Section 3041.3 to use therapeutic pharmaceutical agents under subdivision (d) of Section 3041.

(10) Submits any other information as specified by the board to the extent it is required for licensure by examination under this chapter.

(11) Files an application on a form prescribed by the board, with an acknowledgment by the person executed under penalty of perjury and automatic forfeiture of license, of the following:

(A) That the information provided by the person to the board is true and correct, to the best of his or her knowledge and belief.

(B) That the person has not been convicted of an offense involving conduct that would violate Section 810.

(12) Pays an application fee in an amount equal to the application fee prescribed pursuant to subdivision (a) of Section 3152.

(13) Has successfully passed the board's jurisprudence examination.

(b) If the board finds that the competency of a candidate for licensure pursuant to this section is in question, the board may require the passage of a written, practical, or clinical examination or completion of additional continuing education or coursework.

(c) In cases where the person establishes, to the board's satisfaction, that he or she has been displaced by a federally declared emergency and cannot relocate to his or her state of practice within a reasonable time without economic hardship, the board may reduce or waive the fees required by paragraph (12) of subdivision (a).

(d) Any license issued pursuant to this section shall expire as provided in Section 3146, and may be renewed as provided in this chapter, subject to the same conditions as other licenses issued under this chapter.

(e) The term "in good standing," as used in this section, means that a person under this section:

(1) Is not currently under investigation nor has been charged with an offense for any act substantially related to the practice of optometry by any public agency, nor entered into any consent agreement or subject to an administrative decision that contains conditions placed by an agency upon a person's professional conduct or practice, including any voluntary surrender of license, nor been the subject of an adverse judgment resulting from the practice of optometry that the board determines constitutes evidence of a pattern of incompetence or negligence.

(2) Has no physical or mental impairment related to drugs or alcohol, and has not been found mentally incompetent by a licensed psychologist or licensed psychiatrist so that the person is unable to undertake the practice of optometry in a manner consistent with the safety of a patient or the public.

(Amended by Stats. 2017, Ch. 564, Sec. 7.5. (AB 1708) Effective January 1, 2018.)

3059

(a) It is the intent of the Legislature that the public health and safety would be served by requiring all holders of licenses to practice optometry granted under this chapter to continue their education after receiving their licenses. The board shall adopt regulations that require, as a condition to the renewal thereof, that all holders of licenses submit proof satisfactory to the board that they have informed themselves of the developments in the practice of optometry occurring since the original issuance of their licenses by pursuing one or more courses of study satisfactory to the board or by other means deemed equivalent by the board.

(b) The board may, in accordance with the intent of this section, make exceptions from continuing education requirements for reasons of health, military service, or other good cause.

(c) If for good cause compliance cannot be met for the current year, the board may grant exemption of compliance for that year, provided that a plan of future compliance that includes current requirements as well as makeup of previous requirements is approved by the board.

(d) The board may require that proof of compliance with this section be submitted on an annual or biennial basis as determined by the board.

(e) An optometrist certified to use therapeutic pharmaceutical agents pursuant to Section 3041.3 shall complete a total of 50 hours of continuing education every two years in order to renew his or her certificate. Thirty-five of the required 50 hours of continuing education shall be on the diagnosis, treatment, and management of ocular disease in any combination of the following areas:

(1) Glaucoma.

(2) Ocular infection.

(3) Ocular inflammation.

(4) Topical steroids.

(5) Systemic medication.

(6) Pain medication, including the risks of addiction associated with the use of Schedule II drugs.

(f) The board shall encourage every optometrist to take a course or courses in pharmacology and pharmaceuticals as part of his or her continuing education.

(g) The board shall consider requiring courses in child abuse detection to be taken by those licensees whose practices are such that there is a likelihood of contact with abused or neglected children.

(h) The board shall consider requiring courses in elder abuse detection to be taken by those licensees whose practices are such that there is a likelihood of contact with abused or neglected elder persons.

(Amended by Stats. 2018, Ch. 693, Sec. 9. (SB 1109) Effective January 1, 2019.)

3060

The board shall periodically develop and disseminate to all persons licensed to practice optometry information and educational material regarding all of the following:

(a) The detection of child abuse and neglect. The board shall consult with the Office of Child Abuse Prevention in developing the materials distributed pursuant to this subdivision.

(b) The detection of elder abuse and neglect. The board shall consult with the Adult Protective Services Division of the State Department of Social Services in developing the materials distributed pursuant to this subdivision.

(Added by Stats. 1997, Ch. 556, Sec. 3. Effective January 1, 1998.)

ARTICLE 4. REGISTRATION

3070

(a) Before engaging in the practice of optometry, each licensed optometrist shall notify the board in writing of the address or addresses where he or she is to engage in the practice of optometry and, also, of any changes in his or her place of practice. After providing the address or addresses and place of practice information to the board, a licensed optometrist shall obtain a statement of licensure from the board to be placed in all practice locations other than an optometrist's principal place of practice. The practice of optometry is the performing or the controlling of any of the acts set forth in Section 3041.

(b) A licensed optometrist is not required to provide the notification described in subdivision (a) if he or she engages in the temporary practice of optometry. "Temporary practice" is defined as the practice of optometry at locations other than the optometrist's principal place of practice for not more than five calendar days during a 30-day period, and not more than 36 days within a calendar year. This limitation shall apply to all practice locations where the licensed optometrist is engaging in temporary practice, not to each practice location individually. If the time period of the temporary practice needs to be extended for any reason, the licensed optometrist shall submit an application for a statement of licensure to the board pursuant to Section 1506 of Title 16 of the California Code of Regulations.

(c) Notwithstanding Section 3075, an optometrist engaging in the temporary practice of optometry at a location described in subdivision (b) shall carry and present upon demand evidence of his or her licensure but shall not be required to post his or her current license or other evidence of current license status issued by the board.

(d) In addition to the information required by Section 3076, a receipt issued to a patient by an optometrist engaging in the temporary practice of optometry at a location described in subdivision (b) shall contain the address of the optometrist's primary practice location and the temporary practice location where the services were provided.

(Amended by Stats. 2018, Ch. 334, Sec. 1. (SB 1386) Effective January 1, 2019.)

3070.1

(a) For purposes of this section, the following terms have the following meanings:

(1) "Health facility" means a health facility, as defined in Section 1250 of the Health and Safety Code, exclusive of a hospital defined in subdivision (a) or (b) of that section.

(2) "Residential care facility" means a residential facility, as defined in paragraph (1) of subdivision (a) of Section 1502 of the Health and Safety Code, licensed by the State Department of Social Services, including, but not limited to, the following:

(A) Adult residential facilities.

(B) Adult residential facilities for persons with special health care needs.

(C) Residential care facilities for the chronically ill.

(D) Residential care facilities for the elderly.

(E) Continuing care retirement communities.

(F) Social rehabilitation facilities.

(3) "Home residence" means the primary residence of an individual who is restricted by a disabling physical or mental condition. "Home residence" does not include a health facility, as defined in Section 1250 of the Health and Safety Code, or a community care facility, as defined in subdivision (a) of Section 1502 of the Health and Safety Code, but does include an individual condominium unit, apartment, single-family home, cooperative unit, mobilehome, or trailer, if it is used as a residence.

(b) (1) An optometrist who is certified as a therapeutic pharmaceutical agent pursuant to Section 3041.3 may, in the form and manner prescribed by the board, submit an application to the board for a home residence permit, and pay all applicable fees prescribed in Section 3152. The board shall, upon application and payment of the fee prescribed in Section 3152, issue a home residence permit to an optometrist certified as a therapeutic pharmaceutical agent pursuant to Section 3041.3. A home residence permit authorizes the holder to engage in the practice of optometry at a home residence as specified in this section.

(2) A home residence permit shall expire on the same date the licensee's optometry license expires. A home residence optometrist may renew the permit by submitting an application, in the form and manner prescribed by the board, to the board for renewal, and paying any applicable fees prescribed in Section 3152.

(3) A person engaging in the temporary practice of optometry, as defined in subdivision (b) of Section 3070, is not required to obtain a home residence permit in order to engage in the temporary practice of optometry at a home residence.

(c) An optometrist may engage in the practice of optometry at any health facility or residential care facility, and in a home residence, if all of the following requirements are satisfied:

(1) The optometrist maintains a primary business office, separate from the health facility, residential care facility, or home residence, that meets all of the following requirements:

(A) Is open to the public during normal business hours by telephone and for purposes of billing services or access to patient records.

(B) Is licensed to the optometrist or the employer of the optometrist as a local business with the city or county in which it is located.

(C) Is registered by the optometrist with the Board of Optometry.

(D) Is owned or leased by the optometrist or by the employer of the optometrist.

(E) Is not located in or connected with a residential dwelling.

(2) The optometrist maintains or discloses patient records in the following manner:

(A) Records are maintained and made available to the patient in such a way that the type and extent of services provided to the patient are conspicuously disclosed. The disclosure of records shall be made at or near the time services are rendered and shall be maintained at the primary business office specified in paragraph (1).

(B) The optometrist complies with all federal and state laws and regulations regarding the maintenance and protection of medical records, including, but not limited to, the federal Health Insurance Portability and Accountability Act of 1996 (42 U.S.C. Sec. 300gg).

(C) Pursuant to Section 3007, the optometrist keeps all necessary records for a minimum of seven years from the date of service in order to disclose fully the extent of services furnished to a patient. Any information included on a printed copy of an original document to a patient shall be certified by the optometrist as being true, accurate, and complete.

(D) If a prescription is issued to a patient, records shall be maintained for each prescription as part of the patient's chart, including all of the following information about the optometrist:

(i) Name.

(ii) Optometrist license number.

(iii) The place of practice and the primary business office.

(iv) Description of the goods and services for which the patient is charged and the amount charged.

(E) A copy of any referral or order requesting optometric services for a patient from the health facility's or residential care facility's administrator, director of social services, the attending physician and surgeon, the patient, or a family member shall be kept in the patient's medical record.

(3) The optometrist possesses and appropriately uses the instruments and equipment required for all optometric services and procedures performed within the health facility, residential care facility, or home residence.

(4) The optometrist provides each patient and, if applicable, the patient's caregiver, a consumer notice prescribed by the board that includes the following:

(A) The name, license number, primary telephone number, and primary business address of the optometrist.

(B) Information for filing a complaint with the board.

(d) An optometrist who satisfies all of the requirements in this section for the practice of optometry at a health facility, residential care facility, or home residence shall not be required to comply with Section 3070 with regard to providing notification to the board of each health facility, residential care facility, or home residence at which the optometrist practices.

(e) Before engaging in the practice of optometry at a home residence, an optometrist shall provide each patient and, if applicable, the patient's caregiver, both of the following:

(1) A consumer notice prescribed by the board that includes any information the board deems appropriate to safeguard the public from substandard optometric care, fraud, and other violations of the act. The patient, or, if applicable, the patient's caregiver, shall sign the consumer notice.

(2) An authorization to release the patient's medical information related to the optometrist's provision of optometry services to the board. The authorization shall disclose that the patient's authorization to release medical information to the board is voluntary and that the medical information shall be used by the board only to investigate complaints and to conduct the board's enforcement duties under the act.

(f) An optometrist subject to subdivision (e) shall maintain in the patient's file a copy of the signed consumer notice described in paragraph (1) of, and, if signed, the signed authorization described in paragraph (2) of, subdivision (e).

(g) The board may adopt regulations to conduct quality assurance reviews for optometrists engaging in the practice of optometry at a home residence.

(Amended by Stats. 2019, Ch. 425, Sec. 1. (AB 458) Effective January 1, 2020.)

3070.2

(a) As used in this section, "mobile optometric office" means a trailer, van, or other means of transportation in which the practice of optometry, as defined in Section 3041, is performed and which is not affiliated with an approved optometry school in California.

(b) This section shall not apply to any of the following:

(1) Optometric services provided remotely by an approved optometry school in California that meets the requirements of Section 1507 of Title 16 of the California Code of Regulations.

(2) A licensee engaged in the practice of optometry at a facility defined in paragraph (1), (2), or (3) of subdivision (a) of Section 3070.1.

(3) A federally qualified health center, as defined in Section 1396d(l)(2)(B) of Title 42 of the United States Code.

(4) A nonprofit or charitable organization exempt from taxation pursuant to Section 501(c)(3), 501(c)(4), or 501(c)(6) of the Internal Revenue Code (26 U.S.C. Sec. 501(c)(3), 501(c)(4), or 501(c)(6)), which utilizes the volunteer services of licensees engaging in the temporary practice of optometry pursuant to subdivision (b) of Section 3070.

(5) A free clinic, as defined in subparagraph (B) of paragraph (1) of subdivision (a) of Section 1204 of the Health and Safety Code, which is operated by a clinic corporation, as defined in paragraph (3) of subdivision (b) of Section 1200 of the Health and Safety Code.

(6) A specialized vision health care service plan, as defined in subdivision (f) of Section 1345 of the Health and Safety Code, formed and existing pursuant to the provisions of the Nonprofit Corporation Law (Division 2 (commencing with Section 5000) of Title 1 of the Corporations Code).

(c) The ownership and operation of a mobile optometric office shall be limited to a nonprofit or charitable organization that is exempt from taxation pursuant to Section 501(c)(3) or 501(c)(4) of the United States Internal Revenue Code that provides optometric services to patients regardless of the patient's ability to pay.

(1) The owner and operator of a mobile optometric office shall register with the board. The owner and operator of a mobile optometric office and the optometrist providing services shall not accept payment for services other than those provided through the Medi-Cal program or through any of the state's programs under the Children's Health Insurance Program (CHIP) under Title XIX (42 U.S.C. Sec. 1396 et seq.), or Title XXI (42 U.S.C. Sec. 1397aa et seq.), of the Social Security Act.

(2) The medical operations of the mobile optometric office shall be directed by a licensed optometrist and in every phase shall be under the exclusive control of the licensed optometrist, including the selection and supervision of optometric staff, the scheduling of patients, the amount of time the optometrist or optician spends with patients, the fees charged for optometric products and services, the examination procedures, the treatment provided to patients, and the followup care pursuant to this section.

(3) The owner and operator of a mobile optometric office shall not operate more than 12 mobile optometric offices within the first renewal period of two years, but may operate more than 12 offices after the first renewal period is complete.

(d) An owner and operator who has obtained approval from the board pursuant to paragraph (1) of subdivision (c) and wishes to operate a mobile optometric office shall apply for a permit from the board before beginning operation of each mobile optometric office. The application shall be made on a board-prescribed form that requests any information the board deems appropriate to register a mobile optometric office pursuant to this section. The form shall be accompanied by a nonrefundable fee of four hundred seventy-two dollars ($472). The board may increase the fee, as necessary to cover the reasonable regulatory costs of administration, to not more than six hundred dollars ($600).

(1) Upon approval of the permit, the board shall issue a unique identifying number for each mobile optometric office that shall be used in all reporting by the owner and operator to the board.

(2) Upon approval, the permit shall be valid until the next renewal date of the owner and operator registration.

(3) Mobile optometric office permits are specific to the vehicle registered with the board. Permits are not transferrable.

(4) An owner and operator may apply for renewal of the mobile optometric office permit by attesting to compliance with the requirements of this section and payment of the biennial renewal fee prescribed by the board.

(e) The owner and operator of the mobile optometric office registering with the board pursuant to subdivision (c) shall provide the following information to the board:

(1) The description of services to be rendered within the mobile optometric office.

(2) The names and optometry license numbers of optometrists, registration numbers of opticians, and names of any other persons who are providing patient care, as described in Section 2544.

(3) The dates of operation and cities or counties served.

(4) A description of how followup care will be provided.

(5) A catalog of complaints, if any.

(6) Articles of incorporation or acknowledgment of intent to operate and employer identification number demonstrating the owner and operator is a nonprofit or charitable organization that is exempt from taxation pursuant

to Section 501(c)(3) or 501(c)(4) of the Internal Revenue Code.

(7) Any other information the board deems appropriate to safeguard the public from substandard optometric care, fraud, or other violation of this chapter.

(f) The owner and operator of the mobile optometric office, on a form prescribed by the board, shall file a quarterly report containing the following information:

(1) A list of all visits made by each mobile optometric office, including dates of operation, address, care provided, and names and license numbers of optometrists and opticians who provided care.

(2) A summary of all complaints received by each mobile optometric office, the disposition of those complaints, and referral information.

(3) An updated and current list of licensed optometrists, registered opticians, and any other persons who have provided care within each mobile optometric office since the last reporting period.

(4) An updated and current list of licensed optometrists who are available for followup care as a result of a complaint on a volunteer basis or who accept Medi-Cal payments.

(5) Any other information the board deems appropriate to safeguard the public from substandard optometric care, fraud, or other violation of this chapter.

(g) The owner and operator of the mobile optometric office shall notify the board of any change to the information provided to the board pursuant to subdivision (d) within 14 days.

(h) (1) The owner and operator of the mobile optometric office shall provide each patient and, if applicable, the patient's caregiver or guardian, a consumer notice prescribed by the board that includes the following:

(A) The name, license number, and contact information for the optometrist.

(B) Optometrists providing services at a mobile optometric office are regulated by the board and the contact information for filing a complaint with the board.

(C) Information on how to obtain a copy of the patient's medical information.

(D) Information on followup care available for the patient, including a list of available Medi-Cal or volunteer optometrists. This list shall be updated every six months and is subject to the inspection by the board.

(E) Any other information the board deems appropriate to safeguard the public from substandard optometric care, fraud, or other violation of this chapter.

(2) The optometrist shall maintain a copy of the consumer notice described in paragraph (1) in the patient's medical record.

(3) Upon request by the patient's caregiver or guardian, a copy of the prescription made for the patient shall be provided.

(i) Any person who is employed by the owner and operator of the mobile optometric office to drive or transport the vehicle shall possess a valid driver's license.

(j) By January 1, 2023, the board shall adopt regulations establishing a registry for the owners and operators of mobile optometric offices and shall set a registration fee at an amount not to exceed the reasonable regulatory costs of administration.

(k) The board may adopt regulations to conduct quality assurance reviews for the owner and operator of a mobile optometric office and optometrists engaging in the practice of optometry at a mobile optometric office.

(l) The board shall not bring an enforcement action against an owner and operator of a mobile optometric office based solely on its affiliation status with an approved optometry school in California for remotely providing optometric service before January 1, 2023.

(m) The owner and operator of a mobile optometric office shall maintain records in the following manner, which shall be made available to the board upon request for inspection:

(1) Records are maintained and made available to the patient in such a way that the type and extent of services provided to the patient are conspicuously disclosed. The disclosure of records shall be made at or near the time services are rendered and shall be maintained at the primary business office specified.

(2) The owner and operator of a mobile optometric office complies with all federal and state laws and regulations regarding the maintenance and protection of medical records, including, but not limited to, the federal Health Insurance Portability and Accountability Act of 1996 (42 U.S.C. Sec. 300gg).

(3) Pursuant to Section 3007, the owner and operator of the mobile optometric office keeps all necessary records for a minimum of seven years from the date of service in order to disclose fully the extent of services furnished to a patient. Any information included on a printed copy of an original document to a patient shall be certified by the owner and operator of the mobile optometric office as being true, accurate, and complete.

(4) If a prescription is issued to a patient, records shall be maintained for each prescription as part of the patient's chart, including all of the following information about the optometrist:

(A) Name.

(B) Optometrist license number.

(C) The place of practice and the primary business office.

(D) Description of the goods and services for which the patient is charged and the amount charged. If no charge was made to the patient, a description of the goods and services provided.

(5) The owners and operators of the mobile optometric offices shall maintain accurate records of the mobile optometric offices, including vehicle registration numbers and the year, make, and model of each trailer or van.

(n) Any licensed optometrist who provides patient care in conjunction with a mobile optometric office shall obtain a statement of licensure pursuant to subdivision (a) of Section 3070 with the mobile optometric office's address as registered with the board. If the licensee is not practicing optometry at a location other than with the owner and operator of the mobile optometric office, then the licensee shall list as their primary address of record the owner and operator of the mobile optometric office's address as registered with the board.

(o) All examinations performed at the mobile optometric office shall be performed by a licensed optometrist who is certified to use therapeutic pharmaceutical agents pursuant to Section 3041.3.

(p) This section does not apply to optometry services defined in Section 3070.1.

(q) This section shall remain in effect only until July 1, 2025, and as of that date is repealed.

(Amended by Stats. 2023, Ch. 487, Sec. 1. (SB 502) Effective January 1, 2024. Repealed as of July 1, 2025, by its own provisions.)

3075

An optometrist shall post in each location where he or she practices optometry, in an area that is likely to be seen by all patients who use the office, his or her current license or other evidence of current license status issued by the board. The board may charge a fee as specified in Section 3152 for each issuance of evidence of current licensure.

(Amended by Stats. 2007, Ch. 276, Sec. 3. Effective January 1, 2008.)

3076

A licensed optometrist shall deliver to each patient that makes a payment to the practice, excluding insurance copayments and deductibles, a receipt that contains all of the following information:

(a) His or her name.

(b) The number of his or her optometrist license.

(c) His or her place of practice.

(d) A description of the goods and services for which the patient is charged and the amount charged.

(Amended by Stats. 2005, Ch. 393, Sec. 2. Effective January 1, 2006.)

3077

As used in this section, "office" means any office or other place for the practice of optometry, including but not limited to vans, trailers, or other mobile equipment.

(a) No person, singly or in combination with others, may have an office unless that person is licensed to practice optometry under this chapter or the registered owner and operator of a nonprofit mobile optometric office as set out in this chapter.

(b) No optometrist, and no two or more optometrists jointly, may have more than 11 offices.

(c) Any failure to comply with the provisions of this section shall result in the suspension of the optometrist license of each optometrist who, individually or with others, has an office. An optometrist license so suspended shall not be restored except upon compliance with those provisions and the payment of the fee prescribed by this chapter for restoration of a license after suspension for failure to comply with this section.

(d) The board shall have the power to adopt, amend, and repeal rules and regulations to carry out the provisions of this section.

(e) Notwithstanding any other provision of this section, neither an optometrist nor an individual practice association shall be deemed to have an additional office solely by reason of the optometrist's participation in an individual practice association or the individual practice association's creation or operation. As used in this subdivision, the term "individual practice association" means an entity that meets all of the following requirements:

(1) Complies with the definition of an optometric corporation in Section 3160.

(2) Operates primarily for the purpose of securing contracts with health care service plans or other third-party payers that make available eye/vision services to enrollees or subscribers through a panel of optometrists.

(3) Contracts with optometrists to serve on the panel of optometrists, but does not obtain an ownership interest in, or otherwise exercise control over, the respective optometric practices of those optometrists on the panel.

(f) For purposes of Section 3070.2, "office" shall include a van, trailer, or mobile equipment owned and operated by a mobile optometric office.

(Amended by Stats. 2020, Ch. 121, Sec. 10. (AB 896) Effective September 24, 2020.)

3078

(a) It is unlawful to practice optometry under a false or assumed name, or to use a false or assumed name in connection with the practice of optometry, or to make use of any false or assumed name in connection with the name of a person licensed pursuant to this chapter. However, the board may issue written permits authorizing an individual optometrist or an optometric group or optometric corporation to use a name specified in the permit in connection with its practice if, and only if, the board finds to its satisfaction all of the following:

(1) The place or establishment, or the portion thereof, in which the applicant or applicants practice, is owned or leased by the applicant or applicants, and the practice conducted at that place or establishment, or portion thereof, is wholly owned and entirely controlled by the applicant or applicants. However, if the applicant or applicants are practicing optometry in a community clinic, as defined in subdivision (a) of Section 1204 of the Health and Safety Code, this subdivision shall not apply.

(2) The name under which the applicant or applicants propose to operate is in the judgment of the board not deceptive or inimical to enabling a rational choice for the consumer public and contains at least one of the following designations: "optometry" or "optometric." However, if the applicant or applicants are practicing optometry in a community clinic, as defined in subdivision (a) of Section 1204 of the Health and Safety Code, this subdivision shall not apply. In no case shall the name under which the applicant or applicants propose to operate contain the name or names of any of the optometrists practicing in the community clinic.

(3) The names of all optometrists practicing at the location designated in the application are displayed in a conspicuous place for the public to see, not only at the location, but also in any advertising permitted by law.

(4) No charges that could result in revocation or suspension of an optometrist's license to practice optometry are pending against any optometrist practicing at the location.

(b) Permits issued under this section by the board shall expire and become invalid unless renewed at the times and in the manner provided in Article 7 (commencing with Section 3145) for the renewal of licenses issued under this chapter.

(c) A permit issued under this section may be revoked or suspended at any time that the board finds that any one of the requirements for original issuance of a permit, other than under paragraph (4) of subdivision (a), is no longer being fulfilled by the individual optometrist, optometric corporation, or optometric group to whom the permit was issued. Proceedings for revocation or suspension shall be governed by the Administrative Procedure Act.

(d) If the board revokes or suspends the license to practice optometry of an individual optometrist or any member of a corporation or group to whom a permit has been issued under this section, the revocation or suspension shall also constitute revocation or suspension, as the case may be, of the permit.

(Amended by Stats. 2007, Ch. 276, Sec. 4. Effective January 1, 2008.)

ARTICLE 5. REVOCATION AND SUSPENSION

3090

Except as otherwise provided by law, the board may take action against all persons guilty of violating this chapter or any of the regulations adopted by the board. The board shall enforce and administer this article as to licenseholders, including those who hold a retired license, a license with a retired volunteer designation, an inactive license issued pursuant to Article 9 (commencing with Section 700) of Chapter 1, or a temporary license, and the board shall have all the powers granted in this chapter for these purposes, including, but not limited to, investigating complaints from the public, other licensees, health care facilities, other licensing agencies, or any other source suggesting that an optometrist may be guilty of violating this chapter or any of the regulations adopted by the board.

(Amended by Stats. 2021, Ch. 219, Sec. 3. (SB 509) Effective September 22, 2021.)

3090.5

The board may revoke a license issued to a licensee upon a decision, made in a proceeding as provided in Section 3092, that contains a finding of fact of either of the following:

(a) The licensee has engaged in an act of sexual abuse, misconduct, or relations with a patient, as described in paragraph (2) of subdivision (m) of Section 3110.

(b) The licensee has been convicted of a crime described in paragraph (3) of subdivision (m) of Section 3110.

(Added by Stats. 2013, Ch. 516, Sec. 17. (SB 305) Effective January 1, 2014.)

3091

(a) The board may deny an optometrist license to any applicant guilty of unprofessional conduct or of any cause that would subject a licensee to revocation or suspension of his or her license; or, the board in its sole discretion, may issue a probationary license to an applicant subject to terms and conditions, including, but not limited to, any of the following conditions of probation:

(1) Practice limited to a supervised, structured environment in which the licensee's activities shall be supervised by another optometrist licensed by the board.

(2) Total or partial restrictions on drug prescribing privileges for controlled substances.

(3) Continuing medical or psychiatric treatment.

(4) Ongoing participation in a specified rehabilitation program.

(5) Enrollment and successful completion of a clinical training program.

(6) Abstention from the use of alcohol or drugs.

(7) Restrictions against engaging in certain types of optometry practice.

(8) Compliance with all provisions of this chapter.

(9) Any other terms and conditions deemed appropriate by the board.

(b) The board may modify or terminate the terms and conditions imposed on the probationary license if the licensee petitions for modification or termination of terms and conditions of probation. A licensee shall not petition for modification or termination of terms and conditions until one year has passed from the effective date of the decision granting the probationary license.

(Added by Stats. 2005, Ch. 393, Sec. 6. Effective January 1, 2006.)

3092

All proceedings against a licensee for any violation of this chapter or any of the regulations adopted by the board, or against an applicant for licensure for unprofessional conduct or cause, shall be conducted in accordance with the Administrative Procedure Act (Chapter 5 (commencing with Section 11500) of Part 1 of Division 3 of Title 2 of the Government Code) except as provided in this chapter, and shall be prosecuted by the Attorney General's office.

(Added by Stats. 2005, Ch. 393, Sec. 7. Effective January 1, 2006.)

3093

Before setting aside the revocation or suspension of any optometrist license, the board may require the applicant to pass the regular examination given for applicants for an optometrist license.

(Amended by Stats. 2013, Ch. 473, Sec. 11. (SB 821) Effective January 1, 2014.)

3094

In addition to other proceedings provided for in this chapter, whenever any person has engaged, or is about to engage, in any acts or practices that constitute, or will constitute, an offense against this chapter, the superior court in and for the county wherein the acts or practices take place, or are about to take place, may issue an injunction, or other appropriate order, restraining that conduct on application of the board, the Attorney General, the district attorney of the county, or on application of 10 or more persons holding licenses issued under this chapter.

The proceedings under this section shall be governed by Chapter 3 (commencing with Section 525) of Title 7 of Part 2 of the Code of Civil Procedure.

(Added by renumbering Section 3131 by Stats. 2005, Ch. 393, Sec. 37. Effective January 1, 2006.)

3095

In accordance with Section 125.9, the board may establish a system for the issuance of citations, and the assessment of administrative fines, as deemed appropriate by the board.

(Added by renumbering Section 3135 by Stats. 2005, Ch. 393, Sec. 38. Effective January 1, 2006.)

3096

(a) A licensee may be ordered to undergo a professional competency examination if, after investigation and review by the Board of Optometry, there is reasonable cause to believe that the licensee is unable to practice optometry with reasonable skill and safety to patients. Reasonable cause shall be demonstrated by one or more of the following:

(1) A single incident of gross negligence.

(2) A pattern of inappropriate prescribing.

(3) An act of incompetence or negligence causing death or serious bodily injury.

(4) A pattern of substandard care.

(b) The results of a competency examination shall be admissible as direct evidence and may be considered relevant in any subsequent disciplinary or interim proceeding against the

licensee taking the examination, and, assuming those results are determined to be relevant, shall be considered together with other relevant evidence in making a final determination.

(Added by renumbering Section 3090.1 by Stats. 2005, Ch. 393, Sec. 5. Effective January 1, 2006.)

3097

The sending of a solicitor from house to house or the soliciting from house to house by the holder of an optometrist license constitutes a cause to revoke or suspend his or her license.

(Added by renumbering Section 3096 by Stats. 2005, Ch. 393, Sec. 10. Effective January 1, 2006.)

3098

When the holder uses the title of "Doctor" or "Dr." as a prefix to his or her name, without using the word "optometrist" as a suffix to his or her name or in connection with it, or, without holding a diploma from an accredited school of optometry, the letters "Opt. D." or "O.D." as a suffix to his or her name, it constitutes a cause to revoke or suspend his or her optometrist license.

(Amended by Stats. 2013, Ch. 473, Sec. 12. (SB 821) Effective January 1, 2014.)

3099

No optometrist shall advertise or otherwise hold himself or herself out to be a specialist in eye disease and the treatment thereof.

(Added by renumbering Section 3096.5 by Stats. 2005, Ch. 393, Sec. 11. Effective January 1, 2006.)

3100

The holding out as having a special knowledge of optometry, as defined in this chapter, by the holder of a license, constitutes a cause to revoke or suspend his or her license.

(Added by renumbering Section 3099 by Stats. 2005, Ch. 393, Sec. 15. Effective January 1, 2006.)

3101

It is unlawful to advertise by displaying a sign or otherwise or hold himself or herself out to be an optometrist without having at the time of so doing a valid unrevoked license from the board.

(Added by renumbering Section 3128 by Stats. 2005, Ch. 393, Sec. 34. Effective January 1, 2006.)

3102

It is unlawful to advertise as being free or without cost the furnishing of optometric services where these services are contingent upon payment or other exchange of consideration for goods or other services offered by the provider, unless that contingency is fully disclosed in the same advertisement.

(Amended by Stats. 2006, Ch. 302, Sec. 4. Effective January 1, 2007.)

3103

It is unlawful to include in any advertisement relating to the sale or disposition of goggles, sunglasses, colored glasses, or occupational eye-protective devices, any words or figures that advertise or have a tendency to advertise the practice of optometry.

This section does not prohibit the advertising of the practice of optometry by a licensed optometrist in the manner permitted by law.

(Amended by Stats. 2013, Ch. 473, Sec. 13. (SB 821) Effective January 1, 2014.)

3104

The employing of what are known as "cappers" or "steerers" to obtain business constitutes unprofessional conduct.

(Added by renumbering Section 3100 by Stats. 2005, Ch. 393, Sec. 16. Effective January 1, 2006.)

3105

Altering or modifying the medical record of any person, with fraudulent intent, or creating any false medical record, with fraudulent intent, constitutes unprofessional conduct. In addition to any other disciplinary action, the California State Board of Optometry may impose a civil penalty of five hundred dollars ($500) for a violation of this section.

(Amended by Stats. 2021, Ch. 630, Sec. 86. (AB 1534) Effective January 1, 2022.)

3106

Knowingly making or signing any license, certificate, or other document directly or indirectly related to the practice of optometry that falsely represents the existence or nonexistence of a state of facts constitutes unprofessional conduct.

(Amended by Stats. 2013, Ch. 473, Sec. 14. (SB 821) Effective January 1, 2014.)

3107

It is unlawful to use or attempt to use any license or certificate issued by the board that has been purchased, fraudulently issued, counterfeited, or issued by mistake, as a valid license or certificate.

(Amended by Stats. 2013, Ch. 473, Sec. 15. (SB 821) Effective January 1, 2014.)

3108

When the holder is suffering from a contagious or infectious disease, it constitutes a cause to suspend his or her license during the period of continuance of that disease.

(Added by renumbering Section 3097 by Stats. 2005, Ch. 393, Sec. 14. Effective January 1, 2006.)

3109

Directly or indirectly accepting employment to practice optometry from any person not having a valid, unrevoked license as an optometrist or from any company or corporation constitutes unprofessional conduct. Except as provided in this chapter, no optometrist may, singly or jointly with others, be incorporated or become incorporated when the purpose or a purpose of the corporation is to practice optometry or to conduct the practice of optometry.

The terms "accepting employment to practice optometry" as used in this section shall not be construed so as to prevent a licensed optometrist from practicing optometry upon an individual patient.

Notwithstanding the provisions of this section or the provisions of any other law, a licensed optometrist may be employed to practice optometry by a physician and surgeon who holds a license under this division or by a health care service plan pursuant to the provisions of Chapter 2.2 (commencing with Section 1340) of Division 2 of the Health and Safety Code.

(Amended by Stats. 2021, Ch. 630, Sec. 87. (AB 1534) Effective January 1, 2022.)

3110

The board may take action against any licensee who is charged with unprofessional conduct, and may deny an application for a license if the applicant has committed unprofessional conduct. In addition to other provisions of this article, unprofessional conduct includes, but is not limited to, the following:

(a) Violating or attempting to violate, directly or indirectly assisting in or abetting the violation of, or conspiring to violate any provision of this chapter or any of the rules and regulations adopted by the board pursuant to this chapter.

(b) Gross negligence.

(c) Repeated negligent acts. To be repeated, there must be two or more negligent acts or omissions.

(d) Incompetence.

(e) The commission of fraud, misrepresentation, or any act involving dishonesty or corruption, that is substantially related to the qualifications, functions, or duties of an optometrist.

(f) Any action or conduct that would have warranted the denial of a license.

(g) The use of advertising relating to optometry that violates Section 651 or 17500.

(h) Denial of licensure, revocation, suspension, restriction, or any other disciplinary action against a health care professional license by another state or territory of the United States, by any other governmental agency, or by another California health care professional licensing board. A certified copy of the decision or judgment shall be conclusive evidence of that action.

(i) Procuring his or her license by fraud, misrepresentation, or mistake.

(j) Making or giving any false statement or information in connection with the application for issuance of a license.

(k) Conviction of a felony or of any offense substantially related to the qualifications, functions, and duties of an optometrist, in which event the record of the conviction shall be conclusive evidence thereof.

(l) Administering to himself or herself any controlled substance or using any of the dangerous drugs specified in Section 4022, or using alcoholic beverages to the extent, or in a manner, as to be dangerous or injurious to the person applying for a license or holding a license under this chapter, or to any other person, or to the public, or, to the extent that the use impairs the ability of the person applying for or holding a license to conduct with safety to the public the practice authorized by the license, or the conviction of a misdemeanor or felony involving the use, consumption, or self-administration of any of the substances referred to in this subdivision, or any combination thereof.

(m) (1) Committing or soliciting an act punishable as a sexually related crime, if that act or solicitation is substantially related to the qualifications, functions, or duties of an optometrist.

(2) Committing any act of sexual abuse, misconduct, or relations with a patient. The commission of and conviction for any act of sexual abuse, sexual misconduct, or attempted sexual misconduct, whether or not with a patient, shall be considered a crime substantially related to the qualifications, functions, or duties of a licensee. This paragraph shall not apply to sexual contact between any person licensed under this chapter and his or her spouse or person in an equivalent domestic relationship when that licensee provides optometry treatment to his or her spouse or person in an equivalent domestic relationship.

(3) Conviction of a crime that requires the person to register as a sex offender pursuant to Chapter 5.5 (commencing with Section 290) of Title 9 of Part 1 of the Penal Code. A conviction within the meaning of this paragraph means a plea or verdict of guilty or a conviction following a plea of nolo contendere. A conviction described in this paragraph shall be considered a crime substantially related to the qualifications, functions, or duties of a licensee.

(n) Repeated acts of excessive prescribing, furnishing, or administering of controlled substances or dangerous drugs specified in Section 4022, or repeated acts of excessive treatment.

(o) Repeated acts of excessive use of diagnostic or therapeutic procedures, or repeated acts of excessive use of diagnostic or treatment facilities.

(p) The prescribing, furnishing, or administering of controlled substances or drugs specified in Section 4022, or treatment without a good faith prior examination of the patient and optometric reason.

(q) The failure to maintain adequate and accurate records relating to the provision of services to his or her patients.

(r) Performing, or holding oneself out as being able to perform, or offering to perform, any professional services beyond the scope of the license authorized by this chapter.

(s) The practice of optometry without a valid, unrevoked, unexpired license.

(t) The employing, directly or indirectly, of any suspended or unlicensed optometrist to perform any work for which an optometry license is required.

(u) Permitting another person to use the licensee's optometry license for any purpose.

(v) Altering with fraudulent intent a license issued by the board, or using a fraudulently altered license, permit certification or any registration issued by the board.

(w) Except for good cause, the knowing failure to protect patients by failing to follow infection control guidelines of the board, thereby risking transmission of bloodborne infectious diseases from optometrist to patient, from patient to patient, or from patient to optometrist. In administering this subdivision, the board shall consider the standards, regulations, and guidelines of the State Department of Public Health developed pursuant to Section 1250.11 of the Health and Safety Code and the standards, guidelines, and regulations pursuant to the California Occupational Safety and Health Act of 1973 (Part 1 (commencing with Section 6300) of Division 5 of the Labor Code) for preventing the transmission of HIV, hepatitis B, and other bloodborne pathogens in health care settings. As necessary, the board may consult with the Medical Board of California, the California Board of Podiatric Medicine, the Board of Registered Nursing, and the Board of Vocational Nursing and Psychiatric Technicians of the State of California, to encourage appropriate consistency in the implementation of this subdivision.

(x) Failure or refusal to comply with a request for the clinical records of a patient, that is accompanied by that patient's written authorization for release of records to the board, within 15 days of receiving the request and authorization, unless the licensee is unable to provide the documents within this time period for good cause.

(y) Failure to refer a patient to an appropriate physician and surgeon if an examination of the eyes indicates a substantial likelihood of any pathology that requires the attention of that physician and surgeon.

(Amended by Stats. 2017, Ch. 549, Sec. 8. (AB 443) Effective January 1, 2018.)

3111

It is unprofessional conduct and a violation of this chapter for a person licensed under this chapter to violate, attempt to violate, assist in the violation of, or conspire to violate the Moscone-Knox Professional Corporation Act (Part 4 (commencing with Section 13400) of Division 3 of Title 1 of the Corporations Code), this article, or any regulation adopted pursuant to those provisions.

(Added by Stats. 2006, Ch. 564, Sec. 2. Effective January 1, 2007.)

3112

(a) An optometrist shall not knowingly provide optometric services to any patient who scheduled their appointment for optometry services through any individual, corporation, or firm engaged in the business of filling prescriptions that is not properly registered with the California State Board of Optometry as required by Section 2564.90.

(b) An optometrist shall not knowingly enter into a lease or other written agreement giving rise to a direct or indirect landlord-tenant relationship with any individual, corporation, or firm engaged in the business of filling prescriptions that is not properly registered with the California State Board of Optometry as required by Section 2564.90.

(Added by Stats. 2021, Ch. 630, Sec. 88. (AB 1534) Effective January 1, 2022.)

ARTICLE 6. OFFENSES AGAINST THE CHAPTER

3120

Any person who violates any of the provisions of this chapter is guilty of a misdemeanor and, upon conviction thereof, shall be punished by imprisonment in the county jail not less than ten days nor more than one year, or by a fine of not less than one hundred dollars nor more than one thousand five hundred dollars, or by both such fine and imprisonment.

(Added by Stats. 1937, Ch. 423.)

3137

(a) Except as otherwise provided in this section, any accusation filed against a licensee pursuant to Section 11503 of the Government Code for the violation of any provision of this chapter shall be filed within three years after the board discovers the act or omission alleged as the ground for disciplinary action, or within seven years after the act or omission alleged as the ground for disciplinary action occurs, whichever occurs first.

(b) An accusation filed against a licensee pursuant to Section 11503 of the Government Code alleging fraud or willful misrepresentation is not subject to the limitation in subdivision (a).

(c) An accusation filed against a licensee pursuant to Section 11503 of the Government Code alleging unprofessional conduct based on incompetence, gross negligence, or repeated negligent acts of the licensee is not subject to the limitation in subdivision (a) upon proof that the licensee intentionally concealed from discovery his or her incompetence, gross negligence, or repeated negligent acts.

(d) If an alleged act or omission involves any conduct described in Section 726 committed on a minor, the 10-year limitations period in subdivision (e) shall be tolled until the minor reaches the age of majority.

(e) An accusation filed against a licensee pursuant to Section 11503 of the Government Code alleging conduct described in Section 726 shall be filed within three years after the board discovers the act or omission alleged as the ground for disciplinary action, or within 10 years after the act or omission alleged as the ground for disciplinary action occurs, whichever occurs first. This subdivision shall apply to a complaint alleging conduct received by the board on and after January 1, 2006.

(f) In any allegation, accusation, or proceeding described in this section, the limitations period in subdivision (a) shall be tolled for the period during which material evidence necessary for prosecuting or determining whether a disciplinary action would be appropriate is unavailable to the board due to an ongoing criminal investigation.

(Added by Stats. 2005, Ch. 186, Sec. 1. Effective January 1, 2006.)

ARTICLE 7. REVENUE

3145

There is the Optometry Fund in the State Treasury. Unless otherwise provided, all money collected under the authority of this chapter shall be paid into this fund, and shall be available, upon appropriation of the Legislature, to carry out the purposes of this chapter. The board shall not maintain a reserve balance in the fund that is greater than six months of the appropriated operating expenses of the board in any fiscal year.

(Amended by Stats. 2017, Ch. 564, Sec. 9. (AB 1708) Effective January 1, 2018.)

3145.5

Administrative fines collected pursuant to Section 3095 shall be deposited in the Optometry Fund. It is the legislative intent that moneys collected as fines and deposited in the fund be used by the board primarily for enforcement purposes.

(Amended by Stats. 2005, Ch. 393, Sec. 39. Effective January 1, 2006.)

3146

An optometric license issued under this chapter expires at midnight on the last day of the month in which the license was issued during the second year of a two-year term if not renewed. To renew an unexpired license, the optometrist shall apply for renewal on a form prescribed by the board and pay the renewal fee prescribed by this chapter.

(Amended by Stats. 2018, Ch. 703, Sec. 25. (SB 1491) Effective January 1, 2019.)

3147

(a) Except as otherwise provided by Section 114, an expired optometrist license may be renewed at any time within three years after its expiration, and a retired license issued for less than three years may be reactivated to active status, by filing an application for renewal or reactivation on a form prescribed by the board, paying all accrued and unpaid renewal fees or reactivation fees determined by the board, paying any delinquency fees prescribed by the board, and submitting proof of completion of the required number of hours of continuing education for the last two years, as prescribed by the board pursuant to Section 3059. Renewal or reactivation to active status under this section shall be effective on the date on which all of those requirements are satisfied. If so renewed or reactivated to active status, the license shall continue as provided in Sections 3146 and 3147.5.

(b) Expired statements of licensure, branch office licenses, and fictitious name permits issued pursuant to Sections 3070, 3077, and 3078, respectively, may be renewed at any time by filing an application for renewal, paying all accrued and unpaid renewal fees, and paying any delinquency fees prescribed by the board.

(Amended by Stats. 2018, Ch. 571, Sec. 18. (SB 1480) Effective January 1, 2019.)

3147.5

A license that has been suspended is subject to expiration and shall be renewed as provided in this article, but renewal does not entitle the holder of a suspended license to engage in the practice of optometry, or in any other activity or conduct in violation of the order or judgment by which the license was suspended.

A license that has been revoked is subject to expiration, but it may not be renewed. If a revoked license is reinstated after it has expired, a reinstatement fee of 150 percent of the renewal fee shall be assessed.

(Amended by Stats. 2005, Ch. 393, Sec. 42. Effective January 1, 2006.)

3147.6

Except as otherwise provided by Section 114, a license that is not renewed within three years after its expiration may be restored, and a retired license issued for more than three years may be reactivated to active status, if no fact, circumstance, or condition exists that, if the license were restored, would justify its revocation or suspension, provided all of the following conditions are met:

(a) The holder of the expired license or retired license is not subject to denial of a license under Section 480.

(b) The holder of the expired license or retired license applies in writing for its restoration or reactivation on a form prescribed by the board.

(c) The holder of the expired license or retired license pays the fee or fees as would be required of him or her if he or she were then applying for a license for the first time.

(d) The holder of the expired license or retired license satisfactorily passes both of the following examinations:

(1) The National Board of Examiners in Optometry's Clinical Skills examination

or other clinical examination approved by the board.

(2) The board's jurisprudence examination.

(e) After taking and satisfactorily passing the examinations identified in subdivision (d), the holder of the expired license or retired license pays a restoration fee equal to the sum of the license renewal fee in effect on the last regular renewal date for licenses or a reactivation fee determined by the board, and any delinquency fees prescribed by the board.

(Amended by Stats. 2012, Ch. 359, Sec. 4. (SB 1215) Effective January 1, 2013.)

3147.7

The provisions of Section 3147.6 shall not apply to a person holding a license that has not been renewed within three years of expiration, if the person provides satisfactory proof that he or she holds an active license from another state and meets all of the following conditions:

(a) Is not subject to denial of a license under Section 480.

(b) Applies in writing for restoration of the license on a form prescribed by the board.

(c) Pays all accrued and unpaid renewal fees and any delinquency fees prescribed by the board.

(d) Submits proof of completion of the required number of hours of continuing education for the last two years.

(e) Takes and satisfactorily passes the board's jurisprudence examination.

(Amended by Stats. 2010, Ch. 653, Sec. 17. (SB 1489) Effective January 1, 2011.)

3148

From each fee for the renewal of a license for the biennial renewal of a license, there shall be paid the sum of sixteen dollars ($16) by the Director of Consumer Affairs to the University of California. This sum shall be used at and by the University of California solely for the advancement of optometrical research and the maintenance and support of the department at the university in which the science of optometry is taught.

The balance of each renewal fee shall be paid into the Optometry Fund.

(Amended by Stats. 2005, Ch. 393, Sec. 45. Effective January 1, 2006.)

3150

The department may make all necessary disbursements to carry out the provisions of this chapter.

(Amended by Stats. 2005, Ch. 393, Sec. 46. Effective January 1, 2006.)

3151

(a) The board shall issue, upon application and payment of the fee described in Section 3152, a retired license to an optometrist who holds a license that is current and active.

(b) A licensee who has been issued a retired license is exempt from continuing education requirements pursuant to Section 3059. The holder of a retired license shall not be required to renew that license.

(c) The holder of a retired license shall not engage in the practice of optometry.

(d) An optometrist holding a retired license shall only be permitted to use the titles "retired optometrist" or "optometrist, retired."

(e) The holder of a retired license issued for less than three years may reactivate the license to active status if he or she meets the requirements of Section 3147.

(f) The holder of a retired license issued for more than three years may reactivate the license to active status if he or she satisfies the requirements in Section 3147.6.

(Added by Stats. 2012, Ch. 359, Sec. 5. (SB 1215) Effective January 1, 2013.)

3151.1

(a) The board shall issue, upon application and payment of the fee described in Section 3152, a license with retired volunteer service designation to an optometrist who satisfies any of the following:

(1) The applicant holds any of the following:

(A) A retired license issued within the last three years.

(B) A license that has not been renewed and has expired within the last three years.

(C) A license that is current and active.

(2) The applicant holds either of the following, and the applicant certifies on the application that he or she has completed an additional 50 hours of formal continuing optometric education coursework:

(A) A retired license issued more than three, but less than five, years ago.

(B) A license that has not been renewed and has expired more than three, but less than five, years ago.

(3) The applicant holds either of the following, and satisfies the requirements set forth in subdivisions (a) to (d), inclusive, of Section 3147.6:

(A) A retired license issued more than five years ago.

(B) A license that has not been renewed and has expired more than five years ago.

(b) The board shall not issue a license pursuant to this section to an applicant whose application would be subject to denial pursuant to Section 480.

(c) The applicant shall certify on the application that the sole purpose of the license with retired volunteer service designation is to provide voluntary, unpaid optometric services at health fairs, vision screenings, and public service eye programs.

(d) The holder of the retired license with volunteer service designation shall submit a biennial renewal application, with a fee fixed by this chapter and certify on each renewal that the required number of continuing education hours pursuant to Section 3059 were completed, and certify that the sole purpose of the retired license with volunteer service designation is to provide voluntary, unpaid services as described in subdivision (c). Pursuant to Section 3146, the license expires at midnight on the last day of the licenseholder's birth month every two years if not renewed.

(Amended by Stats. 2015, Ch. 125, Sec. 1. (AB 1253) Effective January 1, 2016.)

3152

The amounts of fees and penalties prescribed by this chapter shall be established by the board in amounts not greater than those specified in the following schedule:

(a) The fee for applicants applying for a license shall not exceed two hundred seventy-five dollars ($275).

(b) The fee for renewal of an optometric license shall not exceed five hundred dollars ($500).

(c) The annual fee for the renewal of a branch office license shall not exceed seventy-five dollars ($75).

(d) The fee for a branch office license shall not exceed seventy-five dollars ($75).

(e) The penalty for failure to pay the annual fee for renewal of a branch office license shall not exceed twenty-five dollars ($25).

(f) The fee for issuance of a license or upon change of name authorized by law of a person holding a license under this chapter shall not exceed twenty-five dollars ($25).

(g) The delinquency fee for renewal of an optometric license shall not exceed fifty dollars ($50).

(h) The application fee for a certificate to perform lacrimal irrigation and dilation shall not exceed fifty dollars ($50).

(i) The application fee for a certificate to treat glaucoma shall not exceed fifty dollars ($50).

(j) The fee for approval of a continuing education course shall not exceed one hundred dollars ($100).

(k) The fee for issuance of a statement of licensure shall not exceed forty dollars ($40).

(l) The fee for biennial renewal of a statement of licensure shall not exceed forty dollars ($40).

(m) The delinquency fee for renewal of a statement of licensure shall not exceed twenty dollars ($20).

(n) The application fee for a fictitious name permit shall not exceed fifty dollars ($50).

(o) The renewal fee for a fictitious name permit shall not exceed fifty dollars ($50).

(p) The delinquency fee for renewal of a fictitious name permit shall not exceed twenty-five dollars ($25).

(q) The fee for a retired license shall not exceed twenty-five dollars ($25).

(r) The fee for a retired license with volunteer designation shall not exceed fifty dollars ($50).

(s) The biennial renewal fee for a retired license with volunteer designation shall not exceed fifty dollars ($50).

(t) The application fee for a certificate to administer immunizations shall not exceed fifty dollars ($50).

(u) The application fee for a home residence permit is fifty dollars ($50). The board may increase the fee to not more than one hundred dollars ($100).

(v) The renewal fee for a home residence permit is fifty dollars ($50). The board may increase the fee to not more than one hundred dollars ($100).

(w) The delinquency fee for a home residence permit is twenty-five dollars ($25). The board may increase the fee to not more than one hundred dollars ($100).

(x) The endorsement fee is forty dollars ($40). The board may increase the fee, as necessary to cover the reasonable regulatory costs of administration, to not more than sixty dollars ($60).

(Amended by Stats. 2021, Ch. 630, Sec. 89. (AB 1534) Effective January 1, 2022.)

3152.5

The board may require each applicant for a certificate to use therapeutic pharmaceutical agents, pursuant to Section 3041.3, to pay an application fee, and may require each licenseholder to pay a renewal fee. The application fee and the renewal fee shall not exceed the actual costs to the board of the reviewing and processing of the application for a license or renewal of a license, monitoring the practice by licenseholders, and enforcing the provisions of law governing the use of therapeutic pharmaceutical agents, the diagnosis and treatment of certain conditions, and the performance of certain procedures by persons certified to use therapeutic pharmaceutical agents.

(Amended by Stats. 2005, Ch. 393, Sec. 48. Effective January 1, 2006.)

ARTICLE 8. OPTOMETRIC CORPORATIONS

3160

An optometric corporation is a corporation that is authorized to render professional services, as described in Sections 13401 and 13401.5 of the Corporations Code, if that corporation and its shareholders, officers, directors, and employees rendering professional services who are physicians and surgeons, psychologists, registered nurses, optometrists, or podiatrists are in compliance with the Moscone-Knox Professional Corporation Act as contained in Part 4 (commencing with Section 13400) of Division 3 of Title 1 of the Corporations Code, the provisions of this article, and all other statutes and regulations now or hereafter enacted or adopted pertaining to the corporation and the conduct of its affairs. With respect to an optometric corporation, the governmental agency referred to in the Moscone-Knox Professional Corporation Act is the California State Board of Optometry.

(Amended by Stats. 2021, Ch. 630, Sec. 90. (AB 1534) Effective January 1, 2022.)

3163

Except as provided in Section 3078, the name of an optometric corporation and any name or names under which it may be rendering professional services shall contain and be restricted to the name or the last name of one or more of the present, prospective, or former shareholders and shall include the words optometric corporation or wording or abbreviations denoting corporate existence, provided that the articles of incorporation shall be amended to delete the name of a former shareholder from the name of the corporation within two years from the date the former shareholder dies or otherwise ceases to be a shareholder.

(Amended by Stats. 2013, Ch. 473, Sec. 17. (SB 821) Effective January 1, 2014.)

3164

Except as provided in Sections 13401.5 and 13403 of the Corporations Code, each director, shareholder, and officer of an optometric corporation shall be a licensed person as defined in the Moscone-Knox Professional Corporation Act.

(Amended by Stats. 1981, Ch. 621, Sec. 4.)

3165

The income of an optometric corporation attributable to professional services rendered while a shareholder is a disqualified person (as defined in the Moscone-Knox Professional Corporation Act) shall not in any manner accrue to the benefit of such shareholder for his shares in the optometric corporation.

(Added by Stats. 1970, Ch. 1265.)

3166

An optometric corporation shall not do or fail to do an act the doing of which or the failure to do which would constitute unprofessional conduct under any statute, rule, or regulation. In conducting its practice, an optometric corporation shall observe and be bound by statutes, rules, and regulations to the same extent as a person holding a license under Section 3055.

(Amended by Stats. 2006, Ch. 564, Sec. 7. Effective January 1, 2007.)

3167

The board may formulate and enforce rules and regulations to carry out the purposes and objectives of this article, including rules and regulations requiring (a) that the articles of incorporation or bylaws of an optometric corporation shall include a provision whereby the capital stock of such corporation owned by a disqualified person (as defined in the Moscone-Knox Professional Corporation Act), or a deceased person shall be sold to the corporation or to the remaining shareholders of such corporation within such time as such rules and regulations may provide; and (b) that an optometric corporation as a condition of obtaining a certificate pursuant to the Moscone-Knox Professional Corporation Act and this article shall provide adequate security by insurance or otherwise for claims against it by its patients arising out of the rendering of professional services.

(Added by Stats. 1970, Ch. 1265.)

CALIFORNIA CODE OF REGULATIONS

TITLE 16: PROFESSIONAL AND VOCATIONAL REGULATIONS

DIVISION 13.5. REGISTERED DISPENSING OPTICIANS OF THE CALIFORNIA STATE BOARD OF OPTOMETRY

ARTICLE 1. GENERAL PROVISIONS

1399.200. CITATION

This chapter may be cited and referred to as the "Registered Dispensing Optician Regulations."

Credits

Note: Authority cited and Reference: Section 2558, Business and Professions Code.

HISTORY

1. New section filed 4-12-79; effective thirtieth day thereafter (Register 79, No. 15).

2. Repealer of Chapter 13.5 (Articles 1-10, Sections 1399.200-1399.355, not consecutive), and new Chapter 13.5 (Articles 1-8, Sections 1399.200-1399.285, not consecutive) filed 8-3-83; effective thirtieth day thereafter (Register 83, No. 32). For prior history, see Registers 83, No. 18; 83, No. 8; 82, No. 17; 80, No. 6; 79, No. 15; 78, No. 33; 77, No. 51; 76, No. 49; and 75, No. 11.

3. Change without regulatory effect amending division heading filed 2-26-2001 pursuant to section 100, title 1, California Code of Regulations (Register 2001, No. 9).

4. Change without regulatory effect amending division heading filed 10-23-2019 pursuant to section 100, title 1, California Code of Regulations (Register 2019, No. 43).

This database is current through 8/30/24 Register 2024, No. 35.

1399.201. LOCATION OF PRINCIPAL OFFICE

The principal office of the California State Board of Optometry for the purpose of the administration of the registered dispensing optician program is located at 2450 Del Paso Road, Suite 105, Sacramento, California 95834.

Credits

Note: Authority cited: Section 2558, Business and Professions Code. Reference: Section 2554, Business and Professions Code.

HISTORY

1. Change without regulatory effect amending section filed 11-24-97 pursuant to section 100, title 1, California Code of Regulations (Register 97, No. 48).

2. Change without regulatory effect amending section filed 10-23-2019 pursuant to section 100, title 1, California Code of Regulations (Register 2019, No. 43).

This database is current through 8/30/24 Register 2024, No. 35.

1399.203. DEFINITIONS

For the purposes of the regulations contained in this Chapter, the term:

(a) "Board" means the California State Board of Optometry.

(b) "Division" means the California State Board of Optometry.

(c) "Code" means the Business and Professions Code.

(d) "Engaging in the business of a dispensing optician" means the filling of prescriptions of licensed physicians and surgeons or optometrists for prescription lenses, and as incidental to the filling of such prescriptions:

(1) Using a keratometer to measure the curvature of the cornea of the eye;

(2) Converting a compounded prescription for spectacle lens by means of an algebraic formula in order to (a) compensate for the different vertex distance between the eye and the refractionist's test lens and between the eye and lens actually dispensed or, (b) to determine the appropriate power of contact lenses in accordance with such prescription;

(3) Taking facial measurements, fitting and adjusting prescription lenses, and fitting and adjusting spectacle frames.

(f) "Personal knowledge," as used in Section 2552(b) of the code, means knowledge of the affiant which is not based on hearsay.

(g) "Physician and Surgeon" means a physician and surgeon, holding a valid certificate issued by the Medical Board of California to practice medicine in the State of California.

(h) "Prescription," as used in Chapter 5.5, Division 2 of the code, means:

(1) A written order from a physician and surgeon or optometrist for spectacle or contact lenses, or

(2) An oral order from a physician and surgeon or optometrist for spectacle or contact lenses if such order is reduced to writing and a copy of such writing is sent to the prescribing physician or optometrist prior to the delivery of the lenses to the patient.

Credits

Note: Authority cited: Section 2558, Business and Professions Code. Reference: Sections 2550, 2552 and 2558, Business and Professions Code.

HISTORY

1. Change without regulatory effect repealing subsection (e) filed 8-22-94 pursuant to section 100, title 1, California Code of Regulations (Register 94, No. 34).

2. Change without regulatory effect amending section filed 11-24-97 pursuant to section 100, title 1, California Code of Regulations (Register 97, No. 48).

3. Change without regulatory effect amending subsections (a), (b) and (g) filed 10-23-2019 pursuant to section 100, title 1, California Code of Regulations (Register 2019, No. 43).

This database is current through 8/30/24 Register 2024, No. 35.

1399.204. DELEGATION OF FUNCTIONS

Except for those powers reserved exclusively to the "agency itself" under the Administrative Procedure Act (Section 11500 et seq. of the Government Code), the division delegates and confers upon the executive officer of the board, or his or her designee, all functions necessary to the dispatch of business of the division in connection with investigative and administrative proceedings under the jurisdiction of the division.

Credits

Note: Authority cited: Section 2558, Business and Professions Code. Reference: Section 2555, Business and Professions Code; and 11500, Government Code.

HISTORY

1. Change without regulatory effect amending section filed 11-24-97 pursuant to section 100, title 1, California Code of Regulations (Register 97, No. 48).

2. Change without regulatory effect amending section filed 2-26-2001 pursuant to section 100, title 1, California Code of Regulations (Register 2001, No. 9).

3. Change without regulatory effect amending section filed 10-23-2019 pursuant to section 100, title 1, California Code of Regulations (Register 2019, No. 43).

This database is current through 8/30/24 Register 2024, No. 35.

ARTICLE 2. APPLICATIONS

1399.220. APPLICATIONS FOR REGISTRATION

All applications shall be submitted on a form provided by the division, accompanied by such evidence, statements or documents as therein required, and filed with the division at its principal office with the required fee.

Credits

Note: Authority cited: Section 2558, Business and Professions Code. Reference: Section 2555, Business and Professions Code; and 11500, Government Code.

HISTORY

1. Change without regulatory effect amending section filed 8-16-90 pursuant to section 100 title 1, California Code of Regulations (Register 90, No. 42).

This database is current through 8/30/24 Register 2024, No. 35.

1399.221. DENIAL OF APPLICATIONS

In the event an application is denied pursuant to Section 2552 or 2553.6 of the code, the division shall notify the applicant in writing within thirty days of the deficiencies or reasons for denial, and of the procedure for requesting a hearing on the denial.

Credits

Note: Authority cited: Section 2558, Business and Professions Code. Reference: Sections 2552, 2553 and 2553.6, Business and Professions Code.

This database is current through 8/30/24 Register 2024, No. 35.

1399.222. RENEWAL APPLICATIONS

A renewal application will be submitted on a form provided by the division accompanied by the renewal fee and filed with the division at its office in Sacramento prior to the expiration date of the registration.

Credits

Note: Authority cited: Section 2558, Business and Professions Code. Reference: Section 2554, Business and Professions Code.

This database is current through 8/30/24 Register 2024, No. 35.

1399.223. ABANDONMENT OF APPLICATION

An applicant shall be deemed to have abandoned an application if he or she does not complete the requirements for registration within one year from the date on which the application was filed. An application submitted subsequent to an abandoned application shall be treated as a new application.

Credits

Note: Authority cited: Section 2558, Business and Professions Code. Reference:

Section 2551, Business and Professions Code.

This database is current through 8/30/24 Register 2024, No. 35.

ARTICLE 3. PRESCRIPTIONS FOR OPHTHALMIC DEVICES

1399.230. ORAL PRESCRIPTIONS

If an oral prescription or order is received for lenses the order shall be reduced to writing and a copy of such writing sent to the prescribing physician or optometrist prior to the delivery of the lenses to the patient.

Credits

Note: Authority cited: Section 2558, Business and Professions Code. Reference: Section 2550, Business and Professions Code.

This database is current through 8/30/24 Register 2024, No. 35.

1399.231. RETENTION OF RECORDS

All written prescriptions or oral prescriptions which have been reduced to writing shall be retained for three years after the dates such prescriptions have been filed.

Credits

Note: Authority cited: Section 2558, Business and Professions Code. Reference: Sections 2550, 2555 and 2556, Business and Professions Code.

This database is current through 8/30/24 Register 2024, No. 35.

1399.232. OPHTHALMIC DEVICES

The minimum quality standards for prescription ophthalmic devices sold, dispensed or furnished by registered dispensing opticians are the current standards of the American National Standard Institute Z80.1 and Z80.2.

Credits

Note: Authority cited: Section 2541.3, Business and Professions Code. Reference: Section 2541.3, Business and Professions Code.

This database is current through 8/30/24 Register 2024, No. 35.

1399.233. EVALUATION OF CONTACT LENSES

In accordance with Section 2562 of the Code, a registered contact lens dispenser shall ensure that a written statement is enclosed with each contact lens container which directs the person named in the contact lens prescription to return to the prescribing physician or optometrist for an evaluation within 60 days.

Credits

Note: Authority cited: Section 2558, Business and Professions Code. Reference: Section 2562, Business and Professions Code.

HISTORY

1. New section filed 5-17-95; operative 6-16-95 (Register 95, No. 20).

This database is current through 8/30/24 Register 2024, No. 35.

ARTICLE 4. CHANGES OF BUSINESS NAME, BUSINESS ADDRESS, OR OWNERSHIP

1399.240. CHANGE OF BUSINESS NAME OR ADDRESS

A registrant shall report to the division in writing within ten working days any change of the business name or address. The division shall change its records accordingly, and shall notify the registrant in writing of the change. There is no fee for recording such a change.

Credits

Note: Authority cited: Section 2558, Business and Professions Code. Reference: Sections 2553 and 2554, Business and Professions Code.

This database is current through 8/30/24 Register 2024, No. 35.

1399.242. CHANGE OF OWNERSHIP

The division shall be promptly notified by the registrant when there is a change in the ownership of the registrant, and the certificate of registration shall immediately be returned to the division for cancellation. No new certificate of registration shall be issued until the previous certificate is cancelled. If there is such a change, the new registrant shall file a new application and pay the prescribed application and initial registration fees.

Credits

Note: Authority cited: Section 2558, Business and Professions Code. Reference: Sections 2551 and 2553, Business and Professions Code.

This database is current through 8/30/24 Register 2024, No. 35.

ARTICLE 5. ADVERTISING

1399.250. ADVERTISING

A registered dispensing optician may advertise the provision of any ophthalmic goods or services authorized to be provided by such registration in a manner authorized by Section 651 of the code so long as such advertising does not promote the excessive or unnecessary use of such services.

Credits

Note: Authority cited: Sections 651 and 2558, Business and Professions Code. Reference: Sections 651, 2556 and 17500, Business and Professions Code.

This database is current through 8/30/24 Register 2024, No. 35.

1399.251. ADVERTISEMENT FOR EYE EXAMINATION

It is unprofessional conduct for a registered dispensing optician to advertise a price or fee for a visual eye examination or a complete medical eye examination or to otherwise advertise the furnishing of the services of an optometrist or a physician and surgeon.

Credits

Note: Authority cited: Sections 651 and 2558, Business and Professions Code. Reference: Sections 651, 2540, 2556 and 17500, Business and Professions Code.

This database is current through 8/30/24 Register 2024, No. 35.

1399.252. ADVERTISING REQUIREMENTS

Registered dispensing opticians shall include the names under which they are registered in all advertising in connection with the business of dispensing optician. For purposes of this chapter, advertising includes classified directories and solicitations to the public.

Credits

Note: Authority cited: Sections 651 and 2558, Business and Professions Code. Reference: Sections 651, 2556 and 2558, Business and Professions Code.

This database is current through 8/30/24 Register 2024, No. 35.

ARTICLE 6. FEES

1399.260. REGISTERED DISPENSING OPHTHALMIC BUSINESS FEES

(a) The initial application fee shall be $200.

(b) The initial registration fee shall be $300.

(c) The biennial renewal fee shall be $300.

(d) The delinquency fee shall be fifty dollars ($50).

Credits

Note: Authority cited: Section 2567, Business and Professions Code. Reference: Section 2565, Business and Professions Code.

HISTORY

1. Amendment of section heading and section filed 11-28-2000; operative 12-28-2000 (Register 2000, No. 48).

2. Amendment of section heading, section and Note filed 12-26-2023; operative 7-1-2024 pursuant to Government Code section 11343.4(b)(2) (Register 2023, No. 52).

This database is current through 8/30/24 Register 2024, No. 35.

1399.261. CONTACT LENS DISPENSER FEES

(a) The initial application fee shall be $200.

(b) The initial registration fee shall be $300.

(c) The biennial renewal fee shall be $300.

(d) The delinquency fee shall be fifty dollars ($50).

Credits

Note: Authority cited: Section 2567, Business and Professions Code. Reference: Section 2566, Business and Professions Code.

HISTORY

1. Amendment filed 11-28-2000; operative 12-28-2000 (Register 2000, No. 48).

2. Amendment of section and Note filed 12-26-2023; operative 7-1-2024 pursuant to Government Code section 11343.4(b)(2) (Register 2023, No. 52).

This database is current through 8/30/24 Register 2024, No. 35.

1399.262. REFUND OF APPLICATION FEE

Any applicant for registration as a contact lens dispenser who does not meet the requirements for registration shall be refunded $50.00 upon written request.

Credits

Note: Authority cited: Section 2558, Business and Professions Code. Reference: Section 2566, Business and Professions Code.

This database is current through 8/30/24 Register 2024, No. 35.

1399.263. SPECTACLE LENS DISPENSER FEES

(a) The initial application fee shall be $200.

(b) The initial registration fee shall be $300.

(c) The biennial renewal fee shall be $300.

(d) The delinquency fee shall be fifty dollars ($50).

Credits

Note: Authority cited: Section 2567, Business and Professions Code. Reference: Section 2566.1, Business and Professions Code.

HISTORY

1. New section filed 11-28-2000; operative 12-28-2000 (Register 2000, No. 48).

2. Amendment of section and Note filed 12-26-2023; operative 7-1-2024 pursuant to Government Code section 11343.4(b)(2) (Register 2023, No. 52).

This database is current through 8/30/24 Register 2024, No. 35.

ARTICLE 7. ENFORCEMENT

1399.270. SUBSTANTIAL RELATIONSHIP CRITERIA

(a) For the purpose of denial, suspension, or revocation of the registration of a dispensing optician pursuant to Section 141, Division 1.5 (commencing with Section 475), or Section 2555.1 of the code, a crime, professional misconduct, or act shall be considered substantially related to the qualifications, functions, and duties of a dispensing optician if, to a substantial degree, it evidences present or potential unfitness of a dispensing optician to perform the functions authorized by the registration in a manner consistent with the public health, safety, or welfare.

(b) In making the substantial relationship determination required under subdivision (a) for a crime, the Board shall consider the following criteria:

(1) The nature and gravity of the offense;

(2) The number of years elapsed since the date of the offense; and

(3) The nature and duties of the registration type sought or held by the person.

(c) For purposes of subdivision (a), substantially related crimes, professional misconduct, or acts shall include, but are not limited to, the following:

(1) Any violation of the provisions of Article 6, Chapter 1, Division 2 of the code relating to dispensing opticians.

(2) Any violation of the provisions of Chapter 5.4, Division 2 of the code.

(3) Any violation of the provisions of Chapter 5.5, Division 2, of the code.

(4) Any act involving theft, dishonesty, fraud, or deceit.

(5) Any act involving assaultive or abusive conduct as defined in Penal Code section 11160(d).

(6) Any act involving sexual misconduct as defined in Business and Professions Code section 726(a).

Credits

Note: Authority cited: Sections 481 and 2558, Business and Professions Code. Reference: Sections 141, 480, 481, 488, 490, 493 and 726, Business and Professions Code; and Section 11160, Penal Code.

HISTORY

1. Amendment of section and Note filed 2-25-2021; operative 2-25-2021 pursuant to Government Code section 11343.4(b)(3) (Register 2021, No. 9). (Filing deadline specified in Government Code section 11349.3(a) extended 60 calendar days pursuant to Executive Order N-40-20 and an additional 60 calendar days pursuant to Executive Order N-71-20.)

This database is current through 8/30/24 Register 2024

1399.271. CRITERIA FOR DENIAL AND REINSTATEMENT OF REGISTRATION

(a) When considering the denial of a registration under Section 480 of the code on the ground that the applicant has been convicted of a crime, the Board shall consider whether the applicant has made a showing of rehabilitation if the applicant completed the criminal sentence at issue without a violation of parole or probation. In making this determination, the Board shall consider the following criteria:

(1) The circumstances, nature, and gravity of the crime(s).

(2) The length(s) of time that has elapsed since the criminal conduct and the completion of probation.

(3) Whether the applicant is a repeat offender of the same or similar crime(s), and the total criminal record.

(4) The terms or conditions of parole or probation and the extent to which they bear on the applicant's rehabilitation.

(b) If the applicant has not completed the criminal sentence at issue without a violation of parole or probation, the Board determines that the applicant did not make a showing of rehabilitation based on the criteria in subdivision (a), the denial is based on professional misconduct, or when considering a petition for reinstatement under Section 11522 of the code, the Board shall apply the following criteria in evaluating the applicant's rehabilitation:

(1) The nature and gravity of the act(s), professional misconduct, or crime(s) under consideration as grounds for denial.

(2) Evidence of any act(s), professional misconduct, or crime(s) committed subsequent to the act(s), professional misconduct, or crime(s) under consideration as grounds for denial.

(3) The time that has elapsed since commission of the act(s), professional misconduct, or crime(s) referred to in subdivision (b)(1) or (b)(2).

(4) The criteria in subdivision (a)(1) through (a)(4), as applicable.

(5) Evidence, if any, of rehabilitation submitted by the applicant.

Credits

Note: Authority cited: Sections 481, 482 and 2558, Business and Professions Code. Reference: Sections 480, 481, 482, 488 and 493, Business and Professions Code.

HISTORY

1. Amendment of section and Note filed 2-25-2021; operative 2-25-2021 pursuant to Government Code section 11343.4(b)(3) (Register 2021, No. 9). (Filing deadline specified in Government Code section 11349.3(a) extended 60 calendar days pursuant to Executive Order N-40-20 and an additional 60 calendar days pursuant to Executive Order N-71-20.)

This database is current through 8/30/24 Register 2024

1399.272. REHABILITATION CRITERIA FOR SUSPENSIONS AND REVOCATIONS

(a) When considering the suspension or revocation of a registration on the grounds that the registrant has been convicted of a crime, the Board shall consider whether the registrant made a showing of rehabilitation if the registrant completed the criminal sentence at issue without a violation of parole or probation. In making this determination, the Board shall consider the following criteria:

(1) The circumstances, nature, and gravity of the crime(s).

(2) The length(s) of time that has elapsed since the criminal conduct and the completion of probation.

(3) Whether the registrant is a repeat offender of the same or similar crime(s), and the total criminal record.

(4) The terms or conditions of parole or probation and the extent to which they bear on the registrant's rehabilitation.

(b) If the registrant has not completed the criminal sentence at issue without a violation of parole or probation, the Board determines that the registrant did not make the showing of rehabilitation based on the criteria in subdivision (a), the suspension or revocation is based on a disciplinary action as described in Section 141 of the code, or the suspension or revocation is based on one or more of the grounds specified in Sections 2555, 2555.1, 2559.3, or 2563 of the code, the Board shall apply the following criteria in evaluating the registrant's rehabilitation:

(1) Nature and gravity of the act(s), disciplinary action(s), or crime(s).

(2) Total criminal record.

(3) The time that has elapsed since commission of the act(s), disciplinary action(s), or crime(s).

(4) Whether the registrant has complied with any or all terms of parole, probation, restitution, or other sanctions lawfully imposed against the registrant.

(5) The criteria in subdivision (a)(1) through (a)(4), as applicable.

(6) If applicable, evidence of dismissal proceedings pursuant to Section 1203.4 of the Penal Code.

(7) Evidence, if any, of rehabilitation submitted by the registrant.

Credits

Note: Authority cited: Sections 481, 482 and 2558, Business and Professions Code. Reference: Sections 141, 481, 482, 488, 490, 493, 2555, 2555.1, 2559.3 and 2563, Business and Professions Code.

HISTORY

1. Amendment of section and Note filed 2-25-2021; operative 2-25-2021 pursuant to Government Code section 11343.4(b)(3) (Register 2021, No. 9). (Filing deadline specified in Government Code section 11349.3(a) extended 60 calendar days pursuant to Executive Order N-40-20 and an additional 60 calendar days pursuant to Executive Order N-71-20.)

This database is current through 8/30/24 Register 2024, No. 35.

1399.274. DEFINITIONS

As used in Sections 1399.275 through 1399.279, inclusive.

(a) "Chief of licensing" means the executive officer of the board, or his or her designee.

(b) "Optician" means a registered dispensing optician, and a registered spectacle lens dispenser or a registered contact lens dispenser, as applicable.

Credits

Note: Authority cited: Sections 125.9 and 2558, Business and Professions Code. Reference: Sections 2550 and 2550.1, Business and Professions Code.

HISTORY

1. New section filed 6-12-89; operative 7-12-89 (Register 89, No. 25).

2. Change without regulatory effect amending subsection (a) and Note filed 2-26-2001 pursuant to section 100, title 1, California Code of Regulations (Register 2001, No. 9).

3. Change without regulatory effect amending subsection (a) filed 10-23-2019 pursuant to section 100, title 1, California Code of Regulations (Register 2019, No. 43).

This database is current through 8/30/24 Register 2024, No. 35.

1399.275. CITATIONS AND FINES

(a) The chief of licensing is authorized to issue citations containing orders of abatement and fines for violations by opticians of the provisions of law referred to in this section.

(b) A citation shall be issued whenever any fine is levied or any order of abatement is issued. Each citation shall be in writing and shall describe with particularity the nature and facts of the violation, including a reference to the statute or regulations alleged to have been violated. The citation shall be served upon the individual personally or by certified mail.

Credits

Note: Authority cited: Sections 125.9 and 2558, Business and Professions Code. Reference: Section 125.9, Business and Professions Code.

HISTORY

1. New section filed 6-12-89; operative 7-12-89 (Register 89, No. 25).

2. Change without regulatory effect amending subsection (a) and Note filed 2-26-2001 pursuant to section 100, title 1, California Code of Regulations (Register 2001, No. 9).

This database is current through 8/30/24 Register 2024, No. 35.

1399.276. AMOUNT OF FINES

The amount of any fine to be levied by the chief of licensing shall take into consideration the factors listed in subdivision (b) (3) of Section 125.9 of the code and shall be within the range set forth in each subsection below.

(a) The fine for a violation of the following provisions shall be from $1100 to $2500:

(1) Business and Professions Code Section 810;

(2) Business and Professions Code Section 2542;

(3) Business and Professions Code Section 2553;

(4) Business and Professions Code Section 2556.5;

(5) Business and Professions Code Section 2559.1;

(6) Business and Professions Code Section 2559.2(e);

(7) Business and Professions Code Section 2560.

(b) The fine for a violation of the following provisions shall be from $100 to $1000:

(1) Business and Professions Code Section 650;

(2) Business and Professions Code Section 651;

(3) Business and Professions Code Section 654;

(4) Business and Professions Code Section 655;

(5) Business and Professions Code Section 2540;

(6) Business and Professions Code Section 2541.3;

(7) Business and Professions Code Section 2543;

(8) Business and Professions Code Section 2553.6;

(9) Business and Professions Code Section 2554;

(10) Business and Professions Code Section 2556;

(11) Business and Professions Code Section 2562;

(12) Business and Professions Code Section 2564.5;

(13) Title 16 Cal. Code Reg. Section 1399.230;

(14) Title 16 Cal. Code Reg. Section 1399.231;

(15) Title 16 Cal. Code Reg. Section 1399.232;

(16) Title 16 Cal. Code Reg. Section 1399.240;

(17) Title 16 Cal. Code Reg. Section 1399.242;

(18) Title 16 Cal. Code Reg. Section 1399.251;

(19) Title 16 Cal. Code Reg. Section 1399.252.

(c) In her or his discretion, the chief of licensing may issue an order of abatement without levying a fine for the first violation of any provision set forth in subsection (b).

(d) The sanctions authorized under this section shall be separate from and in addition to any other civil or criminal remedies.

Credits

Note: Authority cited: Sections 125.9 and 2558, Business and Professions Code.

Reference: Section 125.9, Business and Professions Code.

HISTORY

1. New section filed 6-12-89; operative 7-12-89 (Register 89, No. 25).

2. New subsections (a)(3)-(4), subsection renumbering, and new subsection (a)(6) and subsection renumbering filed 3-11-96; operative 4-10-96 (Register 96, No. 11).

3. Change without regulatory effect amending first paragraph, subsection (c) and Note filed 2-26-2001 pursuant to section 100, title 1, California Code of Regulations (Register 2001, No. 9).

This database is current through 8/30/24 Register 2024, No. 35.

1399.277. COMPLIANCE WITH ORDERS OF ABATEMENT

(a) If a cited optician who has been issued an order of abatement is unable to complete the correction within the time set forth in the citation because of conditions beyond his or her control after the exercise of reasonable diligence, the person cited may request an extension of time from the chief of licensing in which to complete the correction. Such a request shall be in writing and shall be made within the time set forth for abatement.

(b) When an order of abatement is not contested or if the order is appealed and the optician cited does not prevail, failure to abate the violation charged within the time allowed shall constitute a violation and failure to comply with the order of abatement. An order of abatement shall either be personally served or mailed by certified mail, return receipt requested. The time allowed for the abatement of a violation shall begin the first day after the order of abatement has been served or received. Such failure may result in disciplinary action being taken by the division or other appropriate judicial relief being taken against the optician cited.

Credits

Note: Authority cited: Sections 125.9 and 2558, Business and Professions Code. Reference: Section 125.9, Business and Professions Code.

HISTORY

1. New section filed 6-12-89; operative 7-12-89 (Register 89, No. 25).

2. Change without regulatory effect amending subsection (a) and Note filed 2-26-2001 pursuant to section 100, title 1, California Code of Regulations (Register 2001, No. 9).

This database is current through 8/30/24 Register 2024, No. 35.

1399.278. CITATIONS FOR UNLICENSED PRACTICE

The chief of licensing is authorized to issue citations containing orders of abatement and fines against persons, partnerships, corporations or associations who are performing or who have performed services for which registration as an optician is required under Chapters 5.4 and 5.5 of Division 2 of the Code. Each citation issued shall contain an order of abatement. Where appropriate the chief of licensing shall levy a fine for such unlicensed activity in accordance with subdivision (b) (3) of Section 125.9 of the code. The provisions of Sections 1399.275 and 1399.277 shall apply to the issuance of citations for unlicensed activity under this subsection. The sanctions authorized under this section shall be separate from and in addition to any other civil or criminal remedies.

Credits

Note: Authority cited: Sections 125.9 and 2558, Business and Professions Code. Reference: Section 125.9, Business and Professions Code.

HISTORY

1. New section filed 6-12-89; operative 7-12-89 (Register 89, No. 25).

2. Change without regulatory effect amending section and Note filed 2-26-2001 pursuant to section 100, title 1, California Code of Regulations (Register 2001, No. 9).

This database is current through 8/30/24 Register 2024, No. 35.

1399.279. CONTEST OF CITATIONS

(a) In addition to requesting a hearing provided for in subdivision (b) (4) of Section 125.9 of the code, the optician cited may, within ten (10) days after service or receipt of the citation, notify the chief of licensing in writing of his or her request for an informal conference with the chief of licensing regarding the acts charged in the citation. The time allowed for the request shall begin the first day after the citation has been served or received.

(b) The chief of licensing shall hold, within 30 days from the receipt of the request, an informal conference with the optician cited for his or her legal counsel or authorized representative. At the conclusion of the informal conference the chief of licensing may affirm, modify or dismiss the citation, including any fine levied or order of abatement issued. The chief of licensing shall state in writing the reasons for his or her action and serve or mail, as provided in subsection (b) of Section 1399.277, a copy of his or her findings and decision to the optician cited within ten days from the date of the informal conference. This decision shall be deemed to be a final order with regard to the citation issued, including the fine levied and the order of abatement.

(c) The optician cited does not waive his or her request for a hearing to contest a citation by requesting an informal conference after which the citation is affirmed by the chief of licensing. If the citation is dismissed after the informal conference, the request for a hearing on the matter of the citation shall be deemed to be withdrawn. If the citation, including any fine levied or order of abatement, is modified, the citation originally issued shall be considered withdrawn and new citation issued. If a hearing is requested for the subsequent citation, it shall be requested within 30 days in accordance with subdivision (b) (4) of Section 125.9.

Credits

Note: Authority cited: Sections 125.9 and 2558, Business and Professions Code. Reference: Section 125.9, Business and Professions Code.

HISTORY

1. New section filed 6-12-89; operative 7-12-89 (Register 89, No. 25).

2. Change without regulatory effect amending section and Note filed 2-26-2001 pursuant to section 100, title 1, California Code of Regulations (Register 2001, No. 9).

This database is current through 8/30/24 Register 2024, No. 35.

ARTICLE 8. OPTICAL DISPENSING EDUCATIONAL PROGRAMS [REPEALED]

1399.280. SUBSTITUTE FOR EXPERIENCE [REPEALED]

Credits

Note: Authority cited: Section 2558, Business and Professions Code. Reference: Section 2553, Business and Professions Code; and 11500, Government Code.

HISTORY

1. Change without regulatory effect repealing section filed 8-16-90 pursuant to section 100, title 1, California Code of Regulations (Register 90, No. 42).

This database is current through 8/30/24 Register 2024, No. 35.

1399.281. DEFINITION [REPEALED]

Credits

Note: Authority cited: Section 2558, Business and Professions Code. Reference: Section 2553, Business and Professions Code; and 11500, Government Code.

HISTORY

1. Change without regulatory effect repealing section filed 8-16-90 pursuant to section 100, title 1, California Code of Regulations (Register 90, No. 42).

This database is current through 8/30/24 Register 2024, No. 35.

1399.282. REQUIREMENTS FOR APPROVAL OF A PROGRAM. [REPEALED]

Credits

Note: Authority cited: Section 2558, Business and Professions Code. Reference: Section 2552, Business and Professions Code.

HISTORY

1. Change without regulatory effect repealing section filed 8-16-90 pursuant to section 100, title 1, California Code of Regulations (Register 90, No. 42).

2. Editorial correction deleting text and adding History 1 (Register 94, No. 32).

This database is current through 8/30/24 Register 2024, No. 35.

1399.283. DOCUMENTATION REQUIRED FOR APPROVAL [REPEALED]

Credits

Note: Authority cited: Section 2558, Business and Professions Code. Reference: Section 2552, Business and Professions Code.

HISTORY

1. Change without regulatory effect repealing section filed 8-16-90 pursuant to section 100, title 1, California Code of Regulations (Register 90, No. 42).

This database is current through 8/30/24 Register 2024, No. 35.

1399.284. NOTIFICATION OF PROGRAM CHANGES [REPEALED]

Credits

Note: Authority cited: Section 2558, Business and Professions Code. Reference: Section 2552, Business and Professions Code.

HISTORY

1. Change without regulatory effect repealing section filed 8-16-90 pursuant to section 100, title 1, California Code of Regulations (Register 90, No. 42).

This database is current through 8/30/24 Register 2024, No. 35.

1399.285. SUSPENSION OR REVOCATION OF APPROVAL [REPEALED]

Credits

Note: Authority cited: Section 2558, Business and Professions Code. Reference: Section 2552, Business and Professions Code.

HISTORY

1. Change without regulatory effect repealing section filed 8-16-90 pursuant to section 100, title 1, California Code of Regulations (Register 90, No. 42).

This database is current through 8/30/24 Register 2024, No. 35.

DIVISION 15: BOARD OF OPTOMETRY

ARTICLE 1. GENERAL PROVISIONS

1500. LOCATION OF OFFICES. [REPEALED]

Credits

Note: Authority cited: Section 3025, Business and Professions Code. Reference: Section 3026, Business and Professions Code.

HISTORY

1. Amendment filed 3-3-78; effective thirtieth day thereafter (Register 78, No. 9.)

2. Repealer filed 10-25-83; effective thirtieth day thereafter (Register 83, No. 44).

This database is current through 10/4/24 Register 2024, No. 40.

1501. TENSES, GENDER, AND NUMBER. [REPEALED]

Credits

Note: Authority cited: Section 3025, Business and Professions Code. Reference: Section 3025, Business and Professions Code.

HISTORY

1. Amendment filed 3-3-78; effective thirtieth day thereafter (Register 78, No. 9.)

2. Repealer filed 10-25-83; effective thirtieth day thereafter (Register 83, No. 44).

This database is current through 10/4/24 Register 2024, No. 40.

1501.1. DEFINITIONS.

For the purpose of the rules and regulations contained in this chapter, the following definitions shall apply:

(a) The term "Board" means State Board of Optometry.

(b) The term "code" means, unless otherwise designated, Business and Professions Code.

(c) The term "office," as defined in Section 3077 of the code, means any office or other place for the practice of optometry.

Credits

Note: Additional authority cited: Sections 3025, 3025.5, and 3077, Business and Professions Code. Reference: Section 3077, Business and Professions Code.

HISTORY

1. New section filed 1-31-64; effective thirtieth day thereafter (Register 64, No. 3).

2. Amendment of subsection (c) filed 3-3-78; effective thirtieth day thereafter (Register 78, No. 9.)

This database is current through 10/4/24 Register 2024, No. 40.

1502. DELEGATION OF CERTAIN FUNCTIONS

The power and discretion conferred by law upon the Board to receive and file accusations; issue notices of hearing, statements to respondent and statements of issues; receive and file notices of defense; determine the time and place of hearings under Section 11508 of the Government Code; issue subpoenas and subpoenas duces tecum; set and calendar cases for hearing and perform other functions necessary to the business-like dispatch of the business of the Board in connection with proceedings under the provisions of Sections 11500 through 11528 of the Government Code, prior to the hearing of such proceedings; and the certification and delivery or mailing of copies of decisions under Section 11518 of said code are hereby delegated to and conferred upon the executive officer.

Credits

Note: Authority cited: Section 3025, Business and Professions Code. Reference: Section 3027, Business and Professions Code.

HISTORY

1. Amendment filed 12-1-83; effective thirtieth day thereafter (Register 83, No. 49).

2. Amendment filed 3-15-94; operative 4-14-94 (Register 94, No. 11).

This database is current through 10/4/24 Register 2024, No. 40

ARTICLE 2. LOCATION OF PRACTICE

§1505. NOTIFICATION OF INTENTION TO ENGAGE IN PRACTICE

(a) The notification of intention to engage in the practice of optometry which is required by Section 3070 of the code shall be addressed to the Board at its office in Sacramento.

(b) Such notification of intention to engage in the practice of optometry includes notifying the Board of intention to accept employment to practice optometry, the name or names of the optometrist or optometrists, or those who by law may employ an optometrist and the address or addresses of the office or offices at which the licensee will be employed. If the licensee will engage in the practice of optometry exclusively at a mobile optometric office, then the licensee shall comply with the notice requirements in subdivision (n) of Section 3070.2 of the code.

(c) Such notification of intention to engage in the practice of optometry includes notifying the Board prior to the establishment of any office or offices to practice optometry of the intention to establish such office or offices and the location or locations to be occupied.

Credits

Note: Authority cited: Section 3025, Business and Professions Code. Reference: Sections 3070, 3070.2 and 3077, Business and Professions Code.

HISTORY

1. Amendment filed 1-31-64; effective thirtieth day thereafter (Register 64, No. 3).

2. Amendment filed 3-3-78; effective thirtieth day thereafter (Register 78, No. 9).

3. Amendment filed 12-1-83; effective thirtieth day thereafter (Register 83, No. 49).

4. Change without regulatory effect amending subsection (b) filed 1-6-2010 pursuant to section 100, title 1, California Code of Regulations (Register 2010, No. 2).

5. Amendment of subsection (b) and NOTE filed 10-9-2024; operative 10/9/2024 pursuant to Government Code section 11343.4(b)(3) (Register 2024, No. 41).

This database is current through 10/9/24.

1506. CERTIFICATES – POSTING.

(a) A certificate of registration, i.e., original wall certificate, is an original certificate of registration and license to practice optometry in California granted by the Board to a natural person who has qualified for the same pursuant to the provisions of Chapter 7 of Division 2 of the Code and it may not be assigned or transferred to another person but shall; notwithstanding whether it is replaced by a certification of the issuance of a certificate of registration, i.e., duplicate wall certificate, as provided by subdivision (b) of this section; remain valid and in force unless it is revoked or suspended and not reinstated or it is expired and not renewed or restored.

(b) A certification of the issuance of a certificate of registration is a certification by the Board that the person named thereon to whom it is conveyed is the holder of the certificate of registration designated thereon and shall be issued to such person as prima facie evidence that such person is the holder of such certificate of registration designated thereon and to replace the same or a previous certification of the issuance of a certificate of registration issued to the same person, provided that:

(1) There is furnished proof satisfactory to the Board of a change in name authorized by law of such person or of the loss of, destruction of or severe damage to such certificate of registration or previous certification of the issuance of such certificate of registration.

(2) Such certificate of registration or previous certification of the issuance of such certificate of registration is, unless it is lost or destroyed, surrendered to the Board.

(3) There is payment of the fee prescribed by Section 3152(h) of the code for the issuance of a certification of registration.

(c) The principal place of practice of an optometrist shall be deemed by the Board to be that office, other than his/her branch office or offices, wherein he/she owns, singly or jointly with any others, the practice of optometry, provided however:

(1) Where the optometrist does not own a practice, singly or jointly with any others, but practices optometry in a single office as an employee, that office shall be his/her principal place of practice.

(2) Where the optometrist does not own a practice, singly or jointly with any others, but practices optometry in two or more offices as an employee, he/she shall inform the Board in writing as to which of such offices shall be deemed his/her principal place of practice.

(d) When the optometrist owns, singly or jointly with any others, the practice of optometry in more than one office or is employed to practice optometry in more than one office and it is infeasible to have his/her certificate posted in more than one of such offices, he/she shall have a numbered statement of licensure issued by the Board and signed by its executive officer conspicuously posted in each of such additional offices wherein he/she owns, singly or jointly with any others, the practice of optometry or wherein he/she practices optometry as an employee, provided that:

(1) He/she shall first send a written request to the Board for such statement of licensure or statements of licensure and shall include in such request the exact location of the office wherein it or each of them is to be posted in lieu of his/her certificate.

(2) He/she shall not have a statement of licensure posted in any office other than as authorized by such statement of licensure.

(3) A statement of licensure shall not be altered or assigned.

(4) A statement of licensure is to be immediately surrendered to the Board by the optometrist to whom it is issued upon the occurrence of any of the following:

(A) His/her certificate becomes expired, is suspended or is revoked.

(B) He/she terminates ownership of the practice or his/her employment to practice optometry in the office wherein he/she is authorized by such statement of licensure to post the same in lieu of his/her certificate.

(C) The office wherein he/she is authorized by such statement of licensure to post the same becomes the only office wherein he/she has ownership of the practice and/or practices optometry as an employee.

Credits

Note: Authority cited: Section 3025, Business and Professions Code. Reference: Section 3075, Business and Professions Code.

HISTORY

1. Amendment filed 6-28-67; effective thirtieth day thereafter (Register 67, No. 26).

2. Amendment filed 8-7-69; effective thirtieth day thereafter (Register 69, No. 32).

3. Amendment filed 3-3-78; effective thirtieth day thereafter (Register 78, No. 9.)

4. Amendment filed 10-25-83; effective thirtieth day thereafter (Register 83, No. 44).

This database is current through 10/4/24 Register 2024, No. 40.

1507. EXTENDED OPTOMETRIC CLINICAL FACILITIES.

(a) As used in this regulation "extended optometric clinical facility" means and includes any clinical facility employed by an approved optometry school for instruction in optometry which exists outside or beyond the walls, boundaries, or precincts of the primary campus of the approved optometry school, and in which optometric services are rendered.

(b) It is the intent of this section to provide a procedure whereby an extended optometric clinical facility may be identified, qualified and approved by the Board as an adjunct to, and an extension of, the clinical department of an approved optometry school.

(c) Optometric services provided by optometry students at undergraduate and graduate levels in an extended optometric clinical facility shall constitute a part of the optometric education program.

(d) Approved optometry schools shall register extended optometric clinical facilities with the Board. Such registration shall be accompanied with information supplied by the optometry school pertaining to faculty supervision, scope of practice to be rendered, name and location of the facility, date operation will commence, discipline of which such instruction is a part, and a brief description of the equipment and facilities available. The foregoing information shall be supplemented with a copy of the agreement between the approved optometry school or parent university and the affiliated institution establishing the relationship. Any change in the information initially provided to the Board shall be communicated to the Board.

(e) Mobile optometric facilities may only function as a part of a school teaching program as approved by the Board.

(f) The itinerary of the mobile optometric unit must be submitted to the Board with 30 days prior notice.

Credits

Note: Authority cited: Sections 3023.1, 3025 and 3077, Business and Professions Code. Reference: Sections 3023, 3023.1 and 3077, Business and Professions Code.

HISTORY

1. New section filed 5-11-73; effective thirtieth day thereafter (Register 73, No. 19).

2. Amendment filed 12-1-83; effective thirtieth day thereafter (Register 83, No. 49).

This database is current through 10/4/24 Register 2024, No. 40.

1507.1. MOBILE OPTOMETRIC FACILITIES. [REPEALED]

Credits

Note: Authority cited: Section 3025, Business and Professions Code. Reference: Sections 3023, 3023.1 and 3077, Business and Professions Code.

HISTORY

1. New section filed 5-11-73; effective thirtieth day thereafter (Register 73, No. 19).

2. Repealer filed 10-25-83; effective thirtieth day thereafter (Register 83, No. 44).

This database is current through 10/4/24 Register 2024, No. 40.

1507.5. HOME RESIDENCE PERMITS

(a) A licensed optometrist, who is certified to use therapeutic pharmaceutical agents pursuant to Business and Professions Code section 3041.3 and seeks to obtain a home residence permit pursuant to section 3070.1, shall complete an application which shall be accompanied by payment of the fee pursuant to Section 1524 in this Article. The initial home residence permit shall be in effect until the licensee's optometry license renewal date. The application shall require the following information:

(1) First, Middle and Last Name;

(2) Address of the optometrist's primary business office, that the optometrist maintains pursuant to Business and Professions Code section 3070.1(c)(1);

(3) Primary business office telephone Number;

(4) Email address;

(5) Current license number;

(6) A declaration by the applicant, under the penalty of perjury, that the information provided including any accompanying documents is true and accurate, and that the applicant understands and agrees that any misstatements of material facts may be cause for denial of the application and discipline by the board; and

(7) A declaration by the applicant, under the penalty of perjury, that the applicant will comply with all state and federal recordkeeping, reporting, and patient record disclosure requirements, including requirements as set forth in Section 3070.1(c).

(b) A licensed optometrist who seeks to renew a home residence permit shall complete a renewal application which shall be accompanied by payment of the fee pursuant to Section 1524 in this Article. The renewal permit shall expire on the same date the license's optometry license expires. The application shall require the following information:

(1) First, Middle and Last Name;

(2) Address of the optometrist's primary business office, which the optometrist maintains pursuant to Business and Professions Code section 3041.3(c)(1);

(3) Primary business office telephone number;

(4) Email address;

(5) License number;

(6) A declaration by the applicant, under the penalty of perjury, that the information provided including any accompanying documents is true and accurate, and that the applicant understands and agrees that any misstatements of material facts may be cause for denial of the application and discipline by the board; and

(7) A declaration by the applicant, under the penalty of perjury, that the applicant will comply with all state and federal recordkeeping, reporting, and patient record disclosure requirements, including requirements as set forth in Business and Professions Code section 3070.1(c).

(c) Consumer notice.

(1) Each patient, and if applicable the patient's caregiver, shall be issued a consumer notice. A copy of the consumer notice may be provided either in-person or electronically.

(2) The notice shall be in a minimum of 14-point font and must contain the following information:

(A) The name, license number, email address, telephone number, primary business address and normal business hours of the optometrist;

(B) At a minimum, the additional following information:

CONSUMER NOTICE

The practice of optometry in California is regulated by the California State Board of Optometry. The Board of Optometry receives and investigates all consumer complaints involving the practice of optometry. Complaints or grievances involving a California-licensed optometrist or optician should be directed in writing to:

CALIFORNIA DEPARTMENT OF CONSUMER AFFAIRS
BOARD OF OPTOMETRY
2540 DEL PASO ROAD, SUITE 105
SACRAMENTO, CA 95834
PHONE: 1-866-585-2666 OR 916-575-7170
EMAIL: OPTOMETRY@DCA.CA.GOV
WEBSITE: OPTOMETRY.CA.GOV

PRESCRIPTIONS

Optometrists are required to provide patients with a copy of their ophthalmic lens prescriptions as follows:

- Spectacle prescriptions: Release upon completion of exam.
- Contact lens prescriptions: Release upon completion of exam or upon completion of the fitting process.

VOLUNTARY RELEASE OF PATIENT'S MEDICAL INFORMATION

The patient may choose to release their medical information related to the optometrist's provision of optometry services to the Board of Optometry. This authorization is voluntary, and the medical information will only be used to investigate complaints and to conduct the Board of Optometry's enforcement duties under Optometry Practice Act.

(3) Each patient, or the patient's caregiver if applicable, must sign and acknowledge that they have received the consumer notice. The signature must be accompanied by a printed patient or patient caregiver's name. The signed acknowledgement must be retained in the patient's file.

(d) The authorization provided by the optometrist to the patient, and if applicable the patient's caregiver to release the patient's medical information to the Board of Optometry shall be signed separately from the signature required in subdivision (c)(3) above.

Credits

Note: Authority cited: Sections 3025 and 3070.1, Business and Professions Code. Reference: Section 3070.1, Business and Professions Code.

HISTORY

1. New section filed 10-21-2024; operative 10-21-2024 pursuant to Government Code section 11343.4(b)(3) (Register 2024, No. 43).

This database is current through 10/18/24 Register 2024, No. 42.

ARTICLE 2.5. SPONSORED FREE HEALTH-CARE EVENTS — REQUIREMENTS FOR EXEMPTION [REPEALED]

1508. DEFINITIONS. [REPEALED]

Credits

Note: Authority cited: Sections 901 and 3025, Business and Professions Code. Reference: Section 901, Business and Professions Code.

HISTORY

1. New article 2.5 (sections 1508-1508.3) and section filed 4-15-2013; operative 4-15-2013 pursuant to Government Code section 11343.4(b)(3) (Register 2013, No. 16).

2. Change without regulatory effect repealing article 2.5 (sections 1508-1508.3) and repealing section filed 10-

23-2019 pursuant to section 100, title 1, California Code of Regulations (Register 2019, No. 43).

This database is current through 10/4/24 Register 2024, No. 40.

1508.1. SPONSORING ENTITY REGISTRATION AND RECORDKEEPING REQUIREMENTS. [REPEALED]

Credits

Note: Authority cited: Sections 901 and 3025, Business and Professions Code. Reference: Section 901, Business and Professions Code.

HISTORY

1. New section filed 4-15-2013; operative 4-15-2013 pursuant to Government Code section 11343.4(b)(3) (Register 2013, No. 16).

2. Change without regulatory effect amending subsections (a) and (b) filed 4-21-2014 pursuant to section 100, title 1, California Code of Regulations (Register 2014, No. 17).

3. Change without regulatory effect amending subsections (a) and (b) filed 1-4-2017 pursuant to section 100, title 1, California Code of Regulations (Register 2017, No. 1).

4. Change without regulatory effect repealing section filed 10-23-2019 pursuant to section 100, title 1, California Code of Regulations (Register 2019, No. 43).

This database is current through 10/4/24 Register 2024, No. 40.

1508.2. OUT-OF-STATE PRACTITIONER AUTHORIZATION TO PARTICIPATE IN SPONSORED EVENT [REPEALED]

Credits

Note: Authority cited: Sections 144, 901 and 3025, Business and Professions Code. Reference: Sections 144, 480 and 901, Business and Professions Code.

HISTORY

1. New section filed 4-15-2013; operative 4-15-2013 pursuant to Government Code section 11343.4(b)(3) (Register 2013, No. 16).

2. Change without regulatory effect repealing section filed 10-23-2019 pursuant to section 100, title 1, California Code of Regulations (Register 2019, No. 43).

This database is current through 10/4/24 Register 2024, No. 40.

1508.3. TERMINATION OF AUTHORIZATION AND APPEAL [REPEALED]

Credits

Note: Authority cited: Sections 901 and 3025, Business and Professions Code. Reference: Section 901, Business and Professions Code.

HISTORY

1. New section filed 4-15-2013; operative 4-15-2013 pursuant to Government Code section 11343.4(b)(3) (Register 2013, No. 16).

2. Change without regulatory effect repealing section filed 10-23-2019 pursuant to section 100, title 1, California Code of Regulations (Register 2019, No. 43).

This database is current through 10/4/24 Register 2024, No. 40.

ARTICLE 3. PROFESSIONAL RULES

1510. PROFESSIONAL INEFFICIENCY

Inefficiency in the profession is indicated by the failure to use, or the lack of proficiency in the use of the ophthalmoscope, the retinoscope, the ophthalmometer (or keratometer), tonometer, biomicroscope, any one of the modern refracting instruments such as the phoroptor, refractor, etc., or the phorometer-trial frame containing phoria and duction measuring elements or a multicelled trial frame, trial lenses, and prisms, in the conduct of an ocular examination; the failure to make and keep an accurate record of findings; lack of familiarity with, or neglect to use, a tangent screen or perimeter or campimeter; and the failure to make a careful record of the findings when the need of the information these instruments afford is definitely indicated.

Credits

Note: Authority cited: Sections 3025 and 3025.5, Business and Professions Code. Reference: Sections 3025.5 and 3090, Business and Professions Code.

HISTORY

1. Amendment filed 12-1-83; effective thirtieth day thereafter (Register 83, No. 49).

This database is current through 10/4/24 Register 2024, No. 40.

1511. USE OF PREFIX OR SUFFIX. [REPEALED]

Credits

Note: Authority cited: Section 3025, Business and Professions Code. Reference: Section 3098, Business and Professions Code.

HISTORY

1. Amendment filed 1-31-64; effective thirtieth day thereafter (Register 64, No. 3).

2. Repealer filed 10-25-83; effective thirtieth day thereafter (Register 83, No. 44).

This database is current through 10/4/24 Register 2024, No. 40.

1512. REPRESENTATION OF EXCEPTIONAL PROFICIENCY

(a) No title, subtitle, or phrase shall be used which conveys the impression of exceptional proficiency in any phase of optometric practice except as provided in Section 651(h) of the Code.

(b) There shall be no statements in advertising tending to imply that the use of some particular system or procedure in the examination of the eyes and their functions, is superior to or safer than that taught in accredited schools and constituting the legally defined and accepted practice of optometry.

Credits

Note: Authority cited: Sections 651 and 3025, Business and Professions Code. Reference: Section 651, Business and Professions Code.

HISTORY

1. Amendment filed 10-25-83; effective thirtieth day thereafter (Register 83, No. 44).

This database is current through 10/4/24 Register 2024, No. 40.

1513. REGISTERED NAME ONLY

All signs, cards, stationery or other advertising must clearly and prominently identify the individual optometrist or optometrists.

Credits

Note: Authority cited: Sections 651 and 3025, Business and Professions Code. Reference: Sections 651 and 3125, Business and Professions Code.

HISTORY

1. Amendment filed 1-31-64; effective thirtieth day thereafter (Register 64, No. 3).

2. Amendment filed 4-3-75; effective thirtieth day thereafter (Register 75, No. 14).

3. Amendment filed 12-1-83; effective thirtieth day thereafter (Register 83, No. 49).

This database is current through 10/4/24 Register 2024, No. 40.

1514. RENTING SPACE FROM AND PRACTICING ON PREMISES OF COMMERCIAL (MERCANTILE) CONCERN

Where an optometrist rents or leases space from and practices optometry on the premises of a commercial (mercantile) concern, all of the following conditions shall be met:

(a) The practice shall be owned by the optometrist and in every phase be under his/her exclusive control. The patient records shall be the sole property of the optometrist and free from any involvement with a person unlicensed to practice optometry. The optometrist shall make every effort to provide for emergency referrals.

(b) The rented space shall be definite and apart from space occupied by other occupants of the premises and shall have a sign designating that the rented space is occupied by an optometrist or optometrists.

(c) All signs, advertising, and display shall likewise be separate and distinct from that of the other occupants and have the optometrist's name and the word "optometrist" prominently displayed in connection therewith.

(d) There shall be no legends as "Optical Department," "Optometrical Department," "Optical Shoppe," or others of similar import, displayed on any part of the premises or in any advertising.

(e) There shall be no linking of the optometrist's name, or practice, in advertising or in any other manner with that of the commercial (mercantile) concern from whom he/she is leasing space.

Credits

Note: Authority cited: Sections 3025 and 3025.5, Business and Professions Code. Reference: Sections 651 and 3025, Business and Professions Code.

HISTORY

1. Amendment filed 12-1-83; effective thirtieth day thereafter (Register 83, No. 49).

2. Amendment of subsection (b) filed 9-25-2012; operative 10-25-2012 (Register 2012, No. 39).

This database is current through 10/4/24 Register 2024, No. 40.

1515. ADVERTISING OF SERVICES. [REPEALED]

Credits

Note: Authority cited: Section 651, Business and Professions Code. Reference: Sections 651, 651.3, 3129 and 17500, Business and Professions Code.

HISTORY

1. Amendment filed 3-3-78; effective thirtieth day thereafter (Register 78, No. 9.)

2. New subsection (c) filed 2-15-80; effective thirtieth day thereafter (Register 80, No. 7).

3. Amendment filed 12-1-83; effective thirtieth day thereafter (Register 83, No. 49).

4. Change without regulatory effect repealing section filed 3-13-2006 pursuant to section 100, title 1, California Code of Regulations (Register 2006, No. 11).

This database is current through 10/4/24 Register 2024, No. 40.

1516. APPLICATION REVIEW AND CRITERIA FOR REHABILITATION

(a) In addition to any other requirements for licensure, whenever it reasonably appears that an applicant may be unable to practice optometry safely because his or her ability to practice may be impaired due to mental or physical illness affecting competency, the Board may require the applicant to be examined by one or more physicians and surgeons or psychologists designated by the Board. The applicant shall pay the full cost of the examination. An applicant's failure to comply with the requirement shall render his or her application incomplete. If after receiving the report of the evaluation the Board determines that the applicant is unable to safely practice, the Board may deny the application. The report of the evaluation shall be made available to the applicant.

(b) Denial of a license.

(1) When considering the denial of a license under Section 480 of the Code on the grounds that the applicant has been convicted of a crime, the Board shall consider whether the applicant has made a showing of rehabilitation if the applicant completed the criminal sentence at issue without a violation of parole or probation. In making this determination, the Board shall consider the following criteria:

(A) The circumstances, nature, and gravity of the crime(s).

(B) The length(s) of time that has elapsed since the criminal conduct and the completion of probation.

(C) Whether the applicant is a repeat offender of the same or similar crime(s), and the total criminal record.

(D) The terms or conditions of parole or probation and the extent to which they bear on the applicant's rehabilitation.

(2) If the applicant has not completed the criminal sentence at issue without a violation of parole or probation, the Board determines that the applicant did not make the showing of rehabilitation based on the criteria in subdivision (b)(1), the denial is based on professional misconduct, or the denial is based on one or more of the grounds specified in Sections 3091 or 3110 of the code, the Board shall apply the following criteria in evaluating the applicant's rehabilitation:

(A) The nature and gravity of the act(s), professional misconduct, or crime(s) under consideration as grounds for denial.

(B) Evidence of any act(s), professional misconduct, or crime(s) committed subsequent to the act(s), professional misconduct, or crime(s) under consideration as grounds for denial.

(C) The time that has elapsed since commission of the act(s), professional misconduct, or crime(s) referred to in subdivision (b)(2)(A) or (B).

(D) Whether the applicant has complied with any terms of parole, probation, restitution, or any other sanctions lawfully imposed against the applicant.

(E) The criteria in subdivision (b)(1)(A) through (D), as applicable.

(F) Evidence, if any, of rehabilitation submitted by the applicant.

(c) Suspension or revocation of a license.

(1) When considering the suspension or revocation of a license on the grounds that the licensee has been convicted of a crime, the Board shall consider whether the licensee has made a showing or rehabilitation if the licensee completed the criminal sentence at issue without a violation of parole or probation. In making this determination, the Board shall consider the following criteria:

(A) The circumstances, nature, and gravity of the crime(s).

(B) The length(s) of time that has elapsed since the criminal conduct and the completion of probation.

(C) Whether the licensee is a repeat offender of the same or similar crime(s), and the total criminal record.

(D) The terms or conditions of parole or probation and the extent to which they bear on the licensee's rehabilitation.

(2) If the licensee has not completed the criminal sentence at issue without a violation of parole or probation, the Board determines that the licensee did not make a showing of rehabilitation based on the criteria in subdivision (c)(1), the suspension or revocation is based on a disciplinary action as described in Section 141 of the code, or the suspension or revocation is based on one or more of the grounds specified in Sections 3090.5, 3097, 3100, or 3110 of the code, the Board shall apply the following criteria in evaluating whether licensee's rehabilitation:

(A) Nature and gravity of the act(s), disciplinary action(s), or crime(s).

(B) Total criminal record.

(C) The time that has elapsed since commission of the act(s), disciplinary action(s), or crime(s).

(D) Whether the licensee has complied with any terms of parole, probation, restitution, or any other sanctions lawfully imposed against the licensee.

(E) The criteria in subdivision (c)(1)(A) through (D), as applicable.

(F) If applicable, evidence of dismissal proceedings pursuant to Section 1203.4 of the Penal Code.

(G) Evidence, if any, of rehabilitation submitted by the licensee.

(f) When considering a petition for reinstatement of a license under Section 11522 of the Government Code, the Board shall evaluate evidence of rehabilitation submitted by the petitioner, considering those criteria of rehabilitation specified in subdivision (c)(2).

Credits

Note: Authority cited: Sections 481, 482, 3025, 3056 and 3057, Business and Professions Code. Reference: Sections 141, 480, 481, 482, 488, 490, 493, 3056, 3057, 3090.5, 3091, 3097, 3100 and 3110, Business and Professions Code; and Section 11522, Government Code.

HISTORY

1. New section filed 5-11-73; effective thirtieth day thereafter (Register 73, No. 19).

2. Amendment filed 2-4-75 as an emergency; effective upon filing (Register 75, No. 6).

3. Certificate of Compliance filed 3-28-75 (Register 75, No. 13).

4. Amendment filed 10-25-83; effective thirtieth day thereafter (Register 83, No. 44).

5. Amendment of section heading, section and Note filed 12-6-2016; operative 4-1-2017 (Register 2016, No. 50).

6. Amendment of section and Note filed 2-25-2021; operative 2-25-2021 pursuant to Government Code section 11343.4(b)(3) (Register 2021, No. 9). (Filing deadline specified in Government Code section 11349.3(a) extended 60 calendar days pursuant to Executive Order N-40-20 and an additional 60 calendar days pursuant to Executive Order N-71-20.)

This database is current through 10/4/24 Register 2024, No. 40.

1517. SUBSTANTIAL RELATIONSHIP CRITERIA.

(a) For the purpose of denial, suspension, or revocation of the certificate of registration of an optometrist pursuant to Section 141, Division 1.5 (commencing with Section 475), or Section 3110 of the Code, a crime, professional misconduct, or act shall be considered to be substantially related to the qualifications, functions, and duties of an optometrist if, to a substantial degree, it evidences present or potential unfitness of an optometrist to perform the functions authorized by the certificate of registration in a manner consistent with the public health, safety, or welfare.

(b) In making the substantial relationship determination required under subdivision (a) for a crime, the Board shall consider the following criteria:

(1) The nature and gravity of the offense;

(2) The number of years elapsed since the date of the offense; and

(3) The nature and duties of an optometrist.

(c) For purposes of subdivision (a), substantially related crimes, professional misconduct, or acts shall include, but are not limited to, the following:

(1) Any violation of the provisions of Article 2, Chapter 1, Division 2 of the Code (Sections 525 et seq. of the Code).

(2) Any violation of the provisions of Article 6, Chapter 1, Division 2 of the Code (Sections 650 et. seq. of the Code) except Sections 651.4 and 654.

(3) Any violation of the provisions of Chapter 5.4, Division 2 of the Code (Sections 2540 et seq. of the Code).

(4) Any violation of the provisions of Chapter 7, Division 2 of the Code (Sections 3000 et seq. of the Code).

(5) Any act involving theft, dishonesty, fraud, or deceit.

(6) Any act involving assaultive or abusive conduct as defined in Penal Code section 11160.

(7) Any act involving sexual misconduct as defined in Business Code section 726(a).

Credits

Note: Authority cited: Section 481 and 3025, Business and Professions Code. Reference: Sections 141, 480, 481, 490, 493, 726 and 3110, Business and Professions Code; and Section 11160, Penal Code.

HISTORY

1. New section filed 2-4-75 as an emergency; effective upon filing (Register 75, No. 6).

2. Certificate of Compliance filed 3-28-75 (Register 75, No. 13).

3. Amendment filed 10-25-83; effective thirtieth day thereafter (Register 83, No. 44).

4. Amendment of section and Note filed 2-25-2021; operative 2-25-2021 pursuant to Government Code section 11343.4(b)(3) (Register 2021, No. 9). (Filing deadline specified in Government Code section 11349.3(a) extended 60 calendar days pursuant to Executive Order N-40-20 and an additional 60 calendar days pursuant to Executive Order N-71-20.)

This database is current through 10/4/24 Register 2024, No. 40.

1518. FICTITIOUS OR GROUP NAMES.

(a) Applications for a permit to use a fictitious or group name shall be submitted on a form provided by the Board containing such information as is required therein, and accompanied by the initial permit fee of $50. The permit shall be renewed annually with a renewal fee of $50 due on January 31 each year. Failure to renew a fictitious name permit in a timely manner will result in a $25 delinquency fee added to the renewal fee.

(b) No permit shall be issued authorizing the use of a name which is deceptive or inimical to enabling a rational choice for the consumer public and which does not contain at least one of the following designations: "optometry" or "optometric." In considering whether a name is deceptive or inimical to enabling a rational choice for the consumer public the Board may consider, among other things, whether it has a tendency to deceive the public or is so similar to a name previously authorized in the same geographical area as to be deceptive or misleading.

(c) When an optometrist or optometrists acquire the ownership in an optometric practice of another optometrist or other optometrists, the successor optometrist or optometrists may use in connection with such practice the name or names of the predecessor optometrist or optometrists for a reasonable time not in excess of two years thereafter providing:

(1) The acquisition of the ownership in the practice of the predecessor optometrist or optometrists includes permission to use his/her or their names.

(2) The acquisition of the ownership includes the active patient records and prescription files of the practice.

(3) In any signs, professional cards, envelopes, billheads, letterheads, or advertising of any nature, the name or names of the successor optometrist or optometrists shall appear first and be followed by the term "succeeding," "successor to," or "formerly" and then the name or names of the predecessor optometrist or optometrists which shall not appear in letters larger than the letters in the name or names of the successor optometrist or optometrists.

Credits

Note: Authority cited: Section 3078, Business and Professions Code. Reference: Sections 3078, 3152 and 3163, Business and Professions Code.

HISTORY

1. New section filed 3-3-78; effective thirtieth day thereafter (Register 78, No. 9.)

2. Amendment of subsection (b) and repealer of subsections (c) and (d) filed 2-15-80; effective thirtieth day thereafter (Register 80, No. 7).

3. Amendment filed 12-1-83; effective thirtieth day thereafter (Register 83, No. 49).

4. Amendment of subsection (a) and Note filed 2-8-2011; operative 3-10-2011 (Register 2011, No. 6).

This database is current through 10/4/24 Register 2024, No. 40.

1519. OPHTHALMIC DEVICE STANDARDS.

The minimum quality standards for prescription ophthalmic devices sold, dispensed or furnished by licensed optometrists shall be the 1972 standards of the American National Standards Institute Z80.1 and Z80.2.

Credits

Note: Authority cited: Section 2541.3, Business and Professions Code. Reference: Section 2541.3, Business and Professions Code.

HISTORY

1. New section filed 11-17-76; effective thirtieth day thereafter (Register 76, No. 47).

This database is current through 10/4/24 Register 2024, No. 40.

ARTICLE 4. SANITARY AND/OR HYGIENIC FACILITIES—STANDARDS GOVERNING SERVICES

1520. INFECTION CONTROL GUIDELINES

(a) Optometrists and staff, which also includes assistants in the office of an optometrist, must comply with all the applicable Standard Precautions.

(b) Standard Precautions combine the major features of Universal Precautions and Body Substance Isolation and are based on the principle that all blood, body fluids, secretions, excretions (except sweat), non-intact skin, and mucus membranes may contain transmissible infectious agents. All contact with these substances is treated as if known to be infectious for Human Immunodeficiency Virus (HIV), Hepatitis, and other transmissible infectious agents. Standard Precautions are also intended to protect patients by ensuring that optometric staff do not carry infectious agents to patients on their hands or via equipment used when providing optometric services. Standard Precautions must be used in the care of all patients, regardless of suspected or confirmed infection status, and in all settings wherein optometric services are provided. Standard Precautions include:

(1) Proper Hand Hygiene

(A) Each office shall have a hand washing facility that is entirely within the confines of the premises or space occupied by such office and not elsewhere, and which shall be for the exclusive use of the optometrist or optometrists practicing in such office and his/her or their assistants and patients and shall not be used by other persons.

(B) For the purpose of this section, a hand washing facility is a facility affording, at minimum, the following:

1. A wash basin or sink with hot and cold running water which complies with Title 24, California Administrative Code, Part 5 (commencing with Section P100).

2. Liquid hand washing detergent in a dispensing device.

3. Single service sanitary towels in a dispensing device or a sanitary hot-air blower hand drying apparatus.

(C) Hand washing facilities shall be maintained in a condition of cleanliness and good repair.

(D) The optometrists and staff shall maintain at all times a high standard of cleanliness and personal hygiene in order to ensure proper patient care.

(E) The optometrists and staff shall avoid unnecessary touching of face, nose, and surfaces in close proximity to the patient to prevent both contamination of clean hands from environmental surfaces and transmission of pathogens from contaminated hands to surfaces, when providing optometric services.

(F) When hands are visibly soiled, hands shall be washed with soap and water for a 20-second scrub and 10-second rinse or an antimicrobial hand wash. If hands are not visibly soiled, an acceptable alternative of hand decontamination is with an alcohol-based hand rub (except in cases of spores, as described below).

(G) Hands shall be washed or decontaminated as follows:

1. Before having direct contact with any patient, immediately after a procedure (such as eye examinations or other procedures involving contact with tears), and in between patients.

2. After removing gloves, ensure that hands will not carry potential infectious material that might have penetrated through unrecognized cuts or lacerations in the gloves, or that could contaminate the hands during glove removal.

3. Artificial fingernails or extenders shall not be worn if duties include direct contact with patients at high risk for infection and associated adverse outcomes.

(H) After each patient session ends, hands must be washed with soap and water or an antimicrobial hand wash if contact with spores (including but not limited to C. difficile or Bacillus anthracis) is likely to have occurred. The physical action of washing and rinsing hands in such circumstances is required because alcohols, chlorhexidine, iodophors, and other antiseptic agents have poor activity against spores.

(I) If an optometrist or staff member has exudative lesions or weeping dermatitis of the hand, direct patient care and the handling of patient care equipment by the person with the condition must stop until the condition resolves.

(2) Use of Personal Protective Equipment

(A) The optometrists and staff must routinely use gloves to prevent skin exposure when anticipating direct contact with blood or body fluids, mucous membranes, nonintact skin, and other potentially infectious material or surfaces soiled with such fluids.

(B) The optometrists and staff shall discard gloves after contact with each patient to prevent transmission of infectious material.

(C) The optometrists and staff shall change gloves if patient interaction involves touching portable computer keyboards or other mobile equipment that is transported from room to room.

(D) The optometrists and staff shall not reuse gloves.

(E) The optometrists and staff must wear masks, gloves and protective eye wear in situations where blood, respiratory secretions, or contaminated fluids may be sprayed or splashed into the eyes of an optometrist or staff member.

(F) The optometrists and staff must wear masks, gloves and protective eye wear if the optometrist, staff or patient is known or suspected to have a pathogen, which can be transmitted by airborne, contact or droplet routes. If an optometrist or staff member is infected with a pulmonary or other disease that is transmitted by airborne, contact or droplet routes, then that optometrist or staff member must wear a mask, gloves and protective eyewear to protect the patient.

(G) Protective eyewear must be washed and disinfected between each patient or when visibly soiled.

(3) Handling of Sharp Instruments

(A) Precautions must be taken in order to prevent injuries caused by needles, scalpels, and other sharp instruments or devices when:

1. Performing procedures, including but not limited to venipuncture;

2. Cleaning used instruments;

3. Disposing of used needles; and 4. Handling sharp instruments after procedures.

(B) To prevent needle stick injuries, optometrists and staff shall be instructed in the proper handling of needles, including but not limited to when needles must not be recapped, or purposely bent or broken by hand, removed from disposable syringes, or otherwise manipulated by hand.

(C) Optometrists and staff must be instructed to place disposable syringes and needles, scalpel blades and other sharp items in puncture resistant containers following their use. Puncture resistant containers shall be provided and shall be located as close as practical to the area where needles and syringes are in use.

(D) Pursuant to Cal/OSHA's Bloodborne Pathogens Standard, Title 8, Cal. Code Regs., Section 5193, employers governed by this rule must establish, maintain, review and update at least annually and whenever necessary their Exposure Control Plan to reflect changes in technology that eliminate or reduce exposure to bloodborne pathogens, and establish and maintain a Sharps Injury Log. This rule applies to all employers with employees who have occupational exposure to blood or other potentially infectious materials.

(E) Optometrists and staff shall adhere to all federal and state requirements for handling of sharp instruments (including but not limited to the Medical Waste Management Act, California Health and Safety Code sections 117600-118360).

(4) Disinfection Requirements

(A) Germicides and/or disinfectants must be used in order to eliminate most of all pathogenic microorganisms from inanimate objects, such as medical devices or equipment. If there are questions on how to disinfect a particular medical device, the office may contact the manufacturer of the product.

(B) Contact lenses and carrying cases used in trial and follow-up fittings shall be handled in the following manner:

1. Discarding the trial contact lenses is recommended. This procedure however is inapplicable to rigid gas permeable and non-disposable hydrogel trial contact lenses.

2. Disinfecting between each fitting by one of the following regimens:

a. U.S. Food and Drug Administration (FDA) approved chemical disinfection system appropriate for the contact lens type.

b. Heat disinfection.

(C) When using eye drops, optometrists and assistants shall not permit the bottle tip to come into direct contact with the patient's tears or conjunctiva. If the tip touches the patient, the bottle shall be discarded.

(D) Optometrists and staff shall follow employer-established policies and procedures for routine and targeted cleaning of environmental surfaces as indicated by the service-delivery setting, the level of patient contact, and degree of soiling.

(E) Optometrists and staff shall clean and disinfect surfaces that are likely to be contaminated with pathogens, especially those in close proximity to the patient and frequently touched surfaces in the patient care environment.

(c) Optometrists and staff shall comply with all minimum standards for infection control practices issued by local, state, and federal governmental agencies in response to emergency health and safety situations.

Credits

Note: Authority cited: Sections 3010.1, 3025, 3025.5 and 3110, Business and Professions Code. Reference: Sections 2544, 2564.5, 3025.5, 3025.6 and 3110, Business and Professions Code.

HISTORY

1. New Article 4 (Section 1520) filed 131-63; effective thirtieth day thereafter (Register 64. No. 3).

2. Amendment of subsection (d) filed 3-3-78; effective thirtieth day thereafter (Register 78, No. 9.)

3. Amendment filed 12-1-83; effective thirtieth day thereafter (Register 83, No. 49).

4. Amendment of section heading, section and Note filed 12-20-2010; operative 1-19-2011 (Register 2010, No. 52).

This database is current through 10/4/24 Register 2024, No. 40.

ARTICLE 5. APPLICATION FOR LICENSURE EXAMINATION

1523. LICENSURE AND EXAMINATION REQUIREMENTS

(a) (1) Application for licensure as an optometrist shall be made on a form prescribed by the Board (Form 39A-1. Rev. 7-09), which is hereby incorporated by reference, and shall show that the applicant is at least 18 years of age.

(2) Application for licensure by an out of state licensed optometrist as defined in Business and Professions Code Section 3057, shall be made on forms prescribed by the Board (Form OLA-2, Rev. 11/07 and Form LBC-4, rev. 2/07), which are hereby incorporated by reference, and shall show that the applicant is at least 18 years of age.

(b) An application shall be accompanied by the following:

(1) The fees fixed by the Board pursuant to Section 1524 in this Article.

(2) Satisfactory evidence of graduation from an accredited school or college of optometry approved by the Board.

(3) One classifiable set of fingerprints on a form provided by the Board.

(c) An incomplete application shall be returned to the applicant together with a statement setting forth the reason(s) for returning the application and indicating the amount of money, if any, which will be refunded.

(d) Each applicant must achieve passing grades in all Board required examinations before being granted a license to practice optometry.

(e) Permission to take the California Laws and Regulations Examination (CLRE) shall be granted to those applicants who have submitted a paid application.

(f) Licensure shall be contingent on the applicants passing the Clinical Skills portion of the National Board of Examiners in Optometry examination as provided in Section 1531 in this Article and passing the CLRE.

(g) Admission into the examinations shall not limit the Board's authority to seek from an applicant additional information deemed necessary to evaluate the applicant's qualifications for licensure.

Credits

Note: Authority cited: Sections 3025, 3044, 3045 and 3057, Business and Professions Code. Reference: Sections 3044, 3045 and 3057, Business and Professions Code.

HISTORY

1. New article 5 (sections 1523-1524) and section filed 5-12-97; operative 6-11-97 (Register 97, No. 20). For prior history, see Register 83, No. 44.

2. Amendment of section heading, redesignation of subsection (a) as new subsection (a)(1) and new subsection (a)(2), amendment of subsections (b)-(b)(1) and amendment of Note filed 11-7-2007; operative 11-7-2007 pursuant to Government Code section 11343.4 (Register 2007, No. 45).

3. Amendment filed 2-8-2011; operative 3-10-2011 (Register 2011, No. 6).

This database is current through 10/4/24 Register 2024, No. 40.

1524. FEES

The following fees are established:

(a) Application fee for certificate of registration as an optometrist by examination $275

(b) Biennial renewal of a certificate of registration as an optometrist $500

(c) Delinquency fee for failing to renew a certificate of registration timely $50

(d) Application fee for a branch office license $75

(e) Annual renewal of a branch office license...$75

(f) Penalty fee for failure to renew a branch office license timely $25

(g) Issuance fee for a certificate of registration or upon change of name of a person holding a certificate of registration $25

(h) Application fee for a fictitious name permit $50

(i) Annual renewal of a fictitious name permit $50

(1) Delinquency fee for failure to renew a fictitious name permit timely..........$25

(j) Application fee for a statement of licensure $40

(1) Biennial renewal of a statement of licensure $40

(2) Penalty fee for failure to renew a statement of licensure timely $20

(k) Application fee for a certificate to use therapeutic pharmaceutical agents ..$25

(l) Application fee for approval of a continuing education course $100

(m) Application fee for a certificate to treat primary open angle glaucoma..........$50

(n) Application fee for a certificate to perform lacrimal irrigation and dilation.....$50

(o) Application fee for a retired license $25

(p) Application fee for a retired license with a volunteer designation.............$50

(q) Biennial renewal for a retired license with a volunteer designation............$50

(r) Application fee for a certificate to operate as an owner and operator of a mobile optometric office $360

(s) Biennial renewal fee for a certificate to operate as an owner and operator of a mobile optometric office................$360

(t) Delinquency fee for failure to renew a certificate to operate as an owner and operator of a mobile optometric office ..$150

(u) Application fee for a mobile optometric office permit $472

(v) Biennial renewal fee for a mobile optometric office permit $472

(w) Delinquency fee for failure to renew a mobile optometric office permit $150

(x) Application fee for a home residence permit is $50

(y) Renewal fee for a home residence permit is $50

(z) Delinquency fee for a home residence permit is $25

Credit

Note: Authority cited: Sections 3025, 3044, 3075, 3152 and 3152.5, Business and Professions Code. Reference: Sections 163.5, 3055, 3070.1, 3070.2, 3075, 3078, 3151, 3151.1, 3152 and 3152.5, Business and Professions Code.

HISTORY

1. New section filed 5-12-97; operative 6-11-97 (Register 97, No. 20).

2. Amendment of subsections (b)-(e) and (h)-(i), new subsections (i)(1), (j)(1)-(2) and (l)-(n) and amendment of Note filed 4-28-2009; operative 4-28-2009 pursuant to Government Code section 11343.4 (Register 2009, No. 18).

3. New subsections (o)-(q) and amendment of Note filed 1-7-2014; operative 4-1-2014 (Register 2014, No. 2).

4. Amendment of subsections (b) and (l)-(n) filed 12-26-2023; operative 7-1-2024 pursuant to Government Code section 11343.4(b)(2) (Register 2023, No. 52).

5. New subsections (r)-(w) and amendment of Note filed 10-9-2024; operative 10-9-2024 pursuant to Government Code section 11343.4(b)(3) (Register 2024, No. 41).

6. New subsections (x)-(z) and amendment of Note filed 10-21-2024; operative 10-21-2024 pursuant to Government Code section 11343.4(b)(3) (Register 2024, No. 43).

This database is current through 10/18/24 Register 2024, No. 42.

ARTICLE 5.1. FINGERPRINT REQUIREMENTS

1525. OPTOMETRIST LICENSE RENEWAL

(a) A license issued pursuant to Business and Professions Code Section 3055 expires at midnight on the last day of the licensee's birth month following its original issuance and thereafter at midnight on the last day of the licensee's birth month every two years if not renewed.

(b) A renewal for licensure as an optometrist shall be made on a form prescribed by the Board (Form R1POPT, Rev. 3-10), which is hereby incorporated by reference, and shall be accompanied by the fee specified in Section 1524 and filed with the Board at its office in Sacramento.

(c) Failure to provide all of the information required by this section renders any application for renewal incomplete and not eligible for renewal.

(d) Failure of a licensee to comply with subdivision (b) is grounds for disciplinary action by the board against the license.

Credits

Note: Authority cited: Sections 3010.1, 3010.5, 3024 and 3025, Business and Professions Code. Reference: Sections 3055, 3056, 3059 and 3110, Business and Professions Code; and Section 11105, Penal Code.

HISTORY

1. New article 5.1 (sections 1525-1525.2) and section filed 6-21-2010; operative 6-21-2010 pursuant to Government Code section 11343.4 (Register 2010, No. 26).

This database is current through 10/4/24 Register 2024, No. 40.

1525.1. FINGERPRINT REQUIREMENTS

(a) As a condition of renewal for a licensee who was initially licensed prior to April 1, 2007, such licensee shall furnish to the Department of Justice a full set of fingerprints for the purpose of conducting a criminal history record check and to undergo a state and federal criminal offender record information search conducted through the Department of Justice.

(1) The licensee shall pay any costs for furnishing the fingerprints to the Department of Justice and conducting the searches.

(2) A licensee shall certify when applying for renewal whether his or her fingerprints have been furnished to the Department of Justice in compliance with this section.

(3) This requirement is waived if the license is renewed in an inactive status, or if the licensee is actively serving in the military outside the country. The board shall not return a license to active status until the licensee has complied with subsection (a).

(4) A licensee shall retain, for at least three years from the renewal date, either a receipt showing the electronic transmission of his or her fingerprints to the Department of Justice or a receipt evidencing that the licensee's fingerprints were taken.

(b) As a condition of renewal, a licensee shall disclose whether, since the licensee last applied for renewal, he or she has been convicted of any violation of the law in this or any other state and, the United States, and its territories, military court, or other country, omitting traffic infractions under $300 not involving alcohol, dangerous drugs, or controlled substances.

(c) As a condition of renewal, a licensee shall disclose whether, since the licensee last applied for renewal, he or she has been denied a license or had a license disciplined by another licensing authority of this state, of another state, of any agency of the federal government, or of another country.

(d) Failure to comply with the requirements of this section renders any application for renewal incomplete and the license will not be renewed until the licensee demonstrates compliance with all requirements.

(e) Failure to furnish a full set of fingerprints to the Department of Justice as required by this section on or before the date required for renewal of a license is grounds for discipline by the Board.

(f) As a condition of petitioning the board for reinstatement of a revoked or surrendered license or registration, an applicant shall comply with subsection (a).

Credits

Note: Authority cited: Sections 144, 3010.1, 3010.5, 3024 and 3025, Business and Professions Code. Reference: Section 3110, Business and Professions Code; and Section 11105, Penal Code.

HISTORY

1. New section filed 6-21-2010; operative 6-21-2010 pursuant to Government Code section 11343.4 (Register 2010, No. 26).

2. Amendment of subsection (a) filed 9-25-2012; operative 10-25-2012 (Register 2012, No. 39).

This database is current through 10/4/24 Register 2024, No. 40.

1525.2. RESPONSE TO BOARD INQUIRY

If the board or its designee asks a licensee to provide criminal history information, a licensee shall respond to that request within 30 days. The licensee shall make available all documents and other records requested and shall respond with accurate information. Failure to comply with the requirements of this section is grounds for discipline by the board.

Credits

Note: Authority cited: Sections 3010.1, 3010.5, 3024 and 3025, Business and Professions Code. Reference: Sections 144, 3055, 3056, 3059 and 3110, Business and Professions Code; and Section 11105, Penal Code.

HISTORY

1. New section filed 6-21-2010; operative 6-21-2010 pursuant to Government Code section 11343.4 (Register 2010, No. 26).

This database is current through 10/4/24 Register 2024, No. 40.

ARTICLE 6. EXAMINATIONS

1526. PROOF OF CARDIOPULMONARY RESUSCITATION CERTIFICATION (CPR) [REPEALED]

Credits

Note: Authority cited: Sections 3025 and 3053, Business and Professions Code. Reference: Sections 3023.1, 3053 and 3059, Business and Professions Code.

HISTORY

1. New section filed 2-21-89; operative 3-23-89 (Register 89, No. 10).

2. Repealer filed 5-8-96; operative 6-7-96 (Register 96, No. 19).

This database is current through 10/4/24 Register 2024, No. 40.

1530. EXAMINATION RESULTS. [REPEALED]

Credits

Note: Authority cited: Sections 3025, 3053 and 3054, Business and Professions Code. Reference: Sections 3053 and 3054, Business and Professions Code.

HISTORY

1. New Article 6 (Sections 1530-1535) filed 5-4-67 as an emergency; effective upon filing (Register 67, No. 18).

2. Article 6 (Sections 1530 through 1535) refiled 6-28-67; effective thirtieth day thereafter (Register 67, No. 26).

3. Amendment of subsections (d) and (e) filed 1-24-80; effective thirtieth day thereafter (Register 80, No. 4).

4. Amendment filed 10-25-83; effective thirtieth day thereafter (Register 83, No. 44).

5. Repealer and new section filed 5-8-96; operative 6-7-96 (Register 96, No. 19).

6. Change without regulatory effect repealing section filed 3-14-2006 pursuant

to section 100, title 1, California Code of Regulations (Register 2006, No. 11).

This database is current through 10/4/24 Register 2024, No. 40.

1530.1. QUALIFICATIONS OF FOREIGN GRADUATES

Applicants who meet the requirements of Section 3057.5 of the Code shall be admitted to the examination upon furnishing satisfactory evidence that the course of instruction completed is reasonably equivalent, as determined by the Board, to the course of instruction given by a school accredited by the Board; provided, however, that an applicant who is unable to furnish satisfactory evidence of equivalency may take those courses or subjects, in an accredited school or in another program of instruction acceptable to the Board, which would remedy areas of deficiency.

Credits

Note: Authority cited: Sections 3023.1 and 3025, Business and Professions Code. Reference: Sections 3023.1, 3025, 3047, 3050 and 3057.5, Business and Professions Code.

HISTORY

1. New section filed 7-26-72 as an emergency; effective upon filing (Register 72, No. 31).

2. Certificate of Compliance filed 11-22-72 (Register 72, No. 48). 3. Repealer of subsection (d) filed 1-24-80; effective thirtieth day thereafter (Register 80, No. 4).

4. Amendment filed 12-1-83; effective thirtieth day thereafter (Register 83, No. 49).

5. Amendment filed 5-6-86; effective thirtieth day thereafter (Register 86, No. 19).

This database is current through 10/4/24 Register 2024, No. 40.

1531. LICENSURE EXAMINATION

(a) The licensure examinations are composed of:

Section I – Applied Basic Science written cognitive examination approved by the Board and developed by the National Board of Examiners in Optometry (NBEO).

Section II – Patient Assessment and Management/Treatment and Management of Ocular Disease examination developed by the NBEO.

Section III – Clinical Skills Examination developed by the NBEO.

Section IV – California Laws and Regulations Examination developed and administered by the Board or its contractor.

(b) All examinations for licensure developed by the NBEO and the Board prior to January 2010 may be accepted on a case by case basis in the evaluation of an applicant's qualifications for licensure.

Credits

Note: Authority cited: Sections 3025, 3041.2 and 3053, Business and Professions Code. Reference: Sections 3041.2 and 3053, Business and Professions Code.

HISTORY

1. Amendment filed 11-22-77; effective thirtieth day thereafter (Register 77, No. 48).

2. Amendment filed 5-20-83; effective upon filing pursuant to Government Code Section 11346.2(d) (Register 83, No. 21).

3. Amendment filed 8-9-84; effective upon filing pursuant to Government Code Section 11346.2(d) (Register 84, No. 32).

4. Amendment of subsection (d) filed 2-21-89; operative 3-23-89 (Register 89, No. 10).

5. Amendment of section heading, section and Note filed 5-8-96; operative 6-7-96 (Register 96, No. 19).

6. Amendment of section and Note filed 6-24-97; operative 7-24-97 (Register 97, No. 26).

7. Amendment filed 1-28-2002; operative 1-28-2002 pursuant to Government Code section 11343.4 (Register 2002, No. 5).

8. Amendment filed 2-8-2011; operative 3-10-2011 (Register 2011, No. 6).

This database is current through 10/4/24 Register 2024, No. 40.

1532. RE-EXAMINATION.

An applicant who has failed to pass either section II of the National Board of Examiners in Optometry (NBEO) examination or the California Laws and Regulations Examination after a period of five consecutive calendar years from the date of the first examination, must retake sections II and III of the NBEO examination and the California Laws and Regulations Examination.

Credits

Note: Authority cited: Section 3025, Business and Professions Code. Reference: Section 3054, Business and Professions Code.

HISTORY

1. Amendment filed 4-3-75; effective thirtieth day thereafter (Register 75, No. 14).

2. Editorial correction (Register 75, No. 30).

3. Amendment of subsection (b) filed 1-24-80; effective thirtieth day thereafter (Register 80, No. 4).

4. Amendment filed 12-1-83; effective thirtieth day thereafter (Register 83, No. 49).

5. Amendment of subsections (a) and (b) filed 5-8-96; operative 6-7-96 (Register 96, No. 19).

6. Amendment filed 6-24-97; operative 7-24-97 (Register 97, No. 26).

7. Amendment of section and Note filed 2-8-2011; operative 3-10-2011 (Register 2011, No. 6).

This database is current through 10/4/24 Register 2024, No. 40.

1533. RE-SCORING OF CALIFORNIA LAWS AND REGULATIONS EXAMINATION

Any person who fails to pass the California Laws and Regulations Examination may request that the examination be re-scored by the Board. The request shall be submitted in writing and mailed to the principal office of the Board. The request shall be postmarked no later than 75 days after the date the examination results are mailed.

Credits

Note: Authority cited: Section 3025, Business and Professions Code. Reference: Section 3054, Business and Professions Code.

HISTORY

1. Amendment filed 12-1-83; effective thirtieth day thereafter (Register 83, No. 49).

2. Amendment filed 2-21-89; operative 3-23-89 (Register 89, No. 10).

3. Amendment of first paragraph and subsections (a), (b), (d), (f) and (g) filed 5-8-96; operative 6-7-96 (Register 96, No. 19).

4. Amendment of section heading and first paragraph and repealer of subsections (a)-(i) filed 7-5-2001; operative 8-4-2001 (Register 2001, No. 27).

5. Amendment of section heading, section and Note filed 2-8-2011; operative 3-10-2011 (Register 2011, No. 6).

This database is current through 10/4/24 Register 2024, No. 40.

1533.1. EXAMINATION APPEALS [REPEALED]

Credits

Note: Authority cited: Section 3025, Business and Professions Code. Reference: Section 3025, Business and Professions Code.

HISTORY

1. New section filed 10-11-89; operative 11-10-89 (Register 89, No. 41).

2. Repealer filed 4-25-2001; operative 5-25-2001 (Register 2001, No. 17).

This database is current through 10/4/24 Register 2024, No. 40.

1534. NATIONAL BOARD OF EXAMINERS IN OPTOMETRY (NBO) [REPEALED]

Credits

Note: Authority cited: Section 3025, Business and Professions Code. Reference: Section 3053, Business and Professions Code.

HISTORY

1. Amendment of subsection (c) filed 1-24-80; effective thirtieth day thereafter (Register 80, No. 4).

2. Repealer filed 10-25-83; effective thirtieth day thereafter (Register 83, No. 44).

This database is current through 10/4/24 Register 2024, No. 40.

1535. EXAMINATION REQUIREMENTS [REPEALED]

Credits

Note: Authority cited: Sections 3025, 3041.2 and 3053, Business and Professions Code. Reference: Sections 3041.2 and 3053, Business and Professions Code.

HISTORY

1. Amendment filed 8-7-69; effective thirtieth day thereafter (Register 69, No. 32).

2. Amendment filed 11-22-77; effective thirtieth day thereafter (Register 77, No. 48).

3. Amendment filed 4-20-81; effective thirtieth day thereafter (Register 81, No. 17).

4. Amendment filed 5-20-83; effective upon filing pursuant to Government Code Section 11346.2(d) (Register 83, No. 21).

5. Amendment filed 2-21-89; operative 3-23-89 (Register 89, No. 10).

6. Editorial correction of printing error of History No. 5 filing date (Register 89, No. 20).

7. Amendment of section heading and former subsection (a), and repealer of subsection designations and former section (b) filed 5-8-96; operative 6-7-96 (Register 96, No. 19.

8. Repealer filed 6-24-97; operative 7-24-97 (Register 97, No. 26).

This database is current through 10/4/24 Register 2024, No. 40.

ARTICLE 6.5. CONTINUING OPTOMETRIC EDUCATION

1536. CONTINUING OPTOMETRIC EDUCATION; PURPOSE AND REQUIREMENTS

(a) Except as otherwise provided in Section 1536(b), each licensee shall complete 40 hours of formal continuing optometric education course work within the two years immediately preceding the license expiration date. Such course work shall be subject to Board approval. Up to eight hours of course work may be in the area of patient care management or ethics in the practice of optometry. Business management courses are not accepted by the Board.

(b) An optometrist certified to use therapeutic pharmaceutical agents pursuant to Business and Professions Code

Section 3041.3 shall complete a total of 50 hours of continuing optometric education every two years in order to renew their license. Thirty-five of the required 50 hours of continuing optometric education shall be on the diagnosis, treatment and management of ocular disease and consistent with Business and Professions Code section 3059, subdivision (e).

(c)(1) Up to 25 hours of required biennial course work may be accomplished by using any or all of the following alternative methods:

(A) Documented and accredited self study through correspondence or an electronic medium that is completed by successfully passing a test of the subject matter. The test may include: (1) an interactive test where the licensee submits answers electronically to the educational provider and receives instant feedback on whether the answer chosen by the licensee is correct and why, and whether they have passed the test; or (2) through self-assessment testing (open-book tests that are completed by the licensee, submitted to the provider, graded, and returned to the licensee with correct answers).

For the purposes of this section, "self-study" means a form of learning that does not offer participatory interaction between the licensee and the instructor during the instructional period. This may be accomplished via the following methods:

1. Audio or video pre-recorded teleconferences, webinars, seminars, podcasts, broadcasts, or lectures via the internet.

2. CD-ROMs played on a computer.

3. Digital video discs.

4. Books or materials as part of an independent or home study program.

5. Programs or applications on a data-enabled device, such as a computer, tablet, or cellular phone specifically designed for this purpose.

(B) Teaching of continuing optometric education courses if attendance at such course would also qualify for such credit, providing none are duplicate courses within the two-year period.

(C) Writing articles that have been published in optometric journals, magazines or newspapers, pertaining to the practice of optometry (or in other scientific, learned, refereed journals on topics pertinent to optometry), providing no articles are duplicates. One hour of credit will be granted for each full page of printing or the equivalent thereof.

(D) A full day's live attendance at a California State Board of Optometry Board meeting as verified by the Board. Every two hours of open session equates to one hour of credit, up to a maximum of four credit hours.

(E) Completion of a course to receive certification in cardiopulmonary resuscitation (CPR) from the American Red Cross, the American Heart Association, or other association approved by the Board. Up to four credit hours shall be granted for this course.

(F) Any continuing education course approved for category 1 of the American Medical Association or category 1A of the American Osteopathic Association Continued Medical Education credits that contributes to the advancement of professional skill and knowledge in the practice of optometry.

(G) Participation as a subject matter expert in the creation of the Board's California Laws and Regulation Examination. Subject matter experts will receive one hour of continuing education credit for each hour attending a Board sponsored workshop, not to exceed twelve credits per renewal cycle.

(2) All remaining hours of continuing optometric education shall be obtained through live and interactive course study. For purposes of this section, live and interactive course study is defined as:

(A) In-person lectures, in-person workshops, in-person demonstrations, or in-person classroom studies which allow participatory interaction between the licensee and the instructor during the instructional period; or

(B) Lectures, webinars, workshops or audio or video conferences delivered via the internet or computer networks in real time, which means online meetings with participatory interaction between the licensee and the instructor presenting the content during the instructional period at the same time.

(d) A credit hour is defined as one classroom hour, usually a 50-minute period, but no less than that.

(e) Continuing optometric education programs which are approved as meeting the required standards of the Board include the following:

(1) Continuing optometric education courses officially sponsored or recognized by any accredited school or college of optometry. For the purposes of this section, "accredited" means recognition from an accrediting agency recognized by the Secretary of the United States Department of Education.

(2) Continuing optometric education courses provided by any national or state affiliate of the American Optometric Association, the American Academy of Optometry, or the Optometric Extension Program.

(3) Continuing optometric education courses or activities approved by the Association of Regulatory Boards of Optometry committee known as COPE (Council on Optometric Practitioner Education).

(f) Other continuing optometric education courses shall be approved by the Board upon meeting the criteria set forth in paragraph (g) below, and after submission of the fee in Section 1524(l), a completed Continuing Education Course Approval Application (Form CE-01, Rev. 8/22), hereby incorporated by reference, course schedule, topical outline of subject matter, and curriculum vitae of all instructors or lecturers involved. Form CE-01 shall be submitted to the Board not less than 45 days prior to the commencement of the program. The Board may, upon application of any licensee and for good cause shown, waive the requirement for submission of advance information and request for prior approval. Nothing herein shall permit the Board to approve a continuing optometric education course which has not complied with the criteria set forth in paragraph (g) below. Course approvals shall be valid for two years from the date as approved by the Board. Each individual course shall be assigned a course approval number by the Board.

(g) The criteria for judging and approving continuing education courses by the Board for continuing optometric education credit will be determined on the following bases:

(1) Whether the program is likely to contribute to the advancement of professional skills and knowledge in the practice of optometry, including the following subject matter areas:

(A) Patient care management,

(B) Ocular and systemic signs or symptoms of related disease,

(C) Child abuse detection,

(D) Clinical optometry,

(E) Ethics in the practice of optometry,

(F) Elder abuse detection,

(G) Pharmacology/Schedule II drug prescribing and abuse prevention,

(H) Any categories in the diagnosis, treatment, and management of ocular disease as set forth in Section 3059(e) of the Business and Professions Code.

(2) Whether the instructors, lecturers, and others participating in the presentation are recognized by the Board as being qualified in their field.

(3) Whether the proposed course is open to all optometrists licensed in this State.

(4) Whether the provider of any mandatory continuing optometric education course agrees to maintain and furnish to the Board and/or attending licensee such records of course content, dates and places of the course, course completion certificates as specified in subdivision (h), and attendance as the Board requires, for a period of at least four years from the date of course presentation.

(5) The provider does not use the Board's letterhead, seal, or logo on any course certificates, advertising, or solicitation.

(6) If the proposed course is live and interactive as defined in subsection (d), whether the proposed course has measures for participatory interaction, including participant attendance reports, in-content quizzes, participant polls, real time participant video requirements, and records of participant log in and log out times.

(h) Proof of continuing optometric education course attendance shall be provided in a form and manner specified in writing by the Board and distributed to all licensed optometrists in this State. Certification of continuing optometric education course attendance shall be submitted by the licensee to the Board upon request, and shall contain the following minimal information:

(1) Name of the sponsoring organization.

(2) Name, signature, practice address, and license number of the attending licensee.

(3) Subject or title of the course.

(4) Number of continuing optometric education hours provided for attending the course.

(5) Date the course was provided.

(6) Location where the course was provided.

(7) Name(s) and signature(s) of the course instructor(s).

(8) Such other evidence of course content or attendance as the Board may deem necessary.

(9) Course approval number as assigned by the Board, if applicable.

(10) Whether the course was pre-recorded or live.

A certificate of course completion generated by the continuing optometric education provider is required to be issued to any licensee who completes any continuing optometric education course approved by the Board pursuant to the above.

The Board will also recognize and utilize the Association of Regulatory Boards in Optometry's online Optometric Education (OE) Tracker system as proof of continuing education course attendance.

(i) The following licensees shall be exempt from the requirements of this section:

(1) Any licensee serving in the regular armed forces of the United States during any part of the two years immediately preceding the license expiration date.

(2) Any licensee who is renewing an active license for the first time, if they graduated from an accredited school or college of optometry less than one year from the date of initial licensure.

(3) Those licensees as the Board, in its discretion, determines were unable to

complete sufficient hours of continuing optometric education courses due to illness, incapacity, or other unavoidable circumstances. An extension may be granted if the Board, in its discretion, determines that good cause exists for the licensee's failure to complete the requisite hours of continuing optometric education.

(j) The Board, in its discretion, may exempt from the continuing optometric education requirements of this section licensees who for health reasons or other good cause cannot meet these requirements. Licensees requesting an exemption shall complete a Continuing Education Exemption Request (Form CE-E, Rev 2/2016) and submit it, along with all required supporting information, to the Board for its consideration at least thirty (30) days prior to the expiration of the license.

(1) The Board may deny a request for exemption but at its discretion may grant the licensee an extension of up to one year to obtain the necessary continuing optometric education.

(2) A licensee whose requests for an exemption is denied and an extension is not granted shall otherwise comply with the provision of this section.

(k) The Board may conduct an audit of any licensee's attendance of a continuing optometric education course as a means of verifying compliance with this section. A licensee shall maintain all course completion certificates on file which are used for renewal purposes for a period of four (4) years from the license renewal date and shall provide these records to the Board upon request or in the event of an audit, if requested, within ten (10) days of the date of the Board's written request for such records.

(l) Licensees that are glaucoma certified pursuant to BPC section 1571 shall be required to complete 10 hours of glaucoma specific optometric continuing education every license renewal period. These 10 hours shall be part of the required 35 hours on the diagnosis, treatment and management of ocular disease.

(m) A licensee may not repeat for credit the same course more than once within the two-year renewal timeframe.

Credits

Note: Authority cited: Section 3059, Business and Professions Code. Reference: Section 3059, Business and Professions Code.

HISTORY

1. New section filed 2-21-89; operative 3-23-89 (Register 89, No. 10).

2. Amendment of subsections (a) and (d), new subsection (d)(3), and amendment of subsections (e), (f), (f)(2), (f)(4), (g), (g)(8), (h)(2), (h)(3) and (i), and new subsection (j) and amendment of Note filed 5-8-96; operative 6-7-96 (Register 96, No. 19).

3. Amendment filed 12-22-2004; operative 1-21-2005 (Register 2004, No. 52).

4. Amendment of section and Note filed 5-18-2011; operative 6-17-2011 (Register 2011, No. 20).

5. Amendment of subsection (c)(4), new subsections (c)(6)-(7), amendment of subsections (f) and (g)(1), repealer of subsection (i)(2), subsection renumbering, new subsection (i)(3)-(j)(2) and (l) and subsection relettering filed 11-9-2016; operative 1-1-2017 (Register 2016, No. 46).

6. Amendment filed 8-23-2023; operative 8-23-2023 pursuant to Government Code section 11343.4(b)(3) (Register 2023, No. 34).

This database is current through 10/4/24 Register 2024, No. 40.

ARTICLE 7. OPTOMETRIC CORPORATIONS

1540. CITATION OF RULES [REPEALED]

Credits

Note: Authority cited: Sections 3025 and 3167, Business and Professions Code. Reference: Section 3025, Business and Professions Code.

HISTORY

1. New Article 7 (# 1540 through 1550) filed 9-27-71; effective thirtieth day thereafter (Register 71, No. 40).

2. Repealer filed 10-25-83; effective thirtieth day thereafter (Register 83, No. 44).

This database is current through 10/4/24 Register 2024, No. 40.

1541. DEFINITIONS [REPEALED]

Credits

Note: Authority cited: Section 3167, Business and Professions Code. Reference: Section 13410, Corporations Code.

HISTORY

1. Change without regulatory effect repealing Section 1541 (Register 88, No. 15).

This database is current through 10/4/24 Register 2024, No. 40.

1542. PROFESSIONAL RELATIONSHIPS, RESPONSIBILITIES, AND CONDUCT NOT AFFECTED [REPEALED]

Credits

Note: Authority cited: Section 3167, Business and Professions Code. Reference: Section 13410, Corporations Code.

HISTORY

1. Change without regulatory effect repealing Section 1542 (Register 88, No. 15).

This database is current through 10/4/24 Register 2024, No. 40.

1543. OFFICE FOR FILING [REPEALED]

Credits

Note: Authority cited: Sections 3025 and 3167, Business and Professions Code. Reference: Section 3025, Business and Professions Code.

HISTORY

1. Repealer filed 10-25-83; effective thirtieth day thereafter (Register 83, No. 44).

This database is current through 10/4/24 Register 2024, No. 40.

1544. APPLICATION; REVIEW OF REFUSAL TO APPROVE

(a) An applicant corporation shall file with the Board an application for Certificate of Registration on a form furnished by the Board, which shall be signed and verified by an officer of the corporation who is a licensed person and be accompanied by a fee not to exceed two hundred dollars ($200).

(b) The Board, within a reasonable time after an application for registration is submitted to it, shall either approve the application and issue a Certificate of Registration or refuse to approve the application and notify the applicant corporation of the reasons therefor.

(c) The Board may delegate to its executive officer, or other official or employee of the Board, its authority under Section 3161, Business and Professions Code, to review and approve applications for registration and to issue Certificates of Registration.

(d) Any applicant corporation whose application has been disapproved by the Board may request a hearing pursuant to Government Code Section 11504. The hearing shall be conducted pursuant to the Administrative Procedure Act (Government Code Sections 11502-11528).

(e) No applicant corporation shall hold itself out or engage in nor shall it render any professional services unless and until a Certificate of Registration has been issued.

Credits

Note: Authority cited: Section 3167, Business and Professions Code. Reference: Sections 3160-3167, Business and Professions Code; and Section 13401, Corporations Code.

HISTORY

1. Amendment of subsections (a) and (c) filed 2-2-79; effective thirtieth day thereafter (Register 79, No. 5).

2. Change without regulatory effect of Note (Register 88, No. 15).

This database is current through 10/4/24 Register 2024, No. 40.

1545. REQUIREMENTS FOR ISSUANCE OF CERTIFICATE OF REGISTRATION [REPEALED]

Credits

Note: Authority cited: Sections 3025 and 3167, Business and Professions Code. Reference: Section 3025, Business and Professions Code.

HISTORY

1. Repealer filed 10-25-83; effective thirtieth day thereafter (Register 83, No. 44).

This database is current through 10/4/24 Register 2024, No. 40.

1546. NAME OF CORPORATION

(a) Except as provided in Section 1518, the name of the corporation shall contain and be restricted to:

(1) The name or last name of one or more of the present, prospective, or former shareholders, and

(2) One of the following designations denoting corporate existence: "Optometric Corporation," "Optometry Corporation," "Corporation," "Professional Corporation," "Prof. Corp.," "Corp.," "Incorporated," "Inc.," "Optometric Corp.," "Optometry Corp.," "Professional Optometric Corporation," "Professional Optometry Corporation," "Professional Optometric Corp.," or "Professional Optometry Corp.."

(b) The letters "Opt.D." or "O.D." or the word "optometrist" may be used in the corporate name providing that any person using such designation shall be the holder of a diploma from an accredited school of optometry. Some examples of such usage are: "Doctor John Doe, O.D., Inc." or "Dr. James Smith, O.D. and Dr. John Doe, O.D., Optometric Corporation."

Credits

Note: Authority cited: Sections 3025 and 3167, Business and Professions Code. Reference: Sections 3098 and 3163, Business and Professions Code.

HISTORY

1. Amendment filed 4-3-75; effective thirtieth day thereafter (Register 75, No. 14).

2. Amendment filed 3-3-78; effective thirtieth day thereafter (Register 78, No. 9).

3. Amendment of subsection (a) filed 4-20-81; effective thirtieth day thereafter (Register 81, No. 17).

4. Amendment filed 12-1-83; effective thirtieth day thereafter (Register 83, No. 49).

This database is current through 10/4/24 Register 2024, No. 40.

1547. SECURITY FOR CLAIMS AGAINST AN OPTOMETRIC CORPORATION

(a) When an optometric corporation provides security by means of insurance for claims against it by its patients, the security shall consist of a policy or policies of insurance insuring the corporation against liability imposed upon it by law for damages arising out of claims against it by its patients arising out of the rendering of, or failure to render, optometric services by the corporation in an amount of each claim of at least

$50,000 multiplied by the number of employed licensed persons rendering such optometric services and an aggregate maximum limit of liability per policy year of at least $150,000 multiplied by the number of such employees, provided that the maximum coverage shall not be required to exceed $150,000 for each claim and $450,000 for all claims during the policy year, and provided further that the deductible portion of such insurance shall not exceed $5,000 multiplied by the number of such employees.

(b) All shareholders of the corporation shall be jointly and severally liable for all claims established against the corporation by its patients arising out of the rendering of, or failure to render, optometric services up to the minimum amounts specified for insurance under subdivision (a) hereof except during periods of time when the corporation shall provide and maintain insurance for claims against it by its patients arising out of the rendering of, or failure to render, optometric services. Said insurance, when provided, shall meet the minimum standards established in subdivision (a) above.

This database is current through 10/4/24 Register 2024, No. 40.

1548. SHARES: OWNERSHIP AND TRANSFER

(a) The shares of an optometric corporation may be issued only to a natural person licensed to practice optometry and may be transferred only to a natural person licensed to practice optometry or to the issuing corporation.

(b) Where there are two or more shareholders in an optometric corporation and one of the shareholders:

(1) Dies, or

(2) Becomes a disqualified person as defined in Section 13401(d) of the Corporations Code, for a period exceeding ninety (90) days, his/her shares shall be sold and transferred to a natural person licensed to practice optometry or to the issuing optometric corporation, on such terms as are agreed upon. Such sale or transfer shall not be later than six (6) months after any such death and not later than ninety (90) days after the date he/she became a disqualified person.

(c) A corporation and its shareholders may, but need not, agree that shares sold to it by a person who becomes a disqualified person may be resold to such person if and when he/she again ceases to become a disqualified person.

(d) The restrictions of subdivision (a) and, if appropriate, subdivision (b) of this section shall be set forth in the corporation's bylaws or articles of incorporation.

(e) The income of an optometric corporation attributable to optometric services rendered while a shareholder is a disqualified person shall not in any manner accrue to the benefit of such shareholder or his/her shares.

(f) The share certificates of an optometric corporation shall contain either:

(1) An appropriate legend setting forth the restriction of subdivision (a), and where applicable, the restriction of subdivision (b), or

(2) An appropriate legend stating that ownership and transfer of the shares are restricted and specifically referring to an identified section of the by-laws or articles of incorporation of the corporation wherein the restrictions are set forth.

Credits

Note: Authority cited: Section 3167, Business and Professions Code. Reference: Sections 3160, 3164 and 3167, Business and Professions Code; and Sections 13401, 13401.5, 13406 and 13407, Corporations Code.

HISTORY

1. Amendment filed 10-25-83; effective thirtieth day thereafter (Register 83, No. 44).

This database is current through 10/4/24 Register 2024, No. 40.

1549. CERTIFICATE OF REGISTRATION: CONTINUING VALIDITY: REPORTS

(a) A Certificate of Registration shall continue in effect until it is suspended or revoked. Such certificate may be suspended or revoked for any of the grounds permitted by law.

(b) By May 31 of each year, each optometric corporation shall file with the Board a report on a form provided by the Board reflecting its status as of May 1 and including such information pertaining to its qualifications and compliance with the statutes, rules and regulations of the Board as the Board may require.

(c) Each optometric corporation shall file a special report, on a form provided by the Board, within 30 days of any change of the officers, directors, shareholders, places of practice, by-laws, articles of incorporation, corporate name.

(d) Each annual report filed hereunder shall be accompanied by a filing fee not to exceed $50.00.

(e) Each special report filed hereunder shall be accompanied by a filing fee not to exceed $15.00.

Credits

Note: Authority cited: Section 3167, Business and Professions Code. Reference: Sections 3160-3167, Business and Professions Code; and Section 13401, Corporations Code.

HISTORY

1. Amendment of subsection (c) filed 3-3-78; effective thirtieth day thereafter (Register 78, No. 9.)

2. Amendment of subsections (d) and (e) filed 2-2-79; effective thirtieth day thereafter (Register 79, No. 5).

3. Change without regulatory effect of Note (Register 88, No. 15).

This database is current through 10/4/24 Register 2024, No. 40.

1550. BRANCH OFFICES

An optometric corporation is subject to the provisions of Section 3077 of the Code. When any optometric corporation duly registered hereunder desires to have a branch office within the meaning of that code section, it shall, prior to the opening of any branch office, make application therefor to the Board and receive permission in writing from the Board to have such branch office.

This database is current through 10/4/24 Register 2024, No. 40.

ARTICLE 8. TOPICAL PHARMACEUTICAL AGENTS

1560. DEFINITIONS [REPEALED]

Credits

Note: Authority cited: Sections 3025 and 3041, Business and Professions Code. Reference: Section 3041, Business and Professions Code.

HISTORY

1. New Article 8 (Sections 1560-1563) filed 11-22-77; effective thirtieth day thereafter (Register 77, No. 48).

2. Amendment filed 10-25-83; effective thirtieth day thereafter (Register 83, No. 44).

3. New subsection (a)(3)(d) filed 6-20-96; operative 7-20-96 (Register 96, No. 25).

4. Repealer filed 4-6-2001; operative 5-6-2001 (Register 2001, No. 14).

This database is current through 10/4/24 Register 2024, No. 40.

1561. TOPICAL PHARMACEUTICAL AGENTS USAGE—PURPOSE AND REQUIREMENTS

(a) The purpose of this article is to implement Business and Professions Code Section 3041.2, as added to said code by chapter 418 of the 1976 statutes. Only those optometrists meeting the requirements of this article may use topical pharmaceutical agents in the examination of human eyes.

(b) In order to use topical pharmaceutical agents in the examination of human eyes, an optometrist must:

(1) complete a course in pharmacology approved by the Board or have equivalent experience satisfactory to the Board; and

(2) provide evidence of taking and passing either:

(A) both the Applied Basic Science and Clinical Skills sections of the NBEO examination as it was constituted beginning in January 2010; or

(B) a pharmacology examination equivalent to subdivision (b)(1) above and administered by an accredited school or college of optometry.

(c) The Board will issue a Diagnostic Pharmaceutical Agents certification to optometrists fulfilling the requirements of subsection (b) authorizing them to use topical pharmaceutical agents.

Credits

Note: Authority cited: Sections 3025, 3041.2 and 3053, Business and Professions Code. Reference: Sections 3041 and 3041.2, Business and Professions Code.

HISTORY

1. Amendment filed 5-20-83; effective upon filing pursuant to Government Code Section 11346.2(d) (Register 83, No. 21).

2. Amendment of subsection (b) filed 5-8-89; operative 6-7-89 (Register 89, No. 27).

3. Amendment of section and Note filed 2-8-2011; operative 3-10-2011 (Register 2011, No. 6).

This database is current through 10/4/24 Register 2024, No. 40.

1562. PHARMACOLOGY COURSES

(a) In order to be approved by the Board, a course in pharmacology must include instruction in general pharmacology, ocular pharmacology, and in ocular pharmacology applied to relevant clinical procedures. The course must be at least 55 hours in length and be subdivided as follows:

General Pharmacology .....15 hours

Ocular Pharmacology ....20 hours

Clinical Laboratory (ocular pharmacology applied to relevant clinical procedures) ....20 hours

(b) Approval by the Board shall be required of all pharmacology course instructors.

This database is current through 10/4/24 Register 2024, No. 40.

1563. PHARMACOLOGY EXAMINATION

(a) The pharmacology course examination shall cover coursework in general pharmacology, ocular pharmacology, and ocular pharmacology with relevant clinical procedures and shall be given in conjunction with the annual optometrist licensure examination or when otherwise designated by the Board.

(b) The examination fee shall not exceed thirty-five dollars ($35).

(c) The procedure specified in Section 1533 will be used for requests to inspect examination papers or to appeal examination scores.

Credits

Note: Authority cited: Section 3153, Business and Professions Code. Reference: Sections 3041.1 and 3041.2, Business and Professions Code; Sections 1560, 1561 and 1562, California Administrative Code.

HISTORY

1. Amendment of subsection (b) filed 2-2-79; effective thirtieth day thereafter (Register 79, No. 5).

This database is current through 10/4/24 Register 2024, No. 40.

ARTICLE 9. APPLICATION PROCESSING TIMELINES

1564. REVIEW OF OPTOMETRIST APPLICATIONS; PROCESSING TIME

(a) The Board shall inform in writing an applicant for licensure as an optometrist within 45 days of receipt of the application whether the application is complete and accepted for filing or is deficient and what specific information is required.

(b) The Board shall inform in writing an applicant for licensure as an optometrist within 120 days after completion of the application, of its decision whether the applicant meets the requirements for licensure. "Completion of the application" means that a completed application form together with all required information, documentation and fees have been filed by the applicant (This period may be extended by that time necessary for retaking or rescheduling an examination or if the applicant is delayed in obtaining or completing any required professional experience or clinical training.)

(c) The minimum, median and maximum processing times for an application for licensure as an optometrist from the time of receipt of the initial application until the Board makes a final decision on the application are:

(1) Minimum—1 day

(2) Median—30 days

(3) Maximum—120 days

(These processing times apply to those applicants who take and pass the first available licensing examination.)

Credits

Note: Authority cited: Section 3025, Business and Professions Code; and Section 15376, Government Code. Reference: Section 15376, Government Code.

HISTORY

1. New Article 9 (Sections 1564 and 1564.1) filed 8-9-84; effective upon filing pursuant to Government Code Section 11346.2(d) (Register 84, No. 32).

This database is current through 10/4/24 Register 2024, No. 40.

1564.1. REVIEW OF FICTITIOUS NAME PERMIT APPLICATIONS; PROCESSING TIME

(a) The Board shall in writing inform an applicant for a permit for a fictitious name within 45 days from receipt of the application whether the application is complete and accepted for filing or is deficient and what specific information is required.

(b) The Board shall inform in writing an applicant for a permit for a fictitious name within 120 days after completion of the application, of its decision whether the applicant meets the requirements for a fictitious name permit. "Completion of the application" means that a completed application form together with all required information, documentation and fees have been filed by the applicant.

(c) The minimum, median and maximum processing times for a fictitious name permit from the time of receipt of the initial application until the Board makes a final decision on the application are:

(1) Minimum—7 days

(2) Median—30 days

(3) Maximum—120 days

Credits

Note: Authority cited: Section 3025, Business and Professions Code; and Section 15376, Government Code. Reference: Section 15376, Government Code.

This database is current through 10/4/24 Register 2024, No. 40.

ARTICLE 10. PRESCRIPTIONS

1565. PRESCRIPTION STANDARDS: INFORMATION REQUIRED

(a) Any prescription or order by an optometrist comprising written specifications for ophthalmic lenses pursuant to an eye examination must contain the following minimal information: name, address, telephone number and license number of the issuing optometrist; his/her signature; issue date and expiration date; and patient's name.

Credits

Note: Authority cited: Sections 3025 and 3025.5, Business and Professions Code. Reference: Sections 3025.5 and 3041, Business and Professions Code.

HISTORY

1. New section filed 2-21-89; operative 3-23-89 (Register 89, No. 10).

This database is current through 10/4/24 Register 2024, No. 40.

1566. RELEASE OF PRESCRIPTIONS: NOTICE REQUIRED

At each office there shall be posted in a conspicuous place a notice which shall clearly state the legal requirements regarding the release of all corrective lens prescriptions and such notice shall at a minimum contain the following information:

CONSUMER NOTICE

Eye doctors are required to provide patients with a copy of their ophthalmic lens prescriptions as follows:

- Spectacle prescriptions: Release upon completion of exam.
- Contact lens prescriptions: Release upon completion of exam or upon completion of the fitting process.

Credits

Note: Authority cited: Sections 3025, 3025.5 and 3090, Business and Professions Code. Reference: Sections 2541.2, 3025, 3025.5 and 3090, Business and Professions Code; and Title 16 CFR 315.3, 456.1 and 456.2.

HISTORY

1. New section filed 3-15-94; operative 4-14-94 (Register 94, No. 11).

2. Amendment of section and Note filed 3-10-2006; operative 4-9-2006 (Register 2006, No. 10).

This database is current through 10/4/24 Register 2024, No. 40.

1566.1. CONSUMER INFORMATION

The "CONSUMER NOTICE" specified in Section 1566 shall also contain the following consumer information:

The practice of optometry in California is regulated by the Board of Optometry. The Board of Optometry receives and investigates all consumer complaints involving the practice of optometry. Complaints or grievances involving a California-licensed optometrist, should be directed to:

BOARD OF OPTOMETRY
DEPARTMENT OF CONSUMER AFFAIRS
2450 DEL PASO ROAD, SUITE 105
SACRAMENTO, CA 95834

PHONE: 1-866-585-2666 OR
(916) 575-7170
EMAIL: optometry@dca.ca.gov
INTERNET: www.optometry.ca.gov

Credits

Note: Authority cited: Section 3025, Business and Professions Code. Reference: Section 3025.5, Business and Professions Code.

HISTORY

1. New section filed 8-12-99; operative 9-11-99 (Register 99, No. 33).

2. Amendment filed 3-10-2006; operative 4-9-2006 (Register 2006, No. 10).

3. Change without regulatory effect amending section filed 1-14-2013 pursuant to section 100, title 1, California Code of Regulations (Register 2013, No. 3).

This database is current through 10/4/24 Register 2024, No. 40.

ARTICLE 11. THERAPEUTIC PHARMACEUTICAL AGENTS

1567. DEFINITIONS

As used in this Article:

(a) "Infectious" means a type of lesion suspected to be caused by a pathogen.

(b) "NBEO" is the acronym for the National Board of Examiners in Optometry.

(c) "Peripheral Infectious Corneal Ulcers" means those infectious corneal ulcers limited to the area of the eye that lies outside the central 5mm diameter of the cornea.

(d) "Preceptorship service" means 65 hours of training in the diagnosis and treatment of ocular, systemic disease completed in no less than two months nor more than one year in one or more ophthalmologist's office(s) or optometric clinic(s). Preceptor's service shall be authorized by an accredited optometry school or college or recognized ophthalmological residency review committee in California. Preceptors shall be California-licensed ophthalmologists certified by the American Board of Medical Specialties and must be in good standing with the Medical Board of California.

(e) "Referral" means the primary responsibility for the treatment of a patient is transferred from the TPA optometrist to a consulting ophthalmologist.

(f) "Therapeutic Pharmaceutical Agents" includes mydriatics, cycloplegics, anesthetics, agents used for the reversal of mydriasis, topical lubricants, topical antiallergy agents, topical steroidal antiallergy agents, topical nonsteroidal and steroidal antiinflammatories, topical antibiotic agents, topical hyperosmotics, topical antiglaucoma agents (use pursuant to the certification process defined in Business and Professions Code section 3041, subdivision (f)), oral antihistaminines, prescription oral nonsteroidal antiinflammatory agents, oral antibiotics limited to tetracyclines, dicloxacillin, amoxicillin, amoxicillin with clavulanate, erythromycin, clarythromycin, cephalexin, cephadroxil, cefaclor, trimethoprim with sulfamethoxazole, ciprofloxacin, and azithromycin (use limited to the eyelid infection and chlamydial disease, topical antiviral medication and oral acyclovir) use specified in Business and Professions Code section 3041, subdivision (c)(12), non-controlled substance oral analgesics, codeine with compounds and hydrocodone with compounds (use limited to three days) and topical miotics for diagnostic purposes and nonprescription medications.

(g) "TMOD" is the acronym for the "Treatment and Management of Ocular Disease" examination administered by the National Board of Examiners in Optometry. Passage of this examination is mandatory for certain TPA certification applicants.

(h) "TPA" is the acronym for Therapeutic Pharmaceutical Agents.

(i) "TPA certified optometrist" means a California licensed optometrist who has met all of the requirements for certification set forth by the State Board of Optometry to use Therapeutic Pharmaceutical Agents in his or her optometric practice.

(j) "Treat" means the use of therapeutic pharmaceutical agents, as described in Business and Professions Code section 3041, subdivision (c), and the procedures described in subdivision (e).

(k) "Approval" means to certify a TPA certified optometrist to perform lacrimal irrigation and dilation of patients over the age of 12 years pursuant to Business and Professions Code section 3041, subdivision (e)(6).

Credits

Note: Authority cited: Sections 3025, 3025.5 and 3041.2, Business and Professions Code. Reference: Sections 3027.5, 3041, 3041.1, 3041.3, 3059, 3096.5, 3108, 3109, 3152.5, 4033, 4036, 4051 and 4052, Business and Professions Code.

HISTORY

1. New article 11 (sections 1567-1570) and section filed 7-7-97; operative 8-6-97 (Register 97, No. 28).

2. Amendment of subsection (e) and new subsections (j)-(k) filed 12-20-2004; operative 1-19-2005 (Register 2004, No. 52).

This database is current through 10/4/24 Register 2024, No. 40.

1568. THERAPEUTIC PHARMACEUTICAL AGENTS USAGE—PURPOSE AND REQUIREMENTS

Only those optometrists meeting the requirements of this Article may apply for TPA Certification to use Therapeutic Pharmaceutical Agents. The Application for TPA Certification (Form TPA-1 Rev. 4/96), which is hereby incorporated by reference, may be obtained from the Board's Headquarters office. Requirements for TPA certification are as follows:

(a) If the applicant is licensed to practice optometry in California and graduated from an accredited school of optometry prior to January 1, 1992:

(1) Completion of an 80-hour TPA didactic course provided either by the University of California at Berkeley School of Optometry or the Southern California College of Optometry or recognized ophthalmological residency review committee or at an accredited school or college located outside of California as provided in Section 1570 in this Article.

(2) Pass the examination given at the conclusion of the TPA course.

(3) Pass the TMOD component of the NBEO administered after July 1, 1992.

(4) Complete 20 hours of self directed study in the treatment and management of ocular, systemic disease.

(5) Complete a 65-hour preceptorship service as defined in Section 1567 in this Article.

(b) If the applicant is a licensed optometrist in California and graduated from an accredited school of optometry after January 1, 1992 but before January 1, 1996:

(1) Complete 20 hours of self directed study in the treatment and management of ocular, systemic disease.

(2) Complete a 65-hour preceptorship service as defined in Section 1567 in this Article.

(c) If the applicant is a graduate from an accredited school of optometry after January 1, 1996:

(1) Obtain a California optometrist license.

(2) Be certified by an accredited school of optometry that the applicant is

competent in the diagnosis, treatment, and management of ocular, systemic disease.

(3) Be certified by an accredited school of optometry that the applicant has completed 10 hours of experience with an ophthalmologist.

(d) If the applicant is licensed outside California and graduated from an accredited school of optometry before January 1, 1992:

(1) Obtain a California optometrist license.

(2) Completion of an 80-hour TPA didactic course provided either by University of California at Berkeley School of Optometry or Southern California College of Optometry or recognized ophthalmological residency review committee or at an out-of-state school as provided in Section 1570 in this Article.

(3) Pass the examination given at the conclusion of the TPA course.

(4) Pass the TMOD component of the NBEO administered after July 1, 1992.

(5) Complete 20 hours of self directed study in the treatment and management of ocular, systemic disease.

(6) Complete a 65-hour preceptorship service as defined in Section 1567 in this Article.

(e) If the applicant is licensed outside California and graduated from an accredited school of optometry after January 1, 1992 but prior to January 1, 1996:

(1) Obtain a California optometrist license.

(2) Complete 20 hours of self directed study in the treatment and of management of ocular, systemic disease.

(3) Complete a 65-hour preceptorship service as defined in Section 1567 in this Article.

(f) If the applicant is licensed in a state outside of California, graduated from an accredited school of optometry prior to January 1, 1992 and has practiced in that state, or on a reservation or a facility supported and maintained by the United States government with a TPA license:

(1) Obtain a California optometrist license.

(2) Pass the TMOD component of the NBEO administered after July 1, 1992.

(3) Complete a 65-hour preceptorship service as defined in Section 1567 in this Article.

(g) If the applicant is licensed in a state outside of California, graduated from an accredited school of optometry after January 1, 1992 but before January 1, 1996 and has practiced in that state or on a reservation or a facility supported and maintained by the United States government with a TPA license:

(1) Complete 20 hours of self directed study in the treatment and of management of ocular, systemic disease.

(2) Complete a 65-hour preceptorship service as defined in Section 1567 in this Article.

(h) All TPA certified optometrists pursuant to this Article must complete 50 hours of continuing education in order to renew licensure. Thirty-five of the required hours shall be in the diagnosis, treatment and management of ocular, and systemic disease consistent with Business and Professions Code section 3059, subdivision (f).

(i) If the applicant is licensed in a state outside of California and requests that the 65-hour preceptorship service requirement contained in subdivisions (e), (f) and (g) be waived based on their optometric practice experience using TPA in another state, the Board, as authorized under Business and Professions Code Section 3041.3(d)(1), shall deem the experience as equivalent to the 65-hour preceptorship service required in California provided the following conditions are met:

1. Applicant is licensed in good standing in their state of licensure.

2. Applicant has graduated from an accredited school of optometry before January 1, 1996.

3. Applicant has met the requirements to treat with therapeutic pharmaceutical agents in their state of licensure.

4. Applicant has been practicing optometry in their state of licensure using therapeutic pharmaceutical agents for 5 continuous years immediately preceding the submission of their application.

Credits

Note: Authority cited: Sections 3025 and 3041.2, Business and Professions Code. Reference: Sections 3041.3 and 3059, Business and Professions Code.

HISTORY

1. New section filed 7-7-97; operative 8-6-97 (Register 97, No. 28).

2. Amendment of subsection (h) filed 12-20-2004; operative 1-19-2005 (Register 2004, No. 52).

3. New subsection (i) and amendment of Note filed 7-3-2008; operative 7-3-2008 pursuant to Government Code section 11343.4 (Register 2008, No. 27).

This database is current through 10/4/24 Register 2024, No. 40.

1569. SCOPE OF PRACTICE [REPEALED]

Credits

Note: Authority cited: Sections 3025 and 3041.2, Business and Professions Code. Reference: Sections 2266, 3027.5, 3041, 3041.1, 3108 and 3109, Business and Professions Code.

HISTORY

1. New section filed 7-7-97; operative 8-6-97 (Register 97, No. 28).

2. Amendment filed 12-20-2004; operative 1-19-2005 (Register 2004, No. 52).

3. Repealer filed 7-21-2010; operative 8-20-2010 (Register 2010, No. 30).

This database is current through 10/4/24 Register 2024, No. 40.

1570. EDUCATIONAL EQUIVALENCY

Didactic courses at the following schools and colleges of optometry shall be considered equivalent to those given in California:

(a) University of Alabama at Birmingham
School of Optometry
Birmingham, Alabama

(b) University of Waterloo
School of Optometry
Ontario, Canada

(c) Nova Southeastern University
College of Optometry
North Miami Beach, Florida

(d) Illinois College of Optometry
Chicago, IL

(e) Indiana University
School of Optometry
Bloomington, Indiana

(f) New England College of Optometry
Boston, Massachusetts

(g) Ferris State University
College of Optometry
Big Rapids, Michigan

(h) University of Missouri
School of Optometry
St. Louis, Missouri

(i) State University of New York
State College of Optometry
New York, New York

(j) The Ohio State University
College of Optometry
Columbus, Ohio

(k) Northeastern State University
College of Optometry
Tahlequah, Oklahoma

(l) Pacific University
College of Optometry
Forest Grove, Oregon

(m) Pennsylvania College of Optometry
Philadelphia, Pennsylvania

(n) Southern College of Optometry
Memphis, Tennessee

(o) University of Houston
College of Optometry
Houston, Texas

Credits

Note: Authority cited: Sections 3025 and 3041.2, Business and Professions Code. Reference: Sections 3041.1 and 3041.3, Business and Professions Code.

HISTORY

1. New section filed 7-7-97; operative 8-6-97 (Register 97, No. 28).

This database is current through 10/4/24 Register 2024, No. 40.

1571. REQUIREMENTS FOR GLAUCOMA CERTIFICATION

(a) Only optometrists meeting the requirements of this Article may apply for certification for the treatment of glaucoma as described in subdivision (j) of Section 3041, in patients over 18 years of age. The optometrist shall:

(1) Hold an active license as an optometrist in California in good standing with the State Board of Optometry (Board);

(2) Be certified to use Therapeutic Pharmaceutical Agents (TPA) pursuant to Section 3041.3;

(3) Complete a didactic course of no less than 24 hours in the diagnosis, pharmacological and other treatment and management of glaucoma. The following topics may be covered in the course:

(A) Anatomy and physiology of glaucoma

(B) Classification of glaucoma

(C) Pharmacology in glaucoma therapy

(D) Diagnosis of glaucoma including risk factors analysis

(E) Medical and surgical treatment

(F) Participant performance assessment; and

(4) Complete a Case Management Requirement where a minimum of 25 individual patients are each prospectively treated for a minimum of 12 consecutive months. For purposes of this section, "treat" means properly evaluating the patient, performing all necessary tests, diagnosing the patient, recognizing the type of glaucoma within a licensee's scope of practice, creating a treatment plan with proposed medications and target pressures, ongoing monitoring and reevaluation of the patient's condition, and making timely referrals to an ophthalmologist when appropriate. The following options may be chosen in any combination to fulfill this requirement:

(A) Case Management Course: Completion of a 16-hour case management course developed cooperatively by the accredited California schools and colleges of optometry and approved by the Board, with at least 15 cases of moderate to advanced complexity. The course may be conducted live, over the Internet, or by use of telemedicine. One hour of the program will be used for a final competency examination. Although the Case Management Course does not involve treatment of patients, completion of the 16-hour Case Management Course is equivalent to prospectively treating 15 individual patients for 12 consecutive months. Therefore, completion of the 16-hour Case Management Course will count as a 15-patient credit towards the Case Management Requirement. The full course must be completed to receive the 15-patient credit. The course must include the following topics/conditions:

1. Presentation of conditions/cases that licensees may treat:

a. All primary open-angle glaucoma;

b. Exfoliation and pigmentary glaucoma.

2. Presentation of conditions/cases that licensees may not treat, but must recognize and refer to the appropriate physician and/or surgeon such as:

a. Pseudoglaucoma with vascular, malignant, or compressive etiologies;

b. Secondary glaucoma;

c. Traumatic glaucoma;

d. Infective or inflammatory glaucoma;

e. Appropriate evaluation and analysis for medical or surgical consultation;

f. In an emergency, if possible, stabilization of acute attack of angle closure and immediate referral of the patient.

(B) Grand Rounds Program: Completion of a 16-hour grand rounds program developed cooperatively by the accredited California schools and colleges of optometry and approved by the Board, wherein participants will evaluate and create a management plan for live patients. Completion of the 16-hour Grand Rounds Program is equivalent to prospectively treating 15 individual patients for 12 consecutive months. Therefore, the 16-hour Grand Rounds Program will count as a 15-patient credit towards the Case Management Requirement. The full program must be completed to receive the 15-patient credit. Patients must be evaluated in person. The program must include the following:

1. Presentation of various patient types such as: glaucoma suspects; narrow angle, primary open angle glaucoma (early, moderate, late); and secondary open angle glaucoma such as pigment dispersion and pseudoexfoliation. Patient data, including but not limited to, visual acuities, intra-ocular pressures, visual fields, imaging, and pachymetry, will be available on-site and presented upon request;

2. Examination of patients, evaluation of data and test results, and commitment to a tentative diagnosis, treatment, and management plan;

3. Participation in group discussion of the cases with instructor feedback;

4. Attendance of follow-up meetings (within the 16-hour program requirement) where the same or different patients will be reviewed via serial data, including but not limited to visual fields and imaging photos.

(C) Preceptorship Program: Completion of a preceptorship program where each patient must be initially evaluated by the licensee and co-managed with a preceptor. Each patient must be prospectively treated for a minimum of 12 consecutive months. A preceptor for purposes of this section is defined as:

1. A California licensed, Board certified ophthalmologist in good standing; or

2. A California licensed optometrist in good standing, who has been glaucoma certified for two or more years.

Preceptors shall confirm the diagnosis and treatment plan, and then approve the therapeutic goals and management plan for each patient. Consultation with the preceptor must occur at appropriate clinical intervals or when the therapeutic goals are not achieved. Clinical data will be exchanged at appropriate intervals determined by the preceptor and the licensee. Telemedicine and electronic exchange of information may be used as agreed upon by the preceptor and the licensee. Each patient that is seen by the optometrist in the program will count as a 1-patient credit towards the Case Management Requirement.

(b) Licensees who completed their education from an accredited school or college of optometry on or after May 1, 2008, are exempt from the didactic course and case management requirements of this Section, provided they submit proof of graduation from that institution to the Board.

(c) Licensees who graduated from an accredited school or college of optometry prior to May 1, 2000, and who have not completed a didactic course of no less than 24 hours will be required to take the 24-hour course indicated in subsection (a). Licensees who graduated from an accredited school or college of optometry after May 1, 2000, are exempt from the didactic course requirement of this Section.

(d) Licensees who graduated from an accredited school or college of optometry prior to May 1, 2008, and who have taken a didactic course of no less than 24 hours, but not completed the case management requirement under SB 929 [Stats. 2000, ch. 676, 3], will be required to complete the Case Management Requirement indicated in subsection (a).

(e) Licensees who started the process for certification to treat glaucoma under SB 929 [Stats. 2000, ch. 676, 3] but will not complete the requirements by December 31, 2009, may apply all patients who have been co-managed prospectively for at least 12 consecutive months towards the Case Management Requirement indicated in subsection (a).

Credits

Note: Authority cited: Sections 3025, 3041 and 3059, Business and Professions Code. Reference: Sections 3041 and 3041.3, Business and Professions Code.

HISTORY

1. New section filed 12-9-2010; operative 1-8-2011 (Register 2010, No. 50).

2. Repealer of subsection (b), subsection relettering and amendment of Note filed 11-9-2016; operative 1-1-2017 (Register 2016, No. 46).

This database is current through 10/4/24 Register 2024, No. 40.

ARTICLE 12. ENFORCEMENT

1575. UNIFORM STANDARDS RELATED TO SUBSTANCE ABUSE AND DISCIPLINARY GUIDELINES

In reaching a decision on a disciplinary action under the Administrative Procedures Act (Government Code Section 11400 et seq.), the Board of Optometry shall comply with the "Uniform Standards Related to Substance Abuse" (Uniform Standards) and consider the "Disciplinary Guidelines" (DG-4, 5-2012) which are hereby incorporated by reference. The Disciplinary Guidelines apply to all disciplinary matters; the Uniform Standards apply to a substance-abusing licensee.

(a) Subject to subdivision (b), deviation from the Disciplinary Guidelines, including the standard terms of probation, is appropriate where the Board, in its sole discretion, determines that the facts of the particular case warrant such a deviation--for example: the presence of mitigating factors; the age of the case; evidentiary problems.

(b) If the conduct found to be a violation involves drugs and/or alcohol, the licensee shall be presumed to be a substance-abusing licensee for purposes of Section 315 of the Code. If the licensee does not rebut that presumption, then the Uniform Standards for a substance-abusing licensee shall apply.

Credits

Note: Authority cited: Sections 3025 and 3090, Business and Professions Code; and Section 11400.20, Government Code. Reference: Sections 315, 315.2, 315.4, 480, 3090, 3091 and 3110, Business and Professions Code; and Sections 11400.20 and 11425.50(e), Government Code.

HISTORY

1. New article 12 (section 1575) and section filed 7-30-97; operative 7-30-97 pursuant to Government Code section 11343.4(d) (Register 97, No. 31).

2. Amendment of "Disciplinary Guidelines and Model Disciplinary Orders" (incorporated by reference) and amendment of section filed 4-25-2001; operative 5-25-2001 (Register 2001, No. 17).

3. Amendment of section heading, section and Note filed 2-27-2013; operative 4-1-2013 (Register 2013, No. 9).

This database is current through 10/4/24 Register 2024, No. 40.

ARTICLE 12.5. CITATIONS AND FINES

1576. CITATIONS — CONTENT AND SERVICE

(a) The executive officer of the board, or his/her designee, may issue a citation which may contain an administrative fine and/or order of abatement against a licensee for any violation of law which would be grounds for discipline or for violation of any regulation adopted by the board pursuant hereto.

(b) Each citation shall be in writing and shall describe, with particularity, the nature and facts of each violation specified in the citation, including a reference to the statute(s) or regulation(s) alleged to have been violated.

(c) The citation may contain an assessment of an administrative fine, an order of abatement fixing a reasonable time for abatement of the violation, or both.

(d) The citation shall inform the cited individual of the right to an informal citation conference concerning the matter and the right to an administrative hearing.

(e) The citation shall be served upon the individual personally, or by certified mail in accordance with the provisions of Section 11505(c) of the Government Code.

Credits

Note: Authority cited: Sections 125.9, 3025 and 3135, Business and Professions Code. Reference: Sections 125.9 and 3135, Business and Professions Code.

HISTORY

1. New article 12.5 (sections 1576-1581) and section filed 8-17-99; operative 9-16-99 (Register 99, No. 34).

This database is current through 10/4/24 Register 2024, No. 40.

1577. CITATIONS FOR UNLICENSED PERSONS

The executive officer of the board is authorized to determine when and against whom a citation will be issued and to issue citations containing orders of abatement and fines against persons, as defined in Section 125.9 of the Code, who are performing or who have performed services for which a license is required under the statutes and regulations enforced by the Board of Optometry. Each citation issued for unlicensed activity shall be issued in accordance with Section 1578 of these regulations. The provisions of section 1578 shall apply to the issuance of citations for unlicensed activity under this section. The sanction authorized under this section shall be separate from and in addition to any other civil or criminal remedies.

Credits

Note: Authority cited: Sections 125.9, 148, 3025 and 3135, Business and Professions Code. Reference: Sections 125.9 and 148, Business and Professions Code.

HISTORY

1. New section filed 8-17-99; operative 9-16-99 (Register 99, No. 34).

This database is current through 10/4/24 Register 2024, No. 40.

1578. CITATION FACTORS

In assessing an administrative fine or issuing an order of abatement, the executive officer of the board shall give due consideration to the following factors:

(a) The gravity of the violation. If the violation is of such a nature and/or severity that revocation of the license or restrictions on the license are necessary in order to ensure consumer protection, a citation will not be issued.

(b) The good or bad faith exhibited by the cited person.

(c) The history of previous violations of the same or similar nature.

(d) Evidence that the violation was or was not willful.

(e) The extent to which the cited person has cooperated with the board's investigation.

(f) The extent to which the cited person has mitigated or attempted to mitigate any damage or injury caused by the violation.

(g) Any other factors as justice may require.

Credits

Note: Authority cited: Sections 125.9 and 3025, Business and Professions Code. Reference: Section 125.9, Business and Professions Code.

HISTORY

1. New section filed 8-17-99; operative 9-16-99 (Register 99, No. 34).

This database is current through 10/4/24 Register 2024, No. 40.

1579. CITABLE OFFENSES

(a) The executive officer of the board shall assess fines for citable offenses listed in this section, provided however, in no case shall the total fines exceed $2,500 for each violation. The executive officer shall not impose any duplicate fines for the same violation.

(b) Where citations include an assessment of an administrative fine, they shall be classified according to the nature of the violation and shall indicate the classification on the face.

(c) Class "A" citations involve a person who has engaged in the practice of optometry without a current and valid license, including, but not limited to, acting in the capacity of an optometrist or performing or controlling the practice of optometry as defined in Business and Professions Code section 3041.

A class "A" citation is subject to an administrative fine in an amount not less than one thousand five hundred dollars ($1,500) and not to exceed two thousand five hundred dollars ($2,500) for each violation.

(d) Class "B" citations involve an optometrist who has either:

(1) Violated any statute or regulation which would be grounds for discipline by the Board that has caused non-physical financial harm to a person, or

(2) Has committed a violation that are grounds for issuance of a Class "C" citation and has been issued one or more prior Class "C" citations within the three (3) years immediately preceding the issuance of the citation.

A class "B" citation is subject to an administrative fine in an amount not less than five hundred dollars ($500) and not to exceed two thousand five hundred dollars ($2,500) for each violation.

(e) Class "C" citations involve an optometrist who has violated any statute or regulation which would be grounds for discipline by the Board that did not cause physical or financial harm to a person.

A class "C" citation is subject to an administrative fine in an amount not less than two hundred fifty dollars ($250) and not to exceed two thousand five hundred dollars ($2,500) for each violation.

(f) Notwithstanding the administrative fine amounts specified in subsections (c), (d), and (e), a citation may include a fine between two thousand five hundred and one dollars ($2,501) and five thousand dollars ($5,000) if one or more of the following circumstances apply:

(1) The citation involves a violation that has an immediate relationship to the health and safety of another person;

(2) The cited person has a history of two or more prior citations of the same or similar violations;

(3) The citation involves multiple violations that demonstrate a willful disregard of the law;

(4) The citation involves a violation or violations perpetrated against a senior citizen or disabled person;

(5) The citation involves fraudulent billing submitted to an insurance company, or Medi-Cal or Medi-Care programs;

(g) The sanctions authorized under this section shall be separate from, and in addition to, any other civil or criminal remedies.

Credits

Note: Authority cited: Sections 125.9, 148, 2545 and 3025, Business and Professions Code. Reference: Sections 125.9, 148 and 2545, Business and Professions Code.

HISTORY

1. New section filed 8-17-99; operative 9-16-99 (Register 99, No. 34).

2. Amendment of section and NOTE filed 9-26-2006; operative 10-26-2006 (Register 2006, No. 39).

This database is current through 10/4/24 Register 2024, No. 40.

1580. COMPLIANCE WITH CITATION/ORDER OF ABATEMENT

(a) If the cited person who has been issued an order of abatement is unable to complete the correction within the time set forth in the citation because of conditions beyond his or her control after the exercise of reasonable diligence, the cited person may request an extension of time in which to make the correction from the executive officer of the board. Such a request shall be in writing and shall be made within the time set forth for the abatement.

(b) If a citation or order of abatement is not contested, or if the citation is contested and the cited person does not prevail, failure to abate the violation or to pay the assessed fine within the time allowed shall constitute a violation and a failure to comply with the citation or order of abatement.

(c) Failure to comply with an order of abatement or pay an assessed fine may result in disciplinary action being taken by the board or other appropriate judicial action being taken against the cited person.

(d) If a fine is not paid after a citation has become final, the fine shall be added to the cited person's license or registration renewal fee. A license or registration shall not be renewed without payment of the renewal fee and fine.

Credits

Note: Authority cited: Sections 125.9 and 3025, Business and Professions Code. Reference: Section 125.9, Business and Professions Code.

HISTORY

1. New section filed 8-17-99; operative 9-16-99 (Register 99, No. 34).

This database is current through 10/4/24 Register 2024, No. 40.

1581. CONTESTED CITATIONS

(a) If a cited person wishes to contest the citation, assessment of the administrative fine, or order of abatement, the cited person shall, within thirty (30) days after service of the citation, file in writing a request for an administrative hearing to the executive officer regarding the acts charged in the citation, as provided for in subdivision (b)(4) of Section 125.9 of the Code.

(b) In addition to, or instead of, requesting an administrative hearing, as provided for in subdivision (b)(4) of Section 125.9 of the Code, the cited person may, within thirty (30) days after service of the citation, contest the citation by submitting a written request for an informal citation conference to the executive officer or his/her designee.

(c) Upon receipt of a written request for an informal citation conference, the executive officer or his/her designee shall, within sixty (60) days, hold an informal citation conference with the cited person. The cited person may be accompanied and represented at the informal citation conference by an attorney or other authorized representative.

(d) If an informal citation conference is held, the request for an administrative hearing shall be deemed to be withdrawn and the executive officer or his/her designee may affirm, modify or dismiss the citation, including any fine levied or order of abatement issued, at the conclusion of the informal citation conference. If affirmed or modified, the citation originally issued shall be considered withdrawn and an affirmed or modified citation, including reason for the decision, shall be issued. The affirmed or modified citation shall be mailed to the cited person and his/her legal counsel, if any, within ten (10) days from the date of the informal citation conference.

(e) If a cited person wishes to contest an affirmed or modified citation, the person shall, within thirty (30) days of his or her notification, file in writing a request for an administrative hearing to the executive officer regarding the acts charged in the affirmed or modified citation, in accordance with subdivision (b)(4) of Section 125.9 of the Code.

Credits

Note: Authority cited: Sections 125.0 and 3025, Business and Professions Code. Reference: Section 125.9, Business and Professions Code.

HISTORY

1. New section filed 8-17-99; operative 9-16-99 (Register 99, No. 34).

This database is current through 10/4/24 Register 2024, No. 40.

1582. UNPROFESSIONAL CONDUCT

In addition to the conduct described in Section 3110 of the Code, "unprofessional conduct" also includes, but is not limited to the following:

(a) Failure to cooperate and participate in any Board investigation pending against the licensee. This includes, but is not limited to, failure to respond to a Board request for information or evidence within 15 days of receipt of the request or within the time specified in the request, whichever is later, unless the licensee is unable to provide the information within this time period for good cause. This subsection shall not be construed to deprive a licensee of any privilege guaranteed by the Fifth

Amendment to the Constitution of the United States, or any other constitutional or statutory privileges. This subsection shall not be construed to require a licensee to cooperate with a request that would require the licensee to waive any constitutional or statutory privilege or to comply with a request for information or other matters within an unreasonable period of time in light of the time constraints of the licensee's practice. Any exercise by a licensee of any constitutional or statutory privilege shall not be used against the licensee in a regulatory or disciplinary proceeding against the licensee.

(b) Failure to report to the Board, within 30 days, any of the following:

(1) The bringing of an indictment or information charging a felony against the licensee.

(2) The conviction of the licensee, including any verdict of guilty, or pleas of guilty or no contest, of any felony or misdemeanor.

(3) Any disciplinary action taken by another licensing entity or authority of this state or of another state or an agency of the federal government or the United States military that is related to the practice of optometry.

(c) Failure or refusal to comply with a court order, issued in the enforcement of a subpoena, mandating the release of records to the Board.

Credits

Note: Authority cited: Section 3025, Business and Professions Code. Reference: Sections 480, 3010.1, 3010.5, 3024, 3025, 3090 and 3110, Business and Professions Code.

HISTORY

1. New section filed 12-6-2016; operative 4-1-2017 (Register 2016, No. 50).

This database is current through 10/4/24 Register 2024, No. 40.

ARTICLE 13 - MOBILE OPTOMETRIC OFFICES

§1583. REGISTRATION REQUIREMENTS FOR A CERTIFICATE TO OPERATE; OWNERSHIP AND OPERATION OF MOBILE OPTOMETRIC OFFICES; NOTICE OF CHANGES; ABANDONMENT; GROUNDS FOR DENIAL

(a) An owner and operator of a mobile optometric office who wishes to offer optometric services at a mobile optometric office in this state shall register with the Board prior to offering services to the public by submitting a completed application as prescribed by this section. An owner and operator shall utilize an online portal designated by the Board to submit the application as provided in subdivision (b) for registration for ownership and operation of mobile optometric offices and upon approval will receive a certificate to operate as an owner and operator of a mobile optometric office.

(b) The completed application shall contain the information required in this subdivision and shall be electronically submitted through a web link to the Department of Consumer Affairs' online licensing system entitled "BreEZe" located on the Board's website at: www.optometry.ca.gov. The applicant shall complete the application according to the following requirements:

(1) The owner and operator shall first register for a user account by creating a username and password.

(2) The owner and operator shall provide the following information under penalty of perjury through BreEZe:

(A) Name of the owner and operator's organization (legal name);

(B) Owner and operator's primary physical business address, city, state, zip code, and telephone number;

(C) Owner and operator address of record, city, state, zip code, telephone number, and website address, if applicable;

(D) Name, title, direct telephone number, and email address of the authorized contact person submitting application on behalf of a nonprofit or charitable organization seeking to own and operate a mobile optometric office;

(E) A copy of the articles of incorporation or acknowledgment of intent to operate and employer identification number demonstrating the owner and operator is a nonprofit or charitable organization that is exempt from taxation pursuant to Section 501(c)(3) or Section 501(c)(4) of the Internal Revenue Code. These documents shall be scanned and electronically uploaded to the Board in a PDF format that is attached to the application through BreEZe;

(F) A list of all responsible officers or officials in positions of authority, either elected or designated, as determined by the organization (non-profit or charitable organization) and personally identifying information including:

1. Names and titles of the officers or officials;

2. Address, city, state, and zip code of the officers or officials; and

3. Social security numbers (SSN) or individual taxpayer identification numbers (ITN), business telephone numbers, alternate telephone numbers (if any), and email addresses of each of the officers or officials.

(G) Description of the services that will be rendered within the mobile optometric offices;

(H) Description of how follow-up care for all patients served by the mobile optometric office(s) will be provided.

(I) Electronic Signature: When a signature is required by the particular instructions of any filing to be made through BreEZe, including any attestation under penalty of perjury, an authorized representative of the mobile optometric office shall affix their electronic signature to the filing by typing their name in the signature field and submitting the filing via BreEZe. Submission of a filing in this manner shall constitute evidence of legal signature by any individual whose name is typed in the signature field on the filing.

(3) The application for registration for ownership and operation of mobile optometric offices shall be accompanied by the following:

(A) The non-refundable fee fixed by the Board pursuant to Section 1524 shall be electronically submitted at the time of registration through BreEZe;

(B) Full and complete fingerprints of the applicant's elected or designated responsible officers or officials to the Board for use in conducting criminal background checks through the California Department of Justice and the Federal Bureau of Investigation, in the manner specified, and pursuant to the conditions and requirements set forth, in Section 1585. For the purposes of this section, "responsible officers or officials" means the individuals listed by the applicant as the elected or designated principal officers or officials responsible for the operations of the applicant's organization.

(c) The owner and operator of a mobile optometric office shall report to the Board any change in information provided to the Board within fourteen (14) days of the change including, change of primary business address, responsible officers or officials, records location, and the name and license number of the optometrist responsible for directing medical operations.

(d) An applicant who fails to complete application requirements to register with the Board within one year after being notified by the Board of deficiencies in its application, shall be deemed to have abandoned the application and shall be required to file a new application and meet all registration requirements in effect at the time of reapplication.

(e) An application may be denied if an applicant fails to comply with any of the requirements of this section or Section 3070.2 of the code, or upon the grounds specified in Section 480 of the code. Applicants shall receive written notice of approval or denial from the Board within 60 days from the date the Board receives a completed application. "Completed application" means that all required information, documentation, and fees have been filed by the applicant as required by this article or Section 3070.2 of the code.

Credit

Note: Authority cited: Sections 3025, 3041 and 3070.2, Business and Professions Code. Reference: Sections 27, 30, 31, 142, 144, 163.5, 480, 494.5, 2544, 3041, 3041.3, 3055, 3070, 3070.1 and 3070.2, Business and Professions Code; Sections 1633.2, 1633.7 and 1633.9, Civil Code; and Section 16.5, Government Code.

HISTORY

1. New article 13 (sections 1583-1587) and new section filed 10-9-2024; operative 10/9/2024 pursuant to Government Code section 11343.4(b)(3) (Register 2024, No. 41).

Current through Register 2024 Notice Reg. No. 43, October 25, 2024.

§1584. RENEWAL REQUIREMENTS; CERTIFICATE TO OPERATE A MOBILE OPTOMETRIC OFFICE; GROUNDS FOR DISCIPLINE; REINSTATEMENT OF EXPIRED CERTIFICATE

(a) A certificate to operate a mobile optometric office ("certificate to operate") issued by the Board under Section 1583 shall expire two years after the date of issuance unless renewed by the Board prior to its expiration by meeting the requirements in this section.

(b) To renew a certificate to operate, an owner and operator of a mobile optometric office shall pay the renewal fee set forth in Section 1524 and certify in writing to the Board that it maintains compliance with the following requirements:

(1) Optometric services are provided to patients regardless of the patient's ability to pay;

(2) The owner and operator does not accept payment for services other than those provided to Medi-Cal beneficiaries;

(3) The medical operations of the mobile optometric office are directed by a licensed optometrist and in every phase are under the exclusive control of the licensed optometrist, including the selection and supervision of optometric staff, the scheduling of patients, the amount of time the optometrist spends with patients, the fees charged for optometric products and services, the examination procedures, the treatment provided to patients, and the follow-up care;

(4) The owner and operator of the mobile optometric office provides each patient and, if applicable, the patient's caregiver or guardian, a consumer notice prescribed by the Board in Section 1587 and maintains it in the patient's medical record;

(5) Upon request by the patient's caregiver or guardian, the mobile optometric

office provides a copy of the prescription made for the patient;

(6) Any person who is employed by the owner and operator of the mobile optometric office to drive or transport the vehicle possesses a valid driver's license;

(7) The owner and operator of a mobile optometric office maintains records in the manner prescribed by Section 3070.2 of the code and makes them available to the Board upon request for inspection during normal business hours; and

(8) A licensed optometrist who is certified to use therapeutic pharmaceutical agents pursuant to Section 3041.3 of the code performs all examinations at the mobile optometric office.

(c) Failure to comply with the requirements of this section renders any application for renewal of a certificate to operate incomplete and the certificate will not be renewed until the owner and operator of a mobile optometric office demonstrates compliance with all requirements.

(d) In the event an owner and operator of a mobile optometric office does not renew the certificate to operate as provided in this section, the certificate to operate expires and the owner and operator shall be considered unlicensed. An expired certificate to operate may be reinstated and renewed at any time within three years after its expiration if the owner and operator of the mobile optometric office meets the renewal requirements of this section and pays all accrued and unpaid renewal and delinquency fees in Section 1524.

(e) In order to remain registered with the Board, the owner and operator of a mobile optometric office shall respond to any inquiries by the Board, submit any documents requested by the Board, provide any information requested by the Board, and cooperate in any investigation conducted by the Board regarding compliance with the Board's requirements, including Section 3070.2 of the code. A response to any Board inquiry or request shall be provided within fourteen (14) days of the Board's written request.

Disciplinary actions shall be conducted in accordance with Section 3092 of the code. For purposes of this section, a "disciplinary action" includes revocation, suspension, probation or public reproval.

Credit

Note: Authority cited: Sections 3025, 3041, 3070.2 and 3110, Business and Professions Code. Reference: Sections 142, 144, 163.5, 480, 495, 2544, 3041, 3041.3, 3055, 3070, 3070.1, 3070.2 and 3110, Business and Professions Code.

HISTORY

1. New section filed 10-9-2024; operative 10/9/2024 pursuant to Government Code section 11343.4(b)(3) (Register 2024, No. 41).

Current through Register 2024 Notice Reg. No. 43, October 25, 2024

§1584.5. MOBILE OPTOMETRIC OFFICE PERMITS

(a) An owner and operator who has been issued a certificate to operate by the Board pursuant to Section 1583 ("certificate to operate") and wishes to obtain a permit for a mobile optometric office shall do the following before beginning operation of each mobile optometric office:

(1) Utilize BreEZe to submit a completed mobile optometric office permit application as provided in subdivision (b) in compliance with this section;

(2) Meet the requirements for providing optometric services at each office as provided in this section and Section 3070.2 of the code; and

(3) Receive written approval from the Board, including issuance of a permit

with a unique identifying number as provided in subdivision (c).

(b) The application for mobile optometric office permit shall be completed according to the requirements of this subdivision and shall be electronically submitted through BreEZe. For the application to be deemed complete, the following requirements shall be met:

(1) The owner and operator or responsible representative submitting their application for a mobile optometric office permit shall enter their username and password they created to access BreEZe, as referenced in Section 1584.5(b), and provide the information required by this section.

(2) The owner and operator shall provide the following information under penalty of perjury through BreEZe:

(A) Owner and operator's legal name and certificate to operate number;

(B) Submit a non-refundable registration fee as set forth in Section 1524 for each mobile optometric office;

(C) Identifying information of any licensed optometrist providing services at this mobile optometric office including:

1. Name and optometrist license number;

2. Address of record including city, state, and zip code;

3. If applicable, list the statement of licensure number issued by the Board as required by Section 1506 for each owner of an optometry practice or employees practicing optometry in more than one office;

4. Address of record including city, state, and zip code; and,

5. Direct telephone number.

(D) Mobile optometric office vehicle make, model, and year;

(E) License plate or registration number of the mobile optometric office vehicle;

(F) Information specific to the particular mobile optometric office for which a permit is sought, including;

1. Description of the services to be rendered in the mobile optometric office;

2. Names and license numbers for all optometrists;

3. Names and registration numbers for all opticians who will be providing patient care;

4. Names of any other persons who will be providing patient care as described in Section 2544 of the code;

5. Intended dates of operation;

6. Cities and counties served by the mobile optometric office; and

7. Whether the mobile optometric office has the following;

a. An access ramp or lift or other alternative method, as documented in a written plan, to accommodate patients with access issues;

b. An accessible handwashing facility on the premises. For purposes of this section, "accessible handwashing facilities" means a clean and sanitary sink with clean running water, disinfectant soap, and adequate drying devices such as a towel or electric hand dryer, which is physically separate from a lavatory or bathroom and is accessible to all relevant persons. For purposes of this section, "on the premises" includes accessible facilities that are located at the physical site where the mobile optometric office is providing services.

c. A means of sanitation for optometric equipment.

(G) In addition to the requirements of Section 3070.2 of the code, a mobile optometric office shall also meet the sanitary requirements of Section 1520.

(H) Electronic Signature: When a signature is required by the particular instructions of any filing to be made through BreEZe, including any attestation under penalty of perjury, an authorized, representative of the mobile optometric office shall affix their electronic signature to the filing by typing their name in the signature field and submitting the filing via BreEZe. Submission of a filing in this manner shall constitute evidence of legal signature by any individual whose name is typed in the signature field on the filing.

(c) A separate permit is required for each mobile optometric office operated by each owner and operator with a certificate to operate and no more than twelve permits shall be issued to any owner and operator until after the owner and operator's first renewal period of two years is complete.

(d) Upon approval by the Board, the Board will issue a unique identifying number for each permit. A registrant shall include this number in all correspondence, quarterly reports, or any other communication with the Board. In addition, the unique identifying number for each permit shall be included in all forms of advertisement, solicitation, or other presentments made to the public in connection with the rendition of optometric services at each mobile optometric office, including any advertisement, card, letterhead, telephone listing, Internet Web site, written solicitation or communications to a prospective patient or patients, or contract proposal. For purposes of advertisement, solicitations, and other presentments to the public, a registrant may include any and all permit numbers of the potential mobile optometric offices servicing the location.

(e) Each mobile optometric office permit shall be effective until the expiration date of the owner and operator's certificate to operate.

(f) To renew a mobile optometric office permit, an owner and operator shall pay the renewal fee for each mobile optometric office in Section 1524 and attest in writing to the Board to compliance with the requirements as set forth in Section 3070.2 of the code prior to the expiration of the permit. Renewal shall run concurrently with the owner and operator's certificate to operate and, upon expiration, may be reinstated in accordance with the provisions in Section 1584.

Credit

Note: Authority cited: Sections 137, 3025, 3041 and 3070.2, Business and Professions Code. Reference: Sections 27, 30, 31, 136, 137 and 3070.2, Business and Professions Code; Sections 1633.2, 1633.7 and 1633.9, Civil Code; and Section 16.5, Government Code.

HISTORY

1. New section filed 10-9-2024; operative 10/9/2024 pursuant to Government Code section 11343.4(b)(3) (Register 2024, No. 41).

Current through Register 2024 Notice Reg. No. 43, October 25, 2024.

§1585. FINGERPRINTS AND BACKGROUND CHECKS FOR APPLICANTS TO REGISTER AS AN OWNER AND OPERATOR OF MOBILE OPTOMETRIC OFFICE

(a) All applicants for registration with the Board as an owner and operator of a mobile optometric office must submit fingerprints through the California Department of Justice's ("Department of Justice") electronic fingerprint submission Live Scan Service ("Live Scan") as described in this section.

(b) Applicants must complete the Department of Justice Form "Request for Live Scan Service" form, and submit fingerprinting through Live Scan for its responsible officers or officials. For the purposes of this section, "responsible officers or officials" means the individuals listed in response to subdivision (b)(2)(F) in Section 1583 as the principal officers or officials responsible for the operations of the applicant's organization.

(c) The applicant's responsible officers or officials residing in California must take the form to a Live Scan location to have their fingerprints taken by the operator. The applicant, through its officers, will be required to pay all fingerprint processing fees payable to the Live Scan operator, including the Live Scan operator's "rolling fee," if any, and fees charged by the California Department of Justice, and the Federal Bureau of Investigation. For current information about fingerprint background checks, and Live Scan locations, individuals may visit the Attorney General's website at: https://oag.ca.gov/fingerprints.

(d) Individuals residing outside of California that cannot be fingerprinted electronically through Live Scan in California must have their fingerprints taken at a law enforcement agency in their state of residence, using fingerprint cards. These individuals should complete two fingerprint cards. The applicant should retain the second card, to be used if the first card is determined to be unreadable and rejected by the Department of Justice. Applicants must mail one fingerprint card, together with the California Department of Justice and Federal Bureau of Investigation fees (either personal check drawn on a U.S. bank, money order or certified check), payable to the "California Department of Justice," to:

CALIFORNIA STATE BOARD OF OPTOMETRY
2450 DEL PASO ROAD, SUITE 105
SACRAMENTO, CA 95834

The applicant's responsible officers or officials will be notified if the first card is rejected. If rejected, the applicant's responsible officers or officials must follow the instructions on the rejection letter and submit the second fingerprint card.

(e) No certificate to operate will be issued until the Board receives a response from the Department of Justice for all persons required to submit fingerprint information under Section 144 of the code and this Section, and the Board determines that the applicant with whom the persons fingerprinted are associated merits approval pursuant to the procedures and criteria referenced in Section 1583(e).

Credit

Note: Authority cited: Sections 3025 and 3070.2, Business and Professions Code. Reference: Sections 144 and 3070.2, Business and Professions Code; and Section 11105, Penal Code.

HISTORY

1. New section filed 10-9-2024; operative 10/9/2024 pursuant to Government Code section 11343.4(b)(3) (Register 2024, No. 41).

Current through Register 2024 Notice Reg. No. 43, October 25, 2024.

§1586. OWNER/ OPERATOR QUARTERLY REPORTING REQUIREMENTS

(a) An owner and operator of each mobile optometric office shall utilize BreEZe to submit electronically a completed quarterly report with the Board containing all of the information and in accordance with the requirements set forth by this section. After the owner and operator has been registered with the Board, the information shall be submitted to the Board no later than the third business day of the following months and covering each quarter of operations as a registrant: March, June, September and December. Hardcopy documents will not be accepted.

(b) The information required by this section shall constitute the requirements for submission of a quarterly report to the Board in accordance with Section 3070.2 of the code. An owner and operator's quarterly report shall be electronically submitted through BreEZe and shall include all of the following:

(1) The owner and operator or authorized representative shall enter their username and password to access BreEZe and provide the information required by this section.

(2) The owner and operator shall provide the following information under penalty of perjury through BreEZe:

(A) Name of the owner and operator of the mobile optometric office;

(B) Owner and operator certificate to operate number;

(C) Name, mailing address, telephone number, and email address, if available, of the authorized representative;

(D) Total number of complaints received in the quarter being reported; and

(E) A list of all visits made by each mobile optometric office including:

1. Mobile optometric office permit number;

2. Dates of operation of the mobile optometric office;

3. Physical street address where services were provided;

4. A description of the care provided;

5. Name and registration number of optician(s) who provided care;

6. Name and license numbers of optometrist(s) who provided care;

7. A summary of any complaints received by each mobile optometric office including;

a. Mobile optometric office permit number;

b. Complaint patient name, telephone number, and email address (if available);

c. Service(s) provided at the mobile optometric office and date they were provided;

d. Name and address for the organization being serviced at the mobile optometric office;

e. Contact individual for the organization being serviced by the mobile optometric office;

f. Disposition of the complaints;

g. Referral information of follow-up care provided to the patient (i.e., name of the follow-up provider), if applicable;

h. Updated and current list of licensed optometrists, including their license numbers and the organization for which they provide service, who are available for follow-up care as a result of a complaint on a volunteer basis or who accept Medi-Cal payments.

(F) Electronic Signature: When a signature is required by the particular instructions of any filing to be made through BreEZe, including any attestation under penalty of perjury, an authorized representative of the mobile optometric office shall affix their electronic signature to the filing by typing their name in the signature field and submitting the filing via BreEZe. Submission of a filing in this manner shall constitute evidence of legal signature by any individual whose name is typed in the signature field on the filing.

Credit

Note: Authority cited: Sections 3025, 3041 and 3070.2, Business and Professions Code. Reference: Section 3070.2, Business and Professions Code;

Sections 1633.2, 1633.7 and 1633.9, Civil Code; and Section 16.5, Government Code.

HISTORY

1. New section filed 10-9-2024; operative 10/9/2024 pursuant to Government Code section 11343.4(b)(3) (Register 2024, No. 41).

Current through Register 2024 Notice Reg. No. 43, October 25, 2024.

§1587. PATIENT NOTIFICATION AND RECORDS

(a) Each owner and operator of a mobile optometric office shall meet the requirements in Sections 1566 and 1566.1 requiring the posting of a consumer notice in a conspicuous place in the mobile optometric office.

(b) In addition to the posted notice required by subdivision (a), each owner and operator of a mobile optometric office shall provide each patient, or the patient's caregiver or guardian, a consumer notice in at least 12-point font containing all of the following information:

(1) The name, license number, telephone number, primary business address, and business email address (if any), of the optometrist directing medical operations at the mobile optometric office;

(2) The owner and operator of the mobile optometric office's name, primary business address, telephone number, website or email address (if any), and Board-issued certificate to operate number;

(3) Information on follow-up care available for the patient, including a list of available Medi-Cal or volunteer optometrists; and,

(4) The following information:

NOTICE OF REGULATION AND WHO TO CONTACT REGARDING COMPLAINTS

The operation of mobile optometric offices and optometrists providing services at a mobile optometric office are regulated by the California State Board of Optometry ("Board"). The Board receives and investigates all consumer complaints involving the practice of optometry and opticianry. Complaints or grievances involving the operation of this mobile optometric office or a California-licensed optometrist or optician should be directed in writing to:

BOARD OF OPTOMETRY
CALIFORNIA DEPARTMENT OF CONSUMER AFFAIRS
2450 DEL PASO ROAD, SUITE 105
SACRAMENTO, CA 95834
PHONE: 1-866-585-2666 OR 916-575-7170
EMAIL: OPTOMETRY@DCA.CA.GOV
WEBSITE: OPTOMETRY.CA.GOV

PRESCRIPTIONS

Optometrists are required to provide patients upon request with a copy of their ophthalmic lens prescriptions as follows:

- Spectacle prescriptions: Release upon completion of exam.
- Contact lens prescriptions: Release upon completion of exam or upon completion of the fitting process.

COPIES OF MEDICAL RECORDS

Patients may obtain a copy of their medical records by contacting the owner and operator of this mobile optometric office as listed on this notice.

(c) Each owner and operator of a mobile optometric office shall retain the consumer notice required by subdivision (b) in the patient's medical record, and the optometrist shall record all the following in the medical record:

(1) that the patient, caregiver, or guardian has received the consumer notice; and

(2) the date the optometrist provided the consumer notice to the patient, caregiver, or guardian.

(d) An owner and operator of a mobile optometric office shall maintain at the primary business office in California a copy of all records required by Section 3070.2 of the code and this Article. The records may be maintained in either paper or electronic form.

Credit

Note: Authority cited: Sections 138, 3025, 3041 and 3070.2, Business and Professions Code. Reference: Sections 138, 3041, 3041.3, 3070, 3070.1 and 3070.2, Business and Professions Code.

HISTORY

1. New section filed 10-9-2024; operative 10/9/2024 pursuant to Government Code section 11343.4(b)(3) (Register 2024, No. 41).

Current through Register 2024 Notice Reg. No. 43, October 25, 2024.

CORPORATIONS CODE

TITLE 1: CORPORATIONS

DIVISION 3 CORPORATIONS FOR SPECIFIC PURPOSES

PART 4: PROFESSIONAL CORPORATIONS

13400. CITATION OF PART

This part shall be known and may be cited as the "Moscone-Knox Professional Corporation Act."

(Added by Stats. 1968, Ch. 1375.)

13401. DEFINITIONS

As used in this part:

(a) "Professional services" means any type of professional services that may be lawfully rendered only pursuant to a license, certification, or registration authorized by the Business and Professions Code, the Chiropractic Act, or the Osteopathic Act.

(b) "Professional corporation" means a corporation organized under the General Corporation Law or pursuant to subdivision (b) of Section 13406 that is engaged in rendering professional services in a single profession, except as otherwise authorized in Section 13401.5, pursuant to a certificate of registration issued by the governmental agency regulating the profession as herein provided and that in its practice or business designates itself as a professional or other corporation as may be required by statute. However, any professional corporation or foreign professional corporation rendering professional services by persons duly licensed by the Medical Board of California or any examining committee under the jurisdiction of the board, the Podiatric Medical Board of California, the Osteopathic Medical Board of California, the Dental Board of California, the Dental Hygiene Board of California, the California State Board of Pharmacy, the Veterinary Medical Board, the California Architects Board, the Court Reporters Board of California, the Board of Behavioral Sciences, the Speech-Language Pathology and Audiology and Hearing Aid Dispensers Board, the Board of Registered Nursing, the State Board of Optometry, or the California Board of Occupational Therapy shall not be required to obtain a certificate of registration in order to render those professional services.

(c) "Foreign professional corporation" means a corporation organized under the laws of a state of the United States other than this state that is engaged in a profession of a type for which there is authorization in the Business and Professions Code for the performance of professional services by a foreign professional corporation.

(d) "Licensed person" means any natural person who is duly licensed under the provisions of the Business and Professions Code, the Chiropractic Act, or the Osteopathic Act to render the same professional services as are or will be rendered by the professional corporation or foreign professional corporation of which the person is, or intends to become, an officer, director, shareholder, or employee.

(e) "Disqualified person" means a licensed person who for any reason becomes legally disqualified (temporarily or permanently) to render the professional services that the particular professional corporation or foreign professional corporation of which they are an officer, director, shareholder, or employee is or was rendering.

(Amended by Stats. 2023, Ch. 131, Sec. 24. (AB 1754) Effective January 1, 2024.)

13401.3. PROFESSIONAL SERVICES

As used in this part, "professional services" also means any type of professional services that may be lawfully rendered only pursuant to a license, certification, or registration authorized by the Yacht and Ship Brokers Act (Article 2 (commencing with Section 700) of Chapter 5 of Division 3 of the Harbors and Navigation Code).

(Amended by Stats. 2001, Ch. 597, Sec. 1. Effective January 1, 2002.)

13401.5. LICENSEES AS SHAREHOLDERS, OFFICERS, DIRECTORS, OR EMPLOYEES

Notwithstanding subdivision (d) of Section 13401 and any other provision of law, the following licensed persons may be shareholders, officers, directors, or professional employees of the professional corporations designated in this section so long as the sum of all shares owned by those licensed persons does not exceed 49 percent of the total number of shares of the professional corporation so designated herein, and so long as the number of those licensed persons owning shares in the professional corporation so designated herein does not exceed the number of persons licensed by the governmental agency regulating the designated professional corporation. This section does not limit employment by a professional corporation designated in this section to only those licensed professionals listed under each subdivision. Any person duly licensed under Division 2 (commencing with Section 500) of the Business and Professions Code, the Chiropractic Act, or the Osteopathic Act may be employed to render professional services by a professional corporation designated in this section.

(a) Medical corporation.

(1) Licensed doctors of podiatric medicine.

(2) Licensed psychologists.

(3) Registered nurses.

(4) Licensed optometrists.

(5) Licensed marriage and family therapists.

(6) Licensed clinical social workers.

(7) Licensed physician assistants.

(8) Licensed chiropractors.

(9) Licensed acupuncturists.

(10) Naturopathic doctors.

(11) Licensed professional clinical counselors.

(12) Licensed physical therapists.

(13) Licensed pharmacists.

(14) Licensed midwives.

(15) Licensed occupational therapists.

(b) Podiatric medical corporation.

(1) Licensed physicians and surgeons.

(2) Licensed psychologists.

(3) Registered nurses.

(4) Licensed optometrists.

(5) Licensed chiropractors.

(6) Licensed acupuncturists.

(7) Naturopathic doctors.

(8) Licensed physical therapists.

(c) Psychological corporation.

(1) Licensed physicians and surgeons.

(2) Licensed doctors of podiatric medicine.

(3) Registered nurses.

(4) Licensed optometrists.

(5) Licensed marriage and family therapists.

(6) Licensed clinical social workers.

(7) Licensed chiropractors.

(8) Licensed acupuncturists.

(9) Naturopathic doctors.

(10) Licensed professional clinical counselors.

(11) Licensed midwives.

(d) Speech-language pathology corporation.

(1) Licensed audiologists.

(e) Audiology corporation.

(1) Licensed speech-language pathologists.

(f) Nursing corporation.

(1) Licensed physicians and surgeons.

(2) Licensed doctors of podiatric medicine.

(3) Licensed psychologists.

(4) Licensed optometrists.

(5) Licensed marriage and family therapists.

(6) Licensed clinical social workers.

(7) Licensed physician assistants.

(8) Licensed chiropractors.

(9) Licensed acupuncturists.

(10) Naturopathic doctors.

(11) Licensed professional clinical counselors.

(12) Licensed midwives.

(g) Marriage and family therapist corporation.

(1) Licensed physicians and surgeons.

(2) Licensed psychologists.

(3) Licensed clinical social workers.

(4) Registered nurses.

(5) Licensed chiropractors.

(6) Licensed acupuncturists.

(7) Naturopathic doctors.

(8) Licensed professional clinical counselors.

(9) Licensed midwives.

(h) Licensed clinical social worker corporation.

(1) Licensed physicians and surgeons.

(2) Licensed psychologists.

(3) Licensed marriage and family therapists.

(4) Registered nurses.

(5) Licensed chiropractors.

(6) Licensed acupuncturists.

(7) Naturopathic doctors.

(8) Licensed professional clinical counselors.

(i) Physician assistants corporation.

(1) Licensed physicians and surgeons.

(2) Registered nurses.

(3) Licensed acupuncturists.

(4) Naturopathic doctors.

(5) Licensed midwives.

(j) Optometric corporation.

(1) Licensed physicians and surgeons.

(2) Licensed doctors of podiatric medicine.

(3) Licensed psychologists.

(4) Registered nurses.

(5) Licensed chiropractors.

(6) Licensed acupuncturists.

(7) Naturopathic doctors.

(k) Chiropractic corporation.

(1) Licensed physicians and surgeons.

(2) Licensed doctors of podiatric medicine.

(3) Licensed psychologists.

(4) Registered nurses.

(5) Licensed optometrists.

(6) Licensed marriage and family therapists.

(7) Licensed clinical social workers.

(8) Licensed acupuncturists.

(9) Naturopathic doctors.

(10) Licensed professional clinical counselors.

(11) Licensed midwives.

(l) Acupuncture corporation.

(1) Licensed physicians and surgeons.

(2) Licensed doctors of podiatric medicine.

(3) Licensed psychologists.

(4) Registered nurses.

(5) Licensed optometrists.

(6) Licensed marriage and family therapists.

(7) Licensed clinical social workers.

(8) Licensed physician assistants.

(9) Licensed chiropractors.

(10) Naturopathic doctors.

(11) Licensed professional clinical counselors.

(12) Licensed midwives.

(m) Naturopathic doctor corporation.

(1) Licensed physicians and surgeons.

(2) Licensed psychologists.

(3) Registered nurses.

(4) Licensed physician assistants.

(5) Licensed chiropractors.

(6) Licensed acupuncturists.

(7) Licensed physical therapists.

(8) Licensed doctors of podiatric medicine.

(9) Licensed marriage and family therapists.

(10) Licensed clinical social workers.

(11) Licensed optometrists.

(12) Licensed professional clinical counselors.

(13) Licensed midwives.

(n) Dental corporation.

(1) Licensed physicians and surgeons.

(2) Dental assistants.

(3) Registered dental assistants.

(4) Registered dental assistants in extended functions.

(5) Registered dental hygienists.

(6) Registered dental hygienists in extended functions.

(7) Registered dental hygienists in alternative practice.

(o) Professional clinical counselor corporation.

(1) Licensed physicians and surgeons.

(2) Licensed psychologists.

(3) Licensed clinical social workers.

(4) Licensed marriage and family therapists.

(5) Registered nurses.

(6) Licensed chiropractors.

(7) Licensed acupuncturists.

(8) Naturopathic doctors.

(9) Licensed midwives.

(p) Physical therapy corporation.

(1) Licensed physicians and surgeons.

(2) Licensed doctors of podiatric medicine.

(3) Licensed acupuncturists.

(4) Naturopathic doctors.

(5) Licensed occupational therapists.

(6) Licensed speech-language therapists.

(7) Licensed audiologists.

(8) Registered nurses.

(9) Licensed psychologists.

(10) Licensed physician assistants.

(11) Licensed midwives.

(q) Registered dental hygienist in alternative practice corporation.

(1) Registered dental assistants.

(2) Licensed dentists.

(3) Registered dental hygienists.

(4) Registered dental hygienists in extended functions.

(r) Licensed midwifery corporation.

(1) Licensed physicians and surgeons.

(2) Licensed psychologists.

(3) Registered nurses.

(4) Licensed marriage and family therapists.

(5) Licensed clinical social workers.

(6) Licensed physician assistants.

(7) Licensed chiropractors.

(8) Licensed acupuncturists.

(9) Licensed naturopathic doctors.

(10) Licensed professional clinical counselors.

(11) Licensed physical therapists.

(s) Occupational therapy corporation.

(1) Licensed physicians and surgeons.

(2) Licensed doctors of podiatric medicine.

(3) Licensed acupuncturists.

(4) Naturopathic doctors.

(5) Licensed physical therapists.

(6) Licensed speech-language therapists.

(7) Licensed audiologists.

(8) Registered nurses.

(9) Licensed psychologists.

(10) Licensed physician assistants.

(11) Licensed midwives.

(12) Licensed clinical social workers.

(13) Licensed marriage and family therapists.

(14) Licensed occupational therapy assistants.

(Amended by Stats. 2022, Ch. 290, Sec. 7. (AB 2671) Effective January 1, 2023.)

13402. CORPORATION RENDERING SERVICES OTHER THAN PURSUANT TO THIS PART; CONDUCT OF BUSINESS BY CORPORATION NOT PROFESSIONAL CORPORATION

(a) This part shall not apply to any corporation now in existence or hereafter organized which may lawfully render professional services other than pursuant to this part, nor shall anything herein contained alter or affect any right or privilege, whether under any existing or future provision of the Business and Professions Code or otherwise, in terms permitting or not prohibiting performance of professional services through the use of any form of corporation permitted by the General Corporation Law.

(b) The conduct of a business in this state by a corporation pursuant to a license or registration issued under any state law, except laws relating to taxation, shall not be considered to be the conduct of a business as a professional corporation if the business is conducted by, and the license or registration is issued to, a corporation which is not a professional corporation within the meaning of this part, whether or not a professional corporation could conduct the same business, or portions of the same business, as a professional corporation.

(Amended by Stats. 1988, Ch. 919, Sec. 13.)

13043. GENERAL CORPORATION LAW; APPLICABILITY

The provisions of the General Corporation Law shall apply to professional corporations, except where such provisions are in conflict with or inconsistent with the provisions of this part. A professional corporation which has only one shareholder need have only one director who shall be such shareholder and who shall also serve as the president and treasurer of the corporation. The other officers of the corporation in such situation need not be licensed persons. A professional corporation which has only two shareholders need have only two directors who shall be such shareholders. The two shareholders between them shall fill the offices of president, vice president, secretary and treasurer.

A professional medical corporation may establish in its articles or bylaws the manner in which its directors are selected and removed, their powers, duties, and compensation. Each term of office may not exceed three years. Notwithstanding the foregoing, the articles or bylaws of a professional medical corporation with more than 200 shareholders may provide that directors who are officers of the corporation or who are responsible for the management of all medical services at one or more medical centers may have terms of office, as directors, of up to six years; however, no more than 50 percent of the members of the board, plus one additional member of the board, may have six-year terms of office.

(Amended by Stats. 1980, Ch. 36.)

13404. FORMATION; CERTIFICATE OF REGISTRATION

A corporation may be formed under the General Corporation Law or pursuant to subdivision (b) of Section 13406 for the purposes of qualifying as a professional corporation in the manner provided in this part and rendering professional services. The articles of incorporation of a professional corporation shall contain a specific statement that the corporation is a professional corporation within the meaning of this part. Except as provided in subdivision (b) of Section 13401, no professional corporation shall render professional services in this state without a currently effective certificate of registration issued by the governmental agency regulating the profession in which such corporation is or proposes to be engaged, pursuant to the applicable provisions of the Business and Professions Code or the Chiropractic Act expressly authorizing such professional services to be rendered by a professional corporation.

(Amended by Stats. 1993, Ch. 955, Sec. 6. Effective January 1, 1994.)

13406. PROFESSIONAL CORPORATIONS; STOCK; FINANCIAL STATEMENTS; VOTING; NONPROFIT LAW CORPORATIONS

(a) Subject to the provisions of subdivision (b), shares of capital stock in a professional corporation may be issued only to a licensed person or to a person who is licensed to render the same professional services in the jurisdiction or jurisdictions in which the person practices, and any shares issued in violation of this restriction shall be void. Unless there is a public offering of securities by a professional corporation or by a foreign professional corporation in this state, its financial statements shall be treated by the Commissioner of Financial Protection and Innovation as confidential, except to the extent that such statements shall be subject to subpoena in connection with any judicial or administrative proceeding, and may be admissible in evidence therein. A shareholder of a professional corporation or of a foreign professional corporation qualified to render professional services in this state shall not enter into a voting trust, proxy, or any other arrangement vesting another person (other than another person who is a shareholder of the same corporation) with the authority to exercise the voting power of any or all of the shareholder's shares, and any purported voting trust, proxy, or other arrangement shall be void.

(b) A professional law corporation may be incorporated as a nonprofit public benefit corporation under the Nonprofit Public Benefit Corporation Law under either of the following circumstances:

(1) The corporation is a qualified legal services project or a qualified support center within the meaning of subdivisions (a) and (b) of Section 6213 of the Business and Professions Code.

(2) The professional law corporation otherwise meets all of the requirements and complies with all of the provisions of the Nonprofit Public Benefit Corporation Law, as well as all of the following requirements:

(A) All of the members of the corporation, if it is a membership organization as described in the Nonprofit

Corporation Law, are persons licensed to practice law in California.

(B) All of the members of the professional law corporation's board of directors are persons licensed to practice law in California.

(C) Seventy percent of the clients to whom the corporation provides legal services are lower income persons as defined in Section 50079.5 of the Health and Safety Code, and to other persons who would not otherwise have access to legal services.

(D) The corporation shall not enter into contingency fee contracts with clients.

(c) A professional law corporation incorporated as a nonprofit public benefit corporation that is a recipient in good standing as defined in subdivision (c) of Section 6213 of the Business and Professions Code shall be deemed to have satisfied all of the filing requirements of a professional law corporation under Sections 6161.1, 6162, and 6163 of the Business and Professions Code.

(Amended by Stats. 2022, Ch. 452, Sec. 62. (SB 1498) Effective January 1, 2023.)

13407. TRANSFER OF SHARES; RESTRICTION; PURCHASE BY CORPORATION; SUSPENSION OR REVOCATION OF CERTIFICATE

Shares in a professional corporation or a foreign professional corporation qualified to render professional services in this state may be transferred only to a licensed person, to a shareholder of the same corporation, to a person licensed to practice the same profession in the jurisdiction or jurisdictions in which the person practices, or to a professional corporation, and any transfer in violation of this restriction shall be void, except as provided herein.

A professional corporation may purchase its own shares without regard to any restrictions provided by law upon the repurchase of shares, if at least one share remains issued and outstanding.

If a professional corporation or a foreign professional corporation qualified to render professional services in this state shall fail to acquire all of the shares of a shareholder who is disqualified from rendering professional services in this state or of a deceased shareholder who was, on his or her date of death, licensed to render professional services in this state, or if such a disqualified shareholder or the representative of such a deceased shareholder shall fail to transfer said shares to the corporation, to another shareholder of the corporation, to a person licensed to practice the same profession in the jurisdiction or jurisdictions in which the person practices, or to a licensed person, within 90 days following the date of disqualification, or within six months following the date of death of the shareholder, as the case may be, then the certificate of registration of the corporation may be suspended or revoked by the governmental agency regulating the profession in which the corporation is engaged. In the event of such a suspension or revocation, the corporation shall cease to render professional services in this state.

Notwithstanding any provision in this part, upon the death or incapacity of a dentist, any individual named in subdivision (a) of Section 1625.3 of the Business and Professions Code may employ licensed dentists and dental assistants and charge for their professional services for a period not to exceed 12 months from the date of death or incapacity of the dentist. The employment of licensed dentists and dental assistants shall not be deemed the practice of dentistry within the meaning of Section 1625 of the Business and Professions Code, provided that all of the requirements of Section 1625.4 of the Business and Professions Code are met. If an individual listed in Section 1625.3 of the Business and Professions Code is employing licensed persons and dental assistants, then the shares of a deceased or incapacitated dentist shall be transferred as provided in this section no later than 12 months from the date of death or incapacity of the dentist.

(Amended by Stats. 2007, Ch. 433, Sec. 4. Effective January 1, 2008.)

13408. SPECIFICATIONS OF GROUNDS FOR SUSPENSION OR REVOCATION OF CERTIFICATE

The following shall be grounds for the suspension or revocation of the certificate of registration of a professional corporation or a foreign professional corporation qualified to render professional services in this state: (a) if all shareholders who are licensed persons of such corporation shall at any one time become disqualified persons, or (b) if the sole shareholder shall become a disqualified person, or (c) if such corporation shall knowingly employ or retain in its employment a disqualified person, or (d) if such corporation shall violate any applicable rule or regulation adopted by the governmental agency regulating the profession in which such corporation is engaged, or (e) if such corporation shall violate any statute applicable to a professional corporation or to a foreign professional corporation, or (f) any ground for such suspension or revocation specified in the Business and Professions Code relating to the profession in which such corporation is engaged. In the event of such suspension or revocation of its certificate of registration such corporation shall cease forthwith to render professional services in this state.

(Amended by Stats. 1993, Ch. 910, Sec. 7. Effective January 1, 1994.)

13408.5. CORPORATIONS FORMED SO AS TO CAUSE VIOLATION OF LAW

A professional corporation shall not be formed so as to cause any violation of law, or any applicable rules and regulations, relating to fee splitting, kickbacks, or other similar practices by physicians and surgeons or psychologists, including, but not limited to, Section 650 or subdivision (e) of Section 2960 of the Business and Professions Code. A violation of any such provisions shall be grounds for the suspension or revocation of the certificate of registration of the professional corporation. The Commissioner of Financial Protection and Innovation or the Director of the Department of Managed Health Care may refer any suspected violation of those provisions to the governmental agency regulating the profession in which the corporation is, or proposes to be engaged.

(Amended by Stats. 2022, Ch. 452, Sec. 63. (SB 1498) Effective January 1, 2023.)

13409. NAME OF CORPORATION; PROVISION GOVERNING

(a) Subject to Section 201, a professional corporation may adopt any name permitted by a law expressly applicable to the profession in which the corporation is engaged or by a rule or regulation of the governmental agency regulating that profession. The Secretary of State may require proof by affidavit or otherwise establishing that the name of the professional corporation complies with the requirements of this section and of the law governing the profession in which that professional corporation is engaged. The statements of fact in those affidavits may be accepted by the Secretary of State as sufficient proof of the facts.

(b) Subject to Section 201, a foreign professional corporation qualified to render professional services in this state may transact intrastate business in this state by any name permitted by a law expressly applicable to the profession in which the corporation is engaged, or by a rule or regulation of the governmental agency regulating the rendering of professional services in this state by the corporation. The Secretary of State may require proof by affidavit or otherwise establishing that the name of the foreign professional corporation qualified to render professional services in this state complies with the requirements of this section and of the law governing the profession in which the foreign professional corporation qualified to render professional services in this state proposes to engage in this state. The statements of fact in those affidavits may be accepted by the Secretary of State as sufficient proof of the facts.

(Amended by Stats. 2020, Ch. 361, Sec. 12. (SB 522) Effective January 1, 2021.)

13410. DISCIPLINARY RULES AND REGULATIONS

(a) A professional corporation or a foreign professional corporation qualified to render professional services in this state shall be subject to the applicable rules and regulations adopted by, and all the disciplinary provisions of the Business and Professions Code expressly governing the practice of the profession in this state, and to the powers of, the governmental agency regulating the profession in which such corporation is engaged. Nothing in this part shall affect or impair the disciplinary powers of any such governmental agency over licensed persons or any law, rule or regulation pertaining to the standards for professional conduct of licensed persons or to the professional relationship between any licensed person furnishing professional services and the person receiving such services.

(b) With respect to any foreign professional corporation qualified to render professional services in this state, each such governmental agency shall adopt rules, regulations, and orders as appropriate to restrict or prohibit any disqualified person from doing any of the following:

(1) Being a shareholder, director, officer, or employee of the corporation.

(2) Rendering services in any profession in which he or she is a disqualified person.

(3) Participating in the management of the corporation.

(4) Sharing in the income of the corporation.

(Amended by Stats. 1993, Ch. 910, Sec. 10. Effective January 1, 1994.)

EDUCATION CODE

TITLE 2: ELEMENTARY & SECONDARY EDUCATION

DIVISION 4: INSTRUCTION AND SERVICES

PART 27: PUPILS

CHAPTER 9: PUPIL AND PERSONNEL HEALTH

ARTICLE 4: PHYSICAL EXAMINATION

49452. TESTING; SIGHT AND HEARING

(a) The governing board of a school district shall, subject to Section 49451, provide for the testing of the sight and hearing of each pupil enrolled in the schools of the school district.

(b) The test shall be adequate in nature and shall be given only by any of the following:

(1) By duly qualified supervisors of health employed by the school district.

(2) By certificated employees, registered nurses, or licensed vocational nurses, under the supervision of a credentialed school nurse, of the school district, charter school, or the county superintendent of schools who possess the qualifications prescribed by the Commission on Teacher Credentialing.

(3) By contract with an agency duly authorized to perform those services by the county superintendent of schools of the county in which the school district is located, under guidelines established by the state board.

(4) By accredited schools or colleges of optometry, osteopathic medicine, or medicine.

(c) The records of the tests shall serve as evidence of the need of the pupils for the educational facilities provided physically handicapped individuals. The equipment necessary to conduct the tests may be purchased or rented by governing boards of school districts. The state, any agency, or political subdivision thereof may sell or rent such equipment owned by it to the governing board of a school district upon terms as may be mutually agreeable.

(d) As used in this section, the following definitions apply:

(1) "Credentialed school nurse" means only qualified persons who possess an appropriate credential issued pursuant to Section 44267.5.

(2) "Licensed vocational nurse" means a person licensed pursuant to the provisions of Chapter 6.5 (commencing with Section 2840) of Division 2 of the Business and Professions Code.

(Amended by Stats. 2023, Ch. 853, Sec. 2. (AB 1722) Effective January 1, 2024.)

49455. VISION APPRAISAL

(a) (1) During the kindergarten year or upon first enrollment or entry in a California school district of a pupil at an elementary school, and in grades 2, 5, and 8, the pupil's vision shall be appraised by the school nurse or other authorized person under Section 49452.

(2) A pupil whose first enrollment or entry occurs in grade 4 or 7 shall not be required to be appraised in the year immediately following the pupil's first enrollment or entry.

(b) The vision appraisal shall include tests for near vision, far vision, and color vision; however, color vision shall be appraised once and only on male pupils, and the results of the appraisal shall be entered in the health record of the pupil. Color vision appraisal need not begin until the male pupil has reached the first grade.

(c) The appraisal may be waived, if the pupil's parents so desire, by their presenting of a certificate from a physician and surgeon, a physician assistant practicing in compliance with Chapter 7.7 (commencing with Section 3500) of Division 2 of the Business and Professions Code, or an optometrist setting out the results of a determination of the pupil's vision, including visual acuity and color vision.

(d) A pupil's vision may be appraised by using an eye chart or any other scientifically validated photoscreening test. Photoscreening tests shall be performed, under an agreement with, or the supervision of, an optometrist or ophthalmologist, by the school nurse or a trained individual who meets requirements established by the department.

(e) Continual and regular observation of the pupil's eyes, appearance, behavior, visual performance, and perception that may indicate vision difficulties shall be done by the school nurse and the classroom teacher.

(f) This section shall not apply to a pupil whose parents or guardian file with the principal of the school in which the pupil is enrolling, a statement in writing that they adhere to the faith or teachings of any well-recognized religious sect, denomination, or organization and in accordance with its creed, tenets, or principles depend for healing upon prayer in the practice of their religion.

(g) The department shall adopt guidelines to implement this section, including training requirements and a method of testing for near vision.

(Amended by Stats. 2023, Ch. 853, Sec. 3. (AB 1722) Effective January 1, 2024.)

4955.5. NONPROFIT EYE EXAMINATION PROVIDERS

(a) A local educational agency maintaining kindergarten or any of grades 1 to 12, inclusive, may enter into a memorandum of understanding with a nonprofit eye examination provider to provide eye examinations to pupils at any schoolsite within the local educational agency. Eye examinations provided under this section shall be supplemental to, and shall not replace, the vision screenings provided pursuant to Section 49455, and shall be noninvasive and provided exclusively for the purpose of providing eyeglasses. Examination providers providing eye examinations pursuant to this section shall provide reports to parents and guardians consistent with Section 49456.

(b) (1) Before an eye examination is provided at a schoolsite pursuant to subdivision (a), the local educational agency shall have a memorandum of understanding in place with a nonprofit eye examination provider, including, but not limited to, a nonprofit mobile eye examination provider, and the school shall notify parents and guardians of the upcoming provision of eye examinations at the schoolsite. Notification shall include a form on which a parent or guardian may indicate that they do not consent to an eye examination being provided, pursuant to subdivision (a), to their child. The parent or guardian may opt out of their child receiving an eye examination, pursuant to subdivision (a), by submitting the completed form to the school before an eye examination is provided at the schoolsite. Except as provided in clause (ii) of subparagraph (D) of paragraph (3) of subdivision (d), a parent or guardian who submits a written statement in accordance with Section 49451 is deemed to have opted out of their child receiving an eye examination pursuant to subdivision (a).

(2) No later than March 1, 2023, the department shall develop and post on appropriate department internet websites a model opt-out form for purposes of paragraph (1).

(c) (1) Notwithstanding any other law and subject to paragraph (3), participating licensed health care professionals, including independent contractors of those professionals, shall have immunity from civil and criminal liability, and shall not be subject to disciplinary action by a licensing board, for providing services that are authorized by this section without parent or guardian consent pursuant to this section or Section 49091.12.

(2) Notwithstanding any other law and subject to paragraph (3), participating local educational agencies shall have immunity from civil and criminal liability for providing services that are authorized by this section without parent or guardian consent pursuant to this section or Section 49091.12.

(3) This subdivision does not affect any of the following:

(A) A person's liability for damages caused by an act or omission that constitutes gross negligence or willful or wanton misconduct.

(B) A person's culpability for an act that constitutes a crime and is not specifically authorized by this section.

(C) The ability of a licensing board to take disciplinary action against a licensed health care professional for an act not specifically authorized by this section.

(D) (i) The ability of a parent or guardian, having control or charge of a pupil enrolled in the school, to file an annual written statement pursuant to Section 49451, stating that they do not consent to a physical examination of their child, thereby exempting the pupil from any physical examination, including, but not limited to, the eye examination authorized in this section.

(ii) Notwithstanding the filing of a written statement exempting a child from any physical examination in accordance with Section 49451, a parent or guardian having control or charge of any child enrolled in the school may consent to an eye examination authorized in this section by means of executing a written consent to the examination, a copy of which shall be provided to the parent or guardian and the school.

(d) Eye examination providers providing eye examinations to pupils at a school pursuant to this section are subject to, and shall comply with, Section 51520.

(e) Any nonprofit eye examination provider, participating licensed health care professional, including independent contractors of these professionals, or other entity providing services under this section shall comply with the requirements of Section 45125.1 before interacting with any pupils.

(f) For purposes of this section, the following definitions apply:

(1) "Local educational agency" means a school district, county office of education, or charter school.

(2) "Nonprofit mobile eye examination provider" means a nonprofit owner and operator of a "mobile optometric office," as defined in subdivision (a) of

Section 3070.2 of the Business and Professions Code.

(Added by Stats. 2022, Ch. 911, Sec. 1. (AB 2329) Effective January 1, 2023.)

PART 28: GENERAL INSTRUCTIONAL PROGRAMS

CHAPTER 4: PROHIBITED INSTRUCTIONS

ARTICLE 3: SOLICITATIONS

51520. PROHIBITED SOLICITATIONS ON SCHOOL PREMISES

(a) During school hours, and within one hour before the time of opening and within one hour after the time of closing of school, pupils of the public school shall not be solicited on school premises by teachers or others to subscribe or contribute to the funds of, to become members of, or to work for, any organization not directly under the control of the school authorities, unless the organization is a nonpartisan, charitable organization organized for charitable purposes by an act of Congress or under the laws of the state, the purpose of the solicitation is nonpartisan and charitable, and the solicitation has been approved by the county board of education or by the governing board of the school district in which the school is located.

(b) A licensed dentist who provides voluntary dental health screening programs for pupils on school premises, shall not solicit a pupil, or the pupil's parent or guardian, or encourage, or advise treatment or consultation for the pupil by the licensed dentist, or any entity in which the licensed dentist has a financial interest, for any condition discovered in the course of the dental health screening. It is the intent of the Legislature that no licensed dentist use voluntary dental health screening programs for the generation of referrals or for financial benefit. The Legislature does not intend to deny or limit freedom of choice in the selection of an appropriate dental provider for treatment or consultation.

(c) A licensed optometrist who provides voluntary vision testing programs for pupils on school premises, shall not solicit a pupil, or the pupil's parent or guardian, or encourage, or advise treatment or consultation for the pupil by the licensed optometrist, or any entity in which the licensed optometrist has a financial interest, for any condition discovered in the course of the vision testing. It is the intent of the Legislature that no licensed optometrist use voluntary vision testing programs for the generation of referrals or for financial benefit. The Legislature does not intend to deny freedom of choice in the selection of an appropriate vision care provider for treatment or consultation.

(d) Nothing in this section shall be construed as prohibiting the solicitation of pupils of the public school on school premises by pupils of that school for any otherwise lawful purpose.

(Amended by Stats. 1996, Ch. 83, Sec. 1. Effective January 1, 1997.)

GOVERNMENT CODE

TITLE 1: GENERAL

DIVISION 7: MISCELLANEOUS

CHAPTER 3.5: INSPECTION OF PUBLIC RECORDS [REPEALED]

Note: The California Public Records Act (CPRA) Recodification Act of 2021 reorganized and recodified the CPRA to make it more user-friendly. It repealed Chapter 3.5 of Division 7 and added Division 10: Access to Public Records. The act took effect on January 1, 2023.

ARTICLE 1: GENERAL PROVISIONS

6250. LEGISLATIVE FINDING AND DECLARATION [REPEALED]

HISTORY

1. Amended by Stats. 1970, Ch. 575

2. Repealed as of January 1, 2023, by The California Public Records Act (CPRA) Recodification Act of 2021 [AB 473].

6251. CITATION OF CHAPTER [REPEALED]

HISTORY

1. Added by Stats. 1968, Ch. 1473.

2. Repealed as of January 1, 2023, by The California Public Records Act (CPRA) Recodification Act of 2021 [AB 473].

6252. DEFINITIONS [REPEALED]

As used in this chapter:

(a) "Local agency" includes a county; city, whether general law or chartered; city and county; school district; municipal corporation; district; political subdivision; or any board, commission or agency thereof; other local public agency; or entities that are legislative bodies of a local agency pursuant to subdivisions (c) and (d) of Section 54952.

(b) "Member of the public" means any person, except a member, agent, officer, or employee of a federal, state, or local agency acting within the scope of his or her membership, agency, office, or employment.

(c) "Person" includes any natural person, corporation, partnership, limited liability company, firm, or association.

(d) "Public agency" means any state or local agency.

(e) "Public records" includes any writing containing information relating to the conduct of the public's business prepared, owned, used, or retained by any state or local agency regardless of physical form or characteristics. "Public records" in the custody of, or maintained by, the Governor's office means any writing prepared on or after January 6, 1975.

(f) (1) "State agency" means every state office, officer, department, division, bureau, board, and commission or other state body or agency, except those agencies provided for in Article IV (except Section 20 thereof) or Article VI of the California Constitution.

(2) Notwithstanding paragraph (1) or any other law, "state agency" shall also mean the State Bar of California, as described in Section 6001 of the Business and Professions Code.

(g) "Writing" means any handwriting, typewriting, printing, photostating, photographing, photocopying, transmitting by electronic mail or facsimile, and every other means of recording upon any tangible thing any form of communication or representation, including letters, words, pictures, sounds, or symbols, or combinations thereof, and any record thereby created, regardless of the manner in which the record has been stored.

HISTORY

1. Amended by Stats. 2015, Ch. 537, Sec. 20. (SB 387) Effective January 1, 2016.

2. Repealed as of January 1, 2023, by The California Public Records Act (CPRA) Recodification Act of 2021 [AB 473].

6253. TIME FOR INSPECTION OF PUBLIC RECORDS; "UNUSUAL CIRCUMSTANCES" [REPEALED]

(a) Public records are open to inspection at all times during the office hours of the state or local agency and every person has a right to inspect any public record, except as hereafter provided. Any reasonably segregable portion of a record shall be available for inspection by any person requesting the record after deletion of the portions that are exempted by law.

(b) Except with respect to public records exempt from disclosure by express provisions of law, each state or local agency, upon a request for a copy of records that reasonably describes an identifiable record or records, shall make the records promptly available to any person upon payment of fees covering direct costs of duplication, or a statutory fee if applicable. Upon request, an exact copy shall be provided unless impracticable to do so.

(c) Each agency, upon a request for a copy of records, shall, within 10 days from receipt of the request, determine whether the request, in whole or in part, seeks copies of disclosable public records in the possession of the agency and shall promptly notify the person making the request of the determination and the reasons therefor. In unusual circumstances, the time limit prescribed in this section may be extended by written notice by the head of the agency or their designee to the person making the request, setting forth the reasons for the extension and the date on which a determination is expected to be dispatched. No notice shall specify a date that would result in an extension for more than 14 days. When the agency dispatches the determination, and if the agency determines that the request seeks disclosable public records, the agency shall state the estimated date and time when the records will be made available. As used in this section, "unusual circumstances" means the following, but only to the extent reasonably necessary to the proper processing of the particular request:

(1) The need to search for and collect the requested records from field facilities or other establishments that are separate from the office processing the request.

(2) The need to search for, collect, and appropriately examine a voluminous amount of separate and distinct records that are demanded in a single request.

(3) The need for consultation, which shall be conducted with all practicable speed, with another agency having substantial interest in the determination of the request or among two or more components of the agency having substantial subject matter interest therein.

(4) The need to compile data, to write programming language or a computer program, or to construct a computer report to extract data.

(d) Nothing in this chapter shall be construed to permit an agency to delay or obstruct the inspection or copying of public records.

(1) A requester who inspects a disclosable record on the premises of the agency has the right to use the requester's equipment on those premises, without being charged any fees or costs, to photograph or otherwise copy or reproduce the record in a manner that does not require the equipment to make physical contact with the record, unless the means of copy or reproduction would result in either of the following:

(A) Damage to the record.

(B) Unauthorized access to the agency's computer systems or secured networks by using software, equipment, or any other technology capable of accessing, altering, or compromising the agency's electronic records.

(2) The agency may impose any reasonable limits on the use of the requester's equipment that are necessary to protect the safety of the records or to prevent the copying of records from being an unreasonable burden to the orderly function of the agency and its employees. In addition, the agency may impose any limit that is necessary to maintain the integrity of, or ensure the long-term preservation of, historic or high-value records.

(3) The notification of denial of any request for records required by Section 6255 shall set forth the names and titles or positions of each person responsible for the denial.

(e) Except as otherwise prohibited by law, a state or local agency may adopt requirements for itself that allow for faster, more efficient, or greater access to records than prescribed by the minimum standards set forth in this chapter.

(f) In addition to maintaining public records for public inspection during the office hours of the public agency, a public agency may comply with subdivision (a) by posting any public record on its internet website and, in response to a request for a public record posted on the internet website, directing a member of the public to the location on the internet website where the public record is posted. However, if after the public agency directs a member of the public to the internet website, the member of the public requesting the public record requests a copy of the public record due to an inability to access or reproduce the public record from the internet website, the public agency shall promptly provide a copy of the public record pursuant to subdivision (b).

HISTORY

1. Amended by Stats. 2019, Ch. 695, Sec. 1. (AB 1819) Effective January 1, 2020.

2. Repealed as of January 1, 2023, by The California Public Records Act (CPRA) Recodification Act of 2021 [AB 473].

6253.1. AGENCY TO ASSIST IN INSPECTION OF PUBLIC RECORDS [REPEALED]

(a) When a member of the public requests to inspect a public record or obtain a copy of a public record, the public agency, in order to assist the member of the public make a focused and effective request that reasonably describes an identifiable record or records, shall do all of the following, to the extent reasonable under the circumstances:

(1) Assist the member of the public to identify records and information that are responsive to the request or to the purpose of the request, if stated.

(2) Describe the information technology and physical location in which the records exist.

(3) Provide suggestions for overcoming any practical basis for denying access to the records or information sought.

(b) The requirements of paragraph (1) of subdivision (a) shall be deemed to have been satisfied if the public agency is unable to identify the requested information after making a reasonable effort to elicit additional clarifying information from the requester that will help identify the record or records.

(c) The requirements of subdivision (a) are in addition to any action required of a public agency by Section 6253.

(d) This section shall not apply to a request for public records if any of the following applies:

(1) The public agency makes available the requested records pursuant to Section 6253.

(2) The public agency determines that the request should be denied and bases that determination solely on an exemption listed in Section 6254.

(3) The public agency makes available an index of its records.

HISTORY

1. Added by Stats. 2001, Ch. 355, Sec. 3. Effective January 1, 2002.

2. Repealed as of January 1, 2023, by The California Public Records Act (CPRA) Recodification Act of 2021 [AB 473].

6253.4. RECORDS TO BE MADE AVAILABLE [REPEALED]

(a) Every agency may adopt regulations stating the procedures to be followed when making its records available in accordance with this section.

(b) The following state and local bodies shall establish written guidelines for accessibility of records. A copy of these guidelines shall be posted in a conspicuous public place at the offices of these bodies, and a copy of the guidelines shall be available upon request free of charge to any person requesting that body's records:

(1) Department of Motor Vehicles

(2) Department of Consumer Affairs

(3) Transportation Agency

(4) Bureau of Real Estate

(5) Department of Corrections and Rehabilitation

(6) Division of Juvenile Justice

(7) Department of Justice

(8) Department of Insurance

(9) Department of Business Oversight

(10) Department of Managed Health Care

(11) Secretary of State

(12) State Air Resources Board

(13) Department of Water Resources

(14) Department of Parks and Recreation

(15) San Francisco Bay Conservation and Development Commission

(16) State Board of Equalization

(17) State Department of Health Care Services

(18) Employment Development Department

(19) State Department of Public Health

(20) State Department of Social Services

(21) State Department of State Hospitals

(22) State Department of Developmental Services

(23) Public Employees' Retirement System

(24) Teachers' Retirement Board

(25) Department of Industrial Relations

(26) Department of General Services

(27) Department of Veterans Affairs

(28) Public Utilities Commission

(29) California Coastal Commission

(30) State Water Resources Control Board

(31) San Francisco Bay Area Rapid Transit District

(32) All regional water quality control boards

(33) Los Angeles County Air Pollution Control District

(34) Bay Area Air Pollution Control District

(35) Golden Gate Bridge, Highway and Transportation District

(36) Department of Toxic Substances Control

(37) Office of Environmental Health Hazard Assessment

(c) Guidelines and regulations adopted pursuant to this section shall be consistent with all other sections of this chapter and shall reflect the intention of the Legislature to make the records accessible to the public. The guidelines and regulations adopted pursuant to this section shall not operate to limit the hours public records are open for inspection as prescribed in Section 6253.

HISTORY

1. Amended by Stats. 2018, Ch. 92, Sec. 88. (SB 1289) Effective January 1, 2019.

2. Repealed as of January 1, 2023, by The California Public Records Act (CPRA) Recodification Act of 2021 [AB 473].

6254. RECORDS EXEMPT FROM DISCLOSURE REQUIREMENTS [REPEALED]

Except as provided in Sections 6254.7 and 6254.13, this chapter does not require the disclosure of any of the following records:

(a) Preliminary drafts, notes, or interagency or intra-agency memoranda that are not retained by the public agency in the ordinary course of business, if the public interest in withholding those records clearly outweighs the public interest in disclosure.

(b) Records pertaining to pending litigation to which the public agency is a party, or to claims made pursuant to Division 3.6 (commencing with Section 810), until the pending litigation or claim has been finally adjudicated or otherwise settled.

(c) Personnel, medical, or similar files, the disclosure of which would constitute an unwarranted invasion of personal privacy.

(d) Records contained in or related to any of the following:

(1) Applications filed with any state agency responsible for the regulation or supervision of the issuance of securities or of financial institutions, including, but not limited to, banks, savings and loan associations, industrial loan companies, credit unions, and insurance companies.

(2) Examination, operating, or condition reports prepared by, on behalf of, or for the use of, any state agency referred to in paragraph (1).

(3) Preliminary drafts, notes, or interagency or intra-agency communications prepared by, on behalf of, or for the use of, any state agency referred to in paragraph (1).

(4) Information received in confidence by any state agency referred to in paragraph (1).

(e) Geological and geophysical data, plant production data, and similar information relating to utility systems development, or market or crop reports, that are obtained in confidence from any person.

(f) Records of complaints to, or investigations conducted by, or records of intelligence information or security procedures of, the office of the Attorney General and the Department of Justice, the Office of Emergency Services and any state or local police agency, or any investigatory or security files compiled by any other state or local police agency, or any investigatory or security files compiled by any other state or local agency for correctional, law enforcement, or licensing purposes. However, state and local law enforcement agencies shall disclose the names and addresses of persons involved in, or witnesses other than confidential informants to, the incident, the description of any property involved, the date, time, and location of the incident, all diagrams, statements of the parties involved in the incident, the statements of all witnesses, other than confidential informants, to the victims of an incident, or an authorized representative thereof, an insurance carrier against which a claim has been or might be made, and any person suffering bodily injury or property damage or loss, as the result of the incident caused by arson, burglary, fire, explosion, larceny, robbery, carjacking, vandalism, vehicle theft, or a crime as defined by subdivision (b) of Section 13951, unless the disclosure would endanger the safety of a witness or other person involved in the investigation, or unless disclosure would endanger the successful completion of the investigation or a related investigation. However, this subdivision does not require the disclosure of that portion of those investigative files that reflects the analysis or conclusions of the investigating officer.

Customer lists provided to a state or local police agency by an alarm or security company at the request of the agency shall be construed to be records subject to this subdivision.

Notwithstanding any other provision of this subdivision, state and local law enforcement agencies shall make public the following information, except to the extent that disclosure of a particular item of information would endanger the safety of a person involved in an investigation or would endanger the successful completion of the investigation or a related investigation:

(1) The full name and occupation of every individual arrested by the agency, the individual's physical description including date of birth, color of eyes and hair, sex, height and weight, the time and date of arrest, the time and date of booking, the location of the arrest, the factual circumstances surrounding the arrest, the amount of bail set, the time and manner of release or the location where the individual is currently being held, and all charges the individual is being held upon, including any outstanding warrants from other jurisdictions and parole or probation holds.

(2) (A) Subject to the restrictions imposed by Section 841.5 of the Penal Code, the time, substance, and location of all complaints or requests for assistance received by the agency and the time and nature of the response thereto, including, to the extent the information regarding crimes alleged or committed or any other incident investigated is recorded, the time, date, and location of occurrence, the time and date of the report, the name and age of the victim, the factual circumstances surrounding the crime or incident, and a general description of any injuries, property, or weapons involved. The name of a victim of any crime defined by Section 220, 261, 261.5, 262, 264, 264.1,

265, 266, 266a, 266b, 266c, 266e, 266f, 266j, 267, 269, 273a, 273d, 273.5, 285, 286, 288, 288a, 288.2, 288.3, 288.4, 288.5, 288.7, 289, 422.6, 422.7, 422.75, 646.9, or 647.6 of the Penal Code may be withheld at the victim's request, or at the request of the victim's parent or guardian if the victim is a minor. When a person is the victim of more than one crime, information disclosing that the person is a victim of a crime defined in any of the sections of the Penal Code set forth in this subdivision may be deleted at the request of the victim, or the victim's parent or guardian if the victim is a minor, in making the report of the crime, or of any crime or incident accompanying the crime, available to the public in compliance with the requirements of this paragraph.

(B) Subject to the restrictions imposed by Section 841.5 of the Penal Code, the names and images of a victim of human trafficking, as defined in Section 236.1 of the Penal Code, and of that victim's immediate family, other than a family member who is charged with a criminal offense arising from the same incident, may be withheld at the victim's request until the investigation or any subsequent prosecution is complete. For purposes of this subdivision, "immediate family" shall have the same meaning as that provided in paragraph (3) of subdivision (b) of Section 422.4 of the Penal Code.

(3) Subject to the restrictions of Section 841.5 of the Penal Code and this subdivision, the current address of every individual arrested by the agency and the current address of the victim of a crime, if the requester declares under penalty of perjury that the request is made for a scholarly, journalistic, political, or governmental purpose, or that the request is made for investigation purposes by a licensed private investigator as described in Chapter 11.3 (commencing with Section 7512) of Division 3 of the Business and Professions Code. However, the address of the victim of any crime defined by Section 220, 236.1, 261, 261.5, 262, 264, 264.1, 265, 266, 266a, 266b, 266c, 266e, 266f, 266j, 267, 269, 273a, 273d, 273.5, 285, 286, 288, 288a, 288.2, 288.3, 288.4, 288.5, 288.7, 289, 422.6, 422.7, 422.75, 646.9, or 647.6 of the Penal Code shall remain confidential. Address information obtained pursuant to this paragraph shall not be used directly or indirectly, or furnished to another, to sell a product or service to any individual or group of individuals, and the requester shall execute a declaration to that effect under penalty of perjury. This paragraph shall not be construed to prohibit or limit a scholarly, journalistic, political, or government use of address information obtained pursuant to this paragraph.

(4) Notwithstanding any other provision of this subdivision, commencing July 1, 2019, a video or audio recording that relates to a critical incident, as defined in subparagraph (C), may be withheld only as follows:

(A) (i) During an active criminal or administrative investigation, disclosure of a recording related to a critical incident may be delayed for no longer than 45 calendar days after the date the agency knew or reasonably should have known about the incident, if, based on the facts and circumstances depicted in the recording, disclosure would substantially interfere with the investigation, such as by endangering the safety of a witness or a confidential source. If an agency delays disclosure pursuant to this paragraph, the agency shall provide in writing to the requester the specific basis for the agency's determination that disclosure would substantially interfere with the investigation and the estimated date for disclosure.

(ii) After 45 days from the date the agency knew or reasonably should have known about the incident, and up to one year from that date, the agency may continue to delay disclosure of a recording if the agency demonstrates that disclosure would substantially interfere with the investigation. After one year from the date the agency knew or reasonably should have known about the incident, the agency may continue to delay disclosure of a recording only if the agency demonstrates by clear and convincing evidence that disclosure would substantially interfere with the investigation. If an agency delays disclosure pursuant to this clause, the agency shall promptly provide in writing to the requester the specific basis for the agency's determination that the interest in preventing interference with an active investigation outweighs the public interest in disclosure and provide the estimated date for the disclosure. The agency shall reassess withholding and notify the requester every 30 days. A recording withheld by the agency shall be disclosed promptly when the specific basis for withholding is resolved.

(B) (i) If the agency demonstrates, on the facts of the particular case, that the public interest in withholding a video or audio recording clearly outweighs the public interest in disclosure because the release of the recording would, based on the facts and circumstances depicted in the recording, violate the reasonable expectation of privacy of a subject depicted in the recording, the agency shall provide in writing to the requester the specific basis for the expectation of privacy and the public interest served by withholding the recording and may use redaction technology, including blurring or distorting images or audio, to obscure those specific portions of the recording that protect that interest. However, the redaction shall not interfere with the viewer's ability to fully, completely, and accurately comprehend the events captured in the recording and the recording shall not otherwise be edited or altered.

(ii) Except as provided in clause (iii), if the agency demonstrates that the reasonable expectation of privacy of a subject depicted in the recording cannot adequately be protected through redaction as described in clause (i) and that interest outweighs the public interest in disclosure, the agency may withhold the recording from the public, except that the recording, either redacted as provided in clause (i) or unredacted, shall be disclosed promptly, upon request, to any of the following:

(I) The subject of the recording whose privacy is to be protected, or their authorized representative.

(II) If the subject is a minor, the parent or legal guardian of the subject whose privacy is to be protected.

(III) If the subject whose privacy is to be protected is deceased, an heir, beneficiary, designated immediate family member, or authorized legal representative of the deceased subject whose privacy is to be protected.

(iii) If disclosure pursuant to clause (ii) would substantially interfere with an active criminal or administrative investigation, the agency shall provide in writing to the requester the specific basis for the agency's determination that disclosure would substantially interfere with the investigation, and provide the estimated date for the disclosure of the video or audio recording. Thereafter, the recording may be withheld by the agency for 45 calendar days, subject to extensions as set forth in clause (ii) of subparagraph (A).

(C) For purposes of this paragraph, a video or audio recording relates to a critical incident if it depicts any of the following incidents:

(i) An incident involving the discharge of a firearm at a person by a peace officer or custodial officer.

(ii) An incident in which the use of force by a peace officer or custodial officer against a person resulted in death or in great bodily injury.

(D) An agency may provide greater public access to video or audio recordings than the minimum standards set forth in this paragraph.

(E) This paragraph does not alter, limit, or negate any other rights, remedies, or obligations with respect to public records regarding an incident other than a critical incident as described in subparagraph (C).

(F) For purposes of this paragraph, a peace officer does not include any peace officer employed by the Department of Corrections and Rehabilitation.

(g) Test questions, scoring keys, and other examination data used to administer a licensing examination, examination for employment, or academic examination, except as provided for in Chapter 3 (commencing with Section 99150) of Part 65 of Division 14 of Title 3 of the Education Code.

(h) The contents of real estate appraisals or engineering or feasibility estimates and evaluations made for or by the state or local agency relative to the acquisition of property, or to prospective public supply and construction contracts, until all of the property has been acquired or all of the contract agreement obtained. However, the law of eminent domain shall not be affected by this provision.

(i) Information required from any taxpayer in connection with the collection of local taxes that is received in confidence and the disclosure of the information to other persons would result in unfair competitive disadvantage to the person supplying the information.

(j) Library circulation records kept for the purpose of identifying the borrower of items available in libraries, and library and museum materials made or acquired and presented solely for reference or exhibition purposes. The exemption in this subdivision shall not apply to records of fines imposed on the borrowers.

(k) Records, the disclosure of which is exempted or prohibited pursuant to federal or state law, including, but not limited to, provisions of the Evidence Code relating to privilege.

(l) Correspondence of and to the Governor or employees of the Governor's office or in the custody of or maintained by the Governor's Legal Affairs Secretary. However, public records shall not be transferred to the custody of the Governor's Legal Affairs Secretary to evade the disclosure provisions of this chapter.

(m) In the custody of or maintained by the Legislative Counsel, except those records in the public database maintained by the Legislative Counsel that are described in Section 10248.

(n) Statements of personal worth or personal financial data required by a licensing agency and filed by an applicant with the licensing agency to establish their personal qualification for the license, certificate, or permit applied for.

(o) Financial data contained in applications for financing under Division 27 (commencing with Section 44500) of the Health and Safety Code, if an authorized officer of the California Pollution Control Financing Authority determines that disclosure of the financial data would be competitively injurious to the applicant and the data is required in order to obtain guarantees from the United States Small Business Administration. The California Pollution Control Financing Authority shall adopt rules for review of individual requests for confidentiality under this section and for making available to the public those portions of an application that are subject to disclosure under this chapter.

(p) (1) Records of state agencies related to activities governed by Chapter 10.3 (commencing with Section 3512), Chapter 10.5 (commencing with Section 3525), and Chapter 12 (commencing with Section 3560) of Division 4, and Article 19.5 (commencing with Section 8430) of Chapter 2 of Part 6 of Division 1 of Title 1 of the Education Code, that reveal a state agency's deliberative processes, impressions, evaluations, opinions, recommendations, meeting minutes, research, work products, theories, or strategy, or that provide instruction, advice, or training to employees who do not have full collective bargaining and representation rights under these chapters. This paragraph shall not be construed to limit the disclosure duties of a state agency with respect to any other records relating to the activities governed by the employee relations acts referred to in this paragraph.

(2) Records of local agencies related to activities governed by Chapter 10 (commencing with Section 3500) of Division 4, that reveal a local agency's deliberative processes, impressions, evaluations, opinions, recommendations, meeting minutes, research, work products, theories, or strategy, or that provide instruction, advice, or training to employees who do not have full collective bargaining and representation rights under that chapter. This paragraph shall not be construed to limit the disclosure duties of a local agency with respect to any other records relating to the activities governed by the employee relations act referred to in this paragraph.

(q) (1) Records of state agencies related to activities governed by Article 2.6 (commencing with Section 14081), Article 2.8 (commencing with Section 14087.5), and Article 2.91 (commencing with Section 14089) of Chapter 7 of Part 3 of Division 9 of the Welfare and Institutions Code, that reveal the special negotiator's deliberative processes, discussions, communications, or any other portion of the negotiations with providers of health care services, impressions, opinions, recommendations, meeting minutes, research, work product, theories, or strategy, or that provide instruction, advice, or training to employees.

(2) Except for the portion of a contract containing the rates of payment, contracts for inpatient services entered into pursuant to these articles, on or after April 1, 1984, shall be open to inspection one year after they are fully executed. If a contract for inpatient services that is entered into prior to April 1, 1984, is amended on or after April 1, 1984, the amendment, except for any portion containing the rates of payment, shall be open to inspection one year after it is fully executed. If the California Medical Assistance Commission enters into contracts with health care providers for other than inpatient hospital services, those contracts shall be open to inspection one year after they are fully executed.

(3) Three years after a contract or amendment is open to inspection under this subdivision, the portion of the contract or amendment containing the rates of payment shall be open to inspection.

(4) Notwithstanding any other law, the entire contract or amendment shall be open to inspection by the Joint Legislative Audit Committee and the Legislative Analyst's Office. The committee and that office shall maintain the confidentiality of the contracts and amendments until the time a contract or amendment is fully open to inspection by the public.

(r) Records of Native American graves, cemeteries, and sacred places and records of Native American places, features, and objects described in Sections 5097.9 and 5097.993 of the Public Resources Code maintained by, or in the possession of, the Native American Heritage Commission, another state agency, or a local agency.

(s) A final accreditation report of the Joint Commission on Accreditation of Hospitals that has been transmitted to the State Department of Health Care Services pursuant to subdivision (b) of Section 1282 of the Health and Safety Code.

(t) Records of a local hospital district, formed pursuant to Division 23 (commencing with Section 32000) of the Health and Safety Code, or the records of a municipal hospital, formed pursuant to Article 7 (commencing with Section 37600) or Article 8 (commencing with Section 37650) of Chapter 5 of Part 2 of Division 3 of Title 4 of this code, that relate to any contract with an insurer or nonprofit hospital service plan for inpatient or outpatient services for alternative rates pursuant to Section 10133 of the Insurance Code. However, the record shall be open to inspection within one year after the contract is fully executed.

(u) (1) Information contained in applications for licenses to carry firearms issued pursuant to Section 26150, 26155, 26170, or 26215 of the Penal Code by the sheriff of a county or the chief or other head of a municipal police department that indicates when or where the applicant is vulnerable to attack or that concerns the applicant's medical or psychological history or that of members of their family.

(2) The home address and telephone number of prosecutors, public defenders, peace officers, judges, court commissioners, and magistrates that are set forth in applications for licenses to carry firearms issued pursuant to Section 26150, 26155, 26170, or 26215 of the Penal Code by the sheriff of a county or the chief or other head of a municipal police department.

(3) The home address and telephone number of prosecutors, public defenders, peace officers, judges, court commissioners, and magistrates that are set forth in licenses to carry firearms issued pursuant to Section 26150, 26155, 26170, or 26215 of the Penal Code by the sheriff of a county or the chief or other head of a municipal police department.

(v) (1) Records of the Managed Risk Medical Insurance Board and the State Department of Health Care Services related to activities governed by former Part 6.3 (commencing with Section 12695), former Part 6.5 (commencing with Section 12700), Part 6.6 (commencing with Section 12739.5), or Part 6.7 (commencing with Section 12739.70) of Division 2 of the Insurance Code, or Chapter 2 (commencing with Section 15810) or Chapter 4 (commencing with Section 15870) of Part 3.3 of Division 9 of the Welfare and Institutions Code, and that reveal any of the following:

(A) The deliberative processes, discussions, communications, or any other portion of the negotiations with entities contracting or seeking to contract with the board or the department, entities with which the board or the department is considering a contract, or entities with which the board or department is considering or enters into any other arrangement under which the board or the department provides, receives, or arranges services or reimbursement.

(B) The impressions, opinions, recommendations, meeting minutes, research, work product, theories, or strategy of the board or its staff or the department or its staff, or records that provide instructions, advice, or training to their employees.

(2) (A) Except for the portion of a contract that contains the rates of payment, contracts entered into pursuant to former Part 6.3 (commencing with Section 12695), former Part 6.5 (commencing with Section 12700), Part 6.6 (commencing with Section 12739.5), or Part 6.7 (commencing with Section 12739.70) of Division 2 of the Insurance Code, or Chapter 2 (commencing with Section 15810) or Chapter 4 (commencing with Section 15870) of Part 3.3 of Division 9 of the Welfare and Institutions Code, on or after July 1, 1991, shall be open to inspection one year after their effective dates.

(B) If a contract that is entered into prior to July 1, 1991, is amended on or after July 1, 1991, the amendment, except for any portion containing the rates of payment, shall be open to inspection one year after the effective date of the amendment.

(3) Three years after a contract or amendment is open to inspection pursuant to this subdivision, the portion of the contract or amendment containing the rates of payment shall be open to inspection.

(4) Notwithstanding any other law, the entire contract or amendments to a contract shall be open to inspection by the Joint Legislative Audit Committee. The committee shall maintain the confidentiality of the contracts and amendments thereto, until the contracts or amendments to the contracts are open to inspection pursuant to paragraph (3).

(w) (1) Records of the Managed Risk Medical Insurance Board related to activities governed by Chapter 8 (commencing with Section 10700) of Part 2 of Division 2 of the Insurance Code, and that reveal the deliberative processes, discussions, communications, or any other portion of the negotiations with health plans, or the impressions, opinions, recommendations, meeting minutes, research, work product, theories, or strategy of the board or its staff, or records that provide instructions, advice, or training to employees.

(2) Except for the portion of a contract that contains the rates of payment, contracts for health coverage entered into pursuant to Chapter 8 (commencing with Section 10700) of Part 2 of Division 2 of the Insurance Code, on or after January 1, 1993, shall be open to inspection one year after they have been fully executed.

(3) Notwithstanding any other law, the entire contract or amendments to a contract shall be open to inspection by the Joint Legislative Audit Committee. The committee shall maintain the confidentiality of the contracts and amendments thereto, until the contracts or amendments to the contracts are open to inspection pursuant to paragraph (2).

(x) Financial data contained in applications for registration, or registration renewal, as a service contractor filed with the Director of Consumer Affairs pursuant to Chapter 20 (commencing with Section 9800) of Division 3 of the Business and Professions Code, for the purpose of establishing the service contractor's net worth, or financial data regarding the funded accounts held in escrow for service contracts held in force in this state by a service contractor.

(y) (1) Records of the Managed Risk Medical Insurance Board and the State Department of Health Care Services related to activities governed by Part 6.2 (commencing with Section 12693) or former Part 6.4 (commencing with Section 12699.50) of Division 2 of the Insurance Code or Sections 14005.26 and 14005.27 of, or Chapter 3 (commencing with Section 15850) of Part 3.3 of Division 9 of, the Welfare and Institutions Code, if the records reveal any of the following:

(A) The deliberative processes, discussions, communications, or any other portion of the negotiations with entities contracting or seeking to contract with the board or the department, entities with which the board or department is considering a contract, or entities with which the board or department is considering or enters into any other arrangement under which the board or department provides, receives, or arranges services or reimbursement.

(B) The impressions, opinions, recommendations, meeting minutes, research, work product, theories, or strategy of the board or its staff, or the department or its staff, or records that provide instructions, advice, or training to employees.

(2) (A) Except for the portion of a contract that contains the rates of payment, contracts entered into pursuant to Part 6.2 (commencing with Section 12693) or former Part 6.4 (commencing with Section 12699.50) of Division 2 of the Insurance Code, on or after January 1, 1998, or Sections 14005.26 and 14005.27 of, or Chapter 3 (commencing with Section 15850) of Part 3.3 of Division 9 of, the Welfare and Institutions Code shall be open to inspection one year after their effective dates.

(B) If a contract entered into pursuant to Part 6.2 (commencing with Section 12693) or former Part 6.4 (commencing with Section 12699.50) of Division 2 of the Insurance Code or Sections 14005.26 and 14005.27 of, or Chapter 3 (commencing with Section 15850) of Part 3.3 of Division 9 of, the Welfare and Institutions Code, is amended, the amendment shall be open to inspection one year after the effective date of the amendment.

(3) Three years after a contract or amendment is open to inspection pursuant to this subdivision, the portion of the contract or amendment containing the rates of payment shall be open to inspection.

(4) Notwithstanding any other law, the entire contract or amendments to a contract shall be open to inspection by the Joint Legislative Audit Committee. The committee shall maintain the confidentiality of the contracts and amendments thereto until the contract or amendments to a contract are open to inspection pursuant to paragraph (2) or (3).

(5) The exemption from disclosure provided pursuant to this subdivision for the contracts, deliberative processes, discussions, communications, negotiations, impressions, opinions, recommendations, meeting minutes, research, work product, theories, or strategy of the board or its staff, or the department or its staff, shall also apply to the contracts, deliberative processes, discussions, communications, negotiations, impressions, opinions, recommendations, meeting minutes, research, work product, theories, or strategy of applicants pursuant to former Part 6.4 (commencing with Section 12699.50) of Division 2 of the Insurance Code or Chapter 3 (commencing with Section 15850) of Part 3.3 of Division 9 of the Welfare and Institutions Code.

(z) Records obtained pursuant to paragraph (2) of subdivision (f) of Section 2891.1 of the Public Utilities Code.

(aa) A document prepared by or for a state or local agency that assesses its vulnerability to terrorist attack or other criminal acts intended to disrupt the public agency's operations and that is for distribution or consideration in a closed session.

(ab) Critical infrastructure information, as defined in Section 131(3) of Title 6 of the United States Code, that is voluntarily submitted to the Office of Emergency Services for use by that office, including the identity of the person who or entity that voluntarily submitted the information. As used in this subdivision, "voluntarily submitted" means submitted in the absence of the office exercising any legal authority to compel access to or submission of critical infrastructure information. This subdivision shall not affect the status of information in the possession of any other state or local governmental agency.

(ac) All information provided to the Secretary of State by a person for the purpose of registration in the Advance Health Care Directive Registry, except that those records shall be released at the request of a health care provider, a public guardian, or the registrant's legal representative.

(ad) The following records of the State Compensation Insurance Fund:

(1) Records related to claims pursuant to Chapter 1 (commencing with Section 3200) of Division 4 of the Labor Code, to the extent that confidential medical information or other individually identifiable information would be disclosed.

(2) Records related to the discussions, communications, or any other portion of the negotiations with entities contracting or seeking to contract with the fund, and any related deliberations.

(3) Records related to the impressions, opinions, recommendations, meeting minutes of meetings or sessions that are lawfully closed to the public, research, work product, theories, or strategy of the fund or its staff, on the development of rates, contracting strategy, underwriting, or competitive strategy pursuant to the powers granted to the fund in Chapter 4 (commencing with Section 11770) of Part 3 of Division 2 of the Insurance Code.

(4) Records obtained to provide workers' compensation insurance under Chapter 4 (commencing with Section 11770) of Part 3 of Division 2 of the Insurance Code, including, but not limited to, any medical claims information, policyholder information provided that nothing in this paragraph shall be interpreted to prevent an insurance agent or broker from obtaining proprietary information or other information authorized by law to be obtained by the agent or broker, and information on rates, pricing, and claims handling received from brokers.

(5) (A) Records that are trade secrets pursuant to Section 6276.44, or Article 11 (commencing with Section 1060) of Chapter 4 of Division 8 of the Evidence Code, including, without limitation, instructions, advice, or training provided by the State Compensation Insurance Fund to its board members, officers, and employees regarding the fund's special investigation unit, internal audit unit, and informational security, marketing, rating, pricing, underwriting, claims handling, audits, and collections.

(B) Notwithstanding subparagraph (A), the portions of records containing trade secrets shall be available for review by the Joint Legislative Audit Committee, California State Auditor's Office, Division of Workers' Compensation, and the Department of Insurance to ensure compliance with applicable law.

(6) (A) Internal audits containing proprietary information and the following records that are related to an internal audit:

(i) Personal papers and correspondence of any person providing assistance to the fund when that person has requested in writing that their papers and correspondence be kept private and confidential. Those papers and correspondence shall become public records if the written request is withdrawn, or upon order of the fund.

(ii) Papers, correspondence, memoranda, or any substantive

information pertaining to any audit not completed or an internal audit that contains proprietary information.

(B) Notwithstanding subparagraph (A), the portions of records containing proprietary information, or any information specified in subparagraph (A) shall be available for review by the Joint Legislative Audit Committee, California State Auditor's Office, Division of Workers' Compensation, and the Department of Insurance to ensure compliance with applicable law.

(7) (A) Except as provided in subparagraph (C), contracts entered into pursuant to Chapter 4 (commencing with Section 11770) of Part 3 of Division 2 of the Insurance Code shall be open to inspection one year after the contract has been fully executed.

(B) If a contract entered into pursuant to Chapter 4 (commencing with Section 11770) of Part 3 of Division 2 of the Insurance Code is amended, the amendment shall be open to inspection one year after the amendment has been fully executed.

(C) Three years after a contract or amendment is open to inspection pursuant to this subdivision, the portion of the contract or amendment containing the rates of payment shall be open to inspection.

(D) Notwithstanding any other law, the entire contract or amendments to a contract shall be open to inspection by the Joint Legislative Audit Committee. The committee shall maintain the confidentiality of the contracts and amendments thereto until the contract or amendments to a contract are open to inspection pursuant to this paragraph.

(E) This paragraph is not intended to apply to documents related to contracts with public entities that are not otherwise expressly confidential as to that public entity.

(F) For purposes of this paragraph, "fully executed" means the point in time when all of the necessary parties to the contract have signed the contract.

This section does not prevent any agency from opening its records concerning the administration of the agency to public inspection, unless disclosure is otherwise prohibited by law.

This section does not prevent any health facility from disclosing to a certified bargaining agent relevant financing information pursuant to Section 8 of the National Labor Relations Act (29 U.S.C. Sec. 158).

HISTORY

1. Amended by Stats. 2019, Ch. 385, Sec. 29. (AB 378) Effective January 1, 2020.

2. Repealed as of January 1, 2023, by The California Public Records Act (CPRA) Recodification Act of 2021 [AB 473].

6254.3. CONFIDENTIALITY OF STATE EMPLOYEE HOME ADDRESS AND TELEPHONE NUMBERS [REPEALED]

(Repealed as of January 1, 2023, by The California Public Records Act (CPRA) Recodification Act of 2021 [AB 473].)

6254.32 [REPEALED]

(Repealed as of January 1, 2023, by The California Public Records Act (CPRA) Recodification Act of 2021 [AB 473].)

6254.5. DISCLOSURE OF OTHERWISE EXEMPT RECORDS; EXCEPTIONS [REPEALED]

(Repealed as of January 1, 2023, by The California Public Records Act (CPRA) Recodification Act of 2021 [AB 473].)

6254.8. PUBLIC EMPLOYMENT CONTRACTS AS PUBLIC RECORDS [REPEALED]

(Repealed as of January 1, 2023, by The California Public Records Act (CPRA) Re-codification Act of 2021 [AB 473].)

6255. WITHHOLDING RECORDS FROM INSPECTION; JUSTIFICATION; PUBLIC INTEREST [REPEALED]

(Repealed as of January 1, 2023, by The California Public Records Act (CPRA) Re-codification Act of 2021 [AB 473].)

6258. ENFORCEMENT OF RIGHTS; PROCEEDINGS FOR INJUNCTIVE OR DECLARATORY RELIEF; WRITE OF MANDATE [REPEALED]

(Repealed as of January 1, 2023, by The California Public Records Act (CPRA) Re-codification Act of 2021 [AB 473].)

6259. ORDER TO SHOW CAUSE; IN CAMERA INSPECTION; REVIEWABILITY OF DETERMINATION; COSTS AND ATTORNEY FEES [REPEALED]

(Repealed as of January 1, 2023, by The California Public Records Act (CPRA) Re-codification Act of 2021 [AB 473].)

6260. STATUS OF EXISTING JUDICIAL RECORDS; DISCOVERY OF RIGHTS OF LITIGANTS [REPEALED]

(Repealed as of January 1, 2023, by The California Public Records Act (CPRA) Re-codification Act of 2021 [AB 473].)

6262. DISCLOSURE OF LICENSING COMPLAINT AND INVESTIGATION RECORDS ON REQUEST OF DISTRICT ATTORNEY [REPEALED]

(Repealed as of January 1, 2023, by The California Public Records Act (CPRA) Re-codification Act of 2021 [AB 473].)

6265. STATUS OF RECORDS NOT CHANGED BY DISCLOSURE TO DISTRICT ATTORNEY [REPEALED]

(Repealed as of January 1, 2023, by The California Public Records Act (CPRA) Re-codification Act of 2021 [AB 473].)

DIVISION 10. ACCESS TO PUBLIC RECORDS

PART 1. GENERAL PROVISIONS

CHAPTER 1. PRELIMINARY PROVISIONS

ARTICLE 1. SHORT TITLES

7920.000

This division shall be known and may be cited as the California Public Records Act.

7920.005

This division recodifies the provisions of former Chapter 3.5 (commencing with Section 6250) of Division 7 of this title. The act that added this division, and the act that consists of conforming revisions to reflect the addition of this division, shall be known and may be cited as the "CPRA Recodification Act of 2021."

ARTICLE 2. EFFECT OF RECODIFICATION

7920.100

Nothing in the CPRA Recodification Act of 2021 is intended to substantively change the law relating to inspection of public records. The act is intended to be entirely nonsubstantive in effect. Every provision of this division and every other provision of this act, including, without limitation, every cross-reference in every provision of the act, shall be interpreted consistent with the nonsubstantive intent of the act.

(Added by Stats. 2021, Ch. 614, Sec. 2. (AB 473) Effective January 1, 2022. Operative January 1, 2023, pursuant to Sec. 7931.000.)

7920.105

(a) A provision of this division, or any other provision of the CPRA Recodification Act of 2021, insofar as it is substantially the same as a previously existing provision relating to the same subject matter, shall be considered as a restatement and continuation thereof and not as a new enactment.

(b) A reference in a statute to a previously existing provision that is restated and continued in this division, or in any other provision of the CPRA Recodification Act of 2021, shall, unless a contrary intent appears, be deemed a reference to the restatement and continuation.

(c) A reference in a statute to a provision of this division, or any other provision of the CPRA Recodification Act of 2021, which is substantially the same as a previously existing provision, shall, unless a contrary intent appears, be deemed to include a reference to the previously existing provision.

(Added by Stats. 2021, Ch. 614, Sec. 2. (AB 473) Effective January 1, 2022. Operative January 1, 2023, pursuant to Sec. 7931.000.)

7920.110

(a) A judicial decision interpreting a previously existing provision is relevant in interpreting any provision of this division, or any other provision of the CPRA Recodification Act of 2021, which restates and continues that previously existing provision.

(b) However, in enacting the CPRA Recodification Act of 2021, the Legislature has not evaluated the correctness of any judicial decision interpreting a provision affected by the act.

(c) The CPRA Recodification Act of 2021 is not intended to, and does not, reflect any assessment of any judicial decision interpreting any provision affected by the act.

(Added by Stats. 2021, Ch. 614, Sec. 2. (AB 473) Effective January 1, 2022. Operative January 1, 2023, pursuant to Sec. 7931.000.)

7920.115

(a) An opinion of the Attorney General interpreting a previously existing provision is relevant in interpreting any provision of this division, or any other provision of the CPRA Recodification Act of 2021, which restates and continues that previously existing provision.

(b) However, in enacting the CPRA Recodification Act of 2021, the Legislature has not evaluated the correctness of any Attorney General opinion interpreting a provision affected by the act.

(c) The CPRA Recodification Act of 2021 is not intended to, and does not, reflect any assessment of any Attorney General opinion interpreting any provision affected by the act.

(Added by Stats. 2021, Ch. 614, Sec. 2. (AB 473) Effective January 1, 2022. Operative January 1, 2023, pursuant to Sec. 7931.000.)

7920.120

(a) A judicial decision or Attorney General opinion on the constitutionality of a previously existing provision is relevant in determining the constitutionality of any provision of this division, or any other provision of the CPRA Recodification Act of 2021, which restates and continues that previously existing provision.

(b) However, in enacting the CPRA Recodification Act of 2021, the Legislature has not evaluated the constitutionality of any provision affected by the act, or the correctness of any judicial decision or Attorney General opinion on the constitutionality of any provision affected by the act.

(c) The CPRA Recodification Act of 2021 is not intended to, and does not, reflect any determination of the constitutionality of any provision affected by the act.

(Added by Stats. 2021, Ch. 614, Sec. 2. (AB 473) Effective January 1, 2022. Operative January 1, 2023, pursuant to Sec. 7931.000.)

CHAPTER 2. DEFINITIONS

7920.500

For purposes of Article 3 (commencing with Section 7928.200) of Chapter 14 of Part 5, "elected or appointed official" includes, but is not limited to, all of the following:

(a) A state constitutional officer.

(b) A Member of the Legislature.

(c) A judge or court commissioner.

(d) A district attorney.

(e) A public defender.

(f) A member of a city council.

(g) A member of a board of supervisors.

(h) An appointee of the Governor.

(i) An appointee of the Legislature.

(j) A mayor.

(k) A city attorney.

(l) A police chief or sheriff.

(m) A public safety official.

(n) A state administrative law judge.

(o) A federal judge or federal defender.

(p) A member of the United States Congress or appointee of the President of the United States.

(q) A judge of a federally recognized Indian tribe.

(Amended by Stats. 2023, Ch. 478, Sec. 26. (AB 1756) Effective January 1, 2024.)

7920.505

(a) The following provisions are continuations of provisions that were included in former Section 6254 as that section read when it was repealed by the CPRA Recodification Act of 2021:

(1) Section 7921.500.

(2) Sections 7923.600 to 7923.625, inclusive.

(3) Section 7923.700.

(4) Sections 7923.800 and 7923.805.

(5) Section 7924.505.

(6) Section 7925.000.

(7) Section 7925.005.

(8) Section 7925.010.

(9) Section 7926.000.

(10) Section 7926.100.

(11) Section 7926.200.

(12) Section 7926.210.

(13) Section 7926.220, except the continuation of former Section 6254.14(b).

(14) Section 7926.225, except the continuation of former Section 6254.14(b).

(15) Section 7926.230, except the continuation of former Section 6254.14(b).

(16) Section 7926.235.

(17) Section 7927.000.

(18) Section 7927.100.

(19) Section 7927.200.

(20) Section 7927.300.

(21) Section 7927.500.

(22) Section 7927.700.

(23) Section 7927.705.

(24) Section 7928.000.

(25) Section 7928.100.

(26) Sections 7928.405 and 7928.410.

(27) Section 7928.705.

(28) Section 7929.000.

(29) Section 7929.200.

(30) Section 7929.205.

(31) Chapter 18 (commencing with Section 7929.400) of Part 5.

(32) Section 7929.605.

(b) The provisions listed in subdivision (a) may be referred to as "former Section 6254 provisions."

(c) Subdivision (a) does not include any provision that was first codified in one of the specified numerical ranges after the effective date of the CPRA Recodification Act of 2021.

(Added by Stats. 2021, Ch. 614, Sec. 2. (AB 473) Effective January 1, 2022. Operative January 1, 2023, pursuant to Sec. 7931.000.)

7920.510

As used in this division, "local agency" includes any of the following:

(a) A county.

(b) A city, whether general law or chartered.

(c) A city and county.

(d) A school district.

(e) A municipal corporation.

(f) A district.

(g) A political subdivision.

(h) Any board, commission, or agency of the foregoing.

(i) Another local public agency.

(j) An entity that is a legislative body of a local agency pursuant to subdivision (c) or (d) of Section 54952.

(Added by Stats. 2021, Ch. 614, Sec. 2. (AB 473) Effective January 1, 2022. Operative January 1, 2023, pursuant to Sec. 7931.000.)

7920.515

As used in this division, "member of the public" means any person other than a member, agent, officer, or employee of a federal, state, or local agency who is acting within the scope of that membership, agency, office, or employment.

(Added by Stats. 2021, Ch. 614, Sec. 2. (AB 473) Effective January 1, 2022. Operative January 1, 2023, pursuant to Sec. 7931.000.)

7920.520

As used in this division, "person" includes any natural person, corporation, partnership, limited liability company, firm, or association.

(Added by Stats. 2021, Ch. 614, Sec. 2. (AB 473) Effective January 1, 2022. Operative January 1, 2023, pursuant to Sec. 7931.000.)

7920.525

(a) As used in this division, "public agency" means any state or local agency.

(b) As used in Article 5 (commencing with Section 7926.400) of Chapter 5 of Part 5, "public agency" means an entity specified in subdivision (c) of Section 7926.400.

(Added by Stats. 2021, Ch. 614, Sec. 2. (AB 473) Effective January 1, 2022. Operative January 1, 2023, pursuant to Sec. 7931.000.)

7920.530

(a) As used in this division, "public records" includes any writing containing information relating to the conduct of the public's business prepared, owned, used, or retained by any state or local agency regardless of physical form or characteristics.

(b) "Public records" in the custody of, or maintained by, the Governor's office means any writing prepared on or after January 6, 1975.

(Added by Stats. 2021, Ch. 614, Sec. 2. (AB 473) Effective January 1, 2022. Operative January 1, 2023, pursuant to Sec. 7931.000.)

7920.535

As used in this division, "public safety official" means the following parties, whether active or retired:

(a) A peace officer as defined in Sections 830 to 830.65, inclusive, of the Penal Code, or a person who is not a peace officer, but may exercise the powers of arrest during the course and within the scope of the person's employment pursuant to Section 830.7 of the Penal Code.

(b) A public officer or other person listed in Section 1808.2 or 1808.6 of the Vehicle Code.

(c) An "elected or appointed official" as defined in Section 7920.500.

(d) An attorney employed by the Department of Justice, the State Public Defender, or a county office of the district attorney or public defender, the United States Attorney, or the Federal Public Defender.

(e) A city attorney and an attorney who represents cities in criminal matters.

(f) An employee of the Department of Corrections and Rehabilitation who supervises inmates or is required to have care or custody of a prisoner.

(g) A sworn or nonsworn employee who supervises inmates in a city police department, a county sheriff's office, the Department of the California Highway Patrol, federal, state, or a local detention facility, or a local juvenile hall, camp, ranch, or home, and a probation officer as defined in Section 830.5 of the Penal Code.

(h) A federal prosecutor, a federal criminal investigator, and a National Park Service Ranger working in California.

(i) The surviving spouse or child of a peace officer defined in Section 830 of the Penal Code, if the peace officer died in the line of duty.

(j) State and federal judges and court commissioners.

(k) An employee of the Attorney General, a district attorney, or a public defender who submits verification from the Attorney General, district attorney, or public defender that the employee represents the Attorney General, district attorney, or public defender in matters that routinely place that employee in personal contact with persons under investigation for, charged with, or convicted of, committing criminal acts.

(l) A nonsworn employee of the Department of Justice or a police department or sheriff's office that, in the course of employment, is responsible for collecting, documenting, and preserving physical evidence at crime scenes, testifying in court as an expert witness, and other technical duties, and a nonsworn employee that, in the course of employment, performs a variety of standardized and advanced laboratory procedures in the examination of physical crime evidence, determines their results, and provides expert testimony in court.

(Added by Stats. 2021, Ch. 614, Sec. 2. (AB 473) Effective January 1, 2022. Operative January 1, 2023, pursuant to Sec. 7931.000.)

7920.540

(a) As used in this division, "state agency" means every state office, officer, department, division, bureau, board, and commission or other state body or agency, except those agencies provided for in Article IV (except Section 20 thereof) or Article VI of the California Constitution.

(b) Notwithstanding subdivision (a) or any other law, "state agency" also means the State Bar of California, as described in Section 6001 of the Business and Professions Code.

(Added by Stats. 2021, Ch. 614, Sec. 2. (AB 473) Effective January 1, 2022. Operative January 1, 2023, pursuant to Sec. 7931.000.)

7920.545

As used in this division, "writing" means any handwriting, typewriting, printing, photostating, photographing, photocopying, transmitting by electronic mail or facsimile, and every other means of recording upon any tangible thing any form of communication or representation, including letters, words, pictures, sounds, or symbols, or combinations thereof, and any record thereby created, regardless of the manner in which the record has been stored.

(Added by Stats. 2021, Ch. 614, Sec. 2. (AB 473) Effective January 1, 2022. Operative January 1, 2023, pursuant to Sec. 7931.000.)

PART 2. DISCLOSURE AND EXEMPTIONS GENERALLY

CHAPTER 1. RIGHT OF ACCESS TO PUBLIC RECORDS

7921.000

In enacting this division, the Legislature, mindful of the right of individuals to privacy, finds and declares that access to information concerning the conduct of the people's business is a fundamental and necessary right of every person in this state.

(Added by Stats. 2021, Ch. 614, Sec. 2. (AB 473) Effective January 1, 2022. Operative January 1, 2023, pursuant to Sec. 7931.000.)

7921.005

A state or local agency may not allow another party to control the disclosure of information that is otherwise subject to disclosure pursuant to this division.

(Added by Stats. 2021, Ch. 614, Sec. 2. (AB 473) Effective January 1, 2022. Operative January 1, 2023, pursuant to Sec. 7931.000.)

7921.010

(a) Notwithstanding any other provision of law, no state or local agency shall sell, exchange, furnish, or otherwise provide a public record subject to disclosure pursuant to this division to a private entity in a manner that prevents a state or local agency from providing the record directly pursuant to this division.

(b) Nothing in this section requires a state or local agency to use the State Printer to print public records.

(c) Nothing in this section prevents the destruction of a public record pursuant to law.

(d) This section shall not apply to contracts entered into before January 1, 1996, between the County of Santa Clara and a private entity, for the provision of public records subject to disclosure under this division.

(Added by Stats. 2021, Ch. 614, Sec. 2. (AB 473) Effective January 1, 2022. Operative January 1, 2023, pursuant to Sec. 7931.000.)

CHAPTER 2. GENERAL RULES GOVERNING DISCLOSURE

ARTICLE 1. NONDISCRIMINATION

7921.300

This division does not allow limitations on access to a public record based upon the purpose for which the record is being requested, if the record is otherwise subject to disclosure.

(Added by Stats. 2021, Ch. 614, Sec. 2. (AB 473) Effective January 1, 2022. Operative January 1, 2023, pursuant to Sec. 7931.000.)

7921.305

(a) Notwithstanding the definition of "member of the public" in Section 7920.515, an elected member or officer of any state or local agency is entitled to access to public records of that agency on the same basis as any other person. Nothing in this section shall limit the ability of elected members or officers to access public records permitted by law in the administration of their duties.

(b) This section does not constitute a change in, but is declaratory of, existing law.

(Added by Stats. 2021, Ch. 614, Sec. 2. (AB 473) Effective January 1, 2022. Operative January 1, 2023, pursuant to Sec. 7931.000.)

7921.310

Notwithstanding Section 7921.305 or any other provision of law, when the members of a legislative body of a local agency are authorized to access a writing of the body or of the agency as permitted by law in the administration of their duties, the local agency, as defined in Section 54951, shall not discriminate between or among any of those members as to which writing or portion thereof is made available or when it is made available.

(Added by Stats. 2021, Ch. 614, Sec. 2. (AB 473) Effective January 1, 2022. Operative January 1, 2023, pursuant to Sec. 7931.000.)

ARTICLE 2. VOLUNTARY DISCLOSURE

7921.500

Unless disclosure is otherwise prohibited by law, the provisions listed in Section 7920.505 do not prevent any agency from opening its records concerning the administration of the agency to public inspection.

(Added by Stats. 2021, Ch. 614, Sec. 2. (AB 473) Effective January 1, 2022. Operative January 1, 2023, pursuant to Sec. 7931.000.)

7921.505

(a) As used in this section, "agency" includes a member, agent, officer, or employee of the agency acting within the scope of that membership, agency, office, or employment.

(b) Notwithstanding any other law, if a state or local agency discloses to a member of the public a public record that is otherwise exempt from this division, this disclosure constitutes a waiver of the exemptions specified in:

(1) The provisions listed in Section 7920.505.

(2) Sections 7924.510 and 7924.700.

(3) Other similar provisions of law.

(c) This section, however, does not apply to any of the following disclosures:

(1) A disclosure made pursuant to the Information Practices Act of 1977 (Chapter 1 (commencing with Section 1798) of Title 1.8 of Part 4 of Division 3

of the Civil Code) or a discovery proceeding.

(2) A disclosure made through other legal proceedings or as otherwise required by law.

(3) A disclosure within the scope of disclosure of a statute that limits disclosure of specified writings to certain purposes.

(4) A disclosure not required by law, and prohibited by formal action of an elected legislative body of the local agency that retains the writing.

(5) A disclosure made to a governmental agency that agrees to treat the disclosed material as confidential. Only persons authorized in writing by the person in charge of the agency shall be permitted to obtain the information. Any information obtained by the agency shall only be used for purposes that are consistent with existing law.

(6) A disclosure of records relating to a financial institution or an affiliate thereof, if the disclosure is made to the financial institution or affiliate by a state agency responsible for regulation or supervision of the financial institution or affiliate.

(7) A disclosure of records relating to a person who is subject to the jurisdiction of the Department of Business Oversight, if the disclosure is made to the person who is the subject of the records for the purpose of corrective action by that person, or, if a corporation, to an officer, director, or other key personnel of the corporation for the purpose of corrective action, or to any other person to the extent necessary to obtain information from that person for the purpose of an investigation by the Department of Business Oversight.

(8) A disclosure made by the Commissioner of Business Oversight under Section 450, 452, 8009, or 18396 of the Financial Code.

(9) A disclosure of records relating to a person who is subject to the jurisdiction of the Department of Managed Health Care, if the disclosure is made to the person who is the subject of the records for the purpose of corrective action by that person, or, if a corporation, to an officer, director, or other key personnel of the corporation for the purpose of corrective action, or to any other person to the extent necessary to obtain information from that person for the purpose of an investigation by the Department of Managed Health Care.

(10) A disclosure made through the sharing of information between the Independent System Operator and a state agency.

(Amended by Stats. 2022, Ch. 361, Sec. 2. (SB 1020) Effective January 1, 2023. Operative January 1, 2023, pursuant to Sec. 7931.000.)

ARTICLE 3. DISCLOSURE TO DISTRICT ATTORNEY AND RELATED MATTERS

7921.700

A state or local agency shall allow an inspection or copying of any public record or class of public records not exempted by this division when requested by a district attorney.

(Added by Stats. 2021, Ch. 614, Sec. 2. (AB 473) Effective January 1, 2022. Operative January 1, 2023, pursuant to Sec. 7931.000.)

7921.705

(a) If a district attorney makes a request to a state or local agency to inspect or receive a copy of a public record or class of public records not exempted by this division, and the state or local agency fails or refuses to allow inspection or copying within 10 working days of that request, the district attorney may petition a court of competent jurisdiction to require the state or local agency to allow the requested inspection or copying.

(b) Unless the public interest or good cause in withholding the requested records clearly outweighs the public interest in disclosure, the court may require the public agency to allow the district attorney to inspect or copy those records.

(Added by Stats. 2021, Ch. 614, Sec. 2. (AB 473) Effective January 1, 2022. Operative January 1, 2023, pursuant to Sec. 7931.000.)

7921.710

Disclosure of records to a district attorney under the provisions of this division shall effect no change in the status of the records under any other provision of law.

(Added by Stats. 2021, Ch. 614, Sec. 2. (AB 473) Effective January 1, 2022. Operative January 1, 2023, pursuant to Sec. 7931.000.)

CHAPTER 3. GENERAL RULES GOVERNING EXEMPTIONS FROM DISCLOSURE

ARTICLE 1. JUSTIFICATION FOR WITHHOLDING OF RECORD

7922.000

An agency shall justify withholding any record by demonstrating that the record in question is exempt under express provisions of this division, or that on the facts of the particular case the public interest served by not disclosing the record clearly outweighs the public interest served by disclosure of the record.

(Added by Stats. 2021, Ch. 614, Sec. 2. (AB 473) Effective January 1, 2022. Operative January 1, 2023, pursuant to Sec. 7931.000.)

ARTICLE 2. SOCIAL SECURITY NUMBERS AND RELATED MATTERS

7922.200

(a) It is the intent of the Legislature that, in order to protect against the risk of identity theft, a local agency shall redact social security numbers from a record before disclosing the record to the public pursuant to this division.

(b) Nothing in this division shall be construed to require a local agency to disclose a social security number.

(c) This section does not apply to a record maintained by a county recorder.

(Added by Stats. 2021, Ch. 614, Sec. 2. (AB 473) Effective January 1, 2022. Operative January 1, 2023, pursuant to Sec. 7931.000.)

7922.205

Nothing in this division shall be construed to require the disclosure by a county recorder of any "official record," if a "public record" version of that record is available pursuant to Article 3.5 (commencing with Section 27300) of Chapter 6 of Part 3 of Division 2 of Title 3.

(Added by Stats. 2021, Ch. 614, Sec. 2. (AB 473) Effective January 1, 2022. Operative January 1, 2023, pursuant to Sec. 7931.000.)

7922.210

Nothing in this division shall be construed to require the disclosure by a filing office of any "official filing," if a "public filing" version of that record is available pursuant to Section 9526.5 of the Commercial Code.

(Added by Stats. 2021, Ch. 614, Sec. 2. (AB 473) Effective January 1, 2022. Operative January 1, 2023, pursuant to Sec. 7931.000.)

PART 3. PROCEDURES AND RELATED MATTERS

CHAPTER 1. REQUEST FOR A PUBLIC RECORD

ARTICLE 1. GENERAL PRINCIPLES

7922.500

Nothing in this division shall be construed to permit an agency to delay or obstruct the inspection or copying of public records.

(Added by Stats. 2021, Ch. 614, Sec. 2. (AB 473) Effective January 1, 2022. Operative January 1, 2023, pursuant to Sec. 7931.000.)

7922.505

Except as otherwise prohibited by law, a state or local agency may adopt requirements for itself that allow for faster, more efficient, or greater access to records than prescribed by the minimum standards set forth in this division.

(Added by Stats. 2021, Ch. 614, Sec. 2. (AB 473) Effective January 1, 2022. Operative January 1, 2023, pursuant to Sec. 7931.000.)

ARTICLE 2. PROCEDURAL REQUIREMENTS GENERALLY

7922.525

(a) Public records are open to inspection at all times during the office hours of a state or local agency and every person has a right to inspect any public record, exempted as otherwise provided.

(b) Any reasonably segregable portion of a record shall be available for inspection by any person requesting the record after deletion of the portions that are exempted by law.

(Added by Stats. 2021, Ch. 614, Sec. 2. (AB 473) Effective January 1, 2022. Operative January 1, 2023, pursuant to Sec. 7931.000.)

7922.530

(a) Except with respect to public records exempt from disclosure by express provisions of law, each state or local agency, upon a request for a copy of records that reasonably describes an identifiable record or records, shall make the records promptly available to any person upon payment of fees covering direct costs of duplication, or a statutory fee if applicable. Upon request, an exact copy shall be provided unless impracticable to do so.

(b) A requester who inspects a disclosable record on the premises of the agency has the right to use the requester's equipment on those premises, without being charged any fees or costs, to photograph or otherwise copy or reproduce the record in a manner that does not require the equipment to make physical contact with the record, unless the means of copy or reproduction would result in either of the following:

(1) Damage to the record.

(2) Unauthorized access to the agency's computer systems or secured networks by using software, equipment, or any other technology capable of accessing, altering, or compromising the agency's electronic records.

(c) The agency may impose any reasonable limits on the use of the requester's equipment that are necessary to protect the safety of the records or to prevent the copying of records from being an unreasonable burden to the orderly function of the agency and its employees. In addition, the agency may impose any limit that is necessary to maintain the integrity of, or ensure the long-term preservation of, historic or high-value records.

(Added by Stats. 2021, Ch. 614, Sec. 2. (AB 473) Effective January 1, 2022. Operative January 1, 2023, pursuant to Sec. 7931.000.)

7922.535

(a) Each agency, upon a request for a copy of records, shall, within 10 days from receipt of the request, determine whether the request, in whole or in part, seeks copies of disclosable public records in the possession of the agency and shall promptly notify the person making the request of the determination and the reasons therefor. If the agency determines that the request seeks disclosable public records, the agency shall also state the estimated date and time when the records will be made available.

(b) In unusual circumstances, the time limit prescribed in this article and Article 1 (commencing with Section 7922.500) may be extended by written notice from the head of the agency or a designee to the person making the request, setting forth the reasons for the extension and the date on which a determination is expected to be dispatched. No notice shall specify a date that would result in an extension for more than 14 days.

(c) As used in this section, "unusual circumstances" means the following, but only to the extent reasonably necessary to the proper processing of the particular request:

(1) The need to search for and collect the requested records from field facilities or other establishments that are separate from the office processing the request.

(2) The need to search for, collect, and appropriately examine a voluminous amount of separate and distinct records that are demanded in a single request.

(3) The need for consultation, which shall be conducted with all practicable speed, with another agency having substantial interest in the determination of the request or among two or more components of the agency having substantial subject matter interest therein.

(4) The need to compile data, to write programming language or a computer program, or to construct a computer report to extract data.

(Added by Stats. 2021, Ch. 614, Sec. 2. (AB 473) Effective January 1, 2022. Operative January 1, 2023, pursuant to Sec. 7931.000.)

7922.540

(a) A response to a written request for inspection or copies of public records that includes a determination that the request is denied, in whole or in part, shall be in writing.

(b) The notification of denial shall set forth the names and titles or positions of each person responsible for the denial.

(c) An agency shall justify withholding any record by complying with Section 7922.000.

(Added by Stats. 2021, Ch. 614, Sec. 2. (AB 473) Effective January 1, 2022. Operative January 1, 2023, pursuant to Sec. 7931.000.)

7922.545

(a) In addition to maintaining public records for public inspection during its office hours, a public agency may comply with Section 7922.525 by posting any public record on its internet website and, in response to a request for a public record posted on the internet website, directing a member of the public to the location on the internet website where the public record is posted.

(b) However, if after the public agency directs a member of the public to the internet website, the member of the public requesting the public record requests a copy of the public record due to an inability to access or reproduce the public record from the internet website, the public agency shall promptly provide a copy of the public record pursuant to subdivision (a) of Section 7922.530.

(Added by Stats. 2021, Ch. 614, Sec. 2. (AB 473) Effective January 1, 2022. Operative January 1, 2023, pursuant to Sec. 7931.000.)

ARTICLE 3. INFORMATION IN ELECTRONIC FORMAT

7922.570

(a) Unless otherwise prohibited by law, any agency that has information that constitutes an identifiable public record not exempt from disclosure pursuant to this division that is in an electronic format shall make that information available in an electronic format when requested by any person.

(b) When applicable, the agency shall do the following:

(1) The agency shall make the information available in any electronic format in which it holds the information.

(2) The agency shall provide a copy of an electronic record in the format requested if the requested format is one that the agency has used to create copies for its own use or for provision to other agencies.

(c) If a request is for information in other than electronic format, and the information also is in electronic format, an agency may inform the requester that the information is available in electronic format.

(Added by Stats. 2021, Ch. 614, Sec. 2. (AB 473) Effective January 1, 2022. Operative January 1, 2023, pursuant to Sec. 7931.000.)

7922.575

(a) The cost of duplication of an electronic record pursuant to paragraph (2) of subdivision (b) of Section 7922.570 shall be limited to the direct cost of producing a copy of a record in an electronic format.

(b) Notwithstanding subdivision (a), the requester shall bear the cost of producing a copy of the record, including the cost to construct a record, and the cost of programming and computer services necessary to produce a copy of the record when either of the following applies:

(1) In order to comply with subdivisions (a) and (b) of Section 7922.570, the public agency would be required to produce a copy of an electronic record and the record is one that is produced only at otherwise regularly scheduled intervals.

(2) The request would require data compilation, extraction, or programming to produce the record.

(Added by Stats. 2021, Ch. 614, Sec. 2. (AB 473) Effective January 1, 2022. Operative January 1, 2023, pursuant to Sec. 7931.000.)

7922.580

(a) Nothing in Section 7922.570 or 7922.575 shall be construed to require a public agency to reconstruct a record in an electronic format if the agency no longer has the record available in an electronic format.

(b) Nothing in Section 7922.570 or 7922.575 shall be construed to permit an agency to make information available only in an electronic format.

(c) Nothing in Section 7922.570 or 7922.575 shall be construed to require a public agency to release an electronic record in the electronic form in which it is held by the agency if its release would jeopardize or compromise the security or integrity of the original record or of any proprietary software in which it is maintained.

(d) Nothing in Section 7922.570 or 7922.575 shall be construed to permit public access to records held by any agency to which access is otherwise restricted by statute.

(Added by Stats. 2021, Ch. 614, Sec. 2. (AB 473) Effective January 1, 2022. Operative January 1, 2023, pursuant to Sec. 7931.000.)

7922.585

(a) As used in this section, "computer software" includes computer mapping systems, computer programs, and computer graphics systems.

(b) Computer software developed by a state or local agency is not itself a public record under this division. The agency may sell, lease, or license the software for commercial or noncommercial use.

(c) This section shall not be construed to create an implied warranty on the part of the State of California or any local agency for errors, omissions, or other defects in any computer software as provided pursuant to this section.

(d) Nothing in this section is intended to affect the public record status of information merely because it is stored in a computer. Public records stored in a computer shall be disclosed as required by this division.

(e) Nothing in this section is intended to limit any copyright protections.

(Added by Stats. 2021, Ch. 614, Sec. 2. (AB 473) Effective January 1, 2022. Operative January 1, 2023, pursuant to Sec. 7931.000.)

ARTICLE 4. DUTY TO ASSIST IN FORMULATING REQUEST

7922.600

(a) When a member of the public requests to inspect a public record or obtain a copy of a public record, the public agency, in order to assist the member of the public make a focused and effective request that reasonably describes an identifiable record or records, shall do all of the following, to the extent reasonable under the circumstances:

(1) Assist the member of the public to identify records and information that are responsive to the request or to the purpose of the request, if stated.

(2) Describe the information technology and physical location in which the records exist.

(3) Provide suggestions for overcoming any practical basis for denying access to the records or information sought.

(b) The requirements of paragraph (1) of subdivision (a) shall be deemed to have been satisfied if the public agency is unable to identify the requested information after making a reasonable effort to elicit additional clarifying information from the requester that will help identify the record or records.

(c) The requirements of subdivision (a) are in addition to any action required of a public agency by Article 1 (commencing with Section 7922.500) or Article 2 (commencing with Section 7922.525).

(Added by Stats. 2021, Ch. 614, Sec. 2. (AB 473) Effective January 1, 2022. Operative January 1, 2023, pursuant to Sec. 7931.000.)

7922.605

This article shall not apply to a request for public records if any of the following applies:

(a) The public agency makes the requested records available pursuant to Article 1 (commencing with Section 7922.500) and Article 2 (commencing with Section 7922.525).

(b) The public agency makes an index of its records available.

(c) The public agency determines that the request should be denied and bases that determination solely on an exemption listed in Section 7920.505.

(Added by Stats. 2021, Ch. 614, Sec. 2. (AB 473) Effective January 1, 2022. Operative January 1, 2023, pursuant to Sec. 7931.000.)

CHAPTER 2. AGENCY REGULATIONS, GUIDELINES, SYSTEMS, AND SIMILAR MATTERS

ARTICLE 1. AGENCY REGULATIONS AND GUIDELINES

7922.630

Every agency may adopt regulations in accordance with this article stating the procedures to be followed when making its records available.

(Added by Stats. 2021, Ch. 614, Sec. 2. (AB 473) Effective January 1, 2022. Operative January 1, 2023, pursuant to Sec. 7931.000.)

7922.635

(a) The following state and local bodies shall establish written guidelines for accessibility of records:

(1) All regional water quality control boards.

(2) Bay Area Air Pollution Control District.

(3) California Coastal Commission.

(4) Department of Financial Protection and Innovation.

(5) Department of Consumer Affairs.

(6) Department of Corrections and Rehabilitation.

(7) Department of General Services.

(8) Department of Industrial Relations.

(9) Department of Insurance.

(10) Department of Justice.

(11) Department of Managed Health Care.

(12) Department of Motor Vehicles.

(13) Department of Parks and Recreation.

(14) Department of Real Estate.

(15) Department of Toxic Substances Control.

(16) Department of Veterans Affairs.

(17) Department of Water Resources.

(18) Division of Juvenile Justice.

(19) Employment Development Department.

(20) Golden Gate Bridge, Highway and Transportation District.

(21) Los Angeles County Air Pollution Control District.

(22) Office of Environmental Health Hazard Assessment.

(23) Public Employees' Retirement System.

(24) Public Utilities Commission.

(25) San Francisco Bay Area Rapid Transit District.

(26) San Francisco Bay Conservation and Development Commission.

(27) Secretary of State.

(28) State Air Resources Board.

(29) State Board of Equalization.

(30) State Department of Developmental Services.

(31) State Department of Health Care Services.

(32) State Department of Public Health.

(33) State Department of Social Services.

(34) State Department of State Hospitals.

(35) State Water Resources Control Board.

(36) Teachers' Retirement Board.

(37) Transportation Agency.

(b) A copy of these guidelines shall be posted in a conspicuous public place at the offices of these bodies, and a copy of the guidelines shall be available upon request, free of charge, to any person requesting that body's records.

(Amended by Stats. 2022, Ch. 452, Sec. 178. (SB 1498) Effective January 1, 2023. Operative January 1, 2023, pursuant to Sec. 7931.000.)

7922.640

(a) Guidelines and regulations adopted pursuant to this article shall be consistent with all other sections of this division and shall reflect the intention of the Legislature to make the records accessible to the public.

(b) Guidelines and regulations adopted pursuant to this article shall not operate to limit the hours public records are open for inspection as prescribed in Article 1 (commencing with Section 7922.500) and Article 2 (commencing with Section 7922.525).

(Added by Stats. 2021, Ch. 614, Sec. 2. (AB 473) Effective January 1, 2022. Operative January 1, 2023, pursuant to Sec. 7931.000.)

ARTICLE 2. INTERNET RESOURCES

7922.680

If a local agency, except a school district, maintains an internet resource, including, but not limited to, an internet website, internet web page, or internet web portal, which the local agency describes or titles as "open data," and the local agency voluntarily posts a public record on that internet resource, the local agency shall post the public record in an open format that meets all of the following requirements:

(a) Retrievable, downloadable, indexable, and electronically searchable by commonly used internet search applications.

(b) Platform independent and machine readable.

(c) Available to the public free of charge and without any restriction that would impede the reuse or redistribution of the public record.

(d) Retains the data definitions and structure present when the data was compiled, if applicable.

(Added by Stats. 2021, Ch. 614, Sec. 2. (AB 473) Effective January 1, 2022. Operative January 1, 2023, pursuant to Sec. 7931.000.)

ARTICLE 3. CATALOG OF ENTERPRISE SYSTEMS

7922.700

For purposes of this article:

(a) "Enterprise system" means a software application or computer system that satisfies all of the following conditions:

(1) It collects, stores, exchanges, and analyzes information that the agency uses.

(2) It is a multidepartmental system or a system that contains information collected about the public.

(3) It is a system of record.

(b) An "enterprise system" does not include any of the following:

(1) Information technology security systems, including firewalls and other cybersecurity systems.

(2) Physical access control systems, employee identification management systems, video monitoring, and other physical control systems.

(3) Infrastructure and mechanical control systems, including those that control or manage street lights, electrical, natural gas, or water or sewer functions.

(4) Systems related to 911 dispatch and operation or emergency services.

(5) Systems that would be restricted from disclosure pursuant to Section 7929.210.

(6) The specific records that the information technology system collects, stores, exchanges, or analyzes.

(Added by Stats. 2021, Ch. 614, Sec. 2. (AB 473) Effective January 1, 2022. Operative January 1, 2023, pursuant to Sec. 7931.000.)

7922.705

For purposes of this article, "system of record" means a system that serves as an original source of data within an agency.

(Added by Stats. 2021, Ch. 614, Sec. 2. (AB 473) Effective January 1, 2022. Operative January 1, 2023, pursuant to Sec. 7931.000.)

7922.710

(a) In implementing this division, each local agency, except a local educational agency, shall create a catalog of enterprise systems.

(b) The local agency shall complete and post the catalog as required by this article by July 1, 2016, and thereafter shall update the catalog annually.

(Added by Stats. 2021, Ch. 614, Sec. 2. (AB 473) Effective January 1, 2022. Operative January 1, 2023, pursuant to Sec. 7931.000.)

7922.715

(a) The catalog of enterprise systems required by Section 7922.710 shall be made publicly available upon request in the office of the person or officer designated by the agency's legislative body.

(b) If the agency has an internet website, the catalog shall be posted in a prominent location on the agency's internet website.

(Added by Stats. 2021, Ch. 614, Sec. 2. (AB 473) Effective January 1, 2022. Operative January 1, 2023, pursuant to Sec. 7931.000.)

7922.720

(a) The catalog of enterprise systems required by Section 7922.710 shall disclose a list of the enterprise systems utilized by the agency.

(b) For each system, the catalog shall also disclose all of the following:

(1) Current system vendor.

(2) Current system product.

(3) A brief statement of the system's purpose.

(4) A general description of categories or types of data.

(5) The department that serves as the system's primary custodian.

(6) How frequently system data is collected.

(7) How frequently system data is updated.

(c) If, on the facts of the particular case, the public interest served by not disclosing the information described in paragraph (1) or (2) of subdivision (b) clearly outweighs the public interest served by disclosure of the record, the local agency may instead provide a system name, brief title, or identifier of the system.

(Added by Stats. 2021, Ch. 614, Sec. 2. (AB 473) Effective January 1, 2022. Operative January 1, 2023, pursuant to Sec. 7931.000.)

7922.725

(a) This article shall not be interpreted to limit a person's right to inspect public records pursuant to this division.

(b) Nothing in this article shall be construed to permit public access to records held by an agency to which access is otherwise restricted by statute or to alter the process for requesting a public record, as set forth in this division.

(Added by Stats. 2021, Ch. 614, Sec. 2. (AB 473) Effective January 1, 2022. Operative January 1, 2023, pursuant to Sec. 7931.000.)

PART 4. ENFORCEMENT

CHAPTER 1. GENERAL PRINCIPLES

7923.000

Any person may institute a proceeding for injunctive or declarative relief, or for a writ of mandate, in any court of competent jurisdiction, to enforce that person's right under this division to inspect or receive a copy of any public record or class of public records.

(Added by Stats. 2021, Ch. 614, Sec. 2. (AB 473) Effective January 1, 2022. Operative January 1, 2023, pursuant to Sec. 7931.000.)

7923.005

In a proceeding under Section 7923.000, the court shall set the times for hearings and responsive pleadings with the object of securing a decision as to the matters at issue at the earliest possible time.

(Added by Stats. 2021, Ch. 614, Sec. 2. (AB 473) Effective January 1, 2022. Operative January 1, 2023, pursuant to Sec. 7931.000.)

CHAPTER 2. ENFORCEMENT PROCEDURE

ARTICLE 1. PETITION TO SUPERIOR COURT

7923.100

Whenever it is made to appear, by verified petition to the superior court of the county where the records or some part thereof are situated, that certain public records are being improperly withheld from a member of the public, the court shall order the officer or other person charged with withholding the records to disclose those records or show cause why that person should not do so.

(Added by Stats. 2021, Ch. 614, Sec. 2. (AB 473) Effective January 1, 2022. Operative January 1, 2023, pursuant to Sec. 7931.000.)

7923.105

The court shall decide the case after the court does all of the following:

(a) Examine the record in camera, if permitted by subdivision (b) of Section 915 of the Evidence Code.

(b) Examine any papers filed by the parties.

(c) Consider any oral argument and additional evidence as the court may allow.

(Added by Stats. 2021, Ch. 614, Sec. 2. (AB 473) Effective January 1, 2022. Operative January 1, 2023, pursuant to Sec. 7931.000.)

7923.110

(a) If the court finds that the public official's decision to refuse disclosure is not justified under Section 7922.000 or any provision listed in Section 7920.505, the court shall order the public official to make the record public.

(b) If the court finds that the public official was justified in refusing to make the record public, the court shall return the record to the public official without disclosing its content, together with an order supporting the decision refusing disclosure.

(Added by Stats. 2021, Ch. 614, Sec. 2. (AB 473) Effective January 1, 2022. Operative January 1, 2023, pursuant to Sec. 7931.000.)

7923.115

(a) If the requester prevails in litigation filed pursuant to this chapter, the court shall award court costs and reasonable attorney's fees to the requester. The costs and fees shall be paid by the public agency and shall not become a personal liability of the public official involved.

(b) If the court finds that a requester's case pursuant to this chapter is clearly frivolous, the court shall award court costs and reasonable attorney's fees to the public agency.

(c) This article does not limit a requester's right to obtain fees and costs pursuant to this section or any other law.

(Added by Stats. 2021, Ch. 614, Sec. 2. (AB 473) Effective January 1, 2022. Operative January 1, 2023, pursuant to Sec. 7931.000.)

ARTICLE 2. WRIT REVIEW AND CONTEMPT

7923.500

(a) An order of the court, either directing disclosure by a public official or supporting the decision of the public official refusing disclosure, is not a final judgment or order within the meaning of Section 904.1 of the Code of Civil Procedure from which an appeal may be taken, but shall be immediately reviewable by petition to the appellate court for the issuance of an extraordinary writ.

(b) Upon entry of any order pursuant to this chapter, a party shall, in order to obtain review of the order, file a petition within 20 days after service upon the party of a written notice of entry of the order, or within a further time, not exceeding an additional 20 days, as the trial court may for good cause allow.

(c) If the notice is served by mail, the period within which to file the petition shall be increased by five days.

(d) A stay of an order or judgment shall not be granted unless the petitioning party demonstrates that the party will otherwise sustain irreparable damage and probable success on the merits.

(e) Any person who fails to obey the order of the court shall be cited to show cause why that person is not in contempt of court.

(Added by Stats. 2021, Ch. 614, Sec. 2. (AB 473) Effective January 1, 2022. Operative January 1, 2023, pursuant to Sec. 7931.000.)

PART 5. SPECIFIC TYPES OF PUBLIC RECORDS

CHAPTER 5. HEALTH CARE

ARTICLE 1. ACCREDITATION

7926.000

Except as provided in Sections 7924.510, 7924.700, and 7929.610, this division does not require the disclosure of a final accreditation report of the Joint Commission on Accreditation of Hospitals that has been transmitted to the State Department of Public Health pursuant to subdivision (b) of Section 1282 of the Health and Safety Code.

(Added by Stats. 2021, Ch. 614, Sec. 2. (AB 473) Effective January 1, 2022. Operative January 1, 2023, pursuant to Sec. 7931.000.)

ARTICLE 2. ADVANCE HEALTH CARE DIRECTIVE AND RELATED MATTERS

7926.100

(a) Except as provided in subdivision (b) and in Sections 7924.510, 7924.700, and 7929.610, this division does not require the disclosure of any information that a person provides to the Secretary of State for the purpose of registration in the Advance Health Care Directive Registry.

(b) The information described in subdivision (a) shall be released at the request of a health care provider, a public guardian, or the registrant's legal representative.

(Added by Stats. 2021, Ch. 614, Sec. 2. (AB 473) Effective January 1, 2022. Operative January 1, 2023, pursuant to Sec. 7931.000.)

ARTICLE 3. CONTRACTS AND NEGOTIATIONS

7926.200

The provisions listed in Section 7920.505 do not prevent any health facility from disclosing to a certified bargaining agent relevant financing information pursuant to Section 8 of the National Labor Relations Act (29 U.S.C. Sec. 158).

(Added by Stats. 2021, Ch. 614, Sec. 2. (AB 473) Effective January 1, 2022. Operative January 1, 2023, pursuant to Sec. 7931.000.)

7926.205

(a) Nothing in this division or any other provision of law requires disclosure of records of a health plan that is licensed pursuant to the Knox-Keene Health Care Service Plan Act of 1975 (Chapter 2.2 (commencing with Section 1340) of Division 2 of the Health and Safety Code) and that is governed by a county board of supervisors, whether paper records, records maintained in the management information system, or records in any other form, that relate to provider rate or payment determinations, allocation or distribution methodologies for provider payments, formulae or calculations for these payments, and contract negotiations with providers of health care for alternative rates for a period of three years after the contract is fully executed.

(b) Transmission of the records described in subdivision (a), or the information contained therein in an alternative form, to the board of supervisors is not a waiver of exemption from disclosure. The records and information once transmitted to the board of supervisors remain subject to the exemption described in subdivision (a).

(c) (1) This section does not prevent the Joint Legislative Audit Committee from accessing any records in the exercise of its powers pursuant to Article 1 (commencing with Section 10500) of Chapter 4 of Part 2 of Division 2 of Title 2.

(2) This section does not prevent the Department of Managed Health Care from accessing any records in the exercise of its powers pursuant to Article 1 (commencing with Section 1340) of Chapter 2.2 of Division 2 of the Health and Safety Code.

(Added by Stats. 2021, Ch. 614, Sec. 2. (AB 473) Effective January 1, 2022. Operative January 1, 2023, pursuant to Sec. 7931.000.)

7926.210

(a) Except as provided in subdivision (b) or in Sections 7924.510, 7924.700, and 7929.610, this division does not require disclosure of any records of a local hospital district, formed pursuant to Division 23 (commencing with Section 32000) of the Health and Safety Code, or a municipal hospital, formed pursuant to Article 7 (commencing with Section 37600) or Article 8 (commencing with Section 37650) of Chapter 5 of Part 2 of Division 3 of Title 4, that relate to a contract with an insurer or a nonprofit hospital service plan for inpatient or outpatient services for alternative rates pursuant to Section 10133 of the Insurance Code.

(b) A record described in subdivision (a) shall be open to inspection within one year after the contract is fully executed.

(Added by Stats. 2021, Ch. 614, Sec. 2. (AB 473) Effective January 1, 2022. Operative January 1, 2023, pursuant to Sec. 7931.000.)

7926.215

(a) Except as provided in Sections 7924.510, 7924.700, and the provisions listed in Section 7920.505, this division does not require disclosure of records of the Department of Corrections and Rehabilitation that relate to health care services contract negotiations, and that reveal the deliberative processes, discussions, communications, or any other portion of the negotiations, including, but not limited to, records related to those negotiations, such as meeting minutes, research, work product, theories, or strategy of the department, or its staff, or members of the California Medical Assistance Commission, or its staff, who act in consultation with, or on behalf of, the department.

(b) (1) Except for the portion that contains the rates of payment, a contract for health services entered into by the Department of Corrections and Rehabilitation or the California Medical Assistance Commission on or after July 1, 1993, shall be open to inspection one year after it is fully executed.

(2) If a contract for health services was entered into before July 1, 1993, and amended on or after July 1, 1993, the amendment, except for any portion containing rates of payment, shall be open to inspection one year after it is fully executed.

(c) Three years after a contract or amendment is open to inspection under this section, the portion of the contract or amendment containing the rates of payment shall be open to inspection.

(d) (1) Notwithstanding any other provision of law, including, but not limited to, Section 1060 of the Evidence Code, the entire contract or amendment shall be open to inspection by the California State Auditor's Office, the Joint Legislative Audit Committee, and the Legislative Analyst's Office.

(2) The California State Auditor's Office, the Joint Legislative Audit Committee, and the Legislative Analyst's Office shall maintain the confidentiality of each contract or amendment until

the contract or amendment is fully open to inspection by the public.

(e) It is the intent of the Legislature that the confidentiality of health care provider contracts, and of the contracting process as provided in this section, shall protect the competitive nature of the negotiation process, and shall not affect public access to other information relating to the delivery of health care services.

(Added by Stats. 2021, Ch. 614, Sec. 2. (AB 473) Effective January 1, 2022. Operative January 1, 2023, pursuant to Sec. 7931.000.)

7926.220

(a) Except as provided in Sections 7924.510, 7924.700, and 7929.610, this division does not require disclosure of records of a state agency related to activities governed by Article 2.6 (commencing with Section 14081), Article 2.8 (commencing with Section 14087.5), or Article 2.91 (commencing with Section 14089) of Chapter 7 of Part 3 of Division 9 of the Welfare and Institutions Code, that reveal the special negotiator's deliberative processes, discussions, communications, or any other portion of the negotiations with providers of health care services, impressions, opinions, recommendations, meeting minutes, research, work product, theories, or strategy, or that provide instruction, advice, or training to employees.

(b) (1) Except for the portion containing the rates of payment, a contract for inpatient services entered into pursuant to one of these articles, on or after April 1, 1984, shall be open to inspection one year after it is fully executed.

(2) If a contract for inpatient services was entered into before April 1, 1984, and amended on or after April 1, 1984, the amendment, except for any portion containing the rates of payment, shall be open to inspection one year after it is fully executed.

(3) If the California Medical Assistance Commission enters into a contract with a health care provider for other than inpatient hospital services, the contract shall be open to inspection one year after it is fully executed.

(c) Three years after a contract or amendment is open to inspection under this section, the portion of the contract or amendment containing the rates of payment shall be open to inspection.

(d) (1) Notwithstanding any other law, the entire contract or amendment shall be open to inspection by the California State Auditor's Office, the Joint Legislative Audit Committee, and the Legislative Analyst's Office.

(2) The California State Auditor's Office, the Joint Legislative Audit Committee, and the Legislative Analyst's Office shall maintain the confidentiality of each contract or amendment until the contract or amendment is fully open to inspection by the public.

(Added by Stats. 2021, Ch. 614, Sec. 2. (AB 473) Effective January 1, 2022. Operative January 1, 2023, pursuant to Sec. 7931.000.)

7926.225

(a) Except as provided in Sections 7924.510, 7924.700, and 7929.610, this division does not require disclosure of records of the Managed Risk Medical Insurance Board and the State Department of Health Care Services that relate to activities governed by former Part 6.3 (commencing with Section 12695), former Part 6.5 (commencing with Section 12700), former Part 6.6 (commencing with Section 12739.5), or former Part 6.7 (commencing with Section 12739.70) of Division 2 of the Insurance Code, or Chapter 2 (commencing with Section 15810) or Chapter 4 (commencing with Section 15870) of Part 3.3 of Division 9 of the Welfare and Institutions Code, and that reveal any of the following:

(1) The deliberative processes, discussions, communications, or any other portion of the negotiations with entities contracting or seeking to contract with the board or the department, entities with which the board or the department is considering a contract, or entities with which the board or department is considering or enters into any other arrangement under which the board or the department provides, receives, or arranges services or reimbursement.

(2) The impressions, opinions, recommendations, meeting minutes, research, work product, theories, or strategy of the board or its staff or the department or its staff, or records that provide instructions, advice, or training to their employees.

(b) (1) Except for the portion that contains the rates of payment, a contract entered into pursuant to former Part 6.3 (commencing with Section 12695), former Part 6.5 (commencing with Section 12700), former Part 6.6 (commencing with Section 12739.5), or former Part 6.7 (commencing with Section 12739.70) of Division 2 of the Insurance Code, or Chapter 2 (commencing with Section 15810) or Chapter 4 (commencing with Section 15870) of Part 3.3 of Division 9 of the Welfare and Institutions Code, on or after July 1, 1991, shall be open to inspection one year after its effective date.

(2) If a contract was entered into before July 1, 1991, and amended on or after July 1, 1991, the amendment, except for any portion containing the rates of payment, shall be open to inspection one year after the effective date of the amendment.

(c) Three years after a contract or amendment is open to inspection pursuant to this section, the portion of the contract or amendment containing the rates of payment shall be open to inspection.

(d) (1) Notwithstanding any other law, the entire contract or amendment to a contract shall be open to inspection by the California State Auditor's Office, the Joint Legislative Audit Committee, and the Legislative Analyst's Office.

(2) The California State Auditor's Office, the Joint Legislative Audit Committee, and the Legislative Analyst's Office shall maintain the confidentiality of each contract or amendment until the contract or amendment is open to inspection pursuant to subdivision (c).

(Added by Stats. 2021, Ch. 614, Sec. 2. (AB 473) Effective January 1, 2022. Operative January 1, 2023, pursuant to Sec. 7931.000.)

7926.230

(a) Except as provided in Sections 7924.510, 7924.700, and 7929.610, this division does not require disclosure of records of the Managed Risk Medical Insurance Board and the State Department of Health Care Services related to activities governed by Part 6.2 (commencing with Section 12693) or former Part 6.4 (commencing with Section 12699.50) of Division 2 of the Insurance Code or Sections 14005.26 and 14005.27 of, or Chapter 3 (commencing with Section 15850) of Part 3.3 of Division 9 of, the Welfare and Institutions Code, if the records reveal any of the following:

(1) The deliberative processes, discussions, communications, or any other portion of the negotiations with entities contracting or seeking to contract with the board or the department, entities with which the board or department is considering a contract, or entities with which the board or department is considering or enters into any other arrangement under which the board or department provides, receives, or arranges services or reimbursement.

(2) The impressions, opinions, recommendations, meeting minutes, research, work product, theories, or

strategy of the board or its staff, or the department or its staff, or records that provide instructions, advice, or training to employees.

(b) (1) Except for the portion that contains the rates of payment, a contract entered into pursuant to Part 6.2 (commencing with Section 12693) or former Part 6.4 (commencing with Section 12699.50) of Division 2 of the Insurance Code, on or after January 1, 1998, or Sections 14005.26 and 14005.27 of, or Chapter 3 (commencing with Section 15850) of Part 3.3 of Division 9 of, the Welfare and Institutions Code shall be open to inspection one year after its effective date.

(2) If a contract entered into pursuant to Part 6.2 (commencing with Section 12693) or former Part 6.4 (commencing with Section 12699.50) of Division 2 of the Insurance Code or Sections 14005.26 and 14005.27 of, or Chapter 3 (commencing with Section 15850) of Part 3.3 of Division 9 of, the Welfare and Institutions Code, is amended, the amendment shall be open to inspection one year after the effective date of the amendment.

(c) Three years after a contract or amendment is open to inspection pursuant to this section, the portion of the contract or amendment containing the rates of payment shall be open to inspection.

(d) (1) Notwithstanding any other law, the entire contract or amendments to a contract shall be open to inspection by the California State Auditor's Office, the Joint Legislative Audit Committee, and the Legislative Analyst's Office.

(2) The California State Auditor's Office, the Joint Legislative Audit Committee, and the Legislative Analyst's Office shall maintain the confidentiality of each contract or amendment until the contract or amendment is open to inspection pursuant to subdivision (b) or (c).

(e) The exemption from disclosure provided pursuant to this section for the contracts, deliberative processes, discussions, communications, negotiations, impressions, opinions, recommendations, meeting minutes, research, work product, theories, or strategy of the board or its staff, or the department or its staff, shall also apply to the contracts, deliberative processes, discussions, communications, negotiations, impressions, opinions, recommendations, meeting minutes, research, work product, theories, or strategy of applicants pursuant to former Part 6.4 (commencing with Section 12699.50) of Division 2 of the Insurance Code or Chapter 3 (commencing with Section 15850) of Part 3.3 of Division 9 of the Welfare and Institutions Code.

(Added by Stats. 2021, Ch. 614, Sec. 2. (AB 473) Effective January 1, 2022. Operative January 1, 2023, pursuant to Sec. 7931.000.)

7926.235

(a) Except as provided in Sections 7924.510, 7924.700, and 7929.610, this division does not require disclosure of records of the Managed Risk Medical Insurance Board that relate to activities governed by Chapter 8 (commencing with Section 10700) of Part 2 of Division 2 of the Insurance Code, and that reveal the deliberative processes, discussions, communications, or any other portion of the negotiations with health plans, or the impressions, opinions, recommendations, meeting minutes, research, work product, theories, or strategy of the board or its staff, or records that provide instructions, advice, or training to employees.

(b) Except for the portion that contains the rates of payment, a contract for health coverage entered into pursuant to Chapter 8 (commencing with Section 10700) of Part 2 of Division 2 of the Insurance Code, on or after January 1,

1993, shall be open to inspection one year after it has been fully executed.

(c) (1) Notwithstanding any other law, the entire contract or amendment to a contract shall be open to inspection by the Joint Legislative Audit Committee.

(2) The committee shall maintain the confidentiality of each contract or amendment until the contract or amendment is open to inspection pursuant to subdivision (b).

(Added by Stats. 2021, Ch. 614, Sec. 2. (AB 473) Effective January 1, 2022. Operative January 1, 2023, pursuant to Sec. 7931.000.)

ARTICLE 6. WEBSITES AND RELATED MATTERS

7926.500

In implementing this division, each health care district shall maintain an internet website in accordance with subdivision (b) of Section 32139 of the Health and Safety Code.

(Added by Stats. 2021, Ch. 614, Sec. 2. (AB 473) Effective January 1, 2022. Operative January 1, 2023, pursuant to Sec. 7931.000.)

CHAPTER 8. LITIGATION RECORDS AND SIMILAR MATTERS

7927.200

Except as provided in Sections 7924.510, 7924.700, and 7929.610, this division does not require disclosure of any of the following records:

(a) Records pertaining to pending litigation to which the public agency is a party, until the pending litigation has been finally adjudicated or otherwise settled.

(b) Records pertaining to a claim made pursuant to Division 3.6 (commencing with Section 810), until the pending claim has been finally adjudicated or otherwise settled.

(Added by Stats. 2021, Ch. 614, Sec. 2. (AB 473) Effective January 1, 2022. Operative January 1, 2023, pursuant to Sec. 7931.000.)

7927.205

Nothing in this division or any other provision of law requires disclosure of a memorandum submitted to a state body or to the legislative body of a local agency by its legal counsel pursuant to subdivision (e) of Section 11126 or Section 54956.9 until the pending litigation has been finally adjudicated or otherwise settled. The memorandum is protected by the attorney work-product privilege until the pending litigation has been finally adjudicated or otherwise settled.

(Added by Stats. 2021, Ch. 614, Sec. 2. (AB 473) Effective January 1, 2022. Operative January 1, 2023, pursuant to Sec. 7931.000.)

CHAPTER 10. PERSONAL INFORMATION AND CUSTOMER RECORDS

7927.400

Nothing in this division requires the disclosure of records that relate to electronically collected personal information, as defined by Section 11015.5, that is received, collected, or compiled by a state agency.

(Added by Stats. 2021, Ch. 614, Sec. 2. (AB 473) Effective January 1, 2022. Operative January 1, 2023, pursuant to Sec. 7931.000.)

7927.425

This division does not require the disclosure of the following records and information provided to the Controller's office:

(a) Records related to statements of personal worth or personal financial data, including, but not limited to, wills, trusts, account statements, earnings statements, or other similar records.

(b) Personal information, as defined by subdivision (a) of Section 1798.3 of the Civil Code, within records, including, but not limited to:

(1) Social security number.

(2) Date of birth.

(3) Federal employer identification number, until the Controller has made payment of the property in full to the owner.

(4) Account number, until the Controller has made payment of the property in full to the owner.

(5) Check number, until the Controller has made payment of the property in full to the owner.

(Added by Stats. 2022, Ch. 282, Sec. 7. (AB 2280) Effective January 1, 2023.)

CHAPTER 11. PRELIMINARY DRAFTS AND SIMILAR MATERIALS

7927.500

Except as provided in Sections 7924.510, 7924.700, and 7929.610, this division does not require disclosure of any preliminary drafts, notes, or interagency or intraagency memoranda that are not retained by a public agency in the ordinary course of business, if the public interest in withholding those records clearly outweighs the public interest in disclosure.

(Added by Stats. 2021, Ch. 614, Sec. 2. (AB 473) Effective January 1, 2022. Operative January 1, 2023, pursuant to Sec. 7931.000.)

CHAPTER 12. PRIVATE INDUSTRY

7927.600

Whenever a city and county or a joint powers agency, pursuant to a mandatory statute or charter provision to collect private industry wage data for salary setting purposes, or a contract entered to implement that mandate, is provided this data by the United States Bureau of Labor Statistics on the basis that the identity of private industry employers shall remain confidential, the identity of the employers shall not be open to the public or be admitted as evidence in any action or special proceeding.

(Added by Stats. 2021, Ch. 614, Sec. 2. (AB 473) Effective January 1, 2022. Operative January 1, 2023, pursuant to Sec. 7931.000.)

7927.605

(a) Nothing in this division requires the disclosure of records that are any of the following: corporate financial records, corporate proprietary information including trade secrets, and information relating to siting within the state furnished to a government agency by a private company for the purpose of permitting the agency to work with the company in retaining, locating, or expanding a facility within California.

(b) Except as provided in subdivision (c), incentives offered by a state or a local government agency, if any, shall be disclosed upon communication to the agency or the public of a decision to stay, locate, relocate, or expand, by a company, or upon application by that company to a governmental agency for a general plan amendment, rezone, use permit, building permit, or any other permit, whichever occurs first.

(c) Before publicly disclosing a record that describes state or local incentives offered by an agency to a private business to retain, locate, relocate, or expand the business within California, the agency shall delete information that is exempt pursuant to this section.

(Added by Stats. 2021, Ch. 614, Sec. 2. (AB 473) Effective January 1, 2022. Operative January 1, 2023, pursuant to Sec. 7931.000.)

CHAPTER 13. PRIVATE RECORDS, PRIVILEGED MATERIALS, AND OTHER RECORDS PROTECTED BY LAW FROM DISCLOSURE

7927.700

Except as provided in Sections 7924.510, 7924.700, and 7929.610, this division does not require disclosure of personnel, medical, or similar files, the disclosure of which would constitute an unwarranted invasion of personal privacy.

(Added by Stats. 2021, Ch. 614, Sec. 2. (AB 473) Effective January 1, 2022. Operative January 1, 2023, pursuant to Sec. 7931.000.)

7927.705

Except as provided in Sections 7924.510, 7924.700, and 7929.610, this division does not require disclosure of records, the disclosure of which is exempted or prohibited pursuant to federal or state law, including, but not limited to, provisions of the Evidence Code relating to privilege.

(Added by Stats. 2021, Ch. 614, Sec. 2. (AB 473) Effective January 1, 2022. Operative January 1, 2023, pursuant to Sec. 7931.000.)

PART 6. OTHER EXEMPTIONS FROM DISCLOSURE

CHAPTER 1. INTRODUCTORY PROVISIONS

7930.000

(a) It is the intent of the Legislature to assist members of the public and state and local agencies in identifying exemptions to the California Public Records Act. It is the intent of the Legislature that, after January 1, 1999, each addition or amendment to a statute that exempts any information contained in a public record from disclosure pursuant to Section 7927.705 shall be listed and described in Chapter 2 (commencing with Section 7930.100) pursuant to a bill authorized by a standing committee of the Legislature to be introduced during the first year of each session of the Legislature.

(b) The statutes and constitutional provisions listed in Chapter 2 (commencing with Section 7930.100) may operate to exempt certain records, or portions thereof, from disclosure. The statutes and constitutional provisions listed and described may not be inclusive of all exemptions. The listing of a statute or constitutional provision in Chapter 2 (commencing with Section 7930.100) does not itself create an exemption. Requesters of public records and public agencies are cautioned to review the applicable statute or constitutional provision to determine the extent to which it, in light of the circumstances surrounding the request, exempts public records from disclosure.

(Added by Stats. 2021, Ch. 614, Sec. 2. (AB 473) Effective January 1, 2022. Operative January 1, 2023, pursuant to Sec. 7931.000.)

7930.005

Records or information not required to be disclosed pursuant to Section 7927.705 may include, but shall not be limited to, records or information identified in statutes listed in Chapter 2 (commencing with Section 7930.100).

(Added by Stats. 2021, Ch. 614, Sec. 2. (AB 473) Effective January 1, 2022. Operative January 1, 2023, pursuant to Sec. 7931.000.)

CHAPTER 2. ALPHABETICAL LIST

7930.100

The following constitutional provisions may operate to exempt certain records, or portions thereof, from disclosure pursuant to this division:

Crime victims, confidential information or records, The Victims' Bill of Rights Act of 2008: Marsy's Law, Section 28 of Article I of the California Constitution.

Privacy, inalienable right, Section 1 of Article I of the California Constitution.

(Added by Stats. 2021, Ch. 614, Sec. 2. (AB 473) Effective January 1, 2022. Operative January 1, 2023, pursuant to Sec. 7931.000.)

7930.105

The following provisions may operate to exempt certain records, or portions thereof, from disclosure pursuant to this division:

Acquired immunodeficiency syndrome, blood test results, written authorization not necessary for disclosure, Section 121010, Health and Safety Code.

Acquired immunodeficiency syndrome, blood test subject, compelling identity of, Section 120975, Health and Safety Code.

Acquired immunodeficiency syndrome, confidentiality of personal data of patients in State Department of Public Health programs, Section 120820, Health and Safety Code.

Acquired immunodeficiency syndrome, confidentiality of research records, Sections 121090, 121095, 121115, and 121120, Health and Safety Code.

Acquired immunodeficiency syndrome, confidentiality of vaccine volunteers, Section 121280, Health and Safety Code.

Acquired immunodeficiency syndrome, confidentiality of information obtained in prevention programs at correctional facilities and law enforcement agencies, Sections 7552 and 7554, Penal Code.

Acquired immunodeficiency syndrome, disclosure of results of HIV test, penalties, Section 120980, Health and Safety Code.

Acquired immunodeficiency syndrome, personal information, insurers tests, confidentiality of, Section 799, Insurance Code.

Acquired immunodeficiency syndrome, public safety and testing disclosure, Sections 121065 and 121070, Health and Safety Code.

Acquired Immune Deficiency Syndrome Research and Confidentiality Act, production or discovery of records for use in criminal or civil proceedings against subject prohibited, Section 121100, Health and Safety Code.

Acquired Immune Deficiency Syndrome Public Health Records Confidentiality Act, personally identifying information confidentiality, Section 121025, Health and Safety Code.

Acquired immunodeficiency syndrome, test of criminal defendant pursuant to search warrant requested by victim, confidentiality of, Section 1524.1, Penal Code.

Acquired immunodeficiency syndrome, test results, disclosure to patient's spouse and others, Section 121015, Health and Safety Code.

Acquired immunodeficiency syndrome, test of person under Youth Authority, disclosure of results, Section 1768.9, Welfare and Institutions Code.

Acquired Immune Deficiency Syndrome Research and Confidentiality Act, financial audits or program evaluations, Section 121085, Health and Safety Code.

Acquired Immune Deficiency Syndrome Research and Confidentiality Act, violations, Section 121100, Health and Safety Code.

Acquired Immune Deficiency Syndrome Research and Confidentiality Act, personally identifying research records not to be disclosed, Section 121075, Health and Safety Code.

Acquired Immune Deficiency Syndrome Research and Confidentiality Act, permittee disclosure, Section 121080, Health and Safety Code.

Administrative procedure, adjudicatory hearings, interpreters, Section 11513, this code.

Adoption records, confidentiality of, Section 102730, Health and Safety Code.

Advance Health Care Directive Registry, exemption from disclosure for registration information provided to the Secretary of State, Section 7926.100, this code.

(Added by Stats. 2021, Ch. 614, Sec. 2. (AB 473) Effective January 1, 2022. Operative January 1, 2023, pursuant to Sec. 7931.000.)

7930.110

The following provisions may operate to exempt certain records, or portions thereof, from disclosure pursuant to this division:

Aeronautics Act, reports of investigations and hearings, Section 21693, Public Utilities Code.

Agricultural producers marketing, access to records, Section 59616, Food and Agricultural Code.

Aiding disabled voters, Section 14282, Elections Code.

Air pollution data, confidentiality of trade secrets, Sections 7924.510 and 7924.700, this code, and Sections 42303.2 and 43206, Health and Safety Code.

Air toxics emissions inventory plans, protection of trade secrets, Section 44346, Health and Safety Code.

Alcohol and drug abuse records and records of communicable diseases, confidentiality of, Section 123125, Health and Safety Code.

Alcoholic beverage licensees, confidentiality of corporate proprietary information, Section 25205, Business and Professions Code.

Ambulatory Surgery Data Record, confidentiality of identifying information, Section 128737, Health and Safety Code.

Apiary registration information, confidentiality of, Section 29041, Food and Agricultural Code.

Archaeological site information and reports maintained by state and local agencies, disclosure not required, Section 7927.005, this code.

Arrest not resulting in conviction, disclosure or use of records, Sections 432.7 and 432.8, Labor Code.

Arsonists, registered, confidentiality of certain information, Section 457.1, Penal Code.

Assessor's records, confidentiality of information in, Section 408, Revenue and Taxation Code.

Assessor's records, confidentiality of information in, Section 451, Revenue and Taxation Code.

Assessor's records, display of documents relating to business affairs or property of another, Section 408.2, Revenue and Taxation Code.

Assigned risk plans, rejected applicants, confidentiality of information, Section 11624, Insurance Code.

Attorney applicant, investigation by State Bar, confidentiality of, Section 6060.2, Business and Professions Code.

Attorney applicant, information submitted by applicant and State Bar admission records, confidentiality of, Section 6060.25, Business and Professions Code.

Attorney-client confidential communication, Section 6068, Business and

Professions Code, and Sections 952 and 954, Evidence Code.

Attorney, disciplinary proceedings, confidentiality before formal proceedings, Section 6086.1, Business and Professions Code.

Attorney, disciplinary proceeding, State Bar access to nonpublic court records, Section 6090.6, Business and Professions Code.

Attorney, law corporation, investigation by State Bar, confidentiality of, Section 6168, Business and Professions Code.

Attorney work product confidentiality in administrative adjudication, Section 11507.6, this code.

Attorney, work product, confidentiality of, Section 6202, Business and Professions Code.

Attorney work product, discovery, Chapter 4 (commencing with Section 2018.010) of Title 4 of Part 4, Code of Civil Procedure.

Automated forward facing parking control devices, confidentiality of video imaging records from the devices, Section 40240, Vehicle Code.

Automated traffic enforcement system, confidentiality of photographic records made by the system, Section 21455.5, Vehicle Code.

Automobile Insurance Claims Depository, confidentiality of information, Section 1876.3, Insurance Code.

Automobile insurance, investigation of fraudulent claims, confidential information, Section 1872.8, Insurance Code.

Avocado handler transaction records, confidentiality of information, Section 44984, Food and Agricultural Code.

(Added by Stats. 2021, Ch. 614, Sec. 2. (AB 473) Effective January 1, 2022. Operative January 1, 2023, pursuant to Sec. 7931.000.)

7930.115

The following provisions may operate to exempt certain records, or portions thereof, from disclosure pursuant to this division:

Bank and Corporation Tax, disclosure of information, Article 2 (commencing with Section 19542) of Chapter 7 of Part 10.2 of Division 2, Revenue and Taxation Code.

Bank employees, confidentiality of criminal history information, Section 4990, Financial Code.

Bank reports, confidentiality of, Section 459, Financial Code.

Basic Property Insurance Inspection and Placement Plan, confidential reports, Section 10097, Insurance Code.

Beef Council of California, confidentiality of fee transactions information, Section 64691.1, Food and Agricultural Code.

Bids, confidentiality of, Section 10304, Public Contract Code.

Birth, death, and marriage licenses, confidential information contained in, Sections 102100, 102110, and 102230, Health and Safety Code.

Birth defects, monitoring, confidentiality of information collected, Section 103850, Health and Safety Code.

Birth, live, confidential portion of certificate, Sections 102430, 102475, 103525, and 103590, Health and Safety Code.

Blood tests, confidentiality of hepatitis and AIDS carriers, Section 1603.1, Health and Safety Code.

Blood-alcohol percentage test results, vehicular offenses, confidentiality of, Section 1804, Vehicle Code.

Business and professions licensee exemption for social security number, Section 30, Business and Professions Code.

(Added by Stats. 2021, Ch. 614, Sec. 2. (AB 473) Effective January 1, 2022. Operative January 1, 2023, pursuant to Sec. 7931.000.)

7930.120

The following provisions may operate to exempt certain records, or portions thereof, from disclosure pursuant to this division:

Cable television subscriber information, confidentiality of, Section 637.5, Penal Code.

CalFresh, disclosure of information, Section 18909, Welfare and Institutions Code.

California AIDS Program, personal data, confidentiality, Section 120820, Health and Safety Code.

California Apple Commission, confidentiality of lists of persons, Section 75598, Food and Agricultural Code.

California Apple Commission, confidentiality of proprietary information from producers or handlers, Section 75633, Food and Agricultural Code.

California Asparagus Commission, confidentiality of lists of producers, Section 78262, Food and Agricultural Code.

California Asparagus Commission, confidentiality of proprietary information from producers, Section 78288, Food and Agricultural Code.

California Avocado Commission, confidentiality of information from handlers, Section 67094, Food and Agricultural Code.

California Avocado Commission, confidentiality of proprietary information from handlers, Section 67104, Food and Agricultural Code.

California Cherry Commission, confidentiality of proprietary information from producers, processors, shippers, or grower-handlers, Section 76144, Food and Agricultural Code.

California Children's Services Program, confidentiality of factor replacement therapy contracts, Section 123853, Health and Safety Code.

California Cut Flower Commission, confidentiality of lists of producers, Section 77963, Food and Agricultural Code.

California Cut Flower Commission, confidentiality of proprietary information from producers, Section 77988, Food and Agricultural Code.

California Date Commission, confidentiality of proprietary information from producers and grower-handlers, Section 77843, Food and Agricultural Code.

California Egg Commission, confidentiality of proprietary information from handlers or distributors, Section 75134, Food and Agricultural Code.

California Forest Products Commission, confidentiality of lists of persons, Section 77589, Food and Agricultural Code.

California Forest Products Commission, confidentiality of proprietary information from producers, Section 77624, Food and Agricultural Code.

California Iceberg Lettuce Commission, confidentiality of information from handlers, Section 66624, Food and Agricultural Code.

California Kiwifruit Commission, confidentiality of proprietary information from producers or handlers, Section 68104, Food and Agricultural Code.

California Navel Orange Commission, confidentiality of proprietary information from producers or handlers and lists of producers and handlers, Section 73257, Food and Agricultural Code.

California Pepper Commission, confidentiality of lists of producers and handlers, Section 77298, Food and Agricultural Code.

California Pepper Commission, confidentiality of proprietary information from producers or handlers, Section 77334, Food and Agricultural Code.

California Pistachio Commission, confidentiality of proprietary information from producers or processors, Section 69045, Food and Agricultural Code.

California Salmon Council, confidentiality of fee transactions records, Section 76901.5 of the Food and Agricultural Code.

California Salmon Council, confidentiality of request for list of commercial salmon vessel operators, Section 76950 of the Food and Agricultural Code.

California Seafood Council, confidentiality of fee transaction records, Section 78553, Food and Agricultural Code.

California Seafood Council, confidentiality of information on volume of fish landed, Section 78575, Food and Agricultural Code.

California Sheep Commission, confidentiality of proprietary information from producers or handlers and lists of producers, Section 76343, Food and Agricultural Code.

California State University contract law, bids, questionnaires, and financial statements, Section 10763, Public Contract Code.

California State University Investigation of Reported Improper Governmental Activities Act, confidentiality of investigative audits completed pursuant to the act, Section 89574, Education Code.

California Table Grape Commission, confidentiality of information from shippers, Section 65603, Food and Agricultural Code.

California Tomato Commission, confidentiality of lists of producers, handlers, and others, Section 78679, Food and Agricultural Code.

California Tomato Commission, confidentiality of proprietary information, Section 78704, Food and Agricultural Code.

California Tourism Marketing Act, confidentiality of information pertaining to businesses paying the assessment under the act, Section 13995.54, this code.

California Victim Compensation Board, disclosure not required of records relating to assistance requests under Article 1 (commencing with Section 13950) of Chapter 5 of Part 4 of Division 3 of Title 2 of this code, Section 7923.755, this code.

California Walnut Commission, confidentiality of lists of producers, Section 77101, Food and Agricultural Code.

California Walnut Commission, confidentiality of proprietary information from producers or handlers, Section 77154, Food and Agricultural Code.

California Wheat Commission, confidentiality of proprietary information from handlers and lists of producers, Section 72104, Food and Agricultural Code.

California Wheat Commission, confidentiality of requests for assessment refund, Section 72109, Food and Agricultural Code.

California Wine Commission, confidentiality of proprietary information from producers or vintners, Section 74655, Food and Agricultural Code.

California Winegrape Growers Commission, confidentiality of proprietary information from producers and vintners, Section 74955, Food and Agricultural Code.

(Added by Stats. 2021, Ch. 614, Sec. 2. (AB 473) Effective January 1, 2022. Operative January 1, 2023, pursuant to Sec. 7931.000.)

7930.125

The following provisions may operate to exempt certain records, or portions thereof, from disclosure pursuant to this division:

Cancer registries, confidentiality of information, Section 103885, Health and Safety Code.

Candidate for local nonpartisan elective office, confidentiality of ballot statement, Section 13311, Elections Code.

Child abuse information, exchange by multidisciplinary personnel teams, Section 830, Welfare and Institutions Code.

Child abuse report and those making report, confidentiality of, Sections 11167 and 11167.5, Penal Code.

Child care liability insurance, confidentiality of information, Section 1864, Insurance Code.

Child concealer, confidentiality of address, Section 278.7, Penal Code.

Child custody investigation report, confidentiality of, Section 3111, Family Code.

Child day care facility, nondisclosure of complaint, Section 1596.853, Health and Safety Code.

Child health and disability prevention, confidentiality of health screening and evaluation results, Section 124110, Health and Safety Code.

Child sexual abuse reports, confidentiality of reports filed in a contested proceeding involving child custody or visitation rights, Section 3118, Family Code.

Child support, confidentiality of income tax return, Section 3552, Family Code.

Child support, promise to pay, confidentiality of, Section 7614, Family Code.

Childhood lead poisoning prevention, confidentiality of blood lead findings, Section 124130, Health and Safety Code.

Children and families commission, local, confidentiality of individually identifiable information, Section 130140.1, Health and Safety Code.

Cigarette tax, confidential information, Section 30455, Revenue and Taxation Code.

Civil actions, delayed disclosure for 30 days after complaint filed, Section 482.050, Code of Civil Procedure.

Closed sessions, document assessing vulnerability of state or local agency to disruption by terrorist or other criminal acts, Section 7929.200, this code.

Closed sessions, meetings of local governments, pending litigation, Section 54956.9, this code.

Colorado River Board, confidential information and records, Section 12519, Water Code.

Commercial fishing licensee, confidentiality of records, Section 7923, Fish and Game Code.

Commercial fishing reports, Section 8022, Fish and Game Code.

Community care facilities, confidentiality of client information, Section 1557.5, Health and Safety Code.

Community college employee, candidate examination records, confidentiality of, Section 88093, Education Code.

Community college employee, notice and reasons for nonreemployment, confidentiality, Section 87740, Education Code.

(Added by Stats. 2021, Ch. 614, Sec. 2. (AB 473) Effective January 1, 2022. Operative January 1, 2023, pursuant to Sec. 7931.000.)

7930.130

The following provisions may operate to exempt certain records, or portions thereof, from disclosure pursuant to this division:

Conservatee, confidentiality of the conservatee's report, Section 1826, Probate Code.

Conservatee, estate plan of, confidentiality of, Section 2586, Probate Code.

Conservatee with disability, confidentiality of report, Section 1827.5, Probate Code.

Conservator, confidentiality of conservator's birthdate and driver's license number, Section 1834, Probate Code.

Conservator, supplemental information, confidentiality of, Section 1821, Probate Code.

Conservatorship, court review of, confidentiality of report, Section 1851, Probate Code.

Consumer fraud investigations, access to complaints and investigations, Section 26509, this code.

Consumption or utilization of mineral materials, disclosure of, Section 2207.1, Public Resources Code.

Contractor, evaluations and contractor responses, confidentiality of, Section 10370, Public Contract Code.

Controlled Substance Law violations, confidential information, Section 818.7, this code.

Controlled substance offenders, confidentiality of registration information, Section 11594, Health and Safety Code.

Cooperative Marketing Association, confidential information disclosed to conciliator, Section 54453, Food and Agricultural Code.

Coroner, inquests, subpoena duces tecum, Section 27491.8, this code.

County aid and relief to indigents, confidentiality of investigation, supervision, relief, and rehabilitation records, Section 17006, Welfare and Institutions Code.

County alcohol programs, confidential information and records, Section 11812, Health and Safety Code.

County Employees' Retirement, confidential statements and records, Section 31532, this code.

County mental health system, confidentiality of client information, Section 5610, Welfare and Institutions Code.

County social services, investigation of applicant, confidentiality, Section 18491, Welfare and Institutions Code.

County social services rendered by volunteers, confidentiality of records of recipients, Section 10810, Welfare and Institutions Code.

County special commissions, disclosure of health care peer review and quality assessment records not required, Section 14087.58, Welfare and Institutions Code.

County special commissions, disclosure of records relating to the commission's rates of payment for publicly assisted medical care not required, Section 14087.58, Welfare and Institutions Code.

Court files, access to, restricted for 60 days, Section 1161.2, Code of Civil Procedure.

Court files, access to, restricted for 60 days, Section 1708.85, Civil Code.

Court reporters, confidentiality of records and reporters, Section 68525, this code.

Court-appointed special advocates, confidentiality of information acquired or reviewed, Section 105, Welfare and Institutions Code.

Crane employers, previous business identities, confidentiality of, Section 7383, Labor Code.

Credit unions, confidentiality of investigation and examination reports, Section 14257, Financial Code.

Credit unions, confidentiality of employee criminal history information, Section 14409.2, Financial Code.

Criminal defendant, indigent, confidentiality of request for funds for investigators and experts, Section 987.9, Penal Code.

Criminal offender record information, access to, Sections 11076 and 13202, Penal Code.

Crop reports, confidential, Section 7927.300, this code.

Customer list of chemical manufacturers, formulators, suppliers, distributors, importers, and their agents, the quantities and dates of shipments, and the proportion of a specified chemical within a mixture, confidential, Section 147.2, Labor Code.

Customer list of employment agency, trade secret, Section 16607, Business and Professions Code.

Customer list of telephone answering service, trade secret, Section 16606, Business and Professions Code.

(Added by Stats. 2021, Ch. 614, Sec. 2. (AB 473) Effective January 1, 2022. Operative January 1, 2023, pursuant to Sec. 7931.000.)

7930.135

The following provisions may operate to exempt certain records, or portions thereof, from disclosure pursuant to this division:

Dairy Council of California, confidentiality of ballots, Section 64323, Food and Agricultural Code.

Death, report that physician's or podiatrist's negligence or incompetence may be cause, confidentiality of, Section 802.5, Business and Professions Code.

Dental hygienist drug and alcohol diversion program, confidentiality of records pertaining to treatment, Section 1966.5, Business and Professions Code.

Dentist advertising and referral contract exemption, Section 650.2, Business and Professions Code.

Dentist, alcohol or dangerous drug rehabilitation and diversion, confidentiality of records, Section 1698, Business and Professions Code.

Department of Consumer Affairs licensee exemption for alcohol or dangerous drug treatment and rehabilitation records, Section 156.1, Business and Professions Code.

Department of Human Resources, confidentiality of pay data furnished to, Section 19826.5, this code.

Department of Motor Vehicles, confidentiality of information provided by an insurer, Section 4750.4, Vehicle Code.

Department of Motor Vehicles, confidentiality of the home address of specified persons in the records of the Department of Motor Vehicles, Section 1808.6, Vehicle Code.

Developmentally disabled conservatee, confidentiality of reports and records, Sections 416.8 and 416.18, Health and Safety Code.

Developmentally disabled person, access to information provided by family member, Section 4727, Welfare and Institutions Code.

Developmentally disabled person and person with mental illness, access to and release of information about, by protection and advocacy agency, Section 4903, Welfare and Institutions Code.

Developmentally disabled person, confidentiality of patient records, state agencies, Section 4552.5, Welfare and Institutions Code.

Developmentally disabled person, confidentiality of records and information, Sections 4514 and 4518, Welfare and Institutions Code.

Diesel Fuel Tax information, disclosure prohibited, Section 60609, Revenue and Taxation Code.

Disability compensation, confidential medical records, Section 2714, Unemployment Insurance Code.

Disability insurance, access to registered information, Section 789.7, Insurance Code.

Discrimination complaint to Division of Labor Standards Enforcement, confidentiality of witnesses, Section 98.7, Labor Code.

Dispute resolution participants confidentiality, Section 471.5, Business and Professions Code.

Division of Medi-Cal Fraud and Elder Abuse, confidentiality of complaints, Section 12528, this code.

Division of Workers' Compensation, confidentiality of data obtained by the administrative director and derivative works created by the division, Sections 3201.5, 3201.7, and 3201.9, Labor Code.

Division of Workers' Compensation, individually identifiable information and residence addresses obtained or maintained by the division on workers' compensation claims, confidentiality of, Section 138.7, Labor Code.

Division of Workers' Compensation, individually identifiable information of health care organization patients, confidentiality of, Section 4600.5, Labor Code.

Division of Workers' Compensation, individual workers' compensation claim files and auditor's working papers, confidentiality of, Section 129, Labor Code.

Division of Workers' Compensation, peer review proceedings and employee medical records, confidentiality of, Section 4600.6, Labor Code.

Domestic violence counselor and victim, confidentiality of communication, Sections 1037.2 and 1037.5, Evidence Code.

Driver arrested for traffic violation, notice of reexamination for evidence of incapacity, confidentiality of, Section 40313, Vehicle Code.

Driving school and driving instructor licensee records, confidentiality of, Section 11108, Vehicle Code.

(Added by Stats. 2021, Ch. 614, Sec. 4. (AB 473) Effective January 1, 2022. Operative January 1, 2023, pursuant to Sec. 7931.000.)

7930.140

The following provisions may operate to exempt certain records, or portions thereof, from disclosure pursuant to this division:

Educational psychologist-patient, privileged communication, Section 1010.5, Evidence Code.

Electronic and appliance repair dealer, service contractor, financial data in applications, Section 7925.010, this code.

Electronic Recording Delivery Act of 2004, exemption from disclosure for computer security reports, Section 27394, this code.

Emergency Care Data Record, exemption from disclosure for identifying information, Section 128736, Health and Safety Code.

Emergency Medical Services Fund, patient named, Section 1797.98c, Health and Safety Code.

Emergency medical technicians, confidentiality of disciplinary investigation information, Section 1798.200, Health and Safety Code.

Emergency Medical Technician-Paramedic (EMT-P), exemption from disclosure for records relating to personnel actions against, or resignation of, an EMT-P for disciplinary cause or reason, Section 1799.112, Health and Safety Code.

Eminent domain proceedings, use of state tax returns, Section 1263.520, Code of Civil Procedure.

Employment agency, confidentiality of customer list, Section 16607, Business and Professions Code.

Employment application, nondisclosure of arrest record or certain convictions, Sections 432.7 and 432.8, Labor Code.

Employment Development Department, furnishing materials, Section 307, Unemployment Insurance Code.

Enteral nutrition products, confidentiality of contracts by the State Department of Health Care Services with manufacturers of enteral nutrition products, Section 14105.8, Welfare and Institutions Code.

Equal wage rate violation, confidentiality of complaint, Section 1197.5, Labor Code.

Equalization, State Board of, prohibition against divulging information, Section 15619, this code.

Escrow Agents' Fidelity Corporation, confidentiality of examination and investigation reports, Section 17336, Financial Code.

Escrow agents' confidentiality of reports on violations, Section 17414, Financial Code.

Escrow agents' confidentiality of state summary criminal history information, Section 17414.1, Financial Code.

Estate tax, confidential records and information, Section 14251, Revenue and Taxation Code.

Excessive rates or complaints, reports, Section 1857.9, Insurance Code.

Executive Department, closed sessions and the record of topics discussed, Sections 11126 and 11126.1, this code.

Executive Department, investigations and hearings, confidential nature of information acquired, Section 11183, this code.

(Added by Stats. 2021, Ch. 614, Sec. 2. (AB 473) Effective January 1, 2022. Operative January 1, 2023, pursuant to Sec. 7931.000.)

7930.145

The following provisions may operate to exempt certain records, or portions thereof, from disclosure pursuant to this division:

Family court records, Section 1818, Family Code.

Farm product processor license, confidentiality of financial statements, Section 55523.6, Food and Agricultural Code.

Farm product processor licensee, confidentiality of grape purchases, Section 55601.5, Food and Agricultural Code.

Fee payer information, prohibition against disclosure by the State Board of Equalization and others, Section 55381, Revenue and Taxation Code.

Financial institutions, issuance of securities, reports and records of state agencies, Section 7929.000, this code.

Financial statements of insurers, confidentiality of information received, Section 925.3, Insurance Code.

Financial statements and questionnaires, of prospective bidders for the state, confidentiality of, Section 10165, Public Contract Code.

Financial statements and questionnaires, of prospective bidders for California State University contracts, confidentiality of, Section 10763, Public Contract Code.

Firearms, centralized list of exempted federal firearms licensees, disclosure of information compiled from, Sections 28475 and 28480, Penal Code.

Firearms, centralized list of dealers and licensees, disclosure of information compiled from, Section 26715, Penal Code.

Firearm license applications, Sections 7923.800 and 7923.805, this code.

Firearm sale or transfer, confidentiality of records, Section 28060, Penal Code.

Fishing and hunting licenses, confidentiality of names and addresses contained in records submitted to the Department of Fish and Wildlife to obtain recreational fishing and hunting licenses, Section 1050.6, Fish and Game Code.

Foreign marketing of agricultural products, confidentiality of financial information, Section 58577, Food and Agricultural Code.

Forest fires, anonymity of informants, Section 4417, Public Resources Code.

Foster homes, identifying information, Section 1536, Health and Safety Code.

Franchise Tax Board, access to Franchise Tax Board information by the State Department of Social Services, Section 11025, Welfare and Institutions Code.

Franchise Tax Board, auditing, confidentiality of, Section 90005, this code.

Franchises, applications, and reports filed with Commissioner of Financial Protection and Innovation, disclosure and withholding from public inspection, Section 31504, Corporations Code.

(Amended by Stats. 2022, Ch. 452, Sec. 180. (SB 1498) Effective January 1, 2023. Operative January 1, 2023, pursuant to Sec. 7931.000.)

7930.150

The following provisions may operate to exempt certain records, or portions thereof, from disclosure pursuant to this division:

Gambling Control Act, exemption from disclosure for records of the California Gambling Control Commission and the Department of Justice, Sections 19819 and 19821, Business and Professions Code.

Genetically Handicapped Persons Program, confidentiality of factor replacement therapy contracts, Section 125191, Health and Safety Code.

Governor, correspondence of and to Governor and Governor's office, Section 7928.000, this code.

Governor, transfer of public records in control of, restrictions on public access, Sections 7928.005 and 7928.010, this code.

Grand jury, confidentiality of request for special counsel, Section 936.7, Penal Code.

Grand jury, confidentiality of transcription of indictment or accusation, Section 938.1, Penal Code.

Group Insurance, public employees, Section 53202.25, this code.

Guardianship, confidentiality of report regarding the suitability of the proposed guardian, Section 1543, Probate Code.

Guardianship, disclosure of report and recommendation concerning proposed guardianship of person or estate, Section 1513, Probate Code.

(Added by Stats. 2021, Ch. 614, Sec. 2. (AB 473) Effective January 1, 2022. Operative January 1, 2023, pursuant to Sec. 7931.000.)

7930.155

The following provisions may operate to exempt certain records, or portions thereof, from disclosure pursuant to this division:

Hazardous substance tax information, prohibition against disclosure, Section 43651, Revenue and Taxation Code.

Hazardous waste control, business plans, public inspection, Section 25509, Health and Safety Code.

Hazardous waste control, notice of unlawful hazardous waste disposal, Section 25180.5, Health and Safety Code.

Hazardous waste control, trade secrets, disclosure of information, Sections 25512, 25512.1, and 25538, Health and Safety Code.

Hazardous waste control, trade secrets, procedures for release of information, Sections 78480 to 78495, inclusive, Health and Safety Code.

Hazardous waste generator report, protection of trade secrets, Sections 25244.21 and 25244.23, Health and Safety Code.

Hazardous waste licenseholder disclosure statement, confidentiality of, Section 25186.5, Health and Safety Code.

Hazardous waste recycling, information clearinghouse, confidentiality of trade secrets, Section 25170, Health and Safety Code.

Hazardous waste recycling, list of specified hazardous wastes, trade secrets, Section 25175, Health and Safety Code.

Hazardous waste recycling, trade secrets, confidential nature, Sections 25173 and 25180.5, Health and Safety Code.

Healing arts licensees, central files, confidentiality, Section 800, Business and Professions Code.

Health authorities, special county, confidentiality of records, Sections 14087.35, 14087.36, and 14087.38, Welfare and Institutions Code.

Health care provider disciplinary proceeding, confidentiality of documents, Section 805.1, Business and Professions Code.

Health care service plans, review of quality of care, privileged communications, Sections 1370 and 1380, Health and Safety Code.

Health commissions, special county, confidentiality of peer review proceedings, rates of payment, and trade secrets, Section 14087.31, Welfare and Institutions Code.

Health facilities, patient's rights of confidentiality, subdivision (c) of Section 128745 and Sections 128735, 128736,

128737, 128755, and 128765, Health and Safety Code.

Health personnel, data collection by the Office of Statewide Health Planning and Development, confidentiality of information on individual licentiates, Section 127780, Health and Safety Code.

Health plan governed by a county board of supervisors, exemption from disclosure for records relating to provider rates or payments for a three-year period after execution of the provider contract, Sections 7926.205 and 54956.87, this code.

Hereditary Disorders Act, legislative finding and declaration, confidential information, Sections 124975 and 124980, Health and Safety Code.

Hereditary Disorders Act, rules, regulations, and standards, breach of confidentiality, Section 124980, Health and Safety Code.

HIV, disclosures to blood banks by department or county health officers, Section 1603.1, Health and Safety Code.

Home address of public employees and officers in Department of Motor Vehicles, records, confidentiality of, Sections 1808.2 and 1808.4, Vehicle Code.

Horse racing, horses, blood or urine test sample, confidentiality, Section 19577, Business and Professions Code.

Hospital district and municipal hospital records relating to contracts with insurers and service plans, Section 7926.210, this code.

Hospital final accreditation report, Section 7926.000, this code.

Housing authorities, confidentiality of rosters of tenants, Section 34283, Health and Safety Code.

Housing authorities, confidentiality of applications by prospective or current tenants, Section 34332, Health and Safety Code.

(Amended by Stats. 2022, Ch. 258, Sec. 18. (AB 2327) Effective January 1, 2023. Operative January 1, 2024, pursuant to Sec. 130 of Stats. 2022, Ch. 258.)

7930.160

The following provisions may operate to exempt certain records, or portions thereof, from disclosure pursuant to this division:

Improper governmental activities reporting, confidentiality of identity of person providing information, Section 8547.5, this code.

Improper governmental activities reporting, disclosure of information, Section 8547.6, this code.

Industrial loan companies, confidentiality of financial information, Section 18496, Financial Code.

Industrial loan companies, confidentiality of investigation and examination reports, Section 18394, Financial Code.

Influenza vaccine, trade secret information and information relating to recipient of vaccine, Section 120160, Health and Safety Code.

In forma pauperis litigant, rules governing confidentiality of financial information, Section 68633, this code.

Infrastructure information, exemption from disclosure for information voluntarily submitted to the Office of Emergency Services, Section 7929.205, this code.

In-Home Supportive Services Program, exemption from disclosure for information regarding persons paid by the state to provide in-home supportive services, Section 7926.300, this code.

Initiative, referendum, recall, and other petitions, confidentiality of names of signers, Sections 7924.100, 7924.105, and 7924.110, this code.

Insurance claims analysis, confidentiality of information, Section 1875.16, Insurance Code.

Insurance Commissioner, confidential information, Sections 735.5, 1067.11, 1077.3, and 12919, Insurance Code.

Insurance Commissioner, informal conciliation of complaints, confidential communications, Section 1858.02, Insurance Code.

Insurance Commissioner, information from examination or investigation, confidentiality of, Sections 1215.8, 1433, and 1759.3, Insurance Code.

Insurance Commissioner, writings filed with nondisclosure, Section 855, Insurance Code.

Insurance fraud reporting, information acquired not part of public record, Section 1873.1, Insurance Code.

Insurance licensee, confidential information, Section 1666.5, Insurance Code.

Insurer application information, confidentiality of, Section 925.3, Insurance Code.

Insurer financial analysis ratios and examination synopses, confidentiality of, Section 933, Insurance Code.

Department of Resources Recycling and Recovery information, prohibition against disclosure, Section 45982, Revenue and Taxation Code.

International wills, confidentiality of registration information filed with the Secretary of State, Section 6389, Probate Code.

Intervention in regulatory and ratemaking proceedings, audit of customer seeking and award, Section 1804, Public Utilities Code.

Investigation and security records, exemption from disclosure for records of the Attorney General, the Department of Justice, the Office of Emergency Services, and state and local police agencies, Sections 7923.600 to 7923.630, inclusive, this code.

Investigative consumer reporting agency, limitations on furnishing an investigative consumer report, Section 1786.12, Civil Code.

(Added by Stats. 2021, Ch. 614, Sec. 2. (AB 473) Effective January 1, 2022. Operative January 1, 2023, pursuant to Sec. 7931.000.)

7930.165

The following provisions may operate to exempt certain records, or portions thereof, from disclosure pursuant to this division:

Joint Legislative Ethics Committee, confidentiality of reports and records, Section 8953, this code.

Judicial candidates, confidentiality of communications concerning, Section 12011.5, this code.

Judicial proceedings, confidentiality of employer records of employee absences, Section 230.2, Labor Code.

Jurors' lists, lists of registered voters and licensed drivers as source for, Section 197, Code of Civil Procedure.

Juvenile court proceedings to adjudge a person a dependent child of court, sealing records of, Section 389, Welfare and Institutions Code.

Juvenile criminal records, dissemination to schools, Section 828.1, Welfare and Institutions Code.

Juvenile delinquents, notification of chief of police or sheriff of escape of minor from secure detention facility, Section 1155, Welfare and Institutions Code.

Labor dispute, investigation and mediation records, confidentiality of, Section 3601, this code.

Lanterman-Petris-Short Act, mental health services recipients, confidentiality of information and records, mental health advocate, Sections 5540, 5541, 5542, and 5550, Welfare and Institutions Code.

Law enforcement vehicles, registration disclosure, Section 5003, Vehicle Code.

Legislative Counsel records, Section 7928.100, this code.

Library circulation records and other materials, Sections 7925.000 and 7927.105, this code.

Life and disability insurers, actuarial information, confidentiality of, Section 10489.15, Insurance Code.

Litigation, confidentiality of settlement information, Section 68513, this code.

Local agency legislative body, closed sessions, disclosure of materials, Section 54956.9, this code.

Local government employees, confidentiality of records and claims relating to group insurance, Section 53202.25, this code.

Local summary criminal history information, confidentiality of, Sections 13300 and 13305, Penal Code.

Local agency legislative body, closed session, nondisclosure of minute book, Section 54957.2, this code.

Local agency legislative body, meeting, disclosure of agenda, Section 54957.5, this code.

Long-term health facilities, confidentiality of complaints against, Section 1419, Health and Safety Code.

Long-term health facilities, confidentiality of records retained by State Department of Public Health, Section 1439, Health and Safety Code.

Los Angeles County Tourism Marketing Commission, confidentiality of information obtained from businesses to determine their assessment, Section 13995.108, this code.

(Added by Stats. 2021, Ch. 614, Sec. 2. (AB 473) Effective January 1, 2022. Operative January 1, 2023, pursuant to Sec. 7931.000.)

7930.170

The following provisions may operate to exempt certain records, or portions thereof, from disclosure pursuant to this division:

Managed Risk Medical Insurance Board, negotiations with entities contracting or seeking to contract with the board, Sections 7926.225 and 7926.230, this code.

Mandated blood testing and confidentiality to protect public health, prohibition against compelling identification of test subjects, Section 120975, Health and Safety Code.

Mandated blood testing and confidentiality to protect public health, unauthorized disclosures of identification of test subjects, Sections 1603.1, 1603.3, and 121022, Health and Safety Code.

Mandated blood testing and confidentiality to protect public health, disclosure to patient's spouse, sexual partner, needle sharer, or county health officer, Section 121015, Health and Safety Code.

Manufactured home, mobilehome, floating home, confidentiality of home address of registered owner, Section 18081, Health and Safety Code.

Marital confidential communications, Sections 980, 981, 982, 983, 984, 985, 986, and 987, Evidence Code.

Market reports, confidential, Section 7927.300, this code.

Marketing of commodities, confidentiality of financial information, Section 58781, Food and Agricultural Code.

Marketing orders, confidentiality of processors' or distributors' information, Section 59202, Food and Agricultural Code.

Marriage, confidential, certificate, Section 511, Family Code.

Medi-Cal Benefits Program, confidentiality of information, Section 14100.2, Welfare and Institutions Code.

Medi-Cal Benefits Program, request of department for records or information, Section 14124.89, Welfare and Institutions Code.

Medi-Cal managed care program, exemption from disclosure for financial and utilization data submitted by Medi-Cal managed care health plans to establish rates, Section 14301.1, Welfare and Institutions Code.

Medi-Cal program, exemption from disclosure for best price contracts between the State Department of Health Care Services and drug manufacturers, Section 14105.33, Welfare and Institutions Code.

Medical information, disclosure by provider unless prohibited by patient in writing, Section 56.16, Civil Code.

Medical information, types of information not subject to patient prohibition of disclosure, Section 56.30, Civil Code.

Medical and other hospital committees and peer review bodies, confidentiality of records, Section 1157, Evidence Code.

Medical or dental licensee, action for revocation or suspension due to illness, report, confidentiality of, Section 828, Business and Professions Code.

Medical or dental licensee, disciplinary action, denial or termination of staff privileges, report, confidentiality of, Sections 805, 805.1, and 805.5, Business and Professions Code.

Meetings of state agencies, disclosure of agenda, Section 11125.1, this code.

Mentally abnormal sex offender committed to state hospital, confidentiality of records, Section 4135, Welfare and Institutions Code.

Mentally disordered and developmentally disabled offenders, access to criminal histories of, Section 1620, Penal Code.

Mentally disordered persons, court-ordered evaluation, confidentiality of reports, Section 5202, Welfare and Institutions Code.

Mentally disordered or mentally ill person, confidentiality of written consent to detainment, Section 5326.4, Welfare and Institutions Code.

Mentally disordered or mentally ill person, voluntarily or involuntarily detained and receiving services, confidentiality of records and information, Sections 5328, 5328.15, 5328.2, 5328.4, 5328.8, and 5328.9, Welfare and Institutions Code.

Mentally disordered or mentally ill person, weapons restrictions, confidentiality of information about, Section 8103, Welfare and Institutions Code.

Milk marketing, confidentiality of records, Section 61443, Food and Agricultural Code.

Milk product certification, confidentiality of, Section 62121, Food and Agricultural Code.

Milk, market milk, confidential records and reports, Section 62243, Food and Agricultural Code.

Milk product registration, confidentiality of information, Section 38946, Food and Agricultural Code.

Milk equalization pool plan, confidentiality of producers' voting, Section 62716, Food and Agricultural Code.

Mining report, confidentiality of report containing information relating to mineral production, reserves, or rate of depletion of mining operation, Section 2207, Public Resources Code.

Minor, criminal proceeding testimony closed to public, Section 859.1, Penal Code.

Minors, material depicting sexual conduct, records of suppliers to be kept and made available to law enforcement, Section 1309.5, Labor Code.

Misdemeanor and felony reports by police chiefs and sheriffs to Department of Justice, confidentiality of, Sections 11107 and 11107.5, Penal Code.

Monetary instrument transaction records, confidentiality of, Section 14167, Penal Code.

Missing persons' information, disclosure of, Sections 14204 and 14205, Penal Code.

Morbidity and mortality studies, confidentiality of records, Section 100330, Health and Safety Code.

Motor vehicle accident reports, disclosure, Sections 16005, 20012, and 20014, Vehicle Code.

Motor Vehicles, Department of, public records, exceptions, Sections 1808 to 1808.7, inclusive, Vehicle Code.

Motor vehicle insurance fraud reporting, confidentiality of information acquired, Section 1874.3, Insurance Code.

Motor vehicle liability insurer, data reported to Department of Insurance, confidentiality of, Section 11628, Insurance Code.

Multijurisdictional drug law enforcement agency, closed sessions to discuss criminal investigation, Section 54957.8, this code.

(Added by Stats. 2021, Ch. 614, Sec. 5. (AB 473) Effective January 1, 2022. Operative January 1, 2023, pursuant to Sec. 7931.000.)

7930.175

The following provisions may operate to exempt certain records, or portions thereof, from disclosure pursuant to this division:

Narcotic and drug abuse patients, confidentiality of records, Section 11845.5, Health and Safety Code.

Native American graves, cemeteries, and sacred places, records of, Section 7927.000, this code.

Notary public, confidentiality of application for appointment and commission, Section 8201.5, this code.

Nurse, alcohol or dangerous drug diversion and rehabilitation records, confidentiality of, Section 2770.12, Business and Professions Code.

Obscene matter, defense of scientific or other purpose, confidentiality of recipients, Section 311.8, Penal Code.

Occupational safety and health investigations, confidentiality of complaints and complainants, Section 6309, Labor Code.

Occupational safety and health investigations, confidentiality of trade secrets, Section 6322, Labor Code.

Official information acquired in confidence by public employee, disclosure of, Sections 1040 and 1041, Evidence Code.

Oil and gas, confidentiality of proposals for the drilling of a well, Section 3724.4, Public Resources Code.

Oil and gas, disclosure of onshore and offshore exploratory well records, Section 3234, Public Resources Code.

Oil and gas, disclosure of well records, Section 3752, Public Resources Code.

Oil and gas leases, surveys for permits, confidentiality of information, Section 6826, Public Resources Code.

Oil spill feepayer information, prohibition against disclosure, Section 46751, Revenue and Taxation Code.

Older adults receiving county services, providing information between county agencies, confidentiality of, Section 9401, Welfare and Institutions Code.

Organic food certification organization records, release of, Section 110845, Health and Safety Code.

Osteopathic physician and surgeon, rehabilitation and diversion records, confidentiality of, Section 2369, Business and Professions Code.

(Added by Stats. 2021, Ch. 614, Sec. 2. (AB 473) Effective January 1, 2022. Operative January 1, 2023, pursuant to Sec. 7931.000.)

7930.180

The following provisions may operate to exempt certain records, or portions thereof, from disclosure pursuant to this division:

Parole revocation proceedings, confidentiality of information in reports, Section 3063.5, Penal Code.

Passenger fishing boat licenses, records, Section 7923, Fish and Game Code.

Paternity, acknowledgment, confidentiality of records, Section 102760, Health and Safety Code.

Patient-physician confidential communication, Sections 992 and 994, Evidence Code.

Patient records, confidentiality of, Section 123135, Health and Safety Code.

Payroll records, confidentiality of, Section 1776, Labor Code.

Peace officer personnel records, confidentiality of, Sections 832.7 and 832.8, Penal Code.

Penitential communication between penitent and clergy, Sections 1032 and 1033, Evidence Code.

Personal Care Services Program, exemption from disclosure for information regarding persons paid by the state to provide personal care services, Section 7926.300, this code.

Personal Income Tax, disclosure of information, Article 2 (commencing with Section 19542) of Chapter 7 of Part 10.2 of Division 2, Revenue and Taxation Code.

Personal information, Information Practices Act, prohibitions against disclosure by state agencies, Sections 1798.24 and 1798.75, Civil Code.

Personal information, subpoena of records containing, Section 1985.4, Code of Civil Procedure.

Personal representative, confidentiality of personal representative's birthdate and driver's license number, Section 8404, Probate Code.

Persons formerly classified as mentally abnormal sex offenders committed to a state hospital, confidentiality of records, Section 4135, Welfare and Institutions Code.

Persons with mental health disorders, court-ordered evaluation, confidentiality of reports, Section 5202, Welfare and Institutions Code.

Persons with mental health disorders, confidentiality of written consent to detainment, Section 5326.4, Welfare and Institutions Code.

Persons with mental health disorders voluntarily detained and receiving services, confidentiality of records and information, Sections 5328, 5328.15, 5328.2, 5328.4, 5328.8, and 5328.9, Welfare and Institutions Code.

Persons with mental health disorders, weapons restrictions, confidentiality of information about, Section 8103, Welfare and Institutions Code.

Petition signatures, Section 18650, Elections Code.

Petroleum supply and pricing, confidential information, Sections 25364 and 25366, Public Resources Code.

Pharmacist, alcohol or dangerous drug diversion and rehabilitation records, confidentiality of, Section 4372, Business and Professions Code.

Physical therapist or assistant, records of dangerous drug or alcohol diversion and rehabilitation, confidentiality of, Section 2667, Business and Professions Code.

Physical or mental condition or conviction of controlled substance offense, records in Department of Motor Vehicles, confidentiality of, Section 1808.5, Vehicle Code.

Physician assistant, alcohol or dangerous drug diversion and rehabilitation records, confidentiality of, Section 3534.7, Business and Professions Code.

Physician competency examination, confidentiality of reports, Section 2294, Business and Professions Code.

Physicians and surgeons, confidentiality of reports of patients with a lapse of consciousness disorder, Section 103900, Health and Safety Code.

Physician Services Account, confidentiality of patient names in claims, Section 16956, Welfare and Institutions Code.

Pilots, confidentiality of personal information, Section 1157.1, Harbors and Navigation Code.

Pollution Control Financing Authority, financial data submitted to, Section 7924.505, this code.

Postmortem or autopsy photos, Section 129, Code of Civil Procedure.

(Added by Stats. 2021, Ch. 614, Sec. 2. (AB 473) Effective January 1, 2022. Operative January 1, 2023, pursuant to Sec. 7931.000.)

7930.185

The following provisions may operate to exempt certain records, or portions thereof, from disclosure pursuant to this division:

Pregnancy tests by local public health agencies, confidentiality of, Section 123380, Health and Safety Code.

Pregnant women, confidentiality of blood tests, Section 125105, Health and Safety Code.

Prehospital emergency medical care, release of information, Sections 1797.188 and 1797.189, Health and Safety Code.

Prenatal syphilis tests, confidentiality of, Section 120705, Health and Safety Code.

Prescription drug discounts, confidentiality of corporate proprietary information, Section 130506, Health and Safety Code.

Prisoners, behavioral research on, confidential personal information, Section 3515, Penal Code.

Prisoners, confidentiality of blood tests, Section 7530, Penal Code.

Prisoners, medical testing, confidentiality of records, Sections 7517 and 7540, Penal Code.

Prisoners, transfer from county facility for mental treatment and evaluation, confidentiality of written reasons, Section 4011.6, Penal Code.

Private industry wage data collected by public entity, confidentiality of, Section 7927.600, this code.

Private railroad car tax, confidentiality of information, Section 11655, Revenue and Taxation Code.

Probate referee, disclosure of materials, Section 8908, Probate Code.

Probation officer reports, inspection of, Section 1203.05, Penal Code.

Produce dealer, confidentiality of financial statements, Section 56254, Food and Agricultural Code.

Products liability insurers, transmission of information, Section 1857.9, Insurance Code.

Professional corporations, financial statements, confidentiality of, Section 13406, Corporations Code.

Property on loan to museum, notice of intent to preserve an interest in, not subject to disclosure, Section 1899.5, Civil Code.

Property taxation, confidentiality of change of ownership, Section 481, Revenue and Taxation Code.

Property taxation, confidentiality of exemption claims, Sections 63.1, 69.5, and 408.2, Revenue and Taxation Code.

Property taxation, confidentiality of property information, Section 15641, Government Code and Section 833, Revenue and Taxation Code.

Proprietary information, availability only to the director and other persons authorized by the operator and the owner, Section 2778, Public Resources Code.

Psychologist and client, confidential relations and communications, Section 2918, Business and Professions Code.

Psychotherapist-patient confidential communication, Sections 1012 and 1014, Evidence Code.

Public employees' home addresses and telephone numbers, confidentiality of, Section 7928.300, this code.

Public Employees' Medical and Hospital Care Act, confidentiality of data relating to health care services rendered by participating hospitals to members and annuitants, Section 22854.5, this code.

Public Employees' Retirement System, confidentiality of data filed by member or beneficiary with board of administration, Section 20230, this code.

Public investment funds, exemption from disclosure for records regarding alternative investments, Section 7928.710, this code.

Public school employees organization, confidentiality of proof of majority support submitted to Public Employment Relations Board, Sections 3544, 3544.1, and 3544.5, this code.

Public social services, confidentiality of digest of decisions, Section 10964, Welfare and Institutions Code.

Public social services, confidentiality of information regarding child abuse or elder or dependent persons abuse, Section 10850.1, Welfare and Institutions Code.

Public social services, confidentiality of information regarding eligibility, Section 10850.2, Welfare and Institutions Code.

Public social services, confidentiality of records, Section 10850, Welfare and Institutions Code.

Public social services, disclosure of information to law enforcement agencies, Section 10850.3, Welfare and Institutions Code.

Public social services, disclosure of information to law enforcement agencies regarding deceased applicant or recipient, Section 10850.7, Welfare and Institutions Code.

Public utilities, confidentiality of information, Section 583, Public Utilities Code.

Pupil, confidentiality of personal information, Section 45345, Education Code.

Pupil drug and alcohol use questionnaires, confidentiality of, Section 11605, Health and Safety Code.

Pupil, expulsion hearing, disclosure of testimony of witness and closed session of district board, Section 48918, Education Code.

Pupil, personal information disclosed to school counselor, confidentiality of, Section 49602, Education Code.

Pupil record contents, records of administrative hearing to change contents, confidentiality of, Section 49070, Education Code.

Pupil records, access authorized for specified parties, Section 49076, Education Code.

Pupil records, disclosure in hearing to dismiss or suspend school employee, Section 44944.3, Education Code.

Pupil records, release of directory information to private entities, Sections 49073 and 49073.5, Education Code.

(Added by Stats. 2021, Ch. 614, Sec. 2. (AB 473) Effective January 1, 2022. Operative January 1, 2023, pursuant to Sec. 7931.000.)

7930.190

The following provisions may operate to exempt certain records, or portions thereof, from disclosure pursuant to this division:

Radioactive materials, dissemination of information about transportation of, Section 33002, Vehicle Code.

Railroad infrastructure protection program, disclosure not required for risk assessments filed with the Public Utilities Commission, the Director of Emergency Services, or the Office of Emergency Services, Section 7929.215, this code.

Real estate broker, annual report to Bureau of Real Estate of financial information, confidentiality of, Section 10232.2, Business and Professions Code.

Real property, acquisition by state or local government, information relating to feasibility, Section 7928.705, this code.

Real property, change in ownership statement, confidentiality of, Section 27280, this code.

Records described in Section 1620, Penal Code.

Records of contract purchasers, inspection by public prohibited, Section 85, Military and Veterans Code.

Records of persons committed to a state hospital pursuant to Section 4135, Welfare and Institutions Code.

Registered public obligations, inspection of records of security interests in, Section 5060, this code.

Registration of exempt vehicles, nondisclosure of name of person involved in alleged violation, Section 5003, Vehicle Code.

Rehabilitation, Department of, confidential information, Section 19016, Welfare and Institutions Code.

Reinsurance intermediary-broker license information, confidentiality of, Section 1781.3, Insurance Code.

Relocation assistance, confidential records submitted to a public entity by a business or farm operation, Section 7262, this code.

Rent control ordinance, confidentiality of information concerning accommodations sought to be withdrawn from, Section 7060.4, this code.

Report of probation officer, inspection, copies, Section 1203.05, Penal Code.

Repossession agency licensee application, confidentiality of information, Sections 7503, 7504, and 7506.5, Business and Professions Code.

Reproductive health facilities, disclosure not required for personal information regarding employees, volunteers, board members, owners, partners, officers, and contractors of a reproductive health services facility who have provided requisite notification, Sections 7926.400 to 7926.430, inclusive, this code.

Residence address in any record of Department of Housing and Community Development, confidentiality of, Section 7927.415, this code.

Residence address in any record of Department of Motor Vehicles, confidentiality of, Section 7927.405, this code, and Section 1808.21, Vehicle Code.

Residence and mailing addresses in records of Department of Motor Vehicles, confidentiality of, Section 1810.7, Vehicle Code.

Residential care facilities, confidentiality of resident information, Section 1568.08, Health and Safety Code.

Residential care facilities for the elderly, confidentiality of client information, Section 1569.315, Health and Safety Code.

Resource families, identifying information, Section 16519.55, Welfare and Institutions Code.

Respiratory care practitioner, professional competency examination reports, confidentiality of, Section 3756, Business and Professions Code.

Restraint of trade, civil action by district attorney, confidential memorandum, Section 16750, Business and Professions Code.

Reward by Governor for information leading to arrest and conviction, confidentiality of person supplying information, Section 1547, Penal Code.

(Added by Stats. 2021, Ch. 614, Sec. 2. (AB 473) Effective January 1, 2022. Operative January 1, 2023, pursuant to Sec. 7931.000.)

7930.195

The following provisions may operate to exempt certain records, or portions thereof, from disclosure pursuant to this division:

Safe surrender site, confidentiality of information pertaining to a parent or individual surrendering a child, Section 1255.7, Health and Safety Code.

Sales and use tax, disclosure of information, Section 7056, Revenue and Taxation Code.

Santa Barbara Regional Health Authority, exemption from disclosure for records maintained by the authority regarding negotiated rates for the California Medical Assistance Program, Section 14499.6, Welfare and Institutions Code.

Savings association employees, disclosure of criminal history information, Section 6525, Financial Code.

Savings associations, inspection of records by shareholders, Section 6050, Financial Code.

School district governing board, disciplinary action, disclosure of pupil information, Section 35146, Education Code.

School employee, merit system examination records, confidentiality of, Section 45274, Education Code.

School employee, notice and reasons for hearing on nonreemployment of employee, confidentiality of, Sections 44948.5 and 44949, Education Code.

School meals for needy pupils, confidentiality of records, Section 49558, Education Code.

Sealed records, arrest for misdemeanor, Section 851.7, Penal Code.

Sealed records, misdemeanor convictions, Section 1203.45, Penal Code.

Sealing and destruction of arrest records, determination of innocence, Section 851.8, Penal Code.

Search warrants, special master, Section 1524, Penal Code.

Sex change, confidentiality of birth certificate, Section 103440, Health and Safety Code.

Sex offenders, registration form, Section 290.021, Penal Code.

Sexual assault forms, confidentiality of, Section 13823.5, Penal Code.

Sexual assault counselor and victim, confidential communication, Sections 1035.2, 1035.4, and 1035.8, Evidence Code.

Shorthand reporter's complaint, Section 8010, Business and Professions Code.

Small family day care homes, identifying information, Section 1596.86, Health and Safety Code.

Social security number, applicant for driver's license or identification card, nondisclosure of, Section 1653.5, Vehicle Code, and Section 7922.200, this code.

Social security number, official record or official filing, nondisclosure of, Section 9526.5, Commercial Code, and Sections 7922.205 and 7922.210, this code.

Social Security Number Truncation Program, Article 3.5 (commencing with Section 27300) of Chapter 6 of Part 3 of Division 2 of Title 3, this code.

Social security numbers within records of local agencies, nondisclosure of, Section 7922.200, this code.

(Added by Stats. 2021, Ch. 614, Sec. 2. (AB 473) Effective January 1, 2022. Operative January 1, 2023, pursuant to Sec. 7931.000.)

7930.200

The following provisions may operate to exempt certain records, or portions thereof, from disclosure pursuant to this division:

State agency activities relating to unrepresented employees, Section 7928.405, this code.

State agency activities relating to providers of health care, Section 7927.500, this code.

State Auditor, access to barred records, Section 8545.2, this code.

State Auditor, confidentiality of records, Sections 8545, 8545.1, and 8545.3, this code.

State civil service employee, confidentiality of appeal to State Personnel Board, Section 18952, this code.

State civil service employees, confidentiality of reports, Section 18573, this code.

State civil service examination, confidentiality of application and examination materials, Section 18934, this code.

State Compensation Insurance Fund, exemption from disclosure for various records maintained by the State Compensation Insurance Fund, Sections 7929.400 to 7929.430, inclusive, this code.

State Contract Act, bids, questionnaires and financial statements, Section 10165, Public Contract Code.

State Contract Act, bids, sealing, opening, and reading bids, Section 10304, Public Contract Code.

State Energy Resources Conservation and Development Commission, confidentiality of proprietary information submitted to, Section 25223, Public Resources Code.

State hospital patients, information and records in possession of Superintendent of Public Instruction, confidentiality of, Section 56863, Education Code.

State Long-Term Care Ombudsman, access to government agency records, Section 9723, Welfare and Institutions Code.

State Long-Term Care Ombudsman office, confidentiality of records and files, Section 9725, Welfare and Institutions Code.

State Long-Term Care Ombudsman office, disclosure of information or communications, Section 9715, Welfare and Institutions Code.

State Lottery Evaluation Report, disclosure, Section 8880.46, this code.

State prisoners, exemption from disclosure for surveys by the California Research Bureau of children of female prisoners, Section 7443, Penal Code.

State summary criminal history information, confidentiality of information, Sections 11105, 11105.1, 11105.3, and 11105.4, Penal Code.

State Teachers' Retirement System, confidentiality of information filed with the system by a member, participant, or beneficiary, Section 22306, Education Code.

Sterilization of disabled, confidentiality of evaluation report, Section 1955, Probate Code.

Strawberry marketing information, confidentiality of, Section 63124, Food and Agricultural Code.

Structural pest control licensee records relating to pesticide use, confidentiality of, Section 15205, Food and Agricultural Code.

Student driver, records of physical or mental condition, confidentiality of, Section 12661, Vehicle Code.

Student, community college, information received by school counselor, confidentiality of, Section 72621, Education Code.

Student, community college, records, limitations on release, Section 76243, Education Code.

Student, community college, record contents, records of administrative hearing to change contents, confidentiality of, Section 76232, Education Code.

Student, sexual assault on private higher education institution campus, confidentiality of information, Section 94385, Education Code.

Student, sexual assault on public college or university, confidentiality of information, Section 67385, Education Code.

Sturgeon egg processors, records, Section 10004, Fish and Game Code.

(Added by Stats. 2021, Ch. 614, Sec. 2. (AB 473) Effective January 1, 2022. Operative January 1, 2023, pursuant to Sec. 7931.000.)

7930.205

The following provisions may operate to exempt certain records, or portions thereof, from disclosure pursuant to this division:

Taxpayer information, confidentiality, local taxes, Section 7925.000, this code.

Tax preparer, disclosure of information obtained in business of preparing tax returns, Section 17530.5, Business and Professions Code.

Teacher, credential holder or applicant, information provided to Commission on Teacher Credentialing, confidentiality of, Section 44341, Education Code.

Teacher, certified school personnel examination results, confidentiality of, Section 44289, Education Code.

Telephone answering service customer list, trade secret, Section 16606, Business and Professions Code.

Timber yield tax, disclosure to county assessor, Section 38706, Revenue and Taxation Code.

Timber yield tax, disclosure of information, Section 38705, Revenue and Taxation Code.

Title insurers, confidentiality of notice of noncompliance, Section 12414.14, Insurance Code.

Tobacco products, exemption from disclosure for distribution information provided to the State Department of Public Health, Section 22954, Business and Professions Code.

Tow truck driver, information in records of the Department of the California Highway Patrol, Department of Motor Vehicles, or other agencies, confidentiality of, Sections 2431 and 2432.3, Vehicle Code.

Toxic Substances Control, Department of, inspection of records of, Section 25152.5, Health and Safety Code.

Trade secrets, Section 1060, Evidence Code.

Trade secrets, confidentiality of, occupational safety and health inspections, Section 6322, Labor Code.

Trade secrets, disclosure of public records, Section 3426.7, Civil Code.Trade secrets, food, drugs, cosmetics, nondisclosure, Sections 110165 and 110370, Health and Safety Code.

Trade secrets, protection by Director of Pesticide Regulation, Sections 7924.300 to 7924.335, inclusive, this code.

Trade secrets and proprietary information relating to pesticides, confidentiality of, Sections 14022 and 14023, Food and Agricultural Code.

Trade secrets, protection by Director of Industrial Relations, Section 6396, Labor Code.

Trade secrets relating to hazardous substances, disclosure of, Sections 78480 to 78495, inclusive, and Section 78930, Health and Safety Code.

Traffic violator school licensee records, confidentiality of, Section 11212, Vehicle Code.

Traffic offense, dismissed for participation in driving school or program, record of, confidentiality of, Section 1808.7, Vehicle Code.

Transit districts, questionnaire and financial statement information in bids, Section 99154, Public Utilities Code.

Tribal-state gaming compacts, exemption from disclosure for records of an Indian tribe relating to securitization of annual payments, Section 63048.63, this code.

Trust companies, disclosure of private trust confidential information, Section 1602, Financial Code.

(Amended by Stats. 2022, Ch. 258, Sec. 19. (AB 2327) Effective January 1, 2023. Operative January 1, 2024, pursuant to Sec. 130 of Stats. 2022, Ch. 258.)

7930.210

The following provisions may operate to exempt certain records, or portions thereof, from disclosure pursuant to this division:

Unclaimed property, Controller records of, disclosure, Section 1582, Code of Civil Procedure.

Unemployment compensation, disclosure of confidential information, Section 2111, Unemployment Insurance Code.

Unemployment compensation, information obtained in administration of code, Section 1094, Unemployment Insurance Code.

Unemployment fund contributions, publication of annual tax paid, Section 989, Unemployment Insurance Code.

University of California, exemption from disclosure for information submitted by bidders for award of best value contracts, Section 10506.6, Public Contract Code.

Unsafe working condition, confidentiality of complainant, Section 6309, Labor Code.

Use fuel tax information, disclosure prohibited, Section 9255, Revenue and Taxation Code.

Utility systems development, confidential information, Section 7927.300, this code.

Utility user tax return and payment records, exemption from disclosure, Section 7284.6, Revenue and Taxation Code.

Vehicle registration, confidentiality of information, Section 4750.4, Vehicle Code.

Vehicle accident reports, disclosure of, Sections 16005, 20012, and 20014, Vehicle Code and Section 27177, Streets and Highways Code.

Vehicular offense, record of, confidentiality five years after conviction, Section 1807.5, Vehicle Code.

Veterans Affairs, Department of, confidentiality of records of contract purchasers, Section 85, Military and Veterans Code.

Veterinarian or animal health technician, alcohol or dangerous drugs diversion and rehabilitation records, confidentiality of, Section 4871, Business and Professions Code.

Victims' Legal Resource Center, confidentiality of information and records retained, Section 13897.2, Penal Code.

Voter, affidavit or registration, confidentiality of information contained in, Section 7924.000, this code.

Voter, registration by confidential affidavit, Section 2194, Elections Code.

Voting, secrecy, Section 1050, Evidence Code.

(Added by Stats. 2021, Ch. 614, Sec. 2. (AB 473) Effective January 1, 2022. Operative January 1, 2023, pursuant to Sec. 7931.000.)

7930.215

The following provisions may operate to exempt certain records, or portions thereof, from disclosure pursuant to this division:

Wards and dependent children, inspection of juvenile court documents, Section 827, Welfare and Institutions Code.

Wards, petition for sealing records, Section 781, Welfare and Institutions Code.

Winegrowers of California Commission, confidentiality of producers' or vintners' proprietary information, Sections 74655 and 74955, Food and Agricultural Code.

Workers' Compensation Appeals Board, injury or illness report, confidentiality of, Section 6412, Labor Code.

Workers' compensation insurance, dividend payment to policyholder, confidentiality of information, Section 11739, Insurance Code.

Workers' compensation insurance fraud reporting, confidentiality of information, Section 1877.4, Insurance Code.

Workers' compensation insurer or rating organization, confidentiality of notice of noncompliance, Section 11754, Insurance Code.

Workers' compensation insurer, rating information, confidentiality of, Section 11752.7, Insurance Code.

Workers' compensation, notice to correct noncompliance, Section 11754, Insurance Code.

Workers' compensation, release of information to other governmental agencies, Section 11752.5, Insurance Code.

Workers' compensation, self-insured employers, confidentiality of financial information, Section 3742, Labor Code.

Workplace inspection photographs, confidentiality of, Section 6314, Labor Code.

Youth Authority, parole revocation proceedings, confidentiality of, Section 1767.6, Welfare and Institutions Code.

Youth Authority, release of information in possession of Youth Authority for offenses under Sections 676, 1764.1, and 1764.2, Welfare and Institutions Code.

(Added by Stats. 2021, Ch. 614, Sec. 2. (AB 473) Effective January 1, 2022. Operative January 1, 2023, pursuant to Sec. 7931.000.)

PART 7. OPERATIVE DATE

7931.000

This division shall become operative on January 1, 2023.

(Added by Stats. 2021, Ch. 614, Sec. 2. (AB 473) Effective January 1, 2022.)

TITLE 2: GOVERNMENT OF THE STATE OF CALIFORNIA

DIVISION 3: EXECUTIVE DEPARTMENT

PART 1: STATE DEPARTMENT AND AGENCIES

CHAPTER 1: STATE AGENCIES

ARTICLE 9: MEETINGS

11120. LEGISLATIVE FINDING AND DECLARATION; OPEN PROCEEDINGS; CITATION OF ARTICLE

It is the public policy of this state that public agencies exist to aid in the conduct of the people's business and the proceedings of public agencies be conducted openly so that the public may remain informed.

In enacting this article the Legislature finds and declares that it is the intent of the law that actions of state agencies be taken openly and that their deliberation be conducted openly.

The people of this state do not yield their sovereignty to the agencies which serve them. The people, in delegating authority, do not give their public servants the right to decide what is good for the people to know and what is not good for them to know. The people insist on remaining informed so that they may retain control over the instruments they have created.

This article shall be known and may be cited as the Bagley-Keene Open Meeting Act.

(Amended by Stats. 1981, Ch. 968, Sec. 4.)

11121. "STATE BODY"

As used in this article, "state body" means each of the following:

(a) Every state board, or commission, or similar multimember body of the state that is created by statute or required by law to conduct official meetings and every commission created by executive order.

(b) A board, commission, committee, or similar multimember body that exercises any authority of a state body delegated to it by that state body.

(c) An advisory board, advisory commission, advisory committee, advisory subcommittee, or similar multimember advisory body of a state body, if created by formal action of the state body or of any member of the state body, and if the advisory body so created consists of three or more persons.

(d) A board, commission, committee, or similar multimember body on which a member of a body that is a state body pursuant to this section serves in his or her official capacity as a representative of that state body and that is supported, in whole or in part, by funds provided by the state body, whether the multimember body is organized and operated by the state body or by a private corporation.

(e) Notwithstanding subdivision (a) of Section 11121.1, the State Bar of California, as described in Section 6001 of the Business and Professions Code. This subdivision shall become operative on April 1, 2016.

(Amended by Stats. 2015, Ch. 537, Sec. 22. (SB 387) Effective January 1, 2016.)

11121.1. "STATE BODY": DEFINITION EXCLUSIONS

As used in this article, "state body" does not include any of the following:

(a) Except as provided in subdivision (e) of Section 11121, state agencies provided for in Article VI of the California Constitution.

(b) Districts or other local agencies whose meetings are required to be open to the public pursuant to the Ralph M. Brown Act (Chapter 9 (commencing with Section 54950) of Part 1 of Division 2 of Title 5).

(c) State agencies provided for in Article IV of the California Constitution whose meetings are required to be open to the public pursuant to the Grunsky-Burton Open Meeting Act (Article 2.2 (commencing with Section 9027) of Chapter 1.5 of Part 1 of Division 2 of Title 2).

(d) State agencies when they are conducting proceedings pursuant to Section 3596.

(e) State agencies provided for in Section 109260 of the Health and Safety Code, except as provided in Section 109390 of the Health and Safety Code.

(f) The Credit Union Advisory Committee established pursuant to Section 14380 of the Financial Code.

(Amended by Stats. 2015, Ch. 537, Sec. 23. (SB 387) Effective January 1, 2016.)

11121.9. PROVIDING A COPY OF ARTICLE TO MEMBERS OF STATE BODIES

Each state body shall provide a copy of this article to each member of the state body upon his or her appointment to membership or assumption of office.

(Amended by Stats. 1981, Ch. 968, Sec. 7.1.)

11121.95. DUTIES OF PERSONS WHO HAVEN'T YET ASSUMED STATE OFFICE

Any person appointed or elected to serve as a member of a state body who has not yet assumed the duties of office shall conform his or her conduct to the requirements of this article and shall be treated for purposes of this article as if he or she has already assumed office.

(Added by Stats. 1997, Ch. 949, Sec. 1. Effective January 1, 1998.)

11122. ACTION TAKEN

As used in this article "action taken" means a collective decision made by the members of a state body, a collective commitment or promise by the members of the state body to make a positive or negative decision or an actual vote by the members of a state body when sitting as a body or entity upon a motion, proposal, resolution, order or similar action.

(Amended by Stats. 1981, Ch. 968, Sec. 7.3.)

11122.5. "MEETING"; DIRECT COMMUNICATION PROHIBITIONS; PROHIBITION EXCEPTIONS

(a) As used in this article, "meeting" includes any congregation of a majority of the members of a state body at the same time and place to hear, discuss, or deliberate upon any item that is within the subject matter jurisdiction of the state body to which it pertains.

(b) (1) A majority of the members of a state body shall not, outside of a meeting authorized by this chapter, use a series of communications of any kind, directly or through intermediaries, to discuss, deliberate, or take action on any item of business that is within the subject matter of the state body.

(2) Paragraph (1) shall not be construed to prevent an employee or official of a state agency from engaging in separate conversations or communications outside of a meeting authorized by this chapter with members of a legislative body in order to answer questions or provide information regarding a matter that is within the subject matter jurisdiction of the state

agency, if that person does not communicate to members of the legislative body the comments or position of any other member or members of the legislative body.

(c) The prohibitions of this article do not apply to any of the following:

(1) Individual contacts or conversations between a member of a state body and any other person that do not violate subdivision (b).

(2) (A) The attendance of a majority of the members of a state body at a conference or similar gathering open to the public that involves a discussion of issues of general interest to the public or to public agencies of the type represented by the state body, if a majority of the members do not discuss among themselves, other than as part of the scheduled program, business of a specified nature that is within the subject matter jurisdiction of the state body.

(B) Subparagraph (A) does not allow members of the public free admission to a conference or similar gathering at which the organizers have required other participants or registrants to pay fees or charges as a condition of attendance.

(3) The attendance of a majority of the members of a state body at an open and publicized meeting organized to address a topic of state concern by a person or organization other than the state body, if a majority of the members do not discuss among themselves, other than as part of the scheduled program, business of a specific nature that is within the subject matter jurisdiction of the state body.

(4) The attendance of a majority of the members of a state body at an open and noticed meeting of another state body or of a legislative body of a local agency as defined by Section 54951, if a majority of the members do not discuss among themselves, other than as part of the scheduled meeting, business of a specific nature that is within the subject matter jurisdiction of the other state body.

(5) The attendance of a majority of the members of a state body at a purely social or ceremonial occasion, if a majority of the members do not discuss among themselves business of a specific nature that is within the subject matter jurisdiction of the state body.

(6) The attendance of a majority of the members of a state body at an open and noticed meeting of a standing committee of that body, if the members of the state body who are not members of the standing committee attend only as observers.

(Amended by Stats. 2009, Ch. 150, Sec. 1. (AB 1494) Effective January 1, 2010.)

11123. OPEN MEETING REQUIREMENT FOR STATE BODIES; MEETINGS BY TELECONFERENCE

(a) All meetings of a state body shall be open and public and all persons shall be permitted to attend any meeting of a state body except as otherwise provided in this article.

(b) (1) This article does not prohibit a state body from holding an open or closed meeting by teleconference for the benefit of the public and state body. The meeting or proceeding held by teleconference shall otherwise comply with all applicable requirements or laws relating to a specific type of meeting or proceeding, including the following:

(A) The teleconferencing meeting shall comply with all requirements of this article applicable to other meetings.

(B) The portion of the teleconferenced meeting that is required to be open to the public shall be audible to the public at the location specified in the notice of the meeting.

(C) If the state body elects to conduct a meeting or proceeding by teleconference, it shall post agendas at all teleconference locations and conduct teleconference meetings in a manner that protects the rights of any party or member of the public appearing before the state body. Each teleconference location shall be identified in the notice and agenda of the meeting or proceeding, and each teleconference location shall be accessible to the public. The agenda shall provide an opportunity for members of the public to address the state body directly pursuant to Section 11125.7 at each teleconference location.

(D) All votes taken during a teleconferenced meeting shall be by rollcall.

(E) The portion of the teleconferenced meeting that is closed to the public may not include the consideration of any agenda item being heard pursuant to Section 11125.5.

(F) At least one member of the state body shall be physically present at the location specified in the notice of the meeting.

(2) For the purposes of this subdivision, "teleconference" means a meeting of a state body, the members of which are at different locations, connected by electronic means, through either audio or both audio and video. This section does not prohibit a state body from providing members of the public with additional locations in which the public may observe or address the state body by electronic means, through either audio or both audio and video.

(c) The state body shall publicly report any action taken and the vote or abstention on that action of each member present for the action.

(Amended by Stats. 2014, Ch. 510, Sec. 1. (AB 2720) Effective January 1, 2015.)

11123.1. OPEN AND PUBLIC MEETINGS TO CONFORM TO AMERICANS WITH DISABILITIES ACT

All meetings of a state body that are open and public shall meet the protections and prohibitions contained in Section 202 of the Americans with Disabilities Act of 1990 (42 U.S.C. Sec. 12132), and the federal rules and regulations adopted in implementation thereof.

(Added by Stats. 2002, Ch. 300, Sec. 1. Effective January 1, 2003.)

11123.5. HOLDING OPEN MEETINGS BY TELECONFERENCE [REPEALED AS OF JANUARY 1, 2026]

(a) For purposes of this section, the following definitions apply:

(1) "Participate remotely" means participation in a meeting at a location other than the physical location designated in the agenda of the meeting.

(2) "Remote location" means a location other than the primary physical location designated in the agenda of a meeting.

(3) "Teleconference" has the same meaning as in Section 11123.

(b) In addition to the authorization to hold a meeting by teleconference pursuant to subdivision (b) of Section 11123 or Section 11123.2, any state body that is an advisory board, advisory commission, advisory committee, advisory subcommittee, or similar multimember advisory body may hold an open meeting by teleconference as described in this section, provided the meeting complies with all of the section's requirements and, except as set forth in this section, it also complies with all other applicable requirements of this article.

(c) A member of a state body as described in subdivision (b) who participates in a teleconference meeting from a remote location subject to this section's requirements shall be listed in the minutes of the meeting.

(d) The state body shall provide notice to the public at least 24 hours before the meeting that identifies any member who will participate remotely by posting the notice on its internet website and by emailing notice to any person who has requested notice of meetings of the state body under this article. The location of a member of a state body who will participate remotely is not required to be disclosed in the public notice or email and need not be accessible to the public. The notice of the meeting shall also identify the primary physical meeting location designated pursuant to subdivision (f).

(e) This section does not affect the requirement prescribed by this article that the state body post an agenda of a meeting at least 10 days in advance of the meeting. The agenda shall include information regarding the physical meeting location designated pursuant to subdivision (f), but is not required to disclose information regarding any remote location.

(f) A state body described in subdivision (b) shall designate the primary physical meeting location in the notice of the meeting where members of the public may physically attend the meeting, observe and hear the meeting, and participate. At least one staff member of the state body shall be present at the primary physical meeting location during the meeting. The state body shall post the agenda at the primary physical meeting location, but need not post the agenda at a remote location.

(g) When a member of a state body described in subdivision (b) participates remotely in a meeting subject to this section's requirements, the state body shall provide a means by which the public may remotely hear audio of the meeting or remotely observe the meeting, including, if available, equal access equivalent to members of the state body participating remotely. The applicable teleconference phone number or internet website, or other information indicating how the public can access the meeting remotely, shall be in the 24-hour notice described in subdivision (b) that is available to the public.

(h) (1) Except as provided in paragraph (2), the members of the state body shall visibly appear on camera during the open portion of a meeting that is publicly accessible via the internet or other online platform.

(2) The visual appearance of a member of a state body on camera may cease only when the appearance would be technologically impracticable, including, but not limited to, when the member experiences a lack of reliable broadband or internet connectivity that would be remedied by joining without video, or when the visual display of meeting materials, information, or speakers on the internet or other online platform requires the visual appearance of a member of a state body on camera to cease.

(3) If a member of the body does not appear on camera due to challenges with internet connectivity, the member shall announce the reason for their nonappearance when they turn off their camera.

(i) Upon discovering that a means of remote access required by subdivision (g) has failed during a meeting, the state body described in subdivision (b) shall end or adjourn the meeting in accordance with Section 11128.5. In addition to any other requirements that may apply, the state body shall provide notice of the meeting's end or adjournment on its internet website and by email to any person who has requested notice of meetings of the state body under this article. If the meeting will be adjourned and reconvened on the same day, further notice shall be provided by an automated message on a telephone line posted on the state body's agenda, or by a similar means, that will communicate when the state body intends to reconvene the meeting and how a member of the public may hear audio of the meeting or observe the meeting.

(j) This section does not limit or affect the ability of a state body to hold a teleconference meeting under another provision of this article.

(k) This section shall remain in effect only until January 1, 2026, and as of that date is repealed.

(Amended by Stats. 2023, Ch. 216, Sec. 2. (SB 544) Effective January 1, 2024. Repealed as of January 1, 2026, by its own provisions. See later version added by Sec. 3 of Stats. 2023, Ch. 216.)

11123.5 – [OPERATIVE JANUARY 1, 2026]

(a) In addition to the authorization to hold a meeting by teleconference pursuant to subdivision (b) of Section 11123, any state body that is an advisory board, advisory commission, advisory committee, advisory subcommittee, or similar multimember advisory body may hold an open meeting by teleconference as described in this section, provided the meeting complies with all of the section's requirements and, except as set forth in this section, it also complies with all other applicable requirements of this article.

(b) A member of a state body as described in subdivision (a) who participates in a teleconference meeting from a remote location subject to this section's requirements shall be listed in the minutes of the meeting.

(c) The state body shall provide notice to the public at least 24 hours before the meeting that identifies any member who will participate remotely by posting the notice on its internet website and by emailing notice to any person who has requested notice of meetings of the state body under this article. The location of a member of a state body who will participate remotely is not required to be disclosed in the public notice or email and need not be accessible to the public. The notice of the meeting shall also identify the primary physical meeting location designated pursuant to subdivision (e).

(d) This section does not affect the requirement prescribed by this article that the state body post an agenda of a meeting at least 10 days in advance of the meeting. The agenda shall include information regarding the physical meeting location designated pursuant to subdivision (e), but is not required to disclose information regarding any remote location.

(e) A state body described in subdivision (a) shall designate the primary physical meeting location in the notice of the meeting where members of the public may physically attend the meeting and participate. A quorum of the members of the state body shall be in attendance at the primary physical meeting location, and members of the state body participating remotely shall not count towards establishing a quorum. All decisions taken during a meeting by teleconference shall be by rollcall vote. The state body shall post the agenda at the primary physical meeting location, but need not post the agenda at a remote location.

(f) When a member of a state body described in subdivision (a) participates remotely in a meeting subject to this section's requirements, the state body shall provide a means by which the public may remotely hear audio of the meeting or remotely observe the meeting, including, if available, equal access equivalent to members of the state body participating remotely. The applicable teleconference phone number or internet website, or other information indicating how the public can access the meeting remotely, shall be in the 24-hour notice described in subdivision (a) that is available to the public.

(g) Upon discovering that a means of remote access required by subdivision (f) has failed during a meeting, the state body described in subdivision (a) shall end or adjourn the meeting in accordance with Section 11128.5. In addition to any other requirements that may apply, the state body shall provide notice of the meeting's end or adjournment on its internet website and by email to any person who has requested notice of meetings of the state body under this article. If the meeting will be adjourned and reconvened on the same day, further notice shall be provided by an automated message on a telephone line posted on the state body's agenda, or by a similar means, that will communicate when the state body intends to reconvene the meeting and how a member of the public may hear audio of the meeting or observe the meeting.

(h) For purposes of this section:

(1) "Participate remotely" means participation in a meeting at a location other than the physical location designated in the agenda of the meeting.

(2) "Remote location" means a location other than the primary physical location designated in the agenda of a meeting.

(3) "Teleconference" has the same meaning as in Section 11123.

(i) This section does not limit or affect the ability of a state body to hold a teleconference meeting under another provision of this article.

(j) This section shall become operative on January 1, 2026.

(Repealed (in Sec. 2) and added by Stats. 2023, Ch. 216, Sec. 3. (SB 544) Effective January 1, 2024. Operative January 1, 2026, by its own provisions.)

11124. PROHIBITED CONDITIONS TO ATTENDANCE

(a) No person shall be required, as a condition to attendance at a meeting of a state body, to register their name, to provide other information, to complete a questionnaire, or otherwise to fulfill any condition precedent to their attendance.

(b) If an attendance list, register, questionnaire, or other similar document is posted at or near the entrance to the room where the meeting is to be held, or is circulated to persons present during the meeting, it shall state clearly that the signing, registering, or completion of the document is voluntary, and that all persons may attend the meeting regardless of whether a person signs, registers, or completes the document.

(c) This section does not apply to an internet website or other online platform that may require the submission of information to log into a teleconferenced meeting, provided, however, that a person required to submit such information shall be permitted to submit a pseudonym or other anonymous information when using the internet website or other online platform to attend the meeting.

(Amended by Stats. 2023, Ch. 216, Sec. 4. (SB 544) Effective January 1, 2024.)

11124.1. RECORDING OF PROCEEDINGS; INSPECTION OF RECORDING

(a) Any person attending an open and public meeting of the state body shall have the right to record the proceedings with an audio or video recorder or a still or motion picture camera in the absence of a reasonable finding by the state body that the recording cannot continue without noise, illumination, or obstruction of view that constitutes, or would constitute, a persistent disruption of the proceedings.

(b) Any audio or video recording of an open and public meeting made for whatever purpose by or at the direction of the state body shall be subject to inspection pursuant to the California Public Records Act (Division 10 (commencing with

Section 7920.000) of Title 1), but may be erased or destroyed 30 days after the recording. Any inspection of an audio or video recording shall be provided without charge on equipment made available by the state body.

(c) No state body shall prohibit or otherwise restrict the broadcast of its open and public meetings in the absence of a reasonable finding that the broadcast cannot be accomplished without noise, illumination, or obstruction of view that would constitute a persistent disruption of the proceedings.

(Amended by Stats. 2021, Ch. 615, Sec. 161. (AB 474) Effective January 1, 2022. Operative January 1, 2023, pursuant to Sec. 463 of Stats. 2021, Ch. 615.)

11125. NOTICE OF MEETING

(a) The state body shall provide notice of its meeting to any person who requests that notice in writing. Notice shall be given and also made available on the Internet at least 10 days in advance of the meeting, and shall include the name, address, and telephone number of any person who can provide further information prior to the meeting, but need not include a list of witnesses expected to appear at the meeting. The written notice shall additionally include the address of the Internet site where notices required by this article are made available.

(b) The notice of a meeting of a body that is a state body shall include a specific agenda for the meeting, containing a brief description of the items of business to be transacted or discussed in either open or closed session. A brief general description of an item generally need not exceed 20 words. A description of an item to be transacted or discussed in closed session shall include a citation of the specific statutory authority under which a closed session is being held. No item shall be added to the agenda subsequent to the provision of this notice, unless otherwise permitted by this article.

(c) Notice of a meeting of a state body that complies with this section shall also constitute notice of a meeting of an advisory body of that state body, provided that the business to be discussed by the advisory body is covered by the notice of the meeting of the state body, provided that the specific time and place of the advisory body's meeting is announced during the open and public state body's meeting, and provided that the advisory body's meeting is conducted within a reasonable time of, and nearby, the meeting of the state body.

(d) A person may request, and shall be provided, notice pursuant to subdivision (a) for all meetings of a state body or for a specific meeting or meetings. In addition, at the state body's discretion, a person may request, and may be provided, notice of only those meetings of a state body at which a particular subject or subjects specified in the request will be discussed.

(e) A request for notice of more than one meeting of a state body shall be subject to the provisions of Section 14911.

(f) The notice shall be made available in appropriate alternative formats, as required by Section 202 of the Americans with Disabilities Act of 1990 (42 U.S.C. Sec. 12132), and the federal rules and regulations adopted in implementation thereof, upon request by any person with a disability. The notice shall include information regarding how, to whom, and by when a request for any disability-related modification or accommodation, including auxiliary aids or services may be made by a person with a disability who requires these aids or services in order to participate in the public meeting.

(Amended by Stats. 2002, Ch. 300, Sec. 2. Effective January 1, 2003.)

11125.1. AGENDAS OF PUBLIC MEETINGS AND OTHER "WRITINGS" AS PUBLIC RECORD; EXEMPTION; PUBLIC INSPECTION; ALTERNATIVE FORMAT REQUIREMENTS; FEE

(a) Notwithstanding Section 7922.000 or any other provisions of law, agendas of public meetings and other writings, when distributed to all, or a majority of all, of the members of a state body by any person in connection with a matter subject to discussion or consideration at a public meeting of the body, are disclosable public records under the California Public Records Act (Division 10 (commencing with Section 7920.000) of Title 1), and shall be made available upon request without delay. However, this section shall not include any writing exempt from public disclosure under Section 7924.100, 7924.105, 7924.110, 7924.510, or 7924.700 of this code, any provision listed in Section 7920.505 of this code, or Section 489.1 or 583 of the Public Utilities Code.

(b) Writings that are public records under subdivision (a) and that are distributed to members of the state body prior to or during a meeting, pertaining to any item to be considered during the meeting, shall be made available for public inspection at the meeting if prepared by the state body or a member of the state body, or after the meeting if prepared by some other person. These writings shall be made available in appropriate alternative formats, as required by Section 202 of the Americans with Disabilities Act of 1990 (42 U.S.C. Sec. 12132), and the federal rules and regulations adopted in implementation thereof, upon request by a person with a disability.

(c) In the case of the Franchise Tax Board, prior to that state body taking final action on any item, writings pertaining to that item that are public records under subdivision (a) that are prepared and distributed by the Franchise Tax Board staff or individual members to members of the state body prior to or during a meeting shall be:

(1) Made available for public inspection at that meeting.

(2) Distributed to all persons who request notice in writing pursuant to subdivision (a) of Section 11125.

(3) Made available on the internet.

(d) Prior to the State Board of Equalization taking final action on any item that does not involve a named taxpayer or feepayer, writings pertaining to that item that are public records under subdivision (a) that are prepared and distributed by board staff or individual members to members of the state body prior to or during a meeting shall be:

(1) Made available for public inspection at that meeting.

(2) Distributed to all persons who request or have requested copies of these writings.

(3) Made available on the internet.

(e) Nothing in this section shall be construed to prevent a state body from charging a fee or deposit for a copy of a public record pursuant to Section 7922.530, except that no surcharge shall be imposed on persons with disabilities in violation of Section 202 of the Americans with Disabilities Act of 1990 (42 U.S.C. Sec. 12132), and the federal rules and regulations adopted in implementation thereof. The writings described in subdivision (b) are subject to the requirements of the California Public Records Act (Division 10 (commencing with Section 7920.000) of Title 1), and shall not be construed to limit or delay the public's right to inspect any record required to be disclosed by that act, or to limit the public's right to inspect any record covered by that act. This section shall not be construed to be applicable to any writings solely because they are properly discussed in a closed session of a state body. Nothing in this article shall be construed to require a state body to place any paid advertisement or any other paid notice in any publication.

(f) "Writing" for purposes of this section means "writing" as defined under Section 7920.545.

(Amended by Stats. 2021, Ch. 615, Sec. 162. (AB 474) Effective January 1, 2022. Operative January 1, 2023, pursuant to Sec. 463 of Stats. 2021, Ch. 615.)

11125.2. PUBLIC REPORT OF ACTION TAKEN REGARDING PUBLIC EMPLOYEE

Any state body shall report publicly at a subsequent public meeting any action taken, and any rollcall vote thereon, to appoint, employ, or dismiss a public employee arising out of any closed session of the state body.

(Amended by Stats. 1981, Ch. 968, Sec. 10.3.)

11125.3. CONDITIONS FOR TAKING ACTION ON ITEMS NO APPEARING ON POSTED AGENDA; NOTICE REQUIREMENTS

(a) Notwithstanding Section 11125, a state body may take action on items of business not appearing on the posted agenda under any of the conditions stated below:

(1) Upon a determination by a majority vote of the state body that an emergency situation exists, as defined in Section 11125.5.

(2) Upon a determination by a two-thirds vote of the state body, or, if less than two- thirds of the members are present, a unanimous vote of those members present, that there exists a need to take immediate action and that the need for action came to the attention of the state body subsequent to the agenda being posted as specified in Section 11125.

(b) Notice of the additional item to be considered shall be provided to each member of the state body and to all parties that have requested notice of its meetings as soon as is practicable after a determination of the need to consider the item is made, but shall be delivered in a manner that allows it to be received by the members and by newspapers of general circulation and radio or television stations at least 48 hours before the time of the meeting specified in the notice. Notice shall be made available to newspapers of general circulation and radio or television stations by providing that notice to all national press wire services. Notice shall also be made available on the Internet as soon as is practicable after the decision to consider additional items at a meeting has been made.

(Amended by Stats. 2001, Ch. 243, Sec. 9. Effective January 1, 2002.)

11125.4. PERMISSIBLE PURPOSES FOR SPECIAL MEETINGS; NOTICE; FINDING OF HARDSHIP

(a) A special meeting may be called at any time by the presiding officer of the state body or by a majority of the members of the state body. A special meeting may only be called for one of the following purposes when compliance with the 10-day notice provisions of Section 11125 would impose a substantial hardship on the state body or when immediate action is required to protect the public interest:

(1) To consider "pending litigation" as that term is defined in subdivision (e) of Section 11126.

(2) To consider proposed legislation.

(3) To consider issuance of a legal opinion.

(4) To consider disciplinary action involving a state officer or employee.

(5) To consider the purchase, sale, exchange, or lease of real property.

(6) To consider license examinations and applications.

(7) To consider an action on a loan or grant provided pursuant to Division 31 (commencing with Section 50000) of the Health and Safety Code.

(8) To consider its response to a confidential final draft audit report as permitted by Section 11126.2.

(9) To provide for an interim executive officer of a state body upon the death, incapacity, or vacancy in the office of the executive officer.

(b) When a special meeting is called pursuant to one of the purposes specified in subdivision (a), the state body shall provide notice of the special meeting to each member of the state body and to all parties that have requested notice of its meetings as soon as is practicable after the decision to call a special meeting has been made, but shall deliver the notice in a manner that allows it to be received by the members and by newspapers of general circulation and radio or television stations at least 48 hours before the time of the special meeting specified in the notice. Notice shall be made available to newspapers of general circulation and radio or television stations by providing that notice to all national press wire services. Notice shall also be made available on the Internet within the time periods required by this section. The notice shall specify the time and place of the special meeting and the business to be transacted. The written notice shall additionally specify the address of the Internet Web site where notices required by this article are made available. No other business shall be considered at a special meeting by the state body. The written notice may be dispensed with as to any member who at or prior to the time the meeting convenes files with the clerk or secretary of the state body a written waiver of notice. The waiver may be given by telegram, facsimile transmission, or similar means. The written notice may also be dispensed with as to any member who is actually present at the meeting at the time it convenes. Notice shall be required pursuant to this section regardless of whether any action is taken at the special meeting.

(c) At the commencement of any special meeting, the state body must make a finding in open session that the delay necessitated by providing notice 10 days prior to a meeting as required by Section 11125 would cause a substantial hardship on the body or that immediate action is required to protect the public interest. The finding shall set forth the specific facts that constitute the hardship to the body or the impending harm to the public interest. The finding shall be adopted by a two- thirds vote of the body, or, if less than two-thirds of the members are present, a unanimous vote of those members present. The finding shall be made available on the Internet. Failure to adopt the finding terminates the meeting.

(Amended by Stats. 2007, Ch. 92, Sec. 1. Effective January 1, 2008.)

11125.5. EMERGENCY MEETINGS; NOTIFICATION OF MEDIA

(a) In the case of an emergency situation involving matters upon which prompt action is necessary due to the disruption or threatened disruption of public facilities, a state body may hold an emergency meeting without complying with the 10- day notice requirement of Section 11125 or the 48-hour notice requirement of Section 11125.4.

(b) For purposes of this section, "emergency situation" means any of the following, as determined by a majority of the members of the state body during a meeting prior to the emergency meeting, or at the beginning of the emergency meeting:

(1) Work stoppage or other activity that severely impairs public health or safety, or both.

(2) Crippling disaster that severely impairs public health or safety, or both.

(c) However, newspapers of general circulation and radio or television stations that have requested notice of meetings pursuant to Section 11125 shall be notified by the presiding officer of the state body, or a designee thereof, one hour prior to the emergency meeting by telephone. Notice shall also be made available on the Internet as soon as is practicable after the decision to call the emergency meeting has been made. If telephone services are not functioning, the notice requirements of this section shall be deemed waived, and the presiding officer of the state body, or a designee thereof, shall notify those newspapers, radio stations, or television stations of the fact of the holding of the emergency meeting, the purpose of the meeting, and any action taken at the meeting as soon after the meeting as possible.

(d) The minutes of a meeting called pursuant to this section, a list of persons who the presiding officer of the state body, or a designee thereof, notified or attempted to notify, a copy of the rollcall vote, and any action taken at the meeting shall be posted for a minimum of 10 days in a public place, and also made available on the Internet for a minimum of 10 days, as soon after the meeting as possible.

(Amended by Stats. 1999, Ch. 393, Sec. 3. Effective January 1, 2000. As provided in Sec. 7 of Ch. 393, amendment is to be implemented on July 1, 2001, or other date authorized by Dept. of Information Technology pursuant to Executive Order D-3-99.)

11125.7. OPPORTUNITY FOR PUBLIC TO ADDRESS STATE BODY

(a) Except as otherwise provided in this section, the state body shall provide an opportunity for members of the public to directly address the state body on each agenda item before or during the state body's discussion or consideration of the item. This section is not applicable if the agenda item has already been considered by a committee composed exclusively of members of the state body at a public meeting where interested members of the public were afforded the opportunity to address the committee on the item, before or during the committee's consideration of the item, unless the item has been substantially changed since the committee heard the item, as determined by the state body. Every notice for a special meeting at which action is proposed to be taken on an item shall provide an opportunity for members of the public to directly address the state body concerning that item prior to action on the item. In addition, the notice requirement of Section 11125 shall not preclude the acceptance of testimony at meetings, other than emergency meetings, from members of the public if no action is taken by the state body at the same meeting on matters brought before the body by members of the public.

(b) The state body may adopt reasonable regulations to ensure that the intent of subdivision (a) is carried out, including, but not limited to, regulations limiting the total amount of time allocated for public comment on particular issues and for each individual speaker.

(c) (1) Notwithstanding subdivision (b), when a state body limits time for public comment the state body shall provide at least twice the allotted time to a member of the public who utilizes a translator or other translating technology to ensure that non-English speakers receive the same opportunity to directly address the state body.

(2) Paragraph (1) shall not apply if the state body utilizes simultaneous translation equipment in a manner that allows the state body to hear the translated public testimony simultaneously.

(d) The state body shall not prohibit public criticism of the policies, programs, or services of the state body, or of the acts or omissions of the state body. Nothing in this subdivision shall confer any privilege or protection for expression beyond that otherwise provided by law.

(e) This section is not applicable to any of the following:

(1) Closed sessions held pursuant to Section 11126.

(2) Decisions regarding proceedings held pursuant to Chapter 5 (commencing with Section 11500), relating to administrative adjudication, or to the conduct of those proceedings.

(3) Hearings conducted by the California Victim Compensation Board pursuant to Sections 13963 and 13963.1.

(4) Agenda items that involve decisions of the Public Utilities Commission regarding adjudicatory hearings held pursuant to Chapter 9 (commencing with Section 1701) of Part 1 of Division 1 of the Public Utilities Code. For all other agenda items, the commission shall provide members of the public, other than those who have already participated in the proceedings underlying the agenda item, an opportunity to directly address the commission before or during the commission's consideration of the item.

(Amended by Stats. 2021, Ch. 63, Sec. 1. (AB 1291) Effective January 1, 2022.)

11125.8. IDENTIFICATION OF CRIME VICTIM HAVING CLOSED HEARING ON APPLICATION FOR INDEMNIFICATION; EFFECT OF DISCLOSURE THAT PUBLIC IS EXCLUDED FROM HEARING

(a) Notwithstanding Section 11131.5, in any hearing that the California Victim Compensation Board conducts pursuant to Section 13963.1 and that the applicant or applicant's representative does not request be open to the public, no notice, agenda, announcement, or report required under this article need identify the applicant.

(b) In any hearing that the board conducts pursuant to Section 13963.1 and that the applicant or applicant's representative does not request be open to the public, the board shall disclose that the hearing is being held pursuant to Section 13963.1. That disclosure shall be deemed to satisfy the requirements of subdivision (a) of Section 11126.3.

(Amended by Stats. 2016, Ch. 31, Sec. 72. (SB 836) Effective June 27, 2016.)

11126. CLOSED SESSION ON ISSUES RELATING TO PUBLIC EMPLOYEE; EMPLOYEE'S RIGHT TO PUBLIC HEARING; CLOSED SESSIONS NOT PROHIBITED BY ARTICLE; ABROGATION OF LAWYER-CLIENT PRIVILEGE

(a) (1) This article shall not be construed to prevent a state body from holding closed sessions during a regular or special meeting to consider the appointment, employment, evaluation of performance, or dismissal of a public employee or to hear complaints or charges brought against that employee by another person or employee unless the employee requests a public hearing.

(2) As a condition to holding a closed session on the complaints or charges to consider disciplinary action or to consider dismissal, the employee shall be given written notice of their right to have a public hearing, rather than a closed session, and that notice shall be delivered to the employee personally or by mail at least 24 hours before the time for holding a regular or special meeting. If notice is not given, any disciplinary or other action taken against any employee at the closed session shall be null and void.

(3) The state body also may exclude from any public or closed session, during the examination of a witness, any or all other witnesses in the matter being investigated by the state body.

(4) Following the public hearing or closed session, the body may deliberate on the decision to be reached in a closed session.

(b) For the purposes of this section, "employee" does not include any person who is elected to, or appointed to a public office by, any state body. However, officers of the California State University who receive compensation for their services, other than per diem and ordinary and necessary expenses, shall, when engaged in that capacity, be considered employees. Furthermore, for purposes of this section, the term employee includes a person exempt from civil service pursuant to subdivision (e) of Section 4 of Article VII of the California Constitution.

(c) This article shall not be construed to do any of the following:

(1) Prevent state bodies that administer the licensing of persons engaging in businesses or professions from holding closed sessions to prepare, approve, grade, or administer examinations.

(2) Prevent an advisory body of a state body that administers the licensing of persons engaged in businesses or professions from conducting a closed session to discuss matters that the advisory body has found would constitute an unwarranted invasion of the privacy of an individual licensee or applicant if discussed in an open meeting, provided the advisory body does not include a quorum of the members of the state body it advises. Those matters may include review of an applicant's qualifications for licensure and an inquiry specifically related to the state body's enforcement program concerning an individual licensee or applicant where the inquiry occurs prior to the filing of a civil, criminal, or administrative disciplinary action against the licensee or applicant by the state body.

(3) Prohibit a state body from holding a closed session to deliberate on a decision to be reached in a proceeding required to be conducted pursuant to Chapter 5 (commencing with Section 11500) or similar provisions of law.

(4) Grant a right to enter any correctional institution or the grounds of a correctional institution where that right is not otherwise granted by law, nor shall anything in this article be construed to prevent a state body from holding a closed session when considering and acting upon the determination of a term, parole, or release of any individual or other disposition of an individual case, or if public disclosure of the subjects under discussion or consideration is expressly prohibited by statute.

(5) Prevent any closed session to consider the conferring of honorary degrees, or gifts, donations, and bequests that the donor or proposed donor has requested in writing to be kept confidential.

(6) Prevent the Alcoholic Beverage Control Appeals Board or the Cannabis Control Appeals Panel from holding a closed session for the purpose of holding a deliberative conference as provided in Section 11125.

(7) (A) Prevent a state body from holding closed sessions with its negotiator prior to the purchase, sale, exchange, or lease of real property by or for the state body to give instructions to its negotiator regarding the price and terms of payment for the purchase, sale, exchange, or lease.

(B) However, prior to the closed session, the state body shall hold an open and public session in which it identifies the real property or real properties that the negotiations may concern and the person or persons with whom its negotiator may negotiate.

(C) For purposes of this paragraph, the negotiator may be a member of the state body.

(D) For purposes of this paragraph, "lease" includes renewal or renegotiation of a lease.

(E) This paragraph shall not preclude a state body from holding a closed session for discussions regarding eminent domain proceedings pursuant to subdivision (e).

(8) Prevent the California Postsecondary Education Commission from holding closed sessions to consider matters pertaining to the appointment or termination of the Director of the California Postsecondary Education Commission.

(9) Prevent the Council for Private Postsecondary and Vocational Education from holding closed sessions to consider matters pertaining to the appointment or termination of the Executive Director of the Council for Private Postsecondary and Vocational Education.

(10) Prevent the Franchise Tax Board from holding closed sessions for the purpose of discussion of confidential tax returns or information the public disclosure of which is prohibited by law, or from considering matters pertaining to the appointment or removal of the Executive Officer of the Franchise Tax Board.

(11) Require the Franchise Tax Board to notice or disclose any confidential tax information considered in closed sessions, or documents executed in connection therewith, the public disclosure of which is prohibited pursuant to Article 2 (commencing with Section 19542) of Chapter 7 of Part 10.2 of Division 2 of the Revenue and Taxation Code.

(12) Prevent the Board of State and Community Corrections from holding closed sessions when considering reports of crime conditions under Section 6027 of the Penal Code.

(13) Prevent the State Air Resources Board from holding closed sessions when considering the proprietary specifications and performance data of manufacturers.

(14) Prevent the State Board of Education or the Superintendent of Public Instruction, or any committee advising the board or the Superintendent, from holding closed sessions on those portions of its review of assessment instruments pursuant to Chapter 5 (commencing with Section 60600) of Part 33 of Division 4 of Title 2 of the Education Code during which actual test content is reviewed and discussed. The purpose of this provision is to maintain the confidentiality of the assessments under review.

(15) Prevent the Department of Resources Recycling and Recovery or its auxiliary committees from holding closed sessions for the purpose of discussing confidential tax returns, discussing trade secrets or confidential or proprietary information in its possession, or discussing other data, the public disclosure of which is prohibited by law.

(16) Prevent a state body that invests retirement, pension, or endowment funds from holding closed sessions when considering investment decisions. For purposes of consideration of shareholder voting on corporate stocks held by the state body, closed sessions for the purposes of voting may be held only with respect to election of corporate directors, election of independent auditors, and other financial issues that could have a material effect on the net income of the corporation. For the purpose of real property investment decisions that may be considered in a closed session pursuant to this paragraph, a state body shall also be exempt from the provisions of paragraph

(7) relating to the identification of real properties prior to the closed session.

(17) Prevent a state body, or boards, commissions, administrative officers, or other representatives that may properly be designated by law or by a state body, from holding closed sessions with its representatives in discharging its responsibilities under Chapter 10 (commencing with Section 3500), Chapter 10.3 (commencing with Section 3512), Chapter 10.5 (commencing with Section 3525), or Chapter 10.7 (commencing with Section 3540) of Division 4 of Title 1 as the sessions relate to salaries, salary schedules, or compensation paid in the form of fringe benefits. For the purposes enumerated in the preceding sentence, a state body may also meet with a state conciliator who has intervened in the proceedings.

(18) (A) Prevent a state body from holding closed sessions to consider matters posing a threat or potential threat of criminal or terrorist activity against the personnel, property, buildings, facilities, or equipment, including electronic data, owned, leased, or controlled by the state body, where disclosure of these considerations could compromise or impede the safety or security of the personnel, property, buildings, facilities, or equipment, including electronic data, owned, leased, or controlled by the state body.

(B) Notwithstanding any other law, a state body, at any regular or special meeting, may meet in a closed session pursuant to subparagraph (A) upon a two-thirds vote of the members present at the meeting.

(C) After meeting in closed session pursuant to subparagraph (A), the state body shall reconvene in open session prior to adjournment and report that a closed session was held pursuant to subparagraph (A), the general nature of the matters considered, and whether any action was taken in closed session.

(D) After meeting in closed session pursuant to subparagraph (A), the state body shall submit to the Legislative Analyst written notification stating that it held this closed session, the general reason or reasons for the closed session, the general nature of the matters considered, and whether any action was taken in closed session. The Legislative Analyst shall retain for no less than four years any written notification received from a state body pursuant to this subparagraph.

(19) Prevent the California Sex Offender Management Board from holding a closed session for the purpose of discussing matters pertaining to the application of a sex offender treatment provider for certification pursuant to Sections 290.09 and 9003 of the Penal Code. Those matters may include review of an applicant's qualifications for certification.

(20) (A) Prevent the Research Advisory Panel established in Sections 11480 and 11481 of the Health and Safety Code from holding closed sessions for the purpose of discussing, reviewing, and approving research projects, including applications and amendment applications, that contain sensitive and confidential information, including, but not limited to, trade secrets, intellectual property, or proprietary information in its possession, the public disclosure of which is prohibited by law.

(B) This paragraph shall become inoperative on January 1, 2027.

(d) (1) Notwithstanding any other law, any meeting of the Public Utilities Commission at which the rates of entities under the commission's jurisdiction are changed shall be open and public.

(2) This article shall not be construed to prevent the Public Utilities Commission from holding closed sessions to deliberate on the institution of proceedings, or disciplinary actions against any person or entity under the jurisdiction of the commission.

(e) (1) This article shall not be construed to prevent a state body, based on the advice of its legal counsel, from holding a closed session to confer with, or receive advice from, its legal counsel regarding pending litigation when discussion in open session concerning those matters would prejudice the position of the state body in the litigation.

(2) For purposes of this article, all expressions of the lawyer-client privilege other than those provided in this subdivision are hereby abrogated. This subdivision is the exclusive expression of the lawyer-client privilege for purposes of conducting closed session meetings pursuant to this article. For purposes of this subdivision, litigation shall be considered pending when any of the following circumstances exist:

(A) An adjudicatory proceeding before a court, an administrative body exercising its adjudicatory authority, a hearing officer, or an arbitrator, to which the state body is a party, has been initiated formally.

(B) (i) A point has been reached where, in the opinion of the state body on the advice of its legal counsel, based on existing facts and circumstances, there is a significant exposure to litigation against the state body.

(ii) Based on existing facts and circumstances, the state body is meeting only to decide whether a closed session is authorized pursuant to clause (i).

(C) Based on existing facts and circumstances, the state body has decided to initiate or is deciding whether to initiate litigation.

(3) The legal counsel of the state body shall prepare and submit to it a memorandum stating the specific reasons and legal authority for the closed session. If the closed session is pursuant to subparagraph (A) of paragraph (2), the memorandum shall include the title of the litigation. If the closed session is pursuant to subparagraph (B) or (C) of paragraph (2), the memorandum shall include the existing facts and circumstances on which it is based. The legal counsel shall submit the memorandum to the state body prior to the closed session, if feasible, and in any case no later than one week after the closed session. The memorandum shall be exempt from disclosure pursuant to Section 7927.205.

(4) For purposes of this subdivision, "litigation" includes any adjudicatory proceeding, including eminent domain, before a court, administrative body exercising its adjudicatory authority, hearing officer, or arbitrator.

(5) Disclosure of a memorandum required under this subdivision shall not be deemed as a waiver of the lawyer-client privilege, as provided for under Article 3 (commencing with Section 950) of Chapter 4 of Division 8 of the Evidence Code.

(f) In addition to subdivisions (a), (b), and (c), this article shall not be construed to do any of the following:

(1) Prevent a state body operating under a joint powers agreement for insurance pooling from holding a closed session to discuss a claim for the payment of tort liability or public liability losses incurred by the state body or any member agency under the joint powers agreement.

(2) Prevent the examining committee established by the State Board of Forestry and Fire Protection, pursuant to Section 763 of the Public Resources Code, from conducting a closed session to consider disciplinary action

against an individual professional forester prior to the filing of an accusation against the forester pursuant to Section 11503.

(3) Prevent the enforcement advisory committee established by the California Board of Accountancy pursuant to Section 5020 of the Business and Professions Code from conducting a closed session to consider disciplinary action against an individual accountant prior to the filing of an accusation against the accountant pursuant to Section 11503. This article shall not be construed to prevent the qualifications examining committee established by the California Board of Accountancy pursuant to Section 5023 of the Business and Professions Code from conducting a closed hearing to interview an individual applicant or accountant regarding the applicant's qualifications.

(4) Prevent a state body, as defined in subdivision (b) of Section 11121, from conducting a closed session to consider any matter that properly could be considered in closed session by the state body whose authority it exercises.

(5) Prevent a state body, as defined in subdivision (d) of Section 11121, from conducting a closed session to consider any matter that properly could be considered in a closed session by the body defined as a state body pursuant to subdivision (a) or (b) of Section 11121.

(6) Prevent a state body, as defined in subdivision (c) of Section 11121, from conducting a closed session to consider any matter that properly could be considered in a closed session by the state body it advises.

(7) Prevent the State Board of Equalization from holding closed sessions for either of the following:

(A) When considering matters pertaining to the appointment or removal of the Executive Secretary of the State Board of Equalization.

(B) For the purpose of hearing confidential taxpayer appeals or data, the public disclosure of which is prohibited by law.

(8) Require the State Board of Equalization to disclose any action taken in closed session or documents executed in connection with that action, the public disclosure of which is prohibited by law pursuant to Sections 15619 and 15641 of this code and Sections 833, 7056, 8255, 9255, 11655, 30455, 32455, 38705, 38706, 43651, 45982, 46751, 50159, 55381, and 60609 of the Revenue and Taxation Code.

(9) Prevent the California Earthquake Prediction Evaluation Council, or other body appointed to advise the Director of Emergency Services or the Governor concerning matters relating to volcanic or earthquake predictions, from holding closed sessions when considering the evaluation of possible predictions.

(g) This article does not prevent either of the following:

(1) The Teachers' Retirement Board or the Board of Administration of the Public Employees' Retirement System from holding closed sessions when considering matters pertaining to the recruitment, appointment, employment, or removal of the chief executive officer or when considering matters pertaining to the recruitment or removal of the Chief Investment Officer of the State Teachers' Retirement System or the Public Employees' Retirement System.

(2) The Commission on Teacher Credentialing from holding closed sessions when considering matters relating to the recruitment, appointment, or removal of its executive director.

(h) This article does not prevent the Board of Administration of the Public Employees' Retirement System from holding closed sessions when considering matters relating to the development of rates and competitive strategy for plans offered pursuant to Chapter 15 (commencing with Section 21660) of Part 3 of Division 5 of Title 2.

(i) This article does not prevent the Managed Risk Medical Insurance Board from holding closed sessions when considering matters related to the development of rates and contracting strategy for entities contracting or seeking to contract with the board, entities with which the board is considering a contract, or entities with which the board is considering or enters into any other arrangement under which the board provides, receives, or arranges services or reimbursement, pursuant to Part 6.2 (commencing with Section 12693), former Part 6.3 (commencing with Section 12695), former Part 6.4 (commencing with Section 12699.50), former Part 6.5 (commencing with Section 12700), former Part 6.6 (commencing with Section 12739.5), or former Part 6.7 (commencing with Section 12739.70) of Division 2 of the Insurance Code.

(j) This article shall not be construed to prevent the board of the State Compensation Insurance Fund from holding closed sessions in the following:

(1) When considering matters related to claims pursuant to Chapter 1 (commencing with Section 3200) of Part 1 of Division 4 of the Labor Code, to the extent that confidential medical information or other individually identifiable information would be disclosed.

(2) To the extent that matters related to audits and investigations that have not been completed would be disclosed.

(3) To the extent that an internal audit containing proprietary information would be disclosed.

(4) To the extent that the session would address the development of rates, contracting strategy, underwriting, or competitive strategy, pursuant to the powers granted to the board in Chapter 4 (commencing with Section 11770) of Part 3 of Division 2 of the Insurance Code, when discussion in open session concerning those matters would prejudice the position of the State Compensation Insurance Fund.

(k) The State Compensation Insurance Fund shall comply with the procedures specified in Section 11125.4 of the Government Code with respect to any closed session or meeting authorized by subdivision (j), and in addition shall provide an opportunity for a member of the public to be heard on the issue of the appropriateness of closing the meeting or session.

(Amended by Stats. 2024, Ch. 156, Sec. 1. (AB 2841) Effective July 18, 2024.)

11126.1. MINUTE BOOK OF CLOSED SESSION

The state body shall designate a clerk or other officer or employee of the state body, who shall then attend each closed session of the state body and keep and enter in a minute book a record of topics discussed and decisions made at the meeting. The minute book made pursuant to this section is not a public record subject to inspection pursuant to the California Public Records Act (Division 10 (commencing with Section 7920.000) of Title 1), and shall be kept confidential. The minute book shall be available to members of the state body or, if a violation of this chapter is alleged to have occurred at a closed session, to a court of general jurisdiction. The minute book may, but need not, consist of a recording of the closed session.

(Amended by Stats. 2021, Ch. 615, Sec. 164. (AB 474) Effective January 1, 2022. Operative January 1, 2023, pursuant to Sec. 463 of Stats. 2021, Ch. 615.)

11126.2. CLOSED SESSION FOR RESPONSE TO FINAL DRAFT AUDIT REPORT

(a) Nothing in this article shall be construed to prohibit a state body that has received a confidential final draft audit report from the Bureau of State Audits from holding closed sessions to discuss its response to that report.

(b) After the public release of an audit report by the Bureau of State Audits, if a state body meets to discuss the audit report, it shall do so in an open session unless exempted from that requirement by some other provision of law.

(Added by Stats. 2004, Ch. 576, Sec. 2. Effective January 1, 2005.)

11126.3. DISCLOSURE OF ITEMS TO BE DISCUSSED IN CLOSED SESSION; DISCUSSION OF ADDITIONAL PENDING LITIGATION MATTERS ARISING AFTER DISCLOSURE

(a) Prior to holding any closed session, the state body shall disclose, in an open meeting, the general nature of the item or items to be discussed in the closed session. The disclosure may take the form of a reference to the item or items as they are listed by number or letter on the agenda. If the session is closed pursuant to paragraph (2) of subdivision (d) of Section 11126, the state body shall state the title of, or otherwise specifically identify, the proceeding or disciplinary action contemplated. However, should the body determine that to do so would jeopardize the body's ability to effectuate service of process upon one or more unserved parties if the proceeding or disciplinary action is commenced or that to do so would fail to protect the private economic and business reputation of the person or entity if the proceeding or disciplinary action is not commenced, then the state body shall notice that there will be a closed session and describe in general terms the purpose of that session. If the session is closed pursuant to subparagraph (A) of paragraph (2) of subdivision (e) of Section 11126, the state body shall state the title of, or otherwise specifically identify, the litigation to be discussed unless the body states that to do so would jeopardize the body's ability to effectuate service of process upon one or more unserved parties, or that to do so would jeopardize its ability to conclude existing settlement negotiations to its advantage.

(b) In the closed session, the state body may consider only those matters covered in its disclosure.

(c) The disclosure shall be made as part of the notice provided for the meeting pursuant to Section 11125 or pursuant to subdivision (a) of Section 92032 of the Education Code and of any order or notice required by Section 11129.

(d) If, after the agenda has been published in compliance with this article, any pending litigation (under subdivision (e) of Section 11126) matters arise, the postponement of which will prevent the state body from complying with any statutory, court-ordered, or other legally imposed deadline, the state body may proceed to discuss those matters in closed session and shall publicly announce in the meeting the title of, or otherwise specifically identify, the litigation to be discussed, unless the body states that to do so would jeopardize the body's ability to effectuate service of process upon one or more unserved parties, or that to do so would jeopardize its ability to conclude existing settlement negotiations to its advantage. Such an announcement shall be deemed to comply fully with the requirements of this section.

(e) Nothing in this section shall require or authorize a disclosure of names or other information that would constitute an invasion of privacy or otherwise unnecessarily divulge the particular facts concerning the closed session or the disclosure of which is prohibited by state or federal law.

(f) After any closed session, the state body shall reconvene into open session prior to adjournment and shall make any reports, provide any documentation, and make any other disclosures required by Section 11125.2 of action taken in the closed session.

(g) The announcements required to be made in open session pursuant to this section may be made at the location announced in the agenda for the closed session, as long as the public is allowed to be present at that location for the purpose of hearing the announcement.

(Amended by Stats. 2001, Ch. 243, Sec. 11. Effective January 1, 2002.)

11126.5. CLEARING ROOM WHEN MEETING WILLFULLY INTERRUPTED

In the event that any meeting is willfully interrupted by a group or groups of persons so as to render the orderly conduct of such meeting unfeasible and order cannot be restored by the removal of individuals who are willfully interrupting the meeting the state body conducting the meeting may order the meeting room cleared and continue in session. Nothing in this section shall prohibit the state body from establishing a procedure for readmitting an individual or individuals not responsible for willfully disturbing the orderly conduct of the meeting.

Notwithstanding any other provision of law, only matters appearing on the agenda may be considered in such a session. Representatives of the press or other news media, except those participating in the disturbance, shall be allowed to attend any session held pursuant to this section.

(Amended by Stats. 1981, Ch. 968, Sec. 15.)

11126.7. FEES

No fees may be charged by a state body for providing a notice required by Section 11125 or for carrying out any provision of this article, except as specifically authorized pursuant to this article.

(Amended by Stats. 1981, Ch. 968, Sec. 16.)

11127. STATE BODIES SUBJECT TO ARTICLE

Each provision of this article shall apply to every state body unless the body is specifically excepted from that provision by law or is covered by any other conflicting provision of law.

(Amended by Stats. 1981, Ch. 968, Sec. 17.)

11128. WHEN CLOSED SESSIONS HELD

Each closed session of a state body shall be held only during a regular or special meeting of the body.

(Amended by Stats. 1981, Ch. 968, Sec. 18.)

1128.5. ADJOURNMENT OF MEETINGS; POSTING OF COPY OF ORDER OR NOTICE OF ADJOURNMENT

The state body may adjourn any regular, adjourned regular, special, or adjourned special meeting to a time and place specified in the order of adjournment.

Less than a quorum may so adjourn from time to time. If all members are absent from any regular or adjourned regular meeting, the clerk or secretary of the state body may declare the meeting adjourned to a stated time and place and he or she shall cause a written notice of the adjournment to be given in the same manner as provided in Section 11125.4 for special meetings, unless that notice is waived as provided for special meetings. A copy of the order or notice of adjournment shall be conspicuously posted on or near the door of the place where the regular, adjourned regular, special, or adjourned special meeting was held within 24 hours after the time of the adjournment. When a regular or adjourned regular meeting is adjourned as provided in this section, the resulting adjourned regular meeting is a regular meeting for all purposes. When an order of adjournment of any meeting fails to state the hour at which the adjourned meeting is to be held, it shall be held at the hour specified for regular meetings by law or regulation.

(Added by Stats. 1997, Ch. 949, Sec. 11. Effective January 1, 1998.)

11129. CONTINUANCE OF RECONTINUANCE OF HEARING

Any hearing being held, or noticed or ordered to be held by a state body at any meeting may by order or notice of continuance be continued or recontinued to any subsequent meeting of the state body in the same manner and to the same extent set forth in Section 11128.5 for the adjournment of meetings. A copy of the order or notice of continuance shall be conspicuously posted on or near the door of the place where the hearing was held within 24 hours after the time of the continuance; provided, that if the hearing is continued to a time less than 24 hours after the time specified in the order or notice of hearing, a copy of the order or notice of continuance of hearing shall be posted immediately following the meeting at which the order or declaration of continuance was adopted or made.

(Amended by Stats. 1997, Ch. 949, Sec. 12. Effective January 1, 1998.)

11130. ACTION TO STOP OR PREVENT VIOLATIONS OR ARTICLE; ORDER FOR RECORDING OF CLOSED SESSIONS; DISCOVERY OF RECORDING

(a) The Attorney General, the district attorney, or any interested person may commence an action by mandamus, injunction, or declaratory relief for the purpose of stopping or preventing violations or threatened violations of this article or to determine the applicability of this article to past actions or threatened future action by members of the state body or to determine whether any rule or action by the state body to penalize or otherwise discourage the expression of one or more of its members is valid or invalid under the laws of this state or of the United States, or to compel the state body to audio record its closed sessions as hereinafter provided.

(b) The court in its discretion may, upon a judgment of a violation of Section 11126, order the state body to audio record its closed sessions and preserve the audio recordings for the period and under the terms of security and confidentiality the court deems appropriate.

(c) (1) Each recording so kept shall be immediately labeled with the date of the closed session recorded and the title of the clerk or other officer who shall be custodian of the recording.

(2) The audio recordings shall be subject to the following discovery procedures:

(A) In any case in which discovery or disclosure of the audio recording is sought by the Attorney General, the district attorney, or the plaintiff in a civil action pursuant to this section or Section 11130.3 alleging that a violation of this article has occurred in a closed session that has been recorded pursuant to this section, the party seeking discovery or disclosure shall file a written notice of motion with the appropriate court with notice to the governmental agency that has custody and control of the audio recording. The notice shall be given pursuant to subdivision (b) of Section 1005 of the Code of Civil Procedure.

(B) The notice shall include, in addition to the items required by Section 1010 of the Code of Civil Procedure, all of the following:

(i) Identification of the proceeding in which discovery or disclosure is sought, the party seeking discovery or disclosure, the date and time of the meeting recorded, and the governmental agency that has custody and control of the recording.

(ii) An affidavit that contains specific facts indicating that a violation of the act occurred in the closed session.

(3) If the court, following a review of the motion, finds that there is good cause to believe that a violation has occurred, the court may review, in camera, the recording of that portion of the closed session alleged to have violated the act.

(4) If, following the in camera review, the court concludes that disclosure of a portion of the recording would be likely to materially assist in the resolution of the litigation alleging violation of this article, the court shall, in its discretion, make a certified transcript of the portion of the recording a public exhibit in the proceeding.

(5) Nothing in this section shall permit discovery of communications that are protected by the attorney-client privilege.

(Amended by Stats. 2009, Ch. 88, Sec. 43. (AB 176) Effective January 1, 2010.)

11130.3. CAUSE OF ACTION TO VOID ACTION TAKE BY STATE AGENCY IN VIOLATION OF OPEN MEETING REQUIREMENTS

(a) Any interested person may commence an action by mandamus, injunction, or declaratory relief for the purpose of obtaining a judicial determination that an action taken by a state body in violation of Section 11123 or 11125 is null and void under this section. Any action seeking such a judicial determination shall be commenced within 90 days from the date the action was taken. Nothing in this section shall be construed to prevent a state body from curing or correcting an action challenged pursuant to this section.

(b) An action shall not be determined to be null and void if any of the following conditions exist:

(1) The action taken was in connection with the sale or issuance of notes, bonds, or other evidences of indebtedness or any contract, instrument, or agreement related thereto.

(2) The action taken gave rise to a contractual obligation upon which a party has, in good faith, detrimentally relied.

(3) The action taken was in substantial compliance with Sections 11123 and 11125.

(4) The action taken was in connection with the collection of any tax.

(Amended by Stats. 1999, Ch. 393, Sec. 5. Effective January 1, 2000.)

11130.5. COSTS AND ATTORNEY FEES

A court may award court costs and reasonable attorney's fees to the plaintiff in an action brought pursuant to Section 11130 or 11130.3 where it is found that a state body has violated the provisions of this article. The costs and fees shall be paid by the state body and shall not become a personal liability of any public officer or employee thereof.

A court may award court costs and reasonable attorney's fees to a defendant in any action brought pursuant to Section 11130 or 11130.3 where the defendant has prevailed in a final determination of the action and the court finds that the action was clearly frivolous and totally lacking in merit.

(Amended by Stats. 1985, Ch. 936, Sec. 2.)

11130.7. OFFENSES

Each member of a state body who attends a meeting of that body in violation of any provision of this article, and where the member intends to deprive the public of information to which the member knows or has reason to know the public is entitled under this article, is guilty of a misdemeanor.

(Amended by Stats. 1997, Ch. 949, Sec. 14. Effective January 1, 1998.)

11131. PROHIBITION AGAINST USE OF CERTAIN FACILITIES

No state agency shall conduct any meeting, conference, or other function in any facility that prohibits the admittance of any person, or persons, on the basis of ancestry or any characteristic listed or defined in Section 11135, or that is inaccessible to disabled persons, or where members of the public may not be present without making a payment or purchase. As used in this section, "state agency" means and includes every state body, office, officer, department, division, bureau, board, council, commission, or other state agency.

(Amended by Stats. 2007, Ch. 568, Sec. 32. Effective January 1, 2008.)

11131.5. IDENTIFICATION OF CRIME VICTIM

No notice, agenda, announcement, or report required under this article need identify any victim or alleged victim of crime, tortious sexual conduct, or child abuse unless the identity of the person has been publicly disclosed.

(Added by Stats. 1997, Ch. 949, Sec. 16. Effective January 1, 1998.)

11132. PROHIBITION AGAINST CLOSED SESSIONS EXCEPT AS EXPRESSLY AUTHORIZED

Except as expressly authorized by this article, no closed session may be held by any state body.

(Added by Stats. 1987, Ch. 1320, Sec. 4.)

PART 2.8: DEPARTMENT OF FAIR EMPLOYMENT AND HOUSING

CHAPTER 4: DEFINITIONS

12926. DEFINITIONS

As used in this part in connection with unlawful practices, unless a different meaning clearly appears from the context:

(a) "Affirmative relief" or "prospective relief" includes the authority to order reinstatement of an employee, awards of backpay, reimbursement of out-of-pocket expenses, hiring, transfers, reassignments, grants of tenure, promotions, cease and desist orders, posting of notices, training of personnel, testing, expunging of records, reporting of records, and any other similar relief that is intended to correct unlawful practices under this part.

(b) "Age" refers to the chronological age of any individual who has reached a 40th birthday.

(c) Except as provided by Section 12926.05, "employee" does not include any individual employed by that person's parent, spouse, or child or any individual employed under a special license in a nonprofit sheltered workshop or rehabilitation facility.

(d) "Employer" includes any person regularly employing five or more persons, or any person acting as an agent of an employer, directly or indirectly, the state or any political or civil subdivision of the state, and cities, except as follows:

"Employer" does not include a religious association or corporation not organized for private profit.

(e) "Employment agency" includes any person undertaking for compensation to procure employees or opportunities to work.

(f) "Essential functions" means the fundamental job duties of the employment position the individual with a disability holds or desires. "Essential functions" does not include the marginal functions of the position.

(1) A job function may be considered essential for any of several reasons, including, but not limited to, any one or more of the following:

(A) The function may be essential because the reason the position exists is to perform that function.

(B) The function may be essential because of the limited number of employees available among whom the performance of that job function can be distributed.

(C) The function may be highly specialized, so that the incumbent in the position is hired based on expertise or the ability to perform a particular function.

(2) Evidence of whether a particular function is essential includes, but is not limited to, the following:

(A) The employer's judgment as to which functions are essential.

(B) Written job descriptions prepared before advertising or interviewing applicants for the job.

(C) The amount of time spent on the job performing the function.

(D) The consequences of not requiring the incumbent to perform the function.

(E) The terms of a collective bargaining agreement.

(F) The work experiences of past incumbents in the job.

(G) The current work experience of incumbents in similar jobs.

(g) (1) "Genetic information" means, with respect to any individual, information about any of the following:

(A) The individual's genetic tests.

(B) The genetic tests of family members of the individual.

(C) The manifestation of a disease or disorder in family members of the individual.

(2) "Genetic information" includes any request for, or receipt of, genetic services, or participation in clinical research that includes genetic services, by an individual or any family member of the individual.

(3) "Genetic information" does not include information about the sex or age of any individual.

(h) "Labor organization" includes any organization that exists and is constituted for the purpose, in whole or in part, of collective bargaining or of dealing with employers concerning grievances, terms or conditions of employment, or of other mutual aid or protection.

(i) "Medical condition" means either of the following:

(1) Any health impairment related to or associated with a diagnosis of cancer or a record or history of cancer.

(2) Genetic characteristics. For purposes of this section, "genetic characteristics" means either of the following:

(A) Any scientifically or medically identifiable gene or chromosome, or combination or alteration thereof, that is known to be a cause of a disease or disorder in a person or that person's offspring, or that is determined to be associated with a statistically increased risk of development of a disease or disorder, and that is presently not associated with any symptoms of any disease or disorder.

(B) Inherited characteristics that may derive from the individual or family member, that are known to be a cause of a disease or disorder in a person or that person's offspring, or that are determined to be associated with a statistically increased risk of development of a disease or disorder, and that are presently not associated with any symptoms of any disease or disorder.

(j) "Mental disability" includes, but is not limited to, all of the following:

(1) Having any mental or psychological disorder or condition, such as intellectual disability, organic brain syndrome, emotional or mental illness, or specific learning disabilities, that limits a major life activity. For purposes of this section:

(A) "Limits" shall be determined without regard to mitigating measures, such as medications, assistive devices, or reasonable accommodations, unless the mitigating measure itself limits a major life activity.

(B) A mental or psychological disorder or condition limits a major life activity if it makes the achievement of the major life activity difficult.

(C) "Major life activities" shall be broadly construed and shall include physical, mental, and social activities and working.

(2) Any other mental or psychological disorder or condition not described in paragraph (1) that requires special education or related services.

(3) Having a record or history of a mental or psychological disorder or condition described in paragraph (1) or (2), which is known to the employer or other entity covered by this part.

(4) Being regarded or treated by the employer or other entity covered by this part as having, or having had, any mental condition that makes achievement of a major life activity difficult.

(5) Being regarded or treated by the employer or other entity covered by this part as having, or having had, a mental or psychological disorder or

condition that has no present disabling effect, but that may become a mental disability as described in paragraph (1) or (2).

"Mental disability" does not include sexual behavior disorders, compulsive gambling, kleptomania, pyromania, or psychoactive substance use disorders resulting from the current unlawful use of controlled substances or other drugs.

(k) "Military and veteran status" means a member or veteran of the United States Armed Forces, United States Armed Forces Reserve, the United States National Guard, and the California National Guard.

(l) "On the bases enumerated in this part" means or refers to discrimination on the basis of one or more of the following: race, religious creed, color, national origin, ancestry, physical disability, mental disability, medical condition, genetic information, marital status, sex, age, sexual orientation, or military and veteran status.

(m) "Physical disability" includes, but is not limited to, all of the following:

(1) Having any physiological disease, disorder, condition, cosmetic disfigurement, or anatomical loss that does both of the following:

(A) Affects one or more of the following body systems: neurological, immunological, musculoskeletal, special sense organs, respiratory, including speech organs, cardiovascular, reproductive, digestive, genitourinary, hemic and lymphatic, skin, and endocrine.

(B) Limits a major life activity. For purposes of this section:

(i) "Limits" shall be determined without regard to mitigating measures such as medications, assistive devices, prosthetics, or reasonable accommodations, unless the mitigating measure itself limits a major life activity.

(ii) A physiological disease, disorder, condition, cosmetic disfigurement, or anatomical loss limits a major life activity if it makes the achievement of the major life activity difficult.

(iii) "Major life activities" shall be broadly construed and includes physical, mental, and social activities and working.

(2) Any other health impairment not described in paragraph (1) that requires special education or related services.

(3) Having a record or history of a disease, disorder, condition, cosmetic disfigurement, anatomical loss, or health impairment described in paragraph (1) or (2), which is known to the employer or other entity covered by this part.

(4) Being regarded or treated by the employer or other entity covered by this part as having, or having had, any physical condition that makes achievement of a major life activity difficult.

(5) Being regarded or treated by the employer or other entity covered by this part as having, or having had, a disease, disorder, condition, cosmetic disfigurement, anatomical loss, or health impairment that has no present disabling effect but may become a physical disability as described in paragraph (1) or (2).

(6) "Physical disability" does not include sexual behavior disorders, compulsive gambling, kleptomania, pyromania, or psychoactive substance use disorders resulting from the current unlawful use of controlled substances or other drugs.

(n) Notwithstanding subdivisions (j) and (m), if the definition of "disability" used in the federal Americans with Disabilities Act of 1990 (Public Law 101-336) would result in broader protection of the civil rights of individuals with a mental disability or physical disability, as defined in subdivision (j) or (m), or would include any medical condition not included within those definitions, then that broader protection or coverage shall be deemed incorporated by reference into, and shall prevail over conflicting provisions of, the definitions in subdivisions (j) and (m).

(o) "Race, religious creed, color, national origin, ancestry, physical disability, mental disability, medical condition, genetic information, marital status, sex, age, sexual orientation, or military and veteran status" includes a perception that the person has any of those characteristics or that the person is associated with a person who has, or is perceived to have, any of those characteristics.

(p) "Reasonable accommodation" may include either of the following:

(1) Making existing facilities used by employees readily accessible to, and usable by, individuals with disabilities.

(2) Job restructuring, part-time or modified work schedules, reassignment to a vacant position, acquisition or modification of equipment or devices, adjustment or modifications of examinations, training materials or policies, the provision of qualified readers or interpreters, and other similar accommodations for individuals with disabilities.

(q) "Religious creed," "religion," "religious observance," "religious belief," and "creed" include all aspects of religious belief, observance, and practice, including religious dress and grooming practices. "Religious dress practice" shall be construed broadly to include the wearing or carrying of religious clothing, head or face coverings, jewelry, artifacts, and any other item that is part of an individual observing a religious creed. "Religious grooming practice" shall be construed broadly to include all forms of head, facial, and body hair that are part of an individual observing a religious creed.

(r) (1) "Sex" includes, but is not limited to, the following:

(A) Pregnancy or medical conditions related to pregnancy.

(B) Childbirth or medical conditions related to childbirth.

(C) Breastfeeding or medical conditions related to breastfeeding.

(2) "Sex" also includes, but is not limited to, a person's gender. "Gender" means sex, and includes a person's gender identity and gender expression. "Gender expression" means a person's gender- related appearance and behavior whether or not stereotypically associated with the person's assigned sex at birth.

(s) "Sexual orientation" means heterosexuality, homosexuality, and bisexuality.

(t) "Supervisor" means any individual having the authority, in the interest of the employer, to hire, transfer, suspend, lay off, recall, promote, discharge, assign, reward, or discipline other employees, or the responsibility to direct them, or to adjust their grievances, or effectively to recommend that action, if, in connection with the foregoing, the exercise of that authority is not of a merely routine or clerical nature, but requires the use of independent judgment.

(u) "Undue hardship" means an action requiring significant difficulty or expense, when considered in light of the following factors:

(1) The nature and cost of the accommodation needed.

(2) The overall financial resources of the facilities involved in the provision of the reasonable accommodations, the number of persons employed at the facility, and the effect on expenses and resources or the impact otherwise of these accommodations upon the operation of the facility.

(3) The overall financial resources of the covered entity, the overall size of the business of a covered entity with respect to the number of employees,

and the number, type, and location of its facilities.

(4) The type of operations, including the composition, structure, and functions of the workforce of the entity.

(5) The geographic separateness or administrative or fiscal relationship of the facility or facilities.

(v) "National origin" discrimination includes, but is not limited to, discrimination on the basis of possessing a driver's license granted under Section 12801.9 of the Vehicle Code.

(w) "Race" is inclusive of traits historically associated with race, including, but not limited to, hair texture and protective hairstyles.

(x) "Protective hairstyles" includes, but is not limited to, such hairstyles as braids, locks, and twists.

(Amended by Stats. 2019, Ch. 58, Sec. 3. (SB 188) Effective January 1, 2020.)

CHAPTER 6: DISCRIMINATION PROHIBITED

ARTICLE 1: UNLAWFUL PRACTICES, GENERALLY

12944. DISCRIMINATION BY "LICENSING BOARD"

(a) It shall be unlawful for a licensing board to require any examination or establish any other qualification for licensing that has an adverse impact on any class by virtue of its race, creed, color, national origin or ancestry, sex, gender, gender identity, gender expression, age, medical condition, genetic information, physical disability, mental disability, or sexual orientation, unless the practice can be demonstrated to be job related.

Where the commission, after hearing, determines that an examination is unlawful under this subdivision, the licensing board may continue to use and rely on the examination until such time as judicial review by the superior court of the determination is exhausted.

If an examination or other qualification for licensing is determined to be unlawful under this section, that determination shall not void, limit, repeal, or otherwise affect any right, privilege, status, or responsibility previously conferred upon any person by the examination or by a license issued in reliance on the examination or qualification.

(b) It shall be unlawful for a licensing board to fail or refuse to make reasonable accommodation to an individual's mental or physical disability or medical condition.

(c) It shall be unlawful for any licensing board, unless specifically acting in accordance with federal equal employment opportunity guidelines or regulations approved by the commission, to print or circulate or cause to be printed or circulated any publication, or to make any non-job-related inquiry, either verbal or through use of an application form, which expresses, directly or indirectly, any limitation, specification, or discrimination as to race, religious creed, color, national origin, ancestry, physical disability, mental disability, medical condition, genetic information, sex, gender, gender identity, gender expression, age, or sexual orientation or any intent to make any such limitation, specification, or discrimination. Nothing in this subdivision shall prohibit any licensing board from making, in connection with prospective licensure or certification, an inquiry as to, or a request for information regarding, the physical fitness of applicants if that inquiry or request for information is directly related and pertinent to the license or the licensed position the applicant is applying for. Nothing in this subdivision shall prohibit any licensing board, in connection with prospective examinations, licensure, or certification, from inviting individuals with physical or mental disabilities to request reasonable accommodations or from making inquiries related to reasonable accommodations.

(d) It is unlawful for a licensing board to discriminate against any person because the person has filed a complaint, testified, or assisted in any proceeding under this part.

(e) It is unlawful for any licensing board to fail to keep records of applications for licensing or certification for a period of two years following the date of receipt of the applications.

(f) As used in this section, "licensing board" means any state board, agency, or authority in the Business, Consumer Services, and Housing Agency that has the authority to grant licenses or certificates which are prerequisites to employment eligibility or professional status.

(Amended by Stats. 2012, Ch. 147, Sec. 17. (SB 1039) Effective January 1, 2013. Operative July 1, 2013, by Sec. 23 of Ch. 147.)

12950.1. SEXUAL HARASSMENT TRAINING

(a) (1) By January 1, 2021, an employer having five or more employees shall provide at least two hours of classroom or other effective interactive training and education regarding sexual harassment to all supervisory employees and at least one hour of classroom or other effective interactive training and education regarding sexual harassment to all nonsupervisory employees in California. Thereafter, each employer covered by this section shall provide sexual harassment training and education to each employee in California once every two years. New nonsupervisory employees shall be provided training within six months of hire. New supervisory employees shall be provided training within six months of the assumption of a supervisory position. An employer may provide this training in conjunction with other training provided to the employees. The training may be completed by employees individually or as part of a group presentation, and may be completed in shorter segments, as long as the applicable hourly total requirement is met. An employer who has provided this training and education to an employee in 2019 is not required to provide refresher training and education again until two years thereafter. The training and education required by this section shall include information and practical guidance regarding the federal and state statutory provisions concerning the prohibition against and the prevention and correction of sexual harassment and the remedies available to victims of sexual harassment in employment. The training and education shall also include practical examples aimed at instructing supervisors in the prevention of harassment, discrimination, and retaliation, and shall be presented by trainers or educators with knowledge and expertise in the prevention of harassment, discrimination, and retaliation. The department shall provide a method for employees who have completed the training to save electronically and print a certificate of completion.

(2) An employer shall also include prevention of abusive conduct as a component of the training and education specified in paragraph (1).

(3) An employer shall also provide training inclusive of harassment based on gender identity, gender expression, and sexual orientation as a component of the training and education specified in paragraph (1). The training and education shall include practical examples inclusive of harassment based on gender identity, gender expression, and sexual orientation, and shall be presented by trainers or educators with knowledge and expertise in those areas.

(b) The state shall incorporate the training required by subdivision (a) into the 80 hours of training provided to all new employees pursuant to subdivision (b) of Section 19995.4, using existing resources.

(c) Notwithstanding subdivisions (j) and (k) of Section 12940, a claim that the training and education required by this section did not reach a particular individual or individuals shall not in and of itself result in the liability of any employer to any present or former employee or applicant in any action alleging sexual harassment. Conversely, an employer's compliance with this section does not insulate the employer from liability for sexual harassment of any current or former employee or applicant.

(d) If an employer violates this section, the department may seek an order requiring the employer to comply with these requirements.

(e) The training and education required by this section is intended to establish a minimum threshold and should not discourage or relieve any employer from providing for longer, more frequent, or more elaborate training and education regarding workplace harassment or other forms of unlawful discrimination in order to meet its obligations to take all reasonable steps necessary to prevent and correct harassment and discrimination. This section shall not be construed to override or supersede statutes, including, but not limited to, Section 1684 of the Labor Code, that meet or exceed the training for nonsupervisory employees required under this section.

(f) Except as provided in subdivision (l), beginning January 1, 2021, for seasonal, temporary, or other employees that are hired to work for less than six months, an employer shall provide training within 30 calendar days after the hire date or within 100 hours worked, whichever occurs first. In the case of a temporary employee employed by a temporary services employer, as defined in Section 201.3 of the Labor Code, to perform services for clients, the training shall be provided by the temporary services employer, not the client.

(g) Beginning January 1, 2020, sexual harassment prevention training for migrant and seasonal agricultural workers, as defined in the federal Migrant and Seasonal Agricultural Worker Protection Act (29 U.S.C. 1801, et seq.), shall be consistent with training for nonsupervisory employees pursuant to paragraph (8) of subdivision (a) of Section 1684 of the Labor Code.

(h) (1) For purposes of this section only, "employer" means any person regularly employing five or more persons or regularly receiving the services of five or more persons providing services pursuant to a contract, or any person acting as an agent of an employer, directly or indirectly, the state, or any political or civil subdivision of the state, and cities.

(2) For purposes of this section, "abusive conduct" means conduct of an employer or employee in the workplace, with malice, that a reasonable person would find hostile, offensive, and unrelated to an employer's legitimate business interests. Abusive conduct may include repeated infliction of verbal abuse, such as the use of derogatory remarks, insults, and epithets, verbal or physical conduct that a reasonable person would find threatening, intimidating, or humiliating, or the gratuitous sabotage or undermining of a person's work performance. A single act shall not constitute abusive conduct, unless especially severe and egregious.

(i) For purposes of providing training to employees as required by this section, an employer may develop its own training module or may direct employees to view the online training course referenced in subdivision (j) and this shall be deemed to have complied with and satisfied the employers' obligations as set forth in this section and Section 12950.

(j) The department shall develop or obtain two online training courses on the prevention of sexual harassment in the workplace in accordance with the provisions of this section. The course for nonsupervisory employees shall be one hour in length and the course for supervisory employees shall be two hours in length.

(k) The department shall make the online training courses available on its internet website. The online training courses shall contain an interactive feature that requires the viewer to respond to a question periodically in order for the online training courses to continue to play. Any questions resulting from the online training course described in this subdivision shall be directed to the trainee's employer's human resources department or equally qualified professional rather than the department.

(l) (1) An employer that employs workers pursuant to a multiemployer collective bargaining agreement in the construction industry may satisfy the requirements of subdivision (a) or (f) by demonstrating that the employee has received the training required by subdivision (a) within the past two years under any of the following circumstances:

(A) While the employee was employed by another employer that is also signatory to a multiemployer collective bargaining agreement with the same trade in the building and construction industry.

(B) While the employee was an apprentice registered in a building and construction trades apprenticeship program approved by the Division of Apprenticeship Standards.

(C) Through a building and construction trades apprenticeship program approved by the Division of Apprenticeship Standards, a labor management training trust, or labor management cooperation committee. For purposes of this subdivision, "labor management cooperation committee" shall mean a committee that is established pursuant to Section 175a of Title 29 of the United States Code.

(2) For purposes of this subdivision, "multiemployer collective bargaining agreement" means a bona fide collective bargaining agreement to which multiple employers are signatory, including predecessor and successor agreements.

(3) An employer shall require verification that an employee has undergone prevention of harassment training pursuant to this subdivision within the past two years. The employer shall provide prevention of harassment training pursuant to subdivision (a) for any employee for whom verification cannot be obtained.

(4) A state-approved apprenticeship program, labor management training trust, or labor management cooperation committee shall maintain a certificate of completion of training for each person to whom the entity has provided prevention of harassment training pursuant to this subdivision for a period of not less than four years. The apprenticeship program, labor management training trust, or labor management cooperation committee shall maintain a database of journey-level worker and apprentice training that entity has provided and shall provide verification of an employee's or apprentice's prevention of harassment training status upon the request of an employer that is a party to the multiemployer collective bargaining agreement.

(5) (A) A qualified trainer may provide prevention of harassment training on behalf of an apprenticeship program, labor management training trust, or labor management cooperation committee.

(B) A "qualified trainer," for purposes of this subdivision, is any person who, through a combination of training and experience, has the ability to train employees about the following:

(i) How to identify behavior that may constitute unlawful harassment, discrimination, or retaliation under both California and federal law.

(ii) What steps to take when harassing behavior occurs in the workplace.

(iii) How to report harassment complaints.

(iv) Supervisory employees' obligation to report harassing, discriminatory, or retaliatory behavior of which they become aware.

(v) How to respond to a harassment complaint.

(vi) The employer's obligation to conduct a workplace investigation of a harassment complaint.

(vii) What constitutes retaliation and how to prevent it.

(viii) Essential components of an antiharassment policy.

(ix) The effect of harassment on harassed employees, coworkers, harassers, and employers.

(C) A "qualified trainer" includes, but is not limited to, an attorney admitted to the State Bar of California with at least two years of experience practicing employment law, a human resources professional with at least two years of practical eperience in prevention of harassment training, investigation, and advising employers in the prevention of harassment, or any other person who has received training in the provision of prevention of harassment training from a qualified trainer.

(6) An apprenticeship program, labor management training trust, or labor management cooperation committee may also provide training by use of the online training courses referenced in subdivision (j).

(7) An apprenticeship program, labor management training trust, or labor management cooperation committee shall not incur any liability for providing prevention of harassment training or for maintaining records pursuant to this subdivision.

(Amended by Stats. 2019, Ch. 722, Sec. 1. (SB 530) Effective January 1, 2020.)

12953. UNLAWFUL TO VIOLATE LABOR CODE 432.6

It is an unlawful employment practice for an employer to violate Section 432.6 of the Labor Code.

(Added by Stats. 2019, Ch. 711, Sec. 2. (AB 51) Effective January 1, 2020.)

TITLE 3 GOVERNMENT OF COUNTIES

DIVISION 2: OFFICERS

PART 3: OTHER OFFICERS

CHAPTER 1: DISTRICT ATTORNEY

ARTICLE 1: DUTIES AS PUBLIC PROSECUTOR

26509. CONSUMER FRAUD INVESTIGATIONS; ACCESS BY DISTRICT ATTORNEY TO RECORDS OF OTHER AGENCIES

(a) Notwithstanding any other provision of law, including any provision making records confidential, and including Title 1.8 (commencing with Section 1798) of Part 4 of Division 3 of the Civil Code, the district attorney shall be given access to, and may make copies of, any complaint against a person subject to regulation by a consumer-oriented state agency and any investigation of the person made by the agency, where that person is being investigated by the district attorney regarding possible consumer fraud.

(b) Where the district attorney does not take action with respect to the complaint or investigation, the material shall remain confidential.

(c) Where the release of the material would jeopardize an investigation or other duties of a consumer-oriented state agency, the agency shall have discretion to delay the release of the information.

(d) As used in this section, a consumer-oriented state agency is any state agency that regulates the licensure, certification, or qualification of persons to practice a profession or business within the state, where the regulation is for the protection of consumers who deal with the professionals or businesses. It includes, but is not limited to, all of the following:

(1) The Dental Board of California.

(2) The Medical Board of California.

(3) The State Board of Optometry.

(4) The California State Board of Pharmacy.

(5) The Veterinary Medical Board.

(6) The California Board of Accountancy.

(7) The California Architects Board.

(8) The State Board of Barbering and Cosmetology.

(9) The Board for Professional Engineers and Land Surveyors.

(10) The Contractors' State License Board.

(11) The Funeral Directors and Embalmers Program.

(12) The Structural Pest Control Board.

(13) The Bureau of Home Furnishings and Thermal Insulation.

(14) The Board of Registered Nursing.

(15) The State Board of Chiropractic Examiners.

(16) The Board of Behavioral Science Examiners.

(17) The State Athletic Commission.

(18) The Cemetery Program.

(19) The State Board of Guide Dogs for the Blind.

(20) The Bureau of Security and Investigative Services.

(21) The Court Reporters Board of California.

(22) The Board of Vocational Nursing and Psychiatric Technicians of the State of California.

(23) The Osteopathic Medical Board of California.

(24) The Division of Investigation.

(25) The Bureau of Automotive Repair.

(26) The State Board for Geologists and Geophysicists.

(27) The Department of Alcoholic Beverage Control.

(28) The Department of Insurance.

(29) The Public Utilities Commission.

(30) The State Department of Health Services.

(31) The New Motor Vehicle Board.

(Amended by Stats. 2003, Ch. 325, Sec. 8. Effective January 1, 2004.)

HEALTH AND SAFETY CODE

DIVISION 2 LICENSING PROVISIONS

CHAPTER 2.2: HEALTH CARE SERVICE PLANS

ARTICLE 5: STANDARDS

1367. REQUIREMENTS FOR HEALTH CARE SERVICE PLANS

A health care service plan and, if applicable, a specialized health care service plan shall meet the following requirements:

(a) Facilities located in this state including, but not limited to, clinics, hospitals, and skilled nursing facilities to be utilized by the plan shall be licensed by the State Department of Public Health, where licensure is required by law. Facilities not located in this state shall conform to all licensing and other requirements of the jurisdiction in which they are located.

(b) Personnel employed by or under contract to the plan shall be licensed or certified by their respective board or agency, where licensure or certification is required by law.

(c) Equipment required to be licensed or registered by law shall be so licensed or registered, and the operating personnel for that equipment shall be licensed or certified as required by law.

(d) The plan shall furnish services in a manner providing continuity of care and ready referral of patients to other providers at times as may be appropriate consistent with good professional practice.

(e) (1) All services shall be readily available at reasonable times to each enrollee consistent with good professional practice. To the extent feasible, the plan shall make all services readily accessible to all enrollees consistent with Section 1367.03.

(2) To the extent that telehealth services are appropriately provided through telehealth, as defined in subdivision (a) of Section 2290.5 of the Business and Professions Code, these services shall be considered in determining compliance with Section 1300.67.2 of Title 28 of the California Code of Regulations.

(3) The plan shall make all services accessible and appropriate consistent with Section 1367.04.

(f) The plan shall employ and utilize allied health manpower for the furnishing of services to the extent permitted by law and consistent with good medical practice.

(g) The plan shall have the organizational and administrative capacity to provide services to subscribers and enrollees. The plan shall be able to demonstrate to the department that medical decisions are rendered by qualified medical providers, unhindered by fiscal and administrative management.

(h) (1) Contracts with subscribers and enrollees, including group contracts, and contracts with providers, and other persons furnishing services, equipment, or facilities to or in connection with the plan, shall be fair, reasonable, and consistent with the objectives of this chapter. All contracts with providers shall contain provisions requiring a fast, fair, and cost-effective dispute resolution mechanism under which providers may submit disputes to the plan, and requiring the plan to inform its providers upon contracting with the plan, or upon change to these provisions, of the procedures for processing and resolving disputes, including the location and telephone number where information regarding disputes may be submitted.

(2) A health care service plan shall ensure that a dispute resolution mechanism is accessible to noncontracting providers for the purpose of resolving billing and claims disputes.

(3) On and after January 1, 2002, a health care service plan shall annually submit a report to the department regarding its dispute resolution mechanism. The report shall include information on the number of providers who utilized the dispute resolution mechanism and a summary of the disposition of those disputes.

(i) A health care service plan contract shall provide to subscribers and enrollees all of the basic health care services included in subdivision (b) of Section 1345, except that the director may, for good cause, by rule or order exempt a plan contract or any class of plan contracts from that requirement. The director shall by rule define the scope of each basic health care service that health care service plans are required to provide as a minimum for licensure under this chapter. Nothing in this chapter shall prohibit a health care service plan from charging subscribers or enrollees a copayment or a deductible for a basic health care service consistent with Section 1367.006 or 1367.007, provided that the copayments, deductibles, or other cost sharing are reported to the director and set forth to the subscriber or enrollee pursuant to the disclosure provisions of Section 1363. Nothing in this chapter shall prohibit a health care service plan from setting forth, by contract, limitations on maximum coverage of basic health care services, provided that the limitations are reported to, and held unobjectionable by, the director and set forth to the subscriber or enrollee pursuant to the disclosure provisions of Section 1363.

(j) A health care service plan shall not require registration under the federal Controlled Substances Act (21 U.S.C. Sec. 801 et seq.) as a condition for participation by an optometrist certified to use therapeutic pharmaceutical agents pursuant to Section 3041.3 of the Business and Professions Code.

Nothing in this section shall be construed to permit the director to establish the rates charged subscribers and enrollees for contractual health care services.

The director's enforcement of Article 3.1 (commencing with Section 1357) shall not be deemed to establish the rates charged subscribers and enrollees for contractual health care services.

The obligation of the plan to comply with this chapter shall not be waived when the plan delegates any services that it is required to perform to its medical groups, independent practice associations, or other contracting entities.

(Amended by Stats. 2013, Ch. 316, Sec. 2. (SB 639) Effective January 1, 2014.)

1374.13. TELEHEALTH

(a) For the purposes of this section, the definitions in subdivision (a) of Section 2290.5 of the Business and Professions Code apply.

(b) It is the intent of the Legislature to recognize the practice of telehealth as a legitimate means by which an individual may receive health care services from a health care provider without in-person contact with the health care provider.

(c) A health care service plan shall not require that in-person contact occur between a health care provider and a patient before payment is made for the covered services appropriately provided through telehealth, subject to the terms and conditions of the contract entered into between the enrollee or subscriber and the health care service plan, and between the health care service plan and its participating providers or provider groups, and pursuant to Section 1374.14.

(d) A health care service plan shall not limit the type of setting where services are provided for the patient or by the health care provider before payment is made for the covered services appropriately provided through telehealth, subject to the terms and conditions of the contract entered into between the enrollee or subscriber and the health care service plan, and between the health care service plan and its participating providers or provider groups, and pursuant to Section 1374.14.

(e) This section shall also apply to health care service plan contracts and Medi-Cal managed care plan contracts with the State Department of Health Care Services pursuant to Chapter 7 (commencing with Section 14000) or Chapter 8 (commencing with Section 14200) of Part 3 of Division 9 of the Welfare and Institutions Code.

(f) Notwithstanding any other law, this section does not authorize a health care service plan to require the use of telehealth if the health care provider has determined that it is not appropriate.

(Amended by Stats. 2019, Ch. 867, Sec. 2. (AB 744) Effective January 1, 2020.)

1374.14. HEALTH CARE CONTRACTS; TELEHEALTH

(a) (1) A contract between a health care service plan and a health care provider for the provision of health care services to an enrollee or subscriber shall specify that the health care service plan shall reimburse the treating or consulting health care provider for the diagnosis, consultation, or treatment of an enrollee or subscriber appropriately delivered through telehealth services on the same basis and to the same extent that the health care service plan is responsible for reimbursement for the same service through in-person diagnosis, consultation, or treatment.

(2) This section does not limit the ability of a health care service plan and a health care provider to negotiate the rate of reimbursement for a health care service provided pursuant to a contract subject to this section. Services that are the same, as determined by the provider's description of the service on the claim, shall be reimbursed at the same rate whether provided in person or through telehealth. When negotiating a rate of reimbursement for telehealth services for which no in-person equivalent exists, a health care service plan and the provider shall ensure the rate is consistent with subdivision (h) of Section 1367.

(3) This section does not require telehealth reimbursement to be unbundled from other capitated or bundled, risk-based payments.

(b) (1) A health care service plan contract shall specify that the health care service plan shall provide coverage for health care services appropriately delivered through telehealth services on the same basis and to the same extent that the health care service plan is responsible for coverage for the same service through in-person diagnosis, consultation, or treatment. Coverage shall not be limited only to services delivered by select third-party corporate telehealth providers.

(2) This section does not alter the obligation of a health care service plan to ensure that enrollees have access to all covered services through an adequate network of contracted providers, as required under Sections 1367, 1367.03, and 1367.035, and the regulations promulgated thereunder.

(3) This section does not require a health care service plan to cover telehealth services provided by an out-of-network provider, unless coverage is required under other law.

(c) A health care service plan may offer a contract containing a copayment or coinsurance requirement for a health care service delivered through telehealth services, provided that the copayment or coinsurance does not exceed the copayment or coinsurance applicable if the same services were delivered through in-person diagnosis, consultation, or treatment. This subdivision does not require cost sharing for services provided through telehealth.

(d) Services provided through telehealth and covered pursuant to this chapter shall be subject to the same deductible and annual or lifetime dollar maximum as equivalent services that are not provided through telehealth.

(e) The definitions in subdivision (a) of Section 2290.5 of the Business and Professions Code apply to this section.

(f) This section shall not apply to Medi-Cal managed care plans that contract with the State Department of Health Care Services pursuant to Chapter 7 (commencing with Section 14000) of, Chapter 8 (commencing with Section 14200) of, or Chapter 8.75 (commencing with Section 14591) of, Part 3 of Division 9 of the Welfare and Institutions Code.

(g) The provisions of this section are severable. If any provision of this section or its application is held invalid, that invalidity shall not affect other provisions or applications that can be given effect without the invalid provision or application.

(Amended by Stats. 2021, Ch. 439, Sec. 4. (AB 457) Effective January 1, 2022.)

ARTICLE 9: MISCELLANEOUS

1395. ADVERTISING; CONTRACTS WITH LICENSED PROFESSIONALS; OFFICERS; MISREPRESENTATIONS BY PLAN; COMPLIANCE BY PLAN

(a) Notwithstanding Article 6 (commencing with Section 650) of Chapter 1 of Division 2 of the Business and Professions Code, any health care service plan or specialized health care service plan may, except as limited by this subdivision, solicit or advertise with regard to the cost of subscription or enrollment, facilities and services rendered, provided, however, Article 5 (commencing with Section 600) of Chapter 1 of Division 2 of the Business and Professions Code remains in effect. Any price advertisement shall be exact, without the use of such phrases as "as low as," "and up," "lowest prices" or words or phrases of similar import. Any advertisement that refers to services, or costs for the services, and that uses words of comparison must be based on verifiable data substantiating the comparison. Any health care service plan or specialized health care service plan so advertising shall be prepared to provide information sufficient to establish the accuracy of the comparison. Price advertising shall not be fraudulent, deceitful, or misleading, nor contain any offers of discounts, premiums, gifts, or bait of similar nature. In connection with price advertising, the price for each product or service shall be clearly identifiable. The price advertised for products shall include charges for any related professional services, including dispensing and fitting services, unless the advertisement specifically and clearly indicates otherwise.

(b) Plans licensed under this chapter shall not be deemed to be engaged in the practice of a profession, and may employ, or contract with, any professional licensed pursuant to Division 2 (commencing with Section 500) of the

Business and Professions Code to deliver professional services. Employment by or a contract with a plan as a provider of professional services shall not constitute a ground for disciplinary action against a health professional licensed pursuant to Division 2 (commencing with Section 500) of the Business and Professions Code by a licensing agency regulating a particular health care profession.

(c) A health care service plan licensed under this chapter may directly own, and may directly operate through its professional employees or contracted licensed professionals, offices and subsidiary corporations, including pharmacies that satisfy the requirements of subdivision (d) of Section 4080.5 of the Business and Professions Code, as are necessary to provide health care services to the plan's subscribers and enrollees.

(d) A professional licensed pursuant to the provisions of Division 2 (commencing with Section 500) of the Business and Professions Code who is employed by, or under contract to, a plan may not own or control offices or branch offices beyond those expressly permitted by the provisions of the Business and Professions Code.

(e) Nothing in this chapter shall be construed to repeal, abolish, or diminish the effect of Section 129450 of the Health and Safety Code.

(f) Except as specifically provided in this chapter, nothing in this chapter shall be construed to limit the effect of the laws governing professional corporations, as they appear in applicable provisions of the Business and Professions Code, upon specialized health care service plans.

(g) No representative of a participating health, dental, or vision plan or its subcontractor representative shall in any manner use false or misleading claims to misrepresent itself, the plan, the subcontractor, or the Healthy Families or Medi-Cal program while engaging in application assistance activities that are subject to this section. Notwithstanding any other provision of this chapter, any representative of the health, dental, or vision care plan or of the health, dental, or vision care plan's subcontractor who violates any of the provisions of Section 12693.325 of the Insurance Code shall only be subject to a fine of five hundred dollars ($500) for each of those violations.

(h) A health care service plan shall comply with Section 12693.325 of the Insurance Code and Section 14409 of the Welfare and Institutions Code. In addition to any other disciplinary powers provided by this chapter, if a health care service plan violates any of the provisions of Section 12693.325 of the Insurance Code, the department may prohibit the health care service plan from providing application assistance and contacting applicants pursuant to Section 12693.325 of the Insurance Code.

(Amended by Stats. 2001, Ch. 171, Sec. 2. Effective August 10, 2001.)

1396. MISSTATEMENTS OR OMISSIONS IN DOCUMENTS FILED

It is unlawful for any person willfully to make any untrue statement of material fact in any application, notice, amendment, report, or other submission filed with the director under this chapter or the regulations adopted thereunder, or willfully to omit to state in any application, notice, or report any material fact which is required to be stated therein.

(Amended by Stats. 1999, Ch. 525, Sec. 151. Effective January 1, 2000. Operative July 1, 2000, or sooner, by Sec. 214 of Ch. 525.)

1397. HEARINGS; JUDICIAL REVIEW

(a) Whenever reference is made in this chapter to a hearing before or by the director, the hearing shall be held in accordance with the Administrative Procedure Act (Chapter 5 (commencing with Section 11500) of Part 1 of Division 3 of Title 2 of the Government Code), and the director shall have all of the powers granted under that act.

(b) Every final order, decision, license, or other official act of the director under this chapter is subject to judicial review in accordance with the law.

(Amended by Stats. 1999, Ch. 525, Sec. 152. Effective January 1, 2000. Operative July 1, 2000, or sooner, by Sec. 214 of Ch. 525.)

1397.5. SUMMARY OF COMPLAINTS AGAINST PLANS

(a) The director shall make and file annually with the Department of Managed Health Care as a public record, an aggregate summary of grievances against plans filed with the director by enrollees or subscribers. This summary shall include at least all of the following information:

(1) The total number of grievances filed.

(2) The types of grievances.

(b) The summary set forth in subdivision (a) shall include the following disclaimer:

"THIS INFORMATION IS PROVIDED FOR STATISTICAL PURPOSES ONLY. THE DIRECTOR OF THE DEPARTMENT OF MANAGED CARE HAS NEITHER INVESTIGATED NOR DETERMINED WHETHER THE GRIEVANCES COMPILED WITHIN THIS SUMMARY ARE REASONABLE OR VALID."

(c) Nothing in this section shall require or authorize the disclosure of grievances filed with or received by the director and made confidential pursuant to any other provision of law including, but not limited to, the California Public Records Act (Division 10 (commencing with Section 7920.000) of Title 1 of the Government Code) and the Information Practices Act of 1977 (Chapter 1 (commencing with Section 1798) of Title 1.8 of Part 4 of Division 3 of the Civil Code). Nothing in this section shall affect any other provision of law including, but not limited to, the California Public Records Act and the Information Practices Act of 1977.

(Amended by Stats. 2021, Ch. 615, Sec. 229. (AB 474) Effective January 1, 2022. Operative January 1, 2023, pursuant to Sec. 463 of Stats. 2021, Ch. 615.)

1397.6. CONTRACTS WITH MEDICAL CONSULTANTS

The director may contract with necessary medical consultants to assist with the health care program. These contracts shall be on a noncompetitive bid basis and shall be exempt from Chapter 2 (commencing with Section 10290) of Part 2 of Division 2 of the Public Contract Code.

(Amended by Stats. 1999, Ch. 525, Sec. 154. Effective January 1, 2000. Operative July 1, 2000, or sooner, by Sec. 214 of Ch. 525.)

1398.5. REFERENCES TO PRIOR LAW

All references to the Knox-Mills Health Plan Act (Article 2.5 (commencing with Section 12530) of Chapter 6 of Part 2 of Division 3 of the Government Code), which was repealed by Chapter 941 of the Statutes of 1975, shall be deemed to be references to the Knox-Keene Health Care Service Plan Act of 1975.

(Added by Stats. 1976, Ch. 490.)

1399. SURRENDER OF LICENSE; SUMMARY SUSPENSION OR REVOCATION OF LICENSE

(a) Surrender of a license as a health plan becomes effective 30 days after receipt of an application to surrender the license or within a shorter period of time as the director may determine, unless a revocation or suspension proceeding is pending when the application is filed or a proceeding to revoke or suspend or to impose conditions upon the surrender is instituted within 30 days after the application is filed. If this proceeding is pending or instituted, surrender becomes effective at the time and upon the conditions as the director by order determines.

(b) If the director finds that any plan is no longer in existence, or has ceased to do business or has failed to initiate business activity as a licensee within six months after licensure, or cannot be located after reasonable search, the director may by order summarily revoke the license of the plan.

(c) The director may summarily suspend or revoke the license of a plan upon (1) failure to pay any fee required by this chapter within 15 days after notice by the director that the fee is due and unpaid, (2) failure to file any amendment or report required under this chapter within 15 days after notice by the director that the report is due, (3) failure to maintain any bond or insurance pursuant to Section 1376, (4) failure to maintain a deposit, insurance, or guaranty arrangement pursuant to Section 1377, or (5) failure to maintain a deposit pursuant to Section 1300.76.1 of Title 28 of the California Code of Regulations.

(Amended by Stats. 2009, Ch. 298, Sec. 9. (AB 1540) Effective January 1, 2010.)

1399.1. ADMINISTRATIVE ACTIONS APPLICABLE TO TRANSITIONALLY LICENSED PLANS

(a) All orders and other actions taken by the Commissioner of Corporations pursuant to the authority contained in subdivision (c) of Section 1350 on or before September 30, 1977, and all administrative or judicial decisions or orders relating to the same and all conditions imposed upon the same remain in effect against a plan holding a transitional license.

(b) The Knox-Mills Health Plan Act as in effect prior to its repeal continues to govern all suits, actions, prosecutions or proceedings which are pending or which may be initiated under subdivision (c) of Section 1350 on the basis of facts or circumstances occurring on or before September 30, 1977.

(Amended by Stats. 1999, Ch. 525, Sec. 157. Effective January 1, 2000. Operative July 1, 2000, or sooner, by Sec. 214 of Ch. 525.)

1399.5. LEGISLATIVE INTENT; APPLICATION OF CHAPTER

It is the intent of the Legislature that the provisions of this chapter shall be applicable to any private or public entity or political subdivision which, in return for a prepaid or periodic charge paid by or on behalf of a subscriber or enrollee, provides, administers or otherwise arranges for the provision of health care services, as defined in this chapter, unless such entity is exempted from the provisions of this chapter by, or pursuant to, Section 1343.

(Amended by Stats. 1980, Ch. 628.)

DIVISION 10: UNIFORM CONTROLLED SUBSTANCES ACT

CHAPTER 1: GENERAL PROVISIONS AND DEFINITIONS

11024. "PHYSICIAN," "DENTIST," "PODIATRIST," "PHARMACIST," "VETERINARIAN," AND "OPTOMETRIST"

"Physician," "dentist," "podiatrist," "pharmacist," "veterinarian," and "optometrist" means persons who are licensed to practice their respective professions in this state.

(Amended by Stats. 2000, Ch. 676, Sec. 6. Effective January 1, 2001.)

11026. "PRACTITIONER"

"Practitioner" means any of the following:

(a) A physician, dentist, veterinarian, podiatrist, or pharmacist acting within the scope of a project authorized under Article 1 (commencing with Section 128125) of Chapter 3 of Part 3 of Division 107, a registered nurse acting within the scope of a project authorized under Article 1 (commencing with Section 128125) of Chapter 3 of Part 3 of Division 107, a certified nurse-midwife acting within the scope of Section 2746.51 of the Business and Professions Code, a nurse practitioner acting within the scope of Section 2836.1 of the Business and Professions Code, or a physician assistant acting within the scope of a project authorized under Article 1 (commencing with Section 128125) of Chapter 3 of Part 3 of Division 107 or Section 3502.1 of the Business and Professions Code, or an optometrist acting within the scope of Section 3041 of the Business and Professions Code.

(b) A pharmacy, hospital, or other institution licensed, registered, or otherwise permitted to distribute, dispense, conduct research with respect to, or to administer, a controlled substance in the course of professional practice or research in this state.

(c) A scientific investigator, or other person licensed, registered, or otherwise permitted, to distribute, dispense, conduct research with respect to, or administer, a controlled substance in the course of professional practice or research in this state.

(Amended by Stats. 2001, Ch. 289, Sec. 10. Effective January 1, 2002.)

CHAPTER 4: PRESCRIPTIONS

ARTICLE 1: REQUIREMENTS OF PRESCRIPTIONS

11150. PERSONS PERMITTED TO WRITE PRESCRIPTION

No person other than a physician, dentist, podiatrist, or veterinarian, or naturopathic doctor acting pursuant to Section 3640.7 of the Business and Professions Code, or pharmacist acting within the scope of a project authorized under Article 1 (commencing with Section 128125) of Chapter 3 of Part 3 of Division 107 or within the scope of Section 4052.1, 4052.2, or 4052.6 of the Business and Professions Code, a registered nurse acting within the scope of a project authorized under Article 1 (commencing with Section 128125) of Chapter 3 of Part 3 of Division 107, a certified nurse- midwife acting within the scope of Section 2746.51 of the Business and Professions Code, a nurse practitioner acting within the scope of Section 2836.1 of the Business and Professions Code, a physician assistant acting within the scope of a project authorized under Article 1 (commencing with Section 128125) of Chapter 3 of Part 3 of Division 107 or Section 3502.1 of the Business and Professions Code, a naturopathic doctor acting within the scope of Section 3640.5 of the Business and Professions Code, or an optometrist acting within the scope of Section 3041 of the Business and Professions Code, or an out-of-state prescriber acting pursuant to Section 4005 of the Business and Professions Code shall write or issue a prescription.

(Amended by Stats. 2014, Ch. 319, Sec. 5. (SB 1039) Effective January 1, 2015.)

11161.5. SECURITY PRINTERS FOR CONTROLLED SUBSTANCE PRESCRIPTION FORMS; APPLICATION AND APPROVAL; SECURITY CHECKS; GROUNDS FOR DENIAL; LIST OF APPROVED SECURITY PRINTERS; DUTIES OF SECURITY PRINTER; RECORDS; REVOCATION OF APPROVAL

(a) Prescription forms for controlled substance prescriptions shall be obtained from security printers approved by the Department of Justice.

(b) The department may approve security printer applications after the applicant has provided the following information:

(1) Name, address, and telephone number of the applicant.

(2) Policies and procedures of the applicant for verifying the identity of the prescriber ordering controlled substance prescription forms.

(3) Policies and procedures of the applicant for verifying delivery of controlled substance prescription forms to prescribers.

(4) (A) The location, names, and titles of the applicant's agent for service of process in this state; all principal corporate officers, if any; all managing general partners, if any; and any individual owner, partner, corporate officer, manager, agent, representative, employee, or subcontractor of the applicant who has direct access to, or management or control of, controlled substance prescription forms.

(B) A report containing this information shall be made on an annual basis and within 30 days after any change of office, principal corporate officers, managing general partner, or of any person described in subparagraph (A).

(5) (A) A signed statement indicating whether the applicant, any principal corporate officer, any managing general partner, or any individual owner, partner, corporate officer, manager, agent, representative, employee, or subcontractor of the applicant who has direct access to, or management or control of, controlled substance prescription forms, has ever been convicted of, or pled no contest to, a violation of any law of a foreign country, the United States, or any state, or of any local ordinance.

(B) The department shall provide the applicant and any individual owner, partner, corporate officer, manager, agent, representative, employee, or subcontractor of the applicant who has direct access to, or management or control of, controlled substance prescription forms, with the means and direction to provide fingerprints and related information, in a manner specified by the department, for the purpose of completing state, federal, or foreign criminal background checks.

(C) Any applicant described in subdivision (b) shall submit his or her fingerprint images and related information to the department, for the purpose of the department obtaining information as to the existence and nature of a record of state, federal, or foreign level convictions and state, federal, or foreign level arrests for which the department establishes that the applicant was released on bail or on his or her own recognizance pending trial, as described in subdivision (l) of Section 11105 of the Penal Code. Requests for federal level criminal offender record information received by the department pursuant to this section shall be forwarded to the Federal Bureau of Investigation by the department.

(D) The department shall assess against each security printer applicant a fee determined by the department to be sufficient to cover all processing, maintenance, and investigative costs generated from or associated with completing state, federal, or foreign background checks and inspections of security printers pursuant to this section with respect to that applicant; the fee shall be paid by the applicant at the time he or she submits the security printer application, fingerprints, and related information to the department.

(E) The department shall retain fingerprint impressions and related information for subsequent arrest notification pursuant to Section 11105.2 of the Penal Code for all applicants.

(c) The department may, within 60 calendar days of receipt of the application from the applicant, deny the security printer application.

(d) The department may deny a security printer application on any of the following grounds:

(1) The applicant, any individual owner, partner, corporate officer, manager, agent, representative, employee, or subcontractor for the applicant, who has direct access, management, or control of controlled substance prescription forms, has been convicted of a crime. A conviction within the meaning of this paragraph means a plea or verdict of guilty or a conviction following a plea of nolo contendere. Any action which a board is permitted to take following the establishment of a conviction may be taken when the time for appeal has elapsed, the judgment of conviction has been affirmed on appeal, or when an order granting probation is made suspending the imposition of sentence, irrespective of a subsequent order under the provisions of Section 1203.4 of the Penal Code.

(2) The applicant committed any act involving dishonesty, fraud, or deceit with the intent to substantially benefit

himself, herself, or another, or substantially injure another.

(3) The applicant committed any act that would constitute a violation of this division.

(4) The applicant knowingly made a false statement of fact required to be revealed in the application to produce controlled substance prescription forms.

(5) The department determines that the applicant failed to demonstrate adequate security procedures relating to the production and distribution of controlled substance prescription forms.

(6) The department determines that the applicant has submitted an incomplete application.

(7) As a condition for its approval as a security printer, an applicant shall authorize the Department of Justice to make any examination of the books and records of the applicant, or to visit and inspect the applicant during business hours, to the extent deemed necessary by the board or department to properly enforce this section.

(e) An approved applicant shall submit an exemplar of a controlled substance prescription form, with all security features, to the Department of Justice within 30 days of initial production.

(f) The department shall maintain a list of approved security printers and the department shall make this information available to prescribers and other appropriate government agencies, including the Board of Pharmacy.

(g) Before printing any controlled substance prescription forms, a security printer shall verify with the appropriate licensing board that the prescriber possesses a license and current prescribing privileges which permits the prescribing of controlled substances with the federal Drug Enforcement Administration (DEA).

(h) Controlled substance prescription forms shall be provided directly to the prescriber either in person, by certified mail, or by a means that requires a signature signifying receipt of the package and provision of that signature to the security printer. Controlled substance prescription forms provided in person shall be restricted to established customers. Security printers shall obtain a photo identification from the customer and maintain a log of this information.

Controlled substance prescription forms shall be shipped only to the prescriber's address on file and verified with the federal Drug Enforcement Administration or the Medical Board of California.

(i) Security printers shall retain ordering and delivery records in a readily retrievable manner for individual prescribers for three years.

(j) Security printers shall produce ordering and delivery records upon request by an authorized officer of the law as defined in Section 4017 of the Business and Professions Code.

(k) Security printers shall report any theft or loss of controlled substance prescription forms to the Department of Justice via fax or email within 24 hours of the theft or loss.

(l) (1) The department shall impose restrictions, sanctions, or penalties, subject to subdivisions (m) and (n), against security printers who are not in compliance with this division pursuant to regulations implemented pursuant to this division and shall revoke its approval of a security printer for a violation of this division or action that would permit a denial pursuant to subdivision (d) of this section.

(2) When the department revokes its approval, it shall notify the appropriate licensing boards and remove the security printer from the list of approved security printers.

(m) The following violations by security printers shall be punishable pursuant to subdivision (n):

(1) Failure to comply with the Security Printer Guidelines established by the Security Printer Program as a condition of approval.

(2) Failure to take reasonable precautions to prevent any dishonest act or illegal activity related to the access and control of security prescription forms.

(3) Theft or fraudulent use of a prescriber's identity in order to obtain security prescription forms.

(n) A security printer approved pursuant to subdivision (b) shall be subject to the following penalties for actions leading to the denial of a security printer application specified in subdivision (d) or for a violation specified in subdivision (m):

(1) For a first violation, a fine not to exceed one thousand dollars ($1,000).

(2) For a second or subsequent violation, a fine not to exceed two thousand five hundred dollars ($2,500) for each violation.

(3) For a third or subsequent violation, a filing of an administrative disciplinary action seeking to suspend or revoke security printer approval.

(o) In order to facilitate the standardization of all prescription forms and the serialization of prescription forms with unique identifiers, the Department of Justice may cease issuing new approvals of security printers to the extent necessary to achieve these purposes. The department may, pursuant to regulation, reduce the number of currently approved security printers to no fewer than three vendors. The department shall ensure that any reduction or limitation of approved security printers does not impact the ability of vendors to meet demand for prescription forms.

(Amended by Stats. 2018, Ch. 479, Sec. 2. (AB 1753) Effective January 1, 2019.)

11161.7. INFORMATION ON RESTRICTIONS OF PRESCRIBER'S AUTHORITY TO BE PROVIDED TO PHARMACIES, SECURITY PRINTERS, DEPARTMENT OF JUSTICE, AND BOARD OF PHARMACY

(a) When a prescriber's authority to prescribe controlled substances is restricted by civil, criminal, or administrative action, or by an order of the court issued pursuant to Section 11161, the law enforcement agency or licensing board that sought the restrictions shall provide the name, category of licensure, license number, and the nature of the restrictions imposed on the prescriber to security printers, the Department of Justice, and the Board of Pharmacy.

(b) The Board of Pharmacy shall make available the information required by subdivision (a) to pharmacies and security printers to prevent the dispensing of controlled substance prescriptions issued by the prescriber and the ordering of additional controlled substance prescription forms by the restricted prescriber.

(Added by Stats. 2003, Ch. 406, Sec. 7. Effective January 1, 2004.)

11162.1. FEATURES OF PRINTED PRESCRIPTION FORMS; REQUIREMENTS FOR BATCHES AND WHEN ORDERING FORMS

(a) The prescription forms for controlled substances shall be printed with the following features:

(1) A latent, repetitive "void" pattern shall be printed across the entire front of the prescription blank; if a prescription is scanned or photocopied, the word "void" shall appear in a pattern across the entire front of the prescription.

(2) A watermark shall be printed on the backside of the prescription blank; the watermark shall consist of the words "California Security Prescription."

(3) A chemical void protection that prevents alteration by chemical washing.

(4) A feature printed in thermochromic ink.

(5) An area of opaque writing so that the writing disappears if the prescription is lightened.

(6) A description of the security features included on each prescription form.

(7) (A) Six quantity check off boxes shall be printed on the form so that the prescriber may indicate the quantity by checking the applicable box where the following quantities shall appear:

1–24

25–49

50–74

75–100

101–150

151 and over.

(B) In conjunction with the quantity boxes, a space shall be provided to designate the units referenced in the quantity boxes when the drug is not in tablet or capsule form.

(8) Prescription blanks shall contain a statement printed on the bottom of the prescription blank that the "Prescription is void if the number of drugs prescribed is not noted."

(9) The preprinted name, category of licensure, license number, federal controlled substance registration number, and address of the prescribing practitioner.

(10) Check boxes shall be printed on the form so that the prescriber may indicate the number of refills ordered.

(11) The date of origin of the prescription.

(12) A check box indicating the prescriber's order not to substitute.

(13) An identifying number assigned to the approved security printer by the Department of Justice.

(14) (A) A check box by the name of each prescriber when a prescription form lists multiple prescribers.

(B) Each prescriber who signs the prescription form shall identify themselves as the prescriber by checking the box by the prescriber's name.

(15) A uniquely serialized number, in a manner prescribed by the Department of Justice in accordance with Section 11162.2.

(b) Each batch of controlled substance prescription forms shall have the lot number printed on the form and each form within that batch shall be numbered sequentially beginning with the numeral one.

(c) (1) A prescriber designated by a licensed health care facility, a clinic specified in Section 1200, or a clinic specified in subdivision (a) of Section 1206 that has 25 or more physicians or surgeons may order controlled substance prescription forms for use by prescribers when treating patients in that facility without the information required in paragraph (9) of subdivision (a) or paragraph (3).

(2) Forms ordered pursuant to this subdivision shall have the name, category of licensure, license number, and federal controlled substance registration number of the designated prescriber and the name, address, category of licensure, and license number of the licensed health care facility the clinic specified in Section 1200, or the clinic specified in Section 1206 that has 25 or more physicians or surgeons preprinted on the form. Licensed health care facilities or clinics exempt under Section 1206 are not required to preprint the category of licensure and license number of their facility or clinic.

(3) Forms ordered pursuant to this section shall not be valid prescriptions

without the name, category of licensure, license number, and federal controlled substance registration number of the prescriber on the form.

(4) (A) Except as provided in subparagraph (B), the designated prescriber shall maintain a record of the prescribers to whom the controlled substance prescription forms are issued, that shall include the name, category of licensure, license number, federal controlled substance registration number, and quantity of controlled substance prescription forms issued to each prescriber. The record shall be maintained in the health facility for three years.

(B) Forms ordered pursuant to this subdivision that are printed by a computerized prescription generation system shall not be subject to subparagraph (A) or paragraph (7) of subdivision (a). Forms printed pursuant to this subdivision that are printed by a computerized prescription generation system may contain the prescriber's name, category of professional licensure, license number, federal controlled substance registration number, and the date of the prescription.

(d) Within the next working day following delivery, a security printer shall submit via web-based application, as specified by the Department of Justice, all of the following information for all prescription forms delivered:

(1) Serial numbers of all prescription forms delivered.

(2) All prescriber names and Drug Enforcement Administration Controlled Substance Registration Certificate numbers displayed on the prescription forms.

(3) The delivery shipment recipient names.

(4) The date of delivery.

(Amended by Stats. 2019, Ch. 4, Sec. 1. (AB 149) Effective March 11, 2019.)

11162.6. CONTROLLED SUBSTANCE PRESCRIPTION FORMS; PENALTY FOR COUNTERFEITING, OBTAINING UNDER FALSE PRETENSES, FRAUDULENT PRODUCTION, ETC.

(a) Every person who counterfeits a controlled substance prescription form shall be guilty of a misdemeanor punishable by imprisonment in a county jail for not more than one year, by a fine not exceeding one thousand dollars ($1,000), or by both that imprisonment and fine.

(b) Every person who knowingly possesses a counterfeited controlled substance prescription form shall be guilty of a misdemeanor punishable by imprisonment in a county jail not exceeding six months, by a fine not exceeding one thousand dollars ($1,000), or by both that imprisonment and fine.

(c) Every person who attempts to obtain or obtains a controlled substance prescription form under false pretenses shall be guilty of a misdemeanor punishable by imprisonment in a county jail not exceeding six months, by a fine not exceeding one thousand dollars ($1,000), or by both that imprisonment and fine.

(d) Every person who fraudulently produces controlled substance prescription forms shall be guilty of a misdemeanor punishable by imprisonment in a county jail not exceeding six months, by a fine not exceeding one thousand dollars ($1,000), or by both that imprisonment and fine.

(e) This section shall become operative on July 1, 2004.

(Added by Stats. 2003, Ch. 406, Sec. 10. Effective January 1, 2004. Section operative July 1, 2004, by its own provisions.)

11164. REQUIREMENTS FOR PRESCRIPTIONS; ORAL OR ELECTRONIC PRESCRIPTION; WRITTEN RECORDS

Except as provided in Section 11167, no person shall prescribe a controlled substance, nor shall any person fill, compound, or dispense a prescription for a controlled substance, unless it complies with the requirements of this section.

(a) Each prescription for a controlled substance classified in Schedule II, III, IV, or V, except as authorized by subdivision (b), shall be made on a controlled substance prescription form as specified in Section 11162.1 and shall meet the following requirements:

(1) The prescription shall be signed and dated by the prescriber in ink and shall contain the prescriber's address and telephone number; the name of the ultimate user or research subject, or contact information as determined by the Secretary of the United States Department of Health and Human Services; refill information, such as the number of refills ordered and whether the prescription is a first-time request or a refill; and the name, quantity, strength, and directions for use of the controlled substance prescribed.

(2) The prescription shall also contain the address of the person for whom the controlled substance is prescribed. If the prescriber does not specify this address on the prescription, the pharmacist filling the prescription or an employee acting under the direction of the pharmacist shall write or type the address on the prescription or maintain this information in a readily retrievable form in the pharmacy.

(b) (1) Notwithstanding paragraph (1) of subdivision (a) of Section 11162.1, any controlled substance classified in Schedule III, IV, or V may be dispensed upon an oral or electronically transmitted prescription, which shall be produced in hard copy form and signed and dated by the pharmacist filling the prescription or by any other person expressly authorized by provisions of the Business and Professions Code. Any person who transmits, maintains, or receives any electronically transmitted prescription shall ensure the security, integrity, authority, and confidentiality of the prescription.

(2) The date of issue of the prescription and all the information required for a written prescription by subdivision (a) shall be included in the written record of the prescription; the pharmacist need not include the address, telephone number, license classification, or federal registry number of the prescriber or the address of the patient on the hard copy, if that information is readily retrievable in the pharmacy.

(3) Pursuant to an authorization of the prescriber, any agent of the prescriber on behalf of the prescriber may orally or electronically transmit a prescription for a controlled substance classified in Schedule III, IV, or V, if in these cases the written record of the prescription required by this subdivision specifies the name of the agent of the prescriber transmitting the prescription.

(c) The use of commonly used abbreviations shall not invalidate an otherwise valid prescription.

(d) Notwithstanding subdivisions (a) and (b), prescriptions for a controlled substance classified in Schedule V may be for more than one person in the same family with the same medical need.

(e) (1) Notwithstanding any other law, a prescription written on a prescription form that was otherwise valid prior to January 1, 2019, but that does not comply with paragraph (15) of subdivision (a) of Section 11162.1, or a valid controlled substance prescription form approved by the Department of Justice as of January 1, 2019, is a valid prescription that may be filled, compounded, or dispensed until January 1, 2021.

(2) If the Department of Justice determines that there is an inadequate availability of compliant prescription forms to meet demand on or before the date described in paragraph (1), the department may extend the period during which prescriptions written on noncompliant prescription forms remain valid for a period no longer than an additional six months.

(Amended by Stats. 2019, Ch. 4, Sec. 3. (AB 149) Effective March 11, 2019.)

11164.1. WHEN PRESCRIPTION FOR CONTROLLED SUBSTANCE ISSUED BY PRESCRIBER IN ANOTHER STATE FOR DELIVERY TO PATIENT IN ANOTHER STATE MAY BE DISPENSED BY CALIFORNIA PHARMACY; SUBSTANCES FROM OUT-OF-STATE PRESCRIBERS

(a) (1) Notwithstanding any other law, a prescription for a controlled substance issued by a prescriber in another state for delivery to a patient in another state may be dispensed by a California pharmacy, if the prescription conforms with the requirements for controlled substance prescriptions in the state in which the controlled substance was prescribed.

(2) A prescription for a Schedule II, Schedule III, Schedule IV, or Schedule V controlled substance dispensed pursuant to this subdivision shall be reported by the dispensing pharmacy to the Department of Justice in the manner prescribed by subdivision (d) of Section 11165.

(b) A pharmacy may dispense a prescription for a Schedule III, Schedule IV, or Schedule V controlled substance from an out-of-state prescriber pursuant to Section 4005 of the Business and Professions Code and Section 1717 of Title 16 of the California Code of Regulations.

(c) This section shall become operative on January 1, 2021.

(Repealed (in Sec. 3) and added by Stats. 2019, Ch. 677, Sec. 4. (AB 528) Effective January 1, 2020. Section operative January 1, 2021, by its own provisions.)

11166. WHEN FILING PRESCRIPTION FOR CONTROLLED SUBSTANCE IS PROHIBITED

No person shall fill a prescription for a controlled substance after six months has elapsed from the date written on the prescription by the prescriber. No person shall knowingly fill a mutilated or forged or altered prescription for a controlled substance except for the addition of the address of the person for whom the controlled substance is prescribed as provided by paragraph (3) of subdivision (b) of Section 11164.

(Amended by Stats. 2003, Ch. 406, Sec. 19. Effective January 1, 2004.)

11167. EMERGENCY ORDER FOR CONTROLLED SUBSTANCES; REQUIREMENTS

Notwithstanding subdivision (a) of Section 11164, in an emergency where failure to issue a prescription may result in loss of life or intense suffering, an order for a controlled substance may be dispensed on an oral order, an electronic data transmission order, or a written order not made on a controlled substance form as specified in Section 11162.1, subject to all of the following requirements:

(a) The order contains all information required by subdivision (a) of Section 11164.

(b) Any written order is signed and dated by the prescriber in ink, and the pharmacy reduces any oral or electronic data transmission order to hard copy form prior to dispensing the controlled substance.

(c) The prescriber provides a written prescription on a controlled substance prescription form that meets the requirements of Section 11162.1, by the seventh day following the transmission of the initial order; a postmark by the seventh day following transmission of the initial order shall constitute compliance.

(d) If the prescriber fails to comply with subdivision (c), the pharmacy shall so notify the Department of Justice in writing within 144 hours of the prescriber's failure to do so and shall make and retain a hard copy, readily retrievable record of the prescription, including the date and method of notification of the Department of Justice.

(e) This section shall become operative on January 1, 2005.

(Amended by Stats. 2012, Ch. 867, Sec. 8. (SB 1144) Effective January 1, 2013.)

CHAPTER 5: USE OF CONTROLLED SUBSTANCES

ARTICLE 1: LAWFUL MEDICAL USE OTHER THAN TREATMENT OF ADDICTS

11210. PERMITTED PRESCRIBING, FURNISHING, OR ADMINISTERING CONTROLLED SUBSTANCES BY PRACTITIONERS

A physician, surgeon, dentist, veterinarian, naturopathic doctor acting pursuant to Section 3640.7 of the Business and Professions Code, or podiatrist, or pharmacist acting within the scope of a project authorized under Article 1 (commencing with Section 128125) of Chapter 3 of Part 3 of Division 107 or within the scope of Section 4052.1, 4052.2, or 4052.6 of the Business and Professions Code, or registered nurse acting within the scope of a project authorized under Article 1 (commencing with Section 128125) of Chapter 3 of Part 3 of Division 107, or physician assistant acting within the scope of a project authorized under Article 1 (commencing with Section 128125) of Chapter 3 of Part 3 of Division 107, or naturopathic doctor acting within the scope of Section 3640.5 of the Business and Professions Code, or an optometrist acting within the scope of Section 3041 of the Business and Professions Code may prescribe for, furnish to, or administer controlled substances to his or her patient when the patient is suffering from a disease, ailment, injury, or infirmities attendant upon old age, other than addiction to a controlled substance.

The physician, surgeon, dentist, veterinarian, naturopathic doctor acting pursuant to Section 3640.7 of the Business and Professions Code, or podiatrist, or pharmacist acting within the scope of a project authorized under Article 1 (commencing with Section 128125) of Chapter 3 of Part 3 of Division 107 or within the scope of Section 4052.1, 4052.2, or 4052.6 of the Business and Professions Code, or registered nurse acting within the scope of a project authorized under Article 1 (commencing with Section 128125) of Chapter 3 of Part 3 of Division 107, or physician assistant acting within the scope of a project authorized under Article 1 (commencing with Section 128125) of Chapter 3 of Part 3 of Division 107, or naturopathic doctor acting within the scope of Section 3640.5 of the Business and Professions Code, or an optometrist acting within the scope of Section 3041 of the Business and Professions Code shall prescribe, furnish, or administer controlled substances only when in good faith he or she believes the disease, ailment, injury, or infirmity requires the treatment.

The physician, surgeon, dentist, veterinarian, or naturopathic doctor acting pursuant to Section 3640.7 of the Business and Professions Code, or podiatrist, or pharmacist acting within the scope of a project authorized under Article 1 (commencing with Section 128125) of Chapter 3 of Part 3 of Division 107 or within the scope of Section 4052.1, 4052.2, or 4052.6 of the Business and Professions Code, or registered nurse acting within the scope of a project authorized under Article 1 (commencing with Section 128125) of Chapter 3 of Part 3 of Division 107, or physician assistant acting within the scope of a project authorized under Article 1 (commencing with Section 128125) of Chapter 3 of Part 3 of Division 107, or a naturopathic doctor acting within the scope of Section 3640.5 of the Business and Professions Code, or an optometrist acting within the scope of Section 3041 of the Business and Professions Code shall prescribe, furnish, or administer controlled substances only in the quantity and for the length of time as are reasonably necessary.

(Amended by Stats. 2014, Ch. 319, Sec. 6. (SB 1039) Effective January 1, 2015.)

DIVISION 106: PERSONAL HEALTH CARE (INCLUDING MATERNAL, CHILD, AND ADOLESCENT)

PART 1: GENERAL ADMINISTRATION

CHAPTER 1: PATIENT ACCESS TO HEALTH RECORDS

123100. LEGISLATIVE FINDINGS AND DECLARATIONS

The Legislature finds and declares that every person having ultimate responsibility for decisions respecting his or her own health care also possesses a concomitant right of access to complete information respecting his or her condition and care provided. Similarly, persons having responsibility for decisions respecting the health care of others should, in general, have access to information on the patient's condition and care. It is, therefore, the intent of the Legislature in enacting this chapter to establish procedures for providing access to health care records or summaries of those records by patients and by those persons having responsibility for decisions respecting the health care of others.

(Added by Stats. 1995, Ch. 415, Sec. 8. Effective January 1, 1996.)

123105. DEFINITIONS

As used in this chapter:

(a) "Health care provider" means any of the following:

(1) A health facility licensed pursuant to Chapter 2 (commencing with Section 1250) of Division 2.

(2) A clinic licensed pursuant to Chapter 1 (commencing with Section 1200) of Division 2.

(3) A home health agency licensed pursuant to Chapter 8 (commencing with Section 1725) of Division 2.

(4) A physician and surgeon licensed pursuant to Chapter 5 (commencing with Section 2000) of Division 2 of the Business and Professions Code or pursuant to the Osteopathic Act.

(5) A podiatrist licensed pursuant to Article 22 (commencing with Section 2460) of Chapter 5 of Division 2 of the Business and Professions Code.

(6) A dentist licensed pursuant to Chapter 4 (commencing with Section 1600) of Division 2 of the Business and Professions Code.

(7) A psychologist licensed pursuant to Chapter 6.6 (commencing with Section 2900) of Division 2 of the Business and Professions Code.

(8) An optometrist licensed pursuant to Chapter 7 (commencing with Section 3000) of Division 2 of the Business and Professions Code.

(9) A chiropractor licensed pursuant to the Chiropractic Initiative Act.

(10) A marriage and family therapist licensed pursuant to Chapter 13 (commencing with Section 4980) of Division 2 of the Business and Professions Code.

(11) A clinical social worker licensed pursuant to Chapter 14 (commencing with Section 4990) of Division 2 of the Business and Professions Code.

(12) A physical therapist licensed pursuant to Chapter 5.7 (commencing with Section 2600) of Division 2 of the Business and Professions Code.

(13) An occupational therapist licensed pursuant to Chapter 5.6 (commencing with Section 2570).

(14) A professional clinical counselor licensed pursuant to Chapter 16 (commencing with Section 4999.10) of Division 2 of the Business and Professions Code.

(15) A speech-language pathologist or audiologist licensed pursuant to Chapter 5.3 (commencing with Section 2530) of Division 2 of the Business and Professions Code.

(16) A physician assistant licensed pursuant to Chapter 7.7 (commencing with Section 3500) of Division 2 of the Business and Professions Code.

(17) A nurse practitioner licensed pursuant to Article 8 (commencing with Section 2834) of Chapter 6 of Division 2 of the Business and Professions Code.

(b) "Mental health records" means patient records, or discrete portions thereof, specifically relating to evaluation or treatment of a mental disorder. "Mental health records" includes, but is not limited to, all alcohol and drug abuse records.

(c) "Patient" means a patient or former patient of a health care provider.

(d) "Patient records" means records in any form or medium maintained by, or in the custody or control of, a health care provider relating to the health history, diagnosis, or condition of a patient, or relating to treatment provided or proposed to be provided to the patient. "Patient records" includes only records pertaining to the patient requesting the records or whose representative requests the records. "Patient records" does not include information given in confidence to a health care provider by a person other than another health care provider or the patient, and that material may be removed from any records prior to inspection or copying under Section 123110 or 123115. "Patient records" does not include information contained in aggregate form, such as indices, registers, or logs.

(e) "Patient's representative," "patient's personal representative," or "representative" means any of the following:

(1) A parent or guardian of a minor who is a patient.

(2) The guardian or conservator of the person of an adult patient.

(3) An agent as defined in Section 4607 of the Probate Code, to the extent necessary for the agent to fulfill the duties set forth in Division 4.7 (commencing with Section 4600) of the Probate Code.

(4) The beneficiary as defined in Section 24 of the Probate Code or personal representative as defined in Section 58 of the Probate Code, of a deceased patient.

(f) "Alcohol and drug abuse records" means patient records, or discrete portions thereof, specifically relating to evaluation and treatment of alcoholism or drug abuse.

(Amended by Stats. 2020, Ch. 101, Sec. 1. (AB 2520) Effective January 1, 2021.)

123110. INSPECTION OF RECORDS; COPYING OF RECORDS; VIOLATIONS; CONSTRUCTION OF SECTION

(a) Notwithstanding Section 5328 of the Welfare and Institutions Code, and except as provided in Sections 123115 and 123120, any adult patient of a health care provider, any minor patient authorized by law to consent to medical treatment, and any patient's personal representative shall be entitled to inspect patient records upon presenting to the health care provider a request for those records and upon payment of reasonable costs, as specified in subdivision (j). However, a patient who is a minor shall be entitled to inspect patient records pertaining only to health care of a type for which the minor is lawfully authorized to consent. A health care provider shall permit this inspection during business hours within five working days after receipt of the request. The inspection shall be conducted by the patient or patient's personal representative requesting the inspection, who may be accompanied by one other person of their choosing.

(b) (1) Additionally, any patient or patient's personal representative shall be entitled to a paper or electronic copy of all or any portion of the patient records that they have a right to inspect, upon presenting a request to the health care provider specifying the records to be copied, together with a fee to defray the costs of producing the copy or summary, as specified in subdivision (j). The health care provider shall ensure that the copies are transmitted within 15 days after receiving the request.

(2) The health care provider shall provide the patient or patient's personal representative with a copy of the record in the form and format requested if it is readily producible in the requested form and format, or, if not, in a readable paper copy form or other form and format as agreed to by the health care provider and the patient or patient's personal representative. If the requested patient records are maintained electronically and if the patient or patient's personal representative requests an electronic copy of those records, the health care provider shall provide them in the electronic form and format requested if they are readily producible in that form and format, or, if not, in a readable electronic form and format as agreed to by the health care provider and the patient or patient's personal representative.

(c) Copies of X-rays or tracings derived from electrocardiography, electroencephalography, or electromyography need not be provided to the patient or patient's personal representative under this section, if the original X-rays or tracings are transmitted to another health care provider upon written request of the patient or patient's personal representative and within 15 days after receipt of the request. The request shall specify the name and address of the health care provider to whom the records are to be delivered. All reasonable costs, not exceeding actual costs, incurred by a health care provider in providing copies pursuant to this subdivision may be charged to the patient or representative requesting the copies.

(d) (1) Notwithstanding any provision of this section, and except as provided in Sections 123115 and 123120, a patient, employee of a nonprofit legal services entity representing the patient, or the personal representative of a patient, is entitled to a copy, at no charge, of the relevant portion of the patient's records, upon presenting to the provider a written request, and proof that the records or supporting forms are needed to support a claim or appeal regarding eligibility for a public benefit program, a petition for U nonimmigrant status under the Victims of Trafficking and Violence Protection Act, or a self-petition for lawful permanent residency under the Violence Against Women Act. A public benefit program includes the Medi-Cal program, the In-Home Supportive Services Program, the California Work Opportunity and Responsibility to Kids (CalWORKs) program, Social Security Disability Insurance benefits, Supplemental Security Income/State Supplementary Program for the Aged, Blind and Disabled (SSI/SSP) benefits, federal veterans service-connected compensation and nonservice connected pension disability benefits, CalFresh, the Cash Assistance Program for Aged, Blind, and Disabled Legal Immigrants, and a government-funded housing subsidy or tenant-based housing assistance program.

(2) Although a patient shall not be limited to a single request, the patient, employee of a nonprofit legal services entity representing the patient, or patient's personal representative shall be entitled to no more than one copy of any relevant portion of their record free of charge.

(3) This subdivision shall not apply to any patient who is represented by a private attorney who is paying for the costs related to the patient's claim or appeal, pending the outcome of that claim or appeal. For purposes of this subdivision, "private attorney" means any attorney not employed by a nonprofit legal services entity.

(e) If a patient, employee of a nonprofit legal services entity representing the patient, or the patient's personal representative requests a record pursuant to subdivision (d), the health care provider shall ensure that the copies are transmitted within 30 days after receiving the written request.

(f) This section shall not be construed to preclude a health care provider from requiring reasonable verification of identity prior to permitting inspection or copying of patient records, provided this requirement is not used oppressively or discriminatorily to frustrate or delay compliance with this section. This section does not supersede any rights that a patient or personal representative might otherwise have or exercise under Section 1158 of the Evidence Code or any other provision of law. This chapter does not require a health care provider to retain records longer than required by applicable statutes or administrative regulations.

(g) (1) This chapter shall not be construed to render a health care provider liable for the quality of their records or the copies provided in excess of existing law and regulations with respect to the quality of medical records. A health care provider shall not be liable to the patient or any other person for any consequences that result from disclosure of patient records as required by this chapter. A health care provider shall not discriminate against classes or categories of providers in the transmittal of X-rays or other patient records, or copies of these X-rays or records, to other providers as authorized by this section.

(2) Every health care provider shall adopt policies and establish procedures for the uniform transmittal of X-rays and other patient records that effectively prevent the discrimination described in this subdivision. A health care provider may establish reasonable conditions, including a reasonable deposit fee, to ensure the return of original X-rays transmitted to another health care provider, provided the conditions do not discriminate on the basis of, or in a manner related to, the license of the provider to which the X-rays are transmitted.

(h) Any health care provider described in paragraphs (4) to (10), inclusive, of subdivision (a) of Section 123105 who willfully violates this chapter is guilty of unprofessional conduct. Any health care provider described in paragraphs (1) to (3), inclusive, of subdivision (a) of Section 123105 that willfully violates this chapter is guilty of an infraction punishable by a fine of not more than one hundred dollars ($100). The state agency, board, or commission that issued the health care provider's professional or institutional license shall consider a violation as grounds for disciplinary action with respect to the licensure, including suspension or revocation of the license or certificate.

(i) This section prohibits a health care provider from withholding patient records or summaries of patient records because of an unpaid bill for health care services. Any health care provider who willfully withholds patient records or summaries of patient records because of an unpaid bill for health care services is subject to the sanctions specified in subdivision (h).

(j) (1) Except as provided in subdivision (d), a health care provider may impose a reasonable, cost-based fee for providing a paper or electronic copy or summary of patient records, provided the fee includes only the cost of the following:

(A) Labor for copying the patient records requested by the patient or patient's personal representative, whether in paper or electronic form.

(B) Supplies for creating the paper copy or electronic media if the patient or patient's personal representative requests that the electronic copy be provided on portable media.

(C) Postage, if the patient or patient's personal representative has requested the copy, or the summary or explanation, be mailed.

(D) Preparing an explanation or summary of the patient record, if agreed to by the patient or patient's personal representative.

(2) The fee from a health care provider shall not exceed twenty-five cents ($0.25) per page for paper copies or fifty cents ($0.50) per page for records that are copied from microfilm.

(Amended by Stats. 2023, Ch. 294, Sec. 31. (SB 815) Effective January 1, 2024.)

123111. PATIENT ADDENDUM TO MEDICAL RECORD

(a) A patient who inspects his or her patient records pursuant to Section 123110 has the right to provide to the health care provider a written addendum with respect to any item or statement in his or her records that the patient believes to be incomplete or incorrect. The addendum shall be limited to 250 words per alleged incomplete or incorrect item in the patient's record and shall clearly indicate in writing that the patient requests the addendum to be made a part of his or her record.

(b) The health care provider shall attach the addendum to the patient's records and shall include that addendum if the health care provider makes a disclosure of the allegedly incomplete or incorrect portion of the patient's records to any third party.

(c) The receipt of information in a patient's addendum which contains defamatory or otherwise unlawful language, and the inclusion of this information in the patient's records, in accordance with subdivision (b), shall not, in and of itself, subject the health care provider to liability in any civil, criminal, administrative, or other proceeding.

(d) Subdivision (i) of Section 123110 and Section 123120 are applicable with respect to any violation of this section by a health care provider.

(Amended by Stats. 2018, Ch. 275, Sec. 1. (AB 2088) Effective January 1, 2019.)

123114. FORMS THAT SUPPORT A CLAIM REGARDING ELIGIBILITY FOR A PUBLIC BENEFIT PROGRAM

(a) A health care provider shall not charge a fee to a patient for filling out forms or providing information responsive to forms that support a claim or appeal regarding eligibility for a public benefit program.

(b) A health care provider shall provide information responsive to those portions of the form for which the health care provider has the information necessary to provide a medical opinion. If the health care provider does not have the information necessary to provide a medical opinion, the health care provider may inform the patient if an examination is necessary to obtain the information.

(c) If a health care provider conducts an examination pursuant to subdivision (b), the health care provider shall provide information responsive to those portions of the form for which the health care provider has a medical opinion.

(d) For the purposes of this section, a public benefit program includes the Medi-Cal program, the In-Home Supportive Services Program, the California Work Opportunity and Responsibility to Kids (CalWORKs) program, Social Security Disability Insurance benefits, Supplemental Security Income/State Supplementary Program for the Aged, Blind and Disabled (SSI/SSP) benefits, federal veterans service-connected compensation and nonservice connected pension disability benefits, discharge of a federal student loan based on total and permanent disability, CalFresh, the Cash Assistance Program for Aged, Blind, and Disabled Legal Immigrants, and a government-funded housing subsidy or tenant-based housing assistance program.

(e) Notwithstanding any other law, a health care provider may honor a request to disclose a patient record or complete a public benefit form that contains the written or electronic signature of the patient or the patient's personal representative.

(Added by Stats. 2020, Ch. 101, Sec. 3. (AB 2520) Effective January 1, 2021.)

123120. ACTION TO ENFORCE RIGHT TO INSPECT COPY

Any patient or representative aggrieved by a violation of Section 123110 may, in addition to any other remedy provided by law, bring an action against the health care provider to enforce the obligations prescribed by Section 123110. Any judgment rendered in the action may, in the discretion of the court, include an award of costs and reasonable attorney fees to the prevailing party.

(Added by Stats. 1995, Ch. 415, Sec. 8. Effective January 1, 1996.)

123125. EXCEPTION OF ALCOHOL, DRUG ABUSE AND COMMUNICABLE DISEASE CARRIER RECORDS

(a) This chapter shall not require a health care provider to permit inspection or provide copies of alcohol and drug abuse records where, or in a manner, prohibited by Section 408 of the federal Drug Abuse Office and Treatment Act of 1972 (Public Law 92-255) or Section 333 of the federal Comprehensive Alcohol Abuse and Alcoholism Prevention, Treatment, and Rehabilitation Act of 1970 (Public Law 91- 616), or by regulations adopted pursuant to these federal laws. Alcohol and drug abuse records subject to these federal laws shall also be subject to this chapter, to the extent that these federal laws do not prohibit disclosure of the records. All other alcohol and drug abuse records shall be fully subject to this chapter.

(b) This chapter shall not require a health care provider to permit inspection or provide copies of records or portions of records where or in a manner prohibited by existing law respecting the confidentiality of information regarding communicable disease carriers.

(Added by Stats. 1995, Ch. 415, Sec. 8. Effective January 1, 1996.)

123130. PREPARATION OF SUMMARY OF RECORD; CONFERENCE WITH PATIENT

(a) A health care provider may prepare a summary of the record, according to the requirements of this section, for inspection and copying by a patient. If the health care provider chooses to prepare a summary of the record rather than allowing access to the entire record, he or she shall make the summary of the record available to the patient within 10 working days from the date of the patient's request. However, if more time is needed because the record is of extraordinary length or because the patient was discharged from a licensed health facility within the last 10 days, the health care provider shall notify the patient of this fact and the date that the summary will be completed, but in no case shall more than 30 days elapse between the request by the patient and the delivery of the summary. In preparing the summary of the record the health care provider shall not be obligated to include information that is not contained in the original record.

(b) A health care provider may confer with the patient in an attempt to clarify the patient's purpose and goal in obtaining his or her record. If as a consequence the patient requests information about only certain injuries, illnesses, or episodes, this subdivision shall not require the provider to prepare the summary required by this subdivision for other than the injuries, illnesses, or episodes so requested by the patient. The summary shall contain for each injury, illness, or episode any information included in the record relative to the following:

(1) Chief complaint or complaints including pertinent history.

(2) Findings from consultations and referrals to other health care providers.

(3) Diagnosis, where determined.

(4) Treatment plan and regimen including medications prescribed.

(5) Progress of the treatment.

(6) Prognosis including significant continuing problems or conditions.

(7) Pertinent reports of diagnostic procedures and tests and all discharge summaries.

(8) Objective findings from the most recent physical examination, such as blood pressure, weight, and actual values from routine laboratory tests.

(c) This section shall not be construed to require any medical records to be written or maintained in any manner not otherwise required by law.

(d) The summary shall contain a list of all current medications prescribed, including dosage, and any sensitivities or allergies to medications recorded by the provider.

(e) Subdivision (c) of Section 123110 shall be applicable whether or not the health care provider elects to prepare a summary of the record.

(f) The health care provider may charge no more than a reasonable fee based on actual time and cost for the preparation of the summary. The cost shall be based on a computation of the actual time spent preparing the summary for availability to the patient or the patient's representative. It is the intent of the Legislature that summaries of the records be made available at the lowest possible cost to the patient.

(Added by Stats. 1995, Ch. 415, Sec. 8. Effective January 1, 1996.)

123135. CONSTRUCTION OF CHAPTER

Except as otherwise provided by law, nothing in this chapter shall be construed to grant greater access to individual patient records by any person, firm, association, organization, partnership, business trust, company, corporation, or municipal or other public corporation, or government officer or agency. Therefore, this chapter does not do any of the following:

(a) Relieve employers of the requirements of the Confidentiality of Medical Information Act (Part 2.6 (commencing with Section 56) of Division 1 of the Civil Code).

(b) Relieve any person subject to the Insurance Information and Privacy Protection Act (Article 6.6 (commencing with Section 791) of Chapter 1 of Part 2 of Division 1 of the Insurance Code) from the requirements of that act.

(c) Relieve government agencies of the requirements of the Information Practices Act of 1977 (Title 1.8 (commencing with Section 1798) of Part 4 of Division 3 of the Civil Code).

(Added by Stats. 1995, Ch. 415, Sec. 8. Effective January 1, 1996.)

123140. COMPLETION OF SCREENING PROGRAM; ENVIRONMENTAL ABATEMENT

The Information Practices Act of 1977 (Title 1.8 (commencing with Section 1798) of Part 4 of Division 3 of the Civil Code) shall prevail over this chapter with respect to records maintained by a state agency.

(Added by Stats. 1995, Ch. 415, Sec. 8. Effective January 1, 1996.)

123145. PRESERVATION OF RECORDS AFTER LICENSE CEASES OPERATION; ACTION FOR ABANDONMENT OR RECORDS

(a) Providers of health services that are licensed pursuant to Sections 1205, 1253, 1575 and 1726 have an obligation, if the licensee ceases operation, to preserve records for a minimum of seven years following discharge of the patient, except that the records of unemancipated minors shall be kept at least one year after the minor has reached the age of 18 years, and in any case, not less than seven years.

(b) The department or any person injured as a result of the licensee's abandonment of health records may bring an action in a proper court for the amount of damage suffered as a result thereof. In the event that the licensee is a corporation or partnership that is dissolved, the person injured may take action against that corporation's or partnership's principle officers of record at the time of dissolution.

(c) Abandoned means violating subdivision (a) and leaving patients treated by the licensee without access to medical information to which they are entitled pursuant to Section 123110.

(Added by Stats. 1995, Ch. 415, Sec. 8. Effective January 1, 1996.)

123148. REPORT TO PATIENT OF RESULTS OF CLINICAL LABORATORY TEST

(a) Notwithstanding any other law, a health care professional at whose request a test is performed shall provide or arrange for the provision of the results of a test to the patient who is the subject of the test if so requested by the patient, in oral or written form. The results shall be disclosed in plain language and in oral or written form, except the results may be disclosed in electronic form if requested by the patient unless deemed inappropriate by the health care professional who requested the test. The telephone shall not be considered an electronic form of disclosing test results subject to the limits on electronic disclosure of test results for the purpose of this section.

(b) (1) Consent of the patient to receive their test results by internet posting or other electronic means shall be obtained in a manner consistent with the requirements of Section 56.10 or 56.11 of the Civil Code. In the event that a health care professional arranges for the provision of test results by internet posting or other electronic manner, the results shall be disclosed to a patient in a reasonable time period. Access to test results shall be restricted by the use of a secure personal identification number when the results are disclosed to a patient by internet posting or other electronic manner.

(2) Paragraph (1) shall not prohibit direct communication by internet posting or the use of other electronic means to disclose test results by a treating health care professional who ordered the test for their patient or by a health care professional acting on behalf of,

or with the authorization of, the treating health care professional who ordered the test.

(c) When a patient requests access to their test results by internet posting, the health care professional shall advise the patient of any charges that may be assessed directly to the patient or insurer for the service and that the patient may call the health care professional for a more detailed explanation of the laboratory test results when delivered.

(d) The electronic disclosure of test results under this section shall be in accordance with any applicable federal law governing privacy and security of electronic personal health records. However, any state statute that governs privacy and security of electronic personal health records, shall apply to test results under this section and shall prevail over federal law if federal law permits.

(e) The test results to be reported to the patient pursuant to this section shall be recorded in the patient's medical record, and shall be reported to the patient within a reasonable time period after the test results are received by the health care professional who requested the test.

(f) Notwithstanding subdivision (a), unless the patient requests the disclosure, the health care professional deems this disclosure as an appropriate means, and a health care professional has first discussed in person, by telephone, or by any other means of oral communication, the test results with the patient, in compliance with any other applicable laws, none of the following test results and any other related results shall be disclosed to a patient by internet posting or other electronic means:

(1) (A) A positive HIV test, unless an HIV test subject is anonymously tested and the test result is posted on a secure internet website and can only be viewed with the use of a secure code that can access only a single set of test results and that is provided to the patient at the time of testing. The test result shall be posted only if there is no link to any information that identifies or refers to the subject of the test and the information required pursuant to subdivision (h) of Section 120990 is provided.

(B) Subparagraph (A) does not prevent the disclosure of HIV test results, including viral load and CD4 count test results, to a patient living with HIV by secure internet website or other electronic means if the patient has previously been informed about the results of a positive HIV test pursuant to the requirements of this section.

(2) Presence of antigens indicating a hepatitis infection.

(3) Abusing the use of drugs.

(4) Test results related to routinely processed tissues and imaging scans that reveal a new or recurrent malignancy.

(g) Patient identifiable test results and health information that have been provided under this section shall not be used for any commercial purpose without the consent of the patient, obtained in a manner consistent with the requirements of Section 56.11 of the Civil Code. In no event shall patient identifiable HIV-related test results and health information disclosed in this section be used in violation of subdivision (f) of Section 120980.

(h) A third party to whom test results are disclosed pursuant to this section shall be deemed a provider of administrative services, as that term is used in paragraph (3) of subdivision (c) of Section 56.10 of the Civil Code, and shall be subject to all limitations and penalties applicable to that section.

(i) A patient may not be required to pay a cost, or be charged a fee, for electing to receive their test results in a manner other than by internet posting or other electronic form.

(j) A patient or their physician may revoke consent provided under this section at any time and without penalty, except to the extent that action has been taken in reliance on that consent.

(k) As used in this section, “test” applies to both clinical laboratory tests and imaging scans, such as x-rays, magnetic resonance imaging, ultrasound, or other similar technologies.

(l) As used in this section, “internet posting” includes posting to an online patient portal.

(Amended by Stats. 2022, Ch. 888, Sec. 3. (SB 1419) Effective January 1, 2023.)

LABOR CODE

DIVISION 3: EMPLOYMENT RELATIONS

CHAPTER 2: EMPLOYERS, EMPLOYEES AND DEPENDENTS

ARTICLE 1. THE CONTRACT OF EMPLOYMENT

2750

The contract of employment is a contract by which one, who is called the employer, engages another, who is called the employee, to do something for the benefit of the employer or a third person.

(Enacted by Stats. 1937, Ch. 90.)

2750.3. INDEPENDENT CONTRACTOR DEFINED [REPEALED]

(Repealed by Stats 2020 and replaced by Assembly Bill 2257 (AB 2257).)

ARTICLE 1.5. WORKER STATUS: EMPLOYEES

2775

(a) As used in this article:

(1) "Dynamex" means Dynamex Operations W. Inc. v. Superior Court (2018) 4 Cal.5th 903.

(2) "Borello" means the California Supreme Court's decision in S. G. Borello & Sons, Inc. v. Department of Industrial Relations (1989) 48 Cal.3d 341.

(b) (1) For purposes of this code and the Unemployment Insurance Code, and for the purposes of wage orders of the Industrial Welfare Commission, a person providing labor or services for remuneration shall be considered an employee rather than an independent contractor unless the hiring entity demonstrates that all of the following conditions are satisfied:

(A) The person is free from the control and direction of the hiring entity in connection with the performance of the work, both under the contract for the performance of the work and in fact.

(B) The person performs work that is outside the usual course of the hiring entity's business.

(C) The person is customarily engaged in an independently established trade, occupation, or business of the same nature as that involved in the work performed.

(2) Notwithstanding paragraph (1), any exceptions to the terms "employee," "employer," "employ," or "independent contractor," and any extensions of employer status or liability, that are expressly made by a provision of this code, the Unemployment Insurance Code, or in an applicable order of the Industrial Welfare Commission, including, but not limited to, the definition of "employee" in subdivision 2(E) of Wage Order No. 2, shall remain in effect for the purposes set forth therein.

(3) If a court of law rules that the three-part test in paragraph (1) cannot be applied to a particular context based on grounds other than an express exception to employment status as provided under paragraph (2), then the determination of employee or independent

contractor status in that context shall instead be governed by the California Supreme Court's decision in S. G. Borello & Sons, Inc. v. Department of Industrial Relations (1989) 48 Cal.3d 341 (Borello).

(Added by Stats. 2020, Ch. 38, Sec. 2. (AB 2257) Effective September 4, 2020.)

2776

Section 2775 and the holding in Dynamex do not apply to a bona fide business-to-business contracting relationship, as defined below, under the following conditions:

(a) If an individual acting as a sole proprietor, or a business entity formed as a partnership, limited liability company, limited liability partnership, or corporation ("business service provider") contracts to provide services to another such business or to a public agency or quasi-public corporation ("contracting business"), the determination of employee or independent contractor status of the business services provider shall be governed by Borello, if the contracting business demonstrates that all of the following criteria are satisfied:

(1) The business service provider is free from the control and direction of the contracting business entity in connection with the performance of the work, both under the contract for the performance of the work and in fact.

(2) The business service provider is providing services directly to the contracting business rather than to customers of the contracting business. This subparagraph does not apply if the business service provider's employees are solely performing the services under the contract under the name of the business service provider and the business service provider regularly contracts with other businesses.

(3) The contract with the business service provider is in writing and specifies the payment amount, including any applicable rate of pay, for services to be performed, as well as the due date of payment for such services.

(4) If the work is performed in a jurisdiction that requires the business service provider to have a business license or business tax registration, the business service provider has the required business license or business tax registration.

(5) The business service provider maintains a business location, which may include the business service provider's residence, that is separate from the business or work location of the contracting business.

(6) The business service provider is customarily engaged in an independently established business of the same nature as that involved in the work performed.

(7) The business service provider can contract with other businesses to provide the same or similar services and maintain a clientele without restrictions from the hiring entity.

(8) The business service provider advertises and holds itself out to the public as available to provide the same or similar services.

(9) Consistent with the nature of the work, the business service provider provides its own tools, vehicles, and equipment to perform the services, not including any proprietary materials that may be necessary to perform the services under the contract.

(10) The business service provider can negotiate its own rates.

(11) Consistent with the nature of the work, the business service provider can set its own hours and location of work.

(12) The business service provider is not performing the type of work for which a license from the Contractors' State License Board is required,

pursuant to Chapter 9 (commencing with Section 7000) of Division 3 of the Business and Professions Code.

(b) When two bona fide businesses are contracting with one another under the conditions set forth in subdivision (a), the determination of whether an individual worker who is not acting as a sole proprietor or formed as a business entity, is an employee or independent contractor of the business service provider or contracting business is governed by Section 2775.

(c) This section does not alter or supersede any existing rights under Section 2810.3.

(Added by Stats. 2020, Ch. 38, Sec. 2. (AB 2257) Effective September 4, 2020.)

2777

Section 2775 and the holding in Dynamex do not apply to the relationship between a referral agency and a service provider, as defined below,under the following conditions:

(a) If an individual acting as a sole proprietor, or a business entity formed as a partnership, limited liability company, limited liability partnership, or corporation ("service provider") provides services to clients through a referral agency, the determination of whether the service provider is an employee or independent contractor of the referral agency shall be governed by Borello, if the referral agency demonstrates that all of the following criteria are satisfied:

(1) The service provider is free from the control and direction of the referral agency in connection with the performance of the work for the client, both as a matter of contract and in fact.

(2) If the work for the client is performed in a jurisdiction that requires the service provider to have a business license or business tax registration in order to provide the services under the contract, the service provider shall certify to the referral agency that they have the required business license or business tax registration. The referral agency shall keep the certifications for a period of at least three years. As used in this paragraph:

(A) "Business license" includes a license, tax certificate, fee, or equivalent payment that is required or collected by a local jurisdiction annually, or on some other fixed cycle, as a condition of providing services in the local jurisdiction.

(B) "Local jurisdiction" means a city, county, or city and county, including charter cities.

(3) If the work for the client requires the service provider to hold a state contractor's license pursuant to Chapter 9 (commencing with Section 7000) of Division 3 of the Business and Professions Code, the service provider has the required contractor's license.

(4) If there is an applicable professional licensure, permit, certification, or registration administered or recognized by the state available for the type of work being performed for the client, the service provider shall certify to the referral agency that they have the appropriate professional licensure, permit, certification, or registration. The referral agency shall keep the certifications for a period of at least three years.

(5) The service provider delivers services to the client under the service provider's name, without being required to deliver the services under the name of the referral agency.

(6) The service provider provides its own tools and supplies to perform the services.

(7) The service provider is customarily engaged, or was previously engaged, in an independently established business or trade of the same nature as, or related to, the work performed for the client.

(8) The referral agency does not restrict the service provider from maintaining a clientele and the service provider is free to seek work elsewhere, including through a competing referral agency.

(9) The service provider sets their own hours and terms of work or negotiates their hours and terms of work directly with the client.

(10) Without deduction by the referral agency, the service provider sets their own rates, negotiates their rates with the client through the referral agency, negotiates rates directly with the client, or is free to accept or reject rates set by the client.

(11) The service provider is free to accept or reject clients and contracts, without being penalized in any form by the referral agency. This paragraph does not apply if the service provider accepts a client or contract and then fails to fulfill any of its contractual obligations.

(b) For purposes of this section, the following definitions apply:

(1) "Client" means:

(A) A person who utilizes a referral agency to contract for services from a service provider, or

(B) A business that utilizes a referral agency to contract for services from a service provider that are otherwise not provided on a regular basis by employees at the client's business location, or to contract for services that are outside of the client's usual course of business. Notwithstanding subdivision (a), it is the responsibility of a business that utilizes a referral agency to contract for services, to meet the conditions outlined in this subparagraph.

(2) (A) "Referral agency" is a business that provides clients with referrals for service providers to provide services under a contract, with the exception of services in subparagraph (C).

(B) Under this paragraph, referrals for services shall include, but are not limited to, graphic design, web design, photography, tutoring, consulting, youth sports coaching, caddying, wedding or event planning, services provided by wedding and event vendors, minor home repair, moving, errands, furniture assembly, animal services, dog walking, dog grooming, picture hanging, pool cleaning, yard cleanup, and interpreting services.

(C) Under this paragraph, referrals for services do not include services provided in an industry designated by the Division of Occupational Safety and Health or the Department of Industrial Relations as a high hazard industry pursuant to subparagraph (A) of paragraph (3) of subdivision (e) of Section 6401.7 of the Labor Code or referrals for businesses that provide janitorial, delivery, courier, transportation, trucking, agricultural labor, retail, logging, in-home care, or construction services other than minor home repair.

(3) (A) "Referral agency contract" is the agency's contract with clients and service providers governing the use of its intermediary services described in paragraph (2). The intermediary services provided to the service provider by the referral agency are limited to client referrals and other administrative services ancillary to the service provider's business operation.

(B) A referral agency's contract may include a fee or fees to be paid by the client for utilizing the referral agency. This fee shall not be deducted from the rate set or negotiated by the service provider as set forth in paragraph (10) of subdivision (a).

(4) "Service provider" means an individual acting as a sole proprietor or business entity that agrees to the referral agency's contract and uses the referral agency to connect with clients.

(5) "Tutor" means a person who develops and teaches their own curriculum, teaches curriculum that is proprietarily and privately developed, or provides private instruction or supplemental academic enrichment services by using their own teaching methodology or techniques. A "tutor" does not include an individual who contracts with a local education agency or private school through a referral agency for purposes of teaching students of a public or private school in a classroom setting.

(6) (A) "Youth sports coaching" means services provided by a youth sports coach who develops and implements their own curriculum, which may be subject to requirements of a youth sports league, for an athletic program in which youth who are 18 years of age or younger predominantly participate and that is organized for the purposes of training for and engaging in athletic activity and competition. "Youth sports coaching" does not mean services provided by an individual who contracts with a local education agency or private school through a referral agency for purposes of teaching students of a public or private school.

(7) "Interpreting services" means:

(A) Services provided by a certified or registered interpreter in a language with an available certification or registration through the Judicial Council of California, State Personnel Board, or any other agency or department in the State of California, or through a testing organization, agency, or educational institution approved or recognized by the state, or through the Registry of Interpreters for the Deaf, Certification Commission for Healthcare Interpreters, National Board of Certification for Medical Interpreters, International Association of Conference Interpreters, United States Department of State, or the Administrative Office of the United States Courts.

(B) Services provided by an interpreter in a language without an available certification through the entities listed in subparagraph (A).

(8) "Consulting" means providing substantive insight, information, advice, opinions, or analysis that requires the exercise of discretion and independent judgment and is based on an individual's knowledge or expertise of a particular subject matter or field of study.

(9) "Animal services" means services related to daytime and nighttime pet care including pet boarding under Section 122380 of the Health and Safety Code.

(c) The determination of whether an individual worker is an employee of a service provider or whether an individual worker is an employee of a client is governed by Section 2775.

(Added by Stats. 2020, Ch. 38, Sec. 2. (AB 2257) Effective September 4, 2020.)

2778

(a) Section 2775 and the holding in Dynamex do not apply to a contract for "professional services" as defined below, and instead the determination of whether the individual is an employee or independent contractor shall be governed by Borello if the hiring entity demonstrates that all of the following factors are satisfied:

(1) The individual maintains a business location, which may include the individual's residence, that is separate from the hiring entity. Nothing in this paragraph prohibits an individual from choosing to perform services at the location of the hiring entity.

(2) If work is performed more than six months after the effective date of this section and the work is performed in a jurisdiction that requires the individual to have a business license or business

tax registration, the individual has the required business license or business tax registration in order to provide the services under the contract, in addition to any required professional licenses or permits for the individual to practice in their profession.

(3) The individual has the ability to set or negotiate their own rates for the services performed.

(4) Outside of project completion dates and reasonable business hours, the individual has the ability to set the individual's own hours.

(5) The individual is customarily engaged in the same type of work performed under contract with another hiring entity or holds themselves out to other potential customers as available to perform the same type of work.

(6) The individual customarily and regularly exercises discretion and independent judgment in the performance of the services.

(b) For purposes of this section:

(1) An "individual" includes an individual providing services as a sole proprietor or other business entity.

(2) "Professional services" means services that meet any of the following:

(A) Marketing, provided that the contracted work is original and creative in character and the result of which depends primarily on the invention, imagination, or talent of the individual or work that is an essential part of or necessarily incident to any of the contracted work.

(B) Administrator of human resources, provided that the contracted work is predominantly intellectual and varied in character and is of such character that the output produced or the result accomplished cannot be standardized in relation to a given period of time.

(C) Travel agent services provided by either of the following:

(i) A person regulated by the Attorney General under Article 2.6 (commencing with Section 17550) of Chapter 1 of Part 3 of Division 7 of the Business and Professions Code.

(ii) An individual who is a seller of travel within the meaning of subdivision (a) of Section 17550.1 of the Business and Professions Code and who is exempt from the registration under subdivision (g) of Section 17550.20 of the Business and Professions Code.

(D) Graphic design.

(E) Grant writer.

(F) (i) Fine artist.

(ii) For the purposes of this subparagraph, "fine artist" means an individual who creates works of art to be appreciated primarily or solely for their imaginative, aesthetic, or intellectual content, including drawings, paintings, sculptures, mosaics, works of calligraphy, works of graphic art, crafts, or mixed media.

(G) Services provided by an enrolled agent who is licensed by the United States Department of the Treasury to practice before the Internal Revenue Service pursuant to Part 10 of Subtitle A of Title 31 of the Code of Federal Regulations.

(H) Payment processing agent through an independent sales organization.

(I) Services provided by any of the following:

(i) By a still photographer, photojournalist, videographer, or photo editor who works under a written contract that specifies the rate of pay and obligation to pay by a defined time, as long as the individual providing the services is not directly replacing an employee who performed the same work at the same volume for the hiring entity; the individual does not primarily perform the work at the hiring entity's business location, notwithstanding paragraph (1) of subdivision (a); and the individual is not restricted from working for more than one hiring entity. This subclause is not applicable to a still photographer, photojournalist, videographer, or photo editor who works on motion pictures, which is inclusive of, but is not limited to, theatrical or commercial productions, broadcast news, television, and music videos. Nothing in this section restricts a still photographer, photojournalist, photo editor, or videographer from distributing, licensing, or selling their work product to another business, except as prohibited under copyright laws or workplace collective bargaining agreements.

(ii) To a digital content aggregator by a still photographer, photojournalist, videographer, or photo editor.

(iii) For the purposes of this subparagraph the following definitions apply:

(I) "Photo editor" means an individual who performs services ancillary to the creation of digital content, such as retouching, editing, and keywording.

(II) "Digital content aggregator" means a licensing intermediary that obtains a license or assignment of copyright from a still photographer, photojournalist, videographer, or photo editor for the purposes of distributing that copyright by way of sublicense or assignment, to the intermediary's third-party end users.

(J) Services provided by a freelance writer, translator, editor, copy editor, illustrator, or newspaper cartoonist who works under a written contract that specifies the rate of pay, intellectual property rights, and obligation to pay by a defined time, as long as the individual providing the services is not directly replacing an employee who performed the same work at the same volume for the hiring entity; the individual does not primarily perform the work at the hiring entity's business location, notwithstanding paragraph (1) of subdivision (a); and the individual is not restricted from working for more than one hiring entity.

(K) Services provided by an individual as a content contributor, advisor, producer, narrator, or cartographer for a journal, book, periodical, evaluation, other publication or educational, academic, or instructional work in any format or media, who works under a written contract that specifies the rate of pay, intellectual property rights and obligation to pay by a defined time, as long as the individual providing the services is not directly replacing an employee who performed the same work at the same volume for the hiring entity, the individual does not primarily perform the work at the hiring entity's business location notwithstanding paragraph (1) of subdivision (a); and the individual is not restricted from working for more than one hiring entity.

(L) Services provided by a licensed esthetician, licensed electrologist, licensed manicurist, licensed barber, or licensed cosmetologist provided that the individual:

(i) Sets their own rates, processes their own payments, and is paid directly by clients.

(ii) Sets their own hours of work and has sole discretion to decide the number of clients and which clients for whom they will provide services.

(iii) Has their own book of business and schedules their own appointments.

(iv) Maintains their own business license for the services offered to clients.

(v) If the individual is performing services at the location of the hiring entity, then the individual issues a Form 1099 to the salon or business owner from which they rent their business space.

(vi) This subparagraph shall become inoperative, with respect to licensed manicurists, on January 1, 2025.

(M) A specialized performer hired by a performing arts company or organization to teach a master class for no more than one week. "Master class" means a specialized course for limited duration that is not regularly offered by the hiring entity and is taught by an expert in a recognized field of artistic endeavor who does not work for the hiring entity to teach on a regular basis.

(N) Services provided by an appraiser, as defined in Part 3 (commencing with Section 11300) of Division 4 of the Business and Professions Code.

(O) Registered professional foresters licensed pursuant to Article 3 (commencing with Section 750) of Chapter 2.5 of Division 1 of the Public Resources Code.

(c) Section 2775 and the holding in Dynamex do not apply to the following, which are subject to the Business and Professions Code:

(1) A real estate licensee licensed by the State of California pursuant to Division 4 (commencing with Section 10000) of the Business and Professions Code, for whom the determination of employee or independent contractor status shall be governed by subdivision (b) of Section 10032 of the Business and Professions Code. If that section is not applicable, then this determination shall be governed as follows:

(A) For purposes of unemployment insurance by Section 650 of the Unemployment Insurance Code.

(B) For purposes of workers' compensation by Section 3200 et seq.

(C) For all other purposes in the Labor Code by Borello. The statutorily imposed duties of a responsible broker under Section 10015.1 of the Business and Professions Code are not factors to be considered under the Borello test.

(2) A home inspector, as defined in Section 7195 of the Business and Professions Code, and subject to the provisions of Chapter 9.3 (commencing with Section 7195) of Division 3 of that code.

(3) A repossession agency licensed pursuant to Section 7500.2 of the Business and Professions Code, for whom the determination of employee or independent contractor status shall be governed by Section 7500.2 of the Business and Professions Code, if the repossession agency is free from the control and direction of the hiring person or entity in connection with the performance of the work, both under the contract for the performance of the work and in fact.

(Amended by Stats. 2021, Ch. 422, Sec. 1. (AB 1561) Effective January 1, 2022.)

2779

(a) Section 2775 and the holding in Dynamex do not apply to the relationship between two individuals wherein each individual is acting as a sole proprietor or separate business entity formed as a partnership, limited liability company, limited liability partnership, or corporation performing work pursuant to a contract for purposes of providing services at the location of a single-engagement event, as defined below, under the following conditions:

(1) Neither individual is subject to control and direction by the other, in connection with the performance of the work, both under the contract for the performance of the work and in fact.

(2) Each individual has the ability to negotiate their rate of pay with the other individual.

(3) The written contract between both individuals specifies the total payment for services provided by both individuals at the single-engagement event, and the specific rate paid to each individual.

(4) Each individual maintains their own business location, which may include the individual's personal residence.

(5) Each individual provides their own tools, vehicles, and equipment to perform the services under the contract.

(6) If the work is performed in a jurisdiction that requires an individual to have a business license or business tax registration, then each individual has the required business license or business tax registration.

(7) Each individual is customarily engaged in the same or similar type of work performed under the contract or each individual separately holds themselves out to other potential customers as available to perform the same type of work.

(8) Each individual can contract with other businesses to provide the same or similar services and maintain their own clientele without restrictions.

(b) "Single-engagement event" means a stand-alone non-recurring event in a single location, or a series of events in the same location no more than once a week.

(c) "Services" under this section do not include services provided in an industry designated by the Division of Occupational Safety and Health or the Department of Industrial Relations as a high hazard industry pursuant to subparagraph (A) of paragraph (3) of subdivision (e) of Section 6401.7 or janitorial, delivery, courier, transportation, trucking, agricultural labor, retail, logging, in-home care, or construction services other than minor home repair.

(Added by Stats. 2020, Ch. 38, Sec. 2. (AB 2257) Effective September 4, 2020.)

2780

(a) (1) Section 2775 and the holding in Dynamex do not apply to the following occupations in connection with creating, marketing, promoting, or distributing sound recordings or musical compositions, and instead the holding in Borello shall apply to all of the following:

(A) Recording artists, subject to the below.

(B) Songwriters, lyricists, composers, and proofers.

(C) Managers of recording artists.

(D) Record producers and directors.

(E) Musical engineers and mixers engaged in the creation of sound recordings.

(F) Musicians engaged in the creation of sound recordings, subject to the below.

(G) Vocalists, subject to the below.

(H) Photographers working on recording photo shoots, album covers, and other press and publicity purposes.

(I) Independent radio promoters.

(J) Any other individual engaged to render any creative, production, marketing, or independent music publicist services related primarily to the creation, marketing, promotion, or distribution of sound recordings or musical compositions.

(2) This subdivision shall not apply to any of the following:

(A) Film and television unit production crews, as such term is commonly used in the film and television industries, working on live or recorded performances for audiovisual works, including still photographers and cinematographers.

(B) Publicists who are not independent music publicists.

(3) Notwithstanding Section 2775, paragraphs (1) and (2), and the holding in Dynamex, the terms and conditions of any current or future collective bargaining agreements or contractual agreements between the applicable labor unions and respective employers shall govern the determination of employment status in all events.

(4) The following shall apply to recording artists, musicians, and vocalists:

(A) Recording artists, musicians, and vocalists shall not be precluded from organizing under applicable provisions of labor law, or otherwise exercising rights granted to employees under the National Labor Relations Act (29 U.S.C. Sec. 151 et seq.).

(B) (i) Musicians and vocalists who are not royalty-based participants in the work created during any specific engagement shall be treated as employees solely for purposes of receiving minimum and overtime wages for hours worked during the engagement, as well as any damages and penalties due to the failure to receive minimum or overtime wages. Any such wages, damages, and penalties owed under this subparagraph shall be determined according to the applicable provisions of this code, wage orders of the Industrial Welfare Commission, or applicable local laws.

(ii) "Royalty-based participant" means an individual who has either negotiated for the collection or direct administration of royalties derived from the exploitation of a sound recording or musical composition, or is entitled to control, administer or collect royalties related to the exploitation of a sound recording or musical composition as a co-author or joint owner thereof.

(C) In all events, and notwithstanding subparagraph (B), the terms and conditions of any current or future collective bargaining agreements or contractual agreements between the applicable labor unions and respective employers shall govern the determination of employment status.

(b) (1) Section 2775 and the holding in Dynamex do not apply to a musician or musical group for the purpose of a single-engagement live performance event, and instead the determination of employee or independent contractor status shall be governed by Borello, unless one of the following conditions is met:

(A) The musical group is performing as a symphony orchestra, the musical group is performing at a theme park or amusement park, or a musician is performing in a musical theater production.

(B) The musical group is an event headliner for a performance taking place in a venue location with more than 1,500 attendees.

(C) The musical group is performing at a festival that sells more than 18,000 tickets per day.

(2) This subdivision is inclusive of rehearsals related to the single-engagement live performance event.

(3) As used in this subdivision:

(A) "Event headliner" means the musical group that appears most prominently in an event program, advertisement, or on a marquee.

(B) "Festival" means a single day or multiday event in a single venue location that occurs once a year, featuring performances by various musical groups.

(C) "Musical group" means a solo artist, band, or a group of musicians who perform under a distinct name.

(D) "Musical theater production" means a form of theatrical

performance that combines songs, spoken dialogue, acting, and dance.

(E) "Musician" means an individual performing instrumental, electronic, or vocal music in a live setting.

(F) "Single-engagement live performance event" means a stand-alone musical performance in a single venue location, or a series of performances in the same venue location no more than once a week. This does not include performances that are part of a tour or series of live performances at various locations.

(G) "Venue location" means an indoor or outdoor location used primarily as a space to hold a concert or musical performance. "Venue location" includes, but is not limited to, a restaurant, bar, or brewery that regularly offers live musical entertainment.

(c) Section 2775 and the holding in Dynamex do not apply to the following, and instead, the determination of employee or independent contractor status shall be governed by Borello:

(1) An individual performance artist performing material that is their original work and creative in character and the result of which depends primarily on the individual's invention, imagination, or talent, given all of the following conditions are satisfied:

(A) The individual is free from the control and direction of the hiring entity in connection with the performance of the work, both as a matter of contract and in fact. This includes, and is not limited to, the right for the performer to exercise artistic control over all elements of the performance.

(B) The individual retains the rights to their intellectual property that was created in connection with the performance.

(C) Consistent with the nature of the work, the individual sets their terms of work and has the ability to set or negotiate their rates.

(D) The individual is free to accept or reject each individual performance engagement without being penalized in any form by the hiring entity.

(2) "Individual performance artist" shall include, but is not limited to, an individual performing comedy, improvisation, stage magic, illusion, mime, spoken word, storytelling, or puppetry.

(3) This subdivision does not apply to an individual participating in a theatrical production, or a musician or musical group as defined in subdivision (b).

(4) In all events, notwithstanding paragraph (1), the terms and conditions of any current or future collective bargaining agreements or contractual agreements between the applicable labor unions and respective employer shall govern the determination of employment status.

(Added by Stats. 2020, Ch. 38, Sec. 2. (AB 2257) Effective September 4, 2020.)

2781

Section 2775 and the holding in Dynamex do not apply to the relationship between a contractor and an individual performing work pursuant to a subcontract in the construction industry, and instead the determination of whether the individual is an employee of the contractor shall be governed by Section 2750.5 and by Borello, if the contractor demonstrates that all the following criteria are satisfied:

(a) The subcontract is in writing.

(b) The subcontractor is licensed by the Contractors State License Board and the work is within the scope of that license.

(c) If the subcontractor is domiciled in a jurisdiction that requires the subcontractor to have a business license or business tax registration, the subcontractor has the required business license or business tax registration.

(d) The subcontractor maintains a business location that is separate from the business or work location of the contractor.

(e) The subcontractor has the authority to hire and to fire other persons to provide or to assist in providing the services.

(f) The subcontractor assumes financial responsibility for errors or omissions in labor or services as evidenced by insurance, legally authorized indemnity obligations, performance bonds, or warranties relating to the labor or services being provided.

(g) The subcontractor is customarily engaged in an independently established business of the same nature as that involved in the work performed.

(h) (1) Subdivision (b) shall not apply to a subcontractor providing construction trucking services for which a contractor's license is not required by Chapter 9 (commencing with Section 7000) of Division 3 of the Business and Professions Code, provided that all of the following criteria are satisfied:

(A) The subcontractor is a business entity formed as a sole proprietorship, partnership, limited liability company, limited liability partnership, or corporation.

(B) For work performed after January 1, 2020, the subcontractor is registered with the Department of Industrial Relations as a public works contractor pursuant to Section 1725.5, regardless of whether the subcontract involves public work.

(C) The subcontractor utilizes its own employees to perform the construction trucking services, unless the subcontractor is a sole proprietor who operates their own truck to perform the entire subcontract and holds a valid motor carrier permit issued by the Department of Motor Vehicles.

(D) The subcontractor negotiates and contracts with, and is compensated directly by, the licensed contractor.

(2) For work performed after January 1, 2020, any business entity that provides construction trucking services to a licensed contractor utilizing more than one truck shall be deemed the employer for all drivers of those trucks.

(3) For purposes of this subdivision, "construction trucking services" mean hauling and trucking services provided in the construction industry pursuant to a contract with a licensed contractor utilizing vehicles that require a commercial driver's license to operate or have a gross vehicle weight rating of 26,001 or more pounds.

(4) This subdivision shall only apply to work performed before January 1, 2025.

(5) Nothing in this subdivision prohibits an individual who owns their truck from working as an employee of a trucking company and utilizing that truck in the scope of that employment. An individual employee providing their own truck for use by an employer trucking company shall be reimbursed by the trucking company for the reasonable expense incurred for the use of the employee-owned truck.

(Amended by Stats. 2021, Ch. 422, Sec. 2. (AB 1561) Effective January 1, 2022.)

2782

(a) Section 2775 and the holding in Dynamex do not apply to the relationship between a data aggregator and a research subject, and instead the holding in Borello shall apply, if all of the following conditions are satisfied:

(1) The research subject is free from control and direction with respect to the substance and content of the feedback.

(2) The nature of the feedback requested requires the research subject

to exercise independent judgment and discretion.

(3) The research subject has the ability to reject feedback requests, without being penalized in any form by the data aggregator.

(b) As used in this section:

(1) "Data aggregator" is a business, research institution, or organization that requests and gathers feedback on user interface, products, services, people, concepts, ideas, offerings, or experiences from research subjects willing to provide it.

(2) "Research subject" is any person who willingly engages with a data aggregator in order to provide individualized feedback on user interface, products, services, people, concepts, ideas, offerings, or experiences, and does not engage solely for the purposes of completing individual tasks, except as the tasks relate to providing such feedback.

(Amended by Stats. 2021, Ch. 422, Sec. 3. (AB 1561) Effective January 1, 2022.)

2783

Section 2775 and the holding in Dynamex do not apply to the following occupations as defined in the paragraphs below, and instead, the determination of employee or independent contractor status for individuals in those occupations shall be governed by Borello:

(a) A person or organization that is licensed by the Department of Insurance pursuant to Chapter 5 (commencing with Section 1621), Chapter 6 (commencing with Section 1760), or Chapter 8 (commencing with Section 1831) of Part 2 of Division 1 of the Insurance Code or a person who provides underwriting inspections, premium audits, risk management, claims adjusting, third-party administration consistent with use of the term "third-party administrator," as defined in subdivision (cc) of Section 10112.1 of Title 8 of the California Code of Regulations, or loss control work for the insurance and financial service industries.

(b) A physician and surgeon, dentist, podiatrist, psychologist, or veterinarian licensed by the State of California pursuant to Division 2 (commencing with Section 500) of the Business and Professions Code, performing professional or medical services provided to or by a health care entity, including an entity organized as a sole proprietorship, partnership, or professional corporation as defined in Section 13401 of the Corporations Code. Nothing in this subdivision shall circumvent, undermine, or restrict the rights under federal law to organize and collectively bargain.

(c) An individual who holds an active license from the State of California and is practicing one of the following recognized professions: lawyer, architect, landscape architect, engineer, private investigator, or accountant.

(d) A securities broker-dealer or investment adviser or their agents and representatives that are either of the following:

(1) Registered with the Securities and Exchange Commission or the Financial Industry Regulatory Authority.

(2) Licensed by the State of California under Chapter 2 (commencing with Section 25210) or Chapter 3 (commencing with Section 25230) of Division 1 of Part 3 of Title 4 of the Corporations Code.

(e) A direct sales salesperson as described in Section 650 of the Unemployment Insurance Code, so long as the conditions for exclusion from employment under that section are met.

(f) A manufactured housing salesperson, subject to all obligations under Part 2 (commencing with Section 18000) of Division 13 of the Health and Safety Code, including all regulations promulgated by the Department of Housing and Community Development relating to manufactured home salespersons and all other obligations of manufactured housing salespersons to members of the public. The statutorily imposed duties of a manufactured housing dealer under Section 18060.5 of the Health and Safety Code are not factors to be considered under the Borello test.

(g) A commercial fisher working on an American vessel.

(1) For the purposes of this subdivision:

(A) "American vessel" has the same meaning as defined in Section 125.5 of the Unemployment Insurance Code.

(B) "Commercial fisher" means a person who has a valid, unrevoked commercial fishing license issued pursuant to Article 3 (commencing with Section 7850) of Chapter 1 of Part 3 of Division 6 of the Fish and Game Code.

(C) "Working on an American vessel" means the taking or the attempt to take fish, shellfish, or other fishery resources of the state by any means, and includes each individual aboard an American vessel operated for fishing purposes who participates directly or indirectly in the taking of these raw fishery products, including maintaining the vessel or equipment used aboard the vessel. However, "working on an American vessel" does not apply to anyone aboard a licensed commercial fishing vessel as a visitor or guest who does not directly or indirectly participate in the taking.

(2) For the purposes of this subdivision, a commercial fisher working on an American vessel is eligible for unemployment insurance benefits if they meet the definition of "employment" in Section 609 of the Unemployment Insurance Code and are otherwise eligible for those benefits pursuant to the provisions of the Unemployment Insurance Code.

(3) (A) On or before March 1, 2021, and each March 1 thereafter, the Employment Development Department shall issue an annual report to the Legislature on the use of unemployment insurance in the commercial fishing industry. This report shall include, but not be limited to, all of the following:

(i) Reporting the number of commercial fishers who apply for unemployment insurance benefits.

(ii) The number of commercial fishers who have their claims disputed.

(iii) The number of commercial fishers who have their claims denied.

(iv) The number of commercial fishers who receive unemployment insurance benefits.

(B) The report required by this subparagraph shall be submitted in compliance with Section 9795 of the Government Code.

(4) This subdivision shall become inoperative on January 1, 2026, unless extended by the Legislature.

(h) (1) A newspaper distributor working under contract with a newspaper publisher, as defined in paragraph (2), or a newspaper carrier.

(2) For purposes of this subdivision:

(A) "Newspaper" means a newspaper of general circulation, as defined in Section 6000 or 6008 of the Government Code, and any other publication circulated to the community in general as an extension of or substitute for that newspaper's own publication, whether that publication be designated a "shoppers' guide," as a zoned edition, or otherwise. "Newspaper" may also be a publication that is published in print and that may be posted in a digital format, and distributed periodically at daily, weekly, or other short intervals, for the dissemination of news of a general or local character and of a general or local interest.

(B) "Publisher" means the natural or corporate person that manages the newspaper's business operations, including circulation.

(C) "Newspaper distributor" means a person or entity that contracts with a publisher to distribute newspapers to the community.

(D) "Newspaper carrier" means a person who effects physical delivery of the newspaper to the customer or reader, who is not working as an app-based driver, as defined in Chapter 10.5 (commencing with Section 7448) of Division 3 of the Business and Professions Code, during the time when the newspaper carrier is performing the newspaper delivery services.

(3) (A) On or before March 1, 2022, March 1, 2023, and March 1, 2024, every newspaper publisher or distributor that hires or directly contracts with newspaper carriers shall submit to the Labor and Workforce Development Agency, in a manner prescribed by the agency and in conformity with existing law, the following information related to their workforce for the current year:

(i) The number of carriers for which the publisher or distributor paid payroll taxes in the previous year and the number of carriers for which the publisher or distributor did not pay payroll taxes in the previous year.

(ii) The average wage rate paid to carriers classified as independent contractors and as employees.

(iii) The number of carrier wage claims filed, if any, with the Labor Commissioner or in a court of law.

(B) For the March 1, 2022, reporting date only, every newspaper publisher and distributor shall also report the number of carrier wage claims filed with the Labor Commissioner or in a court of law for the preceding three years.

(C) Information that is submitted shall only be disclosed in accordance with Section 7927.705 of the Government Code, relating to trade secrets or other proprietary business information.

(4) This subdivision shall become inoperative on January 1, 2025, unless extended by the Legislature.

(i) An individual who is engaged by an international exchange visitor program that has obtained and maintains full official designation by the United States Department of State under Part 62 (commencing with Section 62.1) of Title 22 of the Code of Federal Regulations for the purpose of conducting, instead of participating in, international and cultural exchange visitor programs and is in full compliance with Part 62 (commencing with Section 62.1) of Title 22 of the Code of Federal Regulations.

(j) A competition judge with a specialized skill set or expertise providing services that require the exercise of discretion and independent judgment to an organization for the purposes of determining the outcome or enforcing the rules of a competition. This includes, but is not limited to, an amateur umpire or referee.

(Amended by Stats. 2023, Ch. 131, Sec. 141. (AB 1754) Effective January 1, 2024.)

2784

Section 2775 and the holding in Dynamex do not apply to the relationship between a motor club holding a certificate of authority issued pursuant to Chapter 2 (commencing with Section 12160) of Part 5 of Division 2 of the Insurance Code and an individual performing services pursuant to a contract between the motor club and a third party to provide motor club services utilizing the employees and vehicles of the third party and, instead, the determination of whether such an individual is an employee of the motor club shall be governed by Borello, if the motor club demonstrates that the third party is a separate and independent business from the motor club.

(Added by Stats. 2020, Ch. 38, Sec. 2. (AB 2257) Effective September 4, 2020.)

2785

(a) Section 2775 does not constitute a change in, but is declaratory of, existing law with regard to wage orders of the Industrial Welfare Commission and violations of this code relating to wage orders.

(b) Insofar as the application of Sections 2776 to Section 2784 would relieve an employer from liability, those sections shall apply retroactively to existing claims and actions to the maximum extent permitted by law.

(c) Except as provided in subdivisions (a) and (b) of this section, this article shall apply to work performed on or after January 1, 2020.

(d) If a hiring entity can demonstrate compliance with all of conditions set forth in any one of Sections 2776 to 2784, inclusive, then Section 2775 and the holding in Dynamex do not apply to that entity, and instead the determination of an individual's employment status as an employee or independent contractor shall be governed by Borello.

(Added by Stats. 2020, Ch. 38, Sec. 2. (AB 2257) Effective September 4, 2020.)

2786

In addition to any other remedies available, an action for injunctive relief to prevent the continued misclassification of employees as independent contractors may be prosecuted against the putative employer in a court of competent jurisdiction by the Attorney General, by a district attorney, or by a city attorney of a city having a population in excess of 750,000, or by a city attorney in a city and county or, with the consent of the district attorney, by a city prosecutor in a city having a full-time city prosecutor in the name of the people of the State of California upon their own complaint or upon the complaint of a board, officer, person, corporation, or association.

(Added by Stats. 2020, Ch. 38, Sec. 2. (AB 2257) Effective September 4, 2020.)

2787

The provisions of this Article are severable. If any provision of this Article or its application is held invalid, that invalidity shall not affect other provisions or applications that can be given effect without the invalid provision or application.

(Added by Stats. 2020, Ch. 38, Sec. 2. (AB 2257) Effective September 4, 2020.)

DIVISION 4: WORKERS' COMPENSATION AND INSURANCE

PART 1: SCOPE AND OPERATION

CHAPTER 2: EMPLOYERS, EMPLOYEES AND DEPENDENTS

ARTICLE 2: EMPLOYEES

3351. "EMPLOYEE" DEFINITION

"Employee" means every person in the service of an employer under any appointment or contract of hire or apprenticeship, express or implied, oral or written, whether lawfully or unlawfully employed, and includes:

(a) Persons who are not citizens or nationals of the United States and minors.

(b) All elected and appointed paid public officers.

(c) All officers and members of boards of directors of quasi-public or private corporations while rendering actual service for the corporations for pay. An officer or member of a board of directors may elect to be excluded from coverage in accordance with paragraph (16), (18), or (19) of subdivision (a) of Section 3352.

(d) Except as provided in paragraph (8) of subdivision (a) of Section 3352, any person employed by the owner or occupant of a residential dwelling whose duties are incidental to the ownership, maintenance, or use of the dwelling, including the care and supervision of children, or whose duties are personal and not in the course of the trade, business, profession, or occupation of the owner or occupant.

(e) All persons incarcerated in a state penal or correctional institution while engaged in assigned work or employment as defined in paragraph (1) of subdivision (a) of Section 10021 of Title 8 of the California Code of Regulations, or engaged in work performed under contract.

(f) All working members of a partnership or limited liability company receiving wages irrespective of profits from the partnership or limited liability company. A general partner of a partnership or a managing member of a limited liability company may elect to be excluded from coverage in accordance with paragraph (17) of subdivision (a) of Section 3352.

(g) A person who holds the power to revoke a trust, with respect to shares of a private corporation held in trust or general partnership or limited liability company interests held in trust. To the extent that this person is deemed to be an employee described in subdivision (c) or (f), as applicable, the person may also elect to be excluded from coverage as described in subdivision (c) or (f), as applicable, if that person otherwise meets the criteria for exclusion, as described in Section 3352.

(h) A person committed to a state hospital facility under the State Department of State Hospitals, as defined in Section 4100 of the Welfare and Institutions Code, while engaged in and assigned work in a vocation rehabilitation program, including a sheltered workshop.

(i) Beginning on July 1, 2020, any individual who is an employee pursuant to Section 2775. This subdivision shall not apply retroactively.

(Amended by Stats. 2023, Ch. 133, Sec. 1. (AB 1766) Effective January 1, 2024.)

PENAL CODE

PART 4: PREVENTION OF CRIMES AND APPREHENSION OF CRIMINALS

TITLE 1: INVESTIGATION AND CONTROL OF CRIMES AND CRIMINALS

CHAPTER 2: CONTROL OF CRIMES AND CRIMINALS

ARTICLE 2.5: CHILD ABUSE AND NEGLECT REPORTING ACT

11164. CITATION OF ARTICLE; INTENT

(a) This article shall be known and may be cited as the Child Abuse and Neglect Reporting Act.

(b) The intent and purpose of this article is to protect children from abuse and neglect. In any investigation of suspected child abuse or neglect, all persons participating in the investigation of the case shall consider the needs of the child victim and shall do whatever is necessary to prevent psychological harm to the child victim.

(Amended by Stats. 2000, Ch. 916, Sec. 1. Effective January 1, 2001.)

11165. DEFINITION

As used in this article "child" means a person under the age of 18 years.

(Repealed and added by Stats. 1987, Ch. 1459, Sec. 2.)

11165.1. "SEXUAL ABUSE"; "SEXUAL ASSAULT"; "SEXUAL EXPLOITATION"

As used in this article, "sexual abuse" means sexual assault or sexual exploitation as defined by the following:

(a) "Sexual assault" means conduct in violation of one or more of the following sections: Section 261 (rape), subdivision (d) of Section 261.5 (statutory rape), Section 264.1 (rape in concert), Section 285 (incest), Section 286 (sodomy), Section 287 or former Section 288a (oral copulation), subdivision (a) or (b) of, or paragraph (1) of subdivision (c) of, Section 288 (lewd or lascivious acts upon a child), Section 289 (sexual penetration), or Section 647.6 (child molestation). "Sexual assault" for the purposes of this article does not include voluntary conduct in violation of Section 286, 287, or 289, or former Section 288a, if there are no indicators of abuse, unless the conduct is between a person 21 years of age or older and a minor who is under 16 years of age.

(b) Conduct described as "sexual assault" includes, but is not limited to, all of the following:

(1) Penetration, however slight, of the vagina or anal opening of one person by the penis of another person, whether or not there is the emission of semen.

(2) Sexual contact between the genitals or anal opening of one person and the mouth or tongue of another person.

(3) Intrusion by one person into the genitals or anal opening of another person, including the use of an object for this purpose, except that, it does not include acts performed for a valid medical purpose.

(4) The intentional touching of the genitals or intimate parts, including the breasts, genital area, groin, inner thighs, and buttocks, or the clothing covering them, of a child, or of the perpetrator by a child, for purposes of sexual arousal or gratification, except that it does not include acts which may reasonably be construed to be normal caretaker responsibilities; interactions with, or demonstrations of affection for, the child; or acts performed for a valid medical purpose.

(5) The intentional masturbation of the perpetrator's genitals in the presence of a child.

(c) "Sexual exploitation" refers to any of the following:

(1) Conduct involving matter depicting a minor engaged in obscene acts in violation of Section 311.2 (preparing, selling, or distributing obscene matter) or subdivision (a) of Section 311.4 (employment of minor to perform obscene acts).

(2) A person who knowingly promotes, aids, or assists, employs, uses, persuades, induces, or coerces a child, or a person responsible for a child's welfare, who knowingly permits or encourages a child to engage in, or assist others to engage in, prostitution or a live performance involving obscene sexual conduct, or to either pose or model alone or with others for purposes of preparing a film, photograph, negative, slide, drawing, painting, or other pictorial depiction, involving obscene sexual conduct. For the purpose of this section, "person responsible for a child's welfare" means a parent, guardian, foster parent, or a licensed administrator or employee of a public or private residential home, residential school, or other residential institution.

(3) A person who depicts a child in, or who knowingly develops, duplicates, prints, downloads, streams, accesses through any electronic or digital media, or exchanges, a film, photograph, videotape, video recording, negative, or slide in which a child is engaged in an act of obscene sexual conduct, except for those activities by law enforcement and prosecution agencies and other persons described in subdivisions (c) and (e) of Section 311.3.

(d) "Commercial sexual exploitation" refers to either of the following:

(1) The sexual trafficking of a child, as described in subdivision (c) of Section 236.1.

(2) The provision of food, shelter, or payment to a child in exchange for the performance of any sexual act described in this section or subdivision (c) of Section 236.1.

(Amended by Stats. 2020, Ch. 180, Sec. 1. (AB 1145) Effective January 1, 2021.)

11165.3. "WILLFUL HARMING OR INJURING OF A CHILD OR THE ENDANGERING OF THE PERSON OR HEALTH OF A CHILD"

As used in this article, "the willful harming or injuring of a child or the endangering of the person or health of a child," means a situation in which any person willfully causes or permits any child to suffer, or inflicts thereon, unjustifiable physical pain or mental suffering, or having the care or custody of any child, willfully causes or permits the person or health of the child to be placed in a situation in which his or her person or health is endangered.

(Amended by Stats. 2004, Ch. 842, Sec. 1. Effective January 1, 2005.)

11165.6. "CHILD ABUSE OR NEGLECT"

As used in this article, the term "child abuse or neglect" includes physical injury or death inflicted by other than accidental means upon a child by another person, sexual abuse as defined in Section 11165.1, neglect as defined in Section 11165.2, the willful harming or injuring of a child or the endangering of the person or health of a child, as defined in Section 11165.3, and unlawful corporal punishment or injury as defined in Section 11165.4. "Child abuse or neglect" does not include a mutual affray between minors. "Child abuse or neglect" does not include an injury caused by reasonable and necessary force used by a peace officer acting within the course and scope of his or her employment as a peace officer.

(Amended by Stats. 2007, Ch. 393, Sec. 2. Effective January 1, 2008.)

11165.7. "MANDATED REPORTER"; TRAINING

(a) As used in this article, "mandated reporter" is defined as any of the following:

(1) A teacher.

(2) An instructional aide.

(3) A teacher's aide or teacher's assistant employed by a public or private school.

(4) A classified employee of a public school.

(5) An administrative officer or supervisor of child welfare and attendance, or a certificated pupil personnel employee of a public or private school.

(6) An administrator of a public or private day camp.

(7) An administrator or employee of a public or private youth center, youth recreation program, or youth organization.

(8) An administrator, board member, or employee of a public or private organization whose duties require direct contact and supervision of children, including a foster family agency.

(9) An employee of a county office of education or the State Department of Education whose duties bring the employee into contact with children on a regular basis.

(10) A licensee, an administrator, or an employee of a licensed community care or child daycare facility.

(11) A Head Start program teacher.

(12) A licensing worker or licensing evaluator employed by a licensing agency, as defined in Section 11165.11.

(13) A public assistance worker.

(14) An employee of a childcare institution, including, but not limited to, foster parents, group home personnel, and personnel of residential care facilities.

(15) A social worker, probation officer, or parole officer.

(16) An employee of a school district police or security department.

(17) A person who is an administrator or presenter of, or a counselor in, a child abuse prevention program in a public or private school.

(18) A district attorney investigator, inspector, or local child support agency caseworker, unless the investigator, inspector, or caseworker is working with an attorney appointed pursuant to Section 317 of the Welfare and Institutions Code to represent a minor.

(19) A peace officer, as defined in Chapter 4.5 (commencing with Section 830) of Title 3 of Part 2, who is not otherwise described in this section.

(20) A firefighter, except for volunteer firefighters.

(21) A physician and surgeon, psychiatrist, psychologist, dentist, resident, intern, podiatrist, chiropractor, licensed nurse, dental hygienist, optometrist, marriage and family therapist, clinical

social worker, professional clinical counselor, or any other person who is currently licensed under Division 2 (commencing with Section 500) of the Business and Professions Code.

(22) An emergency medical technician I or II, paramedic, or other person certified pursuant to Division 2.5 (commencing with Section 1797) of the Health and Safety Code.

(23) A psychological assistant registered pursuant to Section 2913 of the Business and Professions Code.

(24) A marriage and family therapist trainee, as defined in subdivision (c) of Section 4980.03 of the Business and Professions Code.

(25) An unlicensed associate marriage and family therapist registered under Section 4980.44 of the Business and Professions Code.

(26) A state or county public health employee who treats a minor for venereal disease or any other condition.

(27) A coroner.

(28) A medical examiner or other person who performs autopsies.

(29) A commercial film and photographic print or image processor as specified in subdivision (e) of Section 11166. As used in this article, "commercial film and photographic print or image processor" means a person who develops exposed photographic film into negatives, slides, or prints, or who makes prints from negatives or slides, or who prepares, publishes, produces, develops, duplicates, or prints any representation of information, data, or an image, including, but not limited to, any film, filmstrip, photograph, negative, slide, photocopy, videotape, video laser disc, computer hardware, computer software, computer floppy disk, data storage medium, CD- ROM, computer-generated equipment, or computer-generated image, for compensation. The term includes any employee of that person; it does not include a person who develops film or makes prints or images for a public agency.

(30) A child visitation monitor. As used in this article, "child visitation monitor" means a person who, for financial compensation, acts as a monitor of a visit between a child and another person when the monitoring of that visit has been ordered by a court of law.

(31) An animal control officer or humane society officer. For the purposes of this article, the following terms have the following meanings:

(A) "Animal control officer" means a person employed by a city, county, or city and county for the purpose of enforcing animal control laws or regulations.

(B) "Humane society officer" means a person appointed or employed by a public or private entity as a humane officer who is qualified pursuant to Section 14502 or 14503 of the Corporations Code.

(32) A clergy member, as specified in subdivision (d) of Section 11166. As used in this article, "clergy member" means a priest, minister, rabbi, religious practitioner, or similar functionary of a church, temple, or recognized denomination or organization.

(33) Any custodian of records of a clergy member, as specified in this section and subdivision (d) of Section 11166.

(34) An employee of any police department, county sheriff's department, county probation department, or county welfare department.

(35) An employee or volunteer of a Court Appointed Special Advocate program, as defined in Rule 5.655 of the California Rules of Court.

(36) A custodial officer, as defined in Section 831.5.

(37) A person providing services to a minor child under Section 12300 or

12300.1 of the Welfare and Institutions Code.

(38) An alcohol and drug counselor. As used in this article, an "alcohol and drug counselor" is a person providing counseling, therapy, or other clinical services for a state licensed or certified drug, alcohol, or drug and alcohol treatment program. However, alcohol or drug abuse, or both alcohol and drug abuse, is not, in and of itself, a sufficient basis for reporting child abuse or neglect.

(39) A clinical counselor trainee, as defined in subdivision (g) of Section 4999.12 of the Business and Professions Code.

(40) An associate professional clinical counselor registered under Section

4999.42 of the Business and Professions Code.

(41) An employee or administrator of a public or private postsecondary educational institution, whose duties bring the administrator or employee into contact with children on a regular basis, or who supervises those whose duties bring the administrator or employee into contact with children on a regular basis, as to child abuse or neglect occurring on that institution's premises or at an official activity of, or program conducted by, the institution. Nothing in this paragraph shall be construed as altering the lawyer-client privilege as set forth in Article 3 (commencing with Section 950) of Chapter 4 of Division 8 of the Evidence Code.

(42) An athletic coach, athletic administrator, or athletic director employed by any public or private school that provides any combination of instruction for kindergarten, or grades 1 to 12, inclusive.

(43) (A) A commercial computer technician as specified in subdivision (e) of Section 11166. As used in this article, "commercial computer technician" means a person who works for a company that is in the business of repairing, installing, or otherwise servicing a computer or computer component, including, but not limited to, a computer part, device, memory storage or recording mechanism, auxiliary storage recording or memory capacity, or any other material relating to the operation and maintenance of a computer or computer network system, for a fee. An employer who provides an electronic communications service or a remote computing service to the public shall be deemed to comply with this article if that employer complies with Section 2258A of Title 18 of the United States Code.

(B) An employer of a commercial computer technician may implement internal procedures for facilitating reporting consistent with this article. These procedures may direct employees who are mandated reporters under this paragraph to report materials described in subdivision (e) of Section 11166 to an employee who is designated by the employer to receive the reports. An employee who is designated to receive reports under this subparagraph shall be a commercial computer technician for purposes of this article. A commercial computer technician who makes a report to the designated employee pursuant to this subparagraph shall be deemed to have complied with the requirements of this article and shall be subject to the protections afforded to mandated reporters, including, but not limited to, those protections afforded by Section 11172.

(44) Any athletic coach, including, but not limited to, an assistant coach or a graduate assistant involved in coaching, at public or private postsecondary educational institutions.

(45) An individual certified by a licensed foster family agency as a certified family home, as defined in Section 1506 of the Health and Safety Code.

(46) An individual approved as a resource family, as defined in Section 1517 of the Health and Safety Code and Section 16519.5 of the Welfare and Institutions Code.

(47) A qualified autism service provider, a qualified autism service professional, or a qualified autism service paraprofessional, as defined in Section 1374.73 of the Health and Safety Code and Section 10144.51 of the Insurance Code.

(b) Except as provided in paragraph (35) of subdivision (a), volunteers of public or private organizations whose duties require direct contact with and supervision of children are not mandated reporters but are encouraged to obtain training in the identification and reporting of child abuse and neglect and are further encouraged to report known or suspected instances of child abuse or neglect to an agency specified in Section 11165.9.

(c) Except as provided in subdivision (d), employers are strongly encouraged to provide their employees who are mandated reporters with training in the duties imposed by this article. This training shall include training in child abuse and neglect identification and training in child abuse and neglect reporting. Whether or not employers provide their employees with training in child abuse and neglect identification and reporting, the employers shall provide their employees who are mandated reporters with the statement required pursuant to subdivision (a) of Section 11166.5.

(d) Pursuant to Section 44691 of the Education Code, school districts, county offices of education, state special schools and diagnostic centers operated by the State Department of Education, and charter schools shall annually train their employees and persons working on their behalf specified in subdivision (a) in the duties of mandated reporters under the child abuse reporting laws. The training shall include, but not necessarily be limited to, training in child abuse and neglect identification and child abuse and neglect reporting.

(e) (1) On and after January 1, 2018, pursuant to Section 1596.8662 of the Health and Safety Code, a childcare licensee applicant shall take training in the duties of mandated reporters under the child abuse reporting laws as a condition of licensure, and a childcare administrator or an employee of a licensed child daycare facility shall take training in the duties of mandated reporters during the first 90 days when that administrator or employee is employed by the facility.

(2) A person specified in paragraph (1) who becomes a licensee, administrator, or employee of a licensed child daycare facility shall take renewal mandated reporter training every two years following the date on which that person completed the initial mandated reporter training. The training shall include, but not necessarily be limited to, training in child abuse and neglect identification and child abuse and neglect reporting.

(f) Unless otherwise specifically provided, the absence of training shall not excuse a mandated reporter from the duties imposed by this article.

(g) Public and private organizations are encouraged to provide their volunteers whose duties require direct contact with and supervision of children with training in the identification and reporting of child abuse and neglect.

(Amended by Stats. 2019, Ch. 674, Sec. 1. (AB 189) Effective January 1, 2020.)

11165.9. REPORTS TO AUTHORITIES

Reports of suspected child abuse or neglect shall be made by mandated reporters, or in the case of reports pursuant to Section 11166.05, may be made, to any police department or sheriff's department, not including a school district police or security department, county probation department, if designated by the county to receive mandated reports, or the county welfare department. Any of those agencies shall accept a report of suspected child abuse or neglect whether offered by a mandated reporter or another person, or referred by another agency, even if the agency to whom the report is being made lacks subject matter or geographical jurisdiction to investigate the reported case, unless the agency can immediately electronically transfer the call to an agency with proper jurisdiction. When an agency takes a report about a case of suspected child abuse or neglect in which that agency lacks jurisdiction, the agency shall immediately refer the case by telephone, fax, or electronic transmission to an agency with proper jurisdiction. Agencies that are required to receive reports of suspected child abuse or neglect may not refuse to accept a report of suspected child abuse or neglect from a mandated reporter or another person unless otherwise authorized pursuant to this section, and shall maintain a record of all reports received.

(Amended by Stats. 2006, Ch. 701, Sec. 2. Effective January 1, 2007.)

11166. DUTY TO REPORT

(a) Except as provided in subdivision (d), and in Section 11166.05, a mandated reporter shall make a report to an agency specified in Section 11165.9 whenever the mandated reporter, in the mandated reporter's professional capacity or within the scope of the mandated reporter's employment, has knowledge of or observes a child whom the mandated reporter knows or reasonably suspects has been the victim of child abuse or neglect. The mandated reporter shall make an initial report by telephone to the agency immediately or as soon as is practicably possible, and shall prepare and send, fax, or electronically transmit a written followup report within 36 hours of receiving the information concerning the incident. The mandated reporter may include with the report any nonprivileged documentary evidence the mandated reporter possesses relating to the incident.

(1) For purposes of this article, "reasonable suspicion" means that it is objectively reasonable for a person to entertain a suspicion, based upon facts that could cause a reasonable person in a like position, drawing, when appropriate, on the person's training and experience, to suspect child abuse or neglect. "Reasonable suspicion" does not require certainty that child abuse or neglect has occurred nor does it require a specific medical indication of child abuse or neglect; any "reasonable suspicion" is sufficient. For purposes of this article, the pregnancy of a minor does not, in and of itself, constitute a basis for a reasonable suspicion of sexual abuse.

(2) The agency shall be notified, and a report shall be prepared and sent by fax or electronic transmission, even if the child has expired, regardless of whether or not the possible abuse was a factor contributing to the death, and even if suspected child abuse was discovered during an autopsy.

(3) A report made by a mandated reporter pursuant to this section shall be known as a mandated report.

(b) If, after reasonable efforts, a mandated reporter is unable to submit an initial report by telephone, the mandated reporter shall immediately or as soon as is practicably possible, by fax or electronic transmission, make a one-time automated written report on the form prescribed by the Department of Justice, and shall also be available to respond to a telephone followup call by the agency with which the mandated reporter filed the report. A mandated reporter who files a one-time automated written report because the mandated reporter was unable to submit an initial report by telephone is not required to submit a written followup report.

(1) The one-time automated written report form prescribed by the Department of Justice shall be clearly identifiable so that it is not mistaken for a standard written followup report. In addition, the automated one-time report shall contain a section that allows the mandated reporter to state the reason the initial telephone call was not able to be completed. The reason for the submission of the one-time automated written report in lieu of the procedure prescribed in subdivision (a) shall be captured in the statewide child welfare information system. The department shall work with stakeholders to modify reporting forms and the statewide child welfare information system as is necessary to accommodate the changes enacted by these provisions.

(2) This subdivision shall not become operative until the statewide child welfare information system is updated to capture the information prescribed in this subdivision.

(3) This subdivision shall become inoperative three years after this subdivision becomes operative or on January 1, 2009, whichever occurs first.

(4) This section does not supersede the requirement that a mandated reporter first attempt to make a report via telephone, or that agencies specified in Section 11165.9 accept reports from mandated reporters and other persons as required.

(c) A mandated reporter who fails to report an incident of known or reasonably suspected child abuse or neglect as required by this section is guilty of a misdemeanor punishable by up to six months confinement in a county jail or by a fine of one thousand dollars ($1,000) or by both that imprisonment and fine. If a mandated reporter intentionally conceals the mandated reporter's failure to report an incident known by the mandated reporter to be abuse or severe neglect under this section, the failure to report is a continuing offense until an agency specified in Section 11165.9 discovers the offense.

(d) (1) A clergy member who acquires knowledge or a reasonable suspicion of child abuse or neglect during a penitential communication is not subject to subdivision (a). For the purposes of this subdivision, "penitential communication" means a communication, intended to be in confidence, including, but not limited to, a sacramental confession, made to a clergy member who, in the course of the discipline or practice of the clergy member's church, denomination, or organization, is authorized or accustomed to hear those communications, and under the discipline, tenets, customs, or practices of the clergy member's church, denomination, or organization, has a duty to keep those communications secret.

(2) This subdivision does not modify or limit a clergy member's duty to report known or suspected child abuse or neglect when the clergy member is acting in some other capacity that would otherwise make the clergy member a mandated reporter.

(3) (A) On or before January 1, 2004, a clergy member or any custodian of records for the clergy member may report to an agency specified in Section 11165.9 that the clergy member or any custodian of records for the clergy member, prior to January 1, 1997, in the clergy member's professional capacity or within the scope of the clergy member's employment, other than during a penitential communication, acquired knowledge or had a reasonable suspicion that a child had been the victim of sexual abuse and that the clergy member or any custodian of records for the clergy member did not previously report the abuse to an agency specified

in Section 11165.9. The provisions of Section 11172 shall apply to all reports made pursuant to this paragraph.

(B) This paragraph shall apply even if the victim of the known or suspected abuse has reached the age of majority by the time the required report is made.

(C) The local law enforcement agency shall have jurisdiction to investigate any report of child abuse made pursuant to this paragraph even if the report is made after the victim has reached the age of majority.

(e) (1) A commercial film, photographic print, or image processor who has knowledge of or observes, within the scope of that person's professional capacity or employment, any film, photograph, videotape, negative, slide, or any representation of information, data, or an image, including, but not limited to, any film, filmstrip, photograph, negative, slide, photocopy, videotape, video laser disc, computer hardware, computer software, computer floppy disk, data storage medium, CD-ROM, computer-generated equipment, or computer-generated image depicting a child under 16 years of age engaged in an act of sexual conduct, shall, immediately or as soon as practicably possible, telephonically report the instance of reasonably suspected abuse to the law enforcement agency located in the county in which the images are seen. Within 36 hours of receiving the information concerning the incident, the reporter shall prepare and send, fax, or electronically transmit a written followup report of the incident with a copy of the image or material attached.

(2) A commercial computer technician who has knowledge of or observes, within the scope of the technician's professional capacity or employment, any representation of information, data, or an image, including, but not limited to, any computer hardware, computer software, computer file, computer floppy disk, data storage medium, CD-ROM, computer-generated equipment, or computer-generated image that is retrievable in perceivable form and that is intentionally saved, transmitted, or organized on an electronic medium, depicting a child under 16 years of age engaged in an act of sexual conduct, shall immediately, or as soon as practicably possible, telephonically report the instance of reasonably suspected abuse to the law enforcement agency located in the county in which the images or materials are seen. As soon as practicably possible after receiving the information concerning the incident, the reporter shall prepare and send, fax, or electronically transmit a written followup report of the incident with a brief description of the images or materials.

(3) For purposes of this article, "commercial computer technician" includes an employee designated by an employer to receive reports pursuant to an established reporting process authorized by subparagraph (B) of paragraph (43) of subdivision (a) of Section 11165.7.

(4) As used in this subdivision, "electronic medium" includes, but is not limited to, a recording, CD-ROM, magnetic disk memory, magnetic tape memory, CD, DVD, thumbdrive, or any other computer hardware or media.

(5) As used in this subdivision, "sexual conduct" means any of the following:

(A) Sexual intercourse, including genital-genital, oral-genital, anal-genital, or oral-anal, whether between persons of the same or opposite sex or between humans and animals.

(B) Penetration of the vagina or rectum by any object.

(C) Masturbation for the purpose of sexual stimulation of the viewer.

(D) Sadomasochistic abuse for the purpose of sexual stimulation of the viewer.

(E) Exhibition of the genitals, pubic, or rectal areas of a person for the purpose of sexual stimulation of the viewer.

(f) Any mandated reporter who knows or reasonably suspects that the home or institution in which a child resides is unsuitable for the child because of abuse or neglect of the child shall bring the condition to the attention of the agency to which, and at the same time as, the mandated reporter makes a report of the abuse or neglect pursuant to subdivision (a).

(g) Any other person who has knowledge of or observes a child whom the person knows or reasonably suspects has been a victim of child abuse or neglect may report the known or suspected instance of child abuse or neglect to an agency specified in Section 11165.9. For purposes of this section, "any other person" includes a mandated reporter who acts in the person's private capacity and not in the person's professional capacity or within the scope of the person's employment.

(h) When two or more persons, who are required to report, jointly have knowledge of a known or reasonably suspected instance of child abuse or neglect, and when there is agreement among them, the telephone report may be made by a member of the team selected by mutual agreement and a single report may be made and signed by the selected member of the reporting team. Any member who has knowledge that the member designated to report has failed to do so shall thereafter make the report.

(i) (1) The reporting duties under this section are individual, and no supervisor or administrator may impede or inhibit the reporting duties, and no person making a report shall be subject to any sanction for making the report. However, internal procedures to facilitate reporting and apprise supervisors and administrators of reports may be established provided that they are not inconsistent with this article. An internal policy shall not direct an employee to allow the employee's supervisor to file or process a mandated report under any circumstances.

(2) The internal procedures shall not require any employee required to make reports pursuant to this article to disclose the employee's identity to the employer.

(3) Reporting the information regarding knowledge of or reasonably suspected child abuse or neglect to an employer, supervisor, school principal, school counselor, coworker, or other person shall not be a substitute for making a mandated report to an agency specified in Section 11165.9.

(j) (1) A county probation or welfare department shall immediately, or as soon as practicably possible, report by telephone, fax, or electronic transmission to the law enforcement agency having jurisdiction over the case, to the agency given the responsibility for investigation of cases under Section 300 of the Welfare and Institutions Code, and to the district attorney's office every known or reasonably suspected instance of child abuse or neglect, as defined in Section 11165.6, except acts or omissions coming within subdivision (b) of Section 11165.2, or reports made pursuant to Section 11165.13 based on risk to a child that relates solely to the inability of the parent to provide the child with regular care due to the parent's substance abuse, which shall be reported only to the county welfare or probation department. A county probation or welfare department also shall send by fax or electronic transmission a written report thereof within 36 hours of receiving the information concerning the incident to any agency to which it makes a telephone report under this subdivision.

(2) A county probation or welfare department shall immediately, and in no case in more than 24 hours, report to the law enforcement agency having jurisdiction over the case after receiving information that a child or youth who is receiving child welfare services has been identified as the victim of commercial sexual exploitation, as defined in subdivision (d) of Section 11165.1.

(3) (A) When a child or youth who is receiving child welfare services and who is reasonably believed to be the victim of, or is at risk of being the victim of, commercial sexual exploitation, as defined in Section 11165.1, is missing or has been abducted, the county probation or welfare department shall immediately, or in no case later than 24 hours from receipt of the information, report the incident to the appropriate law enforcement authority for entry into the National Crime Information Center database of the Federal Bureau of Investigation and to the National Center for Missing and Exploited Children (NCMEC).

(B) The report submitted by the county probation or welfare department to law enforcement agencies and NCMEC shall include, where reasonably possible, all of the following:

(i) A photo of the missing or abducted child or youth.

(ii) A description of the child's or youth's physical features, such as height, weight, sex, ethnicity, race, hair color, and eye color.

(iii) Endangerment information, such as the child's or youth's pregnancy status, prescription medications, suicidal tendencies, vulnerability to being sex trafficked, and other health or risk factors, to the extent such information is released in compliance with other applicable laws.

(iv) Information about whether the child or youth is or may be an Indian child, as defined in Section 224.1 of the Welfare and Institutions Code, including the name of the child's tribe.

(C) For each child or youth described in this paragraph, the county probation or welfare department shall maintain regular communication with law enforcement agencies, including tribal law enforcement agencies in the case of an Indian child, and NCMEC in efforts to provide a safe recovery of the missing or abducted child or youth, including by sharing information pertaining to the child's or youth's recovery and circumstances related to the recovery.

(k) A law enforcement agency shall immediately, or as soon as practicably possible, report by telephone, fax, or electronic transmission to the agency given responsibility for investigation of cases under Section 300 of the Welfare and Institutions Code and to the district attorney's office every known or reasonably suspected instance of child abuse or neglect reported to it, except acts or omissions coming within subdivision (b) of Section 11165.2, which shall be reported only to the county welfare or probation department. A law enforcement agency shall report to the county welfare or probation department every known or reasonably suspected instance of child abuse or neglect reported to it that is alleged to have occurred as a result of the action of a person responsible for the child's welfare, or as the result of the failure of a person responsible for the child's welfare to adequately protect the minor from abuse when the person responsible for the child's welfare knew or reasonably should have known that the minor was in danger of abuse. A law enforcement agency also shall send by fax or electronic transmission a written report thereof within 36 hours of receiving the information concerning the incident to any agency to which it makes a telephone report under this subdivision.

(Amended by Stats. 2024, Ch. 46, Sec. 4. (AB 161) Effective July 2, 2024.)

11166.01. PUNISHMENT FOR VIOLATION OF 11166; FAILURE TO REPORT RESULTING IN DEATH OR GREAT BODILY INJURY

(a) Except as provided in subdivision (b), any supervisor or administrator who violates paragraph (1) of subdivision (i) of Section 11166 shall be punished by not more than six months in a county jail, by a fine of not more than one thousand dollars ($1,000), or by both that fine and imprisonment.

(b) Notwithstanding Section 11162 or subdivision (c) of Section 11166, any mandated reporter who willfully fails to report abuse or neglect, or any person who impedes or inhibits a report of abuse or neglect, in violation of this article, where that abuse or neglect results in death or great bodily injury, shall be punished by not more than one year in a county jail, by a fine of not more than five thousand dollars ($5,000), or by both that fine and imprisonment.

(Amended by Stats. 2006, Ch. 901, Sec. 10. Effective January 1, 2007.)

11166.05. SERIOUS EMOTIONAL DAMAGE

Any mandated reporter who has knowledge of or who reasonably suspects that a child is suffering serious emotional damage or is at a substantial risk of suffering serious emotional damage, evidenced by states of being or behavior, including, but not limited to, severe anxiety, depression, withdrawal, or untoward aggressive behavior toward self or others, may make a report to an agency specified in Section 11165.9.

(Amended by Stats. 2004, Ch. 842, Sec. 9. Effective January 1, 2005.)

11167. REQUIRED INFORMATION; CONFIDENTIALITY OF REPORTER'S IDENTITY; ADVISING INDIVIDUAL OF COMPLAINT OR ALLEGATIONS

(a) Reports of known or reasonably suspected child abuse or neglect pursuant to Section 11166 or Section 11166.05 shall include the name, business address, and telephone number of the mandated reporter; the capacity that makes the person a mandated reporter; and the information that gave rise to the knowledge or reasonable suspicion of child abuse or neglect and the source or sources of that information. If a report is made, the following information, if known, shall also be included in the report: the child's name, address, present location, and, if applicable, school, grade, and class; the names, addresses, and telephone numbers of the child's parents or guardians; and the name, address, telephone number, and other relevant personal information about the person or persons who the mandated reporter knows or reasonably suspects to have abused or neglected the child. The mandated reporter shall make a report even if some of this information is not known or is uncertain to them.

(b) Information relevant to the incident of child abuse or neglect and information relevant to a report made pursuant to Section 11166.05 may be given to an investigator from an agency that is investigating the known or suspected case of child abuse or neglect.

(c) Information relevant to the incident of child abuse or neglect, including the investigation report and other pertinent materials, and information relevant to a report made pursuant to Section 11166.05 may be given to the licensing agency when it is investigating a known or suspected case of child abuse or neglect.

(d) (1) The identity of all persons who report under this article shall be confidential and disclosed only among agencies receiving or investigating mandated reports, to the prosecutor in a criminal prosecution or in an action initiated under Section 602 of the Welfare and Institutions Code arising from alleged child abuse, or to counsel appointed pursuant to subdivision (c) of Section 317 of the Welfare and Institutions Code, or to the county counsel or prosecutor in a proceeding under Part 4 (commencing with Section 7800) of Division 12 of the Family Code or Section 300 of the Welfare and Institutions Code, or to a licensing agency when abuse or neglect in out-of-home care is reasonably suspected, or when those persons waive confidentiality, or by court order.

(2) No agency or person listed in this subdivision shall disclose the identity of any person who reports under this article to that person's employer, except with the employee's consent or by court order.

(e) Notwithstanding the confidentiality requirements of this section, a representative of a child protective services agency performing an investigation that results from a report of reasonably suspected child abuse or neglect made pursuant to Section 11166 or Section 11166.05, at the time of the initial contact with the individual who is subject to the investigation, shall advise the individual of the complaints or allegations against them, in a manner that is consistent with laws protecting the identity of the reporter under this article.

(f) (1) An agency specified in Section 11165.9 receiving a report of known or reasonably suspected child abuse or neglect pursuant to subdivision (g) of Section 11166 shall ask the reporter to provide all of the following information in the report:

(A) Their name.

(B) Their telephone number.

(C) The information that gave rise to the knowledge or reasonable suspicion of child abuse or neglect.

(D) The source or sources of the information that gave rise to the knowledge or reasonable suspicion of child abuse or neglect.

(2) If the reporter refuses to provide their name or telephone number, the agency shall make efforts to determine the basis for that refusal and advise the reporter that the identifying information will remain confidential.

(Amended by Stats. 2023, Ch. 434, Sec. 1. (AB 391) Effective January 1, 2024.)

11167.5. CONFIDENTIALITY AND DISCLOSURE OF REPORTS

(a) The reports required by Sections 11166 and 11166.2, or authorized by Section 11166.05, and child abuse or neglect investigative reports that result in a summary report being filed with the Department of Justice pursuant to subdivision (a) of Section 11169 shall be confidential and may be disclosed only as provided in subdivision (b). Any violation of the confidentiality provided by this article is a misdemeanor punishable by imprisonment in a county jail not to exceed six months, by a fine of five hundred dollars ($500), or by both that imprisonment and fine.

(b) Reports of suspected child abuse or neglect and information contained therein may be disclosed only to the following:

(1) Persons or agencies to whom disclosure of the identity of the reporting party is permitted under Section 11167.

(2) Persons or agencies to whom disclosure of information is permitted under subdivision (b) of Section 11170 or subdivision (a) of Section 11170.5.

(3) Persons or agencies with whom investigations of child abuse or neglect

are coordinated under the regulations promulgated under Section 11174.

(4) Multidisciplinary personnel teams as defined in subdivision (d) of Section 18951 of the Welfare and Institutions Code.

(5) Persons or agencies responsible for the licensing of facilities which care for children, as specified in Section 11165.7.

(6) The State Department of Social Services or any county, as specified in paragraph (4) of subdivision (b) of Section 11170, when an individual has applied for a license to operate a community care facility or child daycare facility, or for a certificate of approval to operate a certified family home or resource family home, or for employment or presence in a licensed facility, certified family home, or resource family home, or when a complaint alleges child abuse or neglect by a licensee or employee of, or individual approved to be present in, a licensed facility, certified family home, or resource family home.

(7) Hospital scan teams. As used in this paragraph, "hospital scan team" means a team of three or more persons established by a hospital, or two or more hospitals in the same county, consisting of health care professionals and representatives of law enforcement and child protective services, the members of which are engaged in the identification of child abuse or neglect. The disclosure authorized by this section includes disclosure among all hospital scan teams.

(8) Coroners and medical examiners when conducting a post mortem examination of a child.

(9) The Board of Parole Hearings, which may subpoena an employee of a county welfare department who can provide relevant evidence and reports that both (A) are not unfounded, pursuant to Section 11165.12, and (B) concern only the current incidents upon which parole revocation proceedings are pending against a parolee charged with child abuse or neglect. The reports and information shall be confidential pursuant to subdivision (d) of Section 11167.

(10) Personnel from an agency responsible for making a placement of a child pursuant to Section 361.3 of, and Article 7 (commencing with Section 305) of Chapter 2 of Part 1 of Division 2 of, the Welfare and Institutions Code.

(11) Persons who have been identified by the Department of Justice as listed in the Child Abuse Central Index pursuant to paragraph (7) of subdivision (b) of Section 11170 or subdivision (c) of Section 11170, or persons who have verified with the Department of Justice that they are listed in the Child Abuse Central Index as provided in subdivision (f) of Section 11170. Disclosure under this paragraph is required notwithstanding the California Public Records Act, (Division 10 (commencing with Section 7920.000) of Title 1 of the Government Code). Nothing in this paragraph shall preclude a submitting agency prior to disclosure from redacting any information necessary to maintain confidentiality as required by law.

(12) Out-of-state law enforcement agencies conducting an investigation of child abuse or neglect only when an agency makes the request for reports of suspected child abuse or neglect in writing and on official letterhead, or as designated by the Department of Justice, identifying the suspected abuser or victim by name and date of birth or approximate age. The request shall be signed by the department supervisor of the requesting law enforcement agency. The written request shall cite the out-of-state statute or interstate compact provision that requires that the information contained within these reports is to be disclosed only to law enforcement, prosecutorial entities, or multidisciplinary investigative teams, and shall cite the safeguards in

place to prevent unlawful disclosure provided by the requesting state or the applicable interstate compact provision.

(13) Out-of-state agencies responsible for approving prospective foster or adoptive parents for placement of a child only when the agency makes the request in compliance with the Adam Walsh Child Protection and Safety Act of 2006 (Public Law 109-248). The request shall also cite the safeguards in place to prevent unlawful disclosure provided by the requesting state or the applicable interstate compact provision and indicate that the requesting state shall maintain continual compliance with the requirement in paragraph (20) of subdivision (a) of Section 671 of Title 42 of the United States Code that requires the state have in place safeguards to prevent the unauthorized disclosure of information in any child abuse and neglect registry maintained by the state and prevent the information from being used for a purpose other than the conducting of background checks in foster or adoptive placement cases.

(14) Each chairperson of a county child death review team, or the chairperson's designee, to whom disclosure of information is permitted under this article, relating to the death of one or more children and any prior child abuse or neglect investigation reports maintained involving the same victim, siblings, or suspects. Local child death review teams may share any relevant information regarding case reviews involving child death with other child death review teams.

(c) Authorized persons within county health departments shall be permitted to receive copies of any reports made by health practitioners, as defined in paragraphs (21) to (28), inclusive, of subdivision (a) of Section 11165.7, and pursuant to Section 11165.13, and copies of assessments completed pursuant to Sections 123600 and 123605 of the Health and Safety Code, to the extent permitted by federal law. Any information received pursuant to this subdivision is protected by subdivision (e).

(d) Nothing in this section requires the Department of Justice to disclose information contained in records maintained under Section 11170 or under the regulations promulgated pursuant to Section 11174, except as otherwise provided in this article.

(e) This section shall not be interpreted to allow disclosure of any reports or records relevant to the reports of child abuse or neglect if the disclosure would be prohibited by any other provisions of state or federal law applicable to the reports or records relevant to the reports of child abuse or neglect.

(Amended by Stats. 2021, Ch. 615, Sec. 346. (AB 474) Effective January 1, 2022. Operative January 1, 2023, pursuant to Sec. 463 of Stats. 2021, Ch. 615.)

11172. LIABILITY OF PERSON MAKING REPORT; REIMBURSEMENT BY STATE OF ATTORNEY FEES INCURRED IN DEFENDING ACTION

(a) No mandated reporter shall be civilly or criminally liable for any report required or authorized by this article, and this immunity shall apply even if the mandated reporter acquired the knowledge or reasonable suspicion of child abuse or neglect outside of their professional capacity or outside the scope of their employment. Any other person reporting a known or suspected instance of child abuse or neglect shall not incur civil or criminal liability as a result of any report authorized by this article unless it can be proven that a false report was made and the person knew that the report was false or was made with reckless disregard of the truth or falsity of the report, and any person who makes a report of child abuse or neglect known to be false or with reckless disregard of the truth or falsity of the report is liable for any damages caused. No person required to make a report pursuant to this article, nor any person taking photographs at their direction, shall incur any civil or criminal liability for taking photographs of a suspected victim of child abuse or neglect, or causing photographs to be taken of a suspected victim of child abuse or neglect, without parental consent, or for disseminating the photographs, images, or material with the reports required by this article. However, this section shall not be construed to grant immunity from this liability with respect to any other use of the photographs.

(b) Any person, who, pursuant to a request from a government agency investigating a report of suspected child abuse or neglect, provides the requesting agency with access to the victim of a known or suspected instance of child abuse or neglect shall not incur civil or criminal liability as a result of providing that access.

(c) Any commercial computer technician, and any employer of any commercial computer technician, who, pursuant to a warrant from a law enforcement agency investigating a report of suspected child abuse or neglect, provides the law enforcement agency with a computer or computer component which contains possible evidence of a known or suspected instance of child abuse or neglect, shall not incur civil or criminal liability as a result of providing that computer or computer component to the law enforcement agency.

(d) Any person who, in good faith, provides information or assistance, including medical evaluations or consultations, to an agency specified in Section 11165.9, in connection with a report, investigation, or legal intervention pursuant to a good faith report of child abuse or neglect under this article, shall not incur civil or criminal liability as a result of providing that information or assistance. This subdivision does not grant immunity from liability for an individual who is suspected of committing abuse or neglect of the child who is the subject of the report.

(e) (1) The Legislature finds that even though it has provided immunity from liability to persons required or authorized to make reports pursuant to this article, that immunity does not eliminate the possibility that actions may be brought against those persons based upon required or authorized reports. In order to further limit the financial hardship that those persons may incur as a result of fulfilling their legal responsibilities, it is necessary that they not be unfairly burdened by legal fees incurred in defending those actions. Therefore, a mandated reporter may present a claim to the Department of General Services for reasonable attorney's fees and costs incurred in any action against that person on the basis of making a report required or authorized by this article if the court has dismissed the action upon a demurrer or motion for summary judgment made by that person, or if they prevail in the action. The Department of General Services shall allow that claim if the requirements of this subdivision are met, and the claim shall be paid from an appropriation to be made for that purpose. Attorney's fees awarded pursuant to this section shall not exceed an hourly rate greater than the rate charged by the Attorney General of the State of California at the time the award is made and shall not exceed an aggregate amount of fifty thousand dollars ($50,000).

(2) This subdivision shall not apply if a public entity has provided for the defense of the action pursuant to Section 995 of the Government Code.

(f) A court may award attorney's fees and costs to a commercial film and photographic print processor when a suit is brought against the processor because of a disclosure mandated by this article and the court finds this suit to be frivolous.

(Amended by Stats. 2019, Ch. 777, Sec. 17. (AB 819) Effective January 1, 2020.)

CODE OF FEDERAL REGULATIONS

TITLE 16: COMMERCIAL PRACTICES

CHAPTER 1: FEDERAL TRADE COMMISSION

SUBCHAPTER C: REGULATIONS UNDER SPECIFIC ACTS OF CONGRESS

PART 315. CONTACT LENS RULE

315.1. SCOPE OF REGULATIONS IN THIS PART

This part, which shall be called the "Contact Lens Rule," implements the Fairness to Contact Lens Consumers Act, codified at 15 U.S.C. 7601-7610, which requires that rules be issued to address the release, verification, and sale of contact lens prescriptions. This part specifically governs contact lens prescriptions and related issues. Part 456 of Title 16 governs the availability of eyeglass prescriptions and related issues (the Ophthalmic Practice Rules (Eyeglass Rule)).

315.2. DEFINITIONS

For purposes of this part, the following definitions shall apply:

Business hour means an hour between 9 a.m. and 5 p.m., during a weekday (Monday through Friday), excluding Federal holidays. "Business hour" also may include, at the seller's option, a prescriber's regular business hours on Saturdays, provided that the seller has actual knowledge of these hours. "Business hour" shall be determined based on the time zone of the prescriber.

"Eight (8) business hours" shall be calculated from the time the prescriber receives the prescription verification information from the seller, and shall conclude when eight (8) business hours have elapsed. For verification requests received by a prescriber during non-business hours, the calculation of "eight (8) business hours" shall begin at 9 a.m. on the next weekday that is not a Federal holiday or, if applicable, on Saturday at the beginning of the prescriber's actual business hours.

Commission means the Federal Trade Commission.

Contact lens means any contact lens for which State or Federal law requires a prescription.

Contact lens fitting means the process that begins after an initial eye examination for contact lenses and ends when a successful fit has been achieved or, in the case of a renewal prescription, ends when the prescriber determines that no change in the existing prescription is required, and such term may include:

(1) An examination to determine lens specifications;

(2) Except in the case of a renewal of a contact lens prescription, an initial evaluation of the fit of the contact lens on the eye; and

(3) Medically necessary follow-up examinations.

Contact lens prescription means a prescription, issued in accordance with State and Federal law, that contains sufficient information for the complete and accurate filling of a prescription for contact lenses, including the following:

(1) The name of the patient;

(2) The date of examination;

(3) The issue date and expiration date of prescription;

(4) The name, postal address, telephone number, and facsimile telephone number of prescriber;

(5) The power, material or manufacturer or both of the prescribed contact lens;

(6) The base curve or appropriate designation of the prescribed contact lens;

(7) The diameter, when appropriate, of the prescribed contact lens; and

(8) In the case of a private label contact lens, the name of the manufacturer, trade name of the private label brand, and, if applicable, trade name of equivalent brand name.

Direct communication means completed communication by telephone, facsimile, or electronic mail.

Issue date means the date on which the patient receives a copy of the prescription at the completion of a contact lens fitting.

Ophthalmic goods are contact lenses, eyeglasses, or any component of eyeglasses.

Ophthalmic services are the measuring, fitting, and adjusting of ophthalmic goods subsequent to an eye examination.

Prescriber means, with respect to contact lens prescriptions, an ophthalmologist, optometrist, or other person permitted under State law to issue prescriptions for contact lenses in compliance with any applicable requirements established by the Food and Drug Administration. "Other person," for purposes of this definition, includes a dispensing optician who is permitted under State law to issue prescriptions and who is authorized or permitted under State law to perform contact lens fitting services.

Private label contact lenses mean contact lenses that are sold under the label of a seller where the contact lenses are identical to lenses made by the same manufacturer but sold under the labels of other sellers.

Provide to the patient a copy means giving a patient a copy of his or her contact lens prescription:

(1) On paper; or

(2) In a digital format that can be accessed, downloaded, and printed by the patient. For a copy provided in a digital format, the prescriber shall identify to the patient the specific method or methods of electronic delivery to be used, such as text message, electronic mail, or an online patient portal, and obtain the patient's verifiable affirmative consent to receive a digital copy through the identified method or methods; and maintain records or evidence of a patient's affirmative consent for a period of not less than three years. Such records or evidence shall be available for inspection by the Federal Trade Commission, its employees, and its representatives.

Reasonably understandable volume means at an audible level that renders the message intelligible to the receiving audience.

Slow and deliberate manner means at a rate that renders the message intelligible to the receiving audience.

[69 FR 40508, July 2, 2004, as amended at 85 FR 50717, Aug. 17, 2020]

315.3. AVAILABILITY OF CONTACT LENS PRESCRIPTIONS TO PATIENTS

(a) In general. When a prescriber completes a contact lens fitting, the prescriber:

(1) Whether or not requested by the patient, shall provide to the patient a copy of the contact lens prescription;

(2) Shall, as directed by any person designated to act on behalf of the patient, verify the contact lens prescription by electronic or other means; and

(3) Shall, upon request, provide any person designated to act on behalf of the patient with a copy of the patient's

contact lens prescription by electronic or other means within forty (40) business hours of receipt of the request. A prescriber shall note in the patient's record the name of the requester and the date and time that the prescription was provided to the requester.

(b) Limitations. A prescriber may not:

(1) Require the purchase of contact lenses from the prescriber or from another person as a condition of providing a copy of a prescription under paragraph (a)(1) or (a)(3) of this section or as a condition of verification of a prescription under paragraph (a)(2) of this section;

(2) Require payment in addition to, or as part of, the fee for an eye examination, fitting, and evaluation as a condition of providing a copy of a prescription under paragraph (a)(1) or (a)(3) of this section or as a condition of verification of a prescription under paragraph (a)(2) of this section; or

(3) Require the patient to sign a waiver or release as a condition of releasing or verifying a prescription under paragraph (a)(1), (a)(2), or (a)(3) of this section.

(c) Confirmation of prescription release.

(1) (i) Upon completion of a contact lens fitting, the prescriber shall do one of the following:

(A) Request that the patient acknowledge receipt of the contact lens prescription by signing a statement confirming receipt of the contact lens prescription;

(B) Request that the patient sign a prescriber-retained copy of a contact lens prescription that contains a statement confirming receipt of the contact lens prescription;

(C) Request that the patient sign a prescriber-retained copy of the receipt for the examination that contains a statement confirming receipt of the contact lens prescription; or

(D) If a digital copy of the prescription was provided to the patient (via methods including an online portal, electronic mail, or text message) in compliance with paragraph (a)(1) of this section, retain evidence that the prescription was sent, received, or made accessible, downloadable, and printable.

(ii) If the prescriber elects to confirm prescription release via paragraphs (c)(1)(i)(A), (B), or (C) of this section, the prescriber may, but is not required to, use the statement, "My eye care professional provided me with a copy of my contact lens prescription at the completion of my contact lens fitting" to satisfy the requirement.

(iii) In the event the patient declines to sign a confirmation requested under paragraph (c)(1)(i)(A), (B), or (C) of this section, the prescriber shall note the patient's refusal on the document and sign it.

(2) A prescriber shall maintain the records or evidence required under paragraph (c)(1) of this section for a period of not less than three years. Such records or evidence shall be available for inspection by the Federal Trade Commission, its employees, and its representatives.

(3) Paragraphs (c)(1) and (c)(2) of this section shall not apply to prescribers who do not have a direct or indirect financial interest in the sale of contact lenses, including, but not limited to, through an association, affiliation, or co-location with a contact lens seller.

[69 FR 40508, July 2, 2004, as amended at 85 FR 50717, Aug. 17, 2020]

315.4. LIMITS ON REQUIRING IMMEDIATE PAYMENT

A prescriber may require payment of fees for an eye examination, fitting, and evaluation before the release of a contact lens prescription, but only if the prescriber requires immediate payment in the case of an examination that reveals no requirement for ophthalmic goods. For purposes of the preceding sentence, presentation of proof of insurance coverage for that service shall be deemed to be a payment.

315.5. PRESCRIBER VERIFICATION

(a) Prescription requirement. A seller may sell contact lenses only in accordance with a contact lens prescription for the patient that is:

(1) Presented to the seller by the patient or prescriber directly or by facsimile; or

(2) Verified by direct communication.

(b) Information for verification. When seeking verification of a contact lens prescription, a seller shall provide the prescriber with the following information through direct communication:

(1) The patient's full name and address;

(2) The contact lens power, manufacturer, base curve or appropriate designation, and diameter when appropriate;

(3) The quantity of lenses ordered;

(4) The date of patient request;

(5) The date and time of verification request;

(6) The name of a contact person at the seller's company, including facsimile and telephone numbers; and

(7) If the seller opts to include the prescriber's regular business hours on Saturdays as "business hours" for purposes of paragraph (c)(3) of this section, a clear statement of the prescriber's regular Saturday business hours.

(c) Verification events. A prescription is verified under paragraph (a)(2) of this section only if one of the following occurs:

(1) The prescriber confirms the prescription is accurate by direct communication with the seller;

(2) The prescriber informs the seller through direct communication that the prescription is inaccurate and provides the accurate prescription; or

(3) The prescriber fails to communicate with the seller within eight (8) business hours after receiving from the seller the information described in paragraph (b) of this section. During these eight (8) business hours, the seller shall provide a reasonable opportunity for the prescriber to communicate with the seller concerning the verification request.

(d) Automated telephone verification messages. If a seller verifies prescriptions through calls that use, in whole or in part, an automated message, the seller must:

(1) Record the entire call;

(2) Commence the call by identifying it as a request for prescription verification made in accordance with the Contact Lens Rule;

(3) Deliver the information required by paragraph (b) of this section in a slow and deliberate manner and at a reasonably understandable volume; and

(4) Make the information required by paragraph (b) of this section repeatable at the prescriber's option.

(e) Invalid prescription. If a prescriber informs a seller before the deadline under paragraph (c)(3) of this section that the contact lens prescription is inaccurate, expired, or otherwise invalid, the seller shall not fill the prescription. The prescriber shall specify the basis for the inaccuracy or invalidity of the prescription. If the prescription communicated by the seller to the prescriber is inaccurate, the prescriber shall correct it, and the prescription shall then be deemed verified under paragraph (c)(2) of this section.

(f) No alteration of prescription. A seller may not alter a contact lens prescription. In the context of prescription verification, alteration includes, but is not limited to, providing the prescriber with the name of a manufacturer or brand other than that specified by the patient's prescription, unless such name is provided because the patient entered or orally provided it when asked for the manufacturer or brand listed on the patient's prescription. Notwithstanding the preceding sentences, for private label contact lenses, a seller may substitute for contact lenses specified on a prescription identical contact lenses that the same company manufactures and sells under different labels.

(g) Seller requirement to accept prescription presentation: A seller shall provide a prominent method, and a clear and prominent disclosure of that method, for the patient to present the seller with a copy of the patient's prescription. Such method and the disclosure shall be provided prior to requesting a prescriber's contact information for verification of the prescription; provided, however, in the case of an order placed by telephone, a seller shall comply by providing a disclosure of the method prior to requesting a prescriber's contact information for verification of the prescription. The method to present the prescription shall be provided through (i) the same medium by which the order is placed, or (ii) electronic mail, text message, or file upload.

(h) Recordkeeping requirement—verification requests. A seller shall maintain a record of all direct communications referred to in paragraph (a) of this section. Such record shall consist of the following:

(1) For prescriptions presented to the seller: the prescription itself, or the facsimile version thereof (including an email containing a digital image of the prescription), that was presented to the seller by the patient or prescriber.

(2) For verification requests by the seller:

(i) If the communication occurs via facsimile or e-mail, a copy of the verification request, including the information provided to the prescriber pursuant to paragraph (b) of this section, and confirmation of the completed transmission thereof, including a record of the date and time the request was made;

(ii) If the communication occurs via telephone, a log:

(A) Describing the information provided pursuant to paragraph (b) of this section,

(B) Setting forth the date and time the request was made,

(C) Indicating how the call was completed, and

(D) Listing the names of the individuals who participated in the call.

(iii) If the communication occurs via telephone and uses an automated message, the complete recording required pursuant to paragraph (d)(1) of this section.

(3) For communications from the prescriber, including prescription verifications:

(i) If the communication occurs via facsimile or e-mail, a copy of the communication and a record of the time and date it was received;

(ii) If the communication occurs via telephone, a log describing the information communicated, the date and time that the information was received, and the names of the individuals who participated in the call.

(4) The records required to be maintained under this section shall be maintained for a period of not less than three years, and these records must be available for inspection by the Federal Trade Commission, its employees, and its representatives.

(i) Recordkeeping requirement—Saturday business hours. A seller that exercises its option to include a prescriber's regular Saturday business hours in the time period for a request for a copy of the prescription specified in 315.3(a)(3) or for verification specified in paragraph (c)(3) of this section shall maintain a record of the prescriber's regular Saturday business hours and the basis for the seller's actual knowledge thereof. Such records shall be maintained for a period of not less than three years, and these records must be available for inspection by the Federal Trade Commission, its employees, and its representatives.

[69 FR 40508, July 2, 2004, as amended at 85 FR 50717, Aug. 17, 2020]

315.6 EXPIRATION OF CONTACT LENS PRESCRIPTION

(a) In general. A contact lens prescription shall expire:

(1) On the date specified by the law of the State in which the prescription was written, if that date is one year or more after the issue date of the prescription;

(2) Not less than one year after the issue date of the prescription if such State law specifies no date or specifies a date that is less than one year after the issue date of the prescription; or

(3) Notwithstanding paragraphs (a)(1) and (a)(2) of this section, on the date specified by the prescriber, if that date is based on the medical judgment of the prescriber with respect to the ocular health of the patient.

(b) Special rules for prescriptions of less than one year.

(1) If a prescription expires in less than one year, the specific reasons for the medical judgment referred to in paragraph (a)(3) of this section shall be documented in the patient's medical record with sufficient detail to allow for review by a qualified professional in the field.

(2) The documentation described in the paragraph above shall be maintained for a period of not less than three years, and it must be available for inspection by the Federal Trade Commission, its employees, and its representatives.

(3) No prescriber shall include an expiration date on a prescription that is less than the period of time that he or she recommends for a reexamination of the patient that is medically necessary.

315.7. CONTENT OF ADVERTISEMENTS AND OTHER REPRESENTATIONS

Any person who engages in the manufacture, processing, assembly, sale, offering for sale, or distribution of contact lenses may not represent, by advertisement, sales presentation, or otherwise, that contact lenses may be obtained without a prescription.

315.8. PROHIBITION OF CERTAIN WAIVERS

A prescriber may not place on a prescription, or require the patient to sign, or deliver to the patient, a form or notice waiving or disclaiming the liability or responsibility of the prescriber for the accuracy of the eye examination. The preceding sentence does not impose liability on a prescriber for the ophthalmic goods and services dispensed by another seller pursuant to the prescriber's correctly verified prescription.

315.9. ENFORCEMENT

Any violation of this Rule shall be treated as a violation of a rule under section 18 of the Federal Trade Commission Act, 15 U.S.C. 57a, regarding unfair or deceptive acts or practices, and the Commission will enforce this Rule in the same manner, by the same means, and with the same jurisdiction, powers, and duties as are available to it pursuant to the Federal Trade Commission Act, 15 U.S.C. 41 et seq.

315.10. SEVERABILITY

The provisions of this part are separate and severable from one another. If any provision is stayed or determined to be invalid, it is the Commission's intention that the remaining provisions shall continue in effect.

315.11. EFFECTS ON STATE AND LOCAL LAWS

(a) State and local laws and regulations that establish a prescription expiration date of less than one year or that restrict prescription release or require active verification are preempted.

(b) Any other State or local laws or regulations that are inconsistent with the Act or this part are preempted to the extent of the inconsistency.

SUBCHAPTER D: TRADE REGULATION RULES

PART 456. OPHTHALMIC PRACTICE RULES (EYEGLASS RULE)

456.1. DEFINITIONS

(a) A patient is any person who has had a refractive eye examination.

(b) A refractive eye examination is the process of determining the refractive condition of a person's eyes or the presence of any visual anomaly by the use of objective or subjective tests.

(c) Ophthalmic goods are eyeglasses, or any component of eyeglasses, and contact lenses.

(d) Ophthalmic services are the measuring, fitting, and adjusting of ophthalmic goods subsequent to a refractive eye examination.

(e) An ophthalmologist is any Doctor of Medicine or Osteopathy who performs refractive eye examinations.

(f) An optometrist is any Doctor of Optometry.

(g) A prescription is the written specifications for lenses for eyeglasses which are derived from a refractive eye examination, including all of the information specified by State law, if any, necessary to obtain lenses for eyeglasses.

[57 FR 18822, May 1, 1992, as amended at 89 FR 60774, July 26, 2024]

456.2. SEPARATION OF EXAMINATION AND DISPENSING

It is an unfair act or practice for an ophthalmologist or optometrist to:

(a) (1) Fail to provide to the patient one copy of the patient's prescription immediately after the refractive eye examination is completed and before offering to sell the patient ophthalmic goods, whether or not the prescription is requested by the patient. Such prescription shall be provided:

(i) On paper; or

(ii) In a digital format that can be accessed, downloaded, and printed by the patient, after obtaining verifiable affirmative consent, pursuant to 456.3.

(2) Provided: An ophthalmologist or optometrist may refuse to give the patient a copy of the patient's prescription until the patient has paid for the refractive eye examination, but only if that ophthalmologist or optometrist would have required immediate payment from that patient had the examination revealed that no ophthalmic goods were required. For purposes of the preceding sentence, the presentation of proof of insurance coverage for that service shall be deemed to be a payment;

(b) Condition the availability of a refractive eye examination to any person on a requirement that the patient agree to purchase any ophthalmic goods from the ophthalmologist or optometrist;

(c) Charge the patient any fee in addition to the ophthalmologist's or optometrist's refractive eye examination fee as a condition to releasing the prescription to the patient. Provided: An ophthalmologist or optometrist may charge an additional fee for verifying ophthalmic goods dispensed by another seller when the additional fee is imposed at the time the verification is performed; or

(d) Place on the prescription, or require the patient to sign, or deliver to the patient a form or notice waiving or disclaiming the liability or responsibility of the ophthalmologist or optometrist for the accuracy of the refractive eye examination or the accuracy of the ophthalmic goods and services dispensed by another seller.

[89 FR 60774, July 26, 2024]

456.3. VERIFIABLE AFFIRMATIVE CONSENT TO PROVIDING THE PRESCRIPTION IN A DIGITAL FORMAT.

For a prescription copy provided in a digital format, the prescriber shall:

(a) Identify to the patient the specific method or methods of electronic delivery that will be used, such as text message, electronic mail, or an online patient portal;

(b) Obtain, on paper or in a digital format, the patient's verifiable affirmative consent to receive a digital copy through the identified method or methods; and

(c) Maintain records or evidence of a patient's affirmative consent for a period of not less than three years. Such records or evidence shall be available for inspection by the Federal Trade Commission, its employees, and its representatives.

[89 FR 60774, July 26, 2024]

456.4 CONFIRMATION OF PRESCRIPTION RELEASE

(a) (1) Upon completion of a refractive eye examination, and after providing a copy of the prescription to the patient, the prescriber shall do one of the following:

(i) If a paper copy of the prescription was provided to the patient, request that the patient acknow-ledge receipt of the prescription by signing a separate statement on paper or in a digital format confirming receipt of the prescription; or

(ii) If a digital copy of the prescription was provided to the patient (via methods including an online portal, electronic mail, or text message, and pursuant to 456.3), retain evidence that such prescription was sent, received, or made accessible, downloadable, and printable.

(2) If the prescriber elects to confirm prescription release via paragraph (a)(1)(i) of this section, the prescriber may, but is not required to, use the statement, "My eye care professional provided me with a copy of my prescription at the completion of my examination" to satisfy the requirement.

(3) In the event the patient declines to sign a confirmation requested under paragraph (a)(1)(i) of this section, the prescriber shall note the patient's refusal on the document and sign it.

(b) A prescriber shall maintain the records or evidence required under paragraph (a) of this section for a period of not less than three years. Such records or evidence shall be available for inspection by the Federal Trade Commission, its employees, and its representatives.

(c) Paragraphs (a) and (b) of this section shall not apply to prescribers who do not have a direct or indirect financial interest in the sale of eye wear, including, but not limited to, through an association, affiliation, or co-location with an optical dispenser.

[89 FR 60775, July 26, 2024]

456.5. FEDERAL OR STATE EMPLOYEES

This rule does not apply to ophthalmologists or optometrists employed by any Federal, State or local government entity.

[57 FR 18822, May 1, 1992. Redesignated at 89 FR 60774, July 26, 2024]

456.6. DECLARATION OF COMMISSION INTENT

In prohibiting the use of waivers and disclaimers of liability in 456.2(d), it is not the Commission's intent to impose liability on an ophthalmologist or optometrist for the ophthalmic goods and services dispensed by another seller pursuant to the ophthalmologist's or optometrist's prescription.

[57 FR 18822, May 1, 1992. Redesignated at 89 FR 60774, July 26, 2024]

456.7 RULES APPLICABLE TO PRESCRIPTIONS FOR CONTACT LENSES AND RELATED ISSUES

Rules applicable to prescriptions for contact lenses and related issues may be found at 16 CFR part 315 (Contact Lens Rule).

[69 FR 40511, July 2, 2004. Redesignated at 89 FR 60774, July 26, 2024]

Made in United States
Orlando, FL
04 November 2026

90218966R00292